IN THE STEPS OF
THE TEMPLARS

... THE HISTORY OF THE UNITED ORDERS

IN THE STEPS OF THE TEMPLARS

... THE HISTORY OF THE UNITED ORDERS

BRIAN W. PRICE

A History of The Great Priory of the United Religious,
Military, and Masonic Orders of the Temple
and of St John of Jerusalem, Palestine, Rhodes and Malta
of England and Wales and Provinces Overseas
and
some of the Nine Hundred Years of events
since the founding of The Chivalric Crusading Orders
from which these Masonic Orders drew their inspiration.

Lewis Masonic

First published 2021

ISBN 978 0 85318 596 3

Published by Lewis Masonic
an imprint of Ian Allan Publishing Ltd, Shepperton, Middx TW17 8AS.

Printed in England.

Visit the Lewis Masonic website at www.lewismasonic.co.uk

British Library Cataloguing Data
Price, Brian W.

In The Steps of The Templars: The History of The United Orders
A History of the Great Priory of the United Religious, Military, and Masonic Orders of the Temple and of St John of Jerusalem, Palestine, Rhodes and Malta of England and Wales and Provinces Overseas which were inspired by the Chivalric Crusading Orders founded over 900 years ago in 1118.

1. England. Freemasonry. History Masonic Knights Templar

Contents

ACKNOWLEDGEMENTS

It is almost impossible to catalogue adequately the many individuals to whom grateful thanks are due for their assistance during the past nine years, but sincere appreciation must be given to the staff of the library and museum of United Grand Lodge with particular thanks to Peter Aitkenhead, the staff of Mark Masons' Hall, the Library and Archive staff of Grand Lodge of Ireland, many Provincial Archivists, and Historians of Provincial Priories and individual preceptories, library staff of the Archives in Medina and many regimental archives and museums too numerous to mention, but without whose assistance this work would not have been possible.

To Michael Jenkins of the Order of the Allied Masonic Degrees of Canada for permission to quote from his extensive work on the deployment of the British Army and their Military Lodges. To the Secretary of Quatuor Coronati Lodge No. 2076 for permission to quote from their transactions Ars Quatuor Coronatorum.

Above all I must record for posterity sincere appreciation of John Mandleberg's initial research which kick-started the whole project; to Robin Furber of the Supreme Council of the Ancient and Accepted Rite for access to John Mandleberg's papers after his untimely death early in the project; and to Knight David Casdagli for many, many hundreds of hours of research, and for providing the vital continuity throughout the eight years of the project until his untimely death in January 2019, and to John Hirst for assistance in processing acres of photographic records.

And finally my heartfelt thanks to Julia, my long-suffering wife, who has endured, mostly with good humour, over the nine years of this study, the loss of a bedroom to store several hundred years of documentary and other records which formed the basis for this work.

FOREWORD

Most Eminent Knight Paul Raymond Clement, GCT
Most Eminent and Supreme Grand Master

The publication of this much needed and valuable history will undoubtedly recall to many readers the bi-centenary celebrations of Great Priory in 1991 and the launch of Major Freddie Smyth' s book *Brethren in Chivalry.* It is therefore with great pleasure that I introduce to you this new addition to our Masonic Library from the pen of Wing Commander Brian Price, a recognised Masonic author and historian for over 50 years and one whose vast knowledge and love of the Chivalric Orders shines from every page of this enthralling work.

Man has long craved to know his predecessors as they were going about their daily business and pleasures. In his imagination he has a compelling desire to feel and understand the reality of past ages – reality, if correctly interpreted, is often grander than fiction. As an Order we have long been conscious of our Masonic history and the Chivalric Orders from which our forebears drew their inspiration. This has long tempted many to believe that the Crusading Knights Templars and the Masonic Knights Templar are one and the same, and it has even been said that 'all Masons are Knights Templar.'

This author has attempted to dispel this, and other myths. Painstaking research into fresh archives has uncovered aspects of our history that have not been generally known producing not only a fresh view of the chivalric orders at the time of the Crusades in the Holy Land, but the subsequent inspiration they gave to the many European cultures during the intervening centuries. He also examines many lesser Crusades which influenced the changing cultural environment enabling speculative Freemasonry and the Masonic Chivalric Orders including our own Great Priory to emerge throughout Europe.

Whilst this new work will be of primary interest to members of Great Priory, I am sure it also be a useful work of reference both to a wider Masonic audience and to readers interested in the inspiration provided by our crusading forebears both in the Holy Land and elsewhere across Europe.

Paul R. Clement

PREFACE TO

IN THE STEPS OF THE TEMPLARS
... The History of The United Orders.

The first comprehensive history of the Military and Masonic Orders of Knights Templar and the Knights of Malta in England (The United Orders) was published in 1991 to mark the 200th anniversary of the establishment in England of a Grand Conclave, the original governing body of our United Masonic Orders.[1] In recent years, the Author had several opportunities to discuss this history with Freddie Smyth, and although he was his usual discreet self, it was evident that he would have liked to have had much more time to carry out the research which such an undertaking required. He was further handicapped by the relative paucity of archival material in Mark Masons' Hall in London (from which the English Order is administered today) due to an unfortunate misunderstanding when in 1976 this headquarters moved from Upper Brook Street to the present fine building at 86 St James's Street, and much material was lost.

Since 1991 other material, not available to Freddie Smyth before his death, has come to light, specifically that relating to the effective re-establishment of Grand Conclave after the death of the Duke of Sussex in 1843, and also to the surrender of the *Rosae Crucis* and *Kadosh* Degrees to the Supreme Council of the Ancient and Accepted Rite, the Patent of which dates from 1845. Furthermore, probably due to the pressure of time, there is little in earlier works about events after the 'Great War' – 'World War 1' – of 1914-1918, let alone those after 'World War 2' or about the development of Provinces and the Order overseas. In this completely new work, so far as it has been possible, an attempt has been made to fill in these gaps in the history of the United Orders.

In addition, though none of today's Masonic, Military and Religious Orders can trace any lineal connection with those valiant Knights who fought in the Crusades, the latter were the inspiration of not only many aspects of British and European literature and culture, but also our present United Orders, in the Rituals of which there are many references to the events which took place in 'Outremer'. Not unnaturally the Crusading warriors have a considerable fascination for members of the Orders today, but many published works abound with myths and legends, and this work attempts to dispel these highlighting known errors or ill-advised interpretation. Many Masonic Brethren are keen to talk on 'The Crusades'. It has therefore been considered appropriate to provide a rather lengthier account of these expeditions than has been documented before to assist anyone who in the future may be called upon to give such a talk, at the same time dispelling some of the errors which have crept into even some of our present-day printed rituals.

In the Steps of The Templars is a tribute to Smyth, his Masonic learning, and to his unstinting kindly assistance to his fellow-researchers. It is also a tribute to the meticulous scholarship of John Mandleberg and his lifetime of important contributions to masonic history as John died during the early phase of the writing of this work.

Finally, it cannot be denied that the romance of the Crusades and the history of Templar and Hospitaller Orders are still of major interest today, as throughout much of the 900 years which has passed since the founding of The Poor Fellow-Soldiers of Christ and the Temple of Solomon, and it seems appropriate to record a little of how that romance has come down to us today through many different channels. This work therefore sets out a chronological background to the development of the United Orders, tracing the impact of the Crusading Chivalric Orders throughout Europe where early Freemasonry developed, and Appendix A summarises this time-line.

Part One – The history of the Chivalric Orders of Knighthood from which the modern Masonic, Military and Religious Orders of the Temple and the Hospital obtained their inspiration and have derived their names, together with some of their background.

Part Two – A review of the residual elements of the Chivalric Orders of Knighthood, the global environment which facilitated their survival, and the development of operative and speculative masonry up to the end of the 17th century.

Part Three – The development of the modern speculative Masonic orders of chivalry and the establishment of 'the Great Priory of the United Religious, Military and Masonic Orders of the Temple and of St John of Jerusalem, Palestine, Rhodes and Malta of England and Wales and its Provinces Overseas' up to the end of the 19th century.

Part Four – The expansion of the United Orders and the global situation today

This complex history covers over 900 years since the first recorded founding of the The Poor Fellow-Soldiers of Christ and the Temple of Solomon in AD 1118 and identifies many subsequent developments, one of which are today's Masonic Orders of chivalry.

BRIAN W. PRICE

Part One

THE CHIVALRIC ORDERS OF KNIGHTHOOD

Preamble

This provides a brief history of the Chivalric Orders from which the modern Masonic, Military and Religious Orders of the Temple and the Hospital have derived their names and inspiration, together with some of their traditions and their supposed history.

Whilst the development of the Masonic, Military and Religious Orders of the Temple and the Hospital may be considered to be of primarily English origin its history has in fact been heavily influenced by the culture of some other Nations. Equally, many readers may view the Crusades in the Holy Land as essentially episodes in the history of England and the persecution and demise of the Knights Templar as an interlude in the history of France, but these, although significant, by no means represent the complete picture. An examination of the participants in the Crusades not only reveals a wide variety of religious, military, and commercial interests, but also the direct involvement of most of the European Nations. Of considerable importance is to understand that the Crusades were not ventures which ill-informed detractors have sometimes termed 'Muslim-bashing'; indeed many Crusades were primarily aimed at recovering 'that which was lost' – territory and holy sites in the main; and additionally, historical accounts exist showing the Western Crusaders occasionally formed alliances with Muslim forces.

It will be seen that in addition to English and French crusaders, participants included forces from countries which today are known as Norway and other Scandinavian territories in the North; Portugal, and Spain in the West; Germany, Italy, Hungary, and Armenia in Central Europe; and Mediterranean countries such as Sicily and Cyprus. Additionally trading and commercial centres such as Venice and Genoa, and many off-shoots of the former Roman and Byzantine Empires played an early and important part in the crusades and the subsequent spread of influence around Europe.

The significance is that the impact of the Crusades and the emergence of the Chivalric Orders would be felt across Europe and this would affect not only contemporary history but development over many more recent centuries down to modern times as diverse cultures followed in the steps of the Templars. In particular, as will be shown later, many European Countries would embark on 'lesser crusades', many with religious sanction, and this would effectively perpetuate chivalric ideals well beyond the actual period when the chivalric Knights Templar influence was apparent. Whilst these 'lesser crusades' were generally military ventures, many left long-lasting economic and cultural benefits including the basis for development of many other 'Templar-like' chivalric 'honour systems'. It will also be seen to be highly likely that the transitional environment which developed throughout Europe was one which was sympathetic to the Templar cause and could provide a haven for Templar members who escaped persecution.

This is particularly relevant when considering if, and where, residual Templar elements may have survived and it will be seen later that there have been many suggestions, not only that the chivalric Knights Templar survived in Scotland but also that survivors were instrumental in developing the earliest speculative Freemasonry. Whilst this may not be completely impossible, no evidence has been found to categorically support this concept or to support a long held view advanced by some writers that 'all masons are Knights Templar'.

Throughout, all dates are Anno Domini (AD) unless annotated as referencing another era. The term 'Time Immemorial' should not be taken as implying great antiquity, but is used in accordance with current Masonic usage to infer that a Lodge, Chapter, or Preceptory was in existence before its present sovereign body was established.

To assist today's reader, geographical areas are referenced by modern names although, in many cases, Nations (such as Italy) did not exist as such for most of the historical period covered.

1.1 INTRODUCTION – THE CHIVALRIC KNIGHTHOODS

Our United Masonic Orders of today can claim to have inherited little more than the names of the two knightly fraternities which were formed and developed during the Western occupation of what became known as *Outremer* – the Holy Land of Palestine Overseas.

However, the Crusades in general and the rise of these knightly fraternities in particular did not make a sudden dramatic impact on British culture or seem, at the time, to be at all unusual. The British Isles, and for that matter, the near Continent of Europe had long been an area of conflict and foreign occupation; certainly the culture of Britain, France, and Germany were significantly shaped by the Roman Empire; the incursions of the Vikings; and the Norman Conquest. The latter, in particular, institutionalised the concept of feudal Lordships owning land rather than tribal influence over territories. This in effect extended the concept of control by 'the crown' down a number of levels descending from dukedoms and earldoms, down to lordships at manorial level. In addition to the Royal houses of Europe it was such fiefdoms which supported the Crusades, both with money, grants of land, and military personnel.

Such a historical background had created a popular culture which included not only a hierarchy of landowners but also the concept of a knightly class of chivalric leaders which naturally played an essential part both in developing the combatant arts and leading military activities.

It therefore seemed right to preface the story of events which have occurred in more recent times with an account of the institution and the subsequent development of the Orders of the Hospitallers and of the Templars in the Middle Ages. Furthermore, there is also much popular misconception about the circumstances which led to the despatch from the West of the formidable fighting forces generally referred to as 'Crusaders', and also of what they achieved.

Perhaps it is therefore permissible to sketch first the sequence of those events which led to the difficulties which faced pilgrims wishing to visit the Holy Land, and then to summarise the two and a quarter centuries of armed struggle by which it was intended that these difficulties would be removed, the so-called 'Crusades'. It is then relevant to consider some of the wider impact of the crusading philosophy which resulted in a number of 'lesser crusades' and which affected other European Nations, as it will later emerge that such impacts would also influence Masonic developments.

1.2 THE BACKGROUND TO THE CRUSADES
(Up to AD 1086)

O f the 'Hospitallers' It has been said that "the history of the Order can be traced back so far that it is difficult to name an exact date for its beginning".[2] Although originally the Brethren of the Hospital were concerned solely with the nurture of the sick, the Order subsequently became as active a military participant in the crusading wars as did the Order of the Temple which later was founded specifically as an armed military force. But first it should be said that the lengthy struggles in Palestine in the Middle Ages, generally vaguely referred to as 'The Crusades', did not arise from some sudden spontaneous realisation in Western Europe that the Christian Holy Places were in the hands of those who followed the Faith of Islam. The roots of the Crusades went much further back in history than any such realisation.

In the time of Our Lord, Palestine, then known as Judea, was a Roman Province. When in the year 330 Constantine the Great transferred the capital of the Roman Empire to Constantinople both Syria and Palestine were Byzantine Provinces or 'Themes'. The Council which was held at Chalcedon in 331 deeply divided the Christian Church. Many of the Eastern Christians rejected the Council's affirmative pronouncement on the Dual Nature of Christ, and they became known as 'Monophysites'. This difference of opinion did not interrupt the constant stream of pilgrims which was coming from the West to visit the Holy Places in Palestine. As early as the beginning of the 7th century at the instigation of Pope Gregory I, a hostel had been established in Jerusalem to house Western pilgrims visiting the city.

The Monophysites in Egypt (which was also a Byzantine Province at this time) not only renounced their allegiance to the Eastern Orthodox Church which accepted the decisions taken at Chalcedon, but also their allegiance to the Emperor in Constantinople. On the death of the Orthodox Patriarch Eugenius of Alexandria in 607 only seven Churches in the city were left in the hands of those who believed in the Two Natures of the Incarnate Christ.

Heracles usurped the Imperial throne in Constantinople. He ordered Nicetas, an adopted son of the Governor of Cyprus, to recover Egypt for the Eastern Roman Empire and for the Orthodox Church. Having accomplished the first task, Nicetas gave the second to his half-brother John, whom he appointed Patriarch of Alexandria. John, renouncing forceful persuasion, devoted himself to a saintly life of expansive and all-embracing charity which not only converted many of the Monophysites but caused him to be widely known as 'John the Alms-giver'.

The Muslim Arabs now entered the scene. (The Prophet Muhammad, on whom be Peace, received his first vision of the Angel Gabriel in the same year as the Patriarch John entered Alexandria.) In 614, Shahbaraz, the commander of the army of the Parthian rivals of the Eastern Roman Empire, in a loose alliance with the Arabs, captured first Damascus and then Jerusalem where he allowed the Jewish leader, Nehemiah, to destroy the Christian *Church of the Holy Sepulchre*. Shahbaraz returned to Ctesiphon with the reputed fragments of the True Cross which he had seized. However in the following year the Parthian Governor of Jerusalem permitted the Patriarch John the Alms-giver to send a monk, Ctesippus, to Jerusalem to rebuild the Church of the Holy Sepulchre. Ctesippus also cleared the deserted sites of Calvary and of our Lord's Tomb from the rubbish which covered them.

By 635, Parthia had itself been overwhelmed and was submerged below the rising tide of militant Islam; three years later the Muslim Arabs over-ran Palestine, and the Patriarch Sempronius surrendered Jerusalem to them. The Muslims built a mosque on the *'Dome of the Rock'*, but divided the remainder of the Holy Places inside Jerusalem with the Christians who were generally allowed to live at peace within the City which in time was to form part of the Muslim Baghdad Khalifate. Western Christians resumed their briefly-interrupted Pilgrimages to Jerusalem and for over four hundred years such journeys again became commonplace events. Early in the 9th century the Khalif Haroun al-Raschid of Baghdad even permitted the French King Charlemagne to send workmen to re-build and extend the former pilgrim hostel in Jerusalem.

Two hundred years after this the Arab Empire had become fragmented with many Khalifs each claiming to be the rightful 'Commander of the Faithful' – an Umaiyid Khalif in Spain, an Almoravid in North Africa, and a Buwaihid who had driven out the Abbasids in Baghdad. Palestine was now a Province of the Egyptian Fatimid Khalifate Shiites, who on the whole were friendly to the Christians.

The re-built pilgrim hostel in Jerusalem again became damaged in an uprising. By this time trade with the Christian West had become an important factor in the economic life of both Palestine and Egypt. Western merchants had been permitted to establish trading posts in various places in the Arab-occupied territories. So cordial were the Westerners' commercial relations with the Fatimid Governor of Egypt that in 1048 some merchants from Amalfi obtained permission from him to build a Benedictine Monastery, *Santa Maria Latina*, near the restored *Church of the Holy Sepulchre* in Jerusalem. They also re-built the *Hospice* for the care of sick and needy pilgrims to which they added a chapel dedicated to the former Patriarch, John the Alms-Giver. The monks who cared for the sick in the Hospice called themselves 'Brothers of

St John of Jerusalem', as the Patriarch John the Alms-giver had now become known. The insignia of Amalfi was the eight-pointed white Cross, and this was chosen by the Benedictine monks of *Santa Maria Latina* as their emblem. It has ever since distinguished the Orders and fraternities which have been predicated upon the foundation at Jerusalem. For the time being it was the Byzantines and not the Muslims who were the greatest impediment to pilgrims who wished to visit the Holy City. For example, in 1056 Pope Victor II had to write to the Byzantine Empress Theodora asking her to rescind a tax which she had imposed on pilgrims passing through her territory.

In 1078, Jerusalem was captured from the Fatimid Egyptians by Tutush, a Seljuk Turk who then claimed to rule Syria and Palestine from his capital at Aleppo. With another Turki adventurer, Chaka, occupying Smyrna, and with other principal towns in the hands of local chieftains, and in the absence of the friendly Fatimid frontier posts and their well-policed roads, an unaccompanied Western pilgrim now had little chance of reaching Jerusalem alive.

In 1086, Count Robert I of Flanders was one of the few pilgrims who tried to do so, but he was not unaccompanied. He brought with him a strong-armed escort. He proved that the journey could be done by resolute men with adequate support, but, equally, that there was little chance of an unarmed pilgrim surviving a 'Trip to Jerusalem'.[3]

Count Robert returned home by way of Constantinople where Alexius Comnenus, the latest usurper of the Byzantine Imperial throne, was under pressure, and not only from the Seljuqs in the East. In his western Province of Thrace the Pechanegs from the Russian steppes had defeated a Byzantine army, a defeat from the consequences of which Alexius was saved only by the fortuitous arrival on the scene of the homeward-journeying Robert of Flanders with his armed escort. The Byzantines were desperately short of man-power, and after the Pechanegs had been disposed of, Alexius was persuaded by Robert that large numbers of Western European mercenaries were to be had for the asking, himself promising to supply 1,500. It apparently did not occur to Alexius that many of their leaders would be younger sons of noble families seeking estates for themselves.

1.3 THE FIRST CRUSADE (1086-1099)

Within a few years of the pilgrimage of Robert of Flanders the time seemed to be propitious for the Byzantine Emperor Alexius to attempt to recover his lost Provinces or 'Themes' in Asia Minor from the Seljuqs; he was little concerned with Palestine where the Egyptian Fatimids were preparing to recapture Jerusalem from the Seljuqs who now had no single leader. Since Alexius wanted to draw on the whole of the man-power resources of the West, he sent envoys to the Pope, basing his emotional appeal for help on the plight of Christians persecuted by the Seljuq Turks in Armenia. But he made it clear to his envoys that they were to ask only for mercenaries, who would swear an oath of allegiance to him as their paymaster. He envisaged a political war to recover his lands from the Seljuqs, not a Holy War against Islam. Alexius had, in fact, nothing against the Fatimids whom the Byzantines saw as men of honour with a standard of material and intellectual civilisation at least as high as their own.

Pope Urban II, on the other hand, was seriously disturbed about the interruption of the pilgrim traffic to Jerusalem but little concerned with which brand of infidel was causing it. Furthermore, the Princes of Europe were not only fighting among themselves, but also opposing the Papacy on the Investiture concept – the question of whether an ecclesiastic held ('had been Invested with') the temporalities of his benefice – lands, bridge-tolls etc. – from the Pope or from the lay ruler of his country, and whether he did homage to the latter for them. He was already considering an expedition to the East not only to open the pilgrims' routes, but also because it would divert the European rulers and unite them in a common cause under the Church's leadership. The arrival of the Byzantine envoys at a Papal Council being held at Piacenza in the spring of 1095 seemed a heaven-sent opportunity.

Urban had no interest in recovering the Byzantine themes in Asia Minor nor of relieving the Armenian Christians whom he considered to be near-heretics. However, he correctly judged that an expedition to recover the Holy Places would have an immediate emotional appeal in the west. He therefore summoned a Council of the Church to meet in the Auvergne later in the year. He spent the intervening time touring France to make sure that his intention was widely known.

The Council met at Claremont on 18 November 1095. In addition to the Church dignitaries who had been explicitly summoned to the Council, many laymen came to hear the Pope's message. Urban's proposals for an expedition to Palestine were rapturously received. When he repeated them to the crowd assembled outside the Church of Notre Dame du Port, many spontaneously cried out 'God Wills It!' At the Pope's suggestion those who at once promised to take part attached a Cross to their clothing, not necessarily of red but of any colour which came to hand. He announced that the march to the East would start on 15 August 1096. However, what Urban had set in train was something wholly alien to Byzantine policy.

Urban continued to tour France to preach the Crusade. Others did so unasked, among them Peter, known as 'the Hermit'. He went barefoot, wearing filthy rags, abstaining from meat but drinking wine. His preaching convinced his ill-educated hearers that he spoke from Divine Inspiration. The idea of a Crusade was certainly not his, whatever may be the traditions in some modern Masonic Orders. Preaching the Crusade through North-west France before Christmas 1095 Peter was not only followed by peasants but also by impoverished members of the minor nobility such as Walter, known as 'the Penniless'. It is said that by the time he reached Cologne, six months before the Crusade was due to set out, he had 15,000 followers, and he had to lead them somewhere.

Many, perhaps the majority, of those who were following Peter had little idea of what the Crusade was really about. To them Palestine was a legendary land in which the principal events of their Faith had taken place an unimaginably long time ago. Their knowledge of the Holy City had been clouded by apocalyptic sermons about the Second Coming and the New Jerusalem. But one part of the Church's teachings they knew only too well; their Saviour Christ had been put to death by the Jews. And Jews they also knew well; they were scattered over Western Europe, and most of the potential Crusaders, nobles and peasants alike, were in debt to them, some considerably so.

At the head of his motley band of 'Crusaders' Peter the Hermit followed the contingent led by Walter the Penniless through Hungary towards Constantinople. Neither had made any preparations for feeding his followers who, as best they could, despoiled the countryside where food was scarce at the end of winter. While at least both Peter and Walter and their rabble continued to advance Eastwards, they were followed by other similarly disorganised bands that turned aside to massacre Jews at Trier, at Worms, at Spier, and at Mainz. Peter and Walter the Penniless having started too early, the Byzantines had made no preparations to receive them. Pitched battles took place in Bulgaria in which half Peter's followers were killed. At the end of July the bedraggled survivors arrived at the gates of Constantinople. Alexius was horrified by Peter's followers – these were not the disciplined mercenaries whom he had expected. He hastily sent them across the Bosporus having given them some supplies. Instead of waiting for the main body to arrive, individual bands set out to despoil the country and suffered a defeat at Xerigordon where many of them were massacred. A further massacre took place at Civetot, after which the Byzantine fleet brought back to Constantinople the few hundred survivors of the followers of Peter and Walter.

In the autumn of 1096, Godfrey de Bouillon led towards the East a disciplined force of French Crusaders which arrived at the gates of Constantinople ahead of the main body. He refused to swear allegiance to the Byzantine Emperor, and his forces were escorted across the Bosporus. They were followed by an army led by Bohemond which arrived at Constantinople in April of the following year. Raymond of Toulouse had crossed the Adriatic by boat and was leading his contingent to Constantinople along the almost non-existent roads in the North of Greece. Eventually all the 'official' Crusading forces, initially totalling perhaps 50,000 men, crossed the Bosporus, and the advance towards Jerusalem could commence. Nicaea was captured and then Dorylaeum. The next objective was Antioch. After a long siege this was captured by Bohemond whose forces then themselves had to endure being besieged within Antioch by the relieving Seljuq forces under Kerbogha, whom Bohemond was eventually able to drive off. While these events were taking place, the Egyptian Fatimids had occupied Jerusalem after a six-week siege, driving out the Seljuqs. They rebuilt the walls and improved the defences.

In January 1099, while Bohemond remained in Antioch, and Baldwin, the brother of Godfrey de Bouillon, in Edessa which he had captured, seizing its County as his fief, the remainder of the Crusading forces set out on the last stage of their advance to Jerusalem. Although perhaps as many as a hundred thousand men had by now come to Palestine in the previous two and a half years, Raymond of Toulouse, who led the advance, found himself commanding no more than a thousand Knights and five thousand foot soldiers. His line of advance was far enough to the East to avoid the fortified coastal cities, and by prudent route-selection and careful diplomacy, the Crusading force reached the neighbourhood of Jerusalem by June 1099. On 7 June, from the summit of the hill known to pilgrims as Montjoie, they at last came in sight of the Holy City nearly three years after leaving France.

A first assault on the walls of Jerusalem was repulsed, but then a combined English and Genoese fleet arrived at the port of Acre carrying material with which to build siege engines. With this, catapults, siege-towers and scaling-ladders were constructed. When these were in place the City was entered after twenty-four hard-fought hours. The Fatimid commander and his bodyguard were allowed to march out unharmed, but the Crusaders rampaged through the City slaughtering Jews and Muslims alike. Even those who had taken part were afterwards appalled at the extent of the massacre. When Islamic leaders even today refer to Western armies disparagingly as 'Crusaders', it is this blood-bath which is uppermost in their minds.

The Crusaders having entered Jerusalem there was no ecclesiastic present who could use his spiritual authority to impose a single leader on the victors; the Papal Legate to the Crusade, Cardinal Adhemar, had by now died, as had the Patriarch Symeon of Jerusalem. A Fatimid relieving force was advancing on the City, and the appointment of a single leader had become a matter of urgency. Count Raymond of Toulouse, the Commander of the largest force of Crusaders, declined the offer as he wished to return home, considering that the capture of Jerusalem released him from his Crusader's vow. He offered the Kingdom to Duke Godfrey de Bouillon of Lorraine, who accepted it, taking the title of *Advocatus Sancti Sepulchri*. (It is only much later that chroniclers first record that Godfrey had said that he would not wear a Golden Crown in a City where his Saviour had worn a Crown of Thorns; there is no contemporary evidence for Godfrey having said this.)

For the last action of the First Crusade, the defending forces did not wait for a formal battle to be joined, but made a sortie and over-ran the camp of the Fatimid relieving army on 12 August 1099. They took the numerically superior Egyptian forces by surprise, and although their Commander, Afdhal, escaped and returned to Egypt, such of his forces as survived taking refuge in the frontier town of Ascalon; the Western Crusaders were now the unchallenged rulers of Jerusalem.

1.4 ESTABLISHING THE MILITARY ORDERS
(1100-1144)

One of the first acts of the new ruler of Jerusalem was to restore the Hospice founded by the merchants of Amalfi to the monks and lay-brothers who had served it. Hitherto, the Hospice and the Hospital attached to it had been under the control of the Benedictine Abbot of the monastery of *St Maria Latina*. The Hospice now asserted its independence and the brethren accepted the Augustinian rule of Gerard – 'the Blessed Gerard' – who was probably a Frenchman from Martigues in Provence. They also withdrew their allegiance from John the Alms-giver, and, presumably considering that St John the Baptist would be a more powerful mediator, they placed themselves under his protection. Godfrey de Bouillon gave the Hospitallers the castle of El Silsileh and two bake-houses in Jerusalem.

Many of those who now returned to the West from the First Crusade expressed their gratitude for the assistance which they had received from the Hospital of St John in Jerusalem. As a result, it began to attract 'benefactions'. The earliest deed of which the authenticity is accepted conferred thirteen acres of fields known as Clerkenwell (*Clericorum*) to the Chaplain Robert for the Order of the Hospital, on which to build a Church. This was in 1099, and in the following year Count Sancho of Astarac gave the Estate of Fonsorbes to the Hospital and to the Church of the Holy Sepulchre.

Godfrey, the first Christian King of Jerusalem, died on 18 August 1100. He was succeeded by his brother Count Baldwin of Edessa. The Crusader fiefs which were beginning to be established were becoming collectively known as '*Outremer*'; as well as the Kingdom of Jerusalem and the Counties of Edessa and Antioch, by now they included those of Tripoli and also of Galilee which King Baldwin gave to Hugh of St Omer. Many of the original Crusaders had returned home to their own fiefs, and in response to frantic appeals for more man-power, a few reinforcements had arrived from Europe, each Knight intent on carving out an estate for himself; many failed to reach Palestine, being defeated on the way in unnecessary skirmishes in Asia Minor where they and many of their followers were either killed or carried off as slaves by the Seljuq Turks.

The Brethren of the Hospital were by now well established under the rule of the Blessed Gerard, being known as 'Custodians of the Poor of Christ'. The Order is said to have been confirmed by King Baldwin in 1104.

Baldwin's rule in Jerusalem was a mixed blessing. Militarily he acted with incisive energy but he was less capable as a politician. He carried out punitive raids to prevent Arab and Turkish incursions across his frontiers. For example, when in May 1110 Edessa was besieged by the Baghdad Sultan Muhammad Tapar, King Baldwin led an army to its relief. Having accomplished this he immediately marched South to ward off a threatened Egyptian attack. Tripoli was already in Crusader hands, but by the end of the year both Beirut and Sidon were occupied by 'the Franks' as they were known by their Muslim opponents.

Baldwin also commenced the building of the great stone fortresses which characterised the Frankish occupation of *Outremer*. These were no temporary structures, but large and sophisticated castles built of massive blocks of masoned stone, exhibiting considerable skill in both design and construction. While much of the labouring work can only have been carried out by local labour, professional assistance must have been available. It is hard to disregard the tradition long-held by French operative masons of the *compagnonage* that they provided 'Lodges' which accompanied the Crusaders for this purpose.

In the same year, Baldwin gave the Hospitallers a Charter confirming the gift of the property which Godfrey de Bouillon had made to the Hospice. Their prosperity was increased when the Patriarch of Jerusalem exempted them from paying tithes on their properties. Gifts continued to be made – in Europe the Estate of Fiosolvol as well as several properties in *Outremer*. Pilgrims were again coming to the Holy Land from all parts of Europe, among them the Joint-King of Norway, Sigurd, who is said to have been accompanied by 10,000 Norwegians when he arrived in Jerusalem, thereby earning himself the title of *Jorsalfarer*, the ' Jerusalem Traveller'.

Gerard, the Master of the Hospital, seems to have been a man of extraordinary vision as well as being unusually energetic. It has been suggested that he early saw his embryonic Order to have a role not only as carers for the sick, but also in effect as a travel agency to assist pilgrims from the West to come to the Holy Land. The precise status of the *xenodochea*, or hospices, in Europe which were associated with the Hospital of St John in Jerusalem is far from certain, but by 1113 these had been established at Asti, Messina, Otranto, Pisa, and Taranto and at St Gilles in Provence. Pope Paschal II specifically ratified the possessions of the 'Order of St Gilles' which soon became the first Priory of the Jerusalem Order.

With the exception of Asti and Pisa, all these towns were on the western Mediterranean sea-board, and Gerard may have initiated the custom of pilgrims travelling by sea to those ports in Palestine now held by the Crusaders instead of taking the perilous overland journey, for which purpose the Hospitallers acquired a fleet.

In response to Gerard's request, Pope Paschal promulgated a Bull, *Pie postulatio voluntatis*, dated 13 February 1113, in effect giving Gerard the authority to found a new Order, together with freedom from tithes; this extended to the *xenodochea* which themselves were now known by the style of 'of Jerusalem'. Gerard formally adopted the Augustinian tradition. Paschal also called on all ecclesiastics and nobles in Spain to send alms to Gerard who again changed his own designation – he was now 'Master of the Hospital of St John of Jerusalem and guardian of the poor brethren of our Lord Jesus Christ' – it was to be many years before the head of the Hospitallers was to style himself 'Grand Master'.

Direct evidence is scanty, but it is generally agreed that even at this early date the Brethren of the Hospital customarily wore a red shirt of wool or silk with short sleeves. On the back and front of this were stitched vertical and horizontal strips of white cloth to form a plain Cross; it was not until considerably later that the white eight-pointed cross was worn on the Hospitallers' garments. It is uncertain how early the black mantle was adopted, but it was a common garment for those engaged on charitable service.

In June 1113, the Muslims renewed their attack on the Kingdom of Jerusalem, but although King Baldwin's forces were defeated south of the Sea of Galilee, the Muslims did not follow up their victory.

While Count Baldwin II of Edessa was spending Easter in Jerusalem in 1118, his cousin, King Baldwin I of Jerusalem, died. There was little opposition to Count Baldwin of Edessa succeeding his cousin, taking the curiously limited title of 'King of the Latins in the Holy City of Jerusalem'. At this time while the Hospitallers were concerned with the welfare of Jerusalem-bound pilgrims, they had not considered protecting them by armed force. Soon after King Baldwin II ascended the throne of Jerusalem, Royal recognition was requested for a band of Knights who had dedicated themselves to keeping open the pilgrim roads by force of arms. It must be noted, however, that there is no account of the petition of Hugh de Payens or of other events which led to the foundation of the Templar Order in the contemporary history written by Fulk de Chartres who was the official historian at King Baldwin's Court. The only details of the founding of this Order were set out 50 years later by William of Tyre some of whose statements are manifestly untrue. The highway patrol was evidently not carried out by nine Knights who did not add to their numbers for nine years, because by 1126 the Counts of Anjou and of Champagne had joined the band. The original leader of these Knights was certainly Hugh de Payens,[4] and they included Geoffrey of St Omer, Payen de Montdidier, Archambaud of St Agnan and Geoffrey Bisot or Bizol. They called themselves 'The Poor Fellow-Soldiers of Jesus Christ', and took vows of poverty, chastity and obedience.

King Baldwin II was sufficiently impressed by their ardour and devotion to appreciate the value of such a body. It would make no demands on the Royal

Treasury while carrying out those obligations which he, as King of Jerusalem, was bound to assume in order that pilgrims could safely arrive at the Holy City. As a headquarters Baldwin allocated the Knights a building near the *Dome of the Rock* which stood on the reputed site of the stables of King Solomon. This suggested the more impressive title which the Knights adopted – the Knights of the Temple of King Solomon, soon abbreviated to 'The Knights Templar'. It has been suggested that, to emphasise their renunciation of worldly possessions, the Knights adopted a crest or seal depicting two knights mounted on a single horse. Except as a piece of propaganda this was hardly appropriate, because later Templar Regulations laid down that each Knight should have not one but several horses.[5]

'The Blessed Gerard' died in 1120. That the Brethren chose Raymond de Puy to succeed him may indicate that they already saw the role of the professed brethren to be changing. Raymond was a French Knight who had fought in the First Crusade and it can hardly have been other than under his influence that the Hospitallers emerged as a military Order.

In September 1122 Count Joscelin of Edessa was ambushed and taken prisoner by the Turkish Commander's nephew, Balak, and held to ransom. King Baldwin II of Jerusalem assumed also the Regency of Edessa while negotiations for Joscelin's release were taking place. In the following April Baldwin marched North to attempt to hasten this, but he was himself taken prisoner by Balak while hawking near the River Euphrates. In 1124, matters became confused when the Armenians attempted to release King Baldwin and Count Joscelin from the fortress of Kharpur in which they were both confined. Joscelin managed to escape and ride to Jerusalem to summon the Knights of *Outremer* to release their King, but by this time the Seljuq Turks had recaptured Kharpur and had slaughtered every Christian within it except King Baldwin who was sent to Harran. The King was able to return to Jerusalem after a quarter of a ransom of 80,000 Dinars had been paid, his four-year old daughter Yvette being held as security for the balance of the ransom. The King at once gathered a force of Knights, marched North, and defeated the Seljuqs at Azez, capturing so much loot that he was able with it to pay off the remainder of his ransom and recover his daughter.

By 1126, under the militaristic leadership of Raymond le Puy, the Hospitallers had established themselves in Acre, where they built a Hospital and laid the foundations of a magnificent Cathedral dedicated to St John, 'the first patron and protector of the Order'.

Meanwhile in the West, Bernard of Clairvaux had become one of the most influential ecclesiastics. His principal benefactor had been Count Hugh of Champagne who in 1125 left his County and travelled to Jerusalem where he joined the Knights Templar with whom he already had close ties – Hugh de

Payens had been a vassal of his in France, and André de Montbard was the uncle of his protégé, Bernard of Clairvaux. The enrolment of the Count of Champagne suggested to Hugh de Payens that this was an opportunity to obtain Papal recognition for the Order.[6] If Hugh of Champagne could obtain the support of Bernard of Clairvaux, the latter's influence with the Pope would be sufficient to secure this recognition. André de Montbard was sent to Europe with a letter to this effect. It provided the desired outcome. Bernard received agreement in principle from Pope Honorius II, and summoned Hugh de Payens to a special Council which was held at Troyes in France on 13 January 1128.

Hugh de Payens arrived accompanied by several of his Knights who caused some surprise to the members of the Council. They differed in every respect from the elegant cavaliers of Western Europe. They wore old clothes instead of ostentatiously ornamented robes. They bore no flamboyant devices – their shields were painted an unassuming black. Their hair was cropped short, but their beards grew without restraint unlike the trim facial styles of the members of the Council. With only one known dissenting voice – John, Bishop of Orleans – the Council approved the presentations made to it, and the Legates gave the Order formal recognition.

Bernard of Clairvaux was given the task of writing the Rule for the Order – probably single-handedly he provided the 72 complex Articles of the *Regula pauperum commilitonum Christi*. It was to be a strictly ascetic and celibate community upon which was superimposed the discipline of an organised permanent fighting force. At its head was the Master of the Temple, not yet known as 'The Grand Master', whose rule was not to be absolute but subject to the decisions of a Council of the Order. There were to be Provincial Masters in Western Europe, each supreme in his own country. The Rule specified the black-and-white battle standard, described as *baucent*.[7] Further the Rule laid down that the Knights should pray together, that they must have no contact whatsoever with women, (the Rule making it clear that it was a woman who caused the exclusion of the human race from Paradise), and that only grown men, free, and not in bondage or serfdom, could enter the Order, and then only as an act of free-will. As a Rule blessed by the Church, the Knights must discard their rough costumes, and dress solely in white without ornament. But they were not to fast, or to abandon liquor, for above all they were fighting men who must keep themselves in prime physical condition.

However the Order may later have developed, to pretend that at the time of the Council of Troyes that the Knights were anything but what they appeared to be – honest men prepared to renounce the world to die as Soldiers of Christ – is to develop fantasies which take no account of the genuine spirituality of the times. After the Council, Hugh de Payens toured Europe to raise funds for the Order, having first made over his own estates to it. Among many other donations, in March 1128 Queen Theresa of Portugal gave to the Order the Castle and lands of Soure on the River Mondego.

While Hugh de Payens was in France obtaining Papal sanction for the Order of the Temple, the third of the great charitable Orders had been founded in Jerusalem. As in the case of the Hospitallers, this had its origin in a simple *hospitium* or hospital. It was erected in 1128 by a pious German to relieve necessitous or ill German pilgrims visiting the Holy Places. In time the Order became known as that of 'The Teutonic Knights'.

Before he returned to *Outremer* Hugh visited England as the guest of King Henry I; the Temple in London may have been founded during his visit, but this is uncertain. So considerable was the income from the properties which the Order now possessed, quite apart from the gifts of money and treasure which Hugh was able to send back to Jerusalem, that there is not the slightest need to suppose that the Templars had uncovered some horde of wealth under the stables of King Solomon. It is at least plausible to suppose that rather than the records of such a discovery having been minutely destroyed, such records never existed, no such discovery ever having been made.

King Baldwin II was becoming increasingly concerned about the succession to the throne of Jerusalem. He had four daughters and no sons. His second daughter, Alice, was married to Bohemond II of Antioch, but his eldest daughter, Melisenda was available to marry a suitable European noble who would, through her, inherit the Kingdom. Baldwin therefore sent a delegation to King Louis VI of France to ask him if he could find a suitable candidate; Louis recommended Count Fulk V of Anjou, with whom Baldwin had stayed for some time during his visit to France. Fulk travelled to Jerusalem and married Melisenda at the end of May 1129 with the approval of all concerned, apart from the bride whose opinion does not seem to have been requested. King Baldwin was delighted not only to have such an experienced campaigner as a son-in-law, but also to receive the considerable number of reinforcements which he brought with him. He immediately planned to capture Damascus with their help, but when the Crusaders advanced towards the city in October 1129 their army was decisively defeated by the Seljuqs. Only Baldwin's authority and military skill ensured that a retreat was carried out in such an orderly manner that the main body of the Knights was saved.

The Franks in *Outremer* were now under considerable pressure from Zenghi, the Emir of Aleppo, who wished to regain the rule of the whole of Syria. Count Bohemond II was killed in battle against the Seljuqs. His wife, Alice, the second daughter of King Baldwin, declared herself Regent of the County of Antioch in defiance of the disapproval of her father who by feudal custom had the right to make the appointment. Although Alice asked Zenghi for his help, when Baldwin and Fulk marched on Antioch, the gates of the city were opened to them, and though Baldwin allowed his daughter to retain Latakia which had been part of her dowry, he appointed himself Regent of Antioch.

It might be appropriate to insert here some comments upon the enthusiasm of the Western nobles and people for the Order of the Temple. It had struck some emotional chord which cannot be explained away by postulating that there had been a subterranean conspiracy – 'a third and secret Order behind the known and documented Orders of the Cistercians and the Temple'. For example a Council held at Toulouse in 1130 had as its sole purpose the raising of funds for the Temple. The extant document, listing the names of forty-five donors, records gifts ranging from the income of Churches to small articles of clothing. The Templars received gifts of castles in Germany (Supplingeburg) and Spain (Barbers and Granena), estates in all parts of France, including lands at Baudimont, Foix, Nice and Dole, and property in England in Buckinghamshire, Essex, Hertfordshire and Lincolnshire.

Bernard's 'Rule' for the Order had become an actuality; local 'Masters of the Temple' were now administering Templar property in Aragon, Germany and England as well as in France, remitting the income to Palestine for the upkeep of their Crusading brethren. It was not only riches which the Order acquired; somehow the idea of the Brethren of the Temple fired the popular imagination. Widowed and childless Knights who lacked any monastic vocation found a role for themselves as members of the '*milice du Christ*' and joined the Order in considerable numbers. It was an adult Order; the absence of women and children may have appealed to many who had had enough of the family distractions of contemporary life, but were unwilling to lay aside their hard-won Knightly skills as they would have had to do if they had entered a monastery. Furthermore it appealed to the ingrained feudal sense; if great men such as Count Fulk of Anjou were among its leaders, there was a social cachet in enrolling under their adopted banner. Finally to people to whom at this time the Gospels were part of their daily lives the opportunity to contribute to the defence of the City and Sepulchre of Christ made a direct appeal. To preserve them from the infidel needed no understanding of theological doctrine. To bequeath money for this clear and uncomplicated purpose provided an obvious passport to salvation in the world to come.

Not only the Templars but also the Hospitallers were becoming to some extent integrated into the military forces at the disposal of the King of Jerusalem. It is a matter of dispute how far the appointment of a 'Constable of the Hospital', a position held four years earlier by Durandus (of whom nothing else is known), indicates that by that time the Hospitallers had adopted a military organisation. Two years later, however, Raymond du Puy himself appears to have been campaigning with King Baldwin II.

After ruling the Kingdom of Jerusalem for thirteen years, in the summer of 1131 King Baldwin II held a Council at which he persuaded the Knights in Jerusalem to accept Fulk, Count of Anjou, and Melisenda as his joint-heirs. He died on 31 August, and Fulk and Melisenda were crowned on 14 September 1131.

Bernard of Clairvaux continued to act as the Templars' advocate when the question was raised of the propriety of a militant Order killing in the name of the Christian Church. In an open letter, *Laude Novae Milites*, Bernard satisfied the critics by making clear the distinction between *homicide*, killing men in secular warfare, and *malicide*, the killing of evil men, infidels, in a Crusade. Thus reassured, donors continued to enrich the Templar Order.

By 1136, the Hospitallers had become as powerful a fighting force as the Templars. The only drawback from the point of view of the King of Jerusalem was that each was responsible only to the Pope; King Fulk had to enlist their support as allies and not as vassals. He entrusted the Hospitallers with the town of Beth-Gibelin on the frontier of the Egyptian Fatimid Khalifate, with the three-fold task of protecting the frontier from Fatimid incursions, protecting the local Frankish settlers from Arab raiders, and providing a base from which the town of Ascalon could be menaced. The Master of the Temple, Hugh de Payens, died in the same year and the Knights elected the Seneschal, the Burgundian Robert de Craon, as their new Master.[8]

In 1137 King Fulk was besieged in the Castle of Montferrand after being defeated by the Seljuq Turks under Zenghi during an expedition to assist Count Raymond III of Tripoli. While the Patriarch William of Jerusalem summoned an army to relieve the King, Fulk asked for terms, and was allowed to return to Jerusalem after surrendering Montferrand. Zenghi was more concerned about a powerful Byzantine army advancing on Antioch. In May 1138 Count Raymond of Antioch could not prevent the Byzantine Emperor John II Comnenus entering his city of Antioch and he had little alternative but to give him his allegiance. By accepting this, John Comnenus in effect proclaimed to the whole Eastern Mediterranean world that Byzantium was still the leading power in the region.

Robert de Craon went to Rome where he held a series of meetings with Pope Innocent II. The upshot was an extraordinary extension of the rights and privileges of the Templars which the Pope set out in a letter dated March 1139. Innocent had the temporal vision to appreciate the powerful weapon which a body of professed Knights could place in the hands of the Church, but he saw that it could only act as such if it were no longer constrained by the demands of the civil powers. In his letter, the Pope removed all these constraints. Not only could no ecclesiastic throughout Christendom demand tithes or taxes from the Templars but they were to be the vassals of no one, Baron, Prince or

Emperor, and no one could require them to do homage for their possessions, or ask them to swear any oath of loyalty. Their spiritual allegiance was to be given only to the Pope; their own Priests would be answerable only to the Master of the Order, free of the jurisdiction of any Bishop, Archbishop or Patriarch in whose diocese they might happen to be. No one but the Pope could challenge the actions of any member of the Order, either in Palestine or in their European daughter-houses – this had important consequences when the existence of the Order was threatened by King Philip of France nearly two hundred years later. Well might Pope Innocent say in the preamble to his letter that he was giving the Templars *omne datum optimum* – the best of everything. There was nothing more that he could have given them.

Raymond of Tripoli was having great difficulty maintaining the frontiers of his County from the Seljuq raiders. Since King Fulk had had to cede to them the Castle of Montferrand, the Seljuqs had the more easily been able to advance along the valley known to the Franks as La Boquée the entrance to which it dominated. There was a danger that communications would be cut between Tripoli and the County of Antioch. So successful had the Hospitallers been in defending the Egyptian frontier that Raymond entrusted them with further responsibility for the defence of his borders. He gave them several castles – Château Boquée, Felice, Lac, and Mardebech, together with the partially constructed Hasn el Akrad, known to the Franks as Krak des Chevaliers.

King Fulk died in 1143 as the result of a hunting accident. His heir was his 13-year old son Baldwin, on whose behalf Melisenda claimed the regency. This arrangement was accepted in Jerusalem but the Counts of Antioch and Edessa, now styling themselves 'Princes', felt no enthusiasm for becoming the vassals of a female, and *Outremer* became somewhat disunited at a time when the growing power of Zenghi should have dictated a policy of unity and co-operation. At the same time, in the Bull *Milites Templi*, Pope Lucius II confirmed all the rights and privileges of the Templars.

While Count Joscelin of Edessa was absent, raiding in the direction of Raqqa, Zenghi appeared outside his city's walls, well equipped with siege engines. In spite of the heroic but misguided defence put up by Archbishop Hugh, the Muslims entered the town and butchered all the Frankish defenders, sparing the Armenians and Byzantines because Zengi's only objective was the expulsion of the Franks from *Outremer*. The Kingdom of Jerusalem was only saved from being over-run by the Muslims by an insurrection breaking out in Zengi's own Emirate of Mosul. Melisenda at once sent an appeal for help to the Western powers, but the gravity of the situation seems at first not to have been fully appreciated.

1.5. THE SECOND CRUSADE (1145-1179)

King Louis VII the Young of France was one of the few Western rulers to appreciate the danger which Zenghi posed to their fellow-countrymen in *Outremer*. He persuaded Bernard of Clairvaux to preach a new Crusade, in which Louis himself proposed to take part; this would set out in the early summer of 1147. Before this could take place the position in *Outremer* was somewhat relieved by the assassination of Zenghi by one of his own slaves on 14 September 1146. Encouraged by this, Count Joscelin attempted to recover his town of Edessa. A relieving army destroyed Joscelin's slender forces, though he himself managed to escape. This time the Muslims left Edessa desolate. Sixteen thousand women and children were carried off as slaves and the city was comprehensively looted. What had been one of the most prosperous cities in the Middle East, and which had stood for two thousand years, was left a deserted ruin.

When Bernard of Clairvaux preached the new Crusade to the German Court at Spiers at Christmas 1146, the German Emperor Conrad announced his own intention of taking part. This was not even a mixed blessing; it meant that the Crusade would have two 'leaders', neither of whom would yield priority to the other.

Affairs in *Outremer* were temporarily quiescent. Archbishop Fulcher of Tyre was elected as the new Patriarch of Jerusalem and King Baldwin III confirmed the grant of lands which Robert de St Gilles had given to the Hospital. Meanwhile, at the invitation of the French King, the Carthusian Pope Eugenius III was touring France preaching the new Crusade. The Byzantine Emperor Comnenus wrote to the Pope welcoming the Crusade provided that those taking part would do homage to him for any lands they recovered.

Once again there were local massacres of Jews as the Crusaders set out by the overland route, the Emperor Conrad leaving in May a month before King Louis. At Metz, Louis was joined by an English and Norman contingent. These were not the only Englishmen who intended to take part in the Crusade. As Louis left on the overland route, a fleet of English, Flemish and Frisian ships left Dartmouth on the long sea-voyage to the Holy Land. (They never reached it; they put in at Porto at the mouth of the River Douro, and they were persuaded to remain to assist with expelling the Moors from Iberia, something which successive Popes had said was of equal crusading merit to the recovery of the Holy Land itself. Many never returned home but settled in Portugal after assisting King Alphonso Henriques to recover his capital city of Lisbon.)

The arrival of the Germans at Constantinople was not altogether a happy one, the gross habits of the German soldiers resulting in Greek monasteries being plundered and brawls, which culminated in the murder of some drunken soldiers, breaking out with their Byzantine escort. This deterioration in local relations was unfortunate for the later French arrivals.

On reaching Constantinople the German leaders refused to take the oath of allegiance to Manuel Comnenus, but in spite of this the Emperor hurried them across the Bosporus before they were reinforced by the French contingent. Without waiting for Louis, Conrad then divided his army into two parts, one of which was led by Bishop Otto of Freisingen, with a strong escort with which to protect the large number of non-combatants, towards Attalia on the southern coast of Asia Minor, while Conrad with the main body of fighting men advanced towards Dorylaeum. Even in hostile territory, he took few precautions, and without outposts or pickets the Crusaders were ambushed by a superior Seljuq force, most of the foot-soldiers being killed or captured, the baggage-train lost, while Conrad and his mounted Knights with difficulty fought their way back to the starting point at Nicaea.

Louis arrived at Constantinople at about the same time as this defeat took place. He also refused to take any oath to Manuel Comnenus but was allowed to cross the Bosporus to Chalcedon, and there found that Manuel would send him no supplies until he received the assurances for which he asked. With his army at the point of starvation, Louis had no alternative but to give the required pledges.

The French King was accompanied by his wife, Eleanor with whom he was infatuated, and her ladies, all of whom appeared to consider the Crusade no more than an enjoyable picnic, wearing white robes in imitation of the Templars.

The French and the remainder of Conrad's army were united at Nicaea. Neither monarch would take orders from the other, so a concerted plan was impossible. However Conrad was ill, and returned to Constantinople, where he became on good terms with Manuel Comnenus. Louis was not going to waste his time fighting the Seljuqs in Asia Minor, and marched south towards Smyrna and Ephesus; the German contingent could do little other than follow him.

Louis had to disperse a Turkish force while crossing the River Meander near Antioch-in-Pisidia; the Byzantine garrison commander not only refused him any support but sheltered the fleeing Turks. Later, discipline broke down while the Crusaders were crossing the Taurus Mountains, and Louis handed over the military command to the French Master of the Temple, Everard de Barres, who managed to re-unite the army by imposing rigid Templar discipline. On their arrival at Attalia, where the French army found Bishop

Otto's German contingent, here again the Byzantine garrison commander would neither let them enter the town, nor give them any supplies. King Louis could do no more than send a strong letter of protest to the Byzantine Emperor. He saw no chance of reaching Jerusalem by land. He embarked a few of the army in what vessels he could find, and, leaving seven thousand men behind under the command of the Count of Flanders, sailed South. On 19 March 1148, a few hundred Knights including the Templar contingent landed at the Port of St Simeon near Antioch-in-*Outremer*.

The Second Crusade was now inexorably moving towards its disastrous conclusion. When further ships arrived at the port of Attalia, the Count of Flanders decided to sail at once with the remainder of the Knights instead of waiting for enough vessels to arrive to transport the whole of his forces as he had been ordered to do. Deserted by their leaders and not unnaturally distrustful of the Byzantines, the foot-soldiers and the unarmed pilgrims who had been left behind set off along the road to Antioch, two hundred miles of rough tracks infested by Turkish raiders. Few of them reached their goal; the only remnant of two great armies which had set out from the West was the few hundred Knights being entertained by Prince Raymond of Antioch, the uncle of Queen Eleanor.

Although the Second Crusade had largely been occasioned by the fall of Edessa there was little enthusiasm for attempting to recapture the town. Prince Raymond suggested an attack on Aleppo – this made some strategic sense for the town would provide protection for the North-east frontier of *Outremer*. However when it was learned that the Emperor Conrad had left Constantinople and was *en route* to Jerusalem by sea, King Louis decided that he must go to the Holy City himself, a decision complicated by his wife Eleanor who was having an incestuous *affaire* with her uncle Raymond whom she refused to leave. When the King insisted that she should accompany him, Raymond refused to let his Knights accompany the party.

Louis and Conrad met in Jerusalem in May 1148. A Council decided to attack Damascus, a poor decision by inexperienced campaigners in *Outremer*, for the town offered the Franks little military advantage, and its Emir, Umur, was tolerant of them. There was some slight chance of success, however. The army which advanced towards the town was the largest body of Frankish Knights yet assembled in Palestine. An immediate surprise attack when the vanguard reached Damascus on 24 July might have succeeded although Noor al-Deen, the son of Zenghi, was marching to its relief, Conrad had already decided that when captured it should be the fief of the Count of Flanders – counting their chickens before the eggs were even laid was a besetting fault of the Crusaders. But those who had been long-settled in *Outremer* had no wish to fight to enrich a Fleming. So deep was the division that Louis and

Conrad decided to retire before Noor al-Deen arrived. Seljuqs harassed the knights all the way to Jerusalem, many being killed. This rout, for such it was, deepened the divide between those settled in *Outremer* and those who had recently arrived there. Then the Templars, of all people, were accused of having initiated the retreat and betrayed the Crusaders' cause – the extensive privileges which they had been given by the Pope had hardly made them popular. It was even said that they had received a large bribe from the Emir of Damascus if they abandoned the assault. The unhappy Second Crusade broke up with Christian fighting Christian – Bertrand of Toulouse attacking Raymond of Tripoli whom he blamed for the death of his father, Count Alphonse Jourdain. Raymond sought the help not only of the Emir Umur but even of Noor al-Deen, who overwhelmed Bertrand and his Knights and carried them off as slaves to be sold in the market at Aleppo.

After those Crusaders who had no wish to settle in *Outremer* had gone home to their Western fiefs, fighting continued sporadically on the frontiers of the Kingdom of Jerusalem, so-called. On 29 July 1149 the army of Prince Raymond of Antioch was defeated and subsequently massacred by the Seljuqs at Murad near Afamiya; Raymond's skull, mounted in silver was sent to the Khalif in Baghdad. King Baldwin III assumed the Regency of Antioch until Raymond's son should be of age.

Robert de Craon, the Master of the Temple, had died earlier in the year and was succeeded by Everard de Barres who had led the French Templar reinforcements to *Outremer*. In 1152 Everard resigned and retired to France to live as a simple monk, being succeeded in Jerusalem by Bernard de Trémélai. In the summer of 1152 the Seljuqs prepared to attack Jerusalem while Bernard and King Baldwin III were unsuccessfully attempting to recover Tripoli and Nablus from Noor al-Deen, but were dispersed by the Templar garrison which had been left in the town. It is said that more than 5,000 Turks were drowned attempting to retreat across the River Jordan.

In the following year King Baldwin III laid siege to Ascalon. Everard de Barres stormed a breach in the walls at the head of thirty-nine Templar Knights, but refused to allow others to enter because he wanted the town for the Templars. His force was overcome by the defenders and all forty Knights were hung from the ramparts. André de Montbard was subsequently elected as Master of the Temple.

In 1154, Noor al-Deen captured Damascus from the Emir Umur, and the forces opposing the Frankish occupation of *Outremer* were at last united under a single leader. That this did not lead to the immediate expulsion of the Franks was largely because many of the Crusader Barons had entered into truces with their neighbouring Emirs with whom they then lived in considerable harmony as a landlord in the West would have lived with his neighbours. Christian

Baron and Muslim Emir would hunt together and sometimes hold a joint feast after the chase. In their way of life the settlers in *Outremer* began to adopt many Oriental customs, for example wearing Eastern robes. Several of their womenfolk adopted the veil, giving as an excuse that this protected their complexions from the sun. Be that as it may, the practice saved Muslim embarrassment when the frequent visits were exchanged.

In 1157, the young Prince Raymond of Antioch captured and fortified the northern frontier fortresses of Baghras and Gaston. Noor al-Deen besieged Baghras, King Baldwin and Bertrand de Blanquefort, now Master of the Temple, marched to its relief, and were defeated by the Seljuqs. Three hundred Templars were killed and eighty-eight, including Bertrand, were taken prisoner.

In the following year King Baldwin defeated Noor al-Deen in the North of the country, achieving little militarily, but considerably restoring the morale of the Franks. An expeditionary force sent across the frontier into Egypt was however defeated near Gaza.

King Baldwin III died in Beirut on 19 February 1162. Childless, Baldwin, was succeeded by his younger brother Amalric or Amaury.

In 1164, Noor al-Deen decided that the time had come to recover Egypt. He sent an army commanded by Shirk-uh, whose second-in-Command was the twenty-five year-old Salah al-Deen, known in the West as Saladin. Having defeated the Egyptian army at Bilbeis, they advanced on Cairo and deposed the Egyptian ruler Dirgham, but were unable to capture the citadel. The Wazeer, Shawar, appealed for help to King Amalric. Amalric had no wish to see Egypt under Seljuq rule and responded to Shawar's appeal. Together they besieged Bilbeis into which Shirk-uh had retired. Noor al-Deen set out to relieve the town, defeating on the way the armies of Constantinople and of Antioch which for once had joined forces. Amalric had to raise the siege of Bilbeis because he could not leave Jerusalem open to the advance of Noor al-Deen. Amalric signed a truce with Shirk-uh, and the two armies marched North apparently in perfect amity. Saladin met Frankish Knights for the first time and seems to have had much in common with them.

The Sunni, Noor al-Deen, again attempted to regain Egypt for the Baghdad Khalifate in January 1167. Shawar again appealed for help to King Amalric who marched to Cairo at the head of a large force which included both Templars and Hospitallers. Astonishingly, the Military Orders, whose only *raison d'être* was to drive the infidel out of the Holy Land, were preparing to support a Fatimid Khalif against his Sunni rival. Shirk-uh with two thousand men made a wide circuit to the East to avoid interception by the Franks, and crossed the Nile forty miles South of Cairo. After a minor engagement, in the spring of 1167 Shirk-uh marched North to Alexandria where he appointed Saladin

Governor. He then again marched South to Upper Egypt to recruit reinforcements while Amalric laid siege to Alexandria on the strong walls of which his siege engines made little impression. Amalic had earlier made an alliance with the Italian naval city of Pisa to which he had assigned land in Tyre for the use of their merchants, and the Pisan fleet now blockaded the seaward side of Alexandria. Shirk-uh returned and laid siege to Cairo. The consequent stalemate led to another Truce being signed, the basis of which was that both Franks and Turks should leave Egypt. In addition, the Franks were to receive an annual tribute of one hundred thousand gold pieces from the Egyptians. While the arrangements for the evacuation were being completed Saladin stayed in the Frankish camp both as a hostage and as an honoured guest. He again found that he had much in common with the Christian Knights in the matter of their chivalrous code of honour, and while there is no reliable evidence that while in the Frankish camp Saladin was Knighted by Humphrey de Toron, there is nothing inherently impossible in this story.

Meanwhile the Hospitallers were strengthening their roots in *Outremer*. In January 1166, Prince Bohemond III of Antioch granted their English Master, Gilbert de Assailly, the first Estates which the Order held as a territorial sovereign without the obligation to render feudal dues or duty for them. Acre was now the administrative capital of the Kingdom of Jerusalem, and King Amalric, anxious to maintain his alliance with the Pisans, gave them the same rights there as those that they enjoyed in Tyre. The fragile peace in *Outremer* was interrupted in the summer of 1168, when, although no formal Crusade had been declared, the Count of Nevers arrived in the country with a large force of Crusaders. Having left their wives and families at home they did not wish to sit idly by for a year until perhaps another assault on Egypt might take place. Gilbert d'Assailly proposed that this should be undertaken immediately. All that need be said is that the campaign proved an unmitigated disaster in the course of which Shawar burnt Cairo to the ground in a fire which raged for nearly two months to prevent it falling into the hands of the Franks. The Franks had to retire to Jerusalem in the face of a superior relieving force led by Shirk-uh and Saladin. When Shirk-uh died, Saladin was appointed the Viceroy in Egypt of the Sunni Khalif in Baghdad

In October 1169, yet another attack, this time a combined Frankish and Byzantine expedition, was launched against Egypt. With incompetent leadership this also proved a disaster.

When Gilbert d'Assailly died in 1170, he was succeeded as Master of the Hospital by Caste du Morois. King Amalric gave the Order further extensive Estates on his Northern borders, wishing to see them as a bulwark against not only the Muslims, but also any attempt by Manuel Comnenus to recover his former Provinces.

King Amalric died on 11 July 1174. His dubiously accepted successor was his 13-year-old son, Baldwin, who was a leper. No Regent was appointed, but the government was carried out by a Frenchman, Miles de Plessey, who had been King Amalric's Seneschal. When Saladin prepared to advance into *Outremer*, the longer-established Frankish Baronial families, Arabic-speaking and living in harmony with their neighbours, would not accept Miles de Plessey as their leader and Count Raymond III of Tripoli assumed the Office of Regent, because the leper boy-King Baldwin IV was unable to father children. In 1175, the Italian Baron, the Marquis of Montferrat, was sent for to marry Baldwin's sister Sibylla, and thereby in time to become the ruler in Jerusalem.

In 1177, Saladin's advance on Jerusalem began, but King Baldwin, ill, perhaps even dying, but now ruling in his own right, lacked nothing in spirit. He led five hundred Knights in a charge which dispersed Saladin's forces. Instead of pursuing Saladin at once, Baldwin marched north to Ibelin where he reinforced his army with the Knights there, and only then attacked Saladin's advancing forces, perhaps five times as numerous as his own. He outflanked them, surprised them while they were crossing a gorge, and they fled back to Egypt, Saladin himself only escaping on a racing camel.

With the position temporarily stabilised, both Military Orders came under stern criticism from Pope Alexander III who accused both of them of being more interested in accumulating wealth than in fighting the infidel or caring for the poor and needy. The two Orders had indeed for some time been exercising a jealous rivalry. The unintended effect of the Pope's letter to the two Masters, Odo de St Amand of the Temple, and Roger des Moulins of the Hospital, was to bring about a *rapprochement* between them and for them to sign a pact announcing their intention of working together as the single most important force in *Outremer*, and no longer opposing each other in the Council of Jerusalem.

When the Masters had received the Pope's letter, work had been proceeding on another of the stone-built castles, Chastelet, which dominated a ford in the River Jordan to the South of Armenia in country which it had been agreed in a treaty between King Baldwin III and Saladin should be demilitarised. The Templars said that they were not a party to the Treaty. Chastelet was occupied in April 1179 by 50 Templar Knights and 1,500 mercenaries commanded by the Seneschal of the Order. A first assault by Saladin was unsuccessful, but then he was able to rout the army of Jerusalem in a surprise attack after which he returned to the siege of Chastelet. This time his engines breached the walls, and it was captured on 29 August 1179, all the defenders, whom Saladin considered were in breach of the Treaty, being killed, and the castle razed to the ground. In the following year there was a serious drought, and a general truce, to last for two years, was agreed. While this endured Saladin re-built Cairo.

The truce was prematurely brought to an end when Raymond de Chatillon robbed a peaceful caravan on its way from Mecca to Damascus. Saladin retaliated by marching on Jerusalem. The Frankish army halted him near the Castle of Belvoir, and Saladin retired – his principal interest at this time was not expelling the Franks but seeking greater authority from the Khedive in Baghdad.

1.6 THE THIRD CRUSADE (1183-1197)

For the time being Saladin was experiencing too much trouble from his own Emirs whole-heartedly to turn to attack the Franks. Mosul and Aleppo declared their independence from his rule. While Saladin led the Egyptian Army to their recovery, King Baldwin, desperately ill though he was, led the Army of Jerusalem to the walls of Damascus, plundering Muslim towns on the way. The King was now in the last stages of his debilitating illness. He appointed Guy de Lusignan as his Regent, a man whose only supporters were the Patriarch Heraclius and the Masters of the two Military Orders. Guy's evident incompetence led to his deposition and King Baldwin's nephew, also named Baldwin, was acknowledged as his heir. For the time being King Baldwin resumed the rule of the Kingdom from his sick bed, in spite of Guy's continued support from the Masters of the two Orders. King Baldwin had little option but to banish them both from his Court where they were undermining his authority.

Reynold de Chatillon then tried his hand at dynastic diplomacy in an attempt to unite the Franks of *Outremer*. He arranged for Humphrey de Toron to marry Isabella, a daughter of Queen Maria, the ceremony, attended by the leading figures in *Outremer*, taking place in the great Castle of Kerak at the moment which Saladin chose to besiege the Castle, bombarding it with his heavy siege engines. With King Baldwin carried in a litter – the King lacked nothing in spirit – the Army of Jerusalem led by Count Raymond of Tripoli marched to the relief of Kerak, Saladin withdrawing, unwilling to be caught between the advancing army and the immensely strong fortifications. Raymond then persuaded the Patriarch Heraclius and the Masters of the two Orders to go to Europe to ask for reinforcements for *Outremer*.

The German Emperor Frederick I Barbarossa and Pope Lucius met the delegation from *Outremer* at Verona in September 1184. The Pope's first action was to write a series of letters to Saladin asking him, not unexpectedly with no success, to release his Christian prisoners. Arnold de Terroge died in Verona on the last day of the month. When the news reached Jerusalem, the Templars elected the Seneschal, Gerard de Ridefort, as their new Master, an unfortunate choice as Raymond of Tripoli, the *de facto* Commander of the Royal Army, some years earlier had been bribed to prevent Gerard marrying his intended bride, Lucia de Botrom. Unity was now more than ever necessary. The Byzantine Emperor Andronicus I Comnenus had made a Treaty with Saladin in which he promised to give the Franks of *Outremer* no military help. However, Mosul was still holding out against Saladin who then fell ill. Thus, when King Baldwin the Leper died on 16 March 1185 and his seven-year old nephew was crowned as Baldwin V, Raymond, whom King Baldwin IV had insisted should be Regent for his nephew, was able to conclude a four-year Truce with Saladin.

The delegation seeking help for *Outremer* went to England where they met King Henry II at Reading. The King gave his permission for any of his subjects who wished to take the Cross to do so, but made it clear that he did not propose to lead a Crusade, an example followed shortly afterwards by the French King Louis Augustus.

King Baldwin V of Jerusalem died at Acre at the end of August 1186 shortly before his ninth birthday. Matters became confused. A Council was called at Tiberias, the capital of Raymond of Tripoli, rather than at Jerusalem so as to avoid interference from the dissolute Patriarch Heraclius. While the Templars escorted the dead King's body to Jerusalem, Joscelin de Courtenay occupied Acre with his own troops, proclaimed Sibylla as Queen of Jerusalem, and set off with her for the City, arriving before Raymond of Tripoli realised what had been done behind his back. Heraclius crowned Sibylla who then crowned her husband Guy de Lusignan. It was said that when she did so, Gerard de Ridefort cried out 'The marriage of Lucia de Botrum is paid for by the Crown'. Raymond of Tripoli refused to accept Sibylla as his Queen and retired to his wife's estates in Galilee, where he made a treaty with Saladin that its neutrality should be respected. Many Knights, including Baldwin of Ibelin, Balian's younger brother, took refuge with Count Bohemond III in Antioch. At a time when Saladin, recovered from his illness, had subjugated Mosul and now ruled from the Euphrates to the Nile, *Outremer* was divided as it had never been divided before.

Reynald de Chatillon had retired to Kerak, again unable to accept that the four-year truce with Saladin should in any way restrain his own greed. At the end of 1186 he once more plundered a caravan passing the fortress. He killed the escort and imprisoned the merchants and their families. Saladin exhibited his own sense of honour, by first sending a note to Reynald requesting the return of the captives instead of himself breaking the truce by attacking Kerak. He also wrote to King Guy in Jerusalem asking him to restrain his vassal; only when Guy replied regretting his inability to do so did Saladin prepare to renew the war in *Outremer*. Raymond asked Saladin to respect his County of Tripoli saying that the matter was nothing to do with him. Nothing could have suited Saladin better, and in addition he proposed that when he had defeated Guy, Raymond should become King of the Franks.

In spite of this, Guy was persuaded to send a deputation to Raymond of Tripoli to persuade him to support the common cause against the Muslims. Gerard de Ridefort grudgingly agreed to accompany the Archbishop of Tyre and Roger des Moulins. They left Jerusalem on 29 April 1187 accompanied by one hundred and thirty Knights of the two Orders. The next day, having been joined by forty further Knights, on surmounting the hill beyond Nazareth, they saw Saladin, taking advantage of the neutrality he had arranged with Raymond, at the head of a reconnaissance force of more than seven thousand men. The Frankish Knights made a foolhardy charge down the hill – nothing in their oaths bound them to fight against odds of thirty or forty to one – and only Gerard de Ridefort and two Knights escaped the carnage at the Falls of Cresson. (The Archbishop had remained in Nazareth to celebrate the Feast of Saints Philip and James.) The only good things which came out of this massacre were that Raymond of Tripoli transferred his allegiance to King Guy, and Reynald restrained his greed, abstaining from attacking a caravan escorted by Saladin himself.

King Guy was able to recruit more mercenaries as reinforcements to help meet the expected Muslim attack. He assembled some 13,000 fighting men at Acre including more than a 1,000 Knights and 2,000 other mounted soldiers. Saladin's army was advancing in three columns. One occupied Raymond's capital, Tiberias, where the citadel was held by his wife Sibylla, Raymond himself being with Guy in Acre. Raymond had proposed allowing Saladin to advance without interference across arid country where he would find difficulty in obtaining water for his troops, but Guy was determined to take some action and advanced to the oasis at Sephoria, not far from the Falls of Cresson. Against Raymond's advice, Gerard de Ridefort persuaded Guy to advance to the relief of Tiberias. As he did so, Saladin moved to another oasis, ten miles distant from Sephoria, at Hattin, nestling under a hill known as 'The Horns of Hattin', the traditional site of the Sermon on the Mount. On the morning of 4 July 1187 the Franks found themselves surrounded and suffering heavy casualties from the Muslim arrows. By the end of the day the rearguard on the hill was overwhelmed and the King, Gerard de Ridefort, Reynald de Chatillon and a hundred knights of the two Orders captured. The Knights were cut to pieces where they stood, Reynald de Chatillon was beheaded by Saladin who had sworn to do this himself, and only King Guy, Gerard de Ridefort, and the land-owning Barons were held for ransom. All other prisoners were sent back to Damascus for sale as slaves. The disaster at the Horns of Hattin was complete. Not only this, but the citadel of Tiberias fell on the following day.

The siege of Jerusalem began on 20 September 1187. By the end of the month the Muslim siege-engines had breached the walls. By 2 October terms for a honourable surrender were negotiated, all the Franks were expelled, and those who could pay no ransom were sent to Damascus for sale as slaves.

Saladin's first act was to cleanse '*The Dome of the Rock*' from Christian pollution. However he not only allowed the Church of the Holy Sepulchre to remain intact but acceded to a request from the Byzantine Emperor Isaac II Angelus to allow Byzantines to be its guardians, well aware of the further rift which this would cause between the Eastern and Western Christians.

Then, leaving the strong citadel of Jerusalem invested, well-knowing that in due course it would be starved into surrender, Saladin turned West to recover the sea-port towns. He captured Acre on 14 July 1187. By early August all the coastal towns had fallen with the exception of Tyre and Tripoli. While the remaining strong points sent delegations to Europe urgently requesting assistance, Saladin now adopted the economical tactic of demanding him surrender of various Frankish castles in exchange for high-ranking prisoners whom he held. The Templar fortress of Gaza was exchanged for the Master of the Temple, Gerard de Ridefort. The price of the release of King Guy of Lusignan was Ascalon itself, the garrison of which at first refused to obey the command to surrender. However they made terms with Saladin on 4 September 1187 and were allowed to march to Alexandria from which they were repatriated by the Venetian fleet. Of all the more southerly coastal strongholds, only Tyre now remained in Frankish hands.

When Saladin tried to implement his policy of exchange for the Crusading fortresses in the South-east, he met with less success. He arranged with Stephanie 'the Lady of *Oultrejourdain*' (that is, *Outremer* on the east side of the River Jordan) that she should surrender Montreal and Kerak in exchange for her son, Humphrey de Toron. The garrisons refused to obey her commands, and Saladin had to capture the fortresses by force of arms.

In November 1187, Saladin turned his attention to Tyre whose defender, Conrad of Montferrat, had lost no time in strengthening the defences. With his well-equipped siege-train, Saladin encamped on the landward side of the town while his fleet blockaded the seaward side.

The news of the fall of Jerusalem aroused Europe in a way which the earlier delegations had failed to achieve. Unfortunately, in spite of the urgency of the call for reinforcements, most of the Western European Rulers were too involved with their own affairs to take immediate action. For example, King Henry II of England and King Philip Augustus of France were still distracted by the desultory war in which they had been engaged for several years. One of the few who had no such distractions was Duke Richard of Aquitaine, the eldest son of King Henry of England. A new Crusade was a cause which made a genuine appeal to his flamboyant militancy. His only disquiet was the favour which his father was showing to his younger brother, John.

The shock of learning of the fall of Jerusalem had also caused the premature death of Pope Gregory VIII. Bishop Paul Scolari was elected to succeed him as Pope Clement III and he was Consecrated in the Cathedral of Pisa on 20 December 1187. His first concern was to come to an agreement with the now dominant Senate of the Roman Republic for the Headquarters of the Papacy to return once more to Rome.

In the meantime, Saladin continued the siege of Tyre while detachments of his army dealt with the last of the Christian outposts. Kerak, the former headquarters of the dead Reynald de Chatillon, was captured and all its defenders killed. Count Raymond of Tripoli died before the end of the year. His heir was the young son of Bohemond III of Antioch; for the time being, Saladin respected the neutrality of the County of Tripoli.

At the end of December the defenders of Tyre repulsed a major landward attack, while at the same time Saladin's fleet suffered a defeat at the harbour mouth at the hands of a fleet which had been sent by King William of Sicily, one of the few to respond to the calls for assistance. However, the unhealthy coastal plain was beginning to take its toll of Saladin's army and on 1 January 1188 Saladin raised the siege of Tyre and marched eastwards.

Archbishop Josias of Tyre, the delegate from *Outremer*, met the Kings of England and France at Gisors, and persuaded them, together with Count Philip of Flanders, to join together in a new Crusade. The English, French, and Flemings would unite to form a single army distinguished only by wearing respectively white, green and red crosses. To finance the operation Henry imposed a 'Saladin Tithe' of ten per cent on both income and movables of every one of his lay subjects on both sides of the Channel.

Pope Clement sent Legates to every warring city in Europe exhorting them to lay aside their differences in view of the urgent need to recapture Jerusalem. The German Emperor Frederick Barbarossa responded to the Pope's pleas by taking the Cross at Mainz on 27 March 1188 and later entering into an alliance with the French King. However in spite of his initial enthusiasm, Richard of Aquitaine was now detained by a dispute with Count Raymond of Toulouse. In the meantime Saladin was making progress in his recovery of *Outremer*. One by one he was overcoming Bohemond's strong-points in the County of Antioch until eventually the Count made a truce with him by which Saladin agreed to respect his ownership of no more than the city of Antioch itself and its Port of Saint Symeon.

There were few Templar Knights now still alive in *Outremer*. On his release, the Master of the Temple, Gerard de Ridefort, had gone to Tyre where he insisted on taking over the command of the few survivors from Terric, the Preceptor of Jerusalem. He then refused to take orders from Conrad of Montferrat who was conducting a vigorous and competent defence.

Saladin was behaving towards his noble prisoners with every sign of chivalrous courtesy. Although Montreal and Kerak had not been surrendered and had to be stormed by Saladin's troops, he returned Humphrey de Toron to his mother Stephanie, 'the Lady of *Oultrejourdain*'. Neither had Ascalon obeyed the order to surrender which Sibylla had given, but in July 1188 Saladin restored to her King Guy de Lusignan, her husband, on condition that he swore to return to the West, never again to fight the Muslims. Having sworn, Guy, together with Amalric the Constable and nine other nobles, was allowed to join Sibylla in Tripoli, the defences of which had been reinforced by several hundred Knights who had been brought there by the Sicilian fleet which had earlier defeated Saladin's ships outside Tyre. At the same time the elderly Marquis of Montferrat was allowed to join his son, Conrad, in Tyre.

Some commentators have considered that Saladin acted through enlightened self-interest, calculating that the presence of the returned prisoners would stir up dissension both in Tripoli and in Tyre. Guy soon received Absolution from his Oath; Saladin could hardly have expected him to do otherwise, but he may have thought that the presence of the less than competent Guy would be more of a hindrance than a help to the Franks. Guy insisted on resuming his Crown, which Conrad of Montferrat and his followers considered that he had already forfeited by his defeat at Hattin, his captivity, and his Oath. Intentionally or not, Saladin had effectively split loyalties within the Frankish camp. Even so, the position of the Franks in *Outremer* had become slightly less desperate provided that help arrived from the West while they retained their hold on Antioch, Tyre and Tripoli.

Guy de Lusignan felt impelled to take further action while Saladin was occupied with affairs in the North and in Baghdad. Guy marched south to Tyre where Conrad refused to allow him to enter the city, and Guy had to camp outside its walls. To break the *impasse* and to capture a city from which he could rule, Guy left Tyre, together with Gerard de Rideford, having assembled a force of perhaps 700 Knights and 9,000 foot-soldiers to besiege Acre from the landward side while the combined Sicilian and Pisan fleets blockaded the city from the sea. The Pisans, who had sent ships to the East in support of their old ally, Conrad of Montferrat, were not only renowned sailors, but also well-known for their engineering skills in constructing siege-engines. The siege began on 27 August 1189 Saladin, who was besieging the castle of Beaufort, sent a small force to the relief of Acre. It had to camp in the malaria-infested coastal marshes, being unable to dislodge the besiegers from their more healthy position on the Hill of Turon a mile from the city.

After King Richard's Coronation in London on 3 September 1189 he wasted little time in settling outstanding matters at home, using every means in his power to obtain further money with which to finance a Crusade.

Reinforcements for the Franks were now reaching *Outremer* by sea in ever-increasing numbers. A German and an Italian contingent landed at Tyre. When they went south to assist in the siege of Acre, Conrad of Montferrat agreed to accompany them provided that he did not have to take orders from Guy de Lusignan. Saladin now left only a small force to invest Beaufort, and himself marched to relieve the siege of Acre, but was unable to drive Guy de Lusignan from the Hill of Turon. Gerard de Ridefort was again taken prisoner, and this time he was executed. Saladin, in poor health, withdrew most of his army.

In the meantime, the German Emperor, Frederick Barbarossa, was leading his Crusading army to the East by the overland route. As far as Belgrade he had no problems but he had to force his way through Bulgaria. The Byzantine Emperor Isaac Angelus mistrusted his actions, but eventually made a pact with Frederick that if he would by-pass Constantinople, Isaac Angelus would transport him across the Bosporus and provide supplies for the march through Anatolia.

While Frederick delayed in winter-quarters in Adrianople, still further reinforcements had reached *Outremer*, now including contingents from Flanders, Italy, Denmark and Hungary, and these enabled the investment of Acre to be completed. Saladin had also obtained reinforcements. At the end of October fifty Muslim galleys broke through the blockading Frankish fleet and brought much-needed supplies to Acre.

The German Emperor crossed the Bosporus and resumed his march south. He reached Laodicea by 27 April 1190, after which the flanks and rearguard of the German army were severely harassed by the Seljuq tribesmen. By 10 June 1190 the Crusaders, sweltering in the summer heat in the Cilician Plain, were preparing to cross the River Calycadmus. Having galloped far ahead of his bodyguard it is uncertain whether Frederick's horse stumbled, or whether he deliberatively plunged into the cool water in full armour, but he had drowned before assistance arrived.

The Kings of England and of France had not sufficiently set to rights affairs in their respective Kingdoms to be ready to depart for *Outremer* before 4 July 1190 when King Philip Augustus of France and King Richard of England greeted each other in the great Cathedral at Vézélay; this was even later than had originally been planned but at the last moment all had to be postponed again because of the death in March of Philip's wife, Isabel of Flanders. The following day their combined armies marched to Lyons, after which Philip led the French contingent to Genoa, and Richard the English and Norman forces to Marseilles, at which ports each contingent would respectively embark and sail to a rendezvous at Messina, to which Richard, a bad sailor, travelled by land.

Discouraged by the death of their Emperor many of the German Crusaders returned home. His son, Duke Frederick of Swabia, himself in poor health, struggled on with those who were prepared to prosecute the Crusade. The army suffered heavy casualties traversing the Pass of the Syrian Gates. It was only the remnant of the great German Crusading army which had reached Antioch on 21 June 1190 where they were warmly received by Prince Bohemond III; Conrad of Montferrat also came north to greet the Duke. The corpse of Barbarossa was buried in Antioch Cathedral, and with it the morale of the German army.

During the summer, too impatient to await the measured advance of the English and French Kings, several Nobles from France and Burgundy sailed to Tyre together with their followers. It is said that these amounted to as many as ten thousand more mouths to feed which created considerable problems in provisioning the Frankish garrison. The Castle of Beaufort fell to Saladin in July, and its besiegers rejoined the main body of the Muslims outside Acre.

While his army was sailing from Marseilles, King Richard of England, accompanied by a small escort, made his way overland to Messina where he rejoined the English contingent on its arrival. He was reunited with King Philip at Messina on 15 September. Here matters were far from amicable. Richard was engaged in a furious quarrel with King Tancred of Sicily who had detained his sister Joanna. Richard occupied the town, over which he hoisted his standard, allowing that of King Philip to be flown alongside it. Matters were only partially resolved by the release of Joanna and Tancred's offer of twenty thousand ounces of gold in satisfaction of all Richard's demands. Richard, to whom money was the one cure for all ills, accepted this offer together with a promise that his nephew Prince Arthur of Brittany should be betrothed to one of Tancred's daughters.

All this was a long way from a Crusade to recover Jerusalem. King Philip, in spite of his dislike of Richard, was however extraordinarily conciliatory and amenable. On 8 October he met Richard to arrange the details of the forthcoming campaign. In spite of Philip's long-standing wish that Richard should marry his sister Alice, he accepted that Richard should instead marry Berengaria of Navarre; the English Queen-Dowager, Eleanor, was asked to bring her to Sicily.

The besiegers of Acre were enduring considerable hardships while the English and French armies were enjoying a relatively comfortable time in Sicily. Here a formal Treaty between Richard and Tancred was signed on 11 November 1190, and sent to the Pope for approval. Outside Acre further reinforcements had increased the strength of Saladin whose supply lines were open. On the other hand he was preventing further food-supplies reaching the Franks. Supplies for them could not be landed on the open beaches during the winter storms, but the defenders of Acre were better placed as occasional supply-ships managed to enter the harbour. Two of the leaders of the besiegers were among those who died in early January 1191: Thibaud of Blois and the

German, Frederick of Swabia. For the time being, Saladin was content to let disease and starvation do his work for him; horses of the Christian Knights, ill-supplied with fodder, were daily being slaughtered for food.

This situation was in stark contrast to the lives of the Crusaders in Sicily where King Richard had given a Christmas banquet; in the following month tournaments were organised. However, in the spring, although Saladin had despatched a column which was able to force its way into Acre to reinforce the defenders, the situation of the besiegers was improving; a corn ship had safely unloaded its supplies on the beaches, and Leopold of Austria had arrived accompanied by soldiers from the Rhineland, thus providing a leader for the remnant of Barbarossa's former army.

Pope Clement died at the end of March 1191 and the 85-year old Cardinal Hyacinth Bobo was elected to succeed him, taking the style of Celestine III.

King Richard had now become the firm ally of King Tancred of Sicily, somewhat to the chagrin of King Philip who sailed with his army from Messina on 30 March 1191. A few days later the English Queen-mother arrived in Messina with Berengaria. King Richard sailed on 10 April 1191, accompanied by Berengaria, chaperoned by Richard's sister Joanna.

King Philip arrived off Acre on 20 April, and after disembarking he found himself on excellent terms with his cousin Conrad of Montferrat. They decided to defer any assault until Richard arrived, building new siege-engines in the meantime. King Richard was encountering storms unlike the fair weather from which King Philip had profited. His fleet had to take shelter, first in the lee of Crete, and then anchor off the Island of Rhodes for ten days. Here they learned that three ships, including that carrying Berengaria and Joanna, had arrived off Cyprus which was governed by a Byzantine adventurer, Isaac Ducas Comnenus, who looted the ships and imprisoned the passengers and crews.

Richard, weak from sea sickness, sailed at once for Cyprus, reaching the island on 8 May. Isaac would do no more than release Berengaria and Joanna. The still-queasy Richard had to land with a small force of Knights to attempt to obtain the submission of Isaac Comnenus.

The strong alliance between Philip of France and Conrad of Montserrat alarmed Guy de Lusignan, who sailed to Cyprus accompanied by Bohemond III of Antioch and Humphrey de Toron and a small Templar escort. King Richard agreed to support Guy de Lusignan on condition that he first assisted him to capture the Island of Cyprus. On 12 May Richard married Berengaria and she was crowned Queen of England in the Church of St George at Limassol by the Norman Bishop of Evreux. On the following day, the rest of the English ships having arrived, King Richard and his new found ally began the invasion of Cyprus. While they were occupying Famagusta, messengers arrived from Philip of France asking Richard to leave Cyprus and join him as soon as possible. The hot-tempered Richard saw this as his being sent orders by Philip whom he would not recognise as his superior and he angrily refused to abandon the subjection of Cyprus. In his reply he emphasised the strategic value of Cyprus to the Crusaders, an assessment fully borne out by future events.

Richard's superior forces defeated Isaac Comnenus at Tremithus. Isaac withdrew to his northern fortress of Kantara, encouraged because Richard was still suffering from his sea sickness. However, Guy de Lusignan took command, captured Kyrenia where he took Isaac's wife and daughter prisoner, and laid siege to two more of Isaac's northern castles, upon which Isaac surrendered unconditionally.

Recovered from his sickness, Richard reorganised the government of the island, laid a capital levy of half of their goods on its Byzantine inhabitants, and placed English garrisons in all their castles. He appointed two Justiciars to govern the island as his fief. This was disturbing news for Constantinople. Cyprus was a Byzantine Province; what further annexation might this new powerful army of Crusaders carry out?

The subjection of Cyprus being accomplished, King Richard and Guy de Lusignan arrived off Tyre on 6 June 1191. Conrad of Montferrat had ordered his garrison to refuse to allow them to land, and they sailed on to Acre, landing on the open beach having sunk a Muslim supply-vessel on the way. Isaac Comnenus was handed over to the Master of the Hospital, Garnier de Nablus, the former Prior of the English Province, to be confined in their fortress of Margat. Once more debilitated by sea sickness, Richard caught one of the Levantine fevers.

Partially recovered, Richard was persuaded to try to negotiate with Saladin for the return of Jerusalem on condition that the Crusaders left his other territories intact. Saladin rejected this approach, reminding Richard that he was the junior partner in the expedition. But in any case Richard was now too ill to negotiate with anyone. King Philip, whose popularity with the soldiery was much less than that of Richard, tried to re-establish himself by attacking Acre while Richard was too ill to take part in the action. Perhaps it was Philips leadership which was inadequate; the defenders jeered as the Franks retired and they destroyed the new siege-engines with 'Greek fire'.[9] That Saladin did not follow up this repulse was probably due to his forces equally suffering from the discomfort and disease in the coastal plain.

No new Master of the Temple had been elected since the death of de Ridefort; none of the surviving band of Knights appeared to be of sufficient eminence to replace him. King Richard had been accompanied to the East by his vassal, Robert de Sablé, a widower with estates in Anjou. The Templars awarded him the unusual distinction of inviting him to join the Order, and, on his acceptance, at once electing him their eleventh Master.

In early July 1191 there were inconclusive attacks and counter-attacks between besiegers, besieged, and Saladin's forces outside the besiegers. The defenders of Acre sent a message to Saladin that they were on the point of capitulation, but there was no more that he could do to help them. Richard had used his engineers to mine under one of the towers of the fortress. It was now King Philip who was far from well. Without consulting him, Richard started the assault on 11 July. A breach was opened and on the next day the garrison commander asked for terms. The defenders were allowed to leave with nothing except the clothes in which they stood up. They had to agree that Muslim prisoners were to be ransomed for two hundred thousand pieces of gold, fifteen hundred Christian slaves and a hundred named persons were to be released by Saladin, and a piece of the True Cross, captured at Hattin, was to be returned. All this was agreed in the name of Saladin but without his knowledge or consent, but his sense of honour was such that he considered himself bound by the conditions which his Emirs had made in his name.

The defenders were allowed to march out of Acre without interference. King Philip occupied the old Templar headquarters; King Richard installed Berengaria and Joanna in the Royal Palace. Frederick of Swabia being dead, Duke Leopold V of Austria commanded the German forces and demanded that his flag should fly alongside those of Philip and Richard. Richard saw no need for this, and with his usual lack of foresight had it torn down and thrown into the '*jacques*', the public latrine. Furious, Duke Leopold at once left Acre with all his men and returned home.

Before the campaign started, Philip and Richard had agreed to divide any territorial gains between them. This angered the Templars who wanted their property in Acre restored. A further difficulty was that it was not easily possible to say whether the prisoners and slaves to be returned under the terms of the Agreement were still alive; Saladin was granted more time to discharge this part of the agreement.

The victors of Acre were coming to various political arrangements, most of which were not wholly acceptable to all parties. It was agreed that Guy de Lusignan should be recognised as the ruler of the Frankish lands in Palestine with the empty title of 'King of Jerusalem', and that he should be succeeded by Conrad of Montferrat and his wife Isabella. This did not satisfy Richard of England; Guy was his ally and Conrad was far from friendly with him. Philip of France wanted to return home to stake his claim to the lands formerly held by the Count of Flanders which he claimed as heir to his late wife Isabella. Then, on Philip's departure, while Richard's right to be commander-in-chief of the Crusading armies could hardly be disputed, Conrad refused to serve under him and he left Acre at the end of July ostensibly to attend to his estates in Tyre.

In the middle of August Saladin produced a first instalment of the prisoners which he had agreed to liberate, but without some of those specified by name. Richard refused to accept that Saladin might have difficulty in locating the captives, or that his code of honour would not allow him to default on the agreement. Richard had kept two thousand Muslim prisoners as hostages for the payment of the ransom and the relief of the Christian prisoners. He had them brought out of Acre and butchered in full view of the Muslim army – it is said that the Crusaders were happy to carry out this massacre in view of their own losses. There is no way in which this impetuous slaughter can be justified. It achieved nothing except that from now on Saladin took no Christian prisoners.

Leaving the massacred bodies on the ground as they lay, King Richard marched South from Acre on 22 August 1191 with the Knights Templar at the head of an army of perhaps as many as a hundred thousand men, while the fleet sailed south keeping pace with the marching army. His objective was to sever Saladin's communications with his Egyptian base by occupying Ascalon. Saladin's forces further inland shadowed Richard's advance past Haifa, their archers harassing the rearguard. There was no general engagement until Saladin attacked the Franks in strength as the army passed Arsouf.

Richard's defensive plan, in which the Hospitallers played a prominent part, withstood the onslaught, and Saladin had to retreat towards Jerusalem, doubtless wishing to lure the Crusaders to another Hattin.

There is little doubt that Richard at this time could have recaptured Jerusalem. Its defences were in bad repair, and the morale of his army was high. But both Templars and Hospitallers agreed with him that it would be foolish to do so. Not only would its weakened defences make it as difficult for the Franks to hold as for the Muslims to do so, but as soon as Jerusalem was recovered a large part of Richard's army – perhaps even Richard himself – would return home to the West considering that their reason for taking the Cross had been accomplished. Not only this, but a garrison in Jerusalem would have been isolated. *Outremer* was no longer a country of Frankish fiefs with Jerusalem as its natural capital. Apart from the garrisons at Acre and at Tyre, the only lands held by the Franks were in the Counties of Tripoli and of Antioch far to the North.

Richard only went inland as far as Beit Nuba twelve miles to the north west of Jerusalem. It is said that when the king arrived there he held his shield in front of his face so that he would not see the distant prospect of Jerusalem and be tempted to advance further. He turned back towards Jaffa; Saladin could not run the risk of Ascalon being surrendered as Acre had been, with Richard then dominating his line of communications with Egypt. He marched there himself, evacuated the garrison and destroyed the fortifications. When Richard reached the town, he found only smoking ruins.

For the time being there were no further military confrontations. Instead, while the Franks relaxed in the comfortable surroundings of Jaffa and Acre, various proposals to settle the Palestinian conflict were made, each less likely to be accepted than its predecessor. Richard first proposed that as a condition of his own return to England the Muslims should withdraw to the East of the River Jordan leaving Jerusalem and the whole of *Outremer* to the Franks. When not surprisingly this proposition was rejected, it was then proposed that Saphadin, the son of Saladin, should be King of Jerusalem provided that Saladin recognised the River Jordan as the Eastern frontier of *Outremer*. Then, Richard's sister, Joanna, should marry Saphadin, and receive the coastal fortresses as a dowry, while the Templars and the Hospitallers should regain their former fortresses. The most extraordinary thing about this proposal was that actual negotiations about it commenced, in spite of Joanna's outrage at the suggestion that she should marry an Infidel.

This plan also infuriated Conrad of Montferrat who apparently could not see that its impracticability would prevent it ever being put into effect He then suggested to Saladin that he himself should be King in Jerusalem, with the ownership of Beirut, Tyre and Sidon in exchange for that of Acre and for his assurance that he would not join the Crusaders in any attack on Saladin. Discussions on this also broke down. The idea of a 'Crusade' now differed somewhat from the ambitions of Pope Urban; the barons and Knights with no lands in Western Europe were determined to retain by any means their estates in *Outremer*.

For a year while there were seemingly endless discussions about the future of Palestine. Richard was receiving reports about events in his Kingdom of England. These were making him uneasy and he wanted to return home. He solved the problem of the death of one of his Justiciars in Cyprus by selling the island to the Templars. He held a Council to decide on who should be titular King of Jerusalem, and to his surprise it decided in favour of Conrad de Montferrat in preference to Guy de Lusignan. The Templars solved problems which they at once had in Cyprus by selling it to Guy who thereby acquired a fief.

Conrad was murdered by two Assassins whose paymaster has never been identified. Richard acted quickly. Henry of Champagne was proclaimed as King of Jerusalem, he was betrothed to Conrad's widow, Isabella, who was married to him in the Cathedral of Acre after only a week of widowhood. They made their home in the castle.

During 1192, Richard conducted some minor campaigning against Saladin's outposts. In June he again advanced within sight of Jerusalem, then occupied by Saladin who had received significant reinforcements. On 4 July Richard ordered a retreat to Jaffa. More negotiations with Saladin took place. The problem was Ascalon, the ruins of which Richard refused to give up. In July, with no agreement reached, and Richard preparing to embark his army for the voyage home, Saladin attacked Jaffa and sacked it. Richard counter-attacked by sea and by land. Saladin retired, and more offers and counter-offers were made. Eventually Saladin retired to Jerusalem. Then Richard was persuaded to relent about Ascalon, and a formal five-year Treaty was signed by which the Franks retained the coastal cities from Tyre to Jaffa – 'the Kingdom of Jerusalem' was now a coastal strip a hundred miles long. The Franks withdrew from Ascalon, and the Muslims held Sidon and Beirut, separating the 'Kingdom' from the Counties of Antioch and Tripoli. Unarmed Christian pilgrims were to be allowed to visit the Holy Places and Saladin would permit four Catholic Priests to serve at the Church of the Holy Sepulchre.

King Richard was at last free to return to England. Bad sailor as he was, he took the shortest sea-passage, and started to make the rest of the journey by land. The story of his imprisonment by Duke Leopold of Austria in revenge for the standard thrown into the '*jacques*' and Richard's subsequent ransom and release, is well-known but forms no part of the history of the Crusades.

The situation in *Outremer* remained confused. Saladin died in February 1193, leaving the Franks confined to the narrow coastal strip and Islam united, but it was not long before quarrels broke out among the Muslim rulers. For several years they did not take the offensive against the Franks and Henry of Champagne was able to restore some order in the so-called 'Kingdom of Jerusalem', although, curiously, he was never crowned King.

Nowhere was there greater confusion than in the County of Antioch from which King Leo II of Armenia wished to oust Bohemond. By trickery he managed to take the Count prisoner together with his wife and young son and he then assumed temporary possession of the County. Unable to hold it, Leo returned with his prisoners to his capital of Sis, and the Antiochenes set up a Commune which governed the city, its leaders taking an oath of loyalty to Bohemond's son Raymond.

Robert de Sablé, the Master of the Temple, died in September 1193, and Gilbert Erail, the Deputy Master of the Temple in the West, accepted the Knights' invitation to succeed him. After the Master of the Hospital had died at the Fountains of Cresson six years earlier, the Hospitallers had elected in succession two Masters who had each presided over the Order for less than two years: Armengaud d'Aspe and Garnier de Nablus. In 1193 Geoffrey de Donjon was elected to succeed Garnier. In Europe the Order of the Hospital was inexorably extending its already vast domains.

In the spring of 1194 Henry of Champagne led his army to Antioch and then advanced into Armenia. King Leo realised that by his capture of Bohemond he had gone too far; as a result of the negotiations which followed Henry's arrival at Sis, Bohemond was at once set free. It was agreed that his son Raymond should marry Alice, the heiress to Armenia, her husband Hethoum was fortunately assassinated, so that this wedding could take place, and it was intended that eventually Antioch and Armenia would be united under their joint rule.

The rivalries among the Franks were somewhat lessened after the death of Guy de Lusignan, but when Amalric was summoned from Jaffa to be the ruler of Cyprus he refused to submit to Henry of Champagne. In 1195 he turned to the German Emperor Henry VI who was planning a Crusade, and he accepted the Crown of Cyprus as his vassal.

Matters then became even more than usually confused. In 1197 a German advance guard of the Emperor's Crusade at once insisted on attacking the Muslims in Galilee, and Henry of Champagne had to muster his own Knights to reinforce the German infantry. Saphadin had no wish to fight a pitched battle and withdrew instead of advancing on Acre. In September 1197 Henry of Champagne was killed in an accidental fall from a balcony. In the following year Amalric married the widowed Isabella, and united the Crowns of Cyprus and 'Jerusalem'. Reinforced, the Germans attempted to renew the Crusade but on hearing news of the approach of an Egyptian army, they withdrew to Tyre and embarked for the return journey to Europe with nothing achieved.

1.7 THE FOURTH CRUSADE (1200-1204)

Elsewhere, while in *Outremer* matters were generally quiescent, Pope Innocent III was encouraging the European nobles to make preparations for a new Crusade.

The Venetians were to play a leading part, providing the transports in which the Crusaders would sail east. The Venetians then proposed that Crusaders would be partially excused their payment for these if they would first attack the Dalmatian town of Zara which the Venetians saw as a rival. To the Pope's horror, Zara was attacked and pillaged in November 1202; as it was then too late in the year to sail East, the Crusaders encamped there for the winter. In June 1203, the force was then diverted to the Byzantine capital of Constantinople. The Emperor Alexius fled, and the Crusaders occupied the city. Relations with the citizens deteriorated and in May 1204 the Western Crusaders virtually destroyed the greatest city in Eastern Christendom.

This, perhaps unforeseen sacking of Constantinople has dominated accounts of the Fourth Crusade, which have largely ignored the exploits of one small group of Crusaders which did carry on to the Middle East in an attempt to fulfil the original purpose of the Crusade. This group, numbering some 300 knights, was led by Renard II of Dampierre, arriving in *Outremer* in early 1203. Militarily, a force of 300 was inadequate to attempt an attack on Jerusalem or any other well-defended city; however, this contingent did achieve some success in perpetuating the presence of the Latin states in the Muslim-dominated Middle East.

However, so far as the Holy Land was concerned, The Fourth Crusade must be considered a failure; however, some interesting lessons can be learned. Firstly, given that the Holy City had been in Muslim hands since 1187, the timing of the call was not auspicious. Secondly, the Western Nations of England, France, Germany, and Spain were, at that time occupied on internal matters or international conflicts; not only were England and France engaged in serious territorial disputes but also, Richard I of England who had committed himself to return to the Holy Land to complete the unfinished work started in the Third Crusade, died campaigning in France in 1199. The Fourth Crusade was not therefore a 'Monarch's Crusade'. The third lesson is that, despite not being led by their Kings many lesser-rank nobles 'took up the cross'. These included Simon de Montfort, the French Counts of Champagne, Blois, and Flanders, but notably Geoffrey of Villehardouin (who would author a significant Crusading account:'*Conquest of Constantinople*'.

A failed Crusade maybe but another co-operative international venture.

1.8 THE FIFTH CRUSADE (1204-1220)

As far as *Outremer* was concerned the Fourth Crusade had been an irrelevance. Amalric and Saphadin entered into a six-year Truce in 1204. Amalric died in the following year and his eldest daughter, Maria of Montferrat, succeeded to the throne of the Kingdom, notionally 'of Jerusalem', but more plausibly 'of Acre'. Cyprus again became an independent Kingdom where the Regent Walter of Montbéliard ruled on behalf of Amalric's 10-year old son, Hugh I. It was arranged that an impoverished Knight from Champagne, John de Brienne, should marry Queen Maria 'of Jerusalem'.

The Muslims were too concerned with their own internal affairs to worry overmuch about the coastal strip of Palestine held by the Franks. In July 1210, the Six-years Truce came to an end, but its renewal which Saphadin suggested was opposed only by the Templars who considered it wrong prematurely to commit Maria's proposed husband, but after John arrived in Acre and had married Maria he agreed to a five-year renewal of the Truce to be effective from July 1212. While it was in force, the major differences in *Outremer* involved not the Muslims but Bohemond of Antioch and Leo of Armenia.

In the same year there occurred the disturbing affair of 'The Children's Crusade'. Perhaps as many as thirty thousand children from the South of France followed a boy named Stephen intent on liberating the Holy Places. Merchants arranged for them to take ship, but they never reached Palestine, being taken prisoner by the Muslims, or perhaps sold to them by previous arrangement, and then being sold as slaves in the markets of North Africa, Alexandria or even far-distant Baghdad. Another contingent, also numbering several thousand, which marched South from Germany through Italy for the most part were never heard of again.

Pope Honorius III was anxious that there should be a Fifth Crusade, and informed King John de Brienne of Acre that one was being mustered. One or two contingents arrived in Acre towards the end of 1217. There were a few skirmishes. Then, unassisted by the European reinforcements, King John attacked a recently-constructed Muslim fort on Mount Tabor. He failed to capture it. In the next year further forces arrived from Europe, and it was decided to attack not the Arabs in Palestine but those in Egypt.

The new arrivals were led by Cardinal Pelagius who claimed the command of the Crusade. For three years he conducted a badly organised campaign. The Crusading forces were then visited by, of all people, Francis of Assisi, who went to see the Sultan Al-Khamil in Egypt. He was received courteously as a good man afflicted by God, and was sent back with an honourable escort having achieved nothing. Many of the Crusaders were now returning to the West, but equally reinforcements were still arriving.

The Egyptian Sultan was anxious for peace at any price, and offered Jerusalem, Bethlehem, and the whole of Galilee in exchange for the Crusaders withdrawal from Egypt. King John and many of those recently arrived from Europe wished to accept this, but Pelagius would have none of it, in which he was supported by the Military Orders. Francis of Assisi had played no part in the Truce which had been arranged, and when this fell through the Crusaders assaulted Damietta and captured it, finding the whole garrison sick and unable to defend the town.

As so often happened, divisions among the Crusaders prevented the capture being exploited. Pelagius now saw himself as about to achieve the final destruction of Islam – the Crusaders would conquer all Egypt, but for the moment did no more than rebuild Damietta. Pelagius then attempted to advance in the face of the Nile flood. His army was outnumbered, thousands were killed, retreat was inevitable, Damietta was abandoned, and the Fifth Crusade came to an ignominious and humiliating conclusion.

1.9 THE FINAL PALESTINIAN CRUSADES (1227-1277)

For the next half-century a succession of expeditions, each considering itself to be a Crusade, came from the West to Palestine. The German Emperor Frederick II, Barbarossa's grand-son, led an expedition which, based in Acre, was involved in more diplomacy than fighting. In 1227 Frederick secured a ten year Truce, by which the 'Kingdom of Jerusalem' received Jerusalem and Bethlehem while in the former city the Muslims retained the *Dome of the Rock*. It was an unpopular arrangement – for example the Templars were furious that the Muslims retained the Temple. So unpopular did Frederick become that he was virtually driven from Palestine in the summer of 1229.

Other expeditions were mounted by, for example, King Tibald of Navarre and Duke Richard of Cornwall. The Baghdad Khalifate was over-run by Eastern invaders from Khwarismia. Ten thousand Khwarismian horsemen advanced towards Palestine, by-passed Damascus and on 11 July 1244 forced their way into Jerusalem. After the efforts of 250 years, Jerusalem was now finally lost to the Franks.

The city of Acre became the rallying point for the Franks in the South of *Outremer*. They were joined in an unholy alliance against the Khwarismians and their Egyptian Mameluke allies by the Seljuq armies of Homs and Damascus, The combined force was then augmented by Templar and Hospitaller reinforcements from Western Europe. The armies met near Gaza, the Seljuqs were put to flight, and most of the Franks killed or taken prisoner. In the North of *Outremer* Count Bohemond continued to occupy Tripoli, where he held his Court, and, for the time being, Antioch.

In the meantime King Louis IX ('St. Louis') of France was preparing to fulfil a Crusading vow which he had made many years earlier. He landed at Limassol in Cyprus in September 1248 at the head of a force of Western Knights which included both Templars and Hospitallers. It was again decided to attack Egypt rather than first recover Palestine. In June 1249 Damietta was captured and in December King Louis was able to advance southwards. But after initial success he had to retreat towards Damietta. Before reaching it the Frankish army was overwhelmed by the Egyptians in April 1250, Louis himself being taken prisoner. He was released after ceding Damietta and paying an enormous ransom. He remained temporarily in *Outremer* as its *de facto* ruler amid scenes of chaos as the Muslims warred between themselves, Seljuqs fighting Mamelukes, before he returned to France in July 1254 after a disastrous campaign.

By 1261 the Byzantines, led by Michael Palaeologus, had recovered Constantinople from its weak Latin rulers. Matters in *Outremer* were by now again relatively orderly with the Franks continuing to hold their coastal fortress-towns, but Syria and Palestine were faced with another wave of Eastern invaders, the Mongols under Hulagu Khan. Prince Bohemond of Antioch allied himself with Hulagu against the Egyptian Mamelukes who by 1263 had been led by Baibars to sack first Nazareth and then the suburbs of Acre. Two years later Baibars captured the Templar fortress of Arsuf although Athlit held out against him. Later he captured the fortress of Safed which dominated the Galilean uplands, executing all the Knights who had defended it, and soon afterwards he captured Toron. In March 1268 Jaffa fell to Baibars, as did Beaufort in the following month. He then marched North to attack Antioch which fell in May, many of its inhabitants being slaughtered or being sold into slavery, only a few being allowed to ransom themselves. The northern Frankish forts were abandoned as being indefensible. All that was left of the 'Kingdom of Jerusalem' was the City of Acre, which received support from Cyprus, Tripoli and a few outposts. In 1269 King James I of Aragon had led a small force to Acre but achieved nothing; King Louis IX had planned a new Crusade, but no more was heard of this after his death on a Tunisian expedition in 1270.

The Egyptian Sultan Baibars continued seizing one Frankish outpost after another. The following March the Hospitaller stronghold of *Krak des Chevaliers* fell after bombardment by his siege-engines. Bohemond, still holding Tripoli, contracted a ten-year Truce with Baibars who was probably influenced by the impending arrival of another Crusading army led by Prince Edward, the son of King Henry III of England, in discharge of a vow his ailing father had earlier made. Edward found the Frankish forces in what was left of *Outremer* unable to mount a major offensive against the Muslims; he left for England in September 1272, having arranged a ten years and ten months Truce between Baibars and the government of Acre, now a Commune.

Pope Gregory X held a Council at Lyons in 1275, to try to persuade western Princes to assemble yet another major Crusade. It was soon clear that no such expedition was likely, particularly when King Hugh of Cyprus, who, in spite of the opposition of the Commune, had assumed the title of 'King of Jerusalem', returned to Cyprus. Political confusion ensued. Maria of Antioch sold her rights to the 'Kingdom of Jerusalem' to Charles of Anjou who assumed the title of 'King of Jerusalem' and sent Roger of San Severino as his *bailli* to displace Balian of Ibelin, the appointee of King Hugh of Cyprus. The resulting confusion suited Baibars who could see that it might well eliminate any attempt to reinstate *Outremer* while he was dealing with the Seljuqs and the Mongols. However the continuing threat which Baibars posed to the Franks in *Outremer* ended on his death in July 1277.

1.10 THE END OF *OUTREMER* (1281-1302)

Baibars' ineffective son Baraqa was deposed as Sultan of Egypt by the Mameluke Emir Qalawun who then governed the country ostensibly on behalf of Baraqa's infant brother. Fighting broke out among the Muslims, but the equally disorganised Franks took no advantage of the situation.

Bohemond VII of Antioch fell out with the Templars. Treaties were signed and broken by skirmishes. King Hugh of Cyprus invaded Palestine in an attempt to recover his lost Kingdom. He got no further than Tyre where he died in March 1284. In the following year Qalawun captured the great Hospitaller fortress of Marqab. Henry of Cyprus, who had succeeded his brother Hugh, entered Acre in June 1286 and was accepted as its ruler by the Commune, but with less enthusiasm by the Military Orders. After his coronation as King of Jerusalem in Tyre, in spite of the incipient threat from Qalawun, two weeks of festivities were held in Acre with pageants and tournaments. No sooner were these ended than open hostilities broke out between the Pisans and the Genoese fleets off the Syrian Coast.

When Prince Bohemond VII of Antioch died, his heir was his sister Lucia, who lived in Italy, and the inhabitants of Tripoli offered the city instead to the Dowager Princess Sibylla of Armenia. The arrangement fell through and a Commune was proclaimed. Then Lucia arrived in Acre where she was warmly greeted by the Hospitallers. The Grand Masters went to Tripoli where the Commune insisted that Lucia must recognise it as the rightful government. There were extended negotiations in which Pisan and Genoese commercial interests played a leading part. Then the Venetians, who had strong commercial relations with Egypt, asked Qalawun to settle the dispute as it was disrupting trade, always the prime consideration of the Italian coastal cities. Qalawun led a large Egyptian army into Syria, but, preoccupied with their own internal problems, the Franks took no notice of this until the Egyptians arrived at the gates of Tripoli.

Only then did the inhabitants of Tripoli take matters seriously. Lucia was awarded the supreme authority and reinforcements including Templars and Hospitallers reached the city by land and sea. But when the Muslim siege engines began to pulverise the defences, the Venetians sailed away with all their possessions, followed by the Genoese, and the remaining citizens became panic-stricken. On 26 April 1289 the Egyptians swarmed into the city. Although Lucia managed to escape by sea to Cyprus with the Marshals of the two orders, the Commander of the Temple, Peter of Moncada was killed and every man found by the Muslims in the city was put to death, while all the women and children were carried off as slaves. The massacre completed, the city was razed to the ground.

Soon afterwards King Henry of Cyprus arrived in Acre, and was able to renew the Truce with Qalawun. This may appear remarkable but any thought of the recovery of the Holy Places had long gone, and commercial interests, both of the Franks and of the Muslims predominated – the Templars were bankers for Christians and Muslims alike.

In Western Europe most statesmen were too concerned with their own affairs to heed the pleas of Pope Nicholas IV to relieve the perilous position of their countrymen in the East. The only people to take up the challenge was a rabble from northern Italy conveyed in twenty Venetian galleys, who were joined at sea by five galleys sent by King James of Aragon. However in the peaceful conditions brought about by the Truce the merchants in Acre were not contemplating another attack on the Muslims, and the Galilean harvest had been a good one. When the new 'Crusaders' arrived, they were under no sort of control. They considered that they had come to the East to kill Muslims, they ignored any Truce, and when a riot broke out in Acre they rampaged through the town killing every man with a beard, Muslims and Christians alike. Qalawun demanded that those responsible should be handed over to him; the City Council was prepared to do this, but the townspeople would not allow it. Qalawun decided that the final eviction of the Franks from Palestine was now overdue. He mustered both the Syrian and the Egyptian armies, but before he could launch the attack he fell ill in November 1290 and died six days later. His son, al-Ashraf Khalil, was equal to completing his father's unfinished work. In March of the following year he appeared at the gates of Acre with a large army of horsemen and foot-soldiers – perhaps as many as two hundred thousand altogether – and an immense battery of more than a hundred siege-engines.[10] Some reinforcements, Templars and Hospitallers were sent from Western Europe, and Amalric, the brother of King Henry of Cyprus, arrived in Acre with some Cypriot troops.

Acre was strongly defended with a double line of walls set about with twelve towers. Every citizen was called upon to play his part in the defence although shiploads of old men, women and children were sent to Cyprus. The siege began on 6 April 1301. In early May King Henry of Cyprus arrived with further reinforcements. An attempt to renew the Truce was rejected out of hand by al-Ashraf. By the middle of May, several towers had been mined and collapsed, and the outer wall had been breached. The final assault commenced on 18 May, but the brave resistance put up proved useless. King Henry, his brother Amalric and the severely wounded Grand Master of the Hospital, John de Villiers, were able to embark to return to Cyprus; the Grand Master of the

Temple, William de Beaujeu, had already died of his wounds. Otto of Grandson commandeered several Venetian galleys in which he embarked as many survivors as he could but few could be saved – no more than seven Hospitaller Knights reached Cyprus. By nightfall al-Ashraf was in control of the whole of Acre apart from the building on the edge of the harbour still occupied by the Templars, but eventually this collapsed killing not only its Templar defenders but the Muslims who were assaulting it.

Al-Ashraf destroyed the city that it might never again be a focus of Frankish power. Tyre, Sidon and Beirut soon also fell to his forces. The Templars evacuated their castles of Tortosa and Athlit. The Muslims laid waste the rich farms in the former coastal fiefs, and the dream of *Outremer* vanished as if it never had been. Its memory was kept alive only in Cyprus where the refugees led a miserable life, and it is said that out-of-doors the ladies of the Island wore long black cloaks from head to foot as 'a token of mourning for the death of *Outremer*'.[11]

1.11 MILITARY ORDERS OUTSIDE *OUTREMER* (1302-1307)

There was no prospect of renewing the Christian occupation of Palestine. While Pope Nicholas IV tried to organise a further expedition, the European rulers were too concerned with their own immediate problems, although various far-reaching plans were discussed. Only King Philip le Bel of France gave lip-service to the proposal as part of his plan to secure for himself the great Templar wealth.

The Templars were far from popular, due in a large measure to the secrecy with which they surrounded their every activity. It was already rumoured that within their Preceptories esoteric, possibly heretical or even pagan, rites took place. There were also not wholly unfounded allegations that they had sometimes appeared to find the friendship of their Muslim opponents more congenial than that of Barons recently arrived from Western Europe.

The Military Orders were having to look for another role. Little of the earlier high-minded desire to liberate the Holy Places remained. Their European endowments had made the Orders immensely rich. The trade with the East, passing through such entrepôts as Constantinople, Damascus and Alexandria, was mostly in the hands of the Italian maritime powers –Venice, Genoa, Pisa – but the Templars were the world's bankers. In every major capital in the West, London and Paris, for example, both Hospitallers and Templars maintained substantial treasuries. That of the Templars in Paris could not fail to be a temptation to King Philip le Bel to whom the Temple in Paris was of more importance than the Royal Treasury in the Louvre. His personal valuables were deposited not in the Louvre but in the Temple, and in the chronic financial straits of the French economy Philip used the Templars as his personal money-lenders to whom he was already indebted beyond any hope of repayment. That the Templars were generally unpopular made them an even more attractive target for the King's avarice.

In 1302, by Order of the Convent General, the seven Hospitaller Knights from Acre who had taken refuge in Cyprus had been reinforced from the European Preceptories to bring the strength of the Convent at Limassol to eighty fighting men.[12] In 1306, with the assistance of the Genoese fleet, the Grand Master of the Hospital, Fulkes de Villaret, invaded the Island of Rhodes, a Byzantine fief. Progress was slow, but in spite of reinforcements from Constantinople, the city of Rhodes capitulated after a two-year siege. The Hospitallers abandoned Cyprus, where like the Templars, they were far from popular refugees, and set up their new headquarters behind the strongly fortified walls of the city. In the previous year Pope Clement V had already confirmed the Hospitallers' ownership of Rhodes, and by 1310 they were in full possession of the prosperous island.

At the end of 1304, or possibly early in 1305, a certain Esquiu de Floyrano of Beziers had given evidence before a Synod which was being held in Agen. Esquiu repeated his evidence first before King Jaime II of Aragon and then in front of King Philip in Paris. For the first time specific accusations of improper practices were laid against the Templars in the Languedoc where they held extensive estates. Philip le Bel was only too pleased to hear this evidence besmirching his intended victims. At this time, after the death of Pope Benedict XI almost a year had elapsed without the election of a successor to the Papacy and there was therefore no powerful Pontiff to protect the Knights.

It was essential that a compliant Pope should be elected if Philip le Bel was to carry out his plan of despoiling the Templars. The King sent a powerful delegation to Perugia, where the Conclave was meeting. His chosen candidate was not even a Cardinal, but the Archbishop of Bordeaux, Bertrand de Got. According to one contemporary account, the King's delegation bribed the Cardinals to elect Bertrand. It was certainly after tortuous debate and some misgivings that on 5 June 1305 they did so. Bertrand de Got accepted the Office in his Cathedral of Bordeaux, and then announced that he would be crowned not in Rome but at Toussaint near Vienne on the soil of the Empire. In the event he was persuaded to change his mind, but only for the ceremony to take place instead at Lyon. Before this occurred, Bernard de Got entered into a long series of negotiations with King Philip in complete secrecy in the course of which he is believed to have entered into certain commitments.

There is no doubt that Clement recognised that Philip le Bel was the benefactor who had secured the papacy for him, and he conferred upon the King every Dispensation or 'Grâce' which the latter demanded. He annulled all of Pope Boniface's measures of which the King disapproved. Clement fell ill in the winter of 1306, but although he had recovered by the early spring of the following year, for several weeks he resisted the King's urgent demand for a further private meeting. Before this at last took place King Philip's excommunicated councillor, Nogaret, made detailed accusations against the Templars. Philip brought these forward at his Council and said that he would call upon Pope Clement V to examine them.

He met Clement at Poitiers in April 1307 for private discussions which lasted for six weeks. These again included the prospect of a new Crusade to liberate the Holy Places, something of which Pope Clement never lost sight. As a preliminary to this he summoned the Grand Masters of the Military Orders to a conference in France. Fulkes de Villaret replied that the strengthening of the defences of Rhodes did not allow him to leave the Island for the time being. Jacques de Molay, the Master of the Temple, set out for France with a small escort and no more than sufficient funds for the journey, evidently expecting soon to return to Cyprus.

The Master and the Pope met on 6 June 1307.[13] Jacques de Molay presented two memoranda for which he had been asked. One was concerned with the possible conduct of a Crusade, but with the experience of the past two hundred years of campaigning in the Holy Land, de Molay was more sanguine about recovering the Sacred sites than retaining them.

The second dealt with the Pope's project for a union of the two military Orders.[14] Jacques de Molay analysed the proposal in a carefully balanced way. He admitted that a merger could lead to operating economies. But for several reasons his conclusion was that the maintenance of two separate Orders would provide the best basis for the Crusade which he confidently expected the Pope shortly to preach.

Unfortunately the views of the Master of the Hospital, who might well have supported de Molay, were not available. Only the Temple appeared to be opposing the merger. It seems certain that de Molay's opposition added to the suspicion that the Templars had something to hide. However no hint was given to him at Poitiers that the Templars were under investigation. King Philip had already given his instructions to Nogaret who had arrested two Templar Knights without any disturbance occurring. After the meetings in Poitiers (it is uncertain whether King Philip was present at any of them or not) Jacques de Molay appears to have gone to Paris to attend a meeting of the Order.

1.12 THE SUPPRESSION OF THE KNIGHTS TEMPLAR
(1307-1314)

Pope Clement had little enthusiasm for investigating the accusations against the Templars but on 24 August 1307 he informed King Philip that he had decided to carry out this investigation; instead of referring it to the Inquisition it was to be a stately and measured Papal enquiry, something which might take years rather than months.

This was not what King Philip wanted. He insisted that Nogaret had collected sufficient evidence of heresy for the matter to be handed over to the Inquisition. Pope Clement feebly acquiesced. The King's need for money was becoming more desperate.

Some vestige of legality was necessary if such a well-regarded body as the Temple was to be denounced without popular uproar. First, Nogaret was made Keeper of the Great Seal of France which was handed over to him. With this he could authenticate the instructions for the French civil authorities which he then prepared. These ordered the arrest of the Templars at the proper request of William of Paris, the Inquisitor-General of France; this was pure fiction, no such request or even investigation having been made by him. The statement was however essential to preserve the façade of ecclesiastical legality. It was followed by a long list of the heinous crimes, bestial as well as heretical, which Nogaret alleged that the Templars had committed. Pope Clement was also said to have approved these accusations (which he certainly had not); however to say so removed any claim which might be made of Papal protection. That there could be no question of misunderstanding, the formal Latin was accompanied by a French translation.

By these instructions the Seneschals and their Baillis of France were ordered to arrest on 13 October 1307 not only every Knight Templar, but their Sergeants and their servitors. The Inquisitor-General sent similar instructions to his subordinates in the Languedoc. The utmost secrecy was preserved and the arrests were duly carried out without any warning. The Pope was given no previous notice and only two days before Jacques de Molay had amicably accompanied the King to a funeral. De Molay was arrested in the Paris Temple together with the Preceptors of Normandy, Rheims, Acquitaine and Cyprus. In Paris not more than a dozen Templars avoided arrest. The same day Nogaret announced the arrests and the major charges against the Templars to a meeting of dignitaries in the Cathedral of Notre Dame and on the following day to a larger assembly in the Louvre.

Elsewhere many Templars escaped. According to figures quoted by Baigent and Leigh[15] the numbers of Templars in France at this time were 350 Knights and 930 sergeants, a total of 1280. The Inquisition records refer to only 620 Templars as having been arrested. This could mean that several hundred individuals were still at large after the arrests, including some high ranking Officers; among these in addition to Gerard de Villiers was certainly Imbert Blanke, Master of Auvergne, who took refuge in England.

At this time the Templars maintained a fair-sized fleet, which was involved both in trading on behalf of the Order and in conveying pilgrim-passengers to the East, at one time as many as 6,000 per annum from ports in Spain, France and Italy.[16] Baigent and Leigh make a plausible case for some of these vessels having sailed from ports on the Channel coast, customarily used by the Templar fleet, carrying Knights seeking sanctuary, and to have been able to sail round the North of Ireland to the West Coast of Scotland, without interception by the English fleet, a suggestion which is supported by what are apparently 14th century Templar graves at Kilmartin and other places in the West of Argyllshire.[17] There are, however, other possibilities which are addressed later.

Although not every Templar in France had been arrested, King Philip wrote to the other Princes of Europe demanding that they also carried out arrests so that the Order might be disbanded world-wide. His demand was not enthusiastically received. Most of the Rulers would do nothing without instructions from the Pope himself and these were not forthcoming.

The interrogation of the Templars who had been arrested, both Knights and servitors, took place in the cellars of the Temple in Paris. There is no doubt that the Inquisitors subjected their prisoners to torture. Many of them were elderly men who were still suffering from the mental shock of their unexpected instant arrest. Since this had taken place each had been kept in solitary confinement, unaware of what had happened to his colleagues, or whether the Pope had ordered their arrest or even what charges were to be brought against them. They were confined in comfortless conditions, deprived of sleep by being constantly awakened by their guards. There is no wonder that even the sight of the instruments of torture was sufficient for them to confess to anything required of them. The Inquisitors made sure that the 'confessions' were similar in all respects as far as the matters which they wished to establish were concerned. Heresy had to be proved in order to justify the intervention of the Inquisition. A minority of those examined were Knights – of the 138 examined in Paris many were shepherds, carpenters, millers and ploughmen who had lived under the protection of the Preceptories.

Geoffrey de Charnay admitted to blasphemy but would not admit homosexuality. The examination of Jacques de Molay was personally conducted by William of Paris. De Molay was a broken man, and said whatever William of Paris wanted to hear. As de Charnay had done, he confessed to heresy and blasphemy but also refused to admit to homosexuality. On the following day Jacques de Molay and some of his most senior colleagues were paraded before a large audience of ecclesiastics and scholars in Notre Dame. They repeated the evidence of heresy and blasphemy which they had already given. The Order was now condemned from the lips of its own leaders.

On 27 October Pope Clement wrote to King Philip to say that he knew nothing of what had just occurred other than that the Templars had been arrested and their property had been seized.

It was proving more difficult to prove idolatry than simple blasphemy, because the image which was said to be worshipped was given so many descriptions, and the Inquisition preferred unanimous depositions – the idol was a bearded head known as *Baphomet*, it was a black and white figure, it was a statue known by the Arab word *Yalla*, it was an object made of wood, it was the head of a demon. However 130 depositions, even though many were extracted under torture, gave the King ample grounds for concluding not simply that its members were guilty of heresy but that the Order was rotten to the core. Even so, without Papal sanction the whole process of arrest and interrogation was illegal. Clement at last took action to confer legitimacy on the affair by promulgating the Bull *Pastoralis praeeminentiae* on 22 November 1307. It was ingeniously composed and failed to give Philip all that he wanted. It made it clear that no Apostolic Letters had been sent to the King authorising him to handle the whole affair himself, as Nogaret claimed, and it exhorted the King to leave the Templars to the judgement of the Church. As a result the King allowed custody of the Templar prisoners to be vested in two nominated Cardinals. This gave the Templars fresh hope and many complied with the Grand Master's request to withdraw their confessions.

In January 1308, the property of the English Templars was seized, although only two are known to have been arrested. Many of the dispossessed Knights were given pensions as they had been made penniless. Later, when the King received his copy of the Bull, a few more were arrested but little further action was taken.

Pope Clement was in fact refusing to carry out the extreme measures which the King demanded. Philip began to apply considerable pressure against Clement as he had earlier done against Pope Boniface – to King Philip a Pope who opposed his wishes was, *ipso facto*, a negligent Pope. The King referred the legality of his own actions to the Masters of Law and Theology in the University of Paris. The key to the lengthy series of seven questions which he put to the learned Doctors was whether he had the right to dispose of the

Templars' property and possessions. He was more interested in this than in their persons.

He received the answers in March 1308. They gave him considerably less than he had hoped for. In essence, it was made clear that the punishment of heretics was solely the prerogative of the ecclesiastical authorities. The reply to the question of the disposal of the Templar property was Delphic in the extreme – the custody of the Templars' goods should be undertaken in whatever way might best expedite the purpose for which they had been acquired. This little suited the King who summoned the States-General. It convened in May 1309; not only did many of the Nobles cited to appear fail to attend but neither did many ecclesiastics. The latter were in a difficult position; they were to be asked to condemn a religious Order responsible only to the Pope but which, in spite of the evidence amassed by the Inquisitors, the Pope himself had as yet failed to condemn. After ten days of invective the lay-delegates from the towns, who made up the majority of those present, enthusiastically agreed that the Templars were guilty and deserved to be put to death.

The King then led a considerable concourse of the Third Estate, together with such Bishops and Nobles as had attended, to Poitiers to meet Pope Clement who held a Public Consistory at which the Templars were denounced at length, in French and not in Latin, by William de Plaisians. He concluded by saying that Clement had given the King letters authorising his actions, letters the existence of which the Pope had in fact denied. It was now necessary, he said, for the Pope to make a simple declaration that the Order was guilty – the King and the people demanded it. Clement was not so easily cowed. He said that he refused to act with precipitate haste. He did not doubt the sincerity of King Philip's intentions, but he himself would now proceed with the due process of Curial investigation. Weak Clement may have been, but even this partial defiance, which failed to satisfy Philip, must have involved considerable courage. Nogaret had already physically assaulted Clement's predecessor Boniface for which he had been excommunicated; that in his reply Clement said that he was prepared to suffer martyrdom for his faith may indicate that this prospect had not escaped him. At a further Consistory a week later the King made it plain that if the Pope refused to take action, the secular power would do so. But two weeks later the King again gave the persons of the Templars into the custody of the Church. Several members of the Order were then brought before the Pope. This seemed to mark the beginning of Clement's change of heart, though he still refused to condemn the Order as a whole or to agree that its members should be handed over to the civil power for punishment, or that its senior members should be handed over to the Inquisition, although he pardoned William of Paris for the action which he therefore had prematurely taken. Clement decided that he could no longer delay summoning the General Council of the Church which King Philip had demanded. The Pope then promulgated a Bull which set out one hundred and twenty-seven charges against the Templars, most of them somewhat less than specific. These were to be investigated by Provincial Commissions which were to report to the Council which would convene at Vienne in November 1310.

In November 1309 Jacques de Molay was brought before the Commissioners in Paris. An elderly and not very learned man, he became confused, eventually saying that he could make no defence of the Order against the allegations which the Commissioners made, although he knew nothing of the practices of which it was accused. By February 1310, eighty-one of the 134 who had been interrogated in Paris three years earlier told the Commissioners that they wished to retract their confessions. In spite of the failure of the Grand Master to do so, more than 500 Templars now informed the Commissioners that they wished to come to the defence of the Order. They were asked to choose delegates who could speak on their behalf. Under protest two procurators appeared before the Commission and complained about the difficulty of providing a defence while they were being so ill-treated during their imprisonment. A defence was however put forward, including the telling point that no Templar other than those who had been submitted to torture or had been confronted by it in France had ever confessed to any of the charges. They concluded by stating that the charges were dishonest, shameful and unworthy of belief.

The protestations of innocence were beginning to make some headway with the jurors who were hearing the case. Philip's first reaction was to permit only witnesses of inferior quality who could testify to nothing of substance to take up the time of the Commission. He then ordered the Archbishop of Sens to convene his Provincial Council over the head of the Commission in Paris, making it clear what he expected him to do. Discounting any subsequent evidence, on 12 May 1310 this Provincial Council declared the original confessions to be valid, and that purporting to withdraw them was the ultimate sin of relapsing into heresy. For this there was only one punishment, to be burnt at the stake. The Commissioners of the Paris Tribunal vigorously protested, but the sentence was carried out on two of those accused on the following day. Five others were burnt shortly afterwards, while those who had confessed to nothing were sentenced to life imprisonment. So that the King's message might be abundantly clear, those who had confessed and had not withdrawn their confessions were absolved and set free.

The Commissioners in Paris still saw themselves as discharging a judicial function. When they reported to Pope Clement he suggested that they had done enough, but they insisted that they had not completed their task. Many brethren were now too frightened to give evidence in defence of the Order – in particular, those who had confessed, having been absolved and released, wanted to be involved no more. Philip had made it plain he was little interested in individuals; he wanted the Order destroyed so that some of its property might fall into his hands. So far Pope Clement had obstructed the King's wishes without expressly opposing them, except in that he had reproved Philip for prematurely taking possession of some of the property of the Templars, saying that this should be devoted to a fresh expedition to recover the Holy Land. Now he seemed to think that in other matters as well as the fate of the Temple he should adopt a more conciliatory attitude, for at the end of the previous year the relations between Pope and King had been at a very low ebb. Clement now had taken up residence in Avignon, a town in territory belonging to the King of Naples but which was also a fief of the Emperor. In the hands of these protectors he may have felt more secure and he again made it clear that the Order could not be destroyed without his consent. The Commissioners had their final meeting on 5 June 1311 when they met the King at the Abbey of Maubisson in the presence of many of his advisers. They said that they could obtain no more evidence and it was agreed that their enquiry should come to an end.

Pope Clement opened the General Council of the Church which he had summoned on 16 October 1311 in the Cathedral of Vienne. He announced that the Council had three objectives, of which the first was the suppression of the Order of the Temple. Summaries of the evidence obtained were given to the delegates who took several days to read them. It might have been thought that contradictory statements, given under oath or extracted under torture or the threat of it, were hardly satisfactory evidence, even when supported by depositions from ecclesiastics in countries other than France.

Jacques de Molay hoped to be allowed to defend the Order before the Council in Vienne, but King Philip refused to allow the senior Officers of the Order to attend. When others wished to testify, it was Clement who refused to let them do so. Even so he was anxious that the Council should have the trappings of legality. At the beginning of December he put before the Council three carefully phrased procedural questions regarding the Templars' defence. On a written ballot it was agreed that they should have the opportunity to defend themselves. However Clement's decision on the suppression of the Order had been made and he was now only concerned with the disposal of its property about which there were many differing views. By the end of the year the atmosphere at the Council was less than comfortable. Conditions were not improved by the harsh winter weather. Philip was not only exasperated by the delay, but, worried that the Council might refuse to agree to the dissolution after hearing the defence. He placed as much pressure as he could on Clement. In early March he wrote to him demanding the destruction of the Order forthwith, but, since he had referred the matter to the Council there was little more the Pope could do.

Philip came to Vienne with a strong escort of armed retainers. He attended a Consistory at which he deployed every argument for a quick decision on the dissolution. In the presence of the King the Consistory resolved, by a majority of four-fifths, that they approved the suppression of the Order of Knights Templar without hearing any further defence. The decision was made public on 3 April 1312 in a full Session of the General Council. Clement made it clear that the Order was to be suppressed not because it had been found guilty, but by his own exercise of *plena potestatis* derived from his Apostolic powers. He then read the Bull *Vox in excelso* which formally suppressed the Order.

The Order of the Knights Templar was abolished as a political act. The Council never completed its scrutiny of the evidence nor was it allowed to probe it by cross-examination of witnesses; it never expressed an opinion on its validity. The only Templars to be condemned of heresy, or, indeed, of any other crime, were those who confessed to them under torture or threat of it.

Although the Pope had not as yet given his final judgement, on 3 May 1312 by the Bull *Ad providam* he transferred all the possessions of the Temple to the Hospital with the exception of those in Iberia which were to be used in the war against the Moors. Outside France many of the Templar estates were seized by powerful landowners, and in all probability King Philip appropriated much of the treasure in the Temple in Paris – if nothing else he wrote off the substantial loans which he had received from the Templars. Further, until actual property-transfers had taken place, the King received the revenues of the Templar estates. Not only this, but in recognition of their acquisition of the Templars' property the Hospitallers had to agree to give King Philip 200,000 *livres Tournois* a year for three years.

The principal Officers of the Order, Jacques de Molay, Hugues de Pairaud, Geoffrey de Gonneville, Geoffrey de Charnay and the Vice-Chamberlain were to be held in prison pending Clement's final judgement. By his various actions Clement had regained the King's goodwill and the latter agreed, at least in principle, to the new Crusade which the Pope was anxious to see. This became the principal preoccupation of Pope Clement. He lost interest in the fate of the senior Templar Officers, and delegated his authority to deal with them to three Cardinals. There were to be no further hearings and sentence was to be pronounced on the basis of the evidence already received.

The Cardinals considered the matter for 15 months. On 18 March 1314, without further examination, the four accused were brought on to a platform outside the Cathedral of Notre Dame in Paris and sentenced to life imprisonment. Jacques de Molay and Geoffrey de Charnay vigorously protested that they had not admitted that they had committed any crime, and that they had betrayed their Order only to save their lives at the hands of the torturers. They declared that their Order was holy and righteous and that their confessions, obtained under duress, should be disregarded.

The Commission retired to consider the matter afresh. King Philip acted without delay. He said that the confessions being withdrawn meant that the Jacques de Molay and Geoffrey de Charney were relapsed heretics for which there was but one penalty, the stake, and they must die that day. A pyre was built on a small island in the River Seine. That evening, 18 March 1314, still protesting their innocence they steadfastly died in the flames. The Order of the Temple was finally extinguished.

The Temple in Paris became the Royal Treasury. King Philip le Bel died on 29 November 1314, and Pope Clement V had already died on the previous 20th April.

1.13 LESSER CRUSADES (1147-1571)

King Philip le Bel died on 29 November 1314, and Pope Clement V had already died on the previous 20th April. No more was heard of Pope Clement's proposal of a fresh expedition to recover the Holy Land, but conflict between Muslims and Christians occurred throughout the centuries that followed the dissolution of the Knights Templar Order.

Indeed, throughout the whole period of the conflict in the Holy Land there had been lesser military ventures to combat 'infidel' incursions in a number of European Countries. Some of these involved individuals who had survived the conflicts in the Holy Land and went on to apply their military experience in other roles; some involved the regional elements of the Knights Templar and Knights Hospitaller Orders; some may well have provided a home for former Knights Templar who had fled from persecution in France; and yet others used military forces such as the Teutonic Knights which ceased to have a crusading role after the fall of Acre and which sought an alternative '*raison d'etre*'.

Whilst these are of lesser importance to the history of the Knights Templar and Knights Hospitaller Orders, these, nevertheless have a distinct bearing on the cultural environment of the European Nations in which later Chivalric Orders and Freemasonry developed. A brief review of these 'lesser crusades' is therefore felt to be justified. This is a complex story involving many European Nations, and to place these events in context, the following brief notes are in chronological order.

Lisbon Crusade (1147)
This Crusade resulted in the capture of Lisbon.[18] A fleet filled with English, Flemish, Frisian, and Scottish crusaders bound for the East were forced by storms to put into port in Portugal, where King Alfonso of Portugal persuaded them to aid him besiege Moorish-held Lisbon. They took the city and expelled the Moors from it. Lisbon became part of the Christian Kingdom of Portugal.

Wendish Crusade (1147)
The Wendish Crusade was the first of the Northern Crusades. Pope Eugene extended crusading privileges to Germans campaigning against the pagan Wendish Slavs settled around the Elbe River. According to Bernard of Clairvaux, the goal of the crusade was to battle the pagan Slavs 'until such a time as, by God's help, they shall either be converted or deleted'.[19]

Spanish Crusade (1157-1158)

Muslims had crossed from Africa into Spain in the early part of the 8th century and by 718, had conquered most of the Iberian Peninsula. The Spanish Crusades were initiated in the 11th century by Cluniac monks in northern Spain, amidst a growing hatred of the Moorish infidels. Progressively, led mainly by Burgundians and Normans from France, Christians drove the Moors from north and central Spain in a long series known as the Wars of the Reconquest *(La reconquista)* which intensified religious fanaticism and patriotism.[20]

Almohad Dynasty (1170-1296)

Between 1130 and 1170, the Almohads, a Berber family from Morocco who promoted a puritanical and fundamentalist brand of Islam, ousted Almoravid rulers of north Africa and Spain, and out of reforming zeal initially oppressed Spanish Jews and Christians who took refuge in Christian Portugal, Aragon, and Castile. In 1195, the Almohads defeated King Alfonso VIII of Castile in the Battle of Alarcos, temporarily halting the *Reconquista*. The Christians recovered and in 1212 a Christian coalition from Leon/Castile, Navarra, and Aragon defeated the Almohads in the Battle of Las Navas de Tolosa, and established Seville as its capital. With this, the Almohads were forced back to Africa and their rule in Morocco came to an end 1269.

Baltic Crusade (1193)

The Teutonic Order, originally based on a German order of monks who ran a hospital in Acre, became established as a new Military Order, modelled on the Hospitaller Order of St John. Pope Celestine III calls for a crusade against pagans of the Baltic and the Order of the Teutonic Knights was authorised to wage a permanent crusade in Prussia. Further roles of the Teutonic Order will be examined later.

Livonian Crusade (1198-1212)

The Livonian Crusade took place in present-day Latvia, Lithuania, and Estonia. Pope Innocent III established a new German Military Order, the Brothers of the Sword, to aid in the establishment of Christian rule in Livonia and the pagan Baltic.[21] Danish forces were also involved.

'Sicilian' Crusade (1199)

Pope Innocent III called a crusade against Markward of Anweiler, Margrave of Ancona, Count of Abruzzo in central Italy, and Lord of Palermo in the Kingdom of Sicily. Markward was a supporter of Innocent's enemy, the Hohenstaufen claimant to the German throne Philip of Swabia, and posed a threat both to the Papal States and to the Pope's claim to supremacy over Sicily. This was the first 'political crusade.'

The Albigensian Crusade (1208-29)

The Albigensian Crusade by primarily French forces[22] aimed to root out the heretical or Albigensian sect of Christian Cathars in France.

Baltic 'Transylvanian' Crusades (1211-25)

This Crusade, one of a series of Northern Crusades, called by Pope Celestine III in 1193, sought to subdue pagans in Transylvania as had other Northern Kingdoms including the Scandinavian Countries and Poland which started to subjugate their pagan neighbours at this time.

Swedish Crusades (1239 and 1256)

In these crusades, Swedish forces converted the pagan Finns and Sami and extended agriculture north into formerly nomad-inhabited lands. The Swedish Crusades (probably in either 1239 or 1256, but for propaganda purposes it was subsequently backdated to the 1150s and ascribed to St Eric) resulted in Swedish annexation of most of Finland, which remained Swedish property until it became Russian in 1814.

Finally at the end of the Middle Ages, in the 15th century, there was Swedish involvement in a crusade against the proto-Protestant followers of Jan Hus in Bohemia and a series of crusades in the Balkans against the Ottoman Turks.

Egyptian (or Seventh) Crusade (1248-1254)

From 1248 to 1254, King Louis IX of France organized a crusade against Egypt. This battle, known as the Seventh Crusade, was a failure for Louis.

War of Saint Sabas (1256-1270)

This was essentially a commercial war between the Mediterranean maritime republics of Genoa (aided by Philip of Montfort, Lord of Tyre; John of Arsuf; and the Knights Hospitaller) and Venice (aided by the Count of Jaffa and the Knights Templar). The war began with the murder of a Genoese by a Venetian in a dispute over land owned by the monastery of Saint Sabas in Acre but claimed by both Genoa and Venice.

Syrian or Eighth Crusade (1270-1275)

Under the ruthless Sultan Baybars, the Mamluks demolished Antioch in 1268. In response, Louis organized the Eighth Crusade in 1270. The initial goal was to aid the remaining Crusader states in Syria, but the mission was redirected to Tunis, where Louis died.

Lithuanian Crusades (1280-1435) and Novgorod Crusades (1243- 1435)[23]
The Lithuanian and Novgorod Crusades constituted the last two partly-overlapping phases of the Northern Crusades, admittedly authorised by, and fought on behalf of, the church. They were prosecuted by Saxon, Danish, and Swedish Princes as well as by military orders such as the Teutonic Knights and the Sword Brothers. Their opponents were a range of pagan adversaries including Estonians, Finns (Suomi), Lithuanians, Livonians, Russians, and Wends. By the early 15th century, these ecclesiastical wars, as just one element of a broader process of the expansion throughout medieval Europe, had contributed significantly to extension of the north-eastern frontier of Latin Christendom.

Hungarian Crusade (1314-1354)
Crusade in Hungary against Mongols and Lithuanians originally called by the Pope in 1314, but subsequently renewed by the Papacy in 1325, 1332, 1335, 1352, and 1354.

Italian Crusade (1321)
Italy had seen a series of lesser crusades since 1302, but in 1321 the Papacy proclaimed a specific Crusade in Italy against members of the Este family who ruled several cities, together with Matthew Visconti of Milan and Frederick of Montefeltro, political opponents of the papacy. Although the Crusade was considered successful the continued resistance of the Ghibellines prevented the restoration of papal authority in the region.

Polish Crusades (1325-1369)
Crusade in Poland by The Teutonic Knights against Mongols and Lithuanians originally called by the Pope in 1325, but subsequently renewed by papal order in 1340, 1343, 1351, 1354, 1355, 1363, and 1369.

German Crusade (1328)
Crusade against King Louis IV of Germany.

Bohemian Crusade (1340)
Crusade against heretics in Bohemia.

Finnish Crusade (1348)
Crusade of King Magnus of Sweden against pagans of Finland.

Alexandrian Crusade (1365)

An expedition to Egypt, organised by King Peter I of Cyprus in 1365, resulted in the temporary occupation of Alexandria. After a disorganised and unruly massacre, the Crusaders returned to Cyprus with immense booty. Peter had intended to return, but after a failure to obtain European support the aim was abandoned and Peter died in 1369.

Battle of Kosovo (1386)

During the 14th century Egyptian Mameluk forces took over from the Ottoman Turks as the impetus for Islamic expansion. They invaded most of Asia Minor, extending their influence through Macedonia and Bulgaria to the Danube, defeating Christian Serb forces at the Battle of Kosovo in 1386.

Relief of Constantinople (1396) and Relief of Belgrade (1453-1456) and (1521-1526)

By 1396, the earlier Christian objective of recovering Jerusalem was replaced by the need to relieve Constantinople. An expeditionary force led by King Sigismund of Hungary and Count John of Nevers was defeated at Nicopolis in 1396, and in 1443, a Crusading army instigated by Pope Eugenius IV was annihilated at Varna. Constantinople itself would fall to the Ottoman Turkish forces in 1453.

Pope Nicholas V then preached a new crusade, led by John Capistrano to Hungary where an Ottoman force besieging Belgrade was defeated in 1456.[24] This was only a temporary respite. In 1521 Belgrade did fall, and Hungarian forces finally succumbed five years later at the Battle of Mohacs.

The African Crusades (1415, 1437, and 1458)

The Knights of Aviz, in conjunction with their brother Knights of The Order of Christ, undertook a number of Crusading ventures to Africa. Expeditions in 1415 under King João I, their former Grand Master, and in 1437 under his son Duarte resulted in the conquest of Ceuta and attacks on Tangier, both sanctioned by Papal Bulls[25] as religious Crusades.

These crusading ventures were short-lived, however, and the Crusade in Africa degenerated into an essentially mercantile enterprise. One noted participant in these crusades was Prince Henry the Navigator.

Battle of Lepanto (1571)

Following the surrender of Famagusta in August1571, Turkish forces occupied the Island of Cyprus. The Holy League, founded in 1570, with members drawn from Spain, Venice, and the Papacy, led by Don John of Austria, assembled perhaps the largest fleet ever assembled by Christian forces in the 16th century which sailed from Messina in September 1571. The Turkish fleet of a similar size (about 200 galleys) was encountered in Curzolari in the Bay of Lepanto and battle ensued on 7 October. 180 Turkish galleys were captured and towed by the Christian fleet to Corfu; the rest were either burned or sunk. 15,000 Turks were massacred, 7,000 were taken prisoner, and 20,000 slaves were freed. This was undoubtedly an important Christian victory over the infidels conducted with the similar motivation as the earlier Crusades to the Holy Land.

The Impact of these 'Lesser Crusades'

Assessing the impact of these 'lesser crusades' is not easy since many were inextricably linked to other events, including some of the major events which did merit a title of 'Crusade'. Whilst many of these lesser 'crusades' had commercial or political aims as well as religious motivation, they clearly illustrate not only the widespread distribution of many minor chivalric movements but also the extended period of chivalric influence extensively throughout the whole of Europe. This all illustrates the willingness of the Papacy to call anything a Crusade that suited the politics of indidual Popes.

Motivation other than the acquisition of glory, wealth, and power was also in evidence at an early date; for example in 1107-1110 King Sigurd I of Norway, known as *Sigurðr Jórsalafari* or 'Jerusalem-farer' led a successful crusade of Norwegians before the Second Crusade, and brought back scientific knowledge as well as engineering and military technology such as far stronger castles with round rather than square towers. The Fourth Crusade turned into a sack of Constantinople and creation of Crusader states in Byzantine territories because the crusaders did not otherwise have the money to pay the Venetians for their ships.

Such events also illustrate that the northern European Countries which supported the crusades in the Holy Land then went on to pursue similar activities long after the fall of Acre or indeed the suppression of the Knight Templar Order in France. Clearly, surviving members of the Knight Templar Order who wished to flee from the French oppression of 1307 would have had numerous opportunities throughout Europe to integrate with other organisations and pursue similar military roles.

However, it must not be forgotten that the Knights Templar Order played a decisive role in developing activities such as building, banking, commercial trading, ship-building, and facilitating the movement of pilgrims to and from the Holy Land – in effect modern Tourism. Common sense suggests none of these additional activities would simply cease when the military might of the Order was suppressed, and possible developments will now be examined in

Part Two as an adjunct to the military legacy the Order left behind.

It is interesting to speculate whether wider events would have taken the same course had the Knight Templar Order maintained its widespread influence as a major military force, for the Hospitallers, the Teutonic Knights, the Portuguese Order of Christ, and a number of less military-chivalric-religious orders undoubtedly picked up the mantle of opposing some Islamic forces.

Part Two

THE CULTURAL ENVIRONMENT FOR SURVIVAL

Preamble

Undoubtedly, the fall of Acre in 1291 defines the end of the Holy Land crusades but religious crusades did not cease. The Knights Templar and the Knights Hospitaller were not the only chivalric orders in existence in the early 12th century, and other orders survived to oppose many lesser military 'threats' to Christendom – in particular, from the Turkish Empire throughout the late 13th, 14th, and 15th centuries.

Although many individuals died during the Crusades, numerous knights returned to their homelands, taking back with them evidence of their former activities in the form of trophies of war, looted treasures, religious artefacts and relics, historical accounts, philosophical ideas, and anecdotal stories if not actual documents; and undoubtedly they, or their descendants, had an enduring influence.

Likewise, the formal dissolution of the Knights Templar Order was certainly not the end of the story. Whilst the exact strength of the Order in 1307 may never be known it has been estimated that, during the 13th century the tally of knights, sergeants, serving brothers and priests may have been about 7,000 with many times that number of pensioners, associate members, serving officials and other subjects; few were actually arrested in 1307 and even fewer lost their lives. The Templar holdings in 1307 were widespread, and across Europe totalled something like 880 castles, preceptories, and farms, within an overall total of perhaps as many as 15,000 houses. Most of these were concentrated in the Templar Provinces of England (which included Scotland and Ireland), Portugal, Castile, Leon, Aragon, France, Acquitaine, Provence, Germany, Italy, Sicily, and the Eastern Mediterranean (Antioch and Tripoli).

However, properties existed in most European Capitals where the Templars conducted banking operations, and the Order had holdings in many seaports and on major navigable rivers. Pope Clement V had stipulated, that following their suppression the possessions of the Templar Order throughout Europe should be passed on to the Knights Hospitallers[26], and much survived – some within the custodianship of other chivalric orders with a minority passing to secular institutions. Likewise, most Templar ports and shipyards survived and their large commercial cargo and passenger-carrying vessels and naval ships and galleys certainly did not disappear overnight. Inevitably these would continue to affect the communities in which they were built and perpetuate the memories of their builders. Similarly, the demand for other Templar functions did not cease; their financial and banking roles continued, perhaps through contemporary organisations such as the Hanseatic League; and their role as 'Travel Agents' was undoubtedly perpetuated as pilgrims travelled to Jerusalem and other religious sites throughout the intervening centuries; this was also a time of expanding global trade, political colonisation, and a continuous programme of armed conflict, with huge global movements that facilitated the exchange of ideas between nations and countries.

Social elements seen within the crusading orders were not lost either; the institutionalised development of *auberges* or inns by the Knights of St John in Rhodes and Malta up to 1798, clearly fulfilled social as well as accommodation needs for knights from distant *langues* visiting headquarters and we can assume the other chivalric orders adopted a similar approach. Individual Templars who found haven in other surviving chivalric orders, religious bodies, or commercial, political, and educational institutions would not have lost these social needs. Whilst no evidence has yet been found to prove such factors influenced the emerging speculative Masonic chivalric orders, this cannot be ruled this out.

Certainly such evidence was retained by the descendant families of former Templars, the chivalric orders, and 'honour systems', or religious houses and monasteries. The latter particularly perpetuated such evidence in the form of often-illuminated historical and religious texts, but also through such religious and moral teachings as mystery plays. Religious and cultural reformation was imminent followed by successive industrial revolutions, and these promoted urbanisation and the emergence of universities, industrial organisations, clubs, and societies which required the creation of constitutions, regulations, instructions, and written records. This process was assisted by technological developments such as the printing press, and by emerging historical scholarship and historians who helped perpetuate ideas from the past. This was the environment in which early chivalric Freemasonry emerged; the Masonic 'Old Charges' were devised; traditional histories were compiled to illustrate moral teachings, and lodge procedures and rituals developed.

This part considers this environment within which speculative masonry took root up to the end of the 17th century, setting the scene for the emergence of today's Masonic orders of chivalry in the steps of the Crusaders.

2.1 THE TEMPLARS WHO SURVIVED

At the time of its dissolution the Templar Order was reputed to be extremely wealthy, and copious records exist of its properties – perhaps as many as 15,000 'Templar Houses' – and lands possessed by them in many countries. However, unlike land and property which is fixed, much less is known about the disposition, after that fateful 13 October 1307 of their monetary wealth, their entire maritime fleet, and the individuals engaged in commercial and maritime activities,

Surviving Templar Properties
Many writers on the history of the chivalric orders have touched briefly on the surviving Templar properties, but in 2009 Helen Nicholson listed in great detail[27] the Templar properties in the British Isles mentioned during the trials of the Knights Templar, so expansion of this topic is not a priority here.

However, it is worth stressing that the knightly members of the Templar Order who were identified and persecuted in the first decade of the 14th century would only have been a tiny proportion of those involved with Templar activities.

Whilst many preceptories existed for religious or administrative reasons, many of the lands endowed on the Order were of considerable agricultural importance, and preceptories existed for mainly commercial farming and trading reasons; there is no evidence that the dissolution of the Order significantly affected such operations.

A large element of the Order's work involved maritime operations such as trading in wool and grain and the transport of pilgrims to the Holy Land. Even if members of the Order were persecuted throughout Europe, at any point in time only a small proportion of ships and their crews would be in port; others would be either in foreign ports, or statistically more likely, 'on the high seas'. Hence ports and dockyards and their workforce would be little affected, and there is little evidence to suggest the trading and maritime operations were affected.

Throughout Europe, the Templar Order is credited with developing, perhaps as early as 1150, an embryo banking operation. This used an innovative procedure involving a form of 'letters of credit', an early form of cheques or bankers' drafts, the forerunners of those in use today. Pilgrims or other travellers would deposit deeds and valuables with one Templar house, thus creating a form of 'deposit account' and receive a letter detailing their holdings. These may have used some form of encryption or cypher alphabet based on a Maltese Cross, although some scholars have suggested this was a later innovation. Travellers could then present such letters at other Templar centres *en route* and obtain funds from their account. Thus travellers and pilgrims were less likely to be attacked since they carried fewer valuables. Necessarily this required Templars centres in most major European cities and ports; in some cases, such as Paris and London, these were associated with Templar Provinces and major Preceptories which contained facilities for safeguarding large deposits of wealth.

The Templar Fleet
Much of the Templar activity involved transport not only of pilgrims and supplies to and from the Holy Land, but also of the troops, armour, and horses need to replaces losses in warfare. This involved both northern maritime activities from Britain, Ireland, Germany, the Baltic, and Scandinavia, as well as extensive Mediterranean operations. Consequently, there is no question that the Templar Mediterranean fleet was sizeable; in addition to its primary task of transporting Templar troops and their logistics support between theatres of war, trading was another major task; all these roles required large ships with a sea-going capability. In addition, the Mediterranean was the domain of pirates, and Templar ships would be armed or have armed escorts – typically rowing galleys – to resist such attacks.[28]

The Order was, of course, primarily persecuted in France and it has always been assumed that there was sufficient warning of the impending action by Philip le Bel to allow the French Templar fleet to sail before the fateful day thus avoiding capture by the French King's agents. In particular, it was reported that during the preceding day the Templar treasure from Paris together with a number of high-ranking dignitaries of the Order, including the Treasurer, were transported to the Order's naval base at La Rochelle. The treasure was loaded on to eighteen galleys and never heard of again. King Philip certainly attacked the Templar treasury in Paris, but there is little evidence that he obtained any significant wealth by this action, beyond cancelling the repayment of the extensive loans he had received from the Order.

Despite much speculation over the centuries, no details of the fleet's escape route(s) or final destination(s) have been found. More significant is that, on the dissolution of the Templar Order, when its properties and lands were generally handed over to the Order of the Hospital and The Order of Christ, the disposition of the maritime fleet was not recorded – or at least, not publicised. So what happened to the Templar Fleet?

Some authors have argued that this fleet must have ended up in the Western part of Scotland, but this argument must, be considered at best as one possible option amongst others, or at worst as unproven speculation. This view is simply based on practical considerations of general European activities of the time and the existence of other, perhaps more likely possibilities.

For practical purposes the French Templar fleet would of course have been based in either major Mediterranean ports – primarily Marseilles as the main southern trading hub, or Toulon as the major southern naval base – for the support of activities in the Holy Land, or the major Atlantic ports – primarily La Rochelle and Bordeaux – for trading and transport of Pilgrims. However evidence exists of the Templars using many smaller ports such as Argelès-sur-Mer and Collioure in the former major Templar Province of Aragon situated near the important Templar castle of Château Royal.

The Templar naval organisation would therefore be a highly significant part of the organisation in every country, and not only around the Mediterranean. There is no doubt that the Templar holdings included ports and shipyards both on the coast and on major, navigable rivers as well as commercial cargo carrying vessels and naval ships. The history of the Templar voyages also confirmed that their activities were not solely coastal transits; the Templars were some of the first to use magnetic compasses to aid navigation and they possessed some of the most sophisticated maps of the time.

Taking as a working hypothesis that this sizeable fleet did sail in advance of the French King's actions leaving the French ports in October 1307 where might it have gone? Common sense suggests firstly that only a small part of the Templar fleet would have been in French ports or rivers at the time, and consequently the rest of the fleet would have been at sea or in foreign ports – probably where the French King had little or no influence; and secondly, that any ships that left France would certainly aim to take refuge in destinations where they would not be conspicuous or in countries sympathetic to the French and Papal causes which would render them liable for seizure. In addition, practical considerations would suggest that likely destinations would be where large trading vessels or warlike naval ships would not stand out in isolation, and therefore the possible options become extremely limited.

Examining first the Mediterranean area; in the Western Mediterranean the majority of the large ports were French or in today's Italy and Sicily which would be sympathetic to the Papal cause; the Eastern Mediterranean was under the control of Ottoman forces, the long-term enemies of the Templar Order. Even after the demise of Fatimid Caliphate naval strength that started around the time of the First Crusade the area would be closed to the Templar fleet as the maritime Italian states dominated the Eastern Mediterranean with Venice, Genoa and Pisa becoming particularly powerful. Likewise ports on the North African coast would be hostile under control of Barbary pirates.

The one possible exception was the area controlled then by the Order of the Hospital which, having lost its holding in the Holy Land, had established itself on Eastern Mediterranean Islands. It is therefore unlikely that a sizeable Templar fleet could take refuge in any Mediterranean port unless it was a Hospitaller port, and, of course, it is recorded the Hospitallers maintained a sizeable Mediterranean fleet continuously until 1798.

The European Atlantic coastline does not seem to offer likely havens either; although the King of France had little or no control over most of the ports on the Atlantic seaboard, (the area being under the control of the Duke of Aquitaine – the King of England), the Bay of Biscay would probably have been patrolled by the French Navy based in La Rochelle, Brest, or Bordeaux, and therefore access to northern Spanish Ports would also be precluded; however, access to the southern and western Iberian Peninsular would certainly be a possibility for ships leaving the French Mediterranean ports. Later evidence does suggest at least part of the Templar fleet may have taken this route as the Portuguese Order of Christ certainly inherited Templar holdings and no records imply these did not include ports and ships. Indeed, Portuguese explorers such as Prince Henry the Navigator, Vasco de Gama, and Christopher Columbus undertook far-ranging expeditions with ships sometimes bearing the Templar Red Pattee Cross or Maltese Cross. Evidence also suggests these early explorers had access to Templar maps and maritime records.

Which leaves northern European ports, and here, outside the British Isles the significant controlling body was the Hanseatic League, active from 1260-1570, with not only major ports and a significant commercial fleet, but also a major armed naval element and close connections with the former crusading Order of Teutonic Knights. Records confirm in particular that there were a number of Islands in the Baltic area, including Bornholm, Øland, Gothland, and Østlars which not only provided support bases for the Knight Templar fleet, but also had a similar later role supporting the Teutonic Knights, Livonian Brothers of the Sword, and vessels of the Hanseatic League.[29] Whilst documentary evidence does not confirm specifically that former Knights Templar military and naval personnel formed part of the Hanseatic League, it is certainly possible that large Templar commercial ships and armed galleys would not be seen as conspicuous in both Baltic supply bases and the larger Hanseatic ports. Such ports existed in many Baltic cities and Norwegian, Swedish, and English ports such as Boston, Lincolnshire, Bristol, Bishop's Lynn (now King's Lynn), Hull, Ipswich, Norwich, Yarmouth (now Great Yarmouth), York and in major rivers such as the Thames and Humber. It may be coincidence that these ports and rivers were also where former Templar holdings of major significance were located.

Considering where the Templar treasure might have gone must inevitably evoke similar thoughts; the Templar Order developed banking in many

Northern European cities, as did the Hanseatic League from 1260 onwards and unquestionably large Templar financial holdings would be unnoticeable in cities which were also centres of Hanseatic League banking and which would remain so until the late 16th century.

One particularly interesting suggestion, beloved of certain historians and conspiracy theorists alike, is that the Knights Templar were instrumental in laying the foundations for the Country of Switzerland. Certainly, on 1 August 1291, ten weeks after Acre fell, three small regions of the future Switzerland signed a unification pact.[30] These were the cantons of Uri, Schwyz, and Unterwalden, which formed the core of the Country which developed at exactly the same time as the persecution of the Templars. In particular, sharing a major land border with eastern France, the territory would have been a particularly attractive, mountainous destination for Knight Templar members seeking sanctuary from France. In addition, the city of Sion in the Canton of Valais may have early Templar connections with its two huge fortified castles, at Tourbillion and Valere overlooking the City. Early anecdotes told that the Templars originally established themselves there after fleeing from France, and similar anecdotes about the history of several Swiss Cantons record white-coated knights mysteriously appearing to help against foreign belligerents. It is also intriguing that banking and early clock-making were Templar as well as Swiss activities, and the German Hospitaller *langue*, which then covered the territory which later became Switzerland, contained many former Templar holdings.

Surviving Individuals

Although many individuals died during the Crusades, many knights returned to their homelands, and it is interesting to examine – if only briefly – their later achievements. Whilst the exact numerical strength of the Templars in 1307 may never be accurately known it has been estimated that, during the 13th century the tally of knights, sergeants, serving brothers and priests may have been of the order of 7,000 with many times that number of pensioners, associate members, serving officials and other subjects; few were actually arrested in 1307 and even fewer lost their lives. In 2009 Helen Nicholson listed in great detail[31] 144 individual members of the Templar Order in the British Isles in 1308-1311. Not all of these were interrogated. More to the point, many of the individuals actually captured and interrogated were elderly or decrepit and died before interrogation or trial. Of those who survived, some were pardoned but some, found guilty, spent the rest of their lives in monasteries. It is therefore not specifically the survivors of the Templar trials who would provide later influence on the environment for survival, but their families or families of crusading knights who survived and returned from crusades to use their experience and knowledge to further the development of their home countries.

Finally, it is important to recall that in 1308 Pope Clement V absolved the leaders of the Order in what has become known as the Chinon Parchment[32], a document seemingly not made public at the time. In addition, another document dated 20 August 1308 addressed to Philip IV of France stated that *'absolution had been granted to all those Templars that had confessed to heresy and restored them to the Sacraments and to the unity of the Church'*. The latter document, known to historians[33] at least since the 18th century, likewise did not seem to have been given wide publicity. Consequently, so far as we can tell, the guilt of the Templars remained the official position and would have affected the attitudes to the Order. It is not unreasonable to suppose that this probably resulted in any contact with the Templar Order or individual members would either pass unrecorded, or be carefully concealed, or destroyed at an early date so few documents or other evidence survive today.

In September 2001, Barbara Frale discovered a copy of the Chinon Parchment dated 17-20 August 1308 in the Vatican secret archives. Her findings were published in the Journal of Medieval History in 2004, and in 2007 the Vatican published the document as part of a limited edition of 799 copies.[34] Of similar significance are the records of the Papal Inquisition in Malta which have only been made available to scholars very recently; few of these have been examined in any detail as yet.[35] However, such primary sources are rare, and to gain a realistic perspective it is necessary to examine secondary sources including records of contemporary organisations which, for reasons just explained, will rarely include explicit references to the Templar Order.

2.2 THE ORDER OF CHRIST

The Portuguese Order

Portugal had always been extremely supportive of the Knights Templar Order which was established there from 1128, and when the Order was persecuted in other European states[36] and suppressed in France in 1312, King Denis I refused to take similar action. By exemption from Pope John XXII, Portuguese Templar holdings were kept safe; the Templar Order was not extinguished; and no individuals were persecuted. With Papal approval in 1319[37] the Templar Order was reconstituted as the Order of the Knights of Our Lord Jesus Christ.[38] Later, that order reverted to its original name, the Order of Christ (*Ordem Militar de Cristo*), attracting many gifts and donations in support of their cause; their first significant grant was from Theresa, Countess of Portugal in the year of the Council of Troyes. The Order was granted the possessions of the Knights Templar including the principal holdings of the Castles of Almourol, Idanha, Monsanto, Pombal, Soure, and the town of Tomar, including the Castle, the Convent of the Order of Christ, and the Church of Santa Maria do Olival. Royal patronage followed, with royal princes and nobles assuming Mastership of the Order.

During the 14th century the Iberian peninsula was still dominated by Muslim and Moorish forces, and the brief details on the Lesser Crusades given earlier showed the involvement of this fledgling Order. Although the mission of the military orders in Portugal appeared to diminish significantly after the overthrow of Muslim domination, Portuguese expeditions overseas provided fresh opportunities. An expedition in 1415 under King João I resulted in the conquest of Ceuta; and a similar venture in 1437 under his son Duarte to attack Tangier were sanctioned by Papal Bulls as Crusades, inspired by a religious fervour. The Knights of the Order of Christ, successors of the Knights Templars, achieved deeds of valour under Henrique, brother of King Duarte. In these crusading ventures the Order of Christ was supported by the Military Order of Aviz, but despite such support enthusiasm did not last, and the African Crusade degenerated into an essentially mercantile enterprise.

The Order played a major role in the developing Portuguese maritime global ventures, with several key aspects of their history traceable to a Templar background. The two major maritime trading areas prior to the 12th century were the coastal areas of Northern Europe and the Mediterranean basin; there was little commercial opportunity or incentive for European trade east of the Strait of Gibraltar. This changed with the removal of Muslim occupation of the Iberian peninsula, and promotion of economic growth particularly after the siege of Lisbon in 1147. The Italian states, mainly Venice, Genoa, and Pisa, had dominated eastern Mediterranean trade, but then developments in ship design permitted longer sea voyages[39] with the first direct voyage from Genoa to Flanders in 1277. This was contemporary with Templar maritime activity and it is not unreasonable to consider a matching fleet capability both for trade and transport of pilgrims to the Holy Land. Some better known achievements came under Prince Henry 'the Navigator' – a former participant in the 'African Crusades' – who, following his appointment as Grand Master in 1418, used the wealth of the Order to finance voyages of exploration down the African coast, and after his death in 1460 these continued, eventually reaching around the Cape of Good Hope and to parts of Asia. Significantly, these early expeditions were also sanctioned by Papal Bulls[40] as religious crusades, and early travellers to the New World sailed under the flag of the Order of Christ – a variant of a Maltese Cross.

After the relaxation of the requirements of poverty, chastity, and obedience in the 16th century, the Order ceased to be a religious entity and became one of honour and prestige controlled by the Crown; Queen Maria I secularized the Order in 1789, but in 1910 when the Portuguese monarchy ceased, the Order was extinguished. In 1917, the Order of Christ, the Order of Aviz, and St James of the Sword were constituted as a group of 'Ancient Military Orders', and the Order survives today as a chivalric Order of five classes: Grand Cross; Grand Officer; Commander; Officer; and Knight; the first two classes equate to British knighthoods.

The Papal 'Order of Christ.'
The Pope only allowed creation of the Portuguese Order of Christ if he also could confer it as a Papal Order. Thus, today, there are two branches of 'The Order of Christ': the Portuguese order; and the highest order of the Vatican state. These two branches of the order are the only ones which can legitimately claim direct descent from the Templars, and both still exist.

This may seem inconsistent with Vatican policy bearing in mind the earlier Papal attitude to the Templar Order but, as mentioned earlier, in 1308 Pope Clement V not only absolved the Templar leaders[41], but also wrote (20 August 1308) to Philip IV of France, that *'absolution had been granted to all those Templars that had confessed to heresy and restored them to the Sacraments and to the unity of the Church'*.

It may therefore be seen that in both the Portuguese and Vatican Orders there are clear indications of a continuous environment which allowed chivalric elements and ideas to have come down to the present day very much 'in the steps of the Templars'.

2.3 THE TEUTONIC ORDER AND THE HANSA

The Middle Ages are fixed in the popular consciousness as an epoch of kings and kingdoms. But for much of the medieval period, northern Europe was dominated by two great non-princely powers. One was the military order of crusading knights known as the *Deutsche Orden* or Teutonic Order.[42] The other was the Hanseatic League, a confederation of merchant towns more properly called the *Hansa Teutonoricum*, or German Hansa. At first glance, these two northern powers – a brotherhood of crusader knights and a community of merchants – might seem to have little or nothing in common. In fact, however, the two sprang from the same soil, if not from the same roots; they not only occupied overlapping geographic territories, but were deeply interconnected in a myriad of other ways as well.

As explained earlier, not only are these two organisations contemporary with the Templar Order but also both may well have had connections which cast fresh light on the dissolution of the Templars and their subsequent impact on the modern world. Consequently it is not inappropriate to review the Teutonic Order and the Hanseatic League and their interactions from the 14th century onwards.

The Teutonic Order
Like the better-known Knights of the Temple and Knights of St John of Jerusalem, the Teutonic Knights were members of a military order born of the crusades in about 1190 with their roots in Acre. Unlike these slightly older orders, however, the Teutonic Order maintained a distinct national identity which connected it with Germany. After the Muslims regained control in the Middle-East, the Teutonic Order focussed its activities on rooting out paganism in Europe, starting in Hungary in the early 13th century. In 1230, through the Prussian Crusade, the Wends in the area between the Elbe and Poland were converted to Christianity paving the way for German settlement in that region and allowing the creation of a Monastic State by the Teutonic Knights. Subsequent operations were focussed on the Baltic region with crusades against Baltic pagans and the conversion of Courland, Livonia, and Estonia, eventually resulting in the creation of a feudal state and sole rulership of Prussia.

The Order was commanded by a Grand Master or *Hochmeister* and divided into three provinces (one in southern Germany, one in Prussia, and one in Livonia) each ruled by a provincial commander or *Landmeister*. Each province was further divided into commanderies, or *Komtureis*. In general, the objectives of the Teutonic Knights (again, not necessarily in this order!) were to Christianize the indigenous Baltic peoples; to subjugate those same peoples; and to expand the Order's territories. In fact, while conversion of the non-Christian population was one of the Order's stated objectives, it was not, or at least did not remain, the primary one throughout its history.

The Teutonic Order had its origins in a crusader hospital founded during the siege of Acre in 1190; in 1197 it was formally organized as the Order of Saint Mary of the Germans of Jerusalem, and it gained official Papal recognition in 1199. Although the Teutonic Order, like the Hospitallers and the Knights Templar, began in the Holy Land and had the defeat of the Saracens as its initial aim, it was poorly positioned to become a major force in that part of the world; all the important castles and lands had already been granted to the Hospitallers and Templars, and the Teutonic Order there remained small and poor in consequence.

The Knights wore white surcoats with a black cross, granted by Pope Innocent III in 1205, which survived until modern times, the black cross pattée having been adopted by the Kingdom of Prussia as a military decoration and insignia, and later by Germany as the Iron Cross.

Perhaps fortunately for the Order, the Saracens were not the only non-Christians with lands abutting Christendom. In 1224 a Polish Duke, Conrad of Masovia, asked the Teutonic Order for help in defending his lands against attacks by the pagan *Pruzzi*, or Prussians. The Order, after obtaining guarantees from Emperor Frederick II that it could retain and rule all the lands it conquered, agreed, and in 1230 began its decades-long campaign of conquest in the Baltic. The victorious Teutonic Knights founded Kulm in 1232, Marienwerder in 1233, Thorn in 1234, and Elbing in 1237; by 1239 the Knights '... had reached the coast, and had established a network of fortresses from which they could dominate the whole territory'. In 1237, the Order absorbed a smaller military order, the Brethren of the Sword, which had won lands by crusading in Estonia and Livonia; those territories augmented the Order's holdings.

Further conquests led to the founding of Konigsburg in 1253. By 1308, the Order had won control of the coastal lands west of the Vistula (including Danzig), cutting Poland off from the sea and thereby guaranteeing that its trade with the west would be conducted through Prussian ports. With the conquest of Prussia complete (and the Holy Land irretrievably lost to the crusaders in any case), in 1309 the Order moved its headquarters from Venice to the Prussian fortress of Marienburg and turned its attentions to the Grand Duchy of Lithuania, the last pagan state in Northern Europe.

The Teutonic Order became extremely wealthy from their assimilation of smaller orders, acquisitions, and feudal income. This allowed the hiring of mercenaries from across Europe and the establishment of a significant Baltic fleet supported from bases including several islands; these included Bornholm, Øland, Gothland, and Østlars, previously used by the Knight Templar fleet, ships of the Livonian Brothers of the Sword, and Hanseatic League fleets.

Inevitably this power led to the start of the Order's decline; their aggression brought them into conflict with other Christian states such as Poland and Lithuania who feared territorial encroachment. In 1410, attacks by the joint Polish-Lithuanian army at the Battle of Tennenberg or Grunwald initiated the decline of the Teutonic Order, although its power would only really diminish over the following century.

The Teutonic Order reached its zenith in the late 14th century, when kings and noblemen from all over Europe joined the Order in its campaigns against the Lithuanians, and '... for generations, the highest praise that could be given to a Christian nobleman was that he had become a Knight in Prussia'. However, in 1515 the Holy Roman Emperor Maximillian I withdrew support for the Teutonic Order which then lost significant territory; this was further exacerbated in 1525 when their Grand Master, Albert of Brandenburg, converted to Lutheranism, resigned as Grand Master, and became Duke of Prussia.

After the loss of Prussia in 1525, the Teutonic Knights concentrated on their possessions in the Holy Roman Empire. Since they held no contiguous territory, they developed a three-tiered administrative system under which individual properties were combined into commanderies that were administered by a commander *(Komtur)*. Several commanderies were combined to form a bailiwick headed by a *Landkomtur*. All of the Teutonic Knights' possessions were subordinate to the Grand Master, whose seat was in the Castle of Bad Mergentheim, with an organisation in Germany of twelve bailiwicks: Alden Biesen (in present-day Belgium); Alsace-Burgundy; Austria; Franconia; Hesse; Koblenz; Lorraine; Saxony; Thuringia; Tyrol (*An der Etsch und im Gebirge*); Utrecht; and Westphalia. In addition, the Order administered holdings outside Germany in six bailiwicks: Apulia; Armenia-Cyprus; Bohemia; Lombardy; 'Romania' (in Greece); and Sicily.

By 1497 the Order had lost its possessions in Sicily, mainly through Papal influence, but it retained a house in Venice until 1595 when it was sold and became a diocesan seminary; the Order retained some property in Lombardy, and did, in fact, sustain a form of existence in Roman Catholic areas until stripped of any residual power by Napoleon in 1809 when only the seat of the Grand Master at Mergentheim remained.

Today the Order only survives as an essentially charitable organisation. Purely religious since 1929, the Order now has about 1,000 members, including some 700 Associates and 300 Roman Catholic priests and nuns organized into six provinces (Austria, the Czech Republic, Germany, Italy, Slovakia, and Slovenia) providing spiritual guidance and care for the ill and the aged. In this sense the Teutonic Order has returned to its 12th century objective: the spiritual and physical care of Germans in foreign lands. The current Grand Master, Bruno Platter, is based in Vienna and the Order still confers limited honorary knighthoods.

The Hanseatic League

The Hanseatic League (also known as the *Hansa*) was an alliance of trading guilds that established and maintained a trade monopoly along the coast of Northern Europe, from the Baltic to the North Sea, during the Late Middle Ages and early modern period between the 13th and 17th centuries. Rival cities co-operated within the League to defend themselves from pirates as well as to compete against larger economic powers. It has been suggested that The League was the forerunner of the European Community[43] as a free trade zone and as an organisation which needed to balance wider community interests with those its individual constituent members.

Hansa origins mainly stem from the rebuilding of Lübeck in 1159 after Henry, the Lion of Saxony, had captured it from the Count of Holstein. Lübeck was perhaps the most prominent Hanseatic city and hosted the periodic Hanseatic meetings or *Diets*. The *Hansa* gained strength through negotiating the relaxation of tariffs with many European states, providing mutual protection against piracy and other threats through their individual cities each maintaining a standing maritime force supported by trained pilots, and an infrastructure including harbours and lighthouses. In alliance with Swedish merchants, the Baltic trade was significantly developed and this created a wealthy merchant middle class. Some of the *Hansa* cities such as Danzig, now Gdansk, and Riga were developed directly as Hanseatic trading posts; others such as Elbing, now Elblag, were originally founded by the Teutonic Knights. The Hansa also used Danish islands in the Baltic strategically located along the routes used by northern crusading armies for support of their shipping fleet, including, as mentioned earlier, Bornholm, Øland, Gothland, and Østlars. These islands still preserve evidence of Knight Templar activity, and today, incidentally, provide ports of call for modern tourist cruise ships.

Of immense and lasting significance was the League's military arm, and dominance over the European shipbuilding industry; this was based mainly in Lübeck and in Danzig, and *Hansa* ships were sold widely throughout Europe over a period of nearly four hundred years. It may be significant, however, that although the League as a whole put much effort and money into defence, the military forces were the responsibility of individual *Hansa* cities. Consequently, unlike the military and naval arms of the Templar Order which was perceived to have declared territorial ambitions, there was never a standing *Hansa* army or navy which might have been regarded as a threat to the sovereignty of individual states.

However, like the Templar Order, the League had its own banking arrangements including an exchange mechanism, regulated tariffs, and a Parliament (*Diet*, the *Hansetage*), although this rarely met. The League's earliest trading centres were in Bruges (Flanders), Bergen (Norway), and London (England), which became important enclaves. The London centre, established in 1320, stood west of London Bridge near Upper Thames Street just under a mile east of the Temple Church, and today the site of Cannon Street station. It developed as a walled community with its own warehouses, weigh house, church, offices, and houses, reflecting the importance and scale of the activity.

In 1454, the towns of the Prussian Confederation rose against the dominance of the Teutonic Order and asked for help from King Casimir IV of Poland. Danzig, Thorn, and Elbing were incorporated into the Kingdom of Poland as part of Royal Prussia by the Second Peace of Thorn (1466). Kraków, then the capital of Poland, was also a *Hansa* city. Lesser Hanseatic ports had a representative merchant and warehouses, and in England these existed in Boston, Lincolnshire, Bristol, Bishop's Lynn (now King's Lynn), Hull, Ipswich, Norwich, Yarmouth (now Great Yarmouth), and York. Today, the sole remaining Hanseatic warehouse in England survives at Kings Lynn.

The League primarily traded timber, furs, resin (or tar), flax, honey, wheat, and rye from the east to Flanders and England with wool, cloth (and, increasingly) manufactured goods going in the other direction. Metal ore (principally copper and iron) and herring came southwards from Sweden.

German colonists under strict *Hansa* supervision built numerous *Hansa* cities on and near the east Baltic coast, such as Danzig (Gdansk), Elbing (Elblag), Thorn (Toru), Reval (now Tallinn, Estonia), Riga, and Dorpat (Tartu), some of which still retain many *Hansa* buildings and bear the style of their Hanseatic days. Most were founded under Lübeck law, which provided that they had to appeal in all legal matters to Lübeck's city council. The Livonian Confederation incorporated parts of modern-day Estonia and Latvia and had its own Hanseatic parliament (*Diet*); all of its major towns became members of the Hanseatic League. The dominant language of trade was Middle Low German, a dialect with significant impact for countries involved in the trade, particularly the larger Scandinavian countries.

The League had a fluid structure, but its members shared some characteristics. First, most of the *Hansa* cities either started as independent cities or gained independence through the collective bargaining power of the

League. Such independence remained limited, however. The Hanseatic free imperial cities owed allegiance directly to the Holy Roman Emperor without any intermediate tie to the local nobility. Another similarity involved the cities' strategic locations along trade routes. In fact, at the height of its power in the late 1300s, the merchants of the Hanseatic League succeeded in using their economic clout, and sometimes their military might, to influence imperial policy. The similarity of their allegiance and influence to that of the Knight Templar Order is unmistakeable.

The League also wielded power abroad: between 1368 and 1370, *Hansa* ships unified in the Confederation of Cologne fought successfully against Denmark, and forced King Valdemar IV of Denmark to grant the League 15 percent of the profits from Danish trade (Treaty of Stralsund, 1370) and an effective trade monopoly in Scandinavia. The *Hansa* also waged a vigorous campaign against pirates since trade routes needed protecting and the League's ships sailed well-armed. Between 1392 and 1440, maritime trade of the League faced danger from raids of the Victual Brothers and their descendants, privateers hired in 1392 by Albert of Mecklenburg against Queen Margaret I of Denmark. In the Dutch-Hanseatic War (1438-41), the merchants of Amsterdam sought and eventually won free access to the Baltic and broke the *Hansa* monopoly.

Exclusive trade routes often came at a high price. Most foreign cities confined the *Hansa* traders to certain trading areas and to their own trading posts. They could seldom, if ever, interact with the local inhabitants, except in the matter of actual negotiation. Moreover, many people, merchant and noble alike, envied the power of the League. For example, in London the local merchants exerted continuing pressure for the revocation of the privileges of the League. The refusal of the *Hansa* to offer reciprocal arrangements to their English counterparts exacerbated the tension. King Edward IV of England reconfirmed the league's privileges in the Treaty of Utrecht (1474) despite this hostility, in part thanks to the significant financial contribution the League made to the Yorkist side during the Wars of the Roses. A century later, in 1597, Queen Elizabeth I of England expelled the League from London and its steelyard closed the following year. The very existence of the League and its privileges and monopolies created economic and social tensions that often crept over into rivalry between League members. The parallel with the Knights Templar Order is equally unmistakeable, and it certainly not unreasonable to suggest that the development of the Hanseatic League after 1307 owes much to the earlier power and influence of that body and experience of former Knights.

Like the Teutonic Order, The League reached its zenith in the late 14th century, but survived until the late 16th century, as by then it could no longer deal with its own internal struggles, the social and political changes that accompanied the Protestant Reformation, the rise of Dutch and English merchants, and the incursion of the Ottoman Empire upon its trade routes and upon the Holy Roman Empire itself. Only nine members attended the last formal meeting in 1669 and only three (Lübeck, Hamburg, and Bremen) remained as members until its final demise in 1862.

Connections between the Hansa and the Teutonic Order

The histories of the *Hansa* and the Teutonic Order were intertwined almost from their beginnings. As mentioned above, the Teutonic Order had its origins in a crusader hospital founded during the siege of Acre; the founders were German merchants from the towns of Lübeck and Bremen. In this sense, the Order and the *Hansa* sprang from the same roots; merchants from Lübeck and other North German towns provided the source element for both groups. The conquest of the Baltic territories was also to some extent a cooperative venture; the *Hansa* provided ships and support for the Teutonic Order's conquest of Prussia in the mid-13th century; in turn, the Teutonic Knights provided protection for the merchants of the *Hansa*.

The Gotland Company, a merchant organization considered by many scholars to be a forerunner of the *Hansa*, had had a similar relationship forty years earlier with the Brethren of the Sword in that Order's crusade against Livonia.

More importantly, the links between the two powers were not limited to military matters. Several of the towns that were members of the *Hansa* (Danzig, Elbing, Thorn, Kulm, Koenigsberg and Marienburg) were under the direct authority of the Grand Master of the Teutonic Order, who exercised tight control over them, limiting their freedom of action within the *Hansa*. Moreover, the Grand Master of the Teutonic Order was a member of the *Hansa* in his own right – the only territorial prince to hold such a position.

Its relationship with the Teutonic Order seems to have been a mixed blessing for the *Hansa*. On the one hand, the *Hansa* undoubtedly benefited by the association. Hanseatic domination of Baltic trade was made possible to a great extent by the Order's conquest of previously pagan lands along the Eastern Baltic; the conquering Knights established German settlers in their newly-seized territories, and this expansion led in turn to the expansion of German mercantile influence in the Baltic. The participation in the *Hansa* of the Prussian towns founded by the Order added to the strength of the confederation as a whole, since they controlled western trade with Poland from the early 14th century onwards. There is no doubt that the Order's military might was often extremely useful to the *Hansa*; in addition, its association with a crusading order afforded the *Hansa* a certain amount of reflected prestige.

On the other hand, despite their historical and continuing connections, the two groups had different – and sometimes conflicting – goals, as enumerated above. In fact, the Order's pursuit of its own objectives '… often involved the *Hansa* in enterprises that damaged its commercial interests and embroiled it in quarrels with foreign powers. Although the Order at first contributed to the prosperity of the *Hansa*, it was later one of the factors in its decline'.

The tensions inherent in this uneasy relationship first appeared in the late 14th century when the *Hansa* and the Order were at the zenith of their powers. Both organisations started to experience pressure from outside authorities as had the Templar Order earlier. The *Hansa* entered a period of ever-intensifying trade conflicts with its partners and competitors, England and the Low Countries; the Teutonic Order faced the loss of its *raison d'etre* in 1380 when Lithuanian Grand Duke Jagiello married Polish Queen-Regnant Jadwiga, and agreed as part of the marriage settlement to Christianize his formerly pagan realm.

The Order, undaunted by this loss of a rationale for further crusades, continued to exist and to make war on its neighbours. One historian noted that almost three decades after Lithuania's Christianization, '… the Order found it expedient to claim that it was still conducting a crusade against the heathen …'

Amplified by these external pressures, existing tensions, and conflicts of interest inevitably led to frictions between the two powers. As early as 1378, during a trade dispute with England, the Grand Master of the Order caused the other members of the *Hansa* great anxiety by threatening to arrest all the English merchants in his territories – a move that, as more moderate *Hansa* members pointed out, would simply have resulted in reprisals against merchants quartered in the *Hansa's* London trading station. Nor were the vexations all on the *Hansa's* side. The future Henry IV, who journeyed to the Baltic three times, so 'annoyed the German knights by persistently discussing the rights of English merchants to trade in Prussia' that the Order subsequently discouraged English participation in its crusades!

These frictions continued into the 15th century, which would prove to be a pivotal one for both the *Hansa* and the Order. In 1407, the Hansa, 'apprehensive of the Grand Master's intentions in the Baltic and of his selfish policy,' as instrumental in forcing the Teutonic Order to return the island of Gotland, captured in 1398, to Denmark, with which the *Hansa* was temporarily at peace. Further East, continuing incursions into the Russian hinterlands by the Order's Livonian branch led to tensions between the *Hansa* and the Grand Dukes of Moscow. It may be noted that Grand Duke Ivan the Great, who wanted to expand Russian influence into the Baltic, would later in the century subsequently conquer Novgorod and close the important Hanseatic trading station there.

If the 15th century marked the beginning of a slow decline for the *Hansa*, it would witness a much more dramatic, if not disastrous, downturn in the fortunes of the Teutonic Order. Although Grand Duke Jagiello's marriage to Queen Jadwiga had united the two realms of Poland and Lithuania into a Christian state, the Teutonic Knights distrusted this former enemy; relations between the Order and Poland-Lithuania deteriorated after Jadwiga died in 1399, leaving Jagiello as sole ruler of the combined kingdom. A series of skirmishes with Jagiello and his allies led to war in 1410; Jagiello mobilized an army of about 10,000 and invaded Prussia in July of that year. When the Grand Master chose to attack Jagiello's troops at Tannenberg without waiting for support from the Livonian branch of the Order (the former Brethren of the Sword), he was killed and his forces were crushed. Although the Order itself survived, it never recovered its former military strength, and this in turn affected its position within the *Hansa*.

Increasing pressures and the widening disparity of interests and objectives of both groups led to deepening rifts between the *Hansa* and the Order as the century continued. One result was the mid-15th century 'Thirteen Years' War'; in 1454, the Prussian towns, tired of the Grand Master's iron rule, rebelled and declared war on the Order, offering their allegiance to King Casimir IV of Poland in return for his military support. (Since both the Order and the rebel towns were members, the *Hansa* nominally remained neutral in the conflict.) In 1466, the Order concluded the Treaty of Thorn, which transferred sovereignty over most of the Prussian towns, including Elbing, Thorn, Danzig, and Marienberg, to Poland, and the Grand Master henceforward held East Prussia as a vassal of the Polish king. The rebellion of the towns had effectively brought about the ruin of the Teutonic state in Prussia. The centuries-old connection between the *Hansa* and the Teutonic Order had finally been severed.

Both the Teutonic Order and the *Hansa* survived, in some form, until the 17th century. The last Grand Master of the much-reduced Prussian branch of the Order converted to Protestantism in 1525 and declared the Order's remaining East Prussian possessions to be a hereditary duchy, to be held henceforth by himself and his heirs. The Livonian branch of the Teutonic Order lasted until 1561, when its territories fell to Ivan the Terrible; the south German branch survived until the late 17th century, when members of the Order fought against the Turks at Vienna in 1683 and Zenta in 1697.

The *Hansa* retained its power and prosperity for a century or more before its final demise; it survived the Anglo-Hanseatic war in the late 15th century and, with the Peace of Utrecht in 1474, regained its international status and strengthened its position *vis-a-vis* the English for the next hundred years. Despite this victory, however, the gradual decline continued. The Thirty Years'

War effectively brought an end to the *Hansa,* and the last *Hansetag* was held in 1669.

Impact of Residual Templar Activity

Whilst the intention of the Papal Bull issued by Pope Clement V in 1312 was that Templar possessions and even some surviving Knights would be transferred to the Knights Hospitallers, in the northernmost part of Europe the Teutonic Knights were the dominant former-chivalric Order. Moreover, the major objectives of the Order certainly included imposition of Christianity on a number of Pagan communities. Many of their operations were conducted in conjunction with other northern forces which had a history of participation in the Crusades, and many of their activities received Papal sanction.

No direct evidence has been found that the Templar personnel and Templar holdings in northern Europe were transferred to the Teutonic Order, but it cannot be denied that the widespread control of trading activities and maritime activities in the area would not be significantly changed by the absorption of the Templar fleet or individual Knights. Indeed, existing on the Baltic Island of Bornholm, mentioned earlier, there are Crosses and runic stones similar to Knight Templar artefacts elsewhere, round churches similar in design to Athlit in Palestine and Tomar in Portugal, and evidence of the island's role in the later Wendish and Baltic Crusades. The European political environment suggests that it was more likely that today's lack of evidence reflects either a general, widespread reluctance to record any evidence of associating with the banned Templar Order or else the subsequence destruction of such records.

Likewise, although the Hanseatic League did not have any form of centralised organisation or control, it undoubtedly had a significant effect on European banking. Perhaps of more significance, is that between about 1260 and 1307 both the Templar Order and the Hanseatic League were engaged in important trading and banking activities in the major European cities, and the extensive surviving records of the latter contain no suggestion of conflict between the organisations. Indeed, the history of the Baltic Islands mentioned earlier suggests enduring support for the different and successive regimes.

Finally, the maritime trading activities of the *Hansa* undoubted required both merchant ships and armed vessels as did the trading and personnel transport operation of the Templar Order up to 1307 and those of the Order of Malta as late as 1798.

New World ports have been suggested as possible destinations for the missing Templar fleet, with claims the Templars established commercial trading links as early as 1269, deriving much of their wealth from Mexican silver. It does not seem likely that the ships of the period would have been capable of making such journeys, and certainly if the Templar Order is considered in isolation, but a combined residual Templar – Teutonic – *Hansa* – Scandinavian maritime organisation might be worthy of further study. Such a suggestion might seem unusual, but certainly not improbable, given that the Hanseatic League travelled widely until the late 16th century.

In particularly, although based in the Mediterranean throughout the 14th and 18th centuries the Order of St John did not escape the sweeping changes during the Protestant Reformation which split Western Europe into Protestant and Roman Catholic states. Whilst in several countries, including England, Scotland, and Ireland, the order became essentially dormant, in others, entire *langues*, bailiwicks, or commanderies experienced religious conversions and survive today in a modified form in Germany, the Netherlands, Sweden, and, to a lesser extent, in many other countries. This suggests the different chivalric orders were sympathetic to the needs of the personnel from other orders and provided homes for those in trouble.

There is archaeological evidence that members of the chivalric orders reached the new world at an early date. One example is on a hillside in Westford, Massachusetts, where there is a ledge carrying the carved outline of a medieval Knight. The Knight holds a broken sword, and his shield bears the arms of the Gunn family from Caithness, who were related to the Sinclairs, along with the picture of a ship, a comet, a star, and the sun. The carving is claimed to represent the cousin of Sinclair, Sir James Gunn, who died climbing nearby Prospect Hill with a party to investigate rising smoke seen in the distance. A punched-hole effigy outline shows Gunn's cloak of the Knights Templar, and his sword is dated around 1360. Some historians consider such evidence questionable.

Operative stone masons were employed from a very early date in New France constructing the stone forts of the type seen at Louisbourg, and at Quebec City. A cross of the Order of St John of Jerusalem with date 1647 inscribed within a Templar shield on a keystone-shaped stone was found in 1784 among the debris of the Prioral House of the Order at Quebec.

Although there has been much speculation about the provenance of those events, unquestionably by 1651 the Knights of St John reached the New World. On 21 May 1651, the Order of St John purchased four islands in the Caribbean, and occupied them until 1665. These islands, Saint Barthelemy, Saint Christopher, Saint Croix, and Saint Martin, were purchased from the French *Compagnie des Îles de l'Amérique* which had just been dissolved and in 1665, sold to the French West India Company.

Whilst the full range of trading and other activities of the Knights of St John in the New World is still unknown, the Order certainly engaged in the normal commerce of that time and area. It is not known if the Order used its own vessels for such trade, but the extensive trade and military activity in the region confirms that, by that time, not only the Hanseatic League, but also many other maritime Nations certainly had capable sea-going fleets facilitating both commerce and slave trading. This known history of the Knights of St John in the New World certainly adds weight to the suggestion that a review of combined residual Templar – Teutonic – *Hansa* – Scandinavian maritime organisation would be fruitful.

Livonian Brothers of the Sword (1202-1560)
Closely related to the Teutonic Order was the military order of the Livonian Brothers of the Sword, composed of German 'warrior monks', founded by the Prince Bishop Albert of Riga in 1202, and the Order received Papal Sanction from Pope Innocent III two years later.

The Order had several different names including the Christ Knights, Sword Brethren, The Militia of Christ of Livonia, and the Courland Brethren of the Sword (Latin: *Fratres militiæ Christi Livoniae,* German: *Schwert-brüderorden*). Initially the order was independent but after defeat in 1236 at the Battle of Schaulen (Saule) by the Samogitians and Semigalians the surviving Brothers merged into the Teutonic Order as an autonomous branch known as the Livonian Order. Unlike the Teutonic Order, the Livonian Order was not instituted in the Holy Land but in Riga, Livonia now the Latvian capital. With similar religious motivation to the Teutonic Order, their stated objective was to convert or conquer pagan tribes in the region and defend the Christian community from their attacks. Their main operations were in the coastal region of today's Estonia, Latvia and Lithuania, then often referred to as Courland and although the Order's headquarters was in (today's) Viljandi in Estonia, the Knights occupied several castles in that area.

Officially, their Grand Master was subject to the Catholic bishops, but this allegiance soon became nominal as the Sword Brethren often acted completely independently. During the Livonian Crusade they acquired a reputation for bravery as well as being reckless and difficult to control. From time to time the Order seemingly acted as mercenaries entering into agreements with nearby monarchies; one example occurred in 1218, a supposedly joint operation with King Valdemar II of Denmark but which in effect resulted in the Danes colonising northern Estonia. In 1232 Pope Gregory IX called on the Sword Brethren to aid in the defence of Finland from attacks by the Republic of Novgorod; no records survive of their contribution, but the outcome of the Swedish-led crusade was that Finland became united with the Kingdom of Sweden for the first time.

The northern Crusades resulted in a decrease in the threats from the east and the Sword Brothers directed their attention southwards towards Lithuania. This culminated in the Battle of Saule on 22 September 1236 when some 3,000

Christian forces, led by about fifty-five knights were defeated by a 5,000 strong pagan force. Some estimates put their losses at 2,700, and The Sword Brethren ceased to be an effective fighting force, never again recovering as an independent military religious order.

However, those who survived were absorbed into the Teutonic Knights, although retaining their traditions and leaders. As a branch of the Teutonic Knights they were known as the Livonian Order and, under their own Master (albeit subject to the Teutonic Grand Master), continued to achieve some of their military and religious objectives, reconquering Courland, Livonia and Semigallia. The Order eventually bought the Duchy of Estonia from King Valdemar IV of Denmark and their autonomy helped them survive the secularization of the Teutonic Knights by Albert of Brandenburg following his adoption of Lutheranism in 1525.

The pagans may have been suppressed but Lutheran groups to the south and the Russian Orthodoxy in the east remained constant threats. In 1560 they were again almost wiped out by a massive attack by Russian forces, and although some knights tried to carry on with the assistance of Sigismund II, Augustus, King of Poland and Grand Duke of Lithuania, their hopes were dashed when their Master, Gotthard Kettler, converted to Lutheranism. The Livonian Order thus followed the Teutonic Order and became secularized, and although some territories were retained briefly, these were soon taken over by neighbouring states and the order ceased to exist.

This represents an element of crusader history that is largely unknown outside the Baltic States; Latvia and Lithuania still mark the anniversary of the Battle of Saule (22 September 1236) as a national holiday, recently jointly declaring it the 'Day of Baltic Unity'. Hence the Order, with objectives similar in many respects to the Knights Templar Order, remained an effective Crusader force from 1202 until the late 1560s and not only perpetuated the crusader ideals for a further 250 years after the demise of the Templars, but also conditioned the environment of northern Europe to such ideals in a way still recognised today as being very much 'in the steps of the Templars'.

2.4 THE HOSPITALLERS FIND A HOME
(1315-1798)

King Philip *le Bel* died on 29 November 1314, and Pope Clement V had already died on the previous 20 April. No more was heard of Pope Clement's proposal of a fresh expedition to recover the Holy Land, but his stipulation that the Knights Templar possessions throughout Europe should be passed on to the Knights Hospitallers is a matter that should not be ignored.

The knights of the Order were organised according to the regions from which they came broadly based on ethno-linguistic divisions (ie tongues or *langues*) rather than the political divisions then existing throughout Europe. Originally there were seven *langues* designated as Provence, France, Auvergne, Italy, Aragon (including Navarre), England (including Scotland and Ireland), and Germany. In 1492 when the kingdom of Castille, Léon, and Portugal was formed, an eighth *langue* was constituted. Each *langue* had its own Priories, Bailiwicks, and Commanderies.

The French-speaking organisation was divided into three *langues*: of Auvergne, France, and Provence; the Iberian Peninsular was initially organised as the *langue* of Aragon but in 1462, a *langue* of Castille, Léon, and Portugal was given a separate existence; the Italo-Romance area was designated as the *langue* of Italy; Germanic-speaking Northern Europe, Scandinavia, Hungary, and Poland, and all of the Holy Roman Empire, including its Slavic-speaking parts, was organised as the *langue* of Germany; and the British Isles, including Scotland and Ireland was grouped as the *langue* of England.

So far as a headquarters was concerned, the Hospitallers had little difficulty in acquiring the Templar estates in Cyprus which had been bought from King Richard I in 1191. At the same time on the island of Rhodes the city and castle were being fortified more strongly.

With their enhanced responsibilities to defend the Christian world the Order was swiftly organised including a strong and powerful naval fleet which patrolled the eastern Mediterranean and battled against any threat from Barbary pirates and Ottoman forces. As considered earlier, the harbour at Rhodes was probably the only location in the eastern Mediterranean area where the former-Templar fleet of both trading ships and armed galleys could find a safe haven and remain unnoticed after the suppression of the Templar Order. Likewise the arrival in Rhodes of even large numbers of former Templar personnel, both military and seafaring, would not be remarked upon amidst the other comings and goings of the numerous Hospitaller forces.

By the middle of the 14th century there were four hundred Hospitallers in Rhodes where there was an Inn or *Auberge* for each of the seven *langues*. The Knights colonised the neighbouring islands, holding all the southern Sporades, and confined the Turks to the mainland. During this period the Order also occupied Smyrna on the mainland for three years. In 1365, together with the Venetians and with Knights from Cyprus, the Hospitallers attacked Egypt as being the key to the recovery of Palestine. Having captured, plundered, and virtually destroyed Alexandria, nothing more was achieved, because the Venetians withdrew, unhappy at seeing their trade with Egypt ended.

The fortifications of Rhodes continued to be improved, dominated by a lofty tower which the Grand Master Filibert de Naillac (1396-1421) completed in 1421. A magnificent new Hospital was also built. Today, many of the buildings, castles, and fortifications built by the Hospitallers survive on Rhodes and are important tourist attractions.

In 1451 the Sultan Mahomet II became the Turkish leader. Not only did he capture Constantinople, but he extended his rule over much of Southeast Europe, and in 1479 he prepared to annex Rhodes. In May the following year a formidable force equipped with siege artillery landed on the island. The Grand Master of the Hospitallers, Pierre d'Aubusson, displayed great gallantry during a siege of eighty-nine days during which three assaults were repulsed. Pierre d'Aubusson himself survived a serious wound through the skill of the Order's surgeons, and lived to be made a Cardinal by Pope Innocent VIII in 1489.

After the siege, the walls were further strengthened by being increased in thickness, first to 17 feet and later to 40 feet, the better to withstand iron balls fired from the new bronze cannons.

In 1521 Philippe Villiers de l'Isle Adam was elected Grand Master. In July of that year the defenders of Rhodes numbered some 500 Knights and perhaps three times as many foot soldiers when Soliman the Magnificent led a force of perhaps as many as a hundred thousand men to a renewed siege of the city. This time the principal efforts of the Ottoman Turks were directed to mining under the walls, now too thick to be breached by artillery fire.

After six months the Hospitallers' position became untenable. Having resisted earlier pleas from the inhabitants for him to capitulate, de L'Isle Adam saw that there was no alternative if the Order were to survive. The Turks allowed the garrison to sail from the harbour of Rhodes on 1 January 1523. They took refuge briefly in Candia on the island of Crete before sailing on to Messina in Sicily and then to Civitavecchia on the Italian mainland. They were then given a temporary home at Viterbo by the newly-elected Pope Clement VII who was himself a Knight of the Order.

De L'Isle Adam had no easy task in finding a new headquarters for the Order. By this time there were two power *blocs* in the Mediterranean, one the

Ottoman Turks in the East, who, led by Soliman had advanced as far as the walls of Vienna, and the other Spain, newly liberated from the Moors, ruled by the young Charles V of Aragon and Castile.

The Hospitallers were natural allies of the Spanish King. He therefore offered them the Island of Malta where they would be an obstacle to further Turkish advance, and from whence they might cherish vain hopes of recovering Rhodes. The Knights had no wish to be vassals of Spain, and prevaricated, but in 1527 at Viterbo, it was agreed by a majority vote in the Convent to accept the Spanish offer. There was further delay and the Order was not established in its new home until the end of 1530.

The concept of an Inn or *Auberge* for each *langue,* which had originated in Rhodes, was perpetuated in Malta where *Auberges* were established in Birgu, and a chapel for each *langue* may still be found in St John's Co-Cathedral in Valletta, the Order's conventual church.

The following years saw an uneasy succession of attacks and counter-attacks in the Mediterranean until in 1564 a large Turkish force of some 40,000 men landed on the Island of Malta and besieged the town which the Hospitallers had so strongly fortified. While reinforcements for the defenders were being assembled in Sicily and in Spain, the Grand Master, Jean de la Valette Parisot, had to organise the defence of the citadel of St Elmo with what resources were available to him on the spot. His force hung on, in spite of a savage assault on 23 June, until it inevitably fell after five weeks of bloodshed. But the sieges of the Borgo and the Senglea bought more time until Garcia de Toledo brought sixteen thousand men to the relief of the island on 7 September and drove the Turks to their boats and back to Constantinople. Thereafter the Order of the Hospital was to enjoy the suzerainty of the Island of Malta until Napoleon Buonoparte seized the Island in the summer of 1798.

Whilst the destruction of the Hospitaller headquarters in Malta also resulted in the nominal dissolution of the *langues* the expulsion of the Order from Malta did not in itself destroy the regional structure that had been developed during the four centuries the headquarters had been in Cyprus, Rhodes, Candia (Crete), and Malta. For that matter, although the French forces under Napoleon Buonoparte in the summer of 1798 resulted in the expulsion of the Knights of Malta, this neither resulted in their immediate suppression or expunged them from history; Napoleon permitted many Knights of Malta, together with exiled French Knights, to leave the island, although without their fleet of ships which were taken over by the French navy.

Today there are not only many buildings, castles, and fortifications built by the Hospitallers surviving in Malta, but also considerable traces of the different *langues* still visible there in the form of their Inns or *Auberges.*

An *Auberge d'Auvergne* was built in Birgu about 1531 in the traditional Maltese style, and later incorporated into *Auberge d'Auvergne et Provence*. The building is still intact although its façade has been heavily altered. The *Auberge d'Auvergne* in Valletta was built between the 1570s and 1583 and enlarged in 1783. The building was partially destroyed by aerial bombardment during World War II in 1941, and the ruins were demolished in the 1950s to make way for the Courts of Justice building.

An *Auberge de France* was built in Birgu around 1533 in the traditional Maltese style, to a design of Nicolo Flavari. It was later redesigned by Bartolomeo Genga. It is the second best preserved *Auberge* in Birgu, and it now houses the city's local council. The first *Auberge de France* in Valletta was built in around 1570 to a design of Girolamo Cassar. Parts of the building are still intact although they have been heavily altered. The second *Auberge de France* in Valletta was built in around 1583 in the Mannerist style, also to a design of Cassar. The building was largely destroyed by aerial bombardment in 1942, and the ruins were removed to make way for the Workers' Memorial Building.

An *Auberge de Provence* was built in Birgu around 1531 in the traditional Maltese style, and it was eventually incorporated into *Auberge d'Auvergne et Provence,* which survives today but with minor alterations to its façade. Another *Auberge de Provence* was built in Valletta in the 1570s in the Mannerist style, to a design of Girolamo Cassar. Extensively redesigned in 1638 by Mederico Blondel, the building currently houses the National Museum of Archaeology.

An *Auberge d'Aragon* was built in the traditional Maltese style in Birgu sometime in the 16th century. The building is still intact but its façade has been heavily altered. An *Auberge d'Aragon* was also built in Valletta in 1571 in the Mannerist style, to a design of Girolamo Cassar. It is the only *auberge* in Valletta which still retains its original design, the only alteration being a portico which was added in the 1840s. It now houses the Office of the Deputy Prime Minister and the Parliamentary Secretary for the European Union Presidency which was held by Malta in 2017.

An *Auberge de Castille, Léon, and Portugal* was originally built in Birgu in the 1530s but its location is currently unknown. A second *Auberge* in Birgu was built in around 1555; it still exists, but in a much altered state with few surviving features. An *Auberge de Castille* in Valletta was built between 1571 and 1574, but completely rebuilt between 1741 and 1745. This Baroque-style building now houses the Maltese Prime Minister's office.

An *Auberge d'Italie* was built in Birgu in the 1530s, but it was rebuilt in 1553-54. Little survived aerial bombardment in World War II, but some features were incorporated into the façade of new buildings in the 1960s. The first *Auberge d'Italie* in Valletta was built in 1570-71 also to a design of Girolamo Cassar. It was eventually incorporated into the Hospitaller Grandmaster's Palace. A second *Auberge d'Italie* in Valletta was built in 1574-79 and 1582-95 in the Mannerist style to a design of Cassar and other architects. It was extensively redecorated in the Baroque style in the 1680s. The building currently houses the Malta Tourism Authority, and has recently been restored with plans to convert it into an art museum.

An *Auberge d'Allemagne* was built in Birgu sometime in the 16th century but was largely destroyed by aerial bombardment during World War II; some surviving rooms were integrated into new buildings in the 1960s. An *Auberge d'Allemagne* was built in Valletta between 1571 and 1575 in the Mannerist style, to a design of Girolamo Cassar, but was demolished in 1839 to make way for St Paul's Pro-Cathedral.

An *Auberge d'Angleterre* existed in Birgu, but no English *Auberge* was built in Valletta. The *langue* was reinstituted by Grand Master Emmanuel de Rohan-Polduc in 1784 as the Anglo-Bavarian *langue*, which also included Bavarian and Polish knights. It was housed in *Auberge de Bavière*, which had been built as the private *Palazzo Carniero* in 1696, a building which survives today housing the Government Property Department.

One particularly interesting sidelight on the Knights' travels between the headquarters in Malta and the *langues* is found in an early account of the first known Masonic lodge in Malta. An extant French document dated 14 February 1730 refers to an annual donation of 150 Scudi by Bailiff Wolfgang Philip Gutenberg[44], (Bailiff of Brandenburg in the German langue, and a notable dignitary of the Order of St John), to establish a Lodge to meet at '*Ghajn-tal-Hassilyn*' (The Washers Fountain) at Msida. It is recorded that Gutenberg was regularly in France, and a member of an 'informal' Lodge in France linked to Ramsay. It is thought that the Chevalier Ramsay degrees 'the Scotch degree', 'the Novice', and 'Knight of the Temple', introduced in Paris in 1725 and known to develop into the 'Strict Observance' in Germany from the 1750s, would be the form of development adopted by Gutenberg's Lodge in Malta. There is certainly evidence that early Maltese masons had a lodge named *Parfait Harmonie*, operating under the Marseilles Jurisdiction (*Orient de Marseilles*) with links with the *Orient de Carcassonne* and the *Orient de Toulouse*. The evidence for such links and for possible interest in the Portuguese Order of Christ before 1711 can still be found in the surviving records of the Papal Inquisitor for Malta, Giacomo Carpaccio.[45]

St John's Lodge of Secrecy And Harmony No. 539

A second intriguing sidelight concerns the Knights' involvement with an English Masonic Lodge in Malta. In the Library of Grand Lodge of England, a slim file of early papers about Malta [SN 1136] contains correspondence and a petition from Maltese Brethren to regularise an earlier Independent Lodge with no known charter reported dissolved in 1771. It is recorded that the Brethren re-assembled 2 July 1788 and applied for a Warrant to London, receiving, firstly a Dispensation dated 30 March 1789, and then a Warrant with the same date signed by the Duke of Cumberland. This English Lodge was relatively short-lived, and Grand Lodge records its last payment in 1791 and its erasure at the time of the Union in 1813.

More intriguing though is that the petitioners, and the annual returns up to 1792 listed not only their ranks under the Grand Lodge of England, but also their Titles and Grades in the Order of The Hospital. An early history of Freemasonry in Malta[46] summarised their interest:

'It is not surprising that many (Knights Hospitaller) anxious to discover some practical application of their portentous vows, thought they found it in Freemasonry. Freemasonry itself owes much to the Crusading Orders, and the medieval mystique of the Hospitallers and Templars, their hierarchy, their appeal to the noblest instincts of man, their perfect obedience, their secrecy, seemed an obvious model for those who professed the regeneration of mankind as their object.'

A Lodge existed in Malta, presided over in the 1780s by a Bohemian, Knight Kollowrat, who enjoyed the protection of Joseph II who refused to promulgate in his dominions the Bull of Clement XII condemning Freemasonry. Grand Master Pinto had, during his reign, banished six knights for assisting at masonic meetings, but de Rohan, who had himself been initiated while in Parma as squire to the infant Duke, did not actively prosecute the ban, though he declined to lend his patronage.

In 1785 there were, according to Louis Ovide Doublet, de Rohan's French Secretary, forty adepts, all Knights except himself and an anonymous Maltese, and Knight Kollowrat petitioned the Duke of Cumberland, Grand Master of the London Lodge, for a constitution. He responded in 1789 by the creation of St John's Lodge of Secrecy and Harmony which numbered, so Doublet records, over 400 knights by 1792 and which observed a French Ritual. Every year upon the feast of St John, the Lodge, incognito, provided one young bride in each Valetta parish with a dowry.

Hence, there is no question that speculative Freemasonry was practised by the Hospitallers. In the end, news of its existence reached Rome and the Maltese Inquisitor, Mgr Scotti, was instructed to order its dissolution. Scotti may have been a Mason himself, but he could not ignore orders from Rome, and the Lodge was quietly dissolved around 1792. Its effects were sold to reimburse the treasurer for his expenses in obtaining a Patent from London.

G. E. W. Bridges, The Grand Librarian, commented at one point on their activities writing '*The Masonic Degrees of K T and KM were known at the material date ... The French Craft working was very different from the English.*'

However, there is no reason to suppose that these petitioners for an English Craft warrant were acting in any way different to many other brethren who sort regularity at this time – certainly as far as their Craft activity was concerned.

The French masonic tradition at that time, similar to English *Antients* customs and practices, routinely included degrees beyond the Craft, and a Lodge minute of 2 February 1792 recorded that the Lodge worked Knight of the East, Knight of the Sun, and Rose Croix. It is therefore reasonable to suppose that, in accordance with normal French practice, a Knight Templar degree was also worked. The Petitioners and their Ranks in The Order of Malta as reported in their annual returns to UGLE up to 1792 were[47]

David Sigismond de la Tour du Pin	WM	Grand Cross of the Order of Malta
Antoine de Ligondes	Wdn	*Colonel of the French Regiment of Malta*
Joseph Stagno	Wdn	Knight of the Order of Malta
J B Tommasi		Grand Cross of the Order of Malta
Chs Abel de Loras		Grand Cross of the Order of Malta
Louis Ovide Doublet		(Secretary)
J. Cru di Vintimiglia		Knight of the Order of Malta
Aug Formosa de Fremeaux		(Treasurer)
N F Rouyer		Sovereign Knight [*Chevalier Magistral*] of the Order of Malta

Writing later about this Lodge, the Provincial Grand Master Alexander M. Broadley[48] said 'a very numerous & respectable lodge was founded, almost exclusively confined to the Knights of these Orders, who appear however to have adhered chiefly to their French Rituals, and whose lectures were delivered in that language.'

Whilst it cannot be confirmed absolutely that only Knights Hospitaller were involved, R.W.Bro. Broadley's comment does leave open the possibility that there were some Brethren who identified themselves with the former Order of the Temple. However, it must also be observed that membership of one or both Orders, and their petition to the Grand Lodge of England, cannot be taken as unquestionable evidence that in 1780s these brethren were working anything we would recognise as Freemasonry that had been passed down directly from the earlier chivalric orders. Nevertheless, the historical evidence of brethren engaging in both is extremely suggestive.

One further interesting sidelight on invasion of the Island of Malta by Napoleon which led to the expulsion of the Knights of St John from Malta is the involvement of the British fleet with the recovery of the Island. In 1798, the British naval fleet was anchored off Sicily, and a detachment under the command of Captain Alexander Ball, RN was promptly mobilised to blockade the Island of Malta. Successful relief of the Island was rapidly achieved and Capt. Ball was appointed *de-facto* military Governor of Malta. Contemporary records suggest Capt. Ball was a member of the *Orient de Malta* which was known to work Knight Templar ceremonies.

Outside Malta

Naturally, throughout their history, the knights at headquarters only formed part of the Order, and a high proportion always served in the territorial '*langues*'. The *langues* were nominally dissolved when the Order was expelled from Malta with the French invasion and occupation in 1798, but some elements survived and, consequently, after the demise of the Templars, it was these regional organisations of Order of St John throughout Europe that would play a major part in the custodianship of the former Templar properties.

The *Langues* of Auvergne, France and Provence
Until the end of the 18th century many Scottish members of the Order joined the French *langues,* as the Order was never formally organised on a regional basis in Scotland and the Order in England was generally dormant at that time. Individual members would join one of the six Great Priories into which France was divided: France, Aquitania, and Champagne in the former French-speaking *langues;* The Great Priory of Auvergne in the former Auvergnat-speaking *langue*; or St Gilles and Toulouse in the former Provencal-speaking *langue.*

The *Langue* of Italy
Until the end of the 18th century most of the Englishmen and Irishmen joined the *langue* of Italy, as the Order in England was generally dormant for much of that century. They would join one of the Great Priories established in the regions of Barletta, Capua, Lombardy, Pisa, Rome, Sicily, or Venice.

The *Langue* of Aragon

The *langue* of Aragon was established in 1128 when King Alfonso I of Aragon, having no direct heir, bequeathed part of his property to the Knights Templar. Thereafter the Order gained a number of important castles. Despite local opposition from King James II of Aragon, the Templar Order was suppressed in Aragon under Pope Clement V's Bull.

It is not exactly clear what happened to their holdings, which under the Papal Bull, should have been transferred to the Order of the Hospitallers in Aragon, as happened in other *langues*. The reason is that, although the former *langue* was divided in four Great Priories: Amposta, Castille, Navarra, and Portugal, in Portugal the Knight Templar Order was not extinguished, but, with Papal approval, reconstituted as the Portuguese Order of Christ[49] which presumably took over the Templar holdings and many of the former commanderies.

In 1462, the langue of Castille, Léon, and Portugal was split from that of Aragon.

From the earlier brief accounts of the other Chivalric orders which emerged in the Iberian peninsula it is obvious that the Order of the Hospitallers was by no means dominant in that area, so the history of the development of a later-fragmented Hospitaller *langue* of Aragon remains unclear.

The *Langue* of England

In the 1140s the Priory in Clerkenwell was set up as the English headquarters of the Order's English *langue*. The buildings in Clerkenwell were put to different uses in the years that followed. During the 16th century, they were used as the offices of the Master of the Revels. Thirty of Shakespeare's plays were licensed here. In the 18th century, the Gate was briefly used as a coffee house, run by Richard Hogarth, father of the artist William Hogarth. Dr. Samuel Johnson was given his first job in London at St John's Gate, writing reports for *The Gentleman's Magazine*. At the end of the 18th century, the Gate was used as a public house, *The Old Jerusalem Tavern,* where artists and writers, including Charles Dickens, used to meet.

The Order of Malta in England survived more or less intact in the British Isles until dissolved by King Henry VIII in 1540 when its estates were confiscated by the Crown. The Order of Malta was briefly restored by Queen Mary in 1557, but its lands were re-appropriated again by Queen Elizabeth I in 1559. However Queen Mary's Letters Patent were never revoked, and Queen Elizabeth I never formally dissolved the Order, which could therefore be considered dormant from that date, until resuscitated in 1831.

During its history, several attempts were made to restore the Grand Priory of England, including three unsuccessful attempts:

Around 1639 by Sir Nicholas Fortescue, Knight of Justice (1639); the attempt failed after his death at the Battle of Marston Moor.

Around 1687 by the Duke of Berwick (natural son of James II and Arabella Churchill) who was appointed titular Grand Prior by Grand Master Carafa, and his tenure was followed by his two sons (Peter and Anthony Fitzjames) as Grand Priors.

In 1815 the 54th and last titular Grand Prior of England (Girolama Laparelli) was appointed but died the same year and the Order became dormant.

In 1831 the Order in England was resuscitated, and in 1888 the Order was granted a charter as a British Order of Chivalry by Queen Victoria. In 1946 Pope Pius XII encouraged the Order to restore the Grand Priory in England but this was not done until 1993 with the permission of the Vatican and Matthew Festing was appointed as 55th Grand Prior of England.

The Order was never organised in Scotland and Ireland on a separate regional basis; but despite the Reformation there were always English, Scottish, and Irish Knights of Malta. There exist many legal documents attesting to their role in Scotland and both Orders were represented in the Scottish Parliament by the Preceptors of St John down to the period of the Reformation. A Charter issued by King James IV dated 19 October 1488:

> 'confirmed the grants previously made to the Knights of the Temple and St John and made it clear that both Orders were united under the superintendence of the Preceptor of St John'.[50]

Until the end of the 18th century most of the Englishmen and Irishmen joined the *langue* of Italy, while Scotsmen usually joined the French *langue*.

It is therefore fair to say that the Chivalric Order of St John survived in England for practical purposes from the time of the crusades until the mid-19th century and still survives today in a changed form but with chivalric honour elements which echo its original foundations.

The *Langue* of Germany

The Order of St John settled in Germany during the 12th century with a Hospitaller Commandery established at Duisberg by 1154; early development resulted in the founding of Grand Priories covering the territories of Bohemia-Austria, Dacia (Denmark), Germany (which also had Priories or Commanderies in today's Alsace, the Netherlands, and Switzerland), Hungary, and Poland. All Great Priories were sub-divided into Priories and Commanderies, some of which included the former Templar commanderies of Braunschweig, Süpplingenburg, Tempelhof, and Tempelburg and undoubtedly absorbed many others. It must therefore be assumed that many former Knights Templar found refuge in Germany when the Order was suppressed in France.

In the 16th century, a section of the Grand Priory, the Bailiwick of Brandenburg of the Order, became protestant, under the protection of the *Margraves* of Brandenburg, who were to become Kings of Prussia. The Order continues to the present day.

The Order of St John also settled in Scandinavia in the 12th century and became Protestant in 1530. A new Order of St John in Sweden, formerly part of the German *langue* and Bailiwick of Brandenburg, was re-organised in 1920 as a dependent of the German Order and is now under the protection of the Swedish Crown.

After the Fall of Malta

The invasion of the Island of Malta by Napoleon in 1798 effectively initiated the demise of the ancient division into *langues*. The Order began to reorganize itself and the national associations came into being aligned more or less with national boundaries.

The first national association to be created was the Grand Magistry which was established in Rome in 1834. The Germans founded their first national association in 1859, followed by the British in 1875 and the Italians in 1877.

Grand Priory of Russia

After the fall of Malta in 1798, Napoleon permitted many Knights of Malta to leave the island, and some were given sanctuary in Russia together with exiled French Knights.

These brethren formed a Grand Priory of Russia and elected Tsar Paul I as Grand Master[51], despite the facts that he was not a professed knight of the Order and that the election was invalid. Notwithstanding this, the Tsar accepted the honour and received recognition as *de facto* Grand Master from many Catholic authorities – although not by the Holy See.[52]

Venerable Order of St John

The Sovereign Military Order of Malta exists today as a direct continuation of the medieval Knights Hospitaller, with origins in the *Fraternitas Hospitalaria* hospital founded *circa* 1048 by merchants from the Duchy of Amalfi in the Muristan district of Jerusalem, Fatimid Caliphate, to provide medical care for pilgrims to the Holy Land. Following the conquest of Jerusalem in 1099 during the First Crusade and the loss of the Kingdom of Jerusalem to the Mamluk Sultanate, it became a military order to protect Christians against Islamic persecution and was recognised as sovereign in 1113 by Pope Paschal II. It operated from Cyprus (1291-1310), Rhodes (1310-1523), Malta (1530-1798), over which it was sovereign until the French occupation, and from Palazzo Malta in Rome from 1834 until today, subsequently known under its current name. The order venerates as its patroness the Virgin Mary, under the title 'Our Lady of Mount Philermos'.

Today based in Rome, the proceedings of the Order are governed by its Constitutional Charter and the Order's Code. It is divided internationally into six territorial Grand Priories, six Sub-Priories, and 47 national associations. The six Grand Priories are Rome, Lombardy and Venice, Naples and Sicily, Bohemia, Austria, and England.

The Order of St John settled in the British Isles in the 12th century and, except for a short period during the reign of Queen Mary, it ceased to exist under King Henry VIII.

The Venerable Order developed after an unsuccessful attempt to restore the Order of St John in the United Kingdom in 1830. It was only in 1870 that it was established as a humanitarian foundation. In 1888, the Order was recognised by Queen Victoria not as a State Order but as an Order of the Crown. The Venerable Order has priories and associations in some forty countries, mostly English-speaking. Among all the Orders of St John, this is the only one that has no religious restrictions in its admission procedure.

The Order of St John is still today considered to be an Order of Knighthood, categorised under three classes each divided into sub-classes:

First Class, containing only one category: Knights of Justice or Professed Knights, and the Professed Conventual Chaplains, who take religious vows of poverty, chastity, and obedience and form what amounts to a religious order. Until the 1990s membership in this class was restricted to members of families with noble lineages, but this does not apply today.

Second Class: Knights and Dames in Obedience, similarly restricted until recently; these knights and dames make a promise, rather than a vow, of obedience. This class is subdivided into three categories, namely that of Knight and Dames of Honour and Devotion in Obedience, Knight and Dames of Grace and Devotion in Obedience, and Knight and Dames of Magistral Grace in Obedience.

Third Class, which is subdivided into six categories: Knights of Honour and Devotion, Conventual Chaplains *ad honorem*, Knights of Grace and Devotion, Magistral Chaplains, Knights of Magistral Grace, and Donats of Devotion. Members (male and female) do not have to take vows and the categories require a decreasing history of nobility. Knights of Magistral Grace need not prove any noble line.

Within each class and category of knights are ranks ranging from Bailiff Grand Cross (the highest) through Knight Grand Cross, and Knight.

The Order states that it was the hospitaller role that enabled the Order to survive the end of the crusading era; nevertheless, it retains its military title and traditions. In 1876, Italian Knights of the Sovereign Military Order of Malta[53] formed a modern military unit to provide medical support to the Italian Army; from April 1909 this became a special auxiliary volunteer corps of the Italian Army[54] and has since operated both in wartime and peacetime with medical or paramedical military functions, and in ceremonial functions for the Order, such as standing guard around the coffins of high officers of the Order before and during funeral rites. The Military Corps also operated military hospital trains during both World Wars, and still today operates a modern 28-car hospital train with 192 hospital beds, serviced by a medical staff of 38 medics and paramedics provided by the Order and a technical staff provided by the Italian Army Railway Engineers Regiment. The members of the Order may thus be considered worthy successors to their crusading forebears following both knightly and military roles.

It is, of course, very well known today for its ambulance, first-aid, and nursing services active in many countries, and for its ophthalmic hospital in Jerusalem. It must also be noted that the Eye Hospital of St John in Jerusalem is still, today, the beneficiary of a large proportion of the charitable donations from the United Orders, its subordinate Preceptories, individual Knights, and from many other Masonic bodies with Knight Templar connections world-wide.

Alliance of the Orders of St John of Jerusalem
Apart from the Sovereign Order of Malta, there are other three other Orders of St John which are recognised as orders of knighthood being associated in the Alliance of the Orders of St John. As with the originating hospitaller order, all maintain similar historical traditions and the same mission: giving assistance to the sick and the poor. Specifically, all are different from other National Orders of Knighthood by virtues of their Christian faith and traditions derived from lay Christian Orders. All three Orders are recognised by the sovereign authorities of the countries in which they are based. Briefly, the three constituent

Orders of St John recognised by the Sovereign Order of Malta are:

Bailiwick of Brandenburg of St John and Jerusalem[55]
The Order of St John had settled in Germany during the 12th and 13th centuries, founding a Grand Priory. In the 16th century, a section of the Grand Priory, the Bailiwick of Brandenburg of the Order, became protestant, under the protection of the Margraves of Brandenburg, who later became Kings of Prussia. The Bailiwick maintained friendly relations with the Sovereign Order of Malta. In 1811, it was suppressed by the King of Prussia who then founded the Royal Prussian Order of St John as an order of merit. In 1852, the Order regained the name of Bailiwick of Brandenburg and became a noble Order of Prussia. In 1918, after the fall of the monarchy, it was separated from the State and became independent. It is present in a number of European countries, Canada and the United States and also works in Germany with hospitals and senior nursing homes, and is responsible for an important ambulance service – the *'Johanniter Unfallhilfe'*. It has independent affiliations in Finland, France, Hungary and Switzerland.

Order of St John of the Netherlands[56]
The Order of St John initially spread across the Netherlands in the 12th century. Prussia suppressed the Bailiwick of Brandenburg in 1811, but a number of Dutch members gathered together to refound it in 1852. In 1909, an affiliation was created in the Kingdom of Holland. In 1946, the entity separated from the German Order, becoming annexed to the Dutch Crown, but not as a State Order. Today the Order runs hospitals and hospices and collaborates with the Sovereign Order of Malta in charitable activities.

Order of St John of Sweden[57]
The Order of St John settled in Scandinavia in the 12th century and became Protestant in 1530. In Sweden, the Order of St John belonged initially to the Bailiwick of Brandenburg and was re-organised in 1920 as dependent of the German Order under the protection of the Swedish Crown. It gained independence in 1946, under the protection of the King of Sweden. Today, the Order provides care for the elderly and the sick and collaborates with Swedish hospitals, charitable organisations, and Christian communities. It is also internationally active on behalf of refugees and political prisoners.

The Environment for Survival

Despite the dissolution of the Templar Order, developments in Europe provided an enviroment facilitating the survival of many of their elements; in particular it seems clear that the organisation of the Hospitaller Order into European *'langues'* effectively provided the base from which to administer former Templar holdings. Whilst the military elements have nearly all disappeared, the religious aspects have been perpetuated, usually in a much-modified form, the chivalric honour framework can be found today, and trading and banking elements can be traced within modern institutions.

The Order of St John certainly seemed to fulfil at least some of the original intentions regarding the administration of the Templar holdings, and, together with other chivalric former-crusading orders, also perpetuated their ideals. It can therefore be seen that activities of the Knights of St John provided a historical bridge over the centuries between the suppression of the Templars in 1307 and 1798.

And so it is not inappropriate to look briefly at some of these other chivalric former-crusading orders to see their role in creating the environment for the emergence of speculative chivalric Freemasonry.

2.5 OTHER CRUSADING ORDERS TODAY

The romance associated with the crusading Chivalric Orders of Knighthood has been perpetuated throughout the centuries, and the myths and legends associated with the former crusading Orders still form a significant part of today's culture in many countries of the world. It is therefore appropriate to record some brief notes on modern organisations which have a historical or nominal, although sometimes superficial, connection with the Crusading Orders other than those already covered.

The Hospitaller Order of St Lazarus[58]

The Military and Hospitaller Order of Saint Lazarus of Jerusalem is one of the orders of chivalry to survive the downfall of the Kingdom of Jerusalem and the attempts by the Crusader knights to win control of the Holy Land from the forces of Islam. This ancient Order of Chivalry can trace its roots back to the 4th century when a hospice was established outside the walls of Jerusalem by Greek or Armenian monks under the rule of Saint Basil.

Its particular mission was the care and treatment of lepers and those suffering from skin diseases. In a papal bull dated 1043 at Marseilles, Pope Benedict IX granted privileges to the Order which, five years later, were extended and increased in another papal bull. In 1095, Pope Urban II launched a Crusade to gain possession of the Holy Sites, and it was during this period that the Hospitallers were transformed into a Military Order of Knighthood. Whilst the Knights of Saint John and the Knights Templar were more numerous, and stronger militarily, the Knights of the Order of Saint Lazarus attained prominence in the care and transportation of Knights of any Order who contracted leprosy.

Although the primary focus of the Order was its hospitaller activities, the Knights of Saint Lazarus were militarily involved in many notable battles. At the great debacle of the Christian forces at Acre in 1291 every knight of the Order present was slain, but prior to the fall of the Holy Land, the Order had been given the Royal Château of Boigny, near Orléans, by King Louis VII of France. It was to this estate the headquarters of the Order was moved when the Holy Land was recaptured by the Muslim forces.

In France, in 1609, King Henry IV of France linked it administratively to the Order of Our Lady of Mount Carmel to form the Royal Military and Hospitaller Order of Our Lady of Mount Carmel and Saint Lazarus of Jerusalem, which remained listed as of royal protection in the French Royal

Almanac until 1830. This protection of the Royal house of France was renewed in 2004.

In theory, the Order remained a military one, but with the exception of a brief period in the 17th century it played no military role after 1291. With its dedication to the twin ideals of providing aid to those suffering from leprosy, and defending the Christian faith, by the 12th century, the Order had found its way into Europe and established itself in France, Germany, Italy, Sicily, and the British Isles.

Its first appearance in England was during the troubled reign of King Stephen. A hospital was established at Burton (later called Burton Lazars), near Melton Mowbray in Leicestershire and in 1177, through the offices of Sir Roger de Mowbray, a Royal Charter was granted by King Henry II. The hospital at Burton Lazars became the headquarters of the Order in England.

It was administered by a Master as well as eight knights, and was under the protection of the Blessed Virgin and Saint Lazarus. In succeeding years, many hospitals and commanderies were erected in England and, at one period, the Order possessed as many as ninety-five leper houses throughout the kingdom. The demise of the Order in England came in 1544 when King Henry VIII, having dissolved the religious houses, turned his attention to the Hospitallers. Their properties and wealth were seized and the Order of St Lazarus, and that of Saint John, were proscribed, its members being forbidden to wear the habit or use any distinctive titles. While this marked the close of the Order's activities in England, it was not the end altogether, as English and Scottish Knights of the Roman Catholic faith continued to be admitted to the Order in Europe.

During the Middle Ages, the Order of Saint Lazarus fulfilled a dual mission. As a military power, it operated a flotilla of warships in the Mediterranean to protect important sea routes against pirates and marauders, while, at the same time, the Hospitallers of Saint Lazarus protected and treated the victims of leprosy, which was something of a scourge throughout Europe. In the wars of Louis XIV, the Order of St Lazarus gained many of the possessions of the Order of Teutonic Knights which was abolished in his dominions by King Louis in 1672.

Today the Military and Hospitaller Order of Saint Lazarus of Jerusalem is an international, self-governing, and independent body, having its own Constitution; it may be compared with a kind of electoral kingdom. According to its Constitution, the Order is non-political and ecumenical (or non-denominational). Membership is open to all men and women who are practising members of the Christian faith and in good standing with their particular Church. Its international membership comprises Roman Catholic, Anglican, Lutheran, Orthodox, Methodist and other Christians, upholding in their lives, fortunes, and honour the principles of Christianity. Organized as a Christian Chivalric Order, it is registered in London in accordance with English Law. The Order's Spiritual protector is the Catholic Greek Melkite Patriarch of Antioch, Alexandria, Jerusalem, and All the East.

With the exception of the present Teutonic Order ('*Deutscher Orden*'), the Order of Saint Lazarus is the smallest of the present day orders of Christian chivalry, having approximately 5,000 members across the five continents. Members hold one of 11 grades, the highest eight conferring the honour of Knighthood; four use the honorific Knight Grand Cross, two Knight Commander, and two as Knight.

The Order in England & Wales has since 1 January 2011 been under the jurisdiction of The Grand Bailiwick & Priory of England and Wales. The current Grand Prior is the Rt Hon. Charles Chetwynd-Talbot, 22nd Earl of Shrewsbury & Waterford and premier Earl on the rolls of nobility of England and Ireland.

The Italian branch of the Order was merged in 1572 with the Order of Saint Maurice to form the Order of Saints Maurice and Lazarus under the Royal House of Savoy. The Order exists today.

The Order of Saint James of Altopascio

This Italian Order of Saint James of Altopascio is an almost-forgotten military and hospitaller Order founded by Matilda of Canossa between 1070 and 1080 at Altopascio, a town on the Via Francigena in what is now Tuscany. The earliest verifiable reference dates from a 1084 hospital '*edificatus in locus et finibus ubi dicitur Teupascio*' ('built in the place called Teupascio'). [Teupascio may be a later corruption of Altopascio.]

The Order of Saint James of Altopascio (Italian: *Ordine di San Giacomo d'Altopascio or Ordine dei Frati Ospitalieri di San Jacopo*), also called the Knights of the Tau (*Cavalieri del Tau*) or Hospitallers of Saint James, was a military order, possibly one of the earliest Christian institutions which sought to combine the protection and assistance of pilgrims, the staffing of hospitals, and a military wing. The reputation of the Order's hospitals was such as to attract visitors, both well and sick, including women in childbirth and infants from across Italy. As with the Templars, the Order received exemption from all taxes, any interference lay or ecclesiastical with its property, or the movement of goods as part of its regular business.

Originally the Order was only charged with caring for pilgrims on their way to Rome or the Holy Land, via Italy, but later it covered the Way of Saint James. In time the Order also had responsibility for safeguarding the roads and the bridges from brigands. The Order also had a bell named '*La Smarrita*' that was rung each night from a half hour before sunset to a half hour past to help guide any pilgrim wandering in the woods to safety. This custom was still reported in the time of Giovanni Lami.[59] They maintained a ferry service on the Arno River:

> 'in the territory of Florence and on the high road to Rome, where formerly a heavy tribute was exacted. This road has now been made free by members of the aforesaid Great Hospital and of other hospitals affiliated with it. So that at present all pilgrims and others freely pass there without payment.'

The Order drew its income initially from Tuscany[60] but later the Order spread throughout Italy, Sardinia, and Sicily. By the end of the 12th century the Order reached as far as the Rhône in Provence and had endowments in Bavaria, Burgundy, the Dauphiné, England, Flanders, Germany, Lorraine, Navarre, Portugal, Savoy, and France, where during the reign of Philip IV The Order founded the church and hospital of *Saint-Jacques-du-Hault-Pas* in Paris.

The Order was one of six religious orders suppressed by the bull *Execrabilis* issued by Pius II on 18 January 1459 and their property was transferred to a fledgling Order 'Our Lady of Bethlehem' founded by that same bull:

> Further, we suppress and annul their former ordinances (*ordines*), the names of their associations, their titles of priority (*priorales*) and other dignities, and we decree that henceforth they shall be called, held, and named as of that military order of Saint Mary of Bethlehem.

The suppression, however, was imperfectly carried out, or perhaps was never carried out at all. By the 16th century the Order was exchanging lands in such a way as to build up a compact territory of holdings nearer Altopascio, until, on 14 March 1587, Sixtus V, at the request of the Grand Duke of Tuscany, merged the Order of Altopascio with the Order of Saint Stephen. In France it was finally absorbed into the Order of Saint Lazarus in 1672.

Military Order of Saint Mary of Bethlehem

Following the suppression of the Order of Saint James of Altopascio by Papal order (Bull of Pope Pius II, *Execrabilis* issued on 18 January 1459), a new military-religious and hospitaller order similar to the Knights of St John was created:

> *'Moreover, in this order there shall be brethren and knights and priests as also in the aforesaid Order of Rhodes [Knights of Saint John], and the head of the aforesaid Hospital of Saint Mary of Bethlehem shall be the Master, elected by the brethren in the same way (*pariformiter*) [as in the Order of Rhodes].'*

The Monastic and Military Order of Aviz

The Order of Aviz was founded as a monastic military order, in emulation of such military orders as the Knights Templar, in Portugal in 1146. The fledgling order received a grant of the town of Evora in 1166 from King Afonso, which led to the Knights being first called 'Friars of Santa Maria of Évora' with Pedro Henriques, an illegitimate son of the King's father, as the first Grand Master.

The order adopted a modified Benedictine rule in 1162, and after adopting the castle at Aviz as their headquarters became known as the 'Knights of St Benedict of Aviz'. (*Ordem de São Bento de Aviz*). At an early date the order maintained close relations with Knights of Calatrava in Castile who also transferred some of their holdings in Portugal to them on condition that the Knights of Aviz should be subject to the visitation of their Grand Master. Hence the Knights of Aviz were sometimes regarded as a branch of the Calatravan Order, although they never ceased to have a Portuguese Grand Master, dependent for temporalities on the Portuguese King.

In 1383, following the death of King Ferdinand, war broke out between Castile and Portugal. Following his accession to the throne of Portugal João I, until then Grand Master of the Knights of Aviz, did not allow the knights to recognise Castilian authority; later, when Gonsalvo de Guzman came to Aviz as Visitor, the knights, while according him hospitality, refused to recognise him as a superior. This matter remained a subject of contention until 1431 when, at the Council of Basle, Portugal was declared to be in the wrong. However, the nominal Calatravan right was never exercised, and supreme authority over the Knights of Aviz was maintained by their own Grand Masters until, in 1551, that position was vested in perpetuity in the King of Portugal.

Creating a royal Grand Master brought its own changes; the King used the income of the Order to reward army and navy military service and although the Knights of Aviz were not as wealthy the Knights of Christ, their wealth was still significant, drawing income from 43 commanderies. The religious fervour of the knights vanished, and they separated from their clerical brothers who continued to follow a conventual life. In 1502 Pope Alexander VI, faced with increasing reports of scandalous concubinage, released the military Knights from their vow of celibacy and reluctantly authorised their marriage. In 1551, Julius III allowed them to dispose freely of their personal properties.

Whilst the role of the Portuguese military orders in Portugal effectively changed following the overthrow of Muslim domination, The Knights of Aviz, in conjunction with their brother Knights of Order of Christ, did engage in further Crusading ventures. These arose from the opportunities provided by maritime expeditions; expeditions in 1415 under King João I, their former Grand Master, and in 1437 under his son Duarte resulted in the conquest of Ceuta and attacks on Tangier, both sanctioned by Papal Bulls as religious

Crusades to Africa. Under their leader Prince Fernando the Knights of Aviz, achieved deeds of valour. These crusading ventures were short-lived, however, and the Crusade in Africa degenerated into an essentially mercantile enterprise.

In 1789, the order was reformed and became a secular institution under the direction of Pope Pius VI and Queen Mary I with the title Royal Military Order of Aviz (*Ordem Real Militar de Avis*).

In 1834, when the civil government of Portugal abolished religious orders and monasteries, after the defeat of King Miguel in the Civil War, under the constitutional monarchy the Order lost its properties. The ancient military orders were transformed by the liberal constitution and subsequent legislation into orders of merit. The privileges which once had been an essential part of the membership of the old military orders also ceased, as did the requirement to be of Noble birth which had been necessary for aspirants to the mantle, a requirement confirmed by a decree as recent as 1604.

In 1910, when the Portuguese monarchy ended, the Republic of Portugal abolished all the orders except the Order of the Tower and Sword. However, in 1917, at the end of the Great War, some of these orders were re-established as orders of merit to reward outstanding services to the state, the office of Grand Master belonging to the head of state, the President of the Republic. The Military Order of Aviz, (*Ordem Militar de Avis*) together with the other Portuguese Orders of Merit, had its statutes revised on several occasions, during the First Republic (1910-1926), then in 1962, and again in 1986.

The Military Order of Aviz, together with the Military Orders of Christ and of St James of the Sword form the group of the 'Ancient Military Orders', are governed by a chancellor and a council of eight members, appointed by the President of the Republic, to assist him as Grand Master in all matters concerning the administration of the Order. The Order, ranking immediately below that of the Order of Christ, can only be conferred on military personnel, both Portuguese and foreign, for outstanding service.

One senior British recipient of the Grand Cross of the Order was Admiral of the Fleet The Right Honourable The Earl Mountbatten of Burma, *KG, GCB, OM, GCSI, GCIE, GCVO, DSO, PC, FRS*. [Born Prince Louis Francis Albert Victor Nicholas of Battenberg and second cousin once removed of Queen Elizabeth II.]

The Order of Santiago
The Order of Santiago (Spanish: *Orden de Santiago*), also known as 'The Order of St James of the Sword', was a minor military and religious order in Spain with a similar religious and military background to other orders founded during the time of the Crusades. It was founded in the 12th century, taking its

name from the national patron of Galicia and Spain, *Santiago* (St James the Greater) with three initial objectives: to protect the pilgrims of St James' Way; to defend Christendom; and to remove the Muslim Moors from the Iberian Peninsula.

As a religious institution, the Order has always admitted women as well as men and at one time maintained a number of convents, both male and female.

The Order's military history is linked to that of Spain and Portugal; it assisted in the eviction of the Muslims, sometimes independently but sometimes as part of combined royal armies. One interesting commitment was maritime operations against Muslim forces, and from this was accrued the obligation imposed upon members to undertake six months galley service; this obligation was still known in the 18th century, but rarely served as exemption could be easily bought.

Following the death of the Grand Master Alfonso de Cárdenas in 1493, the Order was incorporated into the Spanish Crown, and still survives today as part of the group of the 'Ancient Military Orders', mentioned earlier.

The Military Order of Calatrava

The Military Order of Calatrava, *(Orden Militar de Calatrava)*, was a major military and religious order in Spain with a similar religious and military background to other orders founded during the time of the Crusades.

The order was originated in 1158 when King Sancho III of Castile ceded the fortress of Calatrava to Raymond, Abbot of the Cistercian monastery of Fitero, with instructions to defend it against the Moors. The order of knights and monks who defended the fort was formally recognized by the pope in 1164, and it became closely affiliated with the Cistercian abbey of Morimond in 1187. The order's headquarters, Calatrava, which lay along the Guadiana River in south-western Castile, fell to the Moors in 1195 but was retaken by the knights in 1212.

At an early date the order maintained close relations with the Knights of Aviz in Portugal and some of the Knights of Calatrava holdings there were transferred to the Knights of Aviz on condition that the latter would be subject to the visitation of their Grand Master.

The order participated in the Christian Reconquest of Andalusia and was rewarded with grants of land in both Castile and Aragon. By the 15th century it had a membership of 200,000 and an annual income of 45,000 ducats.

As the pace of the Reconquest slowed, the order became increasingly involved in Castilian domestic politics. To neutralize this potential threat to the crown, the Spanish monarchs Ferdinand and Isabella, with papal sanction, took over the administration of the order in 1489. From then until its dissolution in the 19th century, the order was little more than an honorary association of Spanish nobles.

The Order of Montesa
The Order of Montesa (*Orden de Montesa*) is a lesser Christian military order, based in the former Templar Province of Aragon with its headquarters in the castle of Montesa. It is important as a direct descendant of the Templars who had become established in Aragon in 1128.

King Alfonso I of Aragon, having no direct heir, bequeathed part of his property to the Knights Templar, and the Order gained a number of important castles.

Despite local opposition from King James II of Aragon, the Templar Order was suppressed in Aragon under Pope Clement V's Bull. King James II then persuaded Pope John XXII to allow reorganisation of Templar properties in Aragon and Valencia, under the control of a new military order of very similar character to the Templar Order with responsibility for guarding his frontiers against Moorish aggression.

On 10 June 1317 Pope John XXII sanctioned it as a new Cistercian order to be based at Montesa. The title was adopted from St George of Montesa, and it gained its founding recruits from the Order of Calatrava on which it remained dependant, although under an independent Grand Master until absorbed by the Spanish Crown under Philip II in 1587.

Pseudo-Chivalric Fraternal Bodies[61]
It is thus clear that various European Nations not only perpetuated crusading ideals in a number of religious and military chivalric orders, but also that these either exist today or existed until comparatively recently, although usually in much modified form as chivalric, religious, or charitable institutions. It is not therefore surprising that in many countries, such orders acted as a template or prototype for psuedo-chivalric bodies.

It is in America particularly that such institutions have developed ever since European colonisation of the Continent. Virtually all developed in the 19th century and generally adopted their 'historical base' or traditions from the (supposed or actual) history of the Knights Templar following the exposure or circulation of Masonic Rituals. So far as this history is concerned there is little of interest other than their role in keeping the crusader traditions in the general public consciousness through names they chose to adopt. These included Royal Templars, Knights of Malta (Rite of 14 Degrees); Knights of St John and Malta; Knights of the Golden Eagle (Ceremonial based on the traditions and history of the Crusaders[62]; Independent Order of Good Templars (1851); Illustrious and Exalted Order of Crusaders.[63]

One typical fraternal institution is the Royal Templars of Temperance[64] formed in 1870 in Buffalo, New York. It resulted from an effort to close saloons on Sundays. Its founder, Cyrus K. Porter, had long been active in Freemasonry, the Odd-Fellows, and the Sons of Temperance. The Royal Templars used rituals adapted from modern Freemasonry, and had nothing to do with the Knights Templar other than the name.

2.6 MEDIEVAL DEVELOPMENTS

Whilst historians are not always in agreement about the interpretation of the term 'medieval' it is taken here to refer to the general period between 1000 and 1599 AD; this period covers, of course, not only the time of the crusades, but also nearly 200 years following the demise of the Templars and the time when some of the earliest 'masonic documents' – *The Old Charges* – appeared.

The Reformation – A Time of Change

It is particularly important to remember that up to this time written material was almost non-existent; most of the population could not read or write and these skills were confined to a small number of clergy and even fewer academics. The transmission of moral teachings, new ideas, or entertainment was therefore by the spoken word or visual drama, and thus church sermons and theatrical productions were far more important than today.

One major factor which influenced the decline of the medieval theatre in Europe was the Protestant Reformation. Undoubtedly, medieval theatre, especially the later morality plays, had revived interest in Greek and Roman dramatists. However, increasing prosperity and city development during the Renaissance ended the itinerant medieval theatre form as permanent theatres were built in many cities. The medieval theatre must therefore be considered as but one link in the chain – but an influential link which laid a firm foundation for introducing and moulding popular attitudes to a range of topics, including a view of past history,

The reformation also brought changes in technology which changed matters dramatically. Perhaps the most influential was the invention of the printing press by Johannes Gutenberg, a German goldsmith who developed, c.1439, a mechanical printing press. This not only enabled printed material to be produced quickly in large quantities, but also it reduced the cost so material became affordable to a mass market. By 1500, printing presses had appeared in most European countries and most major cities, and this, in effect, initiated the demise of the monopoly held by monasteries on the copying of manuscripts.

This timely invention was possibly that with the greatest ever impact on the modern world – timely because of the subsequent dissolution, between 1536 and 1541 under King Henry VIII of monasteries, priories, convents, and friaries in England, Wales, and Ireland, which, *inter alia*, had been a major source of written material – both historical as well as ecclesiastical texts.

It was not just the mechanics of such changes, but the cultural impact as well; not only did this alter the education possibilities for the general populace as never before, but this was a time when formal institutions and guilds appeared, also supplementing the church as *de-facto* repositories of the written word.

Significantly, this was the very period when the oldest 'Masonic' writings – the *Old Charges* – appear to have surfaced in England. The Regius MS of 1390 is well-known as one of the earliest sources of moral instruction to a trade guild with its unequivocal advice to an operative mason of his duty to his master, brethren and to Holy Church. Moreover, specific details, such as the emphasis in 1390 on leading a moral life and respecting the chastity of a master's or fellow's wife and daughter, and the first (Emulation) charge with which today's Masons should be familiar, demonstrate a clear link.[65] However, the Regius MS was a hand written document and therefore of only very limited distribution, as were many other early *Old Charges* some of which would be written specifically for each lodge. The availability of the printed text from the mid-16th century gave undoubted impetus to their distribution and most surviving copies of *Old Charges* are printed versions which undoubtedly entered routine use in lodges; their impact will be considered later.

Similarly, it cannot be denied that Freemasonry in the different countries also reflected the cultures within which the different strands developed, and the English base with its emphasis on operative activities was not mirrored directly in Continental Freemasonry. In particular, it is seen that in Germany legends with a Knight Templar theme became the base for such dramas as the operas of Richard Wagner.

But it not only for the ritual impact that these MSS are important. They influenced the degree structure adopted by Lodges working after the manner of the *Antients,* as, although of an essentially different character, both the Regius MS and the Cooke MSS appear to have been used in the manner of the 'charge after initiation' to instruct candidates in the background to the Craft.[66] Briefly, that background included commentary on the following main steps:

The Legend of the Flood and Noah.

The inventions and development of Noah's children with particular reference to the seven liberal arts and sciences.

The developments of the various crafts with appropriate emphasis on the craft building and the qualifications needed.

Emphasis on 'ritual journeys' and practical journeys to obtain knowledge and experience.

Knowing our *Antient* brethren normally progressed, from the Craft, to the Mark, and the Royal Arch, and then often to the Rose Croix and Knight Templar rites, such a philosophy of specific qualification by examination and experience laid a firm foundation for the development of its members.

By a similar extension, the industrial revolution brought a continuation of these changes; as a higher proportion of the working population moved from rural employment in agriculture to industrial work in the towns, Clubs and Societies developed. Some were concerned with working practices (Trades Unions); some had a social purpose (Friendly Societies and mutual benefit societies); some were developments of established religions and moral organisations; and others reflected education and training. It became fashionable 'to belong' to such Clubs and Societies, and it was in this cultural environment that Freemasonry emerged.

This was also a time when more of the population was on the move; much was concerned with work or military service, but some was for educational and leisure travel. It was also the time Britain and many other countries were engaged in global colonisation. Global colonisation nearly always required military resources – either for initial territorial conquest or subsequent protection of commercial interests. It is an established fact that early masonic activity was spread by military lodges, and evidence exists that military units did have an influence in the development of masonic degrees in many areas; Undoubtedly, their movements, and those of the ships which carried the colonial venturers, traders, and troops between countries, were important vectors for transmission of early Freemasonry as well as other cultural ideas.

The early Knight Templar encampments, commanderies, or preceptories were nearly all in major ports with the clear implication that travellers played a major part in the spread of masonic ideas; however, one area which had some of the earliest masonic development away from major ports was along the line of the Aire-Calder Navigation – a major route connecting the Liverpool and Humber Ports with early road, canal, and railway developments during the industrial revolution. Such transport links provided opportunities for ideas to be exchanged between the area and Ireland, Scotland, Continental Europe and trans-Atlantic trade routes. In particular, records exist of such developments in Dublin as early as 1523 and, with Liverpool and Bristol being the major ports for sea crossings to Ireland, the possibility of early transfer to England cannot be dismissed.

Magna Carta

The romance associated with the crusading Chivalric Orders of Knighthood has been perpetuated throughout the centuries, and the myths and legends associated with the former crusading orders still form a significant part of today's culture in many countries of the world. It is therefore appropriate to record some brief notes on individual families and modern organisations which have a historical or nominal, although sometimes superficial, connection with the Crusading Orders.

Whilst it is tempting to consider the Crusades as the embodiment of ideals and high principle, we must not forget medieval Europe was a land of violence and internal as well as external conflict. This can well be illustrated by concentrating for a moment on developments in Britain and considering the influence of former crusaders on the control of England and the influence, if any, of former crusading knights on political and social developments – even before the dissolution of the Templar Order. One such area of influence is clearly evident in the development of *Magna Carta.*

The *Magna Carta* was an English charter, originally issued in the year 1215, and first passed into law in 1225. The 1297 version, with the long title (originally in Latin) *'The Great Charter of the Liberties of England, and of the Liberties of the Forest'*, still remains on the statute books of England and Wales. At that time in England there was nothing which could be described as a national identity or consciousness; each individual owed fealty to his lord or baron and followed his banner, generally irrespective of where his lord's fealty rested. Under the English Crown in 1215 the control of the country was distributed amongst 236 baronies, comprising 29 ecclesiastical holdings, and 197 lay baronies held by 45 individual barons. Many barons had multiple baronial holdings maintained through 127 castles. Across the Country the 236 baronies were divided into about 7,000 Lordships or *Knight's fees* – or a small estate, town property, or manor generating sufficient income to support a Knight.

The 45 lay barons represented two separate factions; the majority either supported the Crown or remained neutral, being interested only in maintaining their own fiefdoms; but 24, generally speaking related in some way and acting as a clan, opposed the King in open revolt. The twenty-four lay barons and the Mayor of London formed a group which came together to impose *Magna Carta* on King John; these are generally known as the twenty-five *Magna Carta* Sureties. It is relevant to point out that the term 'baron' was generic and that seven of the Sureties were Earls and three were heirs to Earldoms. The significance is that these were part of the senior ruling class in the country, and the lay baronage was not united against King John; even at the next level, the knightly class, a relatively small proportion was in open revolt.

As might be expected, the *Magna Carta* document itself was undoubtedly composed by jurists; indeed, some historians have suggested it may have been based on an earlier *Angevin* Charter – of the French House of Anjou, the descendants of Fulk of Anjou, King of Jerusalem. The principal authors, in addition to practising lawyers, are believed to have been Roger Bigod, a justice in King Richard's reign; Hubert de Burgh, Justiciar of England in 1215, and a Counsellor of King John; William de Huntingfield, a 'justice itinerant' at the time, although not known to be trained as a lawyer; Stephen Langton, Archbishop of Canterbury, who later achieved fame as an ecclesiastical jurist and author of '*The Constitutions of Langton*'; William Marshall, Earl of Pembroke, perhaps one of the most capable men in England, and also a Counsellor of King John; Saher de Quincy, a justice in the years 1211-1214; and Richard de Montfichet, Hereditary Forester of Essex who may have been instrumental in incorporating clauses related to forest laws. The Mayor of London, who later became a Surety, may also have been involved – possibly through the legal establishments in the Capital.

Leaving aside the politics surrounding the creation of this important aspect of British history, the circumstances of its enforcement are of particular interest. The night before travelling to Runnymede to sign the Great Charter, the King stayed in the Temple property in London, and was escorted to the ceremony by Knights Templar. Some writers have speculated that these circumstances were more to ensure the attendance of the King than to ensure his safety or simply provide an honour escort! Certainly it is widely believed that the Master of the Temple in England, Prior Aymeric, was a great influence at this time.

What is a matter of record is that the twenty-five renowned sureties for the observance of the statutes contained in *Magna Carta* were drawn from the Noble families of the Country. Whilst their actual role is not of particular importance to this review, it is interesting to observe that many of these Nobles were serving or former Knights Templar, or had connections with other crusading Orders; in addition, three of the nobles had connections with Hereford, a major Knight Templar stronghold where the first Templar Headquarters, the Commandery of Garway was located. It may also be relevant that seventeen of the sureties have lineal descendants living today and therefore had family members in the mid-18th century, when speculative Freemasonry first developed.

William d'Albini, (or d'Aubigny) Lord of Belvoir Castle, Leicestershire, 1st Earl of Lincoln and 1st Earl of Arundel (c.1109-1236). William is known as the first proven English supporter of the crusader Order of St Lazarus of Jerusalem and before 1146 had granted them land at Wymondham and built a Leper Hospital near his castle in

Norfolk.[67] In 1219 William sailed for the Holy Land to participate in the Fifth Crusade. William's heir was yet another William, who died in 1247 leaving only daughters, one of whom, Isabel, married Robert de Ros (d.1285) of Helmsley, descendant of Robert de Ros, a known English Knight Templar, so linking the d'Albini inheritance to the de Ros family.

Roger Bigod, 2nd Earl of Norfolk and Suffolk (d.1220) Hereditary Steward of the Household and Privy Councillor; Keeper of Hertford Castle, Judge in the King's Court 1195-96, and Chief Judge in 1197; Warden of Romford Forest, 1200. Ambassador to King Philip of France to arrange for King Richard's crusade. Succeeded as Earl by his son Hugh.

Hugh Bigod, Heir to the Earldoms of Norfolk and Suffolk. (d.February 1225) who in 1206 or 1207 had married Matilda, daughter of the future Regent, William Marshal, Earl of Pembroke, who was buried in the Temple Church in London, clearly implying he had been admitted to the Knight Templar Order. Hugh became 5th Earl of Norfolk, 1221, and was Hereditary Steward of the Household, and Hereditary Warden of Romford Forest.

Henry de Bohun (1176-1220) an Anglo-Norman nobleman; Earl of Hereford and Hereditary Constable of England from 1199 to 1220. He died on the Fifth Crusade in the Holy Land on 1 June 1220.

Gilbert de Clare, heir to the earldom of Hertford. (d.1230) Earl Gilbert was an active participant on the baronial side in the civil war that followed in the wake of King John's rejection of Magna Carta. He fought with Louis and the French at the battle of Lincoln in May 1217 and was taken captive. In 1225 he was a witness to Henry III's definitive reissue of Magna Carta. In 1230 he accompanied Henry on his expedition to Brittany, but died on the way back at Penros.

Robert Fitzwalter, Lord of Dunmow Castle, Essex (d.1234) Robert, held the title of 'Marshal of the Army of God and the Holy Church' supposedly led the rebellion resulting in the Magna Carta. In 1219 he sailed for the Holy Land to participate in the Fifth Crusade along with Earl Saer of Winchester and Earl William d'Aubigny of Arundel. They left Genoa in August, shortly after the main crusading force left Brindisi, and arrived in some time in September, although after the main crusading force had been diverted to the siege of Damietta. Fitzwalter, Saer de Quincy and other English crusaders, arrived at the same time as the cardinal legate Pelagius in the autumn of 1219. The town fell into the crusaders' hands on 6 November, and therefore, although not mentioned, Fitzwalter must have taken part in the latter part of the siege. The crusaders remained in Egypt until August 1221, although before that Fitzwalter had gone home sick.

William de Huntingfield, A feudal baron and Sheriff of Norfolk and Suffolk (1210-11). From September 1203, he was a Lord Warden of the Cinque Ports. In the First Barons' War he was an active rebel against King John. He subsequently supported the French invasion of England, and took part in the Fifth Crusade, where he died in 1220 and was succeeded by his elder son Roger.

John de Lacie, Lord of Halton Castle, Cheshire and Lord of Pontefract Castle[68] (d.1240). Took the Cross for the Crusades along with King John in 1214. In May 1218 he embarked for Damietta in Egypt with his overlord, Ranulph, Earl of Chester to join the 5th Crusade (1219-1220). Returned to England in August 1220. Appointed to conduct Alexander II, King of Scotland, to England to meet King Henry III of England in 1229; Lacie died on 22 July 1240 and was buried near his father in the choir of the Cistercian abbey of Stanlaw (Lancs.), his bones being moved to Whalley, when the monks transferred there in the 1290s. His widow, Margaret, daughter of Roger de Quincy (d.1217), eldest son of Saer de Quincy, Earl of Winchester, died in 1266 and was buried in the Hospitallers' church at Clerkenwell, London.

William III de Lanvallei, Lord of Stanway Castle (d.1217), an English landowner, governor of Colchester Castle, and Lord of Walkern. William accompanied King John of England on his expedition to Poitou in 1214 and was present at the truce. He was related to several of the Magna Carta barons.

William de Mowbray, Knight, Lord of Axholme Castle, Lincolnshire (d.1223), Lord of Thirsk, Yorkshire, Constable of York Castle, Seigneur of Montbrai in Normandy, accompanied King Richard on his return from Palestine; fought for Louis VIII of France in the Battle of Lincoln, and taken prisoner 20 May 1217. Present at the Siege of Bytham Castle in 1221.

Saire/Saher de Quincey, Earl of Winchester. Ambassador to Emperor Otto IV in 1212; sent to France with Robert Fitz Walter to offer the English crown to Prince Louis of France; fought for Louis of France in the Battle of Lincoln, taken prisoner 20 May 1217. In 1219 he sailed for the Holy Land to participate in the Fifth Crusade along with Robert Fitzwalter and William d'Aubigny, and arrived in Acre some time in September. Soon after his arrival in Egypt, however, he fell ill, and died on 3 November 1219. In accordance with his instructions, he was buried at Acre and the ashes of his organs returned to England for interment at Garendon Abbey, Leicestershire, of which he was patron.

Robert de Ros, Lord of Hamlake Castle, Yorkshire (c.1182-1226/7), kinsman through marriage of Eustace de Vesci, and the son of Everard de Ros and Rose, née Trussebut, was a Yorkshire lord, the owner of extensive estates centred on Helmsley in the North Riding of Yorkshire and Wark-on-Tweed in Northumberland. He married, at an unknown date, Isabella, a natural (illegitimate) daughter of William the Lion, king of Scotland, and widow of Robert III de Brus. In 1203 he assisted in the king's defence of Normandy, where by descent from his mother he held the hereditary office of bailiff and Constable of Bonneville-sur-Touques. In 1205, he obtained a licence to pledge his lands for crusading, but his role in the Crusades is not recorded, although at some stage he was received into the ranks of the Templars. In 1212 Robert seems to have entered a monastery, but his monastic profession, however, cannot have lasted for long, for on 30 January 1213, John appointed him sheriff of Cumberland. Sometime before 1226 he again retired to a monastery and died that year or in early 1227. He was buried in the Temple Church in London, where exists an effigy sometimes associated with him. Robert, a possible participant in the First Crusade, and a known member of the Templar Order in England has lineal descendants living today (26th Baron de Ros.)

Geoffrey de Saye, A Feudal Baron in Sussex, Lord of Edmonton (Middlesex), West Greenwich, Birling, Cudham and Keston (Kent), Leckhampstead (Buckinghamshire), Kimpton and Sawbridgeworth (Hertfordshire), etc. (d.1230) Known knightly service under King Richard and King John fighting in the defence of Normandy but no known service in the Holy Land. Present at the Siege of Bytham Castle in 1221, Went on pilgrimage to the Holy Land in 1219 and to Santiago de Compostella in Spain in 1223.

Three sureties, whilst drawn from the knightly class are not known to have any personal crusading involvement or Knight Templar Order history:

Richard de Clare, 3rd Earl of Hertford. (d.1217) played a leading part in the negotiations for Magna Carta, being one of the twenty five Barons appointed as guardians. On 9 November 1215, he was one of the commissioners on the part of the Barons to negotiate the peace with the King.

John FitzRobert, Lord of Warkworth Castle, Northumberland with estates distributed across two regions of England, the far north along the Scottish border, and East Anglia and Essex. He accordingly had ties with the two main, but largely separate, groups of barons who rose in opposition to King John in 1216.

Robert de Vere, Knight, heir to the Earldom of Oxford. (d.1221) Robert de Vere, Knt. Hereditary Master Chamberlain of England, Chief Justice Itinerant in Herefordshire, 1220.

All of these *Magna Carta* sureties are known to have had surviving descendants to at least four generations, but the remaining original sureties are believed to have died without known issue:

William de Fortibus, Earl of Albemarle. (d.1241) Descended from a minor French noble family from the village of Fors in Poitou, in 1227 Albemarle went as English ambassador to Antwerp; in 1230 he accompanied Henry on his expedition to Brittany; and in 1241 he set out for the Holy Land, but died at sea, on his way there, on 26 March 1242.

William Hardell, Mayor of the City of London. (d. after 1216 – No known Crusader or Knight Templar history.)

William Malet, Lord of Curry-Mallet, Kilve, Polden, Shepton Mallet and Sutton Mallet (Somerset), Dullingham (Cambridgeshire), Lullingstone (Kent), etc. (d.c.1217). (No known Crusader or Knight Templar history.)

Geoffrey de Mandeville, Earl of Essex and Gloucester (d.1216). (No known Crusader or Knight Templar history.)

William Marshall Jr, heir to the earldom of Pembroke. (d.1231 and buried in the Temple Church in London, clearly implying involvement with the Knight Templar Order.

Roger de Montbegon, Lord of Hornby Castle, Lancashire (d.1226). [Roger de Montbegon was an original Surety but was replaced by Roger de Mowbray. (Neither had known Crusader or Knight Templar history).

Richard de Montfichet, A feudal baron in Essex. (d. after 1258 without any known crusading activity)

Richard de Percy, A feudal baron in Yorkshire (d.1244 without Issue). Early in John's reign Richard served on military expeditions with or for the king, but is not known to have been a Crusader in the Holy Land.

Eustace de Vesci, Lord of Alnwick Castle, Northumberland (d.1216) He served with King Richard I of England in Palestine in 1191.

Thus, of the eight authors of *Magna Carta*, four (Bigod, Huntingfield, Marshall, and de Quincy) were known crusaders or had Knight Templar connections, and no less than 16 or nearly two-thirds of the 25 Sureties had crusading or chivalric experience in the field. The majority of the authors of the Charter and the *Magna Carta* Sureties, can therefore be classed as both military leaders and landed gentry. Whilst contemporary records do not confirm their loftiness of vision or greatness of mind, their experiences enabled them to sense the importance of what Stephen Langton and the drafters of the *Magna Carta* envisaged. The *Magna Carta* established the power of law and is the cornerstone of English constitutional government, and we must be grateful to the Sureties for recognizing *Magna Carta* significance and enforcing it.

Whilst the topic of *Magna Carta* may not be an obvious feature of Knight Templar history, it has clearly significant chivalric elements, and a review of the individuals involved does produce some interesting ideas, in particular by identifying families of crusaders through which may have survived not only a verbal legacy but also knightly honours and even retained historical artefacts. And it is not only English Crusaders who feature in this story, but even the brief notes of the individuals involved with *Magna Carta* and its enforcement reveal involvement with French Crusaders and their descendants who by then had a major influence on English affairs following the Norman Conquest.

It can thus be seen that neither the Crusades nor Crusaders had been forgotten; whilst the high principles ascribed to the crusades may not necessarily have driven the creation of *Magna Carta* itself, the *Magna Carta* Sureties were military leaders and important landowners who influenced its drafting and enforcement, possibly using concepts derived from the 1129 Templar Rule of Saint Bernard which then became the basis for English 'Common Law'.

Whilst this brief glimpse has only considered the background of some 25 individuals, it must be remembered that the 197 lay baronies at the time were held by 45 individual barons; over half the English nobility therefore features in this story. The English baronage was undoubtedly a direct consequence of invasion, repeated warlike conflict, and royal patronage – much resulting from land redistribution before, during, and after successive Crusades. It is therefore fair to say not only that *Magna Carta* established the framework for the rule of law, but also that this pattern had undoubtedly been influenced by the crusading and chivalric experiences of most of the protagonists thus creating the environment for what followed. Later we will see that these same individuals and their families were also influential is establishing Orders of Chivalry and the British honour systems from which the Masonic Orders of Chivalry derived their senior grades.

2.7 ORDERS OF KNIGHTHOOD

Historically, the British, and to a rather lesser extent, other European Nations, developed honour systems headed by Royal Houses which were the 'fount of honour'; whilst many developed in comparatively recent years the prototypes originated at the time of the Crusades or shortly thereafter.

The British Honour system is structured basically under six Orders:

The Orders of the Garter, Thistle, and of St Patrick honoured royals, peers, statesmen, and eminent military commanders;

The Order of the Bath honoured senior military officers and civil servants;

The Order of St Michael and St George honoured diplomats and colonial officials;

The Order of the Star of India and the Order of the Indian Empire honoured Indian rulers and British and Indian officials of the British Indian Empire;

The Royal Victorian Order, in the personal gift of the monarch, honoured those who had personally served the royal family; and

The Order of the British Empire is an order of chivalry, rewarding contributions to the arts and sciences, work with charitable and welfare organisations, and public service outside the Civil service.

Whilst all of these are Orders of Chivalry, only the two most senior grades, Knight Grand Cross and Knight Commander, confer the honour of Knighthood.

Not all the orders have a military requirement although the awards within The Order of the Bath and the Military Division of the Order of the British Empire are usually restricted to military recipients. It is considered significant that the creation of the highest honorific grades within Masonic Chivalric Orders reflect this honour system adopting the same nomenclature of Knight Grand Cross and Knight Commander.

The Most Noble Order of The Garter

The prototype chivalric honour is generally regarded as the Order of the Garter. Although it has been claimed as founded on 23 April 1344, early records having been lost, The Most Noble Order of the Garter is documented as founded in 1348 by Edward III. It is dedicated to the image and arms of Saint George, England's patron saint, and is the only actual honour awarded by the Sovereign, who alone decides on its membership. All other awards, although given by the Sovereign, are decided upon by politicians.

Two principal legends purport to describe the basis for the Order, but perhaps the most favoured one, recounted in a letter to the Annual Register in 1774, records King Richard I while fighting in the Crusades, was inspired in the 12th century by St George the Martyr to tie garters around the legs of his knights who subsequently won the battle. King Edward supposedly recalled the event in the 14th century when he founded the Order.[69]

The Order currently consists of Her Majesty The Queen who is Sovereign of the Order, His Royal Highness The Prince of Wales and 24 Knights Companions. The 25 founder members, listed as knighted in 1344 in *The Complete Peerage*, which states the order was first instituted on 23 April 1344, were:

Edward Plantagenet, The Black Prince, distinguished himself at Battle of Crecy, 26 August 1346

Henry Plantagenet, Duke of Lancaster

Thomas de Beauchamp, Earl of Warwick, Chief Commander at Battle of Crecy, distinguished at Poitiers 1356, became Earl Marshal of England

Jean de Grailly, Kt, distinguished at Poitiers 1356

Ralph, Lord Stafford, esteemed Edward's Commander in France.

William de Montacute, Earl of Salisbury

Roger Mortimer, Earl of March, descendant of Roger and Hugh Bigod, Gilbert de Clare, John de Lacie, and Saire de Quincy, *Magna Carta* Sureties

John, Baron Lisle de Rougement

Bartholemew, Lord Burghersh, descendant of Roger and Hugh Bigod, *Magna Carta* Sureties

John de Beauchamp, descendant of Roger and Hugh Bigod, and Henry de Bohun, *Magna Carta* Sureties

John, Baron Mohun, descendant of William d'Albini and Robert de Ros, *Magna Carta* Sureties

Hugh, Baron Courtenay, descendant of Henry de Bohun, *Magna Carta* Surety

Thomas de Holand, Earl of Kent, descendant of Saire de Quincy, *Magna Carta* Surety

John, Lord Grey of Rotherfield, descendant of Robert Fitzwalter, *Magna Carta* Surety

Roger or Richard Fitz-Simon, Kt served in Flanders, Castile (1344), Aquitaine (1345-6) and as standard bearer of Edward, the Black Prince at the Battle of Crecy (1346).

Miles Stapleton, Kt served at the Siege of Tournai (1340), in Brittany, and at the siege of Calais in 1347.

Thomas Wale, Kt served in Flanders (1339) King Edward III, Brittany (1342) under William De Bohun, Earl of Northampton, and overseas in 1344 with Richard, Earl of Arundel.

Hugh Wrottesley, Kt served in the Low Countries (1338-39) under King Edward III.

Nele Loryng, Kt, a medieval English soldier and diplomat. Served at the Battle of Sluys (1340) and knighted; Calais (1347); by 1351 served as Chamberlain to the Prince of Wales, and with him in Aquitaine (1353); and at Poitiers (1356); Brittany (1359-60), Aquitaine (1366), and later French campaigns.

John Chandos, Kt, a military strategist and possibly the mastermind behind three of the most important English victories of the Hundred Years War: the Battles of Crécy, Poitiers, and Auray. Rewarded as Lieutenant of France, Vice-Chamberlain of England, Viscount of Saint-Sauveur, Constable of Aquitaine.

James, Lord Audley, served in Crecy (1346), at the naval Battle of Winchelsea (1350); France (1354) [attendance upon the Black Prince], Poitiers (1356); France (1359); Led conquering of fortresses of Chaven in Brittany, Ferte-sous-Jouarre, and was present at Calais. Later Governor of Aquitaine and great Seneschal of Poitou.

Oates *(or Otho)* de Holand, descendant of Saire de Quincy, *Magna Carta* Surety, Served Normandy (1346) and fought at the Battle of Caen. Governor of the Channel Islands (1359)

Henry d'Enne *(or Eam)*, Kt, curiously, his listing among Garter Knights has been attributed to his success at jousting, but he afterwards entered service with Edward, the Black Prince.

Sanchet d'Abrichecourt, a French knight.

Walter Paveley, first cousin of Bartholemew, Lord Burghersh, descendant of Roger and Hugh Bigod, *Magna Carta* Sureties; Various French Wars (1342-47); Aquitaine and Languedoc (1355) with the Black Prince and at the battle of Poitiers (1356).

This Most Noble Order[70] therefore seems to have an origin at the time of the crusades; certainly it has been traditionally awarded to the most senior individuals who have shown service to the realm, and it has since provided an archetype order of chivalry which has spanned nine hundred years and undoubtedly formed the template which many other orders have followed.

Other British Chivalric Orders

The other British chivalric order have no known connections with the crusades, although most include military personnel amongst their recipients. The Order of the Bath, and the Order of the British Empire have specific Military Divisions. The Order of St Michael and St George was originally created to recognise distinguished citizens of the Ionian Islands, and Malta, these being important strategic locations for military bases, although towards the end of the 19th century the Order was expanded to reward distinguished service in British territories, and more generally in foreign affairs.

Foreign Orders

Over the nine centuries since the First Crusade, many Chivalric orders have been instituted, but even in the countries which participated in the Crusades, few were based specifically on crusading ideals or concepts of chivalry. Most European countries which developed honour systems followed the Order of the Garter as their prototype without claiming a specific crusader *raison d'etre*. There are two chivalric orders which do, however, claim such affinity:

The Order of the Dragon (Hungary)

The Order of the Dragon (Latin: *Societas Draconistarum*, literally 'Society of the Dragonists')[71] was a chivalric order for selected nobility, founded in 1408 by Sigismund von Luxembourg who was King of Hungary (1387-1437) and later Holy Roman Emperor (1433-1437). It was fashioned after the military orders of the Crusades, requiring its initiates to defend the cross and fight the enemies of Christianity, in particular the Ottoman Empire. The Order seemed to flourish, mainly in Germany and Italy during the first half of the 15th century, but went into decline after Sigismund's death in 1437. Following the Fall of Constantinople in 1453, it continued to play a role in Hungary, Croatia, Albania, Serbia, and Romania which bore the brunt of the Ottoman incursions.

Order of Charles XIII

This Swedish Order,[72] instituted in 1811 by Charles XIII of Sweden[73] confers the honour of Knighthood equivalent to a British Baronetcy, and was based on the traditional history of the Knight Templar Order. It is significant that it may only be awarded to members of the XI Grade of the Norwegian or

Scandinavian Rite of Freemasonry, the higher degrees of which have an essentially Knights Templar background and traditional history; although it is not a Masonic Order, it is sometimes euphemistically referred to as the 'twelfth degree'.[74]

2.8 THE EMERGENCE OF CLUBS AND SOCIETIES

In medieval times, along with the State, the Church must be regarded as the principal archetype organisation; the crusades were one measure of the ever-increasing power of the church in medieval life, with some estimates suggesting that as many as 40,000 clergy were ordained during the 13th century. This was also shown by the spate of cathedral building, common throughout Europe, at the time. These great buildings would often take several generations to complete, spawning whole communities of artisans and craftsmen and offering them jobs for life. A quarter of the land was owned by the Church and monasteries owned large tracts of land farmed by peasants.

The rest of the land was owned by large land owners, many of whom had gained their lands through either service to the Crown or through military activity, including much resulting from the crusades in the Holy Land. It is not surprising that the majority of the population were engaged in the rural agricultural economy with little social activity beyond the church and the large estates.

Few clubs or societies existed before the end of the 14th century. One notable example, however, was the concept of the *auberges* or inns, developed by the Knights of St John in Rhodes and Malta between 1191 and 1798, for knights from distant *langues* visiting headquarters, and we can assume the other chivalric orders adopted a similar approach, as did later military bodies with messes for different military ranks. These all clearly fulfilled social as well as accommodation needs outside the military environment, and must be regarded as the forerunners of social clubs. Whilst early masonic lodges did have a high proportion of military or naval members which influenced lodge organisation and development, no direct evidence has yet been found that members of former chivalric Orders had a similar influence, but this cannot be ruled this out.

Universities

One notably medieval development was the emergence of the earliest universities, most, for practical purposes, traceable back to cathedral or monastic schools. Although many of these had appeared as early as the 6th century it was hundreds of years before any were established as independent seats of learning. With roots in the Christian Church, it is not surprising that some of the earliest universities appeared in (today's) Italy: Bologna (1088); Padua (1222); Naples (1224); Rome (1303); and Pisa (1308). Similar patterns of development occurred in other European Countries: Salamanca (Spain 1134); Coimbra (Portugal 1290); and Paris (France c.1213).[75]

Whilst most were founded by the Christian church, independence was soon achieved, this showing an emerging type of academic institution usually with a collegiate base which furthered social as well as educational changes, many providing a direct link back to medieval times. Within colleges a formal hierarchy also developed with such institutions as Senior and Junior Common Rooms with procedural elements such as formal 'top table dining'.

Over much the same period, with the earliest appearing in the 14th century, Inns of Court appeared where lawyers traditionally lodged, trained, and carried on their profession. Over the centuries, four Inns of Court developed for the training of barristers, while rather more Inns of Chancery, affiliated to the Inns of Court, developed for training of solicitors.

The four Inns of Court, or 'Honourable Societies' are Inner Temple with records since 1320; the Middle Temple (1346); Lincoln's Inn, the largest, (with official records from 1422) and Gray's Inn (with records from 1569, but teaching perhaps from the late 14th century). Middle and Inner Temple are located in the courtyard of the former Knight Templar church, and lawyers there can trace their history back to advising the Templar Order. Like the Universities, the Inns of Court and Chancery granted qualifications, but in addition had formal disciplinary and supervisory functions.

In parallel with the development of formal academic institutions, philosophical clubs and institutions started to appear, some with a scientific, antiquarian, and historical bias. These, too, appeared throughout Western Europe, some examples being the College of Antiquaries (1586); the *Académie Française* (1635); *Deutsche Akademie der Naturforscher Leopoldina* (1652); and The Royal Society (1660).

Trade Guilds

Academic institutions were not the only emerging societies facilitating change. Associations of trading and professional interests developed first into local or regional Trade Guilds during the Middle Ages and then emerged as Livery Companies. The earliest recorded was The Worshipful Company of Mercers, the premier Livery Company of the City of London incorporated under Royal Charter in 1394, ranking first in the order of precedence of the Companies. It is the first of the 'Great Twelve' City Livery Companies.

However, there are companies of even earlier origin, one example being the Worshipful Company of Girdlers (belt and girdle makers) with accorded precedence as No. 23 but a claimed origin of 1327. The Worshipful Companies of Girdlers and Haberdashers are two of the Companies of particular interest to Masonic historians, since they used the *Goose and Gridiron* Tavern in St Paul's Churchyard at the time the Premier Grand Lodge was conceived; indeed the name of the tavern was probably derived from the working tools of both these trades – a Goose being a large, long-necked smoothing iron, and the Gridiron being the frame on which the goose was heated over a fire.

The 'Great Twelve' City Livery companies in order of precedence from 1394 are the Worshipful Companies of Mercers (general merchants); Grocers (spice merchants); Drapers (wool and cloth merchants); Fishmongers; Goldsmiths (bullion dealers); Skinners (fur traders); Merchant Taylors (tailors); Haberdashers (clothiers in sewn and fine materials, e.g. silk & velvet); Salters (traders of salts and chemicals); Ironmongers; Vintners (wine merchants); and Clothworkers. The Worshipful Company of Masons (stonemasons) is accorded Precedence No. 30, having received its Royal Charter in 1677.

These Livery companies, claiming existence from 1327 until today, thus form one of the prototype trade and professional organisations which paralleled the ecclesiastical organisations and universities. Development continues up to the present day and there are today 110 Livery Companies in London alone, many also providing a direct link back to medieval times. It may well be that such were the organisations from which Masonic lodges derived their nomenclature and practices.

Such change-producing emerging societies and organisations, received further impetus following the Dissolution of the Monasteries by Henry VIII between 1536 and 1541. This effectively broke much of the hold of the Church in England, and subsequently resulted in redistribution of land from the Crown to new landowners resulting in alteration of balance of power.

Industrialisation and Social Changes

Industrialisation brought a shift of population from thinly-spread, widely distributed agricultural work-forces to urbanisation. Urbanisation brought a change in social structure; agricultural workers usually stayed reasonably static, lived with their family, stayed within the extended family of large estates patronised by landed gentry, and had the social support of a local village and church. Industrialisation required more mobility; the work force often travelled, building roads, railways, and canals; men were often employed remote from their family; industrial employers were rarely as philanthropic as country landowners; and industrial accidents generated increased requirements for hospital and community care facilities.

This then provided opportunities for social changes – urban communal dwellings and hostels – public houses, social clubs, new churches, friendly societies, credit unions, banks, and urban shops.

As educational levels improved, and working conditions became less feudal, the work force gained more leisure time, and the requirement for Social institutions spread to all levels of society, rather than just the upper and middle classes. This then was the environment where Masonic Lodges took root and thrived, along with social clubs and institutions; sports clubs; Working Men's Clubs; Political and Trades Union Societies. And it was into this social framework that such societies as Antediluvian Order of Buffaloes (1822), Loyal Order of Moose (1888), and Lions International (1916), also emerged, many seemingly following the lead provided by Masonic Lodges.

As a model for the earliest Masonic Lodges, the traditional gentlemen's club seems to be another obvious prototype institution. The oldest clubs in London: White's Club (1693), Boodle's (1762), and Brooks's (1764), were generally for Aristocrats and had political affiliations (Whig or Tory) and did not admit women members; outside London, one of the earliest was The Gentlemens Club of Spalding (1710) – a members-only private learned society which is still active today; however, by 1775 the Royal Thames Yacht Club appeared with fewer restrictions.

The earliest Masonic Lodges were often for the educated, well-off, upper and middle classes, but as they grew in popularity, membership extended across a wider social spectrum. But such changes appeared gradually, and very much in line with the other social changes occurring at the time – and the changes of particular interest are those in the British Isles induced by cultural impacts of Colonialisation, Global Trade, International Conflicts, and Maritime Influence.

2.9 COLONIZATION, GLOBAL TRADE
AND MARITIME INFLUENCE

The time spectrum which we must consider as influencing the development of Freemasonry and the Knight Templar Order, whilst overlapping the medieval period described above, is really a continuous spectrum when it comes to maritime influences. The use by the crusading forces has been discussed elsewhere, and the Knights Templars and Hospitallers both had maritime arms which, at time, had immense influence – not only on military campaigns, but also on trade, religious pilgrimages, banking, and development of ports, shipyards, and coastal towns. Whilst the question of what happened to the Templar fleet in France at the time of the Templar persecution will perhaps never be resolved, it is reasonable to suppose much if not all of the fleet continued to operate under different flags and with an evolving role. It is therefore appropriate to treat maritime developments, not within the artificial framework of 'medieval' or as who conducted operations but to review the resulting effect of continuous maritime evolution which would facilitate the development of Freemasonry.

Colonization Impacts
The maritime activities of the Portuguese Order of Christ, the European Hanseatic League, and the Order of St John have been mentioned elsewhere. However, in addition to trading activities, virtually all the European Nations had colonial and territorial ambitions; some of these resulted in the lesser crusading activities also mentioned earlier.

Colonial ambitions which took them beyond Europe required considerable maritime resources. These ventures were important for introducing a number of significant changes:

The need for ships with seagoing rather than coastal trading capability promoted the development of maritime technology, navigational maps and charts, and skills.

Defence of ships, crews, passengers, and cargoes from pirates and the colonisation of unknown territories involved naval marines and military forces.

Colonialisation required not only consular and diplomatic personnel, and entrepreneurs, but also supporting medical, educational, technical, and administrative staffs and their families.

The social conditions which then evolved in the foreign locations were naturally an extension of home environments. This included organisations such as churches, social and sports clubs, and masonic lodges. However, colonial entrepreneurs included a high proportion of relatively young, single men to whom sports clubs, and masonic lodges appealed particularly.

Return of ships crews and military personnel following short-term deployments, and traders and colonial staffs on leave or at the end of longer-term appointments brought back, not only fresh ideas and cultural elements but also foreign spouses, commercial employees, and servants.

The mix of personnel involved in colonisation ventures was significantly different to the normal home environments. Note only were numbers considerably smaller with a higher proportion of leaders in each of the professions and trades involved, but also unlike the home environments most long sea voyages and overseas colonies had to include a relatively large proportion of military personnel.

The European maritime Nations ventured globally as soon as technology permitted, and as mentioned earlier the Spanish and the Portuguese were in the forefront of global exploration; the exploits of such explorers as Christopher Columbus and Vasco de Gama, and the expeditions promoted by Prince Henry 'The Navigator' are too well-enough documented as to required detailing here, other than to highlight their voyages to the New World, around the African Continent, and to the Middle and Far East.

During the 15th and 16th centuries, this rapidly resulted in British, French, Belgian, and Netherlands colonisation on the African Continent and in the Middle and Far East, and the increase in the flow of goods such as tea, spices, and silk, and peoples.

It is perhaps significant that early Spanish and Portuguese explorers sailed under the Flag of The Portuguese Order of Christ – a White Maltese Cross on a Red Ground – which almost certainly confirmed that their maritime traditions, skill, and military prowess were those inherited directly from the Knights Templar. In contrast, the Nations surrounding the Mediterranean, whilst having undoubted maritime histories, rarely ventured beyond the Mediterranean itself. In 1492, the expeditions initially seeking westward routes to the East Indies as a source of spices, took European explorers to the New

World. Whilst they did not find access to the spice trade, they quickly gained access to gold and silver from Central and South America and the botanical riches of the Caribbean.

The early result was the establishment in the New World of European Colonies by virtually all the European Nations with the lead being taken by Britain, France, and Spain with lesser colonisation by Portugal and The Netherlands and minor interests by the Scandinavian Countries and the Order of St John. But such Colonial Aspirations were not realised easily; although some territorial opposition came from indigenous peoples the majority of opposition came from European competitors also interested in gaining access to resources such as gold, silver, and mineral wealth and raw materials such as Spices, Tobacco, and Cotton. Such colonial and commercial aspirations therefore required naval and military support, often on a considerable scale.

New World exploration also produced new commercial ventures which dramatically altered both global trading and cultural ideas. By far the greatest global impact resulted initially from the development of Sugar, Coffee, Tobacco, and Cotton plantations in the West Indies which created the Slave Trade and high-volume triangular flow of people and goods across the Atlantic: Manufactured goods, including arms, from Europe to Africa; their exchange for slaves then transported to the New World; and then the return of raw materials, Sugar, Coffee, Tobacco, and Cotton to Europe. This dramatically increased the volume of shipping and people. Such global developments not only produced an exchange of goods and peoples but also fresh ideas. Trading also produced more piracy which, in turn meant the increased use of marines and troops to protect ships and trading interests.

Whilst the majority of the ventures in the New World involved small colonies where the occupying Nations easily became a dominant force, the land mass of North America and the emerging territories of America and Canada were a different story. There the indigenous populations were very much in a minority and the greater part of their population were European emigrants. The reasons for this are irrelevant here, other than to make the point that unlike most global colonial ventures, commercial and military competitors were other European Nations.

One example was The Hudson Bay Company. In the 17th century two enterprising Frenchmen – *Radisson* and *des Groseilliers* – discovered a wealth of fur in the interior of today's Canada – north and west of the Great Lakes accessed via the great inland sea that is now named Hudson Bay. Although the fur trade had obvious potential, neither French nor American support for development was forthcoming, and it required the vision and connections of Prince Rupert, cousin of King Charles II, to acquire the Royal Charter which, in May, 1670 granted the lands of the Hudson Bay watershed to 'the Governor and Company of Adventurers of England trading into Hudson Bay.' However, opening up the interior was not simple, and early operations were based in a few forts and outposts on the shores of James and Hudson Bays. Each year, the local indigenous population brought furs to these locations to barter for goods such as knives, kettles, beads, needles, and blankets. By the late 18th century, competition forced expansion further into the interior – mainly along the great rivers of the West – eventually reaching the Pacific Northwest (Oregon, Washington and British Columbia) and the North (Alaska, the Yukon, and the Northwest Territories). Such development required not only trading entrepreneurs but military forces, for the territories of Canada and America were still unstable politically as well as economically.

America and Canada were both theatres of war with Britain and France as the principal antagonists in Canada and, with Spain, in America rather than only European Nations versus Indigenous peoples. This resulted in far fewer cultural changes of a type unknown outside Europe, but social evolution similar to the home environment but with a different pace of change. However, as pointed out earlier, even in America and Canada the colonial populations likewise included a relatively large proportion of military personnel as well as venturers and entrepreneurs.

In some senses, a parallel development to the Hudson Bay Company was the East India Company which, although formed to trade with 'The East Indies' established a firm base in India. Developments on the Indian sub-continent were somewhat different however; unlike most colonies with sparse native populations including America and Canada, the indigenous population of the Indian sub-continent was huge and colonisation could only be achieved with a large military presence. The Indian sub-continent was by no means home to a single Nation, but hundreds of smaller, often-warring, factions, speaking many languages. Introduction of British, and to a much lesser extent, Portuguese commercial interests thus provided something of a unifying and stabilising influence. But it was the tea trade that became significant to our story. In 1600, a group of merchants incorporated themselves into the East India Company which was granted monopoly privileges on all trade with the East Indies by the British Government. Trade started in India, at the port of Surat, in 1608, and by 1615 the British received the right to establish a factory there. Trading posts were established along the east and west coasts of India, and considerable English communities developed around the three towns of Calcutta, Bombay, and Madras. This global trade also created an immense amount of maritime traffic moving not only raw materials including cotton, jute, rice, and tea to Europe and finished goods back to India, but also considerable movements of personnel.

The Company spread Christianity as well as trade, but in order to protect its interests, it had its own military forces in regimental strength. In 1757 Robert Clive, a military official of the Company, defeated the forces of the Nawab of Bengal, Siraj-ud-daulah. Soon after this victory the Company found itself burdened with massive military expenditures and threatening collapse. Lord North's India Bill 1773 restored its position but provided for greater parliamentary control over the Company. The Tea Act was also passed in 1773 to assist the Company, and this resulted in the Boston Tea Party which had, of course, huge implications for the American colony.

Colonisation was not part of the aims of the Trading Companies but their ventures has similar impacts; creating colonies also generated some unlooked-for additional opportunities for commercial maritime movements, one being the use of new lands for prison colonies to which to deport convicts; these also required the use of troops and the movements of colonial administrators.

The East India Company was given a monopoly against other British traders and merchants, but their Charter gave them no privileges against Portuguese, Dutch, or French traders; consequently this led to wars in the East Indies, and much of the 14th to 18th centuries were times of considerable violence and conflict; indeed, over these five hundred years, Britain was almost constantly at war.

Some conflicts have been mentioned as lesser crusades within Europe, but most later conflicts necessarily generated huge maritime movements involving both naval forces and commercial vessels, and it will soon be apparent that ships crews and naval voyages almost certainly had a disproportionate effect on both the spread of Freemasonry in general and on the influence of military lodges which in turn had an immense impact on the spread of chivalric masonry. More details of military conflicts will therefore be included in the chapter on the activities of military lodges.

2.10 CRUSADER ORDERS IN FICTION

There is no doubt that the Crusading Orders of Chivalry have found an enduring place in history through not only historical accounts but also in popular Drama, Theatre, Opera, Poetry, and fiction. Indeed, in the earliest days, poetry and troubadour's songs were perhaps the only records which embodied eye-witness accounts or contemporary recollections of historical events.

Whilst many such records need to be considered with extreme care by historians it is certainly appropriate to consider fictional accounts as worthy of consideration for three specific reasons:

Many fictional writings are, at the time of their composition, the only contemporary accounts of real historical events which might, perhaps, be put in context by later historians.

Many writers use recorded facts, actual historical events, places, and persons as the base for their fictional accounts event though they may include further embellishments, make unsound interpretations, and derive unwarranted conclusions.

Whereas academic scholarship might well be more accurate, such writings are rarely available to a wide audience, and therefore it is popular fiction and the image of historical events as portrayed that reach a wider audience and conditions the general attitudes to the events, places, and persons portrayed.

It is for these reasons that a brief review of some of the Drama, Theatre, Opera, Poetry, and fiction is relevant when assessing the cultural environment both for the survival of the Crusading Chivalric Orders and the attitudes which prevailed at the time of the emergence of Masonic Orders of Chivalry. This is indeed a complex history in its own right, and of course, is with us today to an even greater extent in films, television, video games, and the internet, all conditioning the attitudes of the modern world to past history; but to illustrate this phenomenon the writings up to the close of the 18th century – the effective dawn of chivalric speculative Masonry – will be considered in chronological order by date of compilation rather than the events to which they refer.

Medieval Troubadours

Perhaps, rather curiously some readers may think, an appropriate group of participants with some first hand knowledge of the Crusades are the often-forgotten troubadours. Troubadours, more than musicians of any other genre, responded to the Crusades, probably because several accompanied their patrons on crusader journeys. The name troubadour itself may even have been derived from the Arab '*tarrab*', or minstrel.

Many troubadours were professional musicians, and as travelling minstrels, performed songs, and not simply poems. Troubadour songs form part of a Western tradition of lyric poetry with a history of upholding the ideals of chivalry; this translated neatly into zeal for the similar ideals fuelling the European crusaders. What troubadours brought back from the fighting, if they returned, was reflected in their songs. Our interest is with those troubadours most closely connected with the crusades. The earliest extant troubadour texts come from *Guilhem de Peiteus* (1071-1127), at a time when the Spaniards were imitating Arabian ideas of rhyme and metre, and it appears that European minstrels adopted music that was related to Arabian verse.

Jaufre Rudel de Blaye was a minor nobleman and castellan of Blaye during the second quarter of the 12th century, *Jaufre's* preoccupation with the 'developing cult of vernacular lyric poetry' rivalled his zeal for the ideals of the crusades; he participated in the Second Crusade (1147-1149), and probably died there in 1148. One of his most notable poems alludes to this Crusade in the Holy Land, depicting particularly the feelings of crusaders taking farewell to their loved ones on departure to the crusades including the stanzas:

> For one friendship am I longing because I know no richer joy than this: that she should be good to me, if she made me a gift of her love. And she has a well-fleshed body, soft and fair, with nothing which does not befit it, and her love is good and pleasurable.

> Love, gaily I leave you because now I go seeking my highest good; yet by this much was I fortunate that my heart still rejoices for it. But, for all this, because of my Good Protector who wants me and calls me and accepts me, I must needs restrain my longing.

> And if anyone stays back here in his delights and does not follow God to Bethlehem, I know not how he might ever be worthy of love or come to salvation; for I know and believe that, to my way of thinking, he whom Jesus teaches is sure of certain doctrine.

But not all troubadours put a favourable slant on the crusades. The earliest known professional troubadour, *Marcabru* enjoyed early and sustained patronage of William X, Duke of Acquitaine (c.1127-1137). Upon William's death, however, *Marcabru* wandered in search of patronage and protection, and probably found it from King Alfonso VII of Castile. Alfonso's own participation in the Iberian *Reconquista* of the late 1130s and early 1140s sparked *Marcabru's* composition of the songs '*Pax in nomine Domini'* and his latest datable poems allude to the Second Crusade (1147-1149) in which he probably participated. Much of his work criticizes the moral corruption he perceives, 'the degeneracy of the nobility, the decline of courtly virtues, and the flourishing of their perverted opposites'.

Giraut de Borneil was a professional troubadour, who took part in the Third Crusade in 1191 in company of his patron, Ademar V, Viscount of Limoges. On his return, he travelled extensively in France and Spain, and is credited with some of the most skilful compositions in the whole corpus of troubadour poetry. His work combined technical skill and poetic sensitivity making him a popular performer at many European Courts, as he undoubtedly portrayed the crusading ethic in a most favourable light.

Other Medieval Travellers

In a similar category to the troubadours who could claim actual knowledge of the Crusades, we find a few contemporary accounts of other visitors to the Holy Land. One of some interest is the writings of a German monk – *Theodoric* – who visited the Holy Land between 1168 and 1174, and after visiting '*Outremer'* afterwards compiled a sort of '*Lonely Planet'* guide for travellers to assist pilgrims visiting holy sites.[76] Whilst this may not be strictly fiction, the work is not that of a historian, but does give some interesting commentary, one example being a graphic account of the Castle of Accaron, near the City of Ptolemais:

> 'In this city the Templars have built a large house of admirable workmanship by the seashore, and the Hospitallers likewise have founded a stately house there. Wherever the ships of pilgrims may have landed them, they are all obliged to repair to the harbour of this city to take them home again on their return from Jerusalem. Indeed, in the year when we were there – on the Wednesday in Easter week – we counted eighty ships in the port besides the ship called a "buss", on board of which we sailed thither and returned. Along the road which leads from Jerusalem through the aforementioned places to Ptolemais one meets with many deserted cities and castles, which were destroyed by Vespasian and Titus; but one also sees very strongly fortified castles, which belong to the Templars and Hospitallers.'

Grail Legends

An important early medieval work of interest is that of Perceval, the Story of the Grail (French: *Perceval ou le Conte du Graal*), an unfinished romance of *Chrétien de Troyes*, (1130-c.1193). It was written in Old French during about 1180-90 and dedicated to *Chrétien's* patron Philip, Count of Flanders who died in 1191 crusading at Acre. The story, combining an embryo Arthurian legend, the mythical Fisher King, and the Grail story, recounts the adventures a young knight Perceval, but the story is unfinished perhaps because *Chrétien*, or

Philip, or the source named by Philip, died. It also contains the legend of Gawain, (9,000 lines long but also unfinished.)

Though *Chrétien* did not complete his epic, it had an enormous and lasting impact on the literary world of the Middle Ages. Perceval introduced an enthusiastic Europe to the grail and all versions of the story, including those that made the grail 'Holy', probably derive directly or indirectly from it. The grail in Perceval has the power to heal the Fisher King so it may have been seen as a mystical or holy object by readers.

Wolfram von Eschenbach's Parzival, one of the greatest works of medieval Germany, is based largely on *Chrétien's* poem although *Chrétien's* focus is on knighthood with religious implications while Wolfram focuses mainly on knighthood. Together these works had a huge impact on medieval attitudes to chivalry.

The next medieval writing of crusading interest is *The Song of Roland*[77] a 4,000 line sung French minstrel epic work. It is actually based on the Emperor Charlemagne's army fighting the Muslims in Spain for seven years until the last city standing is Saragossa, held by the Muslim King Marsile. Although the events are set in the Carolingian era the epic was written sometime before 1115, possibly by a poet named Turold around 1040 but with later additions between 1098 and 1115. Some authors have suggested the poem was inspired by the Castilian campaigns of the 1030s, but that it went on to influence attitudes to the Crusades as there appear to be brief references in the poem to events of the First Crusade. Specifically, the work includes three references to '*d'oltre mer*' or '*l'oltremarin*' in connection with Muslims who came from *oltre mer* to fight in Spain and France. *Oltre mer,* in today's French *Outremer*, was a term meaning 'beyond sea' used by Crusaders to refer to Palestine. Whilst this term does not necessarily suggest anything more than such usage was a common French way of referring to the far side of the Mediterranean, the later additions do perhaps suggest the writers had heard stories from the Crusades.[78]

The Arthurian Legend

Medieval secular literature was much concerned with knighthood and chivalry. Two masterpieces of this literature are the *Chanson de Roland* mentioned earlier and the 14th century *Sir Gawain and the Green Knight*. Arthurian legend and the minstrel *chansons* epics furnished bases for many later romances. The work of *Chrétien de Troyes* also had huge influence on European literature with chivalrous and pastoral romances still being widely read in the 16th century attracting satirization by Cervantes in *Don Quixote*.

In the 12th century Geoffrey of Monmouth created an Arthurian legend which appealed to a medieval England. Whilst his basis was not strictly the crusades, Geoffrey was reflecting a fascination with chivalric subjects, as have numerous writers over the course of history. Whether or not Arthur ever existed as a real historical figure is actually irrelevant, and Arthur, his Round Table, and his Camelot were only important as a chivalric framework in which to present ideas appropriate to the culture, place, and time. However, that framework endured and still appears today to epitomise chivalric ideals and influence modern attitudes to knighthood.

Robert de Boron

Robert de Boron was a French poet of the late 12th century who, according to his own poetic writings served one Lord Gautier de Montbéliard who has been identified as a participant in the Fourth Crusade from 1202 until his death in 1212 in the Holy Land. His principal poetic works were poems *Joseph of Arimathea* and *Merlin*, which later had a major impact on versions of the Arthurian legend.

Robert de Boron is credited with incorporating a rework of the *Chrétien de Troyes*, '*Perceval*' legend bringing into prominence the legend of the '*Holy Grail*', in prose with much greater impact than that portrayed in *Chrétien de Troyes's* unfinished '*Perceval*'. Boron's version included the invention of a group of Crusader Knights to guard the Grail, and his version of the Grail myth was later adopted by many British writers.

Medieval Theatre[79]

Earlier it was seen how European activity set the scene for the development of Freemasonry, including the cultural environment which would be encountered by British travellers, not only military forces engaged in conflict and seafarers engaged in global trade, but also those undertaking Court activity, religious pilgrimages, and cultural trips such as 'The Grand Tour' which later became fashionable.

The well-known description of Freemasonry which runs: 'A peculiar system of morality, veiled in allegory and illustrated by symbols' is familiar to many Masons, and as a description of our present practice, it could not be bettered. However, as the The Revd N. Barker Cryer observes in his study of 'Drama and the Craft' in the background of our masonic ancestry, as it emerges in the 14th to the 17th centuries, is that in every respect this is precisely a description which would have fitted our brethren in those ages as well as our own'.[80]

Mystery plays, 'miracle' plays, or 'saints' plays were three components of medieval theatre derived from dramatizing the liturgy of the Roman Catholic Church, primarily to give religious instruction, establish faith, and encourage piety. Miracle plays deal with the lives of the saints and martyrs;[81] Moralities are an offshoot of Miracle Plays with allegorical and ethical, rather than historical, objectives, and Masonic ritual is much the same.

Although most medieval dramas took material from the lives of saints, some more recent than in traditional biblical writings, the more vernacular dramas performed in the Middle Ages did not always present a real account of the life or martyrdom of a saint. This may account for their popularity in such as countries as Germany, Belgium, and the Netherlands where such traditions survive to this day based on clear chivalric legends ranging from St George slaying the dragon to those depicting the crusades and unmistakeable 'crusaders'.

The influence of the crusades may even be found in dance. One activity which can trace its origin to medieval times is the tradition of Morris Dancing (a corruption of 'Moorish Dance'). At least one regional dance, based on a stylised sword fight, records it as an import from Spain where the *moresca* is common, recalling the strife between Christians and Muslims in that country from the 12th to 15th centuries during the lesser crusades.[82] The earliest known and surviving English written mention of Morris dance is dated to 1448, and records the payment of seven shillings to Morris dancers by the Goldsmiths' Company in London. At least three regional variations seem to confirm this early Moorish influence: Border Morris[83] from the English-Welsh border: a vigorous style, traditionally danced with blackened faces; Longsword dancing from Yorkshire and Durham, danced with long, rigid metal or wooden swords; and Rapper from Northumberland and Durham, danced with short flexible sprung steel swords. An interesting feature of some dances is that swords come together at one point interlinked in a 'nut' – form of endless 'knot' similar to the device appearing on Sir Gawain's shield of Arthurian legend – and perhaps a forerunner of the device later used in the Royal Arch.

Such theatrical performances represented a way of converting pre-Chriatian, biblical, and historical stories into a form which was not only entertaining but also instructive in morals, and medieval theatres appeared in most major centres of population. Such centres also saw the emergence of the first Masonic lodges, and it is almost certainly no coincidence that chivalric rituals first appeared in areas with a history of dramatic theatre.

Geoffrey Chaucer(1340?-1400)

Between 1387 and 1400 Geoffrey Chaucer published perhaps one of the most important medieval works, *Canterbury Tales*, in which the narrator of the 'Knight's Tale' '… served with the (Teutonic) Knights'.[84]

It is unlikely such characterisations would be based on first-hand experiences but derived from, at best, anecdotal accounts – possibly from non-English cultures – or, at worst, pure invention. The same may be said about the mystery plays,[85] moralities,[86] and other 15th and 16th century dramas.

However, the way Chaucer introduces knightly characters in his writings sugests individuals and their exploits would be readily appreciated by his readers without further explanation.

Spenser, Edmund (1552?-1599)

Edmund Spenser, in his work Prothalamion (I.1.127) includes a Templar reference in a way that suggests this was well-enough known to his audience as to require no further explanation:

> Where now the studious Lawyer have their bowers, There whilom wont the Templar Knights to bide Till they decay'd through pride.'

Shakespeare, William (1565-1616)

The writings of William Shakespeare are of particular interest when considering the impact of medieval writings on the popular culture of the time, and whilst his work scarcely references a crusader past directly, much of his work include royal, noble, or chivalric themes. He freely alludes to military tactics, castles, weapons, armour, and the injuries associated with conflict as if he had first hand knowledge. However, he is not known to have had any military service, or direct exposure to relevant social and cultural situations. Likewise his plays display knowledge of several European countries and cultures; and yet The Bard never seemed to travel abroad. Consequently, conspiracy theorists often debated ideas as to who actually wrote the Bard's works; perhaps Shakespeare was, in modern terminology, a 'ghost writer' working with knowledgeable contemporaries who had perhaps participated in lesser crusades.

The background to his writing is really irrelevant, but the impact on medieval culture and popular attitudes to chivalry are unquestionable; his writings certainly left his readers and those who saw and heard his performed works with lasting impressions about the contribution of the nobility and the knightly and chivalric classes to modern culture.

Swift, Dean (1746)

In *A Letter from the Grand Mistress of the Female Free-Masons to Mr. Harding the Printer (Anonymous (Dublin, 1724),* the author, later identified as Dean Swift, mentions 'The famous Old Lodge of Kilwinnin' and 'The Knights of St John of Jerusalem' in a way that suggests that they were correlated in popular opinion.

The incident to which Swift refers came from an idea of 1594 when James VI decided to celebrate the birth of Prince Henry Stuart by rebuilding the Chapel Royal at Stirling following the design and dimensions of Solomon's Temple.

He and Schaw sought out and employed the best stonemasons and craftsmen, 'with his Majesty's own person daily overseer' of the construction, and the design produced showed the chapel as an arch-type example of the Scottish Renaissance. The design for the Temple rebuild was related to James's admiration for the crusading orders portrayed in a royal masque. In it, the King; John Erskine, 1st Earl of Mar; and Thomas Erskine played the role of Knights of Malta who took the field against the infidel Turks. With Mar, Schaw, and his Masons in attendance, James knighted sixteen nobles and gave them instructions in their chivalric duties. It was possibly this that gave rise to both the tradition that Scottish Knights of Malta were also Freemasons and also to the later Jacobite Masonic degree which emerged in the lodge at Stirling in 1745.[87]

Larmenius, Johannes Marcus (c.1804), Charter of

One of the most interesting pieces of masonic 'traditional history' purports to record a list of Grand Masters of the Templar Order – the so-called *Charter of Larmenius*.

In about 1911 a large parchment – sometimes described as the *Charta Transmissionis* – was presented to the Great Priory of England and Wales by Brother F. J. W. Crowe.[88] The manuscript, which is now kept in Mark Masons' Hall, lists twenty-two successive Grand Masters of the Knights Templar after Jacques de Molay, ending in 1804 by naming Bernard-Raymond Fabré-Palaprat, who brought the document to light in that year. It is written in a Latin but in codified form allegedly based on an ancient Knights Templar cipher.[89] Analysis of the deciphered code[90] and the discovery circumstances lead most researchers to conclude it is a forgery.

Fabré-Palaprat claimed the charter was originally created by Larmenius in February 1324, some ten years after Grand Mastership of the Knights Templar Order was verbally transmitted to him in March 1314 by Jacques de Molay. According to the charter, Larmenius, a member of The Order of the Temple, became the Preceptor in Cyprus after the Order left the Holy Land in 1295 after the fall of Acre. It is then claimed that when the Grand Master, Jacques de Molay went to Paris in 1305 to meet Philip IV of France and Pope Clement V, Larmenius became Templar Seneschal in charge of the Templar forces in the Mediterranean. As the effective 'second in command' of the Order he assumed the position of Grand Master on the death of de Molay. The document then records Larmenius transmitting the Grand Mastership to Franciscus Theobaldus, the Prior of the Templar Priory in Alexandria, Egypt, and to a line of Grand Masters down to 1804.

The Charter was considered to be a forgery, possibly by a Jesuit priest, Father Bonani, who helped Philippe II, Duke of Orléans to fabricate the document in 1705 to try to confirm the authenticity of an organisation which claimed continuity from the Knights Templar – the *'Societé d'Aloyau'*, and to gain recognition by the Order of Christ in Portugal. Allegedly, following the dissolution of *'Societé d'Aloyau'* during the French Revolution of 1792 and the death of its Grand Master, the Duke Timoléon de Cossé Brissac, massacred at Versailles, the Charter was found in a piece of furniture and showed to Fabré-Palaprat in 1804.

Even if the document was not a complete forgery and may not date from the 14th century, its claim that the list[91] of the individuals to whom the Grand Mastership was allegedly transmitted by an entirely verbal process may well be valid; this would certainly be likely whilst the order was being persecuted. It may be an original authentic manual record with some genuine names, but there are undeniably several historical points where it could have been fraudulently altered. It is curious (in this author's opinion) that surviving contemporary records such as those of the Knights of St John (in Malta to 1798), fail to mention such a record or these names.

However, even if the charter is a forgery or partly fraudulent, it must still be considered to have value as did some of the other documents mentioned earlier in this chapter, and it is worth recalling these:

The charter may be the only contemporary account of a historical process through which the early transmission of the Templar Grand Mastership occurred; possibly indicating that Jacques de Molay realised going to Paris was fraught with danger so causing him to devise a plan for his succession and the future management of the order should his fears be realised.

Notwithstanding possible later embellishment or fraudulent alteration, some persons named may be genuine and although the overall document may now seem fictional leading to a modern view that the charter is entirely forged, this may be an unsound interpretation with unwarranted conclusions. It is also possible the Charter may refer to some independent Order unconnected with today's Freemasonry.

Whereas academic scholarship might well be more accurate, true written evidence is never likely to become available, so the line of Grand Masters may never be verified; nevertheless, the Templar image in this Charter did continue to keep the Order in the public eye during the 18th century.

Finally, and perhaps of greatest importance, Napoleon is actually believed to have accepted that the charter was genuine and one justification for restoring the Templar Order in France in 1804.

Ironclad (2011)

In the modern era films and video games draw heavily on crusading history and it is not appropriate to develop this subject. However, one film (*Ironclad, 2011*) does have an interesting take on Templar history and the *Magna Carta,* portraying the Order of the Temple as one of the main protagonists in the struggle of the English Nobles against King John which resulted in that Charter. The leading character, Thomas Marshall is very loosely based on William Marshall, 2nd Earl of Pembroke.[92]

The Impact of Fiction

These examples of writings over seven centuries certainly confirm both the enduring interest in the crusading chivalric concepts and the interest of writers over the ages in revisiting the story for many reasons. They also confirm that several European cultures accepted and welcomed these works of poetry, drama, theatre, fiction, and even pseudo-historical documents, and never lost their interest in keeping the chivalric, crusading code alive. It is therefore not surprising that the western cultures were amenable to the emergence of not only speculative Craft Freemasonry with its moralistic approach, but also to the re-emergence of those ideals as embodied in chivalric Freemasonry as it dawned.

2.11 THE DAWN OF CHIVALRIC FREEMASONRY

Earlier the emergence during the late medieval period of the Mystery Plays, and earliest printed documents was mentioned. Significantly, this was the very period when the oldest 'masonic' writings – the '*Old Charges*' – appeared in England. The Regius MS of 1390 is well-known as one of the earliest sources of moral instruction to a trade guild. It includes unequivocal advice to an operative mason of his duty to his master, brethren, and the Holy Church, with emphasis on leading a moral life and respecting the chastity of a master's or fellow's wife and daughter, demonstrating a clear link with the Masonic charges familiar today. However, both Mystery Plays and the Regius MS were hand-written documents and therefore of only very limited distribution, as were many other early '*Old Charges*', some of which would be written specifically for each lodge. The availability of the printed text from the mid-16th century gave undoubted impetus to their distribution and most surviving copies of 'old charges' are printed versions which undoubtedly entered routine use in lodges; their impact will be considered later.

But it is not only for the ritual impact that these manuscripts are important. They influenced the degree structure adopted by Lodges working after the manner of the *Antients*, as, although of an essentially different character, both the Regius MS and others such as the Cooke, Colne, and York manuscripts appear to have been used in the manner of the 'charge after initiation' to instruct candidates in the background to the Craft. Briefly, that background started with a commentary on the Legend of the Flood and Noah and the inventions and developments of Noah's children with particular reference to the seven liberal arts and sciences. These charges, obviously prepared for use by artisans, then developed ideas for the various organisations with appropriate emphasis on the artisan crafts and the training and qualifications. This included an emphasis on 'ritual journeys' and practical steps to obtain knowledge and experience, and ultimately 'to seek for that which was lost'.

It was therefore not surprising that progression from the Craft should develop further journeys between Babylon and Jerusalem to 'recover that which had been lost'. Such biblical accounts clearly provided traditional histories which developed logically as extensions to the Craft and Mark becoming not only progressive journeys undertaken in the Royal Arch, but also in the Ancient and Accepted Rite (Rose Croix) and many other European Masonic Rites. It is equally obvious that the successive journeys of the Crusades fall into this genre of '*recovery of that which was lost*'; the Holy

Land Crusades to recover the lost city of Jerusalem and the Temple; and later lesser Crusades to regain Christendom from the hands of 'infidels'. It is therefore equally unsurprising that elements from the Knights Templar and other chivalric Orders should find their way into the traditional histories of speculative chivalric masonic Orders.

Earlier, the concept of global expansion was reviewed in the context of movements round the world and the development of colonial, trade and military links. It is not appropriate in this work to recount the history of Craft Freemasonry which is well-enough documented elsewhere, but nevertheless, there are elements of that history which are relevant to the origin and development of the Chivalric Orders.

Early references to a Masonic Order of Knights Templar using that exact terminology are hard to find, particularly in France where that Order was suppressed. In the absence of irrefutable evidence one has to look firstly at masonic activities using euphemistic or generalised names for possibilities and then to see whether the most promising of these can be regarded as probabilities. However, this in itself is a vast subject, but to set the scene only elements which involve either military or chivalric Masonry will be mentioned briefly, concentrating on the period up to 1769, when, as we shall see later, the first actual Knight Templar minute activity is recorded.

This intriguing journey into chivalric history starts as far back as the year 1314 which actually takes us back to the era of the Crusading Knights Templar, for the traditional history of the Royal Order of Scotland dates its origination to the reign of King David I in the 12th century. Regrettably this must be regarded in many respects as 'masonic traditional history' and although one of the degrees of the Order – The Heredom of Kilwinning – was traditionally established in Judea, in Palestine, the tradition does not claim this was at the time of the Crusades. The other degree of the Order – The Rosy Cross Degree – traditionally has its origin on the field of Bannockburn, on St John's Day in the summer of 1314. It was instituted by King Robert the Bruce, who having in the course of the battle for Scottish independence, received assistance from a body of sixty-three knights who, it has been suggested, may have been original Knights Templar and Freemasons although, today, the archives of the Grand Lodge of Scotland contain no evidence to confirm this. He conferred upon them as a reward for their services the civil rank of Knighthood with a limit of sixty-three on whom the Knighthood might be conferred, a limit which still applies to both the Grand Lodge and its subordinate Provincial Grand Lodges. The Rosy Cross degree, as its name implies, is closely related to the Rose Croix Degree of the Ancient and Accepted (Scottish) Rite.

Scotland has the earliest documented evidence for the organised Freemasonry we recognise today, and by 1560 mention of lodges working 'beyond the Craft'. The Lodge of St Mary's Chapel, No. 1 Edinburgh was constituted before 1598, and it is this lodge which then features in the first recorded initiation on English soil:

> A Lodge was held at Newcastle, by deputation, on behalf of the Lodge of Mary's Chapel, the 20th May, 1641, under commission to Robert Mackey, General Quartermaster of the Armies of Scotland, to receive Sir Robert Moray; amongst those present were General Hamilton and John Mylne .... members of the Lodge of Mary's Chapel.

But this is also of importance as it shows an ostensibly civilian lodge had military members and was either acting as a military lodge travelling with the Scottish Army, or had issued, in today's terminology, a dispensation to allow lodge members to work in Newcastle.

The first recorded initiation of an English Mason was that of Elias Ashmole who recorded in his diary:

> '1646. Oct. 16. 4.30 p.m. – I was made a Free Mason at Warrington, in Lancashire, with Coll. Henry Mainwaring of Karincham. The names of those that were then of the Lodge (were) Mr Rich Penket, Warden; Mr James Collier, Mr Rich Sankey, Henry Littler, John Ellam, Rich Ellam and Hugh Brewer.' [93]

The importance of this is well known in English Craft Masonic history, but what is not often emphasised is that there is a crucial military dimension to this meeting – the fact that, although the initiation took place during a lill between periods of actual fighting, at least two of the brethren present were military officers then engaged in fighting on different sides of the conflicts in that year. The military aspects of such lodges will be further examined in the next chapter.

The year 1659 next comes to our attention as did the Royal Order of Scotland, with the traditional history of the degree of Scottish Master of St Andrew recording that year as the date for its origin. However, it is not this tradition or the precise year that is important, but the fact that this degree repeatedly occurs in a number of forms from the earliest days of speculative masonry; including variants such as 'Scots', 'Scotch', 'Scottish', and foreign equivalents; alternative names appear is two different forms:

> Specific degree names such as Scots Master, Scotch Master, Scots Master of St Andrew, Apprentice-Companion of St Andrew, Scottish Fellow Craft, Scottish Master, Master of St Andrew, *Maitre Ecossais,*

Very Enlightened Brother of St Andrew, Scottish Knight of Saint Andrew and Knight of Saint Andrew.

More generic terms such as *Ecossais Masonry,* Scottish Rite, and Rectified Scottish Rite, and Ancient and Accepted (Scottish) Rite.

These have a common theme: stripped to their bare essentials each embodies the notion that speculative Freemasonry existed at the time of the crusades, was developed within Europe by crusaders returning home, but after the suppression of the Templars in the 12th century, survived in Scotland where the Papal Bull was never promulgated.

However, it was not long after this that a masonic ritual with a speculative Knight Templar content would be recorded[94] – an Old Irish Ritual for Knight Templar Priests in Lancashire dated at 1686. At much the same time[95] there is clear evidence of organised masonic activity in the City of York[96] and reference to an old lodge (also possibly in York around 1693) in the York MS *Old Charges.*[97]

There was also other sporadic activity in the coastal towns in East Yorkshire probably at the same time; by 1705 this resulted in the establishment of the first known lodge in Yorkshire in the seaport town of Scarborough, and although its warranting authority is not known[98] it is widely held to have worked degrees 'beyond the Craft' influenced by seafaring visitors. Elsewhere, Yorkshire Masonry was also being organised as evidenced by 1706 minutes of a Lodge in York.[99]

County Durham was also showing organised lodge activity at an early stage; in 1717 Lodge of Industry No. 48 was constituted, possibly having worked informally well before that date, and minutes from 1725 are recorded at Winlaton. On 24 June 1735 a lodge was warranted at Swalwell (although it also worked elsewhere in County Durham)[100] and evidence exists for this lodge working an English Masters degree. It has been speculated that this may be a local name for the degree of Scottish Master – changed when the degree was carried there by seafaring brethren, but 'English Master' was also used elsewhere as an alternative name for the degree of Intimate Secretary, the sixth degree of the Rite of Perfection.

Clearly northern brethren in Durham, Lancashire, and Yorkshire were working 'beyond the Craft' before 1717 with hints of Knight Templar elements in coastal towns and seaports strongly suggesting the role played by seafaring brethren as early transmitters of new Masonic ideas. Some of the clearest evidence for this next appears in the 1720s when the earliest recognisable documented Freemasonry appeared in French seaports (Bordeaux) with evidence of transmission there from Bristol c.1720 which is not surprising since there has been a long-standing connection with Bordeaux since the late 17th century.[101] The history of Freemasonry in Spain and Gibraltar also suggests the spread of English and Irish Freemasonry to Southern Europe at about the same period.

It was about this time that the term *Ecossais* Masonry was coined in France, despite the fact that there is little documentary evidence that this type of Freemasonry originated in Scotland or had any formal connection with the Grand Lodge of Scotland.[102] The term *Ecossais* may simply have meant 'with Scottish historical references', 'involving Scottish brethren', or even 'from foreign parts' or 'overseas' without meaning Scotland as a Country.[103] Critically, at an early stage, *Ecossais* Masonry included not only the Craft degrees, but also the degrees of Scots Master and Scots Master of St Andrew which, still today, have undoubted Royal Arch and Knight Templar elements.

However, the recent research by Stevenson does put this view in a different light as he advances the theory that Masonic history has been generally led astray by the prevailing misconception that the emergence of Freemasonry took place in England – 'a belief maintained in the face of the overwhelming preponderance of Scottish documentary evidence relating to the process, evidence which is often simultaneously explained away ... and then used in an English context to make up for the lack of English evidence'.[104]

This certainly seems the case with Masonic Knight Templar history which does appear to have clear links with the earliest *Ecossais* degrees. In particular one degree of a specifically chivalric nature was carried to France by Scottish exiles. This first appeared in lodges held in St Germain under the title *Chevalier Ecossais* as an addition to the three symbolic Craft degrees. This degree, also known as Scotch Knight or *Macon Parfait,* was characterised by a specific device or tracing board bearing the image of a lion, wounded by an arrow, and having escaped from the stake to which he had been bound, with the broken rope still about his neck, is represented lying at the mouth of a cave, and occupied with mathematical instruments which are lying near him. A broken crown lies at the foot of the stake. It has been suggested that this alludes to the dethronement, the captivity, the escape and asylum of James II and his hopes of regaining 'that which was lost' by the help of the loyal Brethren. Whilst the tableau is not now interpreted in that way, the image will be recognised by some Masonic brethren today. It is not very certain, however, when this degree was added, whether immediately after King James's abdication, or about the time of the attempt to set his son on the British throne. But it is certain, that in 1716, this and other *Ecossais* degrees of Masonry were not only popular in France but soon appeared throughout Europe.

In England, besides the Durham lodge at Swalwell mentioned earlier, there are records of lodges conferring the degree of 'Scots Master' or 'Scotch

Master' as early as 1733. Old Lodge No. 1 (now Antiquity No. 2) certainly indicates a Scotch Master Masons degree was known in the 1730s in London. Rawlinsons Manuscript List of 1733 shows Lodge No. 115 at the Devil's Tavern, Temple Bar, London described as a 'Scotch Masons Lodge'. Other lodges include a lodge in Bath in 1735, and the French lodge, St *George de l'Observance* No. 49 at Covent Garden in 1736. In Bristol a Scotch Master degree was known by 1740 (Lodge at The Rummer, Bristol).[105]

In France the *Ecossais* degrees soon became an essential part of a number of other rites: The French Rite (7 Degrees); the Adonhiram Rite (12 Degrees); the Rite of Perfection (25 Degrees); and the Rite of Strict Observance which also spread quickly to Germany and Scandinavia

At the same time as *Ecossais* degrees appeared in France a number of 'knightly' degrees emerged, containing ritual elements which survive today within several different degrees and orders. These degrees included Knight of the East, Knight of the Sword or of the East, and Knight of the East and West.

These *Ecossais* and 'knightly' degrees will be examined in a moment, but it is appropriate first to consider the impact of one of the most influential events in France that cannot be ignored when considering how the customs and practices of the Chivalric Orders came to have an influence on speculative Freemasonry: an 'oration' by Andrew Ramsay in Paris in 1737.

Andrew Ramsay was born in 1686 in Edinburgh, the grandson and son of Church of Scotland Episcopalian ministers, and although a theology graduate from the University of Edinburgh, he soon abandoned the idea of becoming a Minister. He travelled to London, ostensibly to learn French, and he soon became acquainted with many important academics and philosophers including Isaac Newton, Dr Desaguliers, and members of the Royal Society. He also showed early military interest and in about 1707 we find him serving with the English auxiliaries in the Netherlands, where he fought under Marlborough during the War of the Spanish succession.[106] Later he gained further military experience through joining the Jacobite army, probably in Glasgow about 1715, then fighting at the battle of Preston (9-14 November, 1715), after which he was captured and imprisoned. After escaping, he was recaptured and held in Wigan jail until he was deported along with other Jacobite prisoners in June 1716 on a ship bound for St Kitts in the West Indies.[107] However, the prisoners either bribed or overwhelmed the crew and were landed in France.

In France he had several employments as a tutor; for some years with the family of the Duke of Turenne, a blood relation of Godfroi de Bouillon, a key player in the First Crusade. During that time he researched and compiled a history of that family during which he undoubtedly gained an understanding of the crusading chivalric orders and their later history, including the Order of

St Lazarus into which he was later inducted thus gaining the chivalric title of *Chevalier*. He became tutor for a short while to the two sons of the Old Pretender, James Edward Stuart, then living in Rome, from whom in 1723 he received a 'Patent of Nobility', and subsequently a 'Jacobite' Baronetcy. Back in Paris, through such contacts, he was socially accepted not only by many in the upper reaches of French society but also by several of the Jacobite followers in exile there. Seven years later, he spent a year in England towards the end of which he was initiated into Freemasonry in London in the Horn Lodge, the Lodge of which Dr Desaguliers was a member. When Ramsay returned to Paris he became heavily involved in Masonic affairs in the city and was soon afterwards appointed Grand Orator in the Grand Lodge of France.

Ramsay was evidently dissatisfied with the historical references with which Anderson had prefaced his 1723 *Book of Constitutions*, and by 1736 he had written his own very different version of the 'Traditional History'. This is generally called '*Ramsay's Oration*' although it is uncertain when and where he actually delivered it; he may well have presented the original version on 26 December 1736 in a 'St. John's Lodge' which was possibly the French Grand Master's Lodge, St Thomas's No. 1, meeting at Epernay. He intended to deliver a modified version of the *Oration* at the meeting of the Grand Lodge of France in Paris on 24 March 1737, but did not do so in the face of the disapproval of Cardinal Fleury, the principal Minister of King Louis XV.[108] In later life, partly through ill-health, he withdrew from active participation in the French Grand Lodge, but circulated copies of his 'Oration' to several people including a Brother Carte, an English Jacobite, to whom he wrote (in English) saying that he had delivered the Oration at various times at 'the accepcion of eight Dukes and peers and two hundred officers of the first rank and highest nobility'.[109] The validity of this statement is uncertain, but within a few years the *Oration* had evidently been widely circulated, and in modern terminology would seem to have been used as a 'charge after initiation'.

The first of the three sections of the *Oration* sets out the nature of the Freemason's Craft and the duties expected of its members. The second section envisages how the Craft might develop in France to the benefit of the world in general and that of France in particular. The third section is a traditional history, as fanciful as anything written by Anderson.

'Higher' Masonic Degrees, being developed at this time in France and in Germany, were the preserve of the Nobility who were unwilling to consider their aristocratic persons to be the heirs of common workmen, the Operative Masons, to whom the Members of the English Craft were quite content to be the successors. In the third section of the *Oration* Ramsay provided for the French nobility that for which they were seeking – more distinguished

Masonic forbears. Initially Ramsay's 'History' was Andersonian in the sense that it traced Freemasonry back to the Hebrew Patriarchs, and claimed that 'Noah, Abraham, the Patriarchs, Moses, Solomon, and Cyrus were the early Grand Masters in our ancient Order' but in later versions Ramsay discounts the debt which the Craft owed to King Solomon – the French nobility were even uneasy about a Royal person having such an intimate relationship with a common workman, Hiram Abif.[110] Ramsay acknowledges that while Freemasonry also owes something to the ancient Mysteries, for example, the Bacchanals, its specific origin can be found in a revival which, he asserts, took place during the time of the Palestinian Crusades.

> At the time of the Crusades in Palestine many Princes, Lords and citizens banded together and vowed to restore the Temple of the Christians in the Holy Land, to employ themselves in bringing back their architecture to its first institution.
>
> Our ancestors, the Crusaders, who were gathered together in the Holy Land from all parts of Christendom, desired in this manner to reunite the individuals of all nations into one Fraternity.....
>
> Our Order, therefore, must not be considered a revival of the Bacchanals, but as an Order founded in remote antiquity, renewed in the Holy Land by our ancestors in order to recall the memory of the most sublime truths amidst the pleasures of society.....
>
> Our Order formed an intimate union with the Knights of St John of Jerusalem. From that time our lodges took the name of Lodges of St John. This union was made after the example of the Israelites when they erected the second Temple who, whilst they handled the trowel and mortar with one hand, in the other held the sword and buckler.....

Having by these means given contemporary French Freemasons suitably noble predecessors, Ramsay explains the traditional Scottish connection, and how French Lodges came to be derived from those in England –

> The Kings, princes and lords returned from Palestine to their own lands and there established divers lodges. At the time of the last Crusade many lodges were already erected in Germany, Italy, Spain, France and, from thence, in Scotland because of the close alliance between the French and the Scots. James, Lord Steward of Scotland, was Grand Master of a Lodge established at Kilwinning in the West of Scotland MCCLXXXVI [1286], shortly after the death of Alexander III, King of Scotland, and one year before John Baliol mounted the throne. This Lord received as Freemasons into his Lodge, the Earls of Gloucester and Ulster, the one English, the other Irish. By degrees, the solemn proceedings in our Lodges were neglected in most places. That is why, of so many historians, only those in Great Britain speak of our Order. Nevertheless it preserved its splendour amongst those Scotsmen to whom the Kings of France confided during many centuries the safeguard of their royal persons.

So that made everything all right for the French aristocracy – they had a distinguished aristocratic descent as Freemasons, and the Craft came to France not necessarily through the hated English, but rather through their well-loved Scottish allies!

It cannot be said whether this was the result which Ramsay intended. He did not 'invent' the Masonic Order of Knights Templar but he cleared the way for numerous higher Chivalric Degrees to become established in France,[111] (and also in Germany) so that the Nobility could take part in the so-called 'Ecossais' Degrees without feeling constrained by any feeling that they were demeaning themselves by associating with the common people; even his idea of working simultaneously wielding a sword and trowel had chivalric overtones – still found today in Royal Arch and some other rituals. It has been said that if the French aristocrats had played cricket with their tenants as those in England did, there might never have been a French Revolution.

The history he outlined had a somewhat less obscure basis than the English Solomonic – Hiramic legend; although he did not mention the Knights Templars specifically, he did mention the Knights of St John and other Crusader elements. Reflection on the content of his oration suggests that, firstly, his failure to mention the Knight Templar was undoubtedly astute in the country which had led, if not instituted, the persecution of that body; and secondly, his choice of Scotland was of one Country where the successive papal bulls which condemned Freemasonry were never promulgated or enforced.

Such a departure from the English 'artisan' base became, not only favoured by the French, and other European Nations, but also by other cultures (such as those in the New World) where, in particular, Nobility and Chivalric honour systems did not exist, and Masonic titles could be considered as one alternative means of peer-recognition.

Whilst his oration did not deny the operative origins on which the English Craft was based, it treated this as a base for further personal development along the lines of other cultural and hierarchical developments; one result was that the 'Master' of a Lodge became the first of a series of grades with increasingly imposing titles drawn from a wide range of recognised cultural systems – from Religious Hierarchy (Prelates, High Priests); from Military Systems (Lieutenants, Captains, Marshals, and Generals); from Nobility (Constables, Earls, Kings, and Emperors). Such a philosophy undoubtedly gave impetus to the emerging masonic degrees with chivalric-sounding rather than artisan titles.

'Knightly-sounding' titles became an early and essential component of Continental Rites including the 'French Rite' of seven degrees which spread rapidly. This rite, contained four further degrees after the Craft:

4. Master Elect   5. **Scottish Master**

6. **Knight of the East**   7.   Sovereign Prince Rose Croix
                                          / Knight of the Eagle

Later, a longer, although relatively short-lived, rite of twelve degrees would emerge – the so-called The Adonhiram Rite with a further nine degrees after the first three of the Craft:

4.   Perfect Master   5.   Elect of Nine
6.   Elect of Perignan   7.   Elect of Fifteen
8.   Minor Architect
9.   Grand Architect, or **Scottish Fellow Craft**
10. **Scottish Master**
11. Knight of the Sword, **Knight of the East**, or of the Eagle
12. Knight of Rose Croix

Significantly, both contained the degrees of Scottish Master (or variants mentioned earlier) and Knight of the East, the latter also appearing throughout Masonry in several different guises; and under a variety of names. Some include Knight of the East in names such as Knight of the East and West and Knight of the Sword or of the East, but others adopt names indicating the nature of the ritual – such as Red Cross of Babylon.

All these rituals are based on a symbolic journey 'to recover that which was lost' and one variant mirrors closely the legend in today's Royal Arch Ritual: a journey to the East from Jerusalem to Babylon, and then the return to the West from Babylon to Jerusalem having made certain recoveries. Some of the variants introduce specific obstacles into the symbolic journey – typically the need to cross a bridge, encounter opposition, and then overcome that resistance. At some stage, rather than this journey being undertaken by one or more 'knights', implying a military environment, the legend became that of (Prince) Zerubbabel returning to Babylon to gain authority to continue work without hindrance and to recover lost sacred vessels and temple furnishing before returning to Jerusalem bringing the descendants of the Jewish peoples.

Similar traditional histories survive today in many other masonic degrees including that of the Ancient and Accepted (Scottish) Rite, Knight Masons of Ireland, and the Order of the Red Cross of Babylon, and clearly suggest that early precursors of today's Royal Arch were visible at this time.

In France, *Ecossais* Lodges created more degrees at a very early date connecting the Scots Masons with the Knights Templar and thus giving rise to the subsequent flood of Templarism. From that time new rites multiplied in France and Germany, but all those of French origin contain knightly and, almost all, Templar, grades.[112]

A statement made before the Inquisition in Lisbon on 1 August 1738 by Hugo O'Kelly, then Master of a local lodge of mainly Irish Brethren which began working about 1733 certainly confirmed degrees 'beyond the Craft' were known at that time.[113]

Records of Craft Freemasonry appear in Scandinavia in 1735, carried there by Count Axel Wrede-Sparre, a Cavalry Officer who during service in France had become a Freemason. In Sweden he brought together some friends, mostly members of the nobility, who similarly had become Freemasons abroad, and founded a Swedish Order of Freemasons. By the early 1750s a significant number of Freemasons existed in Sweden, and progressively members of classes other than nobility had been admitted.

The rite is an important development of the emerging Continental history as it includes not only three Scottish Master degrees and the Knight of the East and Knight of the West degrees but also perhaps the earliest appearance of a Royal Arch Chapter structure and Knight Templar Masonry. In 1756, Carl Friedrich Eckleff established the first St Andrew's lodge in Stockholm to work additional degrees. The Rite consists of eleven degrees, each worked in full, in three different bodies:

St. John's (Craft) degrees (*S:t Johannesloge*):
I   Apprentice (*S:t Johannes Lärling*)
II   Fellow Craft (*S:t Johannes Medbroder*)
III   Master Mason (*S:t Johannes Mästare*)

St Andrew's (Scottish) degrees (*S:t Andreasloge*):
IV-V Apprentice-Companion of St Andrew (S:t Andreas Lärlinge-Medbroder)
VI   Master of St Andrew (S:t Andreas Mästare)

Chapter (Templar) degrees (*Kapitelloge*):
VII   Very Illustrious Brother, Knight of the East (*Riddare av Öster*)
VIII   Most Illustrious Brother, Knight of the West (*Riddare av Väster*)
IX   Enlightened Brothers of St John's Lodge (*S:t Johanneslogens förtrogne bröder och Tempelkommendörer*)
X   Very Enlightened Brothers of St Andrew's Lodge (*S:t Andreaslogens förtrogne Bröder, Riddare av purpurbandet, och Tempelprefekter*)

The final degree is conferred in **Grand Lodge**. (*Stora Landslogen*):
XI   Most Enlightened Brother, Knight Commander of the Red Cross (*Riddare och Kommendör med Röda korset*)

Each degree is worked in full, and in strict sequence over several years or even decades.

A Knight of the West is required to design his own coat of arms, following established heraldic conventions, and the approved coat-of-arms hangs in his

Provincial Grand Lodge. Noticeably this bears a striking similarity to the requirement placed on Squire Novice brethren in the Rectified Scottish Rite before admission to the degree of Knight Beneficent of the Holy City.

The tenth degree is the highest ordinarily attainable; it can be received after roughly twenty-one years of regular attendance and good proficiency in the ritual, but the time between the degrees may be shorter if the member is active and accepts different offices in his lodges. The Rite is still active under royal patronage and closely associated with the Lutheran Church of Sweden. The Swedish system has since spread to Finland (under Swedish control), and also to Norway, Denmark, and Iceland.

The Order also provides an unusual and interesting link to a chivalric honour system as in exceptional, and relatively rare cases, Swedish Freemasons may be considered for the Order of Charles XIII, an order of chivalry, equivalent to a knighthood. The order of chivalry is available only to Knights-Commander of the Red Cross, and is conferred at the Sovereign's pleasure with a membership limited to thirty-three, including three Clerical brethren of the established Lutheran Church. Although sometimes referred to as the 'twelfth degree', the Order of Charles XIII is not a masonic degree or part of the Swedish Rite.

As mentioned earlier, *Ecossais* Lodges existed in England by 1733 and by 1741 *Ecossais* Masonry had also spread to Germany. R. F. Gould recorded:

> In 1741 we find a Scots Lodge at Berlin erected by members of the Three Globes; in 1744 at Hamburg, and, shortly afterwards, a second; in 1747 at Leipzig; in 1753 at Frankfort, etc., etc. But in Germany their development was arrested because they were very soon absorbed by the Clermont system, becoming the stepping-stone to the lowest Chapter Degrees and, shortly after that, the Clermont Chapters were annihilated by the Templar system of the Strict Observance. But between 1742 and 1764 no fewer than forty-seven such Lodges were erected in Germany.

At the same time many surreptitious Lodges sprang up and *Ecossais* Masonry with its chivalric elements remained active until abolished in 1790-91. In 1743 the Masons of Lyons invented the Kadosh degree, with a traditional history related to the vengeance of the Templars, and thus laid the foundation for many Templar Rites. It was at first called Junior Elect; but developed into Elect of Nine, or of Perignan, Elect of Fifteen, Illustrious Master, Grand Inquisitor, Grand Elect, Commander of the Temple, etc.

It was in the mid-1740s that another influential character appeared on the scene – a minor German aristocrat – Karl Gottfried (or Gottleib), Baron von Hund and Alten-Grotkau (1722-1776). Baron von Hund claimed he was made a Freemason and brought into the Order of the Temple around the year 1743 in Paris. It is said that during his stay there he received Masonic degrees[114] which gave him the idea of forming the Strict Observance Rite. At his reception were supposedly Charles Edward Stuart, and William, 4th Earl of Kilmarnock, Grand Master Mason of Scotland (1742-43).[115] The initiation ceremony of von Hund into this Order of the Temple therefore must have taken place in or around 1744-45. Logically it must be presumed that the other so-called Knights Templars present at that meeting were made members prior to 1744. Indeed, there is evidence of Knight Templar meetings in Holyrood Palace from December 1744[116] and even some corroborated[117] evidence of the admission, on 30 September 1745, of Prince Charles Edward Stuart as a Knight Templar. It is also recorded[118] that William Hamilton, a poet of Bangor, escorted Prince Charles into Holyrood Palace (where his installation as Templar Grand Master took place).

There also seems to be no doubt that chivalric degrees were, by then, in existence in Scotland, since By Laws preserved at Stirling record fees to be charged: Excellent and Super-Excellent: five shillings sterling and Knights of Malta: five shillings sterling.[119]

However, circumstantial evidence also suggests Knight Templar working was known in England at the same time; a Nottinghamshire encampment supposedly worked a seven-degree system including Rose Croix, Kadosh and Knights of the Red Cross under the umbrella of Knights Templar. It has also been claimed that the original members of Lodge No. 44A constituted in 1755 (now named Newstead Lodge) were initiated as Knights Templar by 'members of the military' between 1745 and 1755.

The *Rite of Strict Observance,* of which there is a full account in Robert Gould's *History of Freemasonry throughout the World* was based on the concept that at the time of the destruction of the Knights Templars, a number of Knights took refuge in Scotland and there preserved the due succession of the Order. For various reasons these Knights were also said to have joined the Guilds of Masons in that Kingdom and thus to have given rise to the Society of Freemasons. The Great Doctrine laid down for the followers of the Rite was 'that every true Mason is a Knight Templar'.[120] Within the legend of this Order is the assumption that the time was ripe for the Templars to reveal to the world their continued existence and even for them to lay claim to the former properties and privileges of the Order. Although Gould expresses the view that this was fiction, he states that Lodges in British Regiments must have constantly worked side by side with the Lodges under the Strict Observance (which was active before, during, and after the Seven Years War (1756-63). Certainly Gould records that the degree of Knight Templar became a very favourite one in the lodges of the British Army, and by these military and Masonic bodies – who must have derived their knowledge of it from associating with the lodges and brethren under the Strict Observance – the degree was doubtless introduced into England and America.

Baron von Hund carried The Rite of Strict Observance from France to Germany, and assumed Provincial Grand Mastership of the Rite which began to assume greater importance by 1751. Von Hund, giving particular attention to the restoration of the Order of the Temple, considered it his life work. He commenced to make Knights and divided all Europe into nine Provinces, namely: (1) Aragon, (2) Auvergne, (3) Occitania, (4) Leon, (5) Burgundy, (6) Britain, (7) Elbe and Oder, (8) Rhine, and (9) the Archipelago.

The Rite of Strict Observance mirrored the *Ecossais* degrees found in The French Rite of Seven Degrees, the later Adonhiram Rite of Twelve Degrees, and the embryo Rite of Perfection, all which were spreading widely throughout Europe. It had a similar structure of six degrees, namely, (1) Apprentice, (2) Fellow Craft, (3) Master Mason, (4) Scottish Master, (5) Novitiate, and (6) Templar.

The first three degrees covered Ancient Craft Masonry. The fourth degree depicted the method used to preserve the 'lost word', which was cut on a plate of pure metal put into a secure place – and centuries afterwards recovered, so it was asserted. All have elements of the Royal Arch Degree and Chivalric Templarism. Scots Master is the fifth degree of the French Rite and the 13th degree of the Rite of Perfection and both form preparatory degrees to the Templar and Masonic Knighthood degrees which follow. However, the adherents to Rite of Strict Observance pledged allegiance to 'unknown superiors' – hence the name, 'Strict Observance' – and it was not long before it was assumed this higher authority had abandoned the Rite, and Rite commenced a rapid decline. Whilst hard evidence for this is lacking, circumstantially the execution of Lord Kilmarnock and the failure of the Jacobite cause would undoubtedly explain these circumstances.

Von Hund was so successful with his Rite that, for a time, it almost superseded the English-style Freemasonry which had hitherto been active in Germany, and the Rite was taken to several other countries – the Netherlands, Switzerland, Italy and even into Russia, probably reaching its zenith around 1770-80.

Von Hund died at a Convention of the Rite held at Wolfenbüttel in 1778, and soon afterwards the Rite seems to have disappeared in the turmoil of the French Revolution in the 1790s, although it may have survived for a time under the rule of the Prince de Cambacérès in the days of the Emperor Napoleon I. In the preceding half-century the Rite had considerably influenced Freemasonry on the Continent of Europe, and strong elements derived from it can be found today both in the Scottish Rectified Rite and in the Scandinavian Rite.

This outline summary of the Rite of Strict Observance has been set out because it was once considered of possible relevance to the development of the Masonic Order of Knights Templar. It has long been suggested[121] that the Knight Templar element of the Rite was one of the principal origins of the Knight Templar degree entering our British Military Lodges; however, it seems today that this was not really very likely for several reasons:

Firstly, military brethren would not take kindly to a masonic system which required unquestioning obedience to 'unknown superiors' – particularly if these were part of the outlawed Jacobite cause;

Secondly, the Rite of Strict Observance did not seem to be favoured particularly by French and Dutch military units with which the British army also came into repeated contact; and

Thirdly, there is now clear evidence of Knight Templar activity by brethren familiar with *Ecossais* masonry nearly 30 years before the Rite of Strict Observance became popular in the 1760s.

As Gould stated, Lodges in British Regiments must have constantly worked side by side with the Lodges under the Strict Observance, particularly during, and after, the Seven Years War (1756-63). However, the contact with Continental brethren did not only occur during military operations; British Masons are known to have fraternised frequently with their Continental counterparts both as prisoners-of-war and when escorting and guarding captured troops. From about 1755, French, American, and Spanish Prisoners of War are recorded in the British Isles housed in both Prison Ships and land Depots.[122] Up to 1814 some 122,000 French prisoners-of-war were at some time incarcerated in 50 locations throughout England, Scotland and Wales. In many areas, officers and senior personnel were allowed out on parole, and many French Brethren took the opportunity to visit British lodges or even constitute their own French prisoners-of-war Lodges. Evidence exists of French Brethren working the French Rites undoubtedly contributing to the spread of both Templar and Rose Croix rites widely throughout the British Isles. In particular they were welcomed in the Lodges administered after 1751 by the newly-constituted *Antients* Grand Lodge which recognised Masonic working 'beyond the Craft' including Mark, Royal Arch, Knight Templar and Rose Croix degrees.

In the year 1754 a Chapter of Clermont was set up in Paris by a Chevalier de Bonneville, supposedly with brethren from the Royal Court who disagreed with the behaviour of established Parisian lodges. They developed a type of

Templar system, originally devised about 1743 in Lyon and composed initially of six degrees: three Craft (or St John's) degrees, followed by (4) Knight of the Eagle, (5) Illustrious Knight or Templar, (6) Sublime Illustrious Knight. Later more degrees were added.[123] The 'Chapter of Clermont' has often been cited as a possible origin of the English Templar system, but the evidence for this is inconclusive, particularly as its formation was during the turbulent period immediately preceding the Seven Years War (1756-63) when relations with the French were, at the best, somewhat strained, and, as mentioned previously, evidence now suggests Templar Masonry existed well before this.

However, developments of interest were occurring in England at this time; in 1760 the Grand Lodge of All England at York cited a fraternal Degree called 'Knights Templar' above the 3rd degree of Master Mason and before the Royal Arch.[124.] Anecdotal evidence strongly suggests such degrees had been practised in Yorkshire for perhaps fifteen years before that date, often by visiting military lodges passing through the garrison City of York – particularly *en route* to and from Scotland around the time of the Jacobite rebellion of 1745.

By that time there is written evidence of such activity in military lodges; in about 1760, Records of Lodge No. 246(IC) meeting in the 9th Regiment of Foot (Royal Norfolk Regiment) include an issue of a Knight Templar Priest Certificate to Sir Richard Lovelace at Valenciennes, France, and later York records suggest it was this Regiment which carried the degree there.

In the 1760s there was another development with both military and French connections – this time in London with the arrival of Pierre Lambert de Lintot et de Cavirol, an officer in the Volunteer Grenadiers of Normandy, bringing with him a *French Rite of Seven Degrees*

This Masonic system, perhaps more appropriately referred to as *Lintot's Rite of Seven Degrees,* emerged from the fertile brain of Lambert de Lintot who was born in about 1736. Jackson, in discounting the Rite's derivation from the Chapter of Clermont, supposes de Lintot to have adopted his system from a Rite which in his day was operating in France, or alternatively to have created it by bringing together a mixture of degrees. There is some uncertainty about the date at which the Rite came into being. Eric Ward[125] says 'from 1766 or earlier', although it is unlikely to have been so much earlier as to suggest its seventh degree was a major source of our Order of the Temple. In any event, de Lintot's wordy 'Compendium' of his degrees, drawn up in 1782, shows the seventh to have been a hotchpotch of Kadosh, Templar, and many other elements.[126] Perhaps a more plausible origin was the *Ecossais* Lodges mentioned earlier as existing in England in the 1730s.

The impact de Lintot had on London was interesting though; he became Master of a Lodge of previously unattached French Freemasons which had purchased their Warrant, probably formerly that of the Lodge of Integrity, No. 331. This transaction was grudgingly legitimised by the Premier Grand Lodge which disapproved of such purchases. After occupying various positions under Grand Lodge, de Lintot developed his own *Rite of Seven Degrees.* He then became Master, or *Venerable Maitre*, of a Lodge, *St George de L'Observance*, in which capacity he directed the affairs of his Rite. He obtained a Warrant for this Lodge as the Lodge of Perfect Observance No. 1 from Preston's schismatic Grand Lodge South of the River Trent.

De Lintot's Rite of Seven Degrees, included not only the French versions of the Craft degrees and a degree of Perfect Master, but also contained many of the elements of Morin's original Rite of Perfection. The Sixth degree had some affinity with the Rose Croix, while the Seventh was something of a hotchpotch loosely based on the history of the Knights Templar. The three Craft Degrees were conferred in *St George de l'Observance* under the Premier Grand Lodge, while the 'High Degrees' were worked in the Lodge warranted by Preston.

De Lintot's Rite, which survived for little more than a dozen years, was not in itself of great importance. However, during its short life many English Freemasons were initiated into its various degrees, with the result that knowledge of degrees 'beyond the Craft' became more widely disseminated at the time the Templar Order was gaining adherents; it also gave rise to one of the earliest Knights Templar Encampments, that of Observance of the Seven Degrees in London. There is also evidence that the Rite was exported to Ireland where it became part of the Early Grand Rite.

On 10 June 1762 a warrant, probably signed by Francis Drake, Grand Master, was issued to French prisoners-of-war on parole in York[127] by the Grand Lodge of All England at York for Lodge No. 1 ('locally called Frenchman's Lodge') to meet at *The Punch Bowl* in Stonegate. Local anecdotal evidence suggests all the degrees of the French Rite of Seven degrees including Scots Degrees, Rose Croix, and Knight Templar were worked.

The next development of interest is the Rectified Scottish Rite. Although the Rite was formally organised in 1768, the ritual includes a traditional history which cites a date of 1659 for the Creation of an Order of Scottish Master of St Andrew and transmission of Knight Templar traditions in Scotland. Individual lodges are known working the degree from 1733.

The Rite was organised in its present form in Lyon, France, by Jean-Baptiste Willermoz, from a combination of the Rite of Strict Observance, with elements of the mystical doctrine espoused by Martinez de Pasqually and his Order of Knight Masons of the Elect Cohens of the Universe. This brought in mid-18th century French-Christian esotericism, including *Écossais*

Freemasonry, and Franco-German neo-Templarism. As elsewhere, it did not claim any organisational relationship with Scottish Craft Masonry.

This resulted in a Rite of six degrees: the first three being the equivalent of the three Craft degrees; a two-part fourth degree of Scots Master and Scots Master of St Andrew; a fifth degree of Squire Novice; and the sixth degree of Knight Beneficent of the Holy City or *Chevalier Bienfaisant de la Cité Sainte.*

Its traditional history includes the Solomonic and Hiramic legends of the Craft, elements recognisable in today's Royal Arch, and the survival of Knight Templar concepts in Scotland as evinced in other Continental Orders including French *Ecossais* Masonry, the Rite of Strict Observance, and the Rite of Perfection. It bridges the Old Testament and New Testament, as the candidate is guided into the Christian mysteries of the New Law, which forms the basis of spiritual chivalry.

This rite's three craft degrees are practised in regular lodges in France and Switzerland, while respective bodies confer the high grades under the control of Grand Priories of *Chevalier Bienfaisant de la Cité Sainte* (CBCS).

In England, the first three degrees are not worked; the lengthy two-part fourth degree of Scots Master and Scots Master of St Andrew forms the core of the working in lodges of the Rectified Scottish Rite; the fifth and sixth degrees of Squire Novice and Knights Beneficent of the Holy City are respectively worked in regional bodies known as Prefectures, and under The Grand Priory. The Grand Priory of England was constituted in 1937; until 2004 the Rite was controlled by the United Orders, but exists independently today administered from Mark Masons' Hall. Grand Priories also exist in Australia, Belgium, and North America.

Whilst nothing in this history confirms these degrees are derived directly from the Knight Templar Order, the existence today of the degrees of Scots Master and Scots Master of St Andrew does confirm the enduring nature of the *Ecossais* legend with its essential element of Knight Templarism continuing to exist from the 12th century to today in many forms of Masonic traditional history which follow 'in the Steps of the Templars.'

At about the same time, there developed in France a Rite of Perfection, which, following its transfer to the West Indies by Stephen Morin, in 1761 eventually underwent a succession of changes which resulted in today's Ancient and Accepted (Scottish) Rite. The detailed history of this Rite is too complex for a full examination here beyond a mention of those details which parallel the other developments of an obvious chivalric nature.

Before its transfer to the New World this Rite of 25 degrees, perhaps more appropriately referred to as *Morin's Rite*, certainly referenced Orders of Chivalry and included a degree Knight of the Sword or of the East and several others of a specific 'knightly' nature. As with the other Continental rites, great emphasis was placed on 'symbolic journeys in search of that which was lost', key elements of both the emerging Royal Arch and Templar Freemasonry.

However, it was later inclusion of a further eight degrees including some from the Primitive Rite which confirmed its Templar origins. The degree most illustrative of a Templar traditional history was the Grand *Ecossais* of St Andrew. The legend recounts its formation by *Ecossais* brethren who joined the Crusades in the Holy Land under the banner of St Louis, King of France. In Palestine they joined the crusading chivalric Orders, taking the title of Knights of St Andrew, and after the crusades returned to Scotland. Here they formed a number of societies and, for the first time, *Ecossais* lodges. The legend concludes by stating that, for many years, the French ignored true *Ecossais* Masonry but that it was finally introduced to them by '*the Prince of the House of Stuart whom an unhappy event forced to take refuge in France*'.[128]

Whilst this later addition in the New World is probably too late to have been a direct forebear of the modern Knight Templar Rite, the inclusion of these degrees is certainly consistent with the other Continental developments which were emerging from the 1730s onwards. However, under Morin's influence, the Rite spread throughout the West Indies and Caribbean Islands where many British and French military brethren were deployed throughout the 18th century.

We then encounter one of the most interesting of early chivalric developments – also in the New World. At Boston, Massachusetts, a 'St. Andrew's Lodge No. 81' had been established under a Scottish Charter which was very appropriately dated 'St. Andrew's Day, 30 November 1756'. There was also a 'St. Andrew's Royal Arch Lodge' *(sic)* which, although its surviving written records begin only on 18 August 1769, is presumed to have been meeting earlier. In 1762 the Craft Lodge had, without success, asked the Grand Lodge in Edinburgh (at that date there was no such thing as a Grand Chapter anywhere) for a Warrant for the Royal Arch, reporting that 'a sufficient number of us have arrived at that sublime degree'. It is uncertain where they had done this; one possibility was the Lodge at Fredericksburg in Virginia which had made Royal Arch Masons in 1753; other possibilities were British Army Regimental Lodges, which were, at that time and for many years after, working such degrees under the authority of their Irish, Scottish, and *Antients* Warrants.

After studying the Centenary records of St Andrew's [Craft] Lodge, Sir Charles Cameron concluded that the most likely source of the Templar working in 1769 was the Irish lodge in the 29th Foot, that Regiment being in Boston at that time.[129] However, since he reached that conclusion, evidence has come to light which suggest other possibilities and this will be explored in the next chapter.

Turnbull and Denslow considered it likely that one or more military lodges had sponsored and organized the Royal Arch Lodge at Boston, as despite the records of St Andrew's [Craft] Lodge failing to mention it, they claimed to work under that authority and in 1790, (known by then as St Andrew's Royal Arch Chapter), it passed a vote of thanks to the Craft Lodge for the use of their Warrant.[130]

No matter how this is viewed, the Minute of 28 August 1769 records:

William Davis, a Past Master of *Antient* **Lodge No. 58 working in the 14th Regiment of Foot**[131] *'begging to have and receive the Parts belonging to a Royal Arch Mason . . . was accordingly made by receiving the four steps, that of an Excel., Sup., Royal Arch and Kt. Templar'*

Also present at this meeting were two other members of Lodge No. 58, with three of Lodge No. 322 (Irish Constitution) which worked in the 29th Foot and three of the Royal Arch Lodge itself. It seems reasonable to suppose that all save the Candidate had already taken the four steps in their own or other lodges or chapters and were therefore themselves Knights Templar. To know when these advancements occurred would be a valuable addition to our chronology, so movements of military brethren and the interactions between lodges and *Ecossais* Masonry will be explored in the next chapter.

The Camp of Baldwyn at Bristol has sometimes been proposed as a possible starting-point for the history of Templar Masonry, but the first authentic reference to Knights Templar in that City appeared in the Minutes of the Sea Captains Lodge No. 445 for 1783.[132] The *terminus a quo* of the Order must however be earlier as, even discounting Irish references, the St Andrew's Royal Arch Lodge (*sic*) minute of the meeting held in Boston, Massachusetts on 28 August 1769 can hardly be ignored.

It can now safely be suggested that there was no obvious single source for the Masonic Knight Templar degree(s) appearing with British Military brethren in Boston in the late 1760s. Certainly the European *Ecossais* Masonry – particularly the degrees of Scottish Master and Scottish Master of St Andrew – contained an enduring element of today's traditional history, and the various 'knightly' degrees of Knight of the East, *et al*, created the Masonic environment for chivalric Masonry. These two groups of degrees then became core elements of many different rites which not only spread through Europe between 1720 and 1760, but also were carried to the New World, sometimes by European military brethren, but frequently amongst the 300,000 'Scots-Irish' and 'London Irish' who emigrated to for America between 1720 and 1800.[133] These emigrants gravitated towards specific regions, especially Pennsylvania and North & South Carolina. They were instrumental in promoting, if not introducing, *Antients* Freemasonry to America, and from the mid-18th century their lodges mark the westward development of the American frontier.

However, also discernible are chivalric degrees which mirror the earlier crusading knightly structure: A series of 'knightly' degrees and orders; degrees reflecting not only an intermediate chivalric grade of 'Novice' or 'Squire' but also the emergence of degrees specifically reflecting the support to knightly crusaders provided by a 'priestly' grade.

Some Deductions
This historical evidence leads to the following deductions:

> When *Ecossais* Masonry arrived in Europe in the 1720s, it included a traditional history with Scottish and crusading elements, but did not include a specific Knight Templar degree.

> The French Rite from the 1730s onwards contained Scottish Master with crusading elements, and Knight of the East degrees, and although it developed a Rose Croix degree, it stopped short of developing a separate Knight Templar degree.

> When Chevalier Andrew Ramsay compiled his *Oration* in 1737 he was clearly not advocating the creation of a new Knight Templar rite but placing in a new context a degree which was seemingly well known and commonly accepted.

> The Rite of Strict Observance, developed by von Hund in the 1750s did emphasise Knight Templar masonry, but von Hund certainly did not invent it as he claimed he obtained it from Jacobite sources in the 1740s.

> Likewise the Swedish and Scandinavian Rites obtained their Knight Templar elements from France or the German Rite of Strict Observance in the period 1735-50.

> At about the same time there is the appearance of a Priestly Order or the fore-runner of the modern Holy Royal Arch Knight Templar Priest degree clearly reflecting the relevance of the former priestly function which supported the crusading knights; this too specifically assumed the existence of a Knight Templar degree as a prior qualification.

Lambert de Lintot, who developed a Rite of 7 degrees in London in the 1760s, included *Ecossais*, knightly, and Templar elements in his Rite, but again did not develop a specific Knight Templar degree.

Stephen Morin, who set up an *Ecossais* Lodge in Haiti in 1751, exported the French Rite of Perfection to the New World in the 1760s, and further developed, and undoubtedly invented, additional degrees which today form the basis of the Ancient and Accepted (Scottish) Rite (Rose Croix), also stopped short of including a specific Knight Templar degree.

When The Grand Lodge of All England, recognised the Knight Templar degree at York in 1760, evidence existed of earlier working with no suggestion of a new invention there at that time.

And finally, when the Rectified Scottish Rite emerged in the mid-18th century, becoming formally organised as *Chevalier Bienfaisant de la Cite Sainte* (CBCS) in Europe and Knights Beneficent of the Holy City (KBHC) in England it too contained strong *Ecossais* and crusading elements but also stopped short of including a specific Knight Templar degree.

Quite clearly this brief summary shows none of these different initiatives over that half century (1720-70) needed, or felt at liberty, to develop a Knight Templar degree. **Why?** By far the most likely deduction that follows is that

– because one must have already existed and been widespread.

It was mentioned earlier that Ramsay's failure to mention the Knights Templar was undoubtedly astute in the Country which had led, if not instituted, the persecution of that body; and so it is not unreasonable to assume that the existence of a Masonic Knight Templar degree would not be given prominence in France. However no such political constraints applied elsewhere so evidence appears in Germany, Scandinavia, and Switzerland; *Ecossais* Masonry in England in the 1730s, and, of course, circumstantially from Scotland with additional support from the existence of the High Knights Templar of Ireland from the 1740s.

Despite extensive research by many historians – Masonic and non-masonic – no evidence has come to light confirming the exact emergence of a Masonic Templar degree with an unequivocal chivalric Templar origin or its appearance in a location with a known chivalric Templar presence.

So, before leaving the question of exactly how chivalric Freemasonry developed in England, it is instructive to recall how some degrees and orders developed in the earliest years. Masonic lodges usually developed within a framework of one of three motivational situations: Firstly a specific geographical location such as a City, Town, or long-term building project; Secondly, Brethren brought together temporarily producing sometimes unlooked-for opportunities such as long sea voyages, overseas trading ventures, and enforced overnight stops on stage-coach routes; and Thirdly, specific interest groups bringing brethren together, often away from home, including University, School, Learned Society, Professional, and Business activities. This resulted in mainly static lodges with stable, relatively small, memberships working the main Craft, Mark, and later, Royal Arch degrees.

As degrees 'beyond the Craft' appeared, brethren had a problem, at least for the introduction of a new degree, of not having sufficient brethren available with the knowledge to work it. This applied particularly in rural areas, and one solution manifested itself in 'Union Bands' which allowed several lodges to come together to work a new or complicated degree until it became generally familiar. In rural Ireland particularly many such bands existed, and they were known as well in northern England.

Military brethren, whilst having the motivation of both 'opportunity' and 'interest grouping' likewise did not always exist in sufficient numbers to form a viable lodge; as numbers increased, so regimental or other travelling lodges formed. However, this did not overcome the problem of introducing new degrees as in any one military lodge there would undoubtedly be too few brethren to work such a complex degree as Knight Templar. And so, in early times, whilst not forming anything so identifiable as a 'Union Band', except in rare cases, the only way to overcome the problem was to take advantage of the interaction between Regimental and static civil lodges when military opportunities presented themselves.

It is in this mobile environment that the earliest evidence for the chivalric orders might be found, so in the next chapter, not only will military and travelling lodges be considered, but also the opportunities for interactions between brethren and lodges which would facilitate such chivalric development.

2.12 MILITARY LODGES AND EARLY TRAVELS

In the last chapter precise details were given of the first documented account of a Knight Templar ceremony in the New World, in Boston, Massachusetts, where organised Masonry had been established under the Grand Lodge of Scotland on 'St. Andrew's Day, 30 November 1756'.

A 'St. Andrew's Royal Arch Lodge'*(sic)* minute of 28 August 1769 records William Davis,

> *'begging to have and receive the Parts belonging to a Royal Arch Mason . . . was accordingly made by receiving the four steps, that of an Excel., Sup., Royal Arch and Kt. Templar '*

William Davis was a Past Master of *Antient* Lodge No. 58(ECA) working in the 14th Regiment of Foot, and also present at this meeting were two other members of Lodge No. 58(ECA), with three of Lodge No. 322(IC) which worked in the 29th Regiment of Foot. It is appropriate to consider the circumstances by which the majority of the brethren present were visiting from British regimental lodges.[134]

Political, commercial, and territorial ambitions necessarily involve military forces both for initial invasions and for subsequent protection and defence. Understanding the interest shown by military brethren and their military lodges' activity helps appreciate how Freemasonry arrived, from where, and in what form. This too is a vast subject which cannot be explored fully here, and it is primarily relevant to examine military activities up to 1791 when Thomas Dunckerley accepted an invitation from Bristol brethren to become the Knights Templar Grand Master.

However, 'military activities' does not only mean those of British forces; whilst speculative Freemasonry as we know it must be regarded as essentially originating among English-speaking Nations, there is ample evidence of a similar interest amongst military personnel of other Nations. The military forces of many north-European countries contributed to the Crusades in the Holy Land and the widespread 'lesser crusades', and supported the activities of the Knights of St John throughout the 14th to 17th centuries thus showing sustained interest in military and chivalric ventures, so it was not unexpected that these same nations enthusiastically embraced early Freemasonry in general and the chivalric orders in particular.

Any analysis of the distribution of global Freemasonry strongly indicates the earliest organised interest occurred in the British Isles, former British

Colonies, or English-speaking territories, with lesser interest among French, German, and Dutch expatriates. Equally, there is no doubt that such distribution may be traced primarily to military brethren and Masonic Lodges deployed with British forces around the world. The same undoubtedly applies to the development and spread of chivalric Freemasonry, but here we will concentrate on brethren and lodges associated with British forces known to be involved with early Knight Templar activity. Regrettably, such early chivalric Freemasonry is poorly recorded: partly because military Freemasonry itself is relatively poorly documented; mortality rates of military brethren are high in major conflicts; regimental travelling lodges often only existed for a short time; and communications between lodges overseas and their parent Grand Lodges at home were never easy.

The specific factors affecting military brethren and the Masonic Lodges associated with military and naval units are most important to an understanding of how Freemasonry developed, since such factors resulted in Masonic development markedly different from 'static' urban lodges. Early records show that military and naval personnel had not only a significant interest in Freemasonry generally, but also in the Military and Chivalric Orders in particular. One result was that, when activity 'beyond the Craft' first emerged it included a high proportion of military and naval Brethren.

Because of military and naval deployments, individual brethren, even if initiated in 'static' urban lodges, could not maintain their masonic activity when deployed. Consequently, most army regiments and some naval ships obtained warrants for their own 'travelling' Masonic Lodges, the first of which was warranted by the Grand Lodge of Ireland in 1732 to work in the 1st Regiment of Foot (then the Royal Regiment, and later the Royal Scots).

The membership in most military lodges was necessarily small particularly in the 18th and early 19th centuries; only officers and senior non-commissioned officer (SNCO) ranks could read or write and most soldiers and sailors were completely illiterate. Unless together in regimental or battalion strength, officer and SNCO numbers were small, and when dispersed in detachments there might only be one officer and one SNCO deployed. Whilst lodges of perhaps five or six brethren might be able to work Craft ceremonies, other masonic activity was perhaps only possible when a regimental lodge came in contact with either other military lodges, static civilian lodges, or visiting brethren.

Consequently, military brethren did not confine their masonic activity to their own 'travelling' lodges, and whilst many deployments were of course for warlike engagements when opportunities for masonic activity would be relatively few, military life did present many other opportunities:

Most military units were based on a 'home garrison' with personnel static for long periods, recruiting, and training personnel, thus allowing interactions with local lodges;

Overseas deployments often involved long sea voyages with army, navy, and marines personnel confined closely together;

Many deployments resulted in long periods of relative inactivity between periods of actual conflict or guarding overseas territories;

and, finally, the very nature of warfare bought brethren in contact with foreign adversaries – not only during conflict, but also after capture, and in such situations as hospitalisation, and transporting and guarding foreign prisoners-of-war.

The incident in Boston, although an important part of the 18th century emergence of chivalric Freemasonry, must also be viewed within the perspective of a century of global strife; whilst this is not the place to review such military history, the interactions between military forces are considered highly significant and the following major troop deployments appear to be particularly relevant:

1727	Siege of Gibraltar
1742	War of the Austrian Succession
1743	Battle of Dettingen
1745	Battle of Fontenoy
1746	The Jacobite Rebellion and the Battles of Culloden, Falkirk, and Prestonpans.
1755-62	Seven Years' War and the 1759 Battle of Minden
1759-60	Battle of Louisburg and Siege of Quebec
1759-62	Anglo-French conflicts in the Caribbean Theatre
1769-75	Boston and the 1775 Battles during the American War of Independence

The trail will be followed in the European Theatre later, but first it is clearly most relevant to consider the event recorded in Boston on 28 August 1769 and the presence of Lodges No. 58(ECA) and 322(IC) working respectively in the 14th and 29th Regiments of Foot. However, as highlighted earlier, it is not really individual regiments and their relatively small military lodges that are important to consider, but their deployments which allowed interactions between the regiments and their Brethren, and so these will be reviewed together.

It is clear that August 1769 was a period when there was a brief lull in military conflicts where there were many British Army units in Boston including the 59th, and 64th Regiment s of Foot and Artillery Regiment s all of which had regimental lodges; it may also be noted that the 14th, 29th, and 59th Regiments had been together for three years in Halifax, Nova Scotia.

It is not possible to detail the deployments of every regiment here, but to illustrate the complexity, we will examine regimental travels in three phases of interactions:

Between the 14th and 29th Regiments of Foot in Boston in 1769 and their travels in North America immediately preceding that date.

Between the other regiments with which those regiments came in contact and their travels preceding their arrival in the New World.

Theatres of Military operations with known masonic activity beyond the Craft prior to 1769 from which brethren might have gained Knight Templar knowledge.

14th Regiment of Foot
The 14th Regiment, originally raised in Kent in 1685, was deployed to Gibraltar between 1727 and 1742 with contacts with the 2nd, 5th, 7th, 9th, 10th, 18th, 20th, 22nd, 26th, and 29th Regiments during this deployment and, of course, seafaring brethren on transport vessels and Gibraltar residents.

The period 1743-46 saw similar opportunities for complex interactions: in Flanders in 1743 at the Battle of Dettingen with contacts between 1st, 2nd, 3rd, 4th, and 6th Dragoons and 8th, 11th, 12th, 13th, 14th, 20th, 21st, 23rd, 31st, 33rd, and 37th Regiments; and in 1745 at the Battle of Fontenoy with possible contacts between 1st, 2nd, 3rd, and 6th Dragoons and 3rd, 8th, 11th, 12th, 13th, 14th, 19th, 20th, 21st, 23rd, 25th, 28th, 31st, 32nd, 33rd, 34th, 42nd, 46th, 48th, 55th, 62nd Regiments and Dutch Military Field Lodges.

The following year saw the 14th Regiment deployed through Colchester and York to Scotland to counter the Jacobite Uprising, and before and after the Battle of Culloden on 16 April 1746 there were possible contacts between the 10th and 11th Dragoons, Kingston's Light Dragoons, and 1st, 3rd, 4th, 8th, 13th, 14th, 15th, 20th, 21st, 25th, 27th, 34th, 36th, 37th, 48th, and 62nd Regiments of Foot. The same year (1746) at the Battle of Falkirk saw further possible contacts with the 8th, 34th, and 47th Regiments after which the 14th Regiment remained in Scotland until 1750. Thus, in those three years the 14th Regiment had been in contact with at least thirty-two other regiments and had the opportunity for interaction with Naval brethren, Dutch Military Field Lodges, French Brethren, and civilian brethren and lodges when in transit.

By 1752 the 14th Regiment had redeployed to Gibraltar where it remained for seven years with undoubted contacts with the 4th, 6th, 7th, 13th, 21st, 24th,

39th, 53rd, 54th, and 57th Regiments as well as the static resident civil and military lodges. During this time the Regiment had one Irish lodge, No. 211 (IC) [Constituted 1750], and in 1759 acquired a second No. 58 (ECA);

This provides a picture of an active regiment with multiple opportunities for complex contacts with many other regiments and brethren of several lodges between 1727 and the time of arrival in Boston. It is therefore highly likely that the 14th Regiment was instrumental in dispersing Royal Arch and Knight Templar Masonry around Europe as well as to the New World. This and other such complex interactions are illustrated in Appendix B.

Other opportunities for relevant multiple contacts involving the 14th Regiment are also of interest: In 1760-66 in England the Regiment served in Dover, Maidstone, Windsor, and elsewhere in the South of England including a period guarding French prisoners-of-war at Sissinghurst; later there was a period of repeated deployments between Europe and the New World: between 1766-71 to Portsmouth, North America and Canada (Nova Scotia); in 1771-74 to the West Indies, North America (Virginia, Massachusetts, and New York); in 1776 the Regiment returned from USA to Turkey Point near Portsmouth for a few months before returning to the New World; and in 1777-81 it spent another period in the South of England with more guarding of French prisoners-of-war.

1781 saw the Regiment embarked as Marines including relief of Gibraltar and then in 1782-91 it was deployed to Jamaica – also spending time guarding French prisoners-of-war and escorting them back to England.

Over its long history the 14th Regiment has an impressive masonic pedigree including Lodge No.211(IC) [1750 to 1815]; Lodge No. 245(IC) [1754 to 1801]; Lodge No. 58(ECA) [1782 to erasure at The Union 1813]; Union Lodge No. 338(ECA) [1807 to 1832]; and Lodge of Integrity No.771(EC) [1844 to 1890]. In particular Lodge No. 211(IC) was recorded as working Royal Arch and Knight Templar degrees in Canada as early as 1760 as were Lodges with the 29th, 44th, and 59th Regiments.

29th Regiment of Foot

From 1712 to 1746 the 29th Regiment of Foot was either a permanent part of the Gibraltar Garrison or deployed for short periods in Ireland or North America. In the three years preceding their deployment to Boston in 1768 the 29th Regiment served in Halifax, Nova Scotia where they also came in contact with the 14th and 64th Regiments which arrived from Ireland.

At that time, the 29th Regiment had one lodge: Glittering Star Lodge No. 322(IC); R. V. Harris records that, while at Kilkenny in Ireland, Warrant No. 322(IC) was granted in 1759 to George Macartney (WM), Alexander Wilson and Joseph Alcock (Wdns). The warrant was renewed in 1854 and is still extant. Canadian historians record this lodge as working Royal Arch and Knight Templar degrees (1760-68) as were Lodges with 14th, 44th, and 59th Regiments.[135]

After studying the Centenary records of St Andrew's [Craft] Lodge, Sir Charles Cameron concluded that the most likely source of the Templar working in 1769 was the Irish lodge in the 29th Foot, that Regiment being in Boston at that time.[136] The history of the 14th Regiment suggests this may not be the only option; but it certainly appears likely the 29th was one of the military lodges which sponsored and organized the Royal Arch at Boston. Although the records of St Andrew's [Craft] Lodge nowhere mention its existence, in 1790, by which time it was known as St Andrew's Royal Arch Chapter, it acknowledged the earlier use of the Craft Lodge Warrant.[137]

Although the 29th Regiment has a different pattern of activity to the 14th Regiment, it shows similar opportunities for complex interactions between military and civilian lodges and brethren. When the 29th obtained its first warrant during a 1750-65 it was deployed in Ireland including contact with 10th Regiment at Kilkenny in 1758, and service in 1759 at Clonmel, Kilkenny, Cashel, Athy, and Dublin. However much of its service was in Gibraltar where many regiments and seafaring brethren would interact with each other and resident civilian brethren.

The 29th Regiment also saw service in 1761 at Belle Isle allowing possible contacts between 3rd, 9th, 19th, 21st, 26th, 28th, 30th, 33rd, 34th, 36th, 37th, 50th, and 64th Regiments and with many Naval and Artillery personnel [and possibly French Brethren.]

64th Regiment of Foot

In the three years preceding their deployment to Boston in 1768 both the 14th and 29th Regiments served in Halifax, Nova Scotia where they also came in contact with the 64th Regiment which deployed from Ireland. Whilst this is not a treatise on military history, the activities of this Regiment are also illustrative of the intensity and complexity of interactions between regiments at this time.

The Regiment was raised as a 2nd Battalion of the 11th Foot at Southampton on 10 December 1756 before moving to Newcastle-upon-Tyne; in April 1758, then renamed, the 64th Foot was deployed to the West Indies where, on arrival, in 1759, it took part in the unsuccessful attempt to take Martinique and then in the successful invasion of Guadeloupe. The 64th Regiment returned to England in June 1759 severely reduced in numbers by men drafted to other units and by tropical disease. On arrival at Portsmouth only 137 other ranks out of an establishment strength of 790 were fit for duty, though officer cadre was almost up to full strength. Recovery took a long time and after a brief period in Suffolk the Regiment spent three years in the Scottish Highlands, during which time the Regiment acquired a warrant for Lodge No. 106 (SC) [1761]. The Regiment then spent five years in Ireland before sailing for North America in 1768.

The first posting for the 64th Regiment in America was Boston, at the time a centre of discontent and an unhappy posting was a result. In 1770 the Regiment moved to Halifax, Nova Scotia, but in 1772 returned to Boston being stationed at Castle William, an island garrison in Boston harbour. As unrest grew the 64th took part in an incident which lays a claim to the first blood of the American War of Independence being shed in Salem, Massachusetts. On 26 February 1775 a supply of weapons and ammunition was known to be in Salem and the 64th were ordered to seize the weapons, but the mission failed. On the outbreak of hostilities in April 1775, the 64th was still stationed at Castle William and remained there as the garrison throughout the Siege of Boston and did not take part in the Battle of Bunker Hill. When, in March 1776, the British abandoned Boston, the 64th were the last Regiment to depart for Halifax, giving them the distinction of being the last British unit to set foot in the Commonwealth of Massachusetts during the war.

Thus we find three regiments in Boston at one time: 14th Regiment with two lodges, 211 (IC) [1750], and No. 58 (ECA)[1759]; 29th Regiment with Lodge No. 322(IC) [1759]; and 64th Regiment with Lodge No. 106 (SC) [1761]; along with two companies of the 59th Regiment with Lodge No. 243 (IC) [1754]. There were also British Artillery Units deployed in Boston, but the presence of their military lodges or brethren has not been confirmed.[138] A similar comment could apply to the personnel of the two Companies of the 59th Regiment deployed to Boston; at the time the Regiment had one lodge: Lodge No. 243 (IC) [1754] and although it cannot be confirmed the lodge actually worked in Boston, undoubtedly there were brethren in the Regiment.

Moreover, earlier in its history the 59th Regiment is recorded in Norwich in 1741 where there is evidence of a lodge warranted in 1736 later working Ark, Mark, and Link, Royal Arch, and Knight Templar degrees.[139] Whilst such contact may be considered circumstantial, it is certainly possible the brethren in the 59th Regiment also had experienced Knight Templar masonry in Gibraltar particularly before arrival in the New World. Their Craft Lodge is recorded as holding a Knight Templar Conclave as late as February 1820.

These brief examples illustrate clearly the circumstances which led to interactions between military lodges and brethren and 'static' lodges and brethren. Similar situations occurred throughout the 18th century and significantly influenced global Masonic development.

Other incidents in the Boston area show the 1769 deployments to Boston was far from being unique as Appendix B illustrates. Also present at this meeting were two other members of Lodge No. 58(ECA), with three of Lodge No. 322(IC) which worked in the 29th Foot and three of the Royal Arch Lodge itself. It seems reasonable to suppose that all save the Candidate had already taken the four steps in their own or other lodges or chapters, and were therefore themselves Knights Templar.

In a letter the late Philip Crossle, the distinguished Masonic historian and writer of Dublin, said:

I am confident that Lodge No. 322 must have worked all the R.A. and K.T. degrees when in Halifax, NS between 1765 and the year it left for Boston as the K.T. and R.A. are known to have been worked in Ireland from about 1740. It is submitted that the Knight Templar degree having been conferred by these military brethren in Boston in 1769, it is an irresistible inference that the degree was conferred in Halifax in the previous three years, 1765-68, by these Lodges, all of which had come directly to Halifax from Ireland where they all received their warrants and must have conferred the degree.

In a letter from the Recorder of Boston Commandery to the Secretary of Lodge No. 322, he writes:

'According to our earliest records the introduction of Templar Masonry in this hemisphere and its development to its present form and ritual is traceable to Glittering Star" Lodge No. 322.'

… and then goes on:

'On Oct. 1, 1768, several Regiments of British soldiers arrived in Boston, among them the 14th Regiment in which Army Lodge No. 58 (English-Ancients) was held and the 29th Regiment in which Army Lodge No. 322 (Irish) was held. In the second week of November 1768, the 64th Regiment in which was held Army Lodge No. 106 (Scottish) also arrived. These Army Lodges brought to Boston a knowledge of the Temple. They readily held Masonic intercourse with the Lodge of Saint Andrew of Boston. Aug. 28, 1769, almost a year after the arrival of the British troops, a Royal Arch Lodge was formed and worked under the supposed authority of the charter of the Lodge of Saint Andrew. The record of its first meeting is preserved, and from it we learn that ten Brothers were then present, of whom six were soldiers and four were members of the Lodge of Saint Andrew. British soldiers were chosen as the first three officers of the Lodge which seems to imply that soldiers were its moving spirits and were best enabled to do the work.'

The letter states ten brothers were present. The photostat copy of the minutes shows eight, plus the candidate – a soldier of Army Lodge No. 58 (ECA). As the 14th Regiment and Lodge No. 58 (ECA) came to Boston from Halifax at the same time as Lodge No. 322(IC), it supports the probability that these Lodges worked the Knight Templar degree in Halifax and felt they should confer the degree on Bro. Davis, a P.M. of Lodge No. 58(ECA). No doubt it was the intention to confer it before the lodges left Halifax but they left for Boston in a hurry to deal with a political emergency.

As it is clear that the two senior officers of the Royal Arch Chapter, the Master and Senior Warden, were members of Glittering Star Lodge No. 322 (IC) which had been operating in Halifax, Nova Scotia from 1765 to Oct. 1768 and they held the same offices in Halifax in 1768 and in Boston in 1769, it is fair to assume that they had worked the KT degree in Halifax for it was then the practice to work all degrees under the same warrant.

The fact that the Royal Arch Chapter of Saint Andrew's worked under the supposed authority of their Craft warrant is further evidence that they followed Irish practice of working all degrees under the same warrant; the brethren of the Irish Lodges evidently convinced Boston Masons of the Lodge of Saint Andrew that such was the case – three of the six belonging to Lodge No. 322(IC).

Many key opportunities for regimental interactions and liaison with civil static lodges and brethren have been recorded in addition to the 1769 occurrence in Boston, and a few examples will serve to illustrate the complexity.

Canadian history records that the introduction of the Knight Templar Order[140] was undoubtedly due to the activities of the Masonic lodges in three regiments of the British Army, namely, the 14th, 29th, and 59th Regiments. All of these lodges had Irish Craft Warrants, which enabled them to confer any Masonic degree known to them. As the 14th, 29th, and 59th Regiments had been together for three years in Halifax, the inference is irresistible that during the three years of their sojourn in Halifax they had kept up their knowledge and proficiency in these ceremonies, learned before their deployment to the New World, and were able to confer the Royal Arch on sufficient civilian residents to provide adequate numbers to form their own RA Chapter both in Halifax, Nova Scotia and later in Boston, Massachusetts. Of the many military Lodges which worked in the Province, at least five are proven to have been working the Royal Arch, Mark Master and Knight Templar degrees as early as 3 June 1759. On that date, Lodge No. 218(IC) in the 48th Foot issued Certificates believed to be dispensations for civilian members of the Lodge to attend Royal Arch 'Lodges' in New York.

Later, in Halifax in 1782, six brethren conferred the Royal Arch and Knight Templar degrees upon several candidates acting under the authority of the warrant of St John's Lodge, No. 211, now No. 2. The minutes from 1782 to 1806, and from 1839 to 1856, along with other evidence, are still extant and help to establish the origin and continuity of the present day Antiquity Preceptory No. 5, Halifax, Nova Scotia.

Lodge No. 168(SC) in the 17th Foot was working the Royal Arch in

Halifax, Nova Scotia exalted a member of St Andrew's Lodge, Halifax, Nova Scotia and issued a Certificate on 1 May 1784.

Louisburg, the capital of the French Province of *Ile-Royale*, was captured by a New England colonial force assisted by the British fleet on 17 June 1745, and for the next three years nearly 4,000 New England troops were kept in garrison. The New Englanders were gradually sent home, their places being taken by British regiments; Fuller's (29th); three companies of Frampton's (30th); and Warburton's (45th) arrived in 1746; and by Shirley's (50th) and Pepperrell's (66th), formed from the New England troops which had previously served in the capture of the fortress. Frampton's (30th) Regiment had at the time an active Lodge, No. 85(IC), formed in 1738. During the period of occupation there was much coming and going between Louisburg and Boston and the names of many of those on duty in Nova Scotia appear among those present as visitors or candidates in lodges in Boston.[141]

Louisburg features again in our story in 1759 when General James Wolfe sailed from there during the summer of 1759 to attack the French stronghold at **Quebec** with the 15th, 28th, 35th, 43rd, 47th, 48th, 58th, and 78th Regiments, the 2nd and 3rd Battalions of the 60th Regiment, and the Louisburg Grenadiers (formed by detachments from the 1st, 17th, 22nd, 40th, and 56th Regiments). The attack also involved a large part of the British fleet including HMS *Vanguard* with Thomas Dunckerley's Sea Lodge (and 22 ships of the line, 27 frigates and smaller ships, and troop transports carrying 9,000 soldiers) to move British forces to within sixty miles of Quebec. The Battle of the Plains of Abraham took place on 13 September and Quebec City surrendered to British forces on 18 September 1759.

The foregoing list of regiments in Wolfe's army is important from a Masonic perspective because the Masonic Lodges of the 15th, 28th, 43rd, 47th, and 48th Regiments accompanied their regiments to Quebec where they would join the 14th, 29th, and 59th Regiments, also with their lodges, which had been together for three years in Halifax, Nova Scotia.

There were no lodges in the 35th, 58th, and 78th Regiments at this time, although all would later gain Lodges: in the 58th in 1760; in the 78th in 1763; and the 35th in 1769. All the regiments providing detachments for the Louisburg Grenadiers had Lodges except for the 56th Regiment, and although it is likely that the Lodges had remained with the main body of their regiments, individual brethren almost certainly were to be found in the detachments. In Quebec in 1758 there would have been contact between 1st, 15th, 17th, 22nd, 28th, 35th, 40th, 47th, 56th, 58th, 60th, 78th Regiments and Brethren of at least one Canadian Lodge and Regimental Lodges No. 192(IC) [47th (Lascelles' Regiment)]; No. 218(IC) [48th (Webb's Regiment)]; No. 245(IC)

[15th (Amherst's Regiment)]; No. 1 (Louisburg) [28th (Bragg's Regiment), warranted by the (Moderns) Provincial Grand Lodge of Massachusetts]; and a Lodge held in the 43rd (Kennedy's) Regiment, under a Dispensation granted by an Irish Lodge.

A number of French regiments in Quebec also included Brethren and their regiments later had travelling Regimental Lodges[142] including *22e Régiment Guyenne Batt* with Lodge Saint Louis [Founded 1771]; *51e Régiment La Sarre Batt* (Founded La Ferté 1651) with Lodge Pureté [Founded 1767]; *54e Régiment Royal Rousillon* with Lodge Union Fraternelle [Founded 1765]; *Régiment Bearn* with Lodge Constance [Founded 1787]; and *Régiment de Berry* with Lodge Frères d'Armes [Founded 1785]; The constitution dates of these lodges perhaps also indicates the exposure of individual brethren to emerging Freemasonry in that diverse multi-national community and the increased interest due to similar interactions between French Regiments.

Considerable numbers of French, and some American, prisoners-of-war were taken during these North American (and later West Indian) conflicts, and transported to the British Isles. There is no doubt such prisoners-of-war included brethren who thus came into contact with army brethren, marines, and crews in both naval and merchant ships.

But the capture of Quebec was only one success in the continuing North American saga. Gould records[143] that 'the siege of Louisburg (1762-68) has a twofold interest ... this was the last place held by the French against England on the East Coast of America .... and ending with the capture of Newfoundland in 1762 ... and interest in connection with the travelling lodges of Freemasons which accompanied the British Forces.' In the winter of 1759, after the capitulation of what has been termed the 'Gibraltar of America' the warranted Regimental lodges there, to the number of eight or nine, assembled and elected an Acting Grand Master. This temporary measure was succeeded in the following year by one of a more permanent character – with Thomas Dunckerley playing a leading part.

Not even Boston was quiet; as tensions developed in America, more regiments deployed there in 1774-75 with the 4th, 10th, 18th, 22nd, 23rd, 38th, 43rd, 49th, 52nd, 59th, 63rd, 64th Regiments of Foot in the area with many brethren and at least 13 Lodges. Indeed, in Boston alone, during this relatively brief period, at least 38 British Regiments of Foot numbered as follows came together;

1758-59	1, 15, 17, 22, 28, 35, 40, 43, 47, 48, 56, 58, 60, 78
1759-60	1, 3, 4, 26, 32, 34, 35, 40, 43, 46, 54, 55, 63, 64, 65,90
1765-69	14, 29, 59, 64
1775[144]	4, 10, 18, 22, 23, 38, 43, 49, 52, <u>59,</u> 63, 64

Hence it is extremely clear that the interactions of 1769, although very significant because of the surviving Knight Templar minute, are but a small part of the possibilities. Neither the incident in Boston on 28 August 1769, nor indeed the North American theatre should be viewed in isolation but as part of a continuing pattern illustrative of military units deployed overseas in situations conducive to major interactions. This pattern was seen elsewhere in the New World throughout the last half of the 18th century where Anglo-French conflicts ran concurrently in both the Caribbean and in mainland America.

Many of the British regiments, their supporting arms, troopships, and ships of the line deployed repeatedly between Canada/North America, the West Indies, and Europe. Before leaving the New World, it is instructive to consider the concurrent history of military deployments and regimental interactions in the Caribbean theatre between 1750 and 1775.

The Caribbean Theatre (1750-1762)

The Caribbean features in this story because many of the Army and Naval units mentioned earlier in the Louisburg-Quebec conflicts in 1759-62 then deployed to that theatre. However, within the Caribbean Theatre the history of European interaction goes back a long way – at least to the 15th century when Columbus started to exploit the region. By 1700, Spanish, French, and British interests in North America and Canada were extensive, and involved large troop concentrations; any conflicts in the Caribbean theatres are therefore intimately connected with North American developments. Either theatre could be supported by military and naval forces from the other at relatively short notice as compared to obtaining similar support from Europe. Throughout the 18th century European Nations engaged in numerous conflicts affecting the West Indies and other Caribbean territories; the War of the Spanish Succession from 1702 resulted in France ceding its half of Saint Kitts to Great Britain under the Treaty of Utrecht (1713), which partitioned the Spanish empire between European powers.

Later conflicts: the American French and Indian War from 1754, Seven Years War (1756-63), and the 1778-1783 Anglo-French War all created deployments of both British and French troops to and from this region. Particular build-ups took place around 1759 when territories changed hands frequently involving Guadeloupe, St Lucia, St Kitts, and Antigua with British success in the Caribbean during the final years of the war. These operations were invariably not brief, one-off, visits; British Forces made over 70 visits to Martinique, Guadeloupe and Jamaica; 60-69 visits to St Lucia, Cuba, Haiti/San Domingo; 20-59 visits to Barbados Grenada, and St Vincent; and most island territories had multiple deployments. Of peripheral interest is that four Caribbean islands also had a history of ownership and occupation by the Hospitaller Order of St John in the mid 17th century.[145] Undoubtedly the French forces, taking and retaking the same territories demonstrated similar visit patterns, and it must be assumed military brethren on both sides also interacted with resident brethren.

During the build up to the North American conflicts discussed earlier, many regiments had served in the Caribbean Theatre – and this included both British and French regiments and their naval arms. Between 1702 and the end of the Napoleonic War in 1813, some ninety French Regiments of the Line, with Artillery and supporting arms passed through the region – many on several occasions. In addition, Marine units were deployed on Naval Vessels, troopships, and merchant ships and in defence of harbours and barracks. Losses were huge – many through sickness – and many regiments never recovered from their Caribbean experience. The British experience was not dis-similar; by 1799, with deployments to the region of troops from at least eighty-three different regiments. In addition to massive combat losses, peacetime sickness rates were unacceptable – of the order of 2,000 a year – and so tours of duty were short with frequent troop rotations. Other global events dictated frequent movements of British and French forces to and fro between the West Indies, North America, and Europe.

It is French brethren that we thank for the first organised Freemasonry in the region. Freemasonry was popular among military personnel, first being mentioned (by Gould) as an Irish Lodge in a French Regiment in 1690. By 1787, at least seventy-six lodges existed, and more formed later. Within the 90+ French Regiments of the Line that served in the West Indies at least eighty Masonic Lodges have been recorded, with, as mentioned earlier, routine working 'beyond the Craft'.

By 1789 there were close to forty lodges under Grand Orient of France in the Caribbean, half of them in today's Haiti. After the slave revolt of the 1790s most of them closed or moved out to Cuba, Puerto Rico or the Dominican Republic. Whilst this may not seem particularly relevant here today, there was undoubtedly a long history of interactions between both military brethren, civilian Masons, and seafarers sailing between the islands. One noteworthy observation is that from about 1750, when Morin took *Ecossais* Masonry to Haiti, establishment of Craft degrees in this region generally seems to have been concurrent with 'degrees beyond the Craft' – particularly the Rose Croix degree, and this suggests the French Masonry was indeed dominant. Noticeably, records confirm that very senior military brethren of both British and French forces became involved with Freemasonry at an early date.[146] Undoubtedly the Caribbean was an absolutely ideal breeding ground for emerging chivalric Freemasonry.

It must be noted that the *Ecossais* Lodge created by Etienne Morin in Haiti in 1751 and the Rite of Perfection which Morin, a French wine-trader, took to the West Indies in 1761, were probably the most significant events affecting chivalric Freemasonry in the new World. With the authority of the Patent appointing him as 'Inspector' Morin and his colleague Francken nominated a large number of 'Deputy Inspectors'. Among these were several Officers in the British Army, for example Colonel Prevost who was appointed 'Deputy Inspector General for the Windward Isles and the British Army'.

As with the French, Freemasonry was extremely popular within the British forces in the Caribbean; among the 112 regiments of the British Army with recorded service in the Caribbean, all but nine had associated Masonic Lodges: 77 Regiments had 149 Irish Lodges; 53 Regiments had 99 English Lodges; 18 Regiments had 24 Scottish Lodges; and 1 Regiment had a Dutch lodge. Of course, not all of these 273 lodges were there concurrently; some were perhaps inactive in that particular theatre; but many regiments also included brethren who were not members of their regimental lodge.

To illustrate the complexity of interaction related to the earlier North American Louisburg-Quebec conflicts, in the years 1759-62 the British Regiments of Foot deployed to Guadeloupe, Dominica, Martinique, and other Caribbean Islands resulted in more potential contacts between 1st, 3rd, 4th, 26th, 32nd, 34th, 35th, 40th, 43rd, 46th, 54th, 55th, 63rd, 64th, 65th, 90th Regiments, HMS *Vanguard* with Thomas Dunckerley's Sea Lodge, several French Regiments and Lodges, and resident Lodges.

These, together with the long sea-voyages involved, clearly provided opportunities for contacts between brethren; if a little speculation is allowed, the author believes it is most likely that this scenario was where Thomas Dunckerley first encountered Knight Templar Freemasonry in about 1759.

The European Theatre
Although the New World military deployments are undoubtedly important to our story, it is in Europe that we find **most** of our Masonic history and, although not well recorded, early chivalric developments as well. Consequently, it is now appropriate to turn to military influences not only nearer home, but also back further in time.

In 1640, Alexander Hamilton, General of the Artillery and Master of the Ordnance and Ammunition, was admitted as 'Fellow and Master of the Craft' on 20 May 1640 in the Lodge of Edinburgh. This officer held a high command in the expeditionary force sent from Scotland in 1631 to serve under Gustavus Adolphus, King of Sweden, during the Thirty Years' War.

Indeed, the earliest recorded initiations on English soil mentioned earlier had essentially military overtones. The deputation from the Lodge of St Mary's

Chapel, No. 1 Edinburgh, constituted before 1598, an ostensibly civilian lodge, was either acting as a military lodge travelling with the Scottish Army, or had issued, in today's terminology, a dispensation to allow military lodge members to work in Newcastle – in another Country.

> A Lodge was held at Newcastle, by deputation, on behalf of the Lodge of Mary's Chapel, the 20th May, 1641, under commission to Robert Mackey, General Quartermaster of the Armies of Scotland, to receive Sir Robert Moray; amongst those present were General Hamilton and John Mylne..... members of the Lodge of Mary's Chapel.[147]

Before holding the appointment of Quartermaster-General in the Army of the Covenanters, Sir Robert Moray (or Murray) served with distinction in France under Richelieu. He was with the Scottish Army when Charles I sought shelter in the camp of his fellow-countrymen, in May 1646, and planned a scheme for his escape, which, but for the King's want of resolution, must have been crowned with success. After the Restoration he was Secretary of State for Scotland, and one of the founders and the first President of the Royal Society.

Likewise, the initiation of Elias Ashmole in 1646, in Warrington whilst not perhaps a solely military affair, was of immense significance. His diary records:

> '1646. Oct. 16. 4.30 pm. – I was made a Free Mason at Warrington, in Lancashire, with Coll. Henry Mainwaring, of Karincham. The names of those that were then of the Lodge (were) Mr Rich Penket, Warden; Mr James Collier, Mr Rich Sankey, Henry Littler, John Ellam, Rich Ellam and Hugh Brewer.'

The significance was that Col Henry Mainwaring and Elias Ashmole were members of opposing forces engaged in the first English Civil War; Ashmole, then a Captain in Lord Astley's Regiment of Foot was an ordnance officer of the forces of King Charles I; and Colonel Henry Mainwaring, with whom Ashmole was initiated, was a Roundhead parliamentarian; Warrington was at this time a parliamentary stronghold.

This provides clear evidence that Freemasonry was able to transcend political and military allegiances at an early date. Of the others present, Hugh Brewer was possibly the Lancashire yeoman who served in Lord Derby's Royalist Regiment of Horse, and documents also show the Warden, James Collier held a commission as a Captain and was a known Royalist.[148] Amongst the Sloane MSS is a copy of the Masonic Charges on which Ashmole is believed to have been obligated, endorsed in 1646 by Robert Sankey, a member of an old Warrington family.

In passing, Ashmole was one of the founding Fellows of the Royal Society, an important institution mentioned earlier which numbered many early

Freemasons amongst its membership, and whose President was Sir Robert Moray mentioned above. Perhaps as an aside, but of some interest, one writer[149] on the subject of Freemasonry, credits Ashmole with having written 'an elaborate history of the Knight Templars'. This is an error, the full title of his book published in 1672, is *'The Institution, Laws, and Ceremonies of the most noble Order of the Garter'*. The same writer adds: 'It is not impossible that Elias Ashmole may have sought a knowledge of the mysteries of Freemasonry, presuming, perhaps, upon the service it might afford him in preparing his history of chivalry.'

The 18th century when chivalric Freemasonry emerged was a particularly active one militarily in Europe; of specific relevance are the major troop deployments for:

1727	Siege of Gibraltar
1742	War of the Austrian Succession
1743	Battle of Dettingen
1745	Battle of Fontenoy
1746	Battles of Culloden, Falkirk, and Prestonpans.
1755	Seven Years' War (1755-62).
1759	Battle of Minden

Gibraltar

During the build up to the conflicts just discussed, many British regiments and many naval ships served in or staged through Gibraltar which has an intriguing early masonic history of continual interactions between regimental lodges and static lodges – both civil and military.

The British territory of Gibraltar has been of significant military importance for nearly five centuries, and its military strength has been provided by three main elements of the British armed forces:

Firstly the key presence of naval forces and the development of Gibraltar as the major naval base in the Mediterranean before the acquisition of Malta which took over that role after 1799.

Secondly, the positioning of artillery and royal artillery units in Gibraltar both for defence of the territory and to deter aggression at the strategically important western entrance to the Mediterranean.

Lastly, a continued presence by army regiments for defence of the territory against land aggressions and their infrastructure which provided key staging facilities for other forces in transit to and from other Mediterranean theatres of war.

Although its strategic importance goes back many years, it is at the dawn of Freemasonry that the territory is of particular interest as Gibraltar had an early connection with two important military Freemasons: the 1st Earl of Portmore, Colonel of the 2nd Regiment of Foot in 1703, and governor of Gibraltar in 1713; and Lieutenant-General Francis Columbine, governor in 1738. However, Francis Columbine is better known to students of masonry as holding the rank of Colonel in 1725, when occupying the combined offices of Premier Provincial Grand Master of Cheshire, reputedly the oldest Province, and Master of the lodge held at *The Sun*, in Chester, in 1725 – a lodge which may have in its history the earliest hints of Knight Templar Freemasonry in England.

This was a period of European tension which saw significant military forces deployed to Gibraltar. In 1711 the 29th Regiment of Foot (later known as the Worcestershire and Sherwood Foresters Regiment) mentioned earlier was deployed to Gibraltar for two years, but after a period in Ireland (1713-26) the Regiment returned to the garrison remaining there from 1727 to 1745.[150]

It was during this period of build-up that first indications of *Ecossais* Lodges appeared in Continental ports, carried by seafaring brethren, possibly members of Sea Captains' Lodges, on troop transports as well as naval vessels, and it is highly likely *Ecossais* Masonry reached Gibraltar at the same time. The first Lodge to be warranted to work on Gibraltar[151] is believed to have been working unofficially in (or before) 1724.[152] Gibraltar would also have had contact with travellers to and from other Mediterranean ports.

This deployment of the 29th Regiment was part of a notable build up of British forces in 1727 ahead of a conflict often referred to as the Siege of Gibraltar, and during that year twelve Line Regiments were deployed to Gibraltar: the 5th, 13th, 14th, 18th, 20th, 22nd, 25th, 26th, 29th, 36th, 39th, and 55th Regiments of Foot. However, the most significant impact masonically was provided by the resident garrison troops and artillery, which maintained a permanent presence in this important fortress garrison, and which of course they still do today.

The next 'Masonic first' occurred in 1728 when the first military lodge for which any distinct record has been found, the Lodge of St John of Jerusalem No. 51 being established at Gibraltar.[153] Masons in the armed forces speedily introduced their own lodges, and Lodge No. 51 was constituted as a static lodge; however, it is also noticeable that Sea Captains' Lodges and others for seafaring brethren were also founded at the same time, and such lodges as well as individual military brethren were almost certainly instrumental in helping Freemasonry in Gibraltar develop early. Whilst definitive details are lacking, the history of the 29th Regiment with both Irish and Gibraltar connections is suggestive that brethren from that Regiment may have been instrumental in this development.

The early military Freemasonry was probably conducted in Gibraltar as elsewhere on an informal basis without formal authorisation, and it was the Irish invention of the Warrant which made travelling lodges possible. There is little doubt that to the soldier Mason the Warrant of his Lodge held a place in his heart second only to the Colours. The first such warrant was one granted by the Grand Lodge of Ireland to the first Battalion, The Royal Scots, on 7 November 1732. The first issued by Scotland was in 1747 to the Duke of Norfolk's Lodge in the 12th Foot, and Ray Sheppard recorded that over 100 Military Lodges had been formed by the end of 1761. Of these something like seventy-five were warranted by the Grand Lodge of Ireland, four by the Antients and twelve by the Moderns Grand Lodges of England, and nine by the Grand Lodge of Scotland. Of the 100 British Regiments of the Line by the time of the Union in 1813, ninety-four had one or more masonic lodges associated with them and one regiment had, during its history, nine masonic warrants. Lodges were also established in the military and naval support arms such as the Artillery and Marines. Of particular relevance to chivalric masonry is that the Freemasonry worked in lodges warranted by the Grand Lodges of Ireland, Scotland, and the English *Antients* routinely included degrees 'beyond the Craft'.

However, military Freemasonry also introduced three factors that static lodges did not have; the first two are the opportunity to cross international borders, and the ability to transcend political boundaries, and these are clearly demonstrated by the earliest records; the third is the organised involvement with foreign troops arising through escorting and guarding prisoners-of-war, an aspect to be considered more later. Whilst these have no political implications, such contacts are of cultural significance.

The 14th Regiment of Foot, which featured significantly in the 1769 Boston event were garrisoned in Gibraltar from 1733 to 1752 except for a short period (1745-51) deployed to Flanders and Scotland before returning to Gibraltar. Between 1752 and 1759, taking into account garrison duty regiments, Gibraltar provided opportunities for contacts between the 4th, 6th, 7th, 13th, 14th, 21st, 24th, 39th, 53rd, 54th, and 57th Regiments all of which had Masonic lodges associated with them.

However, the mention of Flanders and Scotland introduces the next significant conflicts which generated major troop deployments with more significant opportunities for interactions between regiments. Specifically, military units deployed to Gibraltar, were always close at hand to form part of any forces engaged in the European Theatre and such conflicts clearly illustrate the myriad opportunities, not only for interactions between British units and brethren, but also between British and Foreign units and brethren.

Nevertheless, as mentioned earlier, it was not the actual military conflicts which are important but the periods preceding such conflicts when armies were being assembled and the periods after when troops often became involved with enemy forces – either in hospital, following capture, or when guarding prisoners-of-war. Even these few events took British army and naval forces both repeatedly to the Continent of Europe, and the New World, and back to their home stations, with the inevitable result that military brethren and their lodges became the vector for spreading masonic ideas rapidly around the world.

Military and naval brethren have been recorded in virtually every regiment and in many naval ships – and at an early date; brethren in the army in the 1640s were mentioned earlier, and the first English naval officer who can be identified as a member of the Craft is Admiral Robert Fairfax[154] admitted in York on 7 August 1713. It is also noticeable that Sea Captains' Lodges and others for seafaring brethren were also founded at a very early date.

Tensions in Europe continued, particularly during the War of the Austrian Succession when many British regiments served on the Continent, and by 1743 major troop build-ups were again evident; two conflicts are of particular note as huge concentrations of British troops were involved.

> In 1743 for the Battle of Dettingen with troops involved from the 1st, 2nd, 3rd, 4th, and 6th Dragoons and the 8th, 11th, 12th, 13th, 14th, 20th, 21st, 23rd, 31st, 33rd, and 37th Regiments of Foot.

> In 1745 for the Battle of Fontenoy with troops involved from the 1st, 2nd, 3rd, and 6th Dragoons and the 3rd, 8th, 11th, 12th, 13th, 14th, 19th, 20th, 21st, 23rd, 25th, 28th, 31st, 32nd, 33rd, 34th, 42nd, 46th, 48th, 55th, and 62nd Regiments of Foot and Dutch[155] Military Field Lodges.

However, this was also the time when tensions in Scotland were increasing with the onset of another Jacobite Rebellion of 1745, and it became necessary for regiments to be withdrawn from Flanders for redeployment to Scotland. Several different routes were taken: some regiments moved directly by sea to Edinburgh; others landed at Harwich and other English ports and marched northwards via Norwich, York, Newcastle, and Berwick. Anecdotal and circumstantial evidence suggests some regimental brethren found time for masonic activity *en route*, and some of this involved activity beyond the Craft. Indeed, 1745 minutes of York[156] lodges record visits by Brethren of 14th Regiment *en route* from Fontenoy, Flanders to Culloden[157] – with some suggestion of 'higher degrees' being worked.

The main conflicts in Scotland involving large troop concentrations in 1745-46 were:

The Battle of Culloden (16th April 1746) with involvement of the 10th and 11th Dragoons, Kingston's Light Dragoons, and the 1st, 3rd, 4th, 8th, 13th, 14th, 15th, 20th, 21st, 25th, 27th, 34th, 36th, 37th, 48th, and 62nd Regiments of Foot.

The Battle of Falkirk with involvement by the 8th, 14th, 34th, and 47th Regiments of Foot.

After these conflicts, many regiments remained in Scotland or redeployed to Ireland for security duties, but some returned to Europe for participation between 1755 and 1762 in the Seven Years' War. One typical build-up was in 1759 for the 1 August 1759 Battle of Minden, (an Anglo-Hanoverian vs French conflict) with not only opportunities for interactions between British and German forces, but also contacts between 1st Dragoons, 12th, 23rd, 25th, 37th and 61st Regiments all of which (except possibly the 61st Regiment) were known to have lodges attached at that time).[158]

It is here perhaps that the first contacts with German Military Freemasons occurred as German Military Lodges appeared from about 1745; as with their British and French counterparts, German brethren rapidly embraced the chivalric elements of Freemasonry, with particular interest in the Rite of Strict Observance with its *Ecossais* and Knight Templar degrees. There is no question that British and German brethren worked closely during the latter part of the 18th century, particular in the lead up in to the 1759 Battle of Minden when the Duke of Brunswick led an Anglo-Hanoverian army against the French. It was at one time suggested that these contacts with German brethren were the most likely source of British Knight Templary, but now the evidence suggests that 1759 was too late.

In 1770, The Grand Lodge of All England at York issued its only known Military Warrant – to the 6th (Iniskilling) Regiment of Dragoons – and it is perhaps significant that this was from a Grand Lodge that had recognised Knight Templar degrees for at least ten years before this.

It is perhaps appropriate at this point to reconsider and emphasise the influence of French Freemasonry in the French forces on our history. As with the British Army and Navy so too was Freemasonry popular with French forces; and as recounted earlier, French rituals normally extended beyond the Craft into chivalric Masonry. Briefly the interactions between the British and French forces can be seen to have impacts in four main situations outside those involving actual conflict:

Before, during, and after actual military engagements including extended periods of siege;

After capture when British forces were held by the French;

After capturing French forces when acting as their gaolers or when escorting them between locations including long sea-voyages returning from overseas theatres to the British Isles;

When acting as gaolers or supervising French prisoners-of-war 'on Parole' in British towns or encountering them as visitors to Military or civil lodges.

Such situations arose in consequence of military conflicts but similar interactions were also apparent when British troops occupied territories formerly occupied by the French, and this included many areas, particularly in the New World, where French lodges had been established. However, similar situations occurred after peace was established in both overseas territories and the British Isles.

In the period between 1740 and 1815 large numbers of prisoners-of-war were incarcerated in the British Isles. In 1759, 11,000 prisoners-of-war were located at Knowle near Bristol but the majority were brought to the British Isles during the Revolutionary wars of 1797 to 1814. Most were sent to Britain between 1803 and 1814 with up to 122,000 French prisoners-of-war arriving to be housed in at least 50 locations. Necessarily, the prisoners had to be escorted from the place of capture and subsequently guarded, and both regular troops and militia units carried out this role.

In general terms the soldiers and sailors were incarcerated in large barracks or prisons, some of which were specially built for that purpose, the principal locations being: Forton near Portsmouth housing 4,000 prisoners; Portchester housing 5,000; Perth housing 7,000; Dartmoor housing 6,000; Norman Cross, Peterborough housing 6,000; Portsmouth housed 9,000 in prison hulks in the harbour; and Weedon Barracks in Northamptonshire housed several thousand. The remainder were distributed over the country; almost every town possessing suitable accommodation having its complement. In addition many were housed in decommissioned ships ('hulks') both on the coast and in inland rivers.

Military and Naval officers, and civilians who were entitled to rank as 'Gentlemen' were allowed to reside *'on parole'* within assigned limits and, in many cases, were accommodated with local residents. This is known to have occurred in at least thirty-seven locations. Such individuals were permitted to visit local Masonic lodges or, if sufficient brethren were located where a suitable lodge was not present, it was permissible for them to form their own lodge. Evidence suggests that such lodges worked the French Rite of Seven

Degrees with *Ecossais*, Knight of the East, Rose Croix, and Knight Templar elements, with an undoubted influence on both the military lodges and brethren involved and local civil lodges. Whilst details are scarce, the following activity has been identified and although records may not include precise dates, they do show many widespread locations[159] up to 1814 when most French prisoners-of-war were released for return home. For consistency, details up to 1791 are included with other known pre-Conclave events shown above; the main prisons were widely distributed, and, for example, the following regiments can be linked to prisoner-of-war activities:

> Sissinghurst Castle, Kent Between 1760 and 1766 the 14th Regiment of Foot was deployed to several locations in the South of England including Dover, Maidstone, Windsor, and Sissinghurst Castle in Kent guarding French prisoners-of-war.

> Norman Cross, Peterborough with 77th Regimental records of significance.

Many records exist of interaction between prisoners-of-war and local lodges without being linked to specific military regimental 'guards'; many examples are included in **Appendix B** which consider such activity in the context of the formation of the Grand Conclave.

Finally, of course, prisoners-of-war brethren on parole rarely confined their Masonry to their own prisoner-of-war lodge(s) visiting other military, civil, and foreign lodges – including brethren of opposing forces.

As a footnote to this activity in the British Isles, similar activity did occur in France but on a much smaller scale; indeed one estimate put the number of British internees in France at about 25,000. Whilst there were many brethren amongst these internees the earliest record of an actual lodge being held was in 1805 – Lodge No. 183(ECA) in the 9th Regiment of Foot after a detachment of the Regiment was interned at Valenciennes following a shipwreck on the French coast near Calais. The lodge met until 1814, and Thorp recorded its minutes were still in existence in 1900.[160]

There was likewise a record of activity amongst French prisoners-of-war in Germany. From 1757 prisoners in the fortress of Magdeburg are recorded as visiting and joining a local lodge (*de la Felicite*) and subsequently forming their own lodge there in about 1761. In 1758 the Grand Lodge of the Three Globes in Berlin granted a warrant to Gabriel de Lernais, a French prisoner residing there on parole for a French lodge to meet in that city 'without the right of initiating'.[161] No doubt these events would clearly suggest interaction with the German forces guarding them.

Four lodges are known to have met on naval vessels; their mention is particularly warranted as they operated under the Premier Grand Lodge by virtue of a strange mandate to Thomas Dunckerley, a commissioned gunner. It has been generally alleged that Dunckerley obtained this authority to grant warrants from the Premier Grand Lodge, although such evidence has not yet been found in Grand Lodge archives. In 1760, under this mandate, he installed the first Provincial Grand Master of Canada at Quebec. In the same year he was responsible for establishing a lodge on board HMS *Vanguard*, and he also granted warrants to HMS *Canceaux* and HMS *Guadaloupe* in 1762. There is only one other ship known to have had a warrant which was HMS *Ardent* that gained a warrant in 1810 under the Scottish constitution and formed the Naval Kilwinning Lodge.[162]

The one period of history of seaborne lodges of particular interest relates to the deployment of HMS *Vanguard* and its embarked Sea Lodge in 1759-60 to the West Indies (Guadeloupe), Dominica, Martinique (1761), Havannah (1762). Certainly there were possible contacts between the 1st, 3rd, 4th, 26th, 32nd, 34th, 35th, 40th, 43rd, 46th, 54th, 55th, 63rd, 64th, 65th, and 90th Regiments, a number of French Regiments and military lodges, and resident civilian lodges, many of which had had contacts with regimental lodges and brethren with known Knight Templar activity by the 1760s.

Some ships included active masons in their crews, and, in particular, long sea voyages were precisely the time when lodges embedded within military units could further promulgate the spread of masonry. Hence, it is not in the least surprising that most early Freemasonry throughout the world can trace its origin and subsequent development around seaport towns or major naval dockyards (for example, The Clyde, Bristol, Portsmouth, Devonport, Malta, Chatham, Hull, Newcastle, Bordeaux, Gibraltar, Bombay, Calcutta, Hong Kong, and Sydney). These examples also illustrate known ways in which active brethren in warranted Lodges did move between locations where history shows significant later masonic developments.

The two Irish military lodges are today the last remaining travelling lodges: No. 322 Lodge Glittering Star warranted in the 29th of Foot (Worcestershire's and Sherwood Foresters) on 3 May 1759 travels widely during its Masonic year; and No. 295 St Patrick's is the last truly regimental lodge of the Royal Dragoons (formerly the 4th/7th Dragoon Guards.

The deployments of The First King's Dragoon Guards[163] in 1791 feature in the records of the Ancient York Conclave of Redemption at York. These record a visit by Thomas Dixon [Captain, 1st Dragoon Guards] who intimated that Thomas Dunckerley was about to form a Grand Conclave of which he was to be the first Grand Master. In the same year, the Ancient York Conclave of Redemption received a response to a petition sent to

Thomas Dunckerley at Bristol stating the existence of eight encampments by that date.

Other records of the Ancient York Conclave of Redemption at York are some of the earliest which have survived;[164] in 1791 John Watson received a Warrant for a Conclave or Chapter of Encampment at the City of York from Thomas Dunckerley, Grand Master, dated 11 March 1791. [Signed R. W. Whalley, Grand Chancellor; W. Hannam, Acting Grand Master].

The letter dated 15 June 1791 confirms the appointment by Thomas Dunckerley of Thomas Dixon [Captain, 1st Dragoon Guards] as 'Acting Grand Master for the north District of England' covering Yorkshire, Westmorland, Cumberland, Durham and Northumberland.

To complete this review of early military involvement with chivalric masonry, brief mentions of the British colonies of India and South Africa are relevant.

It is hardly possible to discuss the 18th century movements of British regiments and their lodges without mentioning the sub-continent of India. British Military Forces have been in India since the 17th century, and were engaged in war in Western India by Chatrapati Shivaji (1627-1680); it is also possible that an Irish Lodge was attached to one of the Regiments in those battles, but records do not seem to have survived.

It may be noted that British Military presence was particularly noticeable in Bengal and the Coromandel in the 18th century, the Maratha Confederacy having kept the British successfully away from their territories until the beginning of the 19th century; and consequently, the early Lodges worked in Bengal and the Coromandel.

A famous Irish Lodge No. 128 in the 39th Regiment of Foot was the second founded in Gibraltar, in 1742. It departed for India when the Regiment moved on, and it is said that the first Freemason to be initiated in India was made in this Irish Lodge. The lodge continued in existence until 1872, during which time it was issued with duplicate warrants on no less than three occasions.

On 3 May 1759, Warrant No. 322 was issued to the Masons in the 29th Regiment of Foot (now known as the Worcestershire and Sherwood Foresters Regiment), who formed the Glittering Star Lodge No. 322(IC). The Regiment served in Ireland, North America, India and Burma, Jamaica, Trinidad and Tobago, Palestine, Germany and South Africa over the next 200 years, and of course features earlier in our story.

Formal Freemasonry began in India when a petition was sent to the Grand Lodge of England by a few Brethren, members of the East India Company, in 1728 to constitute a Provincial Grand Lodge in Calcutta (Fort William). The Petition was granted and a Brother Pomfret was empowered to constitute a regular Lodge at Fort William (No. 72) – Lodge Star of the East, which is still in existence. In 1729, Provincial Grand Masters were appointed for 'East India in Bengal' and 'East Indies'. In addition to the English Constitution, several other Grand Lodges formed Lodges in India including

A Dutch Constitution – Lodge Solomon was founded on 7 April 1758 in Bengal by the commander of the merchant fleet of the Netherlands East India Company, Bro. Jacob Larwood Van Chevichaven;

A French Constitution Lodge *Sincere Amite*, at Pondicherry in 1787;

Scottish, Danish, and Irish Constitution lodges also appeared in the early 19th century, but so far records of chivalric activity before 1791 have not come to light.

It is noticeable that the developments in India spawned lodges in the wake of the trading agreements and territorial expansion carried out by the East India Company, and indeed the Provincial Grand Master for East India in Bengal appointed in 1729 was Captain Ralph Farrwinter, an officer of the East India Company.

Such developments bear a striking similarity to the developments in Canada, and the activities of the Hudson Bay Trading Company; and include many other indications of military lodges working beyond the Craft. One such example is that of the lodges in the 17th (Duke of Cambridge's Own) Lancers. This regiment had a pattern of lodges typical of many regiments: Lodge No. 478(IC) [1769-1817]; Lodge No. 285(ECA) [1794-1913]; Lodge No. 361(EC) [1814-28]; and, significantly later Lodge No. 218b(IC) [1873-20 Sep 1883] when the Warrant was surrendered. Curiously it was the two English lodges that have been recorded as working Royal Arch and Knight Templar, and Gould notes[165] that in 1813, in Kiara, in Goojerat, Presidency of Bombay, the Lodge (English) No. 361 had thirty-four members, of whom sixteen were Knights Templar, and 17 were Royal Arch Masons. Twenty-nine were Non-Commissioned Officers and the rest private dragoons. The degrees worked, in addition to 'the three regular steps' were those of Past Master (in the Lodge); Royal Arch; Super-excellent; Mark and Link (in the Chapter); and Knight Templar, St John of Jerusalem, and Knight of Malta (in the Encampment). Whilst this was clearly well after the initiation of the Grand Conclave, the chivalric degrees were still being worked under the Craft warrants, and the foundation of the two English lodges was after this date as well. It would not be unreasonable to suppose British regiments included Knight Templar brethren from a much earlier date; however, despite considerable research, no surviving records of Knight Templar activity in India prior to 1791 have been found.

It would likewise be expected that 18th century military deployments to South Africa would feature in our story as considerable records exist at that time of Irish, Scottish, and Dutch lodges working in that British colony. Typical examples are:

The 8th Light Dragoons served in the Cape from November 1796 until February 1803, and their Lodge No. 280(IC) (Constituted 1757, removed from the Roll 1815) is known to have conferred higher degrees on local brethren.

The 22nd Regiment present in the Cape from May 1800 to December 1802 possessed, in addition to the Scottish Lodge, Moriah (Wedderburns) No. 132 (1767-1809) mentioned earlier, an Irish Lodge No. 251 (Constituted 1754, erased 1817).

The 65th Regiment served in the Cape from February 1801 to February 1803 when it too left for India with Irish Lodge No. 631 (Warranted 1784).

The 71st Foot is recorded in The Cape with an Irish Lodge No. 895 (Warranted 1801 erased in 1858).

The Cape was also visited by another regimental Lodge No. 441(IC) in the 38th Foot (warranted 1765) and the 20th Light Dragoons also had an Irish Lodge (No. 759 warranted 1792).

However, despite current research, no specific records of Knight Templar activity have been found in the Cape colony prior to 1791.

Overall, despite few actual records of chivalric activity surviving, an interesting picture emerges from the observed pattern of military deployments and interactions between the regiments reviewed:

In addition to the four regiments recorded as having Knight Templar working in Boston in 1769, many more regiments had direct contacts with those four regiments after 1769.

A further nineteen regiments without such direct contact, had a pattern of European deployments including Gibraltar with known interactions with lodges working chivalric degrees.

A further eighteen regiments had known deployments in the Caribbean allowing contacts with local and French military lodges known to have worked *Ecossais* degrees, The Rite of Perfection, or the Knightly degrees of the emerging Ancient and Accepted (Scottish) Rite between 1751 and 1791.

A further thirty-five had European deployments with good possibilities of contacts with French, German, and Dutch military units with known military lodges as well as inter-actions with other British regiments and French prisoners-of-war.

These seventy-six regiments had generally returned to the British Isles either temporarily or permanently by 1791.

The Impact on Knights Templar Development

Historians over the last 300 years have been fascinated by the origin of Masonic Knight Templary, and whilst there is perhaps little reason to doubt that, as with most other basic speculative masonry, it was similarly a product of the British Isles, it now seems reasonably certain that its development and global distribution were essentially military by-products.

If, how, and when, the Knight Templar degree was spread is poorly documented, partly because military Freemasonry itself is relatively poorly documented, military mortality rates are high in major conflicts, and regimental travelling lodges often only existed for a short time.

Leaving aside for the moment the question of where in the British Isles the germ of Knight Templary first appeared, it is possible, however, to discern three main possibilities for the origin of Templar degrees in England.

Option 1 A product of a static English organisation or individual (such as de Lintot or later inventions by John Yarker or Robert Wentworth Little (1838-78).

Option 2 A Fully Developed Knight Templar degree invented and sourced overseas and imported by seafaring or military brethren.

Option 3 An embryo constituent of a Masonic Rite such as the *Ecossais* Rite, the French Rite, the rite of Strict Observance, or the Rite of Perfection/Ancient and Accepted Rite which was then developed by British brethren.

So far as Option 1 is concerned, Masonic history does not support such an idea; no other degrees in Freemasonry appeared without some history of their source, even in cases where this was not particularly reputable. Moreover, there is no evidence of an individual claiming credit for such an invention.

When considering Option 2, all the evidence – albeit circumstantial in some cases – suggests some form of an embryo Knight Templar degree started to appear gradually in various English locations as early as 1730 – perhaps earlier. This was certainly before most military lodges were constituted and therefore transfer would have to be through individual brethren, and no such individuals have been identified. On the contrary, the little evidence which does exist suggests such individuals took the degree overseas.

Option 3 – a constituent of an existing Rite or Order is a possible option although the Rite of Strict Observance and the Rite of Perfection seem to have developed well after the first appearance of a Knight Templar degree. Both lodges working the French Rite and *Ecossais* Lodges worked Scottish Master and Scottish Master of St Andrew degrees with traditional histories with crusading or Templar elements. Both also worked Knightly degrees with symbolic journeys which went beyond the craft and later perhaps metamorphosed into the Royal Arch.

Despite earlier suggestions that *Ecossais* degrees had no formal connection with any Scottish organising body, the degrees of Scottish Master and Scottish Master of St Andrew may well have have originated in Scotland, Ireland, or England. These degrees do not appear to have been brought to England by any single event but through a variety of means including:

By seafaring brethren and Sea Captain's Lodges by 1733;

By trading or military brethren returning from other countries, particularly France where development received the impetus of Chevalier Ramsay's oration;

By French prisoners-of-war with experience of one or more of the different Rites worked by French lodges.

Without further evidence, it is therefore not possible to confirm the origin of our Knight Templar degree; however, at this stage a combination of the degrees of Scottish Master of St Andrew and a Knights of the East or Knights of the East and West degree would appear to be a likely possibility.

Earlier the point was made that military lodges were generally very small, and it is fair to say that, although most regiments probably included brethren who did not belong to the 'regimental lodges', not all military brethren would extend their Masonry into the chivalric degrees.

If the experience of the 1769 Boston regiments is a basis, after allowing for high military attrition rates, a reasonable estimate of the number of Knight Templar brethren per regiment might be as low as two or three. It would also be reasonable to observe that, over the three decades before 1791, a similar number might have left active service and returned to the areas where originally recruited. These areas, of course, would include a high proportion in Ireland and Scotland – the source perhaps of half of all British regiments. On this tentative basis, the military impact on English Knight Templary in 1791, could be at least 200 brethren, a potential population for recruitment into the embryo Grand Conclave which will be considered next.

No evidence has come to light which suggests any Masonic source was derived directly from either any former chivalric Knightly organisations or individuals or that the emerging Masonic Knight Templary was specifically associated with any of the many hundreds of known chivalric Knight Templar houses which have been identified either on the Continent of Europe or in the British Isles.[166]

Finally, the existence of Freemasonry among French prisoners-of-war has been well documented in the period 1756 to 1814 and French brethren would certainly have had contact with their Army and Militia guards. French prisoners-of-war lodges have been traced throughout England and Wales in some of the thirty-seven 'Parole towns' It is undoubtedly the case that such lodges not only made Masons, but also conferred degrees, beyond the Craft on local brethren and therefore these must be considered a further source of Knight Templar Masonic knowledge.

2.13 CONCLUSIONS ABOUT CULTURAL CHANGE

T he period during which the crusades occurred was in itself a time of major cultural change; much of the globe had not been explored in 1000 AD although maritime excursions by the Scandinavia peoples had started and Britain, and nearby countries were experiencing, not only the negative effects of Viking raids, but also the positive effects of cultural exchanges, trade, new ideas, the spread of religion, and genetic factors. A brief examination of the last 900 years thus leads to these conclusions.

Europe was a violent environment and most nations were involved with conflict of one sort or another. Multiple conflicts had a history of creating armies of varying sizes, and, likewise the spread of religious ideas generated many different bodies. Consequently, the advent of the crusades must not have seemed, at the time, a particularly new or different activity.

The travels involving the various crusading countries – from Norway in the North to Spain in the South; from Portugal in the West to The Holy Land and Asia Minor in the East, – must have had a major impact on means of transport and logistics generally, and this necessarily created multiple avenues for the exchange of new ideas. The return of forces from the crusades clearly brought specific benefits; building techniques changed; the crusading Orders introduced, in effect, modern banking and also the concept of 'travel agents'; and the military and chivalric framework undoubtedly spawned many of the European 'honour systems'.

The English Domesday survey recorded, in writing, the wealth and life of much of the country. Religious and cultural ideas underwent major developments during the period; the church lost its evident monopoly on production of the written word – later exacerbated by the dissolution of the monasteries and the loss of manuscript production skills and facilities, and medieval theatre supplemented religious sermons in educating a hitherto illiterate populace. Progressively, Mystery Plays were written down, and their care passed to towns and the emerging trade guilds; medieval theatre developed widely; academic and social institutions emerged; and the further development of mechanised printing allowed written work to become available to an increasingly literate population. Institutions developed charters, – formerly the domain of royalty, the church, and the wealthy – and other written texts such as by-laws, and codes of conduct and instructions to members about trades and organisational development. This class of developments included the earliest Masonic *'Old Charges'*. And many social institutions developed

– including Universities, social clubs, friendly societies, professional guilds and later trades unions, and masonic lodges.

The crusades had also promoted travel and this developed greatly as time passed; transportation of large armies promoted the development of large ships, often with sea-going capability; global exploration started in earnest, and the benefits of this included increased trade and, again, the exchange of ideas. The identification of new territories promoted colonisation by the major nations – particularly seafaring ones – resulting in increased military activity to support the emerging trade footholds abroad.

Thus by the end of the 16th century, the cultural environment was ripe for change and multiple institutions were in place to facilitate such change. But these institutions had not forgotten their past, and historical ideas, moral ideals, and even the trappings from the past became readily incorporated. Right from the highest echelons of society such historical bases are readily visible today; the robes, jewels, and ritual of the Orders of Chivalry reflect a crusader past; the Order of the Hospital still exists, albeit in modified form, in many countries; our cultural heritage includes time and effort maintaining Templar and Hospitaller fortifications and churches; and the Crusading Orders have featured in academic dissertations, popular fiction, and a myriad of dramatic productions on stage, film, television, and even video games; this continues to the present day and across the globe.

Speculative Freemasonry emerged as one of the most important intellectual, philosophic, and social movements of the 18th century, a key part of the 'Age of Enlightenment'. Masonic lodges were a specific form of social clubs – mainly for men but also, to a lesser extent, for women – with a creed derived from the myriad teachings of Enlightenment philosophy. They developed and organised, albeit selectively, such philosophical teachings and illustrated them with symbols drawn from many ancient and modern sources; by way of coherent explanation, rituals were developed to make such teachings understandable to initiates and members. From the beginning, it was stressed that Freemasonry was not a religion or a substitute for religion, indeed going beyond the articles of faith of established religions with the aim of replacing them with a coherent, rational set of tenets and ideals.

It is hardly surprising that the Masonic lodges with embryo chivalric elements were well received as part of the emerging culture of the time; indeed, it is clear that individual military brethren played an important part in developing the very earliest lodges. The appearance of regimental and naval lodges with 'travelling warrants' then provided the means of spreading Masonic ideas throughout the 18th century so that military travelling lodges and brethren had not only promoted wide interest in chivalric Masonry, but also were perhaps instrumental in introducing hundreds of military Masonic knights onto the English scene by 1791. This scene will now be examined in the context of a base for the organised chivalric structure that would soon evolve.

Part Three

THE UNITED ORDERS ... TO 1895
THE MASONIC, MILITARY, AND RELIGIOUS ORDERS OF THE TEMPLE AND OF ST JOHN OF JERUSALEM, PALESTINE, RHODES AND MALTA

Early speculative Freemasonry does not appear to have developed from a single source but from multiple, perhaps contemporary sources; it is also apparent that the earliest development was initiated many years before the conventional history of the English Craft suggests. Whilst unequivocal evidence has not yet confirmed an absolute source or starting date for speculative Freemasonry, it is nevertheless clear from historical literature including poetry, plays, operas, and fictional works that an element that we recognise today as 'masonic' has been part of European culture for much longer than the three hundred years recently celebrated by the English Craft.

European culture has been conditioned by warlike activity throughout mankind's recorded history, and the period regarded today as 'the Crusades' is, in the overall perspective of modern developments, only a brief interlude. However, it was perhaps the first period which brought many sovereign nations together in a single venture aimed at recovery of territory occupied by a religious culture seen as inimical to European interests. For this reason alone, the combining of separate national forces into Crusading armies raises the Crusader concept to a level that has continued to appeal to modern man over a period of 900 years – possible placing this in the same emotional category as the development of the Egyptian, Greek, or Roman civilisations and the emergence of the main world religions. The creation of the Hanseatic League produced a similar attitude – a League that has been suggested as the first 'European Community'.

It is therefore not surprising that the development of speculative Freemasonry has not only incorporated, as the source of its moral teachings, traditional histories from a wide variety of historical traditions including the histories of the various Crusades, but also that many other social organisations have adopted the same sources for their inspiration.

Early speculative Freemasonry in the British Isles clearly incorporated traditional histories with Crusading elements from the very earliest time with particular impetus coming from the interest shown in chivalric ideas by military and naval brethren for whom the traditions of the Craft only provided limited fulfilment. This seemed of considerable importance so a number of traditional histories and rituals with chivalric elements in general and Knight Templar themes in particular were examined; however, despite exhaustive reviews no evidence has come to light to suggest our modern rituals had their origins within chivalric knightly orders.

In his introduction to his important earlier work on the history of the Masonic Knight Templar Order[167] Frederick Smyth wrote:

> Although we are in no doubt at all that we are quite correctly celebrating, in the year 1991, the bicentenary of our Great Priory, we have to admit to some difficulty in settling upon a date on which the celebrations could most appropriately take place. In our *Liber Ordinis Templi* there is an excellent list of those who have ruled over us and from this we can see that Thomas Dunckerley is regarded as having assumed the functions of Grand Master in February 1791, although he was not installed as such until 24 June. There was plenty of activity in the intervening period, as a later chapter will tell us.
>
> 1791, therefore, is the year in which a governing organization for our Order came into being. With the exception of the Craft (1717) and the Royal Arch (1766) – and to them in several senses we owe our existence – we are the longest-established Masonic authority in England. It can be claimed of various degrees and Orders that they were being *worked* at an early date but it was not until the 19th century that a Supreme Council for the Ancient and Accepted Rite (1845), a Grand Mark Lodge (1856) and several other sovereign hierarchies were established.
>
> In taking stock, so to speak, of the past two centuries we cannot do so in splendid isolation. Much of our early history is interwoven with that of our sister Great Priories of Ireland and Scotland; a great deal of what we shall be writing of our more recent years affects, or is affected by, what has happened in other countries. This book has therefore something of an international flavour and it is hoped that it will thus be of interest to our brother knights 'wheresoe'er dispersed', but that they will understand and forgive the inevitable absence from this text of much that is familiar in their annals.
>
> Because of our links, however tenuous, with the military knights of he Middle Ages, it is right that we should recall something of their story so far as can properly be done. We can therefore consider how and when the Masonic thread weaves itself into the tapestry and allow it to lead us to the point where our own centuries begin.

Modern speculative Freemasonry now contains a number of degrees and orders with a chivalric or military bias. However, apart from brief references, examination of these is beyond the scope of this work which therefore concentrates on the development of the Great Priory of the United Religious, Military and Masonic Orders of the Temple and of St John of Jerusalem, Palestine, Rhodes and Malta of England and Wales and its Provinces Overseas, which will generally be referred to hereafter as 'The United Orders'.

3.1 THE CAMP OF BALDWYN

One cannot write about the evolution of our present-day Order of Knights Templar in England and Wales without making particular reference to the 'Camp of Baldwyn' in the City of Bristol. Any Masonic historian suffers from a well-nigh universal handicap, the shortage of written records; in some cases because there were matters which it was not considered proper to commit to writing, in others because it was no one's business to take care to preserve what documentary evidence that there was, and yet again because either by accident or by design archival material was destroyed. The Camp of Baldwyn is no different in this respect, but while much has fortunately been preserved, there is nothing that can be relied on to establish when the Camp first met. Their published history records a meeting as Knights Templar at the *Rose & Crown Inn*, Temple Street, Bristol, in January 1772. The principal evidence for this is somewhat oblique, and consists of what at first appears to be no more than a scurrilous item in the news-sheet, *Felix Farley's Bristol Journal,* of 25 January 1772 –

> *On Tuesday last, a young recruiting Party Capt. Turpentine, Lieut. Sweet, Ensign Grogg, Serjeant House, Corporal Hemp, and Drummer Guzzle, took their Departure from the Sea G-d* [168] *in this City, to Breakfast in Bath, from thence to the Cross Hands to Dinner (where they were met by a Carriage laden with Corinthian Brass) and Home to spend the Evening under the Rose*[169] *with the Knights Templars. Considerable Bets were depending upon the Captain, Ensign and Drum's performing this March in 16 Hours, the Lieutenant being a heavy corpulent Man, was allow'd one Hour more (the Serjeant and the Corporal were Volunteers in the Expedition), but the whole Corps arrived in good Order two hours within the Time: the Knowing Ones were taken in.*

Skit or a serious piece of reporting with perhaps names otherwise familiar to the citizens of Bristol concealed under pseudonyms? Whichever it may be, a mention of 'the Knights Templars' would hardly be included unless their existence in the City of Bristol at this time was familiar to at least some of the *Journal's* readership.

Their history also suggests meetings were certainly held earlier than 1772, and by 1780, eight years after this, a body of Knights Templar in Bristol had certainly constituted themselves into 'The Supreme Grand and Royal Encampment of Knights Templar of St John of Jerusalem, Knights Hospitallers and Knights of Malta etc. etc.'. Its Statutes were embodied in a Charter dated 20 December 1780, still preserved in the Baldwyn' archives (Appendix C). Its opening sentence states:

Whereas by Charter of Compact our Encampment is Constituted, the Supreme Grand and Royal Encampment of this Noble Order, with full Power, when Assembled, to issue, publish, and make known to all our loving Knights Companions, whatever may contribute to their knowledge, not inconsistent with its general LAWS.

This statement would appear to indicate the existence of some earlier document by which the pre-eminence of what was to become known as 'The Camp of Baldwyn' was recognised by one or more local bodies of Knights Templar, for example perhaps the 'Camp of Antiquity' in Bath; indeed the latter body appears to have recognised the authority of Baldwyn as late as 1820.[170] No such document or record of any such earlier agreement has, however, ever come to light.

The 1780 Charter first sets out the composition of 'a complete Encampment of this degree' – three principal Officers with the curious titles of 'The Most Eminent Grand Master', 'the Grand Master of the Order', and 'the Grand Master Assistant General', together with two Grand Standard Bearers – 'No regular Encampment of this Degree can consist of a less number than five'. (It is noted that the presiding Officer of an Encampment was known as its 'Grand Master' appears, as will be seen later, also to have been common practice outside Bristol until Thomas Dunckerley erected Grand Conclave in 1791.) The Charter then sets out first the procedure for election to the Order by careful ballot, then the dress and regalia of Knights Companions, the procedure to be observed when an Encampment has been opened, and also that for petitioning for the constitution of a new Encampment, and finally the fees and dues to be paid and other such matters of administrative detail.

In 1780 this document was signed by the chief Officers at the time – 'Joshua Springer, M. E. G. M.; Jno Maddick, G. M. of the O.; Wm. Trotman, G. M. A.; Wm. Lewis, Equerry; Robt. Wasborough, Steward; J. Ferris, Treasurer; Wm. Mason, Gd. Actuary'. Subsequent 'Grand Masters' and other senior Officers appear to have signed the document when they were appointed presumably to indicate their acceptance of the conditions laid down within it, and their intention to act in accordance with them.

Reference has already been made to the earliest conclusive record of the Degree of Knight Templar in Bristol. This is contained in a letter written on 3 April 1783 by the Secretary of the Sea Captains' Lodge addressed to James Heseltine, the Grand Secretary[171] –

The majority of our members being Master Masons are desirous of becoming Royal Arch and Kt. Templars. We shall thank you to inform us if a particular constitution be required for that purpose, or if it may be regularly done under our present one as we would wish never to deviate from the rules & customs of the Grand Lodge.

No record has been found of the Grand Secretary's reply, but that the Sea Captains' Lodge constituted itself into an Encampment is demonstrated by a Minute of 24 November 1790 stating 'Bro. Southey moved that no Brother should appear in this Lodge with the order of Knights Templar provided he acknowledged the present Self-Created Encampment of Knights Templar'.

There was a remarkable similarity between Masonic developments in Bristol and those which were taking place in the East of Ireland, specifically on the opposite coast of Munster, for example, in the port of Youghal from which comes the earliest record of the Royal Arch. The distinguished Irish historian, Dr. Chetwode Crawley, pointed out –

> We have seen that the occurrence of Royal Arch Minutes in Bristol and in Youghal were almost simultaneous. Some connection of a similar kind might be traced in the spread of the Templar Degrees. For the prominence of the High Knights Templar of Ireland in the Dublin Freemasonry of 1774 was followed by the occurrence of the Degree in 1778 at Portsmouth, in a quasi-military Lodge, and by that attempt at Templar organisation in Bristol, which is known as the Charter of 1780 (*vide Appendix C*), while the revived York Grand Lodge, undoubtedly in fraternal relation with the Irish Military Lodges, almost simultaneously recognise the 'Five Degrees' or Orders of Masonry. The sequence seems too close to be accidental.[172]

Certainly by 1780 the Knights Templar Degree was being worked in Bristol and by then the influential figure of Thomas Dunckerley had arrived on the Bristol scene.

3.2 THOMAS DUNCKERLEY

No baptismal Certificate has been found for Thomas Dunckerley who was to play a prominent part in Freemasonry in Bristol before becoming Grand Master of the Order of Knights Templar in England and Wales.

Professor Sommers states Thomas Dunckerley appears to have been born on 23 October 1724,[173] and to be of Welsh descent.[174] Although this seems to support the views of earlier biographers, from the evidence of his apprenticeship registration in 1735 (usually entered into at the age of 14, and unlikely at 11), the circumstances of his joining the Navy, and his own evidence when applying for a Naval pension in 1764 (when he stated on oath that he was 43 years old), it seems more probable that he had been born three years earlier than this.[175]

In later life he convinced himself that he was an illegitimate son of King George II. Indeed, until recently it has been accepted by the majority of his many biographers that he was conceived when his mother, Mary Bolnest, renewed an affair with the then Prince of Wales which allegedly had originally taken place some years before her marriage to Adam Dunckerley. The researches of Professor Sommers perhaps suggest this is less probable.[176]

Mary Bolnest and Adam Dunckerley were married at Houghton in Norfolk on 29 October 1712. Adam Dunckerley was a porter at Somerset House in London. (What he was doing at Houghton, the seat of the Walpole family at the time of Adam's marriage to Mary, is unexplained although several suggestions have been made.) Residence within Somerset House is no evidence for Royal Patronage; indeed, the Somerset House Porters were required to live on the premises, and after Adam Dunckerley died in January 1729 his widow simply continued to occupy his apartment. For a widow to do so as a 'Grace and Favour' lodging seems to have been a common practice, and if any influence was required to achieve Mary Dunckerley's continued occupation of these rooms, it could just as well have been that of one or other member of the Walpole family, Robert Walpole of Houghton Hall or Sir Edward Walpole, for example.

On 1 September 1735 Thomas, the fifth of the six children of Mary Dunckerley, by this time a widow, was registered as an apprentice for seven years to William Simpson, a barber and perruquier of St Martin's in the Fields. The young Thomas appears to have absconded from his master (who threatened legal action against the family on this account) in little more than two years and to have run away to sea. He was then probably 16 years old.

The muster roll of HMS *Namur* records him as an able seaman from 14 April to 4 August 1742. He is next mentioned in Admiralty records on 19 February 1744, when he was appointed schoolmaster on a seventy-gun ship called the *Edinburgh*. On 6 January 1745, the minutes of Trinity House at Deptford record that

> 'Mr Thomas Dunckerley being Examin'd & found Qualify'd to be a School Master in her Majesty's Navy & having produc'd a certificate (as usual) of his Sobriety & good Affection to his Majesty, he was certify'd accordingly.'

In 1746 he was appointed to the sloop *Fortune*, as Gunner, a term equivalent to Chief Gunnery Officer. [Sommers notes that the Sea-gunner Vade Mecum makes clear that Sea-gunners were not directly involved in the firing of the guns which was undertaken by seamen.] He proceeded to posts as Gunner on larger ships, including HMS *Crown* in June 1747 during the Mediterranean voyages of which he wrote letters to Lord Chesterfield with accounts of Gibraltar, Minorca, Leghorn, Bastia, Florenzo on the Island of Corsica,Cagliari on the island of Sardinia, Barcelona, Malaga, Alicante, and Cadiz on the coast of Spain during 1748 and 1749.

His career included service on HMS *Vanguard* as both Gunner and Schoolmaster (1757-61); the 90 gun HMS *Prince (1761-63); HMS Bedford* (1763-64); and HMS *Guadeloupe* (1764-66). Thomas Dunckerley's advancement to the warranted or commissioned rank of gunner and schoolmaster was certainly attributed by him to the patronage of Sir Edward Walpole, writing to him on 1 November 1753 that 'all my preferments in the Royal Navy proceeded from your Recommendations'.[177]

His mother died in 1760, and according to Dunckerley, it was in 1760, while attending his mother's funeral, her neighbour, Mrs Pinkney, told him of her death-bed confession. While her husband was away on the business of the Duke of Devonshire, she had been seduced by the Prince of Wales (later King George II), who was Thomas's natural father.

Being immediately called away to sea, this information was of no immediate use to him. However, on his superannuation in 1764, monies owed to him were not paid due to incomplete paperwork, and he was obliged to pay medical expenses after an accident caused his daughter to require an amputation of the lower leg. This left him in debt, and arranging for his pension to be paid to his family, he took ship with the Frigate HMS *Guadeloupe* to the Mediterranean. The next year, he was put ashore at Marseilles with scurvy. On his recovery, with the help of Captain Ruthven of the HMS *Guadeloupe* and the financial assistance of Freemasons in Gibraltar, Dunckerley managed to lay his case before several persons of rank on his way back to England. Finally, in 1767, his mother's statement was laid before King

George III, who apparently accepted Dunckerley's claim to be the half brother of his father, Frederick, Prince of Wales, the son of George II, and provided an annuity of £100, a sum which some writers have suggested increased later to £800.[178]

According to Professor Sommers 'Dunckerley was permitted to assume his mother's apartments in 1765, a few years after her death but before he laid his claim of kinship before King George III.' There are at least half a dozen disparate accounts of how King George became aware of this extraordinary claim; it is a well-established fact that he did become so aware and he apparently accepted it. Dunckerley was authorised to account himself an 'Esquire', his occupation of the apartment in Somerset House was confirmed, and he was later accommodated in Hampton Court Palace (although this is as likely to have been on the recommendation of the Walpole family as on that of the King).

Dunckerley received £200 a year from the King's Privy Purse[179] from 1767 to 1782 when the present-day 'Civil List' was instituted; the List then became what nowadays would be called 'more transparent' – in other words it was subjected to careful scrutiny – and the payment ceased. As a result Dunckerley appealed to several acquaintances for financial help and the two Royal brothers, George, Prince of Wales, and Frederick, Duke of York, each undertook to pay Dunckerley £100 per annum for the rest of his life. It is not possible to say whether or not they believed Dunckerley's claim, but their generosity allayed any scandal which might have arisen if too many questions had been asked.

After his apparent acknowledgement by King George III, Thomas Dunckerley used a seal featuring the Royal Arms, differenced by a Bend Sinister for bastardy. This seal he used openly upon his Masonic correspondence without reprimand from any quarter until the time of his death.

About 1770 he retired from full-time Naval service, although it is then claimed that he was 'attached' to HMS *Vanguard* from 1765-71, and he may similarly have been associated with HMS *Canceaux* (1768-92) but this may well have been through their lodges rather than naval duties. In the same year, 1770, he entered the Inner Temple to study law, and as late as 1785 he was still declaring his profession as Barrister.

In 1777 he joined the South Hampshire Militia; no Commissioning Records have been found, yet in 1790 he is accorded the rank of Lieutenant[180]; it is therefore possible he used a naval rank of Lieutenant, rather than taking an Army Militia commission.

Thomas died on 10 November 1795 at home in Portsmouth, and he was buried initially at St Mary's Church, Kingston. In the 18th century, this was the parish church for Portsea and Portsmouth Common, and was most likely the church Dunckerley had attended in the 1740s and 1750s when he and his family lived in and around Portsmouth. Thus it was indeed a homecoming, but not the one to which he aspired for his will of 1795 states:

' ... I desire to be decently buried in the Temple Church near the Knights Templars [*sic*] if I should die in London or at Hampton Court.'

When St Mary's Church was rebuilt in the 19th century, all the monuments were moved, leaving the whereabouts of Dunckerley's burial unknown.[181]

Thomas Dunckerley's recollection of his early Masonic career is not clear; in his own writings[182] he states in 1792 that his masonic experience then amounted to 40 years – implying initiation c.1752 – but the following year he implies[183] he was Initiated and Passed in 1747. Other records suggest Thomas Dunckerley was Initiated in 1754 in a Lodge in Plymouth and, according to a letter which he wrote many years later, he had been made a Royal Arch Mason in the same year. Perhaps the most reliable is the Grand Lodge entry for Harmony Lodge No. 474/384 which records his (initiation) age as 30, his Profession as Barrister, and residence at Hampton Court on 11 July 1785 when he joined and recorded his Date of Initiation 10 January 1754 (Lodge Not Stated). It has not been possible, so far, to identify this lodge; Lane has no Plymouth lodges recorded in 1754, and he does not seem to have ever joined an Irish or Scottish Lodge.

Dunckerley was a member of many lodges during his masonic career; Sommers records[184]: Dunckerley, while attached to HMS *Vanguard* (1755-61), joined:

Lodge No. 67	Masons' Arms Tavern, Plymouth Dock	1757
Lodge No. 134	Popes Head Tavern, Plymouth	1757

He appears to have risen as rapidly in the estimation of the Masonic authorities as in that of the Naval ones, and, his maritime career apparently taking him to the other side of the Atlantic Ocean, he received authority from Grand Lodge 'to regulate Masonic affairs in the newly acquired Canadian Provinces' where he was installed, temporarily one must assume, Acting Grand Master of all Warranted Lodges in Quebec. He warranted a Lodge No. 254(ECM) on board the Naval vessel HMS *Vanguard,*[185] and afterwards one on HMS *Prince*, a Lodge which is said later to have come ashore as the Somerset House Lodge.

On HMS *Vanguard* he saw service at the Siege of Quebec which, in 1759 would have brought contact with personnel of the 1st, 15th, 17th, 22nd, 28th, 35th, 40th, 43rd, 47th, 48th, 56th, 58th, 60th, 78th Regiments and brethren of at least one Canadian lodge and Regimental Lodges No. 192(IC)[47th (Lascelles' Regiment)]; No. 218(IC)[48th (Webb's Regiment)]; No.

245(IC)[15th (Amherst's Regiment)]; No. 1 (Louisburg) [28th (Bragg's Regiment), warranted from the Provincial Grand Lodge of Massachusetts (Moderns)]; a Lodge held in the 43rd (Kennedy's Regiment) under a Dispensation granted by an Irish Lodge; and a Lodge held in the Royal Artillery under a Dispensation granted by an Irish lodge. After service in Quebec, HMS *Vanguard* deployed to the West Indies and then returned briefly to England during which time he apparently applied, successfully, to the Premier Grand Lodge of England for authority to to set up Lodges on board HM ships AT SEA. No record of this application has yet been found in Grand Lodge minutes or Library archives.

Dunckerley returned to Quebec in the spring of 1760 on board HMS *Vanguard* seemingly in possession of a personal Patent of Appointment granted to him by the Grand Master of the Premier Grand Lodge of England to regulate Masonic affairs where no Provincial Grand Master had been appointed. It was by virtue of this authority that he installed Colonel Simon Fraser, of the 78th Regiment, as Provincial Grand Master of Quebec. No record of this patent either has yet been found in Grand Lodge minutes.

Besides this well-documented activity in Quebec, it seems that, in this one year (1759-60) in Canada and the Caribbean, Dunckerley could well have had contact with brethren of at least 34 British regiments of Foot.[186] He almost certainly came in contact with members of Lodge No. 211(IC) of the 14th Regiment, Lodge No. 35(IC) of the 28th Regiment, and Lodge No. 205a(IC) of the 35th Regiment with records of Knight Templar activity in the New World; it is therefore likely that it was at this time he first encountered the Knight Templar Rite.

In 1767 Thomas Dunckerley had been appointed the first Provincial Grand Master in the Craft for Hampshire, and this was quickly followed by appointment as Provincial Grand Master for Essex, Dorset and Wiltshire, Gloucestershire and Somerset, and, in 1790, Herefordshire. By 1793 he was concurrently the Provincial Grand Master in the Craft over at least eight Provinces and the Royal Arch Superintendent in and over no fewer than eighteen Provinces. Dunckerley received a Patent as Provincial Grand Master for Bristol in 1784, prior to which Bristol was combined in a single Province with Gloucestershire and Somerset. It is perhaps indicative of Dunckerley's assiduity and popularity that when the one Craft Province was divided into three, Bristol becoming the only English city which was its own Masonic Province, Dunckerley continued to rule each of the three separately.

After this division, at the first Meeting in 1784 of the Provincial Grand Lodge of Gloucestershire, Dunckerley appointed as his Provincial Wardens two of the original signatories of the 1780 Charter, Jonathan Maddick who was for many years WM of the Jehoshaphat[187] Lodge and Joshua Springer who, after his appointment as the first Deputy Provincial Grand Master, was to serve as such for three terms totalling 17 years.

3.3 THE FORMATION AND EARLY YEARS
OF GRAND CONCLAVE

In his Paper '*The Baldwin Rite – An impartial Survey*'Eric Ward, a usually reliable Masonic historian, wrote, unusually without giving any reference to support the statement, that:

> In January 1791, Thomas Dunckerley, being Grand Superintendent of Royal Arch Masons at Bristol was invited by the Knights Templar to be their Grand Master, which he accepted.[188]

The passage is unfortunately ambiguous, for, as has already been noted, before the erection of the Grand Conclave, a Knight in the chair of an encampment of Knights Templar who today would be called 'the Eminent Preceptor', was referred to as the 'Grand Master' of that body. For example John Knight described himself as 'Grand Master' of the St John of Jerusalem Encampment in a letter to Dunckerley as late as 17th August 1791.[189]

In his booklet on the origin and history of our Orders, R. M. Handfield Jones makes a statement similar to that made by Ward, but again without giving other reference, that in 1791:

> The Bristol Knights and many others *from surrounding districts* approached Dunckerley with the suggestion that he should take the lead in forming *a Grand Encampment of Knights Templar for England and Wales. (Author's Italics)*

It seems possible that these two quotations refer to the same event, confusion being caused by the ambiguous use of the term 'Grand Master'. However something of the sort presumably took place in January 1791, for on the following 22 March Dunckerley replied to an undated Petition which he had received from the Conclave of Redemption at York:

> I accept with gratitude the confidence you place in me as Grand Master by the Will of God, of the Most Noble and Exalted Religious and Military Order of Masonic Knights Templar of St John of Jerusalem. I must request that as soon as possible you send to me the Names, Ages, Proffession *(sic)* & Residence of your Encampment as I intend to have a regular Register of our Order. Being Grand Superintendent of Royal Arch Masons at Bristol, I was requested by the Knights Templar in that City (who have had an Encampment Time Immemorial) to accept the office of Grand Master, which I had no sooner complied with than Petitions were sent to me for the same purpose from London 1, Bath 2, the first Regiment of Dragoon Guards 3, Colchester 4, York 5, Dorchester 6, and Biddeford *(sic)* 7. I suppose that there are many more Encampments in England, which with God's permission I may have the happiness to revive & assist.

> It has already been attended with a blessing for I have been *but two months* Grand
> Master & have already 8 Encampments in my care. *(Author's Italics)*

This letter can hardly be interpreted in any way other than that by this time
Thomas Dunckerley considered himself to have been, since the preceding
January, Grand Master (in our sense of the word) of all the Encampments of
the Order of Knights Templar in England and, presumably, Wales.

Indeed, on 24 June 1791, being the Feast of St John the Baptist, the first
Grand Conclave of the Order was held in London and the Installation of
Thomas Dunckerley as Grand Master took place, as was until recently
recorded in each edition of the *Liber Ordinis Templi.*[190] Dunckerley's own
report on the occasion is included in a letter written four days later to the
Conclave at York.

> . . . . *on the 24th inst. I went to town and at 11 in the forenoon I met the Knights at St
> Clement's Church. At noon I opened a Grand Conclave at the Unicorn Tavern, with
> Lieut. General Sir Charles Rainsford, &c. We then made our Offerings for the poor,
> which was sent to the prisoners in the Savoy. Five Knights were install'd. I had
> compiled a Code of Laws from our Antient Statutes; which were unanimously
> approved. At 3, we ate the Bread of Thankfulness and drank the Cup of Cheerfulness.
> I appointed the Grand Officers, gave an exhortation and at 7 we departed in Love and
> Unity, Peace and Harmony.*
>
>   *According to antient usage, I am very soon to be proclaimed on a high hill within
> a triangle of Knights Companions.*[191]

The preamble to the 'Code of Laws from our Antient Statutes', which were
'unanimously approved' at the first meeting of the Grand Conclave stated
that –

> The flourishing state of Symbolic MASONRY, under the protection of his Royal
> Highness the PRINCE OF WALES, Grand Master, and the great increase of Royal
> Arch Chapters, patronized by his Royal Highness the DUKE OF CLARENCE; having
> animated the masonic KNIGHTS TEMPLARS of ST JOHN OF JERUSALEM &c.
> with a desire to revive their ancient, royal, exalted, religious and military order; they
> confederated and unanimously selected their brother and knight companion, Thomas
> Dunckerley, of Hampton Court Palace, in the County of Middlesex, Grand Master of
> the confraternity, under the patronage of his Royal Highness PRINCE EDWARD,
> T.H.E.

The 'Code of Laws' goes on to say:

> 1791, at London, on the Feast of St John the Baptist, a grand and royal conclave was
> held; when the following ancient statutes of the order were revised and enacted.

> The public interests of the confraternity of knights templars, as a collective body, are
> to be regulated by a general convention of all the chapters of encampment on record;

or by their representatives, the respective eminent and (??) captains, commanding columns; who with the most eminent and supreme grand master of the order, attended by his grand officers, compose the grand and royal chapter.

The grand and royal conclave or council of the order is to consist of the grand master and his officers, with the three principals of every chapter.

The high office of grand master is held during his natural life, or until such time, as for particular reason he shall signify his intention to resign.

On the death or resignation of a grand master, the acting grand master is to summon a convocation of the order, who are to select or elect another most eminent and supreme grand master, and at the first convenient opportunity he is to be proclaimed in the ancient manner at a proper place. (sic)

The grand master is to appoint all the grand officers, except the treasurer who is to be elected annually in the grand and royal chapter.

On a vacancy of grand patron of the order, the grand master is to make humble suit, in the name of the confraternity, to a prince of the blood-royal of Great Britain (if a knight of the order) requesting his patronage.

The grand master by his authority may appoint provincial acting grand masters for districts at a distance from the grand metropolis.

A grand and royal chapter is to be convoked annually on the feast of St John the Baptist, in the grand field of encampment at London. The solemnity of the day is to begin with the public worship of the Great Architect of the Universe, and by making offerings for the poor. An exhortation is to be given by the grand orator. The grand officers are to be appointed by the grand master for the ensuing year. The knights companions are to eat the bread of thankfulness, and drink the cup of cheerfulness with their grand officers.

Every regular conclave or chapter of encampment is to be constituted by patent, with the seal of the order, and witnessed by the acting grand master, grand chancellor, and grand scribe and register,[192] for which one pound and six shillings is to be paid, or a sum equal to the fee for installing a knight in the chapter. For as all chapters have authority to make bye laws and regulations, for the good government of the same, provided they are conformable to these ancient statutes, they may enact any sum for the installation of a knight templar, not less than one pound and six shillings.

Every knight companion of the order is to be registered in the grand and royal conclave at London; for which five shillings is to be paid; and a certificate of his register will be delivered or sent to him signed with the seal of the grand master by the second scribe.

According to ancient custom, a complete chapter of the order is to consist of an eminent deputy grand master, two captains commanding columns, two standard–bearers with knights attendants with one or two equerries.

The conclave or council of a chapter is to consist of the five principal officers above mentioned, with the treasurer and scribe.

On all ballots for admission of candidates, one black ball is to exclude. The eminent deputy grand master of a chapter is to be elected annually on the feast of St John the divine, by a majority of the knights, and he is to appoint the other officers, except the treasurer, who is to be elected by the officers and knights companions of the chapter.

The name of the eminent grand master of a chapter, when elected, is to be sent to the most eminent and supreme grand master. If a knight should present himself at any conclave or chapter without his sash and medal with the distinctive marks of the order, he shall not take a seat, or fill any office in that conclave or chapter, unless (for reasons assigned) a dispensation is granted by the eminent D.G.M.

Every knight is to remember that our ancient and royal order is founded on the love of God, benevolence to mankind, and charity to the poor and distressed, the sick and wounded, therefore, after the prayer, (at the opening of the chapter) the poor's-box is to be presented to every knight companion.

The knights companions are to keep with the greatest care the secrets of their election, and work assiduously in the reformation of their morals, never to lose sight of the mysterious steps they have taken, but endeavour to exercise the duties they contain, by a strict fidelity to the grand master, and to the order. They are to reconcile differences between their brethren, not to speak without permission from the eminent D.G.M. after the prayer and opening of the chapter. They are to pay due attention to the working; not to laugh or joke, or to behave unseemly. If a knight neglect to attend his proper chapter after having been duly summoned, he shall be fined according to the Bye-Laws of the said chapter.

The knights in general are to distinguish themselves from the rest of mankind, by their most intimate and perfect union; by their readiness to relieve their brethren in distress, and procuring for them all the happiness in their power.

The standards are to be placed on each side the throne; and are not to be taken out of the chapter, but on particular occasions, by permission from the M. E. & S. grand master.

Every knight is to write his name on the lower corner of his certificate or register for particular reasons, well known to the confraternity; and he is to produce the same on his first visit to a regular constituted chapter, where none are to be admitted but those who are registered in the grand and royal conclave, except knights companions from foreign chapters.

Every chapter is to assemble on the 11th day of March annually, to humble themselves before the great Disposer of all events, with fasting and prayer; and to make their offerings for the poor and needy.

Any subject which is not treated of in the foregoing statutes must be decided by the general rules of masonry, contained in the book of constitutions.

The above laws were read at a grand conclave, June 24th, 1791, and were unanimously approved of.

This 'Code of Laws' contains nothing particularly surprising. It is of interest how closely related to the Royal Arch the Order of Knights Templar is seen to be; reference is made throughout to local gatherings as 'chapters', and in one place their three senior officers are referred to as the 'principals'. Evidently Dunckerley did not see the Order simply as a matter of 'dressing-up' to simulate the Knights of a bygone Order – to him it is apparent that after the glorification of God the Order existed with no other purpose than that of providing relief for the poor.

The only obscure matter is the necessity for every knight to write his name on the lower corner of his certificate or register 'for *particular* reasons well known to the confraternity', a procedure for which we can find no explanation. This was not to be an Order for the mass of the people – the sum for the installation of a Knight Templar was to be 'not less than one pound and six shillings', equivalent approximately to £100-£150 in early 21st century money. It may also be noted that the 'laws' make provision for an 'exhortation' to be given by the 'grand orator' at the annual meeting of Grand Conclave, but nowhere does this individual appear among the list of Grand Officers.

The formal name of the newly constituted Grand Conclave was 'The Grand Conclave of the Royal, Exalted, Religious and Military Order of H.R.D.M. Grand Elected Masonic Knights Templars K.D.S.H of St John of Jerusalem, Palestine, Rhodes etc.' This is an all-embracing title, which includes not only the present Order of Malta which today remains a constituent of the United Orders, but also claiming authority over what are now the 18th and 30th Degrees of the Ancient and Accepted Rite (H.R.D.M. & K.D.S.H.), an influential Order not at this time yet established in England and Wales, Scotland, or Ireland. There is no doubt that prior to 1845 many, if not all, Encampments in England and Wales were conferring '*Rosae Crucis*' and 'Kadosh', as Degrees progressive from the Knight Templar Degree; the Camp of Baldwyn was certainly doing so.

As has already been pointed out, any historian of the Order of Knights Templar finds himself lamenting that there are no definitive records of how the Order came to be established in England, and the lament continues with no less force now that the story has progressed to the early years of Grand Conclave. In this context, there is the additional frustration that many such records as did exist were consumed in 1820 in a disastrous fire at the home in Soho of Robert Gill, Vice-Chancellor at that time. What we know of Dunckerley's term of office has therefore to be pieced together from various secondary sources including his own correspondence.

Fortunately, Dunckerley, acting as his own Vice-Chancellor, wrote a large number of letters to the various Encampments over which he presided, as well as in many cases to their individual members, discharging most conscientiously what he conceived to be his duty towards the Order. This is all the more remarkable when one remembers that he was also communicating with no less devotion with his many Provinces in the Craft and even more in the Royal Arch.

If it were not for this correspondence there would be no record of the way in which the early encampments of the Order were established, and of when, why, and how those which did not long survive had to be removed from the Register. One can only be thankful that not only has the Ancient Conclave of Redemption in York preserved much of its correspondence with the first Grand Master of the Order, but also that, though they were formerly widely scattered, many letters between Dunckerley and John Knight, the 'Grand Master' in the embryonic Encampment at Redruth in Cornwall, have now been brought together.[193] From this latter correspondence with John Knight, the genesis of the Encampment of St John of Jerusalem at Redruth can be discovered in some detail; whether this is typical of the manner in which Dunckerley warranted other Encampments it is impossible to say, but it may be presumed that in each case something at least similar occurred.

John Knight, who lived at Redruth in Cornwall, was born in 1745[194] and was initiated there into the *Druids'*[195] *Lodge of Love and Liberality* in 1766 at the age of 21. In 1775 Knight was Exalted in the *Royal Arch Chapter of Sincerity*, *Peace and Prosperity* at Devonport in which town it is also probable that he was Installed as a Knight Templar, probably in 1776.[196] He was the principal Founder and the first MEZ of the *Druids Royal Arch Chapter of Love and Liberality*.

On 17th August 1791, two months after Dunckerley had been Installed as Grand Master of the Order at the meeting of the Grand Conclave in London, in his capacity as the Provincial Grand Superintendent in and over Cornwall he sent the Warrant for the recently consecrated *Royal Arch Chapter of Love and Liberality* to its Scribe together with a covering letter. John Knight then wrote to Dunckerley –

> We See by your Letter to Bror. Harrison of the 8 July a Point relative to the Royal and Exalted, Religious Order of Knight Templars, and that you are the Most Eminent & Supreme Grand Master. There are some of the order in this place & Bror. Knight of the Druids Chapter has formerly presided as Grand Master. We co'd wish to know the Expence of a Warrant or Dispensation and what Steps it will be necessary to take for the obtaining of the Same.[197]

In his reply dated 26 August, Dunckerley informed John Knight that –

The Price of a Patent for a Conclave & Chapter of Knights Templar is £1.6.0, with five shillings for each Knight, for which Certificates will be sent.

If there are three or more Knights among ye I will grant you a Patent if you send me the first letter of the Pass Word, & last letter of the sacred word.

The establish'd Sash[198] to be worn by every Knight in the Chapter will cost

	6^s -		)
The Gilt Cross	7 - 6		) £1. 1. 0.
& the Statutes	3^s		)
The Silver Star	7 - 6		)[199]

After further correspondence Dunckerley again wrote to John Knight -

To a Patent of Constitution	£1. 6. 0
3 Certificates @ 5^s	0. 15. 0
3 Sashes, 3 Stars and 3 Crosses	3. 6. 0
10 Books of Statutes at 6^d	0. 5. 0
Box, booking etc.	0. 1. 0
Carriage of the Sashes &c from)	
London to Hampton Court)	0. 0. 6
	5. 14. 0

Dear Bror & Knt Compn   Hampton Court Palace

Decr 21 1791

According to your request I send the above. The last letter of the principal word is right therefore when I hear from you in return shall forward what you desire. Let me know the title of your Conclave & the names, Ages & professions of the other Knights.[200]

On 27 January 1792 Dunckerley wrote again, saying in a letter addressed to 'Sir John Knight, Eminent Deputy Grand Master of the Conclave & Chapter of Knights Templar &c. at Redruth, Cornwall' –

Your letter (date unknown) I rec'd the 25th with a Draught for £5.14^s.0^d., which I immediately put in my Bureau, but lost the letter the same day. However I wrote to Town for the Sashes etc. but cannot remember the names of your two Brother Knights, but have sent the Blank Certificates to be filled up. I have also left a Blank for the day on which your first Conclave is to be held. I am concern'd that there is so great distance between us, as it would give me much pleasure to communicate to every Conclave I have constituted, the Masonic Knowledge which I have glean'd in Europe, America and Africa[201] for forty years past. Altho' Mrs. Dunckerley (the Lady Patroness of Knt. Templars) is near 80 years of age, and I am not far from 70, yet we intend (with God's permission) to visit the West of England next summer, and (if we should winter at Plymouth) It is probable that I may have the happiness of conversing with some of the Knts. Comps. from Exeter, Redruth and Biddeford (sic).

I was selected Grand Master, to revive the Order in England in February 1791 and have had the pleasure to constitute the following Conclaves, viz.:

Of 'Observance of the Seven Degrees' London Coffee House, Ludgate Hill
'Redemption'[202]   *York*
'Royal Cumberland'   *Bath, Bear Inn*
'Fortitude'   *First Regiment, Dragoon Guards*
'Trine'   *Biddeford, New Ring of Bells*
'Naval'[203]   *Portsmouth*
'Durnovarian'   *Dorchester, Royal Oak*
'Harmony'   *Salisbury, White Hart*
'Science'   *Salisbury, Parade Coffee House*
'Royal Edward'   *Hereford, Bowling Green*
'St. John of Jerusalem'   *Redruth*

Having provided this useful list for the future historian, Dunckerley goes on to describe the appropriate uniform which he has now given instructions should be worn by the Knights Companions –

My servant having mislaid your letter, you will on receipt of this give me a line with the names of the other Knights, with your days of Meetings, and at what House, and also insert it in your Patent. The Seals should be put on with wafers, and I have sent a Uniform Button and pattern of the cloth for a Frock[204] which I have established to be worn in the several conclaves. The Coat will take 14 Buttons. Ten in front and four for the hips and skirts, with 2 very small Gilt buttons at the opening of each sleeve, and a White Kerseymere Waistcoat and White French basket buttons, with black breeches. A cheap suit of clothes that may be worn by Men of all professions and at any time. I paid the Taylor £4.4s.0d. for my coat and waistcoat. In all the Chapters Cock'd Hats and Cockades are worn with Swords, and black velvet stocks. The Stocks, Cockades and Swords to be kept in a box in each Chapter. Most of the Knights (I have more than 120 register'd) have already appeared in their uniforms, in compliance with my recommendation, and Request; and shall be happy to hear that you add to the numbers, if not attended with inconvenience. This letter is very badly wrote. The sashes &c are come to hand within the hour, and I write hastily that the box may go from London by ye mail coach tomorrow Evening. My wife unites with me in wishing every Success to an Order sacred to the memory of Redemption and you have our hearty Greeting.
                    Your faithful and affectionate Compn. and Bror. Tho Dunckerley.

It is evident from such surviving correspondence[205] that not only was Dunckerley his own administrator, but also that he was not prepared to discharge his duties to the Craft, Royal Arch and Knights Templar solely from his study in Hampton Court. For example, in a letter to John Knight from Southampton dated 27 August 1792, Dunckerley writes –

On the 22nd ultimo I left Hampton Court, & on the 3rd Inst. (on the request of the congregation of this place) laid the first stone of a church to be rebuilt. The 11th, 16th,

& 21ˢᵗ of this month I held Grand Lodges at Shaftesbury in Dorset, City of Bristol, and in Wells, in honor of the Birthdays of the Prince of Wales, Duke of York, & Duke of Clarence. I returned yesterday and rec'd your favour of the 8ᵗʰ.

We should perhaps bear in mind, accustomed as we are to travel widely to meetings at home and abroad in the relative comfort of reliable cars, trains and aircraft, that Dunckerley made his extensive journeys by stage-coaches singularly devoid of comfort along roads which were always rough and often dangerous. In honouring, some of the early Encampments which survive we may perhaps regard them as monuments to the dedication of Thomas Dunckerley. The perils of travel were not the only hardships which Dunckerley suffered; on 9 May 1794 in a letter to John Knight he wrote 'I have been laid up with the Gout in both feet for 3 long months: am now praised be God! getting better.'

Earlier, writing to John Knight on 22 June 1793 Dunckerley said:

I do myself the pleasure to appoint you Provincial Grand Master of Knights Templar for the County of Cornwall which to accept if agreeable you will please to signify your acceptance by return of [?] and let me know if you rec'd the copy of a letter from Prince Edward to me dated Oct. 1792. Next Monday I shall hold a Grand Conclave of the Order at the London Coffee House, Ludgate Hill.

Having replied –

I am duly sensible of the high Honor you do to me in appointing me Provincial Grand Master of Knights Templar for the County of Cornwall which office I accept with sincere thanks ...

John Knight thereafter signed himself 'E.D.G.M. & P.G.M.' – Eminent Deputy Grand Master and Provincial Grand Master.

Perhaps the most surprising communication from Thomas Dunckerley was the printed circular letter dated 11 March 1794 which he sent to all the Encampments under the Grand Conclave over which he now presided at a time when there was a real fear in England that Napoleon Buonoparte was preparing to invade the island. It is addressed to the 'Deputy Grand Masters' of the various Encampments and reads as follows –

As our Nation is preparing to guard against an Invasion from our Enemies, if should they have the temerity to make the attempt, it is become my duty to request and require that such of you as can, without prejudice to your families, do hold yourselves in readiness (as Knights Templars) to unite and be under the command of the officers of the military corps stationed in your respective counties, as may be most convenient taking the name of 'Prince Edward's Loyal Volunteers'. When the important moment arrives, I shall offer my services to the Navy or the Army; and whenever I have the honour to be received, shall inform you of my address; and although we are prevented, by adverse circumstances, from assembling together where I might have the honor and happiness of commanding in person, yet our hearts will be united in the glorious cause, in conformity with the sacred obligations we are under. Let our prayers be addressed to the Throne of grace; that as Christ's faithful soldiers and servants we may be enabled to defend the Christian religion, our gracious Sovereign, our laws, liberties and properties against a rapacious enemy. Let the word of the day be *The Will of God*[206]; and let us remember that a day, an hour of virtuous liberty, is worth a whole eternity of bondage.

The Knights Companions are required to wear the uniform of the corps in which they serve as volunteers, with the Cross of the Order of the Knights Templar on a black riband between two button-holes on the breast of the waistcoat.

(The Circular then goes on more mundanely to set out the arrangements for the Annual Grand Conclave to be held on 11 April 1794.)

Happy as the Knights Companions in Cornwall were to be subject to the new Grand Conclave, there can be little doubt that the members of the Camp of Baldwyn in Bristol had not expected that Thomas Dunckerley would establish the ruling body for the Order in London. For many years by virtue of their long standing constitution and their 'time immemorial' status, they continued to regard themselves as an independent body, a 'Grand Conclave' at least co-equal with that in London over which Dunckerley was now presiding, and which was under no necessity to remit any payments or fees to the latter. They considered themselves bound only by their own established regulations and usages, acknowledging only the personal pre-eminence of the M. E. & S. G. Master.

3.4 GRAND CONCLAVE AFTER THOMAS DUNCKERLEY

After Thomas Dunckerley died in November 1795 temporary charge of the Order's affairs was taken by William Hannam. Hannam was a man of some consequence, being the Provost Marshal of His Majesty's Guards, and who, in 1790, had served as Grand Master of Lintot's Rite of Seven Degrees. Now, signing himself 'Acting Gd. Master', he advised the Encampments of the loss which they had sustained and put forward a suggestion as to his successor –

> Permit me to Point out as the Person Most Eligible to do Honour to the Society The Rt. Hon'ble Lord Rancliffe, who is a Member of the Chapter and Conclave of Observance, the more so from being a Colonel in the Army.

Hannam held the Annual Assembly of the Grand Conclave on 5th July 1795. A sufficiency of the Knights Companions presumably indicated their approval and the noble Lord was elected and installed on 3rd February 1796.

Thomas, the first Lord Rancliffe, cuts a rather insignificant figure in the story of our United Orders and for this we must to some extent blame the scanty records of his Grand Mastership. It is known that he was born Thomas Boothby Parkyns in 1755 into a wealthy family. He followed a parliamentary career, sitting first for Stockbridge in Hampshire and then as the Member for Leicester. When fears arose of a Napoleonic invasion of England, Rancliffe raised the Prince of Wales' Regiment of Fencible Cavalry and it was in command thereof that he gained his Colonel's rank.[207] Rancliffe's Irish peerage entitled him to sit in the House of Lords which he continued to do until his death.

In 1783 Rancliffe was the Provincial Grand Master in the Craft for Nottinghamshire, and six years later he was made additionally responsible for the Provinces of Derbyshire and of Leicestershire and Rutland. In the Royal Arch he became Grand Superintendent of Leicestershire and Rutland in 1793, having already been appointed Second Grand Principal in the previous year. He continued to rule the Province until he became Grand Z in 1794, holding both Offices until his death in 1800. All this would seem to indicate great zeal for the fraternity, but Thorp[208] wrote that

> . . . he does not appear to have taken the slightest personal interest in Masonry in this Province (*Leicestershire)* during the eleven years he presided over it, except on one solitary occasion, namely being present at an Emergency Meeting of St John's Lodge, Leicester, on April 27th 1791, after which he presented the set of silver jewels for the officers, which are still in use.

It is possible that it was to the governance of the Royal Arch and Knight Templary that Rancliffe principally devoted his attention.

Together with the rule of the Order of the Temple, Rancliffe also succeeded to Dunckerley's Grand Commandership in the 'Society of Antient Masons of the Diluvian Order of Royal Ark and Mark Mariners', but it is improbable that he devoted much attention to it. It can be confusing to modern readers who are accustomed to the term 'United Orders' referring to those of the Temple and of the Hospital that Dunckerley himself used to refer to the Knights Templar and the Ark Mariners as the 'United Orders', evidently seeing the latter as the maritime counterpart of the former.

Records show that the Templar Grand Conclave met twice in Rancliffe's first year as Grand Master, but only once in each of the three following. There seems to have been a lack of enthusiasm for the Order on Rancliffe's part. While an Encampment was warranted by him at Ashton-under-Lyne on 12 August 1796, it was to be almost nine years before another came into being. His parliamentary duties and the management of his Irish estates may have occupied much of his time, but in 1799 there was also a period of great uncertainty among Freemasons when the Government was about to pass *The Unlawful Societies Act* 'for the more effectual suppression of Societies established for seditious and treasonable purposes' (39 Geo. III, c.79) until the 4th Duke of Atholl together with Lord Moira persuaded the Government to insert saving clauses for Freemasons' Lodges.

By these clauses, under certain conditions, Freemasonry was exempted from the most draconian of the Act's provisions, an exemption which was embodied in clauses 5 and 6 of the Act:

> 5. And whereas certain Societies have long been accustomed to be holden in the Kingdom under the denomination of Lodges of Freemasons, the meetings whereof have been in great measure directed to charitable purposes; be it therefore enacted that nothing in this Act shall extend to the meetings of any Society or Lodge which shall before the passing of this Act have been usually holden under the said denomination, and in conformity with the rules prevailing among the said Societies of Freemasons.

Clause 6 laid down that this exemption would only apply if two of the members of each 'Society or Lodge' annually certified on oath before a Magistrate that it conformed 'to the rules prevailing among the Societies or Lodges of Freemasonry in the Kingdom', and also deposited with the Clerk of the Peace 'the names and descriptions of all and every the members thereof'.[209]

On the death of Lord Rancliffe in 1800, his Deputy Grand Master, Robert Gill, acted as Grand Master for four years. Gill was a considerable contrast to Lord

Rancliffe. He was active in the Craft, Royal Arch and Knights Templar until his death in 1821, attending many Lodges and Chapters and whenever he did so he was generally apt to seek the opportunity of taking the Chair. Even though Grand Conclave did not meet for several years, for the last four years of Rancliffe's life Gill, who had served as Grand Senior Warden in the *Antient* Grand Lodge, had virtually taken his place as Grand Master of the Order of Knights Templar. During this period Brethren who were upholders of the 'Modern' tradition as well as those who were *'Antients'*, seem to have been able to work in harmony at all levels in the Order of the Temple.[210]

The Duke of Kent, still the Royal Patron of the Order, was representing King George III in Canada until 1803, and it was not until the following year, presumably with the Duke's approval, that Robert Gill sent a circular letter to all the known Encampments, implicitly acknowledging that the Grand Conclave of 1791 had effectively fallen into desuetude, and it was in effect necessary to revive it:

London 23rd October 1804

London 23rd October 1804

Brethren and Sir Knights, It is with infinite concern and regret that I now inform you that the Grand Conclave has been dormant for at least six years, to the great detriment of the Order, and to the Brethren Sir Knights Companions in general.

I am therefore directed by the members of the Encampment No. 20 of the 'Holy Cross of Christ', under our Grand Commander the Duke of Kent (being the only Encampment in London, meeting at the Queen's Arms Tavern, Newgate Street) to state that it is their intention to form and congregate themselves into a Grand Conclave, for a revival thereof, presuming it will meet your concurrence and approbation, as we hope of the other Encampments in the Country.

Permit me therefore, Brother Sir Knights, to request the favour of an immediate reply, on or before the second Monday in next month, being the night of our Encampment, with your Sentiments and Support thereto.

The outcome of this move is amply reported in another letter written less than four months afterwards –

'At a General Meeting held on the 14th of January 1805, a Deputation was appointed to wait upon H.R.H. the Duke of Kent, for the purpose of obtaining his approbation and consent to the drawing up of a Charter of Compact between the Members of the Order and H.R.H. as their Head or Chief. The Deputation had the honour to meet H.R.H. agreeable to his own appointment, on Sunday the 20th January at Kensington Palace when the proposal not only met H.R.H.'s full approbation and consent, but he consented to be nominated Most Eminent and Supreme Grand Master of the Order.

Whereupon another General Meeting was called, and a Committee was appointed to compose and to draw up the Charter of Compact above alluded to, which had been done in as full and ample a manner as possible and which has met with the entire approbation of H.R.H. and wherein he has condescended to be nominated M.E. & S.G.M. of the Order, and the Knights Companions in it are to be the first Grand Officers for the year ensuing, viz.

ROBERT GILL Esq.	Deputy and Acting Grand Master
JAMES HIGGINS MD	First Grand Captain
EVAN LLOYD	Second Grand Captain
WILLIAM DAVIS	Grand Chancellor
JOHN GILBERT	Grand Scribe and Registrar
JAMES MURRAY)	
JOHN SAFFELL)	Grand Standard Bearers

Having thus informed you of the very forward and we trust very pleasing and prosperous state of the Order I would beg leave to advert to some of the Powers and Prerogatives conferred by H.R.H. on the Grand Conclave; the first and most important of which is, that they now have full right and authority to grant Warrants for new Encampments, and to exact from all others a strict account for registering fees; to grant Certificates &c. – Secondly that there is to be an Annual Grand Conclave of Communication to which the Principals of all Encampments are to be invited for the Election of Grand Officers, and for all other general purposes of the Order. Besides there is to be a Quarterly Communication for the purposes of Charity, and to regulate the public business of the Order.

Being thus in possession of our proceedings and of the Powers with which we are invested let us beg that you will be so kind as to favour us with your correspondence, and we will thank you to remit any registering fees, that may be now due, from your Encampment to the Grand Conclave. Addressed to the G.S. and Reg., as under, and we will thank you to send us a list of all the Encampments that you now know of lest we should have omitted sending to all, when you acknowledge receipt of this, which we trust will be immediately after your next meeting.

One more thing I have to inform you of, that it is the request of H.R.H. and is inserted in the body of the Charter that the Jewels and the Regalia are to be worn as follows, viz.: the Grand Commander a Star of eight points with a black Sash over the right shoulder; the Captains a similar Sash with a Star of seven points, Private Companions the same Sash with a Mother of Pearl Cross, and all to wear an Apron bound with black with the proper badge or Skull and Cross-bones displayed thereon; and for the sake of uniformity we think that a Suit of Black and black Sword would be more consistent with the Order than any other dress.

      By Command of the D.G.M. and Grand Officers
          I am, with due respect
              Your Brother and Companion
                JOHN GILBERT G.S. & Reg.

Blackwall
February 14, 1805'

There are several points of interest about this communication. In the first place it is unusual for the Patron of any Masonic body to revert, as it were, to becoming its Grand Master. The Grand Offices were the same minimum number as the Offices in an Encampment, with the addition only of a Grand Chancellor. All Knightly Brethren were to wear an Apron; this was presumably to emphasise that the Order was a Masonic Body which was eligible to be exempted from the provisions of the 1799 Act, for the best known characteristic of Freemasons, then and now, is that they wear aprons. The dress to be worn is described only as a 'suit of black'; there is no reference to Dunckerley's 'frock' with gilt buttons, White Kerseymere Waistcoat, Black Velvet Stock and Cocked Hat. The White Sashes with which Dunckerley had supplied John Knight had now become 'a black sash over the right shoulder' and the Cross then to be worn by all the Knights Companions was 'Gilt' and not 'Mother-of-Pearl'.

The Charter of Compact to which this letter refers is in the archives of Mark Masons' Hall but framed behind glass and somewhat difficult to read. It is a lengthy document which five years later was to be 'revoked, cancelled and annulled'.[211]

The assumption of the Grand Mastership of the Order by the Duke of Kent ended a lengthy period of stagnation and uncertainty. Prince Edward Augustus, who in 1799 had been created Duke of Kent and Strathearn, was in many respects the right man for the job. Born in 1767 he had been initiated in the Union Lodge at Geneva at the age of 23. As was traditionally the practice he was in the same year, 1790, made a Past Grand Master of the Premier Grand Lodge, the 'Moderns', and he was also appointed Provincial Grand Master for Gibraltar and Andalusia. He was on the active list of the Army, and was, it cannot be gainsaid, a martinet whose strictness sometimes got him into trouble with the military authorities at home. It was this characteristic which caused him to be relieved of his command on The Rock and he was posted to North America where he became the Provincial Grand Master for Lower Canada, but this time under the Grand Lodge of the *Antients*. It was from Canada that his correspondence with Dunckerley was dated between 1792 and 1795.

When the Duke returned to England in 1803 Gill was able to enlist his support in reviving the Grand Conclave.[212] It appears that when this was resurrected in 1805, none of those involved were in possession of a copy of the Statutes which had been drawn up by Dunckerley for approval at that first meeting of Grand Conclave on 24 June 1791.

While following the sequence of events by which the governing body of the English Knights Templar was established, it is easy to lose sight of the fact that it was because new Knights were regularly being Installed in Encampments across the country – it was a popular Order for those who could afford it – that a governing body with a proper Constitution was required to preserve at least some measure of uniformity. It is therefore not out of place to interpose here some descriptions of the ceremonies and procedures by which these Installations were carried out in some Encampments, which may perhaps be considered typical.

3.5 EARLY KNIGHT TEMPLAR RITUALS

Regrettably few early rituals in use in the first quarter century of the Order have survived; the earliest surviving ritual found to date is one dated 1773.[213] This contains a detailed Knight Templar working together together with a *Rosae Crucis* or *Ne Plus Ultra* record of eleven brethren admitted to that degree at Falmouth on 30 November 1773. John Knight documented in considerable detail a sequence of twenty-six degrees in which Knight Templar was the 19th and *Ne Plus Ultra* the 26th.

Before that date there were many recorded instances of workings with Knight Templar elements; and the existence of *Ecossais* Lodges in England was noted as early as 1733; Philip Crossle, the Irish historian, stated that the degree was worked in Ireland from about 1740; *Antients* Lodges appeared from 1751 onwards working degrees beyond the Craft under their Craft Warrants; French Rites and the Rite of Perfection developed in France at the same time and were transported to England among French prisoners-of-war and their military escorts and guards not long after; and the Priestly Order and Holy Royal Arch Knight Templar Priest degree sequences appeared by the 1760s. Any of these could well have provided sources for John Knight's *Rosae Crucis* or *Ne Plus Ultra* rites of 1773. A Comparison of John Knight's sequence of degrees with these earlier sources is instructive and is given in Appendix D.

John Knight later extended this sequence to thirty-seven degrees, and although he himself confessed he was dubious about some, he retained the twentieth Degree of 'Mediterranean Pass' and the 21st 'Knight of Malta' in amended versions up to the date of his death in 1828.

1805 John Knight and an Early Cornish Ritual Until his death in 1828 John Knight, who appears to have been something of an autocrat, presided personally over the many Degrees worked at Redruth. These included that of the Order of Knights Templar for which, as previously noted, he had obtained a Warrant from Thomas Dunckerley, who later appointed him Provincial Grand Master for Cornwall. For each of the Degrees over which he presided, including those of the Craft and of the Royal Arch, John Knight transcribed into one or other of a series of Notebooks the ritual as it was worked in Redruth. One particular ritual exists in a small manuscript notebook (18×12cm) held in the John Coombe Masonic Library Hayle, Cornwall, the first entry relating to a meeting held on 11 March 1805 which is perhaps one of the earliest of John Knight's transcriptions of the Degree of Knights

Templar.[214] It contains a list of those present at the Meeting and an extract of the salient details is given in Appendix D.

Some of Knight's note-books contained the Ritual of a single Order or Degree, while others recorded the Ritual of a series of successive progressive Degrees which Knight subsequently incorporated into what was effectively a Redruth 'rite' although it was never referred to as such.

The source of some of these Orders and Degrees is uncertain; none of them were among those promoted by Finch even though in some cases the titles of the Degrees are the same as those which Finch gave to those he propagated. However the earliest rituals of the Craft or 'Blue' Degrees, of the Royal Arch and of the Knights Templar, apparently transcribed before 1805, can only be presumed to record the ceremonies by which John Knight himself was admitted to these Degrees and Order in the last quarter of the 18th century before he became aware of the other Degrees which he later adopted. Further details of this 1805 Cornish Knight Templar Ritual as recorded by John Knight are given in Appendix E.

Possibly in about 1810, and then again shortly before his death in 1828, John Knight transcribed further versions of the Knight Templar Degree, each more sophisticated than that preceding it. On what these modifications are based it is impossible to say; 'Ritual' does not figure in John Knight's correspondence with Dunckerley, and one can only assume that he was enlightened either by visitors to the Encampment of St John or by himself visiting other Encampments; even so it cannot be said how far these changes were aligned with modifications to the ritual carried out elsewhere. It is perhaps important to mention that in John Knight's own writings there is no suggestion that the Redruth Knight Templar ritual was derived from a chivalric Templar source which had been handed down over many generations. Likewise there is no indication of source in other contemporary or later rituals which have survived and which are now mentioned briefly in apparent chronological order.

1791-c.1795 Sheffield Ritual An early knight templar ritual exists in the Societas Rosicruciana in Anglia library in Tapton Hall, Sheffield and was transcribed and edited by Christopher Powell to mark the centenary of that library.[215] The transcription is of a ritual roughly contemporary to Knight's Cornish Ritual but much closer to that with which we are familiar today except for the Scriptural References are of an earlier date suggesting the ritual probably was in use 1791-95. Four key points are of interest:

> The ritual had been written c.1800 into an older notebook which can be dated c.1780 together with a Royal Arch ritual which can be dated to 1780-85;

The ritual mentions the Grand Conclave of England (set up by Thomas Dunckerley in 1791);

The ritual is in four distinct sections in catechetical form (Question and Answer) with the third section, mainly omitted from today's ritual, dealing with events following Christ's betrayal;

Whilst there is nothing to confirm its provenance directly, the language suggests both the Royal Arch and Knight Templar rituals were used in Northern England.[216]

Bro. Powell comments 'that the Sheffield ritual is probably the oldest KT ritual in English that has so far come to light and a lecture in KT of a similar date (1797) is contained in the Tunnah manuscript now in the Library and Museum of Freemasonry in London'.

Early Irish Rituals 1796 and 1804 Philip Crossle, the Irish historian, published transcripts of early Knight Templar rituals, one being that of the Early Grand Encampment of High Knights Templar of Dublin. Whilst many elements of the ceremony are recognisable by an English Knight Templar today, three points are of particular interest:

The candidate is admitted as a Royal Arch Mason, but is examined in his knowledge of the blue Lodge (Craft) including 'Passing the chair'; the degree of Excellent Mason; the degree of Super-Excellent Mason; and the Royal Arch. This seems to confirm the ceremonial observed in 1769 in Boston had an essentially Irish origin.

The candidate, in response to the query 'Whence come you?' responds with 'From where the Light Shineth in Darkness and the Darkness Comprehended it not.' It may be noted that similar phraseology appeared early in Lancashire and other northern Counties in both Knight Templar and other degree rituals suggesting contact with Ireland as a ritual source.

There is no evidence of the qualification adopted by the *Antients* who required a Mark degree before admission to the Royal Arch, which is, perhaps, surprising, since the *Antients* seemingly had an essentially Irish background.

1801 Wigan Ritual A Wigan version of the Ritual of the Early Grand Rite, survives which is dated roughly contemporary with Knight's Cornish Ritual but appears to be much closer to that with which we are familiar today. It is entirely possible the Sheffield and Wigan rituals were derived from a common source. It must be noted that the pre-1801 Ritual from which Thomas Lonsdale Bold copied the 1801 Wigan Ritual, and which which later copied by John Yarker in about 1864, are both likewise not too distant from those known today.

North American Rituals. Detailed rituals were included in Thomas Smith Webb's *Freemasons Monitor* (1808 and a second Edition 1818). The content is similar to that in use today and suggest transfer from Europe to the New World. However there are sufficient differences from English Rituals as to suggest a probable Irish origin; in particular:

> As with the English version, membership of the Royal Arch is an essential qualification with the difference that the American Royal Arch is preceded by the degrees of Mark Master, Passed Master, and Excellent Master or Most Excellent Master. This again suggests Irish or Scottish sources, but the continued inclusion of a Mark qualification suggests a source other than solely Ireland; circumstantially this may be indicative of the degree having originally been transferred to the New World between 1732-1784 by military lodges holding Irish, Scottish, or *Antients* Warrants.

> The American Knight Templar Rite is preceded by a qualification degree of 'Red Cross' – similar in many respects to Irish degrees within the Knight Masons Rite (Knight of the Sword, Knight of the East, and Knight of the East and West extending the RA story similar to the (English) Allied Masonic Degree of Red Cross of Babylon.

> The ritual element associated with the admission as a Pilgrim is far more extensive that the modern English version.

> The Knight of Malta degree precedes that of Knight Templar although the ritual is broadly similar to that used in England.

1825 'Manual of Freemasonry' In 1825 Mr Richard Carlile gave a very detailed description of the Degree in his *'Manual of Freemasonry'* published in London by the printer William Reeves. To knights familiar with New World rituals, there is no question that Carlile used North American material as his source for not only the Knight Templar degree but also for many of the other degrees and orders in his books.

It is of interest to note that when Thomas Dunckerley took control of the Knights Templar Rite in 1791 he did not interfere with the forms of ritual worked by the individual Encampments. However by the 1850's it was considered desirable to introduce some measure of uniformity.

Today with a few well known exceptions, all Preceptories under the 'English jurisdiction' use the ritual book authorised by Great Priory to install candidates into the Order. Today a demonstration team drawn from the Province of Hampshire and Isle of Wight demonstrate, in costume, one of the many and varied ceremonies being worked in Dunckerley's day. This had been produced and directed by the Provincial Prior, who played the part of its author, Richard Carlile.

1840 19th Regiment Ritual A Undated ritual (dated on or before 1840) was copied by T. B. Whytehead, the noted historian, in 1886 from 'an original lent to me by Donald Grant, 19th Regiment, formerly the property of his grandfather who was a prominent Mason in 1840.

Whilst the exact provenance of this ritual is not known the 19th Regiment, with its associated lodges, was active throughout both Europe including Fontenoy (1745) and Belle Isle (1761) and the New World including service in the Caribbean (1759) and had known contact with other regiments with proven Knight Templar activity.

It may also be noted that, from 1782-1875 the 19th Regiment was designated the 1st (Yorkshire, North Riding) Regiment of Foot and that T. B. Whytehead was a prominent Yorkshire Mason.

Standardisation of the Rituals

1851 Ritual Grand Conclave met in 1851 to receive a revised Ritual of the Ceremonies to be carried out in Encampments, an evident necessity in view of the severance of the *Rosae Crucis* and *Kadosh* Degrees. It was resolved that this Ritual should be adopted, and is broadly similar to that in use today.

This Ritual was probably largely (or may even have been wholly) the editing work of John Masson who was appointed First Grand Captain at the meeting. Masson concluded his Report by saying – 'Finally the Grand Chancellor has intimated to Grand Conclave, that as the Ritual it has adopted has received the marked approval, and accordance of Knights Templars, in conformity throughout the Christian world, he has in preparation a System of Examination in Sections with a lecture, in strict accordance with the said Ritual and Masonic History of the Order.'

1863 A Malta Ritual By 1863, Grand Conclave evidently considered that the 'Malta' Rituals, such as they were, should be put in order as that of Knight Templar had been by Masson. 'The Ritual of the Knights of Malta' was 'sanctioned by the Grand Master at the Meeting of the Grand Conclave held on the 8th day of May 1863 and recommended to be adopted by all the Priories'.

1864 Another Wigan Ritual In about 1864 John Yarker documented a pre-1801 Ritual from which Thomas Lonsdale Bold copied the 1801 Wigan Ritual.

1866 Installation Ritual A Ritual of The Ceremony of Installation of an Eminent Prior was approved by the Committee on 1 December 1866.

1876 Report of the Ritual Commission In 1876, the Ritual Commission appointed under the Anglo-Hibernian Convention of 1868 recommended a Knight of the Temple Ritual which was duly adopted.

Thus is seen an extended period (1791-1876) over which our rituals have developed; over many years, commanderies and preceptories were left free to adopt whatever ritual they desired; Dunckerley did not appear to attach importance to this matter and the standardisation which we know today is a fairly recent innovation.

3.6 THE CHARTER OF CONSTITUTION, 1809

We left off the narrative of events in Grand Conclave when in 1805 Robert Gill was able to report the accession of the Duke of Kent to the Grand Mastership of the Order of Knights Templar. No one then involved appeared to have been in possession of a copy of the Statutes or Constitutions which Dunckerley had drawn up for approval at the first meeting of Grand Conclave on 24 June 1791. It was not until 1807 that a copy of these came to light, when, with the full approval of the Duke of Kent, it was possible to elect as Grand Master Waller Rodwell Wright. This allowed the Duke to revert to his more appropriate role of Royal Grand Patron. It took some time for the arrangements to be finalized. When this was completed two years later in 1809, it was done in some style by a 'Charter of Constitution' being beautifully engrossed on parchment or vellum.

This 'Charter' was addressed on behalf of 'His Royal Highness Prince Edward Duke of Kent' to 'The Knights Companions of the Exalted Religious and Military Orders of the Holy Temple and Sepulchre and of St John of Jerusalem HRDM KDSH', these last initials indicating the extent to which the Rose Croix of Heredom and Kadosh Degrees were now firmly established within the Order. The reason for the promulgation of the Charter is given as –

> 'WHEREAS certain of our Brethren, being Knights Companions of the said Religious and Military Order viz. James Higgins MD, Robert Gill, Evan Lloyd, John Gilbert, William Davis, James Murray and John R. Saffell did heretofore present to us in their humble Suit and Petition stating that the antient Grand Conclave of the said Order had for many Years suspended and discontinued its Meetings and that the members thereof were for the most part dead or dispersed without hope of them being again assembled to resume the exercise of their former Function and Privileges and praying that we should be pleased to grant unto them our Charter for the purpose of constituting and forming them into a Supreme Grand Conclave of the said Order AND WHEREAS we in Consideration of the Premises did grant unto them such Charter bearing date the – (*sic*) of March in the year of our Lord One thousand eight hundred and four therein'.[217]

The new Charter then goes on to say that Dunckerley's 1791 Constitutions now having been found, the Charter given in 1804 is hereby revoked, cancelled and annulled, and

> '**THAT WE** . . . . . do hereby ratify and confirm the said Constitutions bearing date the 24th day of June one thousand seven hundred and ninety one in all things whatsoever save and except inasmuch as relates to the amount of the fees to be charged in Warrants of Constitutions and Certificates to be hereafter granted to any Knights Companions of the said Order and the day on which the annual Grand Conclave and

Festival of the said Order is appointed to be holden, which matters so accepted are henceforth to be regulated at the discretion of the Grand Conclave for the time being.'

The Duke then declares that he will now 'accept and take upon us the Style Title and Office of ROYAL GRAND PATRON' and that 'we do hereby approve ratify and confirm' the election which had now taken place two years earlier of Waller Rodwell Wright as Grand Master. Furthermore the Royal Grand Patron confirmed the Grand Officers in their several Offices, namely:

Deputy Grand Master	*John Christian Burckhardt*
1st Grand Captain	*Charles Davis Valentine*
2nd Grand Captain	*Richard Jebb*
Grand Prelate	*The Revd John Frith, DD*
Grand Chancellor	*William Henry White*
Grand Register (sic)	
and Vice Chancellor	*Robert Gill*
Grand Treasurer	*John Gilbert*

This was evidently a considerable step forward, but, to quote,

'when the Bristol Sir Knights elected Bro. Dunckerley to the Grand Mastership of the Order, they never contemplated the abandonment of their position as the Supreme Grand Encampment; and, although they owed him allegiance as their regularly elected Grand Master, they refused to acknowledge the authority of the Grand Conclave in London which was formed under his rule'.[218]

Thomas Dunckerley had been succeeded as local Grand Master by Joshua Springer, and after his resignation, by John Sanders who succeeded him in 1804[219], according to records in the Baldwyn archives quoted by Duckett. In 1809 Baldwyn Encampment communicated with the Grand Conclave in London to obtain acknowledgement of the Rights and Privileges of our Encampment of being from time immemorial.[220] Duckett goes on to say

'the same year, Baldwyn Encampment assented to the rule of London "for so long as the Latter kept to the old customs and usages. Should any deviation from the regular Proceedings take place, then Baldwyn Conclave (sic) would resume their Ancient Independence and Usage as heretofore observed."

In the event for 50 years, initially under the guidance of Knights Husenbeth and Goldwyer, the Camp of Baldwyn went its own way, administering its idiosyncratic 'Rite of Seven Degrees', in spite of occasional attempts to effect a reconciliation.

In addition the Camp of Baldwyn also maintained its right to warrant Encampments and warranted the Percy Encampment in Adelaide, South Australia on 20 August 1858. The encampment was consecrated by the Very

Eminent Knight Percy Wells, who had resigned his Offices as Grand Chancellor and as Provincial Grand Master of Somerset before going to live in the antipodes. As far as is known, it is the only Preceptory other than that of Baldwyn itself authorised to work the Baldwyn Ritual. This Preceptory was transferred to The Great Priory of South Australia when constituted in 1982.

3.7 THE RESURRECTED GRAND CONCLAVE
(PRE-UNION)

The successor of the Duke of Kent as Grand Master, Waller Rodwell Wright, was born at Bury St Edmunds in Suffolk in 1775, and was called to the Bar, thereafter serving twice as the Recorder of his native city (1801-1803 and 1806-1814). From 1803 to 1806 he was Consul-General of the Ionian Islands. Later he became Senior Justice in Malta from 1814 until his death there in 1826 at the comparatively early age of 51.

He was initiated into Freemasonry at Bury St Edmunds in a Lodge which no longer exists, and thereafter joined the Lodge of Antiquity No. 1, now No. 2, and also the Prince of Wales Lodge No. 412 now No. 259, both 'Red Apron' Lodges. In the Royal Arch he was appointed Grand Superintendent in and over Suffolk in 1801 and of Cambridgeshire in 1807, although he made way in the latter for the Reverend George Adam Browne[221] in 1810. The former he retained, for quite long periods *in absentia*, until his death. He also rose to high rank in the Royal Arch, being 'Grand Master J', that is Third Grand Principal, in the Moderns' Grand Chapter in 1802/3 and again in 1806/12.

A somewhat curious appointment in the Craft came his way in 1813 when he was appointed Provincial Grand Master of the Ionian Islands; curious because in the first place he was no longer residing there, and perhaps even more curiously because no English Lodge was formed there until 1861.[222] Before he left England to spend the remainder of his life in Malta he was issued with a Patent as the Island's Provincial Grand Master (the Province had a number of different titles during his stewardship), an office which he retained until his death.

Not only was Wright the Grand Master of the Order of Knights Templar but he was apparently the Founder of the Order of the Red Cross of Palestine, one of several 'Red Cross' Orders the inter-relationships of which it is almost impossible to unravel. However, before he departed for Malta, Wright installed the Duke of Sussex as Grand Master both of the Knights Templar and of the Red Cross of Palestine.

Waller had served the Templars well as their Grand Master. By the end of his term of office there were 48 encampments on the Roll of Grand Conclave; eight of those which were constituted during Wright's Grand Mastership are still working today.[223]

Grand Conclave, having been resurrected and restored to an active role, met before 1812 on several occasions. It appears that it was only to the annual conventions, those at which the Grand Officers of the year were invested, that the Knights throughout the Order were summoned; for the other meetings only the Grand Officers for the year, together with such other members of the Order whose presence was particularly required, were called upon to attend. Of these meetings there are definitive records in the form of printed proceedings from 1807 onwards. After two meetings at St Paul's Coffee House by the Cathedral the next set of Minutes shows that a move had been made to *Freemasons' Tavern* on the site of today's Freemasons' Hall in Great Queen Street.

In the Minutes of the Meeting on 12 April a growing irritation can be sensed with the Lodges and Chapters still claiming the authority to dispense the Chivalric Degrees by virtue of their Craft Warrants.

> '. . . . Several Crafts (sic) Lodges, held in Wigan and Warrington . . . . (having no lawful Warrant of this Order), were clandestinely installing Knights Templars, also a Crafts Lodge at Bury.'

Stern measures were required; the Grand Master waited upon the Royal Grand Patron. H.R.H. was pleased to issue a proclamation, copies of which were distributed to different parts of the country, intended to put a stop to such practices, but it is uncertain how far this succeeded in doing so!

Of perhaps greater interest is the account of the 'Grand Conclave of Emergency of Grand Officers' held on 30 January 1812. When the Royal Grand Patron, the Duke of Kent, arrived, . . . the Grand Officers arranged themselves in due order for his reception: His Highness was afterwards introduced by the two Grand Experts and two Aid du Camps (*sic*), and conducted to the throne in solemn form.

Then the Duke of Sussex arrived and was similarly introduced 'and conducted to his situation at the right of the M.E. Grand Master'. The Minutes of the previous Meeting having been read, the reason for this distinguished attendance became clear.

The Right Honourable Francis, Earl Moira, having been proposed, balloted for, and approved on the 23rd instant, and this meeting having been convoked for the purpose of installing his Lordship, the Noble Earl having therefore attended the Encampment, he was accordingly introduced by the Grand Orator, Provost and Hospitaller, and reported by the Senior Captain of the Lines. His Lordship was afterwards installed a Knight Templar, according to ancient form. The Grand Orator was pleased to explain the rise, progress and principles of the Order.

After this, ... His Royal Highness the Royal Patron was pleased to appoint His Royal Highness Frederick Augustus, Duke of Sussex to be Captain General of the Order. On this somewhat special occasion the Royal Grand Patron appears to have usurped the prerogative of the Grand Master by himself making the appointment, something which may have been the cause of the

Minute-taker becoming confused and recording the forenames of the Duke of Sussex in the wrong order. For the second time in this series of documents duties have been assigned to the 'Grand Orator' without any previous indication that this appointment was numbered among the Grand Officers.

Two Meetings later, on 5 May 1812 the Grand Master, Waller Rodwell Wright, proposed that the Duke of Sussex should succeed him. His proposition, seconded by the Deputy Grand Master, John Burckhardt, was carried unanimously. The Duke of Sussex, who had been born in 1773 the sixth son of King George III and had been Initiated in the Lodge *zur siegenden Wahrheit* in Berlin in 1798, was in some ways a curious choice. The Duke was Grand Master of the 'Modern' Grand Lodge which numbered among its Brethren many fierce opponents of Chivalric degrees such as that of the Knights Templar being included within the profession of 'Pure Antient Masonry'.

The Duke of Sussex was Installed in the Chair at a Meeting on 6 August 1812 to which he was admitted under an Arch of Steel. The Minutes go on to describe the ceremony of Installation in some detail, and also record that

> 'His Royal Highness, in an eloquent speech, returned his thanks to the Knights assembled, assuring them of his zealous attachment to the principles and determination to maintain the privileges, and promote the well-being, of the Order.'

3.8 AFTER THE UNION OF THE GRAND LODGES

In the same year that the Duke of Sussex accepted the Grand Mastership of the Knights Templar he was also appointed Deputy Grand Master of the Premier Grand Lodge, 'the Moderns'. In the following year, 1813, the Union of the two rival Grand Lodges at last came about with the Duke of Sussex as the first Grand Master of the United Grand Lodge of England.

That the Duke, and indeed any brother of the Craft, was entitled, when duly qualified, to attend meetings of the Order of Knights Templar was apparently recognised by the second paragraph of the Second of the Articles of Union which read in full:

> 'pure Ancient Masonry consists of three degrees and no more, viz., those of the Entered Apprentice, the Fellow Craft, and the Master Mason, including the Supreme Order of the Holy Royal Arch.
>
> 'But this article is not intended to prevent any Lodge or Chapter from holding a meeting in any of the degrees of the Orders of Chivalry according to the constitutions of the said Orders.'

Many Lodge and Chapters, and not only those in obedience to the Grand Lodge of the *Antients*, considered that their Warrants entitled them to hold such meetings as were set out in the second paragraph of Article II. Apparently those who drafted the Article were prepared to see such meetings continue. But the Article made no reference to the Orders of Chivalry being administered by Sovereign Masonic Bodies operating independently of the newly formed United Grand Lodge.

This placed the Duke in a difficult position as Grand Master of one such Sovereign body. There were those within the United Grand Lodge who felt strongly that the chivalric Orders were outside the Masonic pale,[224] and who might, if they considered themselves sufficiently provoked, independently revive the Grand Lodge of the Moderns, and thereby destroy the United Grand Lodge which had been so painfully conceived and brought to birth. But while this was undoubtedly a danger, if the Duke of Sussex wished the Order of Knights Templar to survive and to obtain exemption from the provisions of the 1799 Act, the Chivalric Orders had to remain Masonic bodies and to be seen by the authorities as such.

In 1817, four years after the Union of the two Grand Lodges, the 1799 *Unlawful Societies Act* was amended by the passing of *The Seditious Meetings Act*[225] at much the same time as the Supreme Grand Chapter of England was erected. For whatever reason the second paragraph of the second of the Articles of Union (which had become the Preliminary Declaration to the Regulations in the Book of Constitutions of the United Grand Lodge of England) seems to have been quietly swept under the carpet and omitted from later Editions of the Book of Constitutions. By now the Duke of Sussex was leaving the management of the affairs of the Knights Templars in the hands of Robert Gill and of John Christian Burckhardt, the Duke himself maintaining a discreet separation from the Order; as Handfield-Jones puts it, he quietly and unostentatiously concerned himself with no more than unofficial action to keep the Order alive. A meeting of Grand Conclave took place on 31 January 1820, but it was not again summoned for more than twenty years.

It has already been noted that much archival material was lost when the house of Robert Gill in Soho was burnt to the ground in 1820. Gill himself died soon afterwards. For more than twenty years after this the Order of Knights Templar was largely guided by Burckhardt alone who acted *de facto* as what today would be called the 'Pro Grand Master'. Not only was the Duke of Sussex unwilling to offer any provocation to the opponents of Degrees outside the Craft by holding further meetings of Grand Conclave but it was not until 1834 that the he even considered it expedient to put his own name to the Warrant of a newly-formed Encampment. This was the Royal Sussex Encampment at Torquay[226] although by this time Burckhardt, as 'Deputy Grand Master *ad vitam*' seems to have quietly warranted a few other encampments himself.[227]

The Order of the Knights Templar was not the only Christian Order outside the Craft which the Duke of Sussex found something of an embarrassment in his determination to preserve the Union. He had no wish to excite controversy by actively supporting another chivalric order, known in England and Wales as 'The Ancient and Accepted Rite'. However, in 1819, only six years after The Union, while the flames of controversy had not yet died down, a Frenchman Joseph D'Obernay had manoeuvred The Duke into an extremely difficult position.

D'Obernay, the emissary of the French so called '*Prado*' Supreme Council of the Thirty-Third Degree, had first visited Ireland where he had received some support from the Irish Council of Rites which, in that Country, controlled both the Knights Templar and that which later became known as the Eighteenth Rose Croix Degree. The Duke of Leinster, the Grand Master of the Craft in Ireland, gave D'Obernay a letter of introduction to the Duke of Sussex.

Having presented this, D'Obernay then proposed that there should be a Supreme Council of Great Britain of the Ancient and Accepted Rite with the Duke of Sussex at its head. The Duke was on the horns of a dilemma. Rightly or wrongly he accepted the dubious regularity of the *Prado* Supreme Council.

If he openly agreed to set up a British Supreme Council under its auspices, there would be a very real danger that some of the more conservative English Craft Brethren might break away and undo the Union so painfully contrived. But if he refused to establish a Supreme Council of the Thirty-Third Degree, Britain, including England, would be 'unoccupied territory' where the *Prado* Supreme Council itself, under the provisions of the Grand Constitutions of the Ancient Accepted Rite of 1786, would be entitled to establish a Daughter Supreme Council, membership of which would certainly be attractive to many English members of the Craft. Not only this, but, if it were established, there would be nothing to prevent it conferring the three Craft Degrees as well as the Higher Degrees of the Order, and England would again have two different Jurisdictions of Craft Freemasons.

According to the Grand Constitutions of the Ancient and Accepted Rite a Supreme Council comes into being when three Sovereign Grand Inspectors General have been appointed to it. The Duke's solution to the problem with which he was confronted was therefore first formally to agree to the formation of a Supreme Council. D'Obernay then conferred the Thirty-Third degree on the Duke of Sussex and his confidential Masonic secretary Hippolyte da Costa. At the same time the Duke of Leinster had authorised the Duke of Sussex to receive the Degree by proxy on his behalf. The Duke of Sussex first appointed Leinster and da Costa to the newly formed Supreme Council, thus providing the necessary number of three. He then *prevaricated* by informing the Council of the *Prado* that 'it is not proposed to fill the number for the Supreme Council for England, Great Britain, Ireland and the possessions in America and the Indies until everything has been arranged and the location chosen, which has not yet been done'. With himself, Leinster, and da Costa the only members of the Council the Duke then allowed it to wither peacefully on the vine after the 'British' members had accepted Honorary Membership of the *Prado* Council and had reciprocally conferred the corresponding distinction upon their new found French Brethren.

The relevance of this curious proceeding to the history of the Knights Templar in England and Wales is that for many years English Encampments of Knights Templar had been conferring two progressive Degrees, *Rosae Crucis* and *Kadosh* or *Ne Plus Ultra,* over each of which the Grand Conclave exercised little or no control.

These were very similar to, though not identical with, the 18th Rose Croix and the 30th Kadosh Degrees which were worked, *inter alia,* under the several Supreme Councils which were now established around the world in many national territories. In most, if not all, English Knights Templar Encampments under the Grand Conclave it was customary for a Knight Templar to have these two Degrees successively conferred upon him shortly after his Installation.

However, there were many Brethren, notably Dr. Thomas Crucefix, who were not only anxious for a 'real' Supreme Council of the Thirty-Third Degree to be formed in England, but also one which would take under its wing both *Rosae Crucis* and *Ne Plus Ultra* which they considered had no part in the Order of Knights Templar but rightfully belonged to the Ancient and Accepted Rite. During the lifetime of the Duke of Sussex this could be no more than a pipe-dream.

The Duke of Sussex died in 1843.

3.9 AFTER THE DEATH OF THE DUKE OF SUSSEX

When the Duke of Sussex died in 1843 there may have been no more than thirty Encampments of Knights Templar surviving in England, among the most influential of which were probably The Cross of Christ[228], Faith and Fidelity *(Now No. 26)* and Mount Calvary*(Now 'D')* in London, Antiquity *(Now No. 1)* in Bath, and Baldwyn *(Now 'C')* in Bristol. No meeting of Grand Conclave had been summoned for more than twenty years.

The Deputy Grand Master, John Christian Burckhardt was over seventy years old in 1843, and he had no ambitions to succeed the Duke of Sussex as head of the Military, Masonic and Religious Order. There was no other obvious successor, and Burckhardt, as the Deputy Grand Master in charge, took his time before recommending a suitable replacement to his Brother Knights. It was nearly three years after the Duke's death before Burckhardt summoned a meeting of Grand Conclave at which he nominated Colonel Charles Kemeys Kemeys Tynte for election as the Most Eminent and Supreme Grand Master of the Knights Templar of England and Wales.

Charles Tynte had been Installed as a Knight of the Order in London in The Chapter of Observance of the Seven Degrees on 15 March 1818 probably by Burckhardt himself. He had joined William Tucker's Holy Cross Conclave (of which he became the Commander in 1846) at Coryton Park near Axminster many years before its move to Exeter to become the Union and Rougemont Preceptory *(Now 'F')*. Tynte had also previously been appointed by Burckhardt as Provincial Grand Commander for Dorsetshire.

Grand Conclave approved the nomination, and on 2 February 1846 Tynte replied to Burckhardt's 'offer letter' writing, *inter alia:*

> 'I hasten to answer your letter announcing the high Honour proposed to me by the Grand Conclave of "Masonic Knights Templar" in selecting me to Preside over that Order, as Successor to my late Honoured & lamented Royal Friend & Master H.R.H. the Duke of Sussex.
>
> You inform me that "the choice of the Meeting was <u>unanimous</u>." I cannot then hesitate to answer Such a Call, with the Same Spirit of confidence & mutual kindness of feeling with which the Members of the Grand Conclave have honoured me'.[229]

On 26 February 1846 the Grand Conclave confirmed Tynte's Election and he was Installed as Most Eminent and Supreme Grand Master on 3 April 1846. Fresh Statutes of the Order had been prepared and the newly-installed Grand Master approved them at the Meeting. As his Deputy Tynte appointed William

Stuart, who was also a member of The Chapter of Observance of the Seven Degrees. During Tynte's Grand Mastership some thirty Encampments were warranted, the majority of which are still in existence although some of these are no longer part of the English jurisdiction and exist under the Sovereign Great Priories of Australia or Canada.

The revised Statutes, which were printed by command of the Most Eminent and Supreme Grand Master in August 1846 over the name of W. H. White, Grand Chancellor,[230] were divided into 22 serially numbered Articles. These are only briefly reviewed here because seven years later they were superseded by a further revision which clarified some of the more general statements included in 1846. For example, Article VI gave the Grand Master authority to 'appoint Provincial Grand Commanders for districts at a distance from the Metropolis' without specifying what was meant by 'at a distance'. In the matter of the holding a Grand Conclave, the 1809 'Constitutions' had removed the fixed day on which this should be held and left it to be selected by the Knights Companions in Grand Conclave; in Section 1 of Article VII in 1846 it was laid down that:

> A Grand and Royal Chapter is to be convoked annually, at the Friday immediately preceding Good Friday, at three o'clock in the afternoon; the solemnity of the day is to begin with public worship of the Supreme Architect of the Universe and by making offerings for the poor. An exhortation is to be given by the Grand Prelate. The Grand Officers are to be appointed by the Grand Master for the ensuing year. The Knights Companions are to eat the bread of thankfulness and drink the cup of cheerfulness with the Grand Officers. Should the business at any time to be brought before the annual meeting be of such a length, as not conveniently to be disposed of at that meeting, an adjournment may be made for the purpose of proceeding thereon, or it shall be competent to the Most Eminent Grand Master to order a special Grand Conclave to be convened by summons for that purpose.

Evidently in 1846, while the Christian and charitable basis of the Order is stressed as all-important, it was not foreseen in these Statutes that extensive business would be brought before the Annual Meeting of Grand Conclave. It appears to be assumed in the Statutes that 'business' will be confined to little more than the appointment of the Grand Officers (not forgetting the payment of their Fees of Honour, specifically noting that 'Promotion from Second to First Grand Captain entails a repetition of the fee of honour'!) and then the election of the 'committee for general purposes' in which the administration of the Order was evidently to be vested. Indeed, Article VII,6 specifically provides that:

> "as there will be only an annual meeting of Grand Conclave, its *(that is, the Committee's)* regulations shall become law without confirmation unless it shall be

considered advisable by the Grand Master to call an especial Grand Conclave for the purpose of confirmation within one month".

In accordance with the earlier tradition, evidently the annual Meeting of Grand Conclave was seen as a ceremonial rather than an administrative occasion, and the reference to the Knights Companions 'eating the bread of thankfulness and drinking the cup of cheerfulness' presumably does not refer to a secular banquet but rather to formal proceedings analogous to those which then took place in a private Encampment.

Articles VIII – XXI are concerned with affairs in private Chapters of Encampment. Article XXI lays down that

> Every Encampment ought to assemble on the 11th day of March annually, in memory of the martyrdom of Jacques de Molay, to humble themselves before the Great Disposer of Events, and to make offerings for the poor and needy.

At the end of the 1846 Statutes there is a 'Memorandum' stating that 'The articles relating to the costume proper to be worn by Knights Companions, will not be printed until further directions are given by the Grand Master'. In fact it took two further years to provide the Regulations for 'Costume'; perhaps there were problems in reconciling the differing patterns of 'costume' worn in various Encampments.

For the meeting of Grand Conclave on 26 March 1847 the Minutes include no more than the list of officers, which no longer comprises only the five Officers together with the Registrar, Treasurer and Equerries corresponding to those which were customary in a private Encampment. Besides the Grand Master and his Deputy (William Stuart), there were now twenty-nine Grand Offices of which two or three were not filled on this occasion[231].

Burckhardt was still on the active list but had demoted himself to Grand Sub-Prior. The Minutes for the Meeting on 14 April 1848 are similar, except that the newly adopted 'Costume Regulations' are appended to them. This is a pamphlet of three folios, signed by C. B. Clayton, Grand Chancellor.

> An Apron ('Badge') was to be worn, of white kid-skin 13½" by 15½" bordered by a black watered silk ribbon 4" broad. In the centre of the apron 'a Red Cross Paté, in velvet or embroidery'. Attached to the apron 'A belt of black silk velvet, five inches broad in front and three inches broad behind'. At its front the belt had the 'Emblems of Mortality in a triangle', silver for Knights who had not presided over an Encampment, and gold or silver-gilt for all others.

> A black watered-silk ribbon, 4 inches wide, worn over the right shoulder provided a sash or baldric.

The sword was suspended from the sash, the guard to consist of two isosceles triangles, the handle gilt for Officers of Grand Conclave, and black for all other Knights.

The Cross worn by Knights Companions was specified in detail –

Of red and white enamel in gold, swallow-tailed, surmounted by a celestial crown; – to be worn pendant from a Syrian ribbon, two inches broad, the cross to measure diametrically two and a half inches.

The regalia for Grand Officers is 'differenced' by three white stripes on the badge and sash – nothing is said about Provincial Officers, or even of Provincial Grand Commanders of whom there were 7 in 1846.[232] After the final paragraph there is an 'N.B.' –

'These Regulations are to be considered imperative on those only who may henceforth be installed or who may be appointed to Office in Grand Conclave'.

It may therefore be assumed that, for example, the 'Provincial Commanders' had already adopted some form of distinctive 'costume', but, so far as is known, there is no indication of its composition.

These revised Statutes did nothing, however, to address the still outstanding concerns about the relevance of the *Rosae Crucis* and *Kadosh* degrees worked in many, if not most, Knight Templar Encampments, and it is this topic which generates the next major change for the Order.

Very little time had been wasted after the death of the Duke of Sussex in taking steps to establish a Supreme Council of the Ancient and Accepted Rite in England. Even if those concerned had known of its existence (which they may well not have done, so well-hidden had the Duke of Sussex maintained it) the embryonic Council established by the Duke could safely be ignored because, by the Duke's death, it had fallen into desuetude, no longer having the essential membership of three Sovereign Grand Inspectors General.

England could therefore once more be regarded by the outside world as 'unoccupied territory'. Most of those senior English Freemasons who looked forward to the establishment of an English Supreme Council had no wish to see a further invasion by one of the French Councils of doubtful legitimacy. In spite of this it was known that Dr. Henry Beaumont Leeson, Second Grand Captain in the Grand Conclave of Knights Templar in 1848, was already having discussions with one of the French Supreme Councils which the two Jurisdictions in the United States of America, two of the oldest Supreme Councils in the world, considered irregular. On this account Robert Crucefix, at the time incidentally the Master of Ceremonies in Grand Conclave, entered with some urgency into negotiations for a Patent from the Northern Jurisdiction of the USA which was still a Trinitarian Christian body, something which the Supreme Council of the Southern Jurisdiction, – 'the Mother Supreme Council of the World' – had ceased to be.

By 1847 not only had Robert Crucefix received his Patent from America and was establishing the Supreme Council of England ('and Wales' was added later), but also moves were afoot in some of the more influential Knights Templar Encampments to separate out the Degrees of *Rosae Crucis* and *Kadosh*. The so-called 'Council', perhaps more accurately the 'Standing Committee', of the Encampment of Faith and Fidelity in London, had been asked to consider the matter. Its President, Henry Udall, reported the Committee's conclusions to the Encampment Meeting on 31 January 1846 at which the Knights Companions accepted Udall's proposition that the Encampment should be divided into three semi-autonomous components. Henry Udall[233] would be the Grand Superintendent of the Encampment and continue to be President of the Council. Within the Encampment only the Degrees of Knight Templar, Knight of Malta, and Mediterranean Pass would be worked. There would be an 'Illustrious College of Knights Kadosh and *Ne Plus Ultra*' with Richard Lea Wilson as its President, and finally Henry Beaumont Leeson would be 'Most Wise Sovereign of the Sovereign Chapter of Princes Rose Croix'.

The subsequent translation of *Rosae Crucis* and *Kadosh* from Templar Encampments under the Grand Conclave to Rose Croix (18th degree) and to Grand Elected Knight Kadosh (30th degree) under the Supreme Council of the Ancient and Accepted Rite of England must have been eased by many of the first members of the new Supreme Council already being, or were shortly to become, holders of senior Office in Grand Conclave. In 1847 Henry Udall was appointed Second Grand Captain, and in the following year he was succeeded by Henry Leeson. Other early members of the English Supreme Council to hold Office in Grand Conclave were Matthew Dawes, Henry Emly, for many years Grand Almoner, William Tucker, and Captain G. A. Vernon. Perhaps the most influential in effecting the transfer of authority may have been John Astell Deacon Cox, Grand Registrar of Grand Conclave from 1848 to 1860, while also being Grand Secretary General of the Supreme Council from 1857 to 1861.

Thus it was that a seamless transfer could be made, the first Warrant (or 'Patent' as it was then called) for a Rose Croix Chapter under the new Supreme Council being presented to Dr. Leeson at a regular meeting of the Sovereign Chapter of Rose Croix of the Faith and Fidelity Encampment, the Chapter thereby severing its allegiance to Grand Conclave and transferring to the Supreme Council 33° of the Ancient and Accepted Rite.

A similar turn of events took place after Thomas Pryer, another of the earliest members of the Supreme Council, was installed as the successor to

John Harris as Eminent Commander of the Mount Calvary Encampment of Knights Templar on St John's Day, 27 December 1846. As Faith and Fidelity had done, a Committee was set up to consider the future conduct of the 'Superior Degrees' in the Encampment. When its deliberations were reported to the Knights it was resolved to seek a Patent from the Supreme Council for the Rose Croix Chapter; this was presented on 6 June 1848. Other Encampments followed suit with greater or less enthusiasm and for many years new Chapters Rose Croix were seldom Patented other than where there was a Knights Templar Encampment in the neighbourhood. With the exception of 'The Camp of Baldwyn' in Bristol and that of 'Antiquity' in Bath, a complete separation of *Rosae Crucis* and *Kadosh* from the Knights Templar Order was before long painlessly effected.

However, it is not known how much local grief was caused by the separation of these two degrees. It may well have been that the lead given by the London Encampments, and the efforts of those Brethren of the Supreme Council who were also Officers of Grand Conclave, and the leadership by Provincial Grand Commanders resulted in the relatively smooth transition (other than in the Baldwyn and Antiquity Encampments).[234]

However, there were some regional anomalies, one noted example being the Craft Lodge of Prince George (now No. 308) at Bottoms, Stansted in the Calder Valley of Yorkshire. This Craft lodge, despite having close associations with an early Knight Templar Preceptory (Prince Edward Preceptory No. 18 warranted 30 October 1811), continued to work the *Rosa Croix, Ne Plus Ultra,* and other degrees until 1892, and indeed, designated itself as a Supreme Council from c.1860 until accepting the authority of the (London) Supreme Council in 1892. It is not known how many other Craft Lodges adopted a similar view.

It is, perhaps, curious that such a significant alteration in the work of the Encampments and, indeed in the nature of the Order, did not find its way into the Minutes of the Grand Conclave, but nothing is specifically recorded about it at Meetings of Grand Conclave held on 30 March 1849, 22 March 1850, and 11 April 1851.

At the latter meeting the accounts were approved and some minor amendments were made to the Statutes, together with the approval of a Resolution that a copy of the amended Statutes be sent to each Provincial Commander, with no reference to the transfer of the *Rosae Crucis.* However the most important business before Grand Conclave on this occasion was to receive a revised Ritual of the Ceremonies to be carried out in Encampments, an evident necessity in view of the severance of the *Rosae Crucis* and *Kadosh* Degrees.[235] It was resolved that this Ritual should be adopted and that a copy sent to each Provincial Grand Commander and to each Eminent Commander of an Encampment; the latter were each to be charged one guinea (£1.05p.) for it. At the Meeting on 14 May 1852 further changes to the Statutes were approved. At this meeting Captain MacLeod Moore was invested as Second Grand Captain; a few years later he was to figure prominently in the affairs in Canada of both the Order of the Temple and of the Ancient and Accepted Rite.

At the meeting on 15 May 1853, such time as was available was again taken up by a discussion of amendments to the Statutes, but the Minutes also include a copy of the resolution of the Committee that a Testimonial be presented to Colonel Tynte 'in gratitude for the services which he has rendered to the Order and his unceasing exertions to promote its welfare'. The Minutes record that the subscriptions already made by 40 individuals and four Encampments totalled £63.19s.0d, and, in calling for further subscriptions, an engraving of a magnificent silver epergne is included.

An 'especial Grand Conclave' appears to have been held to approve the finally revised Statutes. The title page of the approved version announces them as 'The Statutes for the Government of the Royal Exalted Religious & Military Order of Masonic Knights Templar in England & Wales as Resolved and Agreed on at the Grand Conclave held on the 13th day of July 1853'.

3.10 THE STATUTES OF 1853 AND THEREAFTER

The text of the Statutes of 1853 is preceded by a History of Grand Conclave. Its author refrains from embarking on a traditional history in the Andersonian tradition and does not seek to trace the ancestry of the Masonic Knights Templar back to the medieval Orders; he does not even mention Ramsay, Larmenius, *de Lintot,* or *von Hund*, but takes the position in 1791 as his starting-point:

'The flourishing state of Symbolic Masonry, under the protection of H.R.H. The Prince of Wales (afterwards George IV), Grand Master, and the great increase of Royal Arch-Chapters, patronized by H.R.H. The Duke of Clarence (afterwards William IV) having animated the Masonic Knights Templar, of St John of Jerusalem, &c. with a desire to revive their ancient royal religious and military Order, they confederated and unanimously selected their Brother and Knight Companion, Thomas Dunckerley (sic), of Hampton Court Palace, in the County of Middlesex, Grand Master of the Confraternity under the Patronage of H.R.H. Prince Edward (afterwards Duke of Kent); and on the 24th day of June, 1791, a Grand and Royal Conclave was held, by which the ancient Statutes of the Order were revised, re-enacted and unanimously approved. On the 10th day of April 1809, a Grand and Royal Conclave was held, according to ancient form, under the sanction of H.R.H. Edward Duke of Kent, Royal Grand Patron of the Order, and in the presence of the Most Eminent Grand Master, Waller Rodwell Wright, when the Statutes of the Order, passed on 24th day of June 1791, were revised, and with sundry alterations, confirmed. On the 6th day of August, 1812, H.R.H. the Duke of Sussex was installed Grand Master of the Order, and gave his sanction and approval of the Statutes as revised in 1809. These Statutes were subsequently again revised by Grand Conclave, and with the alterations then made, received the approval and confirmation of the Most Eminent and Supreme Grand Master, Sir Knight Colonel C. K. K. Tynte, on his installation on the 3rd day of April, 1846. And at the Grand Conclave held on the 13th May 1853, it was resolved, that the Statutes then revised and agreed on to be promulgated amongst the Order. The Committee for General Purposes have, therefore, caused this edition of the Statutes to be printed, and have directed that each copy shall be signed at the end thereof by the Grand Chancellor or Grand Vice-Chancellor'.[236]

The Regulations are set out in Sections, each with a series of numbered paragraphs starting at '1' in each Section, which are themselves unnumbered; this makes unambiguous reference to a particular Regulation somewhat difficult. The first Regulation in the first Section, which is headed 'OF THE GRAND CONCLAVE', starts rather splendidly:

1. The public interests of the Order as a collective body shall be regulated by a general convocation of all the Encampments on record in England and Wales and its Dependencies, represented by their respective Eminent Commanders.[237]

The remaining eighteen Regulations in this Section first set out the composition of Grand Conclave; this is followed by the procedure for conducting its Meetings, together with its powers which are described in considerable detail. The next Section deals with the Appointment of Grand Officers, again not forgetting to specify their respective Fees of Honour! This is followed by Sections dealing with the powers of the Grand Master, the Deputy Grand Master, the Provincial Grand Commanders, the Grand Chancellor and the Grand Vice-Chancellor, Grand Treasurer, Grand Registrar and Grand Almoner, none of which contain anything particularly noteworthy.

This is followed by a Section 'OF THE COMMITTEE' in which its composition is set out. Its membership included, in addition to the *ex officio* members whose presence would be expected (Grand Master, Deputy Grand Master, Grand Chancellor, Grand Treasurer, etc.) 'the Very Eminent Provincial Grand Commanders' of whom at this date there were ten,[238] together with four nominees of the Grand Master and five elected by the Grand Conclave.

This committee of twenty-six members, for which it was laid down that there would be five statutory meetings annually, must have constituted a somewhat unmanageable governing body to which the new Statutes gave wide-ranging powers.

There is nothing which occasions much surprise in the following two Sections, 'OF PROVINCIAL GRAND CONCLAVES' and 'OF PRIVATE ENCAMPMENTS', save perhaps that the minimum fee for Installation in an Encampment was increased to what was in those days the large sum of three guineas (£3.15p.).[239]

The Section 'AS TO REGISTRATION AND CERTIFICATES &c.' contains the provisions that each Encampment must procure a Certificate of Registration from Grand Conclave for every Knight installed within it, at a cost of 7s. 6d. (37½ p.); Annual Dues of 1/- (5p.) had to be paid for every member. Grand Officers could receive a Diploma or Certificate from Grand Conclave on payment of 7s. 6d., and 'No Encampment shall grant any private certificate whatsoever to any Knight of the Order . . . . and no Encampment nor any of the members thereof, shall on any pretence whatsoever make any charge or receive any fee for any private Certificate issued by the Encampment' – (which latter is a curious provision if the Encampment was not in any case permitted to issue such a Certificate!).

The Section 'AS TO WARRANTS AND PATENTS OF CONSTITUTION' provided that a petition for a new Encampment had to be signed by at least seven Knights of the Order,[240] and the 'Warrant or Patent' would cost five guineas (£5.25p.) It is perhaps indicative of the need at this time still to encourage Encampments which considered themselves to have 'Time Immemorial' status to come under the Banner of Grand Conclave[241] that

4. Although Encampments take precedence according to the dates of their respective warrants it shall be lawful for the Grand Master to order and direct, in any warrant of confirmation of any Encampment, that such Encampment shall take precedence from such time as the Grand Master shall think fit.

It is perhaps, the final Section 'AS TO COSTUME' which is of most interest today. These new Regulations considerably amended those promulgated in 1846 as if recognising that there was a certain vanity about the outward and visible signs of status even among those who were members of an organisation pre-eminently devoted to humble charitable relief. This now provided that Provincial Grand Commanders were also to be distinguished by three white stripes on sash and apron, and evidently were now recognised as Grand Officers. Provincial Officers 'ranking above the Provincial Grand Chamberlain' were now entitled to have one distinguishing white stripe on sash and apron and, like Grand Officers, to have gilt handles for their swords.

The Crosses, Stars and Jewels, all of which are illustrated, are generally similar to those worn today, other than those badges of office then prescribed for Officers of Grand and Provincial Conclaves and for those of private Encampments. The 'Cloak or mantle' was to be made of 'white camlet, with a cape or hood, on the left shoulder the Cross, in red silk, which the wearer shall be entitled to wear'. For Knights below the rank of present or past Eminent Commander of an Encampment, this Cross was to be a Cross Patée. The Jewels denoting rank were suspended from a collar of black silk watered ribbon (differenced by white stripes according to rank as for the sash or baldric). Except for the Grand Master and his Deputy, and past and present Provincial Commanders (who wore Cross Jewels similar to those worn today) all Officers of Grand Conclave, Provincial Grand Conclaves, and of private Encampments, wore suspended from the collar, 'a red Cross Patée, three inches in diameter, with a white circle in the centre, one inch and a quarter in diameter'. On the white circle was depicted the symbol of the office and it was further directed that 'the names of the respective offices be written on the circle in old English characters'.[242]

The Minutes for the meetings in 1854 and 1855 do not seem to have been printed, but a letter to the Grand Chancellor, Henry Emly, dated 11 April 1854 announced the receipt by the Hugh de Payens Chapter in Canada of its Patent from the Grand Conclave, also enclosing the Roll of Officers with the formidable Captain (as he still was then) MacLeod Moore at their head.

Emly, Grand Chancellor from 1851 to 1854, was succeeded in 1855 by John Masson, John Halsey Law continuing as Grand Vice Chancellor. Masson was evidently a man of great energy apparently with adequate spare time to spend on the affairs of the Order. From the time of his appointment the Minutes of the Proceedings of Grand Conclave were considerably expanded, containing for the first time not only a full statement of the Order's Accounts signed by Masson himself in 1855 (although in the list of Officers Eminent Knight J. N. Tomkins appears as Grand Treasurer) but also a List of Encampments. This list, repeated and up-dated in all subsequent Minutes of Grand Conclave's proceedings, gives very full information about each Encampment – Title, where held, dates of meetings, date of Warrant, and name of 'Eminent Commander per last return'.

In November 1856 the Encampment of Baldwyn again made overtures to the Grand Conclave in London to effect a reconciliation with S. E. Taylor[243], the Deputy Grand Superintendent, being entrusted with the negotiations. On 31 July 1857 the Grand Superintendent, Davyd Nash, reported to a General Convocation of the Order in Bristol that the talks had failed 'owing to the unmasonic and presumptuous conduct of some members of the Grand Conclave' and announced that 'the ancient Grand and Royal Encampment would now be revived by an Encampment from time immemorial under the Constitutions of 1780'.[244] All this was incorporated in what became known as 'The Circular Letter'. It was addressed to the rulers of the Order 'Throughout the Four Quarters of the Globe' and announced 'the revival and re-establishment of the Supreme Grand and Royal Encampment'. The 'Letter' continues by pointing out, *inter alia,*

'From the year 1820 to the year 1844, a period of 24 years, no communication of any kind took place between the Grand Conclave at London and the Baldwyn Encampment at Bristol, the Grand Conclave was in fact, during the whole of that period of 24 years, in a state of abeyance, while during the same period the Order was steadily and prosperously maintained in Bristol, and during a large portion of the same period also in Bath.'

The letter goes on to point out that

'… the Sir Knights of Bristol and Bath took no part in the election of Colonel Tynte as Grand Master and ultimately refused, for reasons deemed by the then members of the Order From Time Immemorial, just and proper, to concur.'

The Circular Letter further stated that the Camp of Antiquity at Bath (which had 'received a large accession of members') together with the Camp of Baldwyn, as the two 'Time Immemorial' Encampments, were 'desirous of uniting themselves in fraternal union' with those 'holding under the London Grand Conclave'. They had been prepared to forgo some of their immemorial rights and privileges if they were received as 'welcome and honoured associates'. The letter then claims that 'the Grand Conclave repulsed this offered alliance and these overtures of friendship, and required that the Encampments of Bristol and Bath should appear as humble petitioners before the Grand Conclave, for recognition and admission to its ranks.'

Inevitably this caused the Camps of Baldwyn and Antiquity to withdraw, and they were then determined 'to live according to the same laws, ordinances, and customs, as their predecessors.' The 'Letter' then also deplored the surrender of the Degree of *Knights Rosae Crucis* 'to another and different Masonic body' which it described as 'selling its birthright for a mess of pottage'. This paragraph of the 'Circular Letter' is transcribed in Appendix F to indicate the real sense of deprivation felt by many Knights Templar at the assumption by the Supreme Council of the Ancient and Accepted Rite of the *Rosae Crucis* and *Kadosh* Degrees, and the tone of the paragraph perhaps makes it even more surprising that this was accomplished with so little difficulty first in London and then in other parts of the country.

Nothing of this finds its way into the printed proceedings of Grand Conclave for 1857, which are similar to those of 1856, except that this time the Grand Treasurer and the Audit Committee have been allowed to sign the Accounts themselves! The blue paper on which the minutes of the proceedings are printed contain a warning in red ink enjoining 'circumspection' in the reception of visiting Knights, who must not only be proved but also must acknowledge fealty to the Grand Master – an acknowledgement that there were problems not only in Bristol and Bath but that they were also beginning to arise in Devon and Cornwall.

The Camp of Baldwyn then demonstrated its claimed independence from the Grand Conclave in London by issuing warrants for Encampments at Birmingham (Camp of Ascalon), Warwick (Holy Rood), Salisbury (Vale Royal), and Highbridge (Jehoshaphat). As a further act of defiance, the (presumably Baldwyn) Degree of Rose Croix was worked at these Encampments. The Camp of Baldwyn also warranted the Percy Encampment in Adelaide, South Australia, consecrated by the Very Eminent Knight Percy Wells, who had resigned his Offices as Grand Chancellor and as Provincial Grand Master of Somerset before going to live in the antipodes. (It is still the only Preceptory other than that of Baldwyn itself authorised to work the Baldwyn Ritual.)

As the Order expanded, Grand Conclave was becoming a more formal body, following the example of the United Grand Lodge of England in the way it ordered its affairs. A further step forward was taken at the Meeting on 14 May 1858, when a Report by the Grand Chancellor was for the first time included in the Proceedings of its Annual meeting. In the Report then given by Masson, the first item was the Indian Mutiny Relief Fund, Grand Conclave adding the sum of Fifty Guineas (£52.50p.) to the donations totalling approximately £120 already received not only from Provinces and Encampments in England but also from the Encampment of Richard Coeur de Lion No. 54 in Canada West.

Masson concluded his Report by saying –

'Finally the Grand Chancellor has intimated to Grand Conclave, that as the Ritual it has adopted has received the marked approval, and accordance of Knights Templars, in conformity throughout the Christian world, he has in preparation a System of Examination in Sections with a lecture, in strict accordance with the said Ritual and Masonic History of the Order, which, under due obligation, he will have pleasure in dedicating to the Most Eminent and Supreme Grand Master, as a mark of his homage and respect, to be accessible, through Provincial Grand Commanders and Eminent Commanders, under his own Sign manual and with such caution and regulation as to the expense, as the Grand Conclave may determine, and whatever surplus may accrue therefrom shall be donated to the Funds of the Grand Conclave.'

Other business transacted at the Meeting included the reduction in the number necessary to form a quorum for an Encampment Meeting (specifically for the benefit of Overseas Encampments in remote places) and the appointment of James Henderson of the Hugh de Payens Encampment in Kingston, Canada, as its Representative near the Grand Encampment of the United States of America, an appointment which was 'cordially appreciated' by W. B. Hubbard, the American Grand Master of Knights Templar, in a long and courteous letter. Hubbard went on to say that since the United States Grand Encampment now accepted the Grand Conclave as the body ruling over the Order in England; they had rejected a note from the Encampment of Baldwyn as being 'in violation of their vows and fealty'. This 'note' was presumably 'The Circular Letter' despatched by Davyd Nash in July 1857.

The Proceedings for 1859 followed the pattern of the preceding year, though with a considerably shorter Report from Masson. 120 new Members of the Order had been registered during the year. No reply had been received from either Baldwyn or from Antiquity to communications announcing their exclusion. Masson added -

The System of Examination in Sections in strict accordance with the Ritual of the Order, which was announced in the last annual Report to be in preparation, has recently by the care and labour of the Grand Chancellor been completed, and the Committee have authorised that officer to issue it at a charge of ten shillings (50p.) to encampments requiring a copy.

He concluded by saying that the Alms Fund had relieved the daughter of an Irish Knight Templar, and the respective widows of an English and of a Scotch (*sic*) Knight.

Grand Conclave was taking faltering steps to persuade the Knights Templar in Bristol to range themselves under its Banner. Its curious first act was to appoint Samuel Bryant 'Provincial Grand Commander of Gloucestershire and Bristol' although there were there no Encampments recognised by the Grand Conclave to rule. Discussions were however taking place; it was even suggested that Grand Conclave should warrant a new Encampment in Bristol itself, but this came to nothing.

The Report in 1860 began with the sad news of John Masson's untimely death. As Grand Chancellor he had done much to put in order the affairs of Grand Conclave, both administratively and by providing a standard ritual with a System of Examination. Masson's successor, John Halsey Law, told Grand Conclave that before his death Masson had intimated that the system of Examination . . . had been found to work so well and instructively, that the receipts exceeded the expense of getting it up … the surplus to form … the foundation of a Special Charity Fund.

'The System of Examination by Sections' had been published as *By the North-West Angle.* It consists of a series of questions and answers, analogous to the 'Lectures' in the three Craft Degrees, by which the Questioner took the Responder through the Ritual of Installation as a Knight Templar, with elaboration and explanation of each stage in the Ceremony. The publication was presented in two parts, one containing the 'Questions' and the other the 'Answers'.

By the North-West Angle was not the only contribution made by John Masson to the enlightenment and education of his Knights Companions. He delivered two lectures, which were subsequently printed, in which he expanded on the history of the two Orders of the Temple and of the Hospital. In the first of these lectures, after defending the Christian Orders against their detractors who said that Antient Freemasonry was completed by the Holy Royal Arch and needed nothing more, he presented an Andersonian history from pre-Christian times, through the Crusades and the subsequent destruction of the Templar Order, drawing attention to what he claimed to be the medieval monkish builders, and finally explaining how the Templars came to take refuge in Scotland. The second Lecture is largely devoted to the histories of the various medieval monkish Orders, and how Templar Masonry was spread in Scotland.[245]

When John Halsey Law succeeded Masson as Grand Chancellor it was evident that as a practising Barrister he would hardly be able to devote as much time to the affairs of the Order as Masson had done. In his Report to the Annual Meeting of Grand Conclave on 9 May 1860 Law said –

> The time has now arrived which your Companions have long anticipated, and which the late Grand Chancellor had himself felt must shortly occur, when the very laborious nature of the Grand Chancellor's office would require a fresh arrangement of his duties

and the appointment of some salaried officer to keep properly the Returns, and answer the numerous applications from existing and contemplated assemblies.

The Most Eminent and Supreme Grand Master, whose concurrence in their views on the subject the Committee are glad to announce, will propose to the Grand Conclave the name of a Knight well known to the Order, Fr. M. H. Shuttleworth, who has most kindly consented to accept the office of Vice Grand Chancellor, and on whom it is proposed the duties as above-mentioned should for the most part devolve. Towards enabling him the better to fulfil the same a proposal for an allowance of an annual sum from the funds of the Grand Conclave will be made to you from the chair.[246]

Charles Kemeys Kemeys Tynte, Most Eminent and Supreme Grand Master, died on 22 November 1860. During his Grand Mastership of some eleven years some fifty new Encampments had been added to the Roll, many of them overseas. Among the Encampments warranted towards the end of his reign was a travelling military Encampment, Excelsior No. 64, Warranted in 1860 in the 21st Regiment of Foot, The Royal North British (that is, 'Scots') Fusiliers, stationed then in Barbados. As with the ambulatory Craft lodges of the day, the postings hither and thither of the commissioned Officers, who for the most part constituted its membership, made it difficult to keep it going. In 1886 the last surviving knightly Fusilier was to return the Warrant to Grand Conclave. The establishment of Encampments abroad was probably accelerated by authorising colonial Provincial Commanders to issue dispensations to Petitioners so they could form and operate their Encampments while the Warrants therefor were being drawn up, signed and sealed and conveyed by whatever means to the Knights in foreign parts.[247]

William Stuart, the Great Sub Prior, was elected to succeed Charles Kemys Kemys Tynte as Grand Master on 21 January 1861 and he was Installed on the following 10 May by John Huyshe. Stuart, a Member of Parliament, the son of an Irish Archbishop, had joined The Chapter of Observance of the Seven Degrees on 16 January 1834, but it is not known when he was installed as a Knight Templar. However he had been a Founder and first Commander of the Watford Encampment in 1840 which eventually took his name and is now the Stuart Preceptory No. 28. Stuart had been the Senior Grand Warden in United Grand Lodge in 1833.

The Installation Ceremony of the new Grand Master was under the direction of W. J. Meymott, the Grand Director of Ceremonies, another Knight who was also prominent in the affairs of the Ancient and Accepted Rite. The wording of the ceremony was not identical with that in use today, but nothing which is nowadays considered essential was omitted, save that the Grand Master when Installed was greeted with 'Nine' and not 'Eleven'. However after he had been presented with his Baton, the Installing Officer went on to say 'Here also is this Abacus, the ancient and mystic staff of your holy predecessors, the commanders of the order'. After the Installation there was a

Banquet at which all the Knights were instructed 'to appear in Aprons, Sashes, Collars & Jewels (not Mantles). The Banners of Encampments & of Sir Kts. to be arranged in the hall before the banquet'.

3.11 THE APPROVED RITUAL OF 'KNIGHT OF MALTA'

Although in the earliest Ritual transcribed by John Knight there had been references to the 'Mediterranean Pass' and the 'Order of the Knights of Malta', little has survived of the Ritual by which they were conferred. At the beginning of the century no more is said than 'Give the Malta Sign and gripe' to the newly dubbed Knight Templar, without explanation, the Order now being John Knight's 20th Degree.

In his later revised Ritual; after the Installation of the candidate as a Knight Templar he is given the Mediterranean Pass which appears to involve little more than a lengthy perambulation followed by the communication of a Sign, Token and Word. This is followed by the 21st Degree, Knight of Malta. The Opening and Closing involved thirty-three Knocks, and the candidate takes a brief Obligation with a curious reference to acting 'in conjunction with my Colleagues of the Seven Nations' – presumably an explicit reference to the other seven of the eight *langues* or tongues into which the Medieval Chivalric Order of the Knights of St John was organised, but there is no hint the ritual was actually derived from any writings of the Knights of St John. After the Obligation, signs and words are communicated, but little detail is given.

One is left with the impression from this, and from other references, that the 'Malta' ceremonies were less developed than that of the Installation as a Knight Templar. Grand Conclave evidently considered that the 'Malta' Rituals, such as they were, should be put in order as that of Knight Templar had been by Masson, and around December 1862 a letter was issued by the Great Vice-Chancellor inviting Preceptories to report on conferring of the Malta Degree, and asking for a copy of the ritual used.

'The Ritual of the Knights of Malta' was 'sanctioned by the Grand Master at the Meeting of the Grand Conclave held on 8 May 1863 and recommended to be adopted by all the Priories'.

This Ritual is unusually detailed as if it were something with which the Knights Companions were unaccustomed; not only are there carefully drawn diagrams of the two tables with the positions of the Officers at each marked, but, for example, the method of laying their swords on the table is carefully illustrated, as is the procedure by which thirty-three Knocks are given at Opening and Closing. With three major exceptions, the procedure in this Ritual, including the conferment of the Mediterranean Pass in the Guard-room, is the same as that carried out today. The only differences of any significance are:

The five 'banners' are not displayed, but three veils, each with a guard, represent the passage of the Mediterranean Sea, and the five challenges ('B.L.D.R.A') are made by the three veil-guards, the First Lieutenant, and the Second Lieutenant.

Much of the oration now given in the 'Lecture' is given to the new Knight by the Eminent Prior as soon as he has created him 'a Knight Hospitaller of St John of Jerusalem, Palestine, Rhodes and Malta'. The 'Langues' are not enumerated in the oration, but the Eminent Prior makes it clear that the admission of the new Knight, habited as a Templar, is because 'When the Order of Knights Templar was suppressed by the cruelty and avarice of Pope Clement the Fifth and of Philip the Fair, King of France, many of those who remained joined themselves to the Knights Hospitaller of St John of Jerusalem.'

In the closing, the Testaments are presented to the Officers of the two Tables, ranged between them, just as is done today, except in the original Ritual they were presented by the Eminent Prior and not by the Reverend Prelate; carefully drawn diagrams again indicating precisely how this is done.

Otherwise, the greater part of the wording, including the questions and answers in the Opening and Closing and the reception of the Candidate, is identical with that used today – in the Rituals of the additional Orders outside the Craft it is not usual to find such a close correspondence between the words used in the mid-19th and the early 21st centuries.

That this Ritual was a novelty is indicated by the reaction in the Masonic Press, in which some correspondents strongly condemned it as a modern invention, but evidently to no avail.

The newly adopted 'Malta' ceremony was demonstrated at the meeting of Grand Conclave in May 1870, in the presence of the Prince of Wales – the first occasion when he displayed any interest in the Order – remaining to watch the new 'Malta' ceremony, his membership of the Higher Degrees of the Swedish Rite evidently being considered an adequate qualification for this.

3.12 RESTORATION OF RELATIONS
WITH THE CAMP OF BALDWYN

In the early years after William Stuart had been installed as Grand Master several contentious matters were outstanding, but none was of greater importance than the restoration of good relations with the Camp of Baldwyn at Bristol (and with that of Antiquity in Bath).

A General Convocation of the Camp of Baldwyn was held on 4 June 1861 at which it was agreed that some senior members of the Camp should once more seek a meeting with the Grand Conclave Committee in London to make clear to them the peculiar customs and practices of the Bristol Knights Templar dating from Time Immemorial. In the following November Grand Conclave agreed that the matter of the Camp of Baldwyn should, under certain conditions, be further discussed, in the hope of its recognition of William Stuart as Grand Master of the Order in England and Wales. Any agreement should be recorded in a 'permanent and legal document' embodying the arrangements. As a result of this on 6 December 1861 Grand Conclave considered 'a draft of a Charter of Union' presented by a delegation from the Camp of Baldwyn. The principal headings were that:

It was accepted that it was desirable that the Camp of Baldwyn and its affiliated bodies should acknowledge the supremacy of the Most Eminent and Supreme Grand Master presiding over the Grand Conclave in London;

For this to be conceded, it would be appropriate that the City and County of Bristol should be constituted as a separate and distinct District Commandery:

'on the grounds of Immemorial Custom' the Baldwyn Encampment should take precedence over all the Encampments on the Roll of the Grand Conclave of England and Wales the affiliated Encampments of Baldwyn should take precedence according to the dates of their existing Warrants.

There was some ambiguity about a further clause which stated that

'fees for Registration in the books of Grand Conclave would not be demanded from any of the affiliated Encampments, without it being stated whether this was only retrospective or whether it would apply to Encampments to be warranted in the future'.

The only obstacle to the acceptance of this document was that it was signed by Davyd Nash 'on behalf of the Encampment of Baldwyn' with the Triple Salem Cross of a 'Most Excellent and Supreme Grand Master'. Grand

Conclave refused to receive a document thus signed; it would have made it appear that it recognised 'the Grand and Royal Conclave in the Camp of Baldwyn' as a co-equal body which it was not prepared to do. The deputation, being as they said under an Oath of Allegiance to Davyd Nash, had no powers to make any alteration to the document unless released by him from their oaths.

The Knights of Baldwyn were sufficiently anxious to be re-united with their estranged brethren that Nash's resignation was called for and, on it being read to the assembled members of the Encampment, Knight Companion W. A. F. Powell was elected as Grand Superintendent of the Camp. This obstacle having been removed, on 9 May 1862 the Committee of Grand Conclave in London

> 'felt certain that every member of the Order will rejoice that Knights so well qualified as the members of those Encampments to fulfil the requirements of Templar Masonry, may now be welcomed by them as integral parts of the same body, and allied to them by the ties of Christian Masonic Fraternity.'[248]

The formal agreement was embodied in 'The Charter of Compact of 1862'. This is a document with a lengthy preamble which recounts, *inter alia,* that the Encampment of Baldwyn was 'constituted by a certain Charter of Compact the date whereof is from 'time immemorial' which was confirmed on 20 December 1780. The Charter sets out seven heads of agreement. (See **Appendix G**)

There is little doubt that this 'Compact' was not seen as wholly satisfactory by all Knights Companions of the Grand Conclave of the Encampment at Bristol 'From Time Immemorial'. Some had hoped that the 'Compact' would be seen as effecting a union of two equal negotiating parties with Baldwyn retaining a greater measure of self-government than as a 'separate and distinct District Commandery' – which would be in effect no more than just another Provincial Priory under the Grand Conclave. So anxious were the members of Grand Conclave to effect a union that further concessions might well have been conceded, but on 9 May 1862 what was done was done, and few would argue that this has not benefited the Order.

However there was little interference by Grand Conclave with Baldwyn's traditional manner of working which, for example, includes the conferring of the Malta Degree in the course of the Knight Templar ceremony. But further than this Baldwyn would continue its historic practice of administering a Rite of Seven Degrees or Orders. These are:

1. The three Degrees of Craft Masonry considered to be one Order

2. The Supreme Degree of the Holy Royal Arch of Jerusalem

3. The Knights of the Nine Elected Masters

4. Scots Knight Grand Architect, the conferment of which is immediately followed by that of the Royal Order of Scots Knights of Kilwinning, not considered to be a separate one of the 'Seven Degrees'.

5. The Knights of The East, The Sword and The Eagle

6. Knights Templar, including the conferment in the course of the ceremony the Mediterranean Pass and the Knights of St John of Jerusalem, Palestine, Rhodes and Malta (the 'Hospitallers')

7. Knights of the Rose Croix of Mount Carmel (since an Agreement dated 7 May 1881 this is worked under the authority of the Supreme Council 33° for England and Wales, etc.)

The whole is presided over by the Most Eminent Grand Superintendent of the Camp of Baldwyn, who is elected by the Knights of the Camp. His name is notified to Great Priory by whom, after due consideration, he is customarily appointed Provincial Prior of the City and County of Bristol[249]. Similarly, since 1881 after similar notification to the Supreme Council of the Ancient and Accepted Rite, under the provisions of the 1881 Agreement he is appointed Inspector General of Baldwyn Chapter, Bristol, by alphabetical coincidence standing at the head of the Inspectors General of Districts.

The reconciliation of 'Baldwyn' having been satisfactorily concluded, early in his Grand Mastership William Stuart was faced with other significant problems, for example a proposal in 1864 to dispense with the Royal Arch qualification for a candidate. This was rejected, but two years later it was put forward in a different guise – either Royal Arch or Rose Croix should be considered sufficient. This also was turned down, not surprisingly because in the historic past Knight Templar had been a preliminary to 'Rosae Crucis' and 'Ne. Plus. Ultra.' and not vice versa[250].

3.13 'THE TRIPARTITE TREATY'

The short-lived 'Tripartite Treaty' originated in discussions between Grand Conclave, the Supreme Council of the Ancient and Accepted Rite, which had received its Patent in 1845, and the Grand Lodge of Mark Master Masons which was erected in 1854. There are few records of the early preliminaries to this union and for these one has to rely considerably upon the Minutes of the Supreme Council of the Ancient and Accepted Rite. In its Minutes in December 1868 it is recorded –

> that as it is desirable that all degrees of Masonry should work together in harmony, it is proposed that this Council should enter into a Treaty of Union with the Grand Mark Lodge of England.

By December 1869 Captain Nathaniel Philips, the Grand Treasurer General of the Supreme Council of the Ancient and Accepted Rite and also the Grand Commander of the Knights Templar Provincial Grand Encampment of Suffolk, was able to report that a 'Convention' had been held with the Grand Master, Canon Portal, and the Grand Secretary, Frederick Binckes, of Grand Mark Lodge. By May 1870 Philips had written to Portal 'What is required is a general Treaty of Alliance between all the recognised bodies, offensive and defensive.'[251] On 12 July 1870 the Supreme Council resolved

> That Treaties be entered into between the Supreme Council, the Grand Lodge, the Grand Conclave of Knights Templar, and the Grand Lodge of Mark Master Masons.

Similar Resolutions were apparently passed by the Grand Conclave and Grand Mark Lodge. To include in the Resolution Grand Lodge, that is the United Grand Lodge of England, was an optimistic bridge too far!

It might be thought curious that Portal, as Head of what was ostensibly a non-Christian Order, that of the Mark Master Masons, should appear so anxious to be in alliance with the two principal avowedly Trinitarian Christian Orders. In fact, Christian nuances in the Mark Degree are not hard to find. Ten years earlier, when Grand Registrar in the Grand Lodge of Mark Master Masons, Portal had been largely responsible for the appointment of a Committee 'to investigate the connection between Mark Masonry and Christianity'. The Report of the Committee stated that there were several such connections, and the Report was ordered to be printed and widely circulated. No action was taken although subsequently Portal entered into a number of discussions. It seems just possible that Canon Portal had some hopes that by the association of 'Mark' with 'K.T.' and the 'A. & A. Rite' there might be more emphasis on the postulated Christian origin of the former.[252]

Another Trinitarian body, known then as 'Rome and Constantine' (Now 'The Masonic and Military Order of the Red Cross of Constantine') was becoming established, or, as its members considered, re-established. Portal was anxious to include this Order also within the Treaty, but the Supreme Council declined at this time to recognise its regularity and the matter was dropped. A proposal to include Yarker's '*A. & P. Rite of Misraim*' was even more firmly turned down by Nathaniel Philips. After further obstacles had been overcome, Plenipotentiaries met to frame the 'Tripartite Treaty'[253] as it came to be known.

In the first Clause it is stated that it was considered 'expedient to enter into certain Articles and Stipulations'. After recording the agreement of the Parties to recognise as the respective Heads of the Orders, the Most Eminent and Supreme Grand Master for the United Orders, the Grand Mark Master for the Mark Degree, and the Supreme Council for 'the Ancient and Accepted Rite of Thirty-three Degrees from and exclusive of the Master Mason and the Royal Arch Degrees up to the Thirty-third', the parties recorded their agreement that

'without the unanimous consent of all the contracting parties formally expressed in writing to ignore and refuse to admit into their respective Convocations Chapters Lodges or by whatever names their meetings be designated any person belonging to any Masonic Order or Degree which shall be in rebellion against any or either of the Contracting Parties or any person who shall hereafter belong to any Masonic Order or Degree not recognised by one or other of the Contracting Parties and not subject to the Judicial Council hereinafter to be described –

Provided always and it is hereby agreed that the Grand Lodge of Mark Master Masons shall be at liberty to ally itself with a governing body to be formed for the purpose of working the following Ancient Masonic Degrees that is to say of "Royal and Select Master", "Excellent Master", "Super Excellent Master" and "Most Excellent Master" without such act being considered an infringement of the present Convention or as obligatory on the Associated Orders to acknowledge or receive as an Associated Body the Governing Body of the hereinbefore mentioned Degrees: Provided always that all Orders or Degrees now claimed or worked by either of the Associated Orders shall be considered as belonging to them.'

In case any disputes should arise between the three Contracting Parties it was agreed that from time to time as necessary a Judicial Council would meet. To this Council each of the Parties would have the right to nominate three members, and it might be summoned by any of the three giving twenty-one days notice together with 'the subject matter of such Meeting, and the Judgment Decree or Sentence of such Council shall be definite and conclusive.'

Not only this, but a member of any of the three Orders convicted of a Masonic offence by his own Order had the right to appeal to this Judicial Committee. Whatever judgement to which the Committee might then come would have to be enforced by each of the Associated Orders. If there were no such appeal, each of the other two Orders would regard 'any act of contumacy punished by one of the Contracting parties' as if it had been dealt with by its own disciplinary authority. The final Clause stated:

> 'The Contracting Parties agree not hereafter otherwise than by mutual consent to recognise any other Jurisdiction whatsoever except the Grand Lodge of England and Grand Chapter of Royal Arch Masons to join any other independent Masonic Order or Degree within any place in England and Wales except as provided in Article I.'

The Convention was ratified by the Supreme Council but there were some fears that so many Members of Grand Conclave had joined 'Rome and Constantine' that there might be difficulty in securing a majority there in the face of a protest against the exclusion of 'Rome and Constantine' from the Treaty. The fears proved groundless as did similar fears about the results of the vote in Mark Grand Lodge. As far as Grand Conclave was concerned it was reported to the Supreme Council:

> 'On 12 of May 1871 the "Treaty of Alliance" was adopted by the Grand Conclave of Knights Templar by a majority of 31 Votes, the numbers being 53 and 21; the opposition was chiefly supported by the unrecognised Degree (as Masonic) of 'Rome and Constantine' to whom the Dep. G. Master, Bro. Huyshe, lent his aid. The majority would have been larger, but many supporters had left after H.R.H. the Prince of Wales retired.'[254]

A satisfactory conclusion in spite of the shaky arithmetic!

3.14 THE ILL-FATED CONVENT GENERAL

So far as the Convent General is concerned, we who enjoy the luxury of hindsight may yet wonder how this untypical and quite extraordinary interlude in the history of our United Orders could have been allowed to proceed past the exploratory stage. These events were set in train over 150 years ago; we may not understand the views of some of the Brother-Knights of the day, but it is impossible to avoid reporting the decisions then made which created such deep divisions among the membership of the Orders.

It is by no means clear how and where it all began, and who generated the spark by which the fuse was lit, but in the years 1867 and 1868 there were 'talks about talks' between 'Plenipotentiaries' of the Grand Masters of the Conclaves of England, Ireland and Scotland. Documents then signed looked ahead to close co-operation, and to the 'interchange of courtesy and hospitality'. Initially this was looked upon as no more than an alliance, and there was no suggestion of uniting the three bodies under a single governing authority. However as the discussions progressed the concept was put forward of doing just this – uniting the three National Grand Conclaves under a single authority to be known as the 'Convent General'.

The Plenipotentiary representative of the Irish Grand Master was his Grand Chancellor, J. F. Townshend; William Stuart, the Grand Master of the English Order, was represented by Patrick MacChombaich de Colquhoun, *QC*, the English Grand Chancellor, who had been appointed to the office following the resignation in 1866 of John Halsey Law who appears to have thrown himself into the task with perhaps misguided over-enthusiasm; but the representative of the Scottish Grand Conclave, who had taken part in the preliminary discussions, withdrew rather than commit his brethren so far. However the English and Irish Plenipotentiaries carried on with making the necessary arrangements for the establishment of a Convent General.

The first task of Townshend and Colquhoun was to draw up an Agreement to which reference is generally made as the 'Anglo-Hibernian Convention' (or simply as 'the Convention'), the final draft of which was dated 27 November 1868. The Third Article of that Convention provided for the appointment of Commissioners who were to agree upon Statutes, Laws, Ordinances, Forms, Rituals, and other matters to be adopted and observed in the respective Jurisdictions. This Article goes on to declare that:

> 'Any future changes of such Statutes, Laws, Ordinances, Forms, Rituals and other matters shall be mutually agreed between the two contracting parties according to the

Constitutions then actually in force. Such Statutes, Laws, Ordinances, Forms, Rituals and other matters having been thus agreed upon by the said Plenipotentiaries, with the assistance of the above-named Commissioners, shall be signed by the Plenipotentiaries herein named and shall on receiving the ratification of the respective Grand Masters be held to be valid and binding on all Templars under the jurisdiction of either or both.'

A draft of the General Statutes was therefore prepared in accordance with this Convention and was signed by the two Plenipotentiaries. One of these Statutes states:

'The Convent General shall be summoned once in every year by the Arch-Chancellor alternately in England and in Ireland on such day as the Grand Master in Council shall determine, of which day not less than four weeks notice shall be given, and all Statutes and Ordinances therein enacted shall be binding on all members of the Order, individually and collectively within the Jurisdiction of the Grand Master.'

and another:

'The Grand Master's assent shall be requisite to the validity of all Statutes, Laws, Rules and Ordinances, or alterations, modifications, additions or cancellations of those existing which thereupon shall forthwith have force, effect and validity, but if he dissent therefrom as aforesaid then neither the same nor any analogues thereto shall be brought forward within the year.'

What is not made clear is the extent of the power and authority of the Grand Conclave to make changes to its own Statutes, and also whether these Statutes superseded the provisions of the 'Anglo-Hibernian Convention'. The latter could be interpreted as providing that any proposed changes must be agreed between the two National Great Priories before they were even submitted to the Convent General.

On 13 December 1872, after little preliminary consultation, the draft containing, *inter alia*, these Articles was presented to the English Grand Conclave through which, in the words of G. E. W. Bridge it was rushed 'in a manner that can only be described as improper'[255]. Bridge goes on to say –

'When the Provinces and Encampments had had time to realize the extent of the changes (presented to them as a fait accompli) they combined and fought them tooth and nail, and the headquarters was [after a couple of years had been allowed for a sort of 'trial run'] flooded with 'Respectful Memorials' (and others less respectful) from all Provinces and from Encampments ranging from Australia and China, throughout England, to the West Indies – all couched in similar terms.'

A typical example addressed to the Very High and Eminent National Great Prior of England is from 'the Sir Knights of the Province of Devon in Provincial Priory assembled' and a printed copy, with its covering letter, would appear to have been sent to every other English Preceptory.[256] Thus were fanned the flames of dissension!

From this and other 'memorials' it is possible to summarize those changes contained in the new Statutes which the Convent General was committed to enforce but which were seen in the English Provinces as being the most objectionable –

1. The omission of the word 'Masonic' from the title of the Order; this was seen as putting it once more at risk under the Unlawful Societies Act of 1799.

2. The claim, hitherto generally dismissed as mythical, that the Masonic Chivalric Orders were actually derived from those of the medieval Knights. This had had the consequence that both the Ritual and consequent procedure had been adjusted to make them more consistent with what the practices of the medieval Templars were believed to have been. The most evident consequence of this was that since it was considered that the Installation of a Knight never took place in the field in medieval times, but always in a Chapel of the Order, the term 'Encampment' was unsuitable and should be superseded.

3. The change, as a consequence, of nomenclature such as 'encampment' to 'preceptory', 'Commander' to 'Preceptor' and others; 'Provincial Encampments' became 'Provincial Priories'.

4. The abolition of 'Past Rank' which meant that a Great or Provincial Officer had to revert to the status of Past Preceptor, or even that of Brother Knight, when his term of office expired. This highly unpopular alteration to the Rules made it necessary for those affected to adjust their regalia to their higher rank for perhaps one year only and then to have to remove the trimmings – probably of concern as much as a matter of *amour propre* as of expense.

5. The creation of Knights Grand Cross and Knights Commander in both England and Ireland was to be at the discretion of the Grand Master of the Convent General, and not at that of the Great Priors – for that was their new title – of each National Conclave, which was now to be a National Great Priory.

6. The concentration of all executive power in the hands of a relatively small number of Officers of Convent General in London, a well-justified grievance if the paucity of signatures in the Attendance Book of Convent General fairly represents the number actually attending.

7. The failure to give adequate warning to all Knights-Companions that the new Constitution was to be presented, passed and put into operation at a meeting of Grand Conclave on 13 December 1872. Many considered there ought to have been more ample opportunity for consideration in the Provinces of the proposed changes together with full discussion thereafter, before these changes were so hastily put to the vote.

These and other protests, which were to continue for many years to come, were ignored by those who were determined on the erection of the Convent

General. In England the proposals had been bull-dozed through the December 1872 especial meeting of the English Grand Conclave (now Great Priory) at which also took place the election at the age of thirty-one of His Royal Highness Albert Edward, Prince of Wales, to be the first (and, as it turned out, the only) Grand Master of the Convent General of England and Wales and of Ireland.

A similar election took place in Dublin on 15 January 1873, even though Irish objections to the new *regime* were hardly less strong than those in England.

So far as the erstwhile Grand Conclave of England was concerned the first consequence was that William Stuart resigned from the Grand Mastership. His Deputy, the Reverend John Huyshe, acted in his stead until 7 April 1873 when the Installation of the Prince of Wales as the Grand Master of the Convent General took place at a meeting held at Willis's Rooms, King Street, St James's, London.[257] Huyshe presided until he had placed the Grand Master on the Throne. The Earl of Limerick, an English Peer as well as an Irish one, was appointed National Great Prior of England in William Stuart's place. The Duke of Leinster was appointed to the corresponding position in Ireland. In addition to the Great Officers in the two National Priories, Brother-Knights were also appointed to hold Office in the 'superior' organisation, the Convent General; the Officers of this body were distinguished by the addition of the much disliked prefix of 'Arch' to their titles – Colquhoun, who had done so much to ensure establishment of the Convent General, became the 'Arch-Registrar', and it is said that his well-recognised role in the creation of the Convent General caused him to be conversationally referred to as the 'arch-villain'!

However, the Knights Templar in Canada took a somewhat different view. For many years there had been English Encampments of Knights Templar in Canada. A Grand Commandery, subject to the English Grand Conclave, had been instituted as long ago as 1824 to oversee them. In 1868 Sovereign status had been requested for this Commandery by (the now Col) MacLeod Moore, who had become a much-respected figure in both the Order of Knights Templar and in the Ancient and Accepted Rite not only in Canada but also in the northern maritime States of the United States of America. Col MacLeod Moore was given the local rank of Grand Prior for Canada by William Stuart, who allowed him to retain some of the dues which had hitherto been transmitted to London. The Canadian Knights Templar did not express a wish wholly to sever their connections with England, and the former Grand Commandery remained as a 'Provincial' Encampment under the Jurisdiction of the English Grand Conclave.

The Canadian Knights Templar, under the rule of Col MacLeod Moore, appear to have considered the new Statutes to be admirable, so much so that they took the initiative in announcing their claim to adhere to the Convent General, making it clear that they wished to do so not as the subordinates of the English Great Priory, but as a distinct third party, the Great Priory of Canada, within the new organisation, a Union which they considered themselves to have freely and voluntarily 'joined'.[258] This proposal did not receive immediate endorsement by the Convent General.

The third meeting of the newly-constituted Convent General took place on 9 May 1873 at the City Terminus Hotel, Cannon Street, London. The Earl of Limerick took the Chair in the absence of the Grand Master, H.R.H. the Prince of Wales (who never attended any further meeting of the Convent General).

On 1 December 1874 a Major Burgess was expelled from the Order of the Temple, at which time the 'Tripartite Treaty' had ostensibly been in force for three years, or so its signatories evidently considered. It appeared to have occurred to no one that the altered status of one of the signatories was of any practical consequence in this respect. In accordance with the provisions of the Treaty Major Burgess exercised his right of appeal to the Judicial Committee for which the Treaty provided. (It is uncertain of what act of contumacy Burgess was accused, but it was most probably too close an association with Yarker and the Rite of Misraim.)

Summons were therefore sent to the two representatives of each of the signatories including General Henry Clerk and Major (as he then was) Shadwell H. Clerke of the A. & A. Rite to attend a meeting of the Judicial Committee to be held at the offices of the Order of the Temple on 11 February 1875. The Summons were reported to the Supreme Council of the A. & A. Rite at its regular meeting on 9 February when the Minutes record that the Council was

'of the opinion that the Tripartite Treaty had been, ipso facto, terminated by the Order of the Temple ceasing to be a Supreme Body on the formation of the Convent General, but they consider that the members should attend under protest without prejudice to further proceedings and it was Resolved that after the Meeting a letter be addressed to the Chancellor of the Order conveying the decisions above recorded.'[259]

Matters then became somewhat confused. In a lengthy letter the Supreme Council gave no indication that it wished to withdraw from the Tripartite Treaty, but rather that appropriate alterations should be made to take account of the altered position of Great Priory. (See **Appendix H.**) In June 1875 Shadwell Clerke corresponded with the Grand Secretary of the Mark Grand Lodge, Frederick Binckes, and with Sir Patrick Colquhoun; the latter seems to have gained the impression that the Supreme Council wished to abrogate the Tripartite Treaty – it is hard to see how Shadwell Clerke's earlier letter could have been thus misinterpreted. Clerke had to write a further strong letter dated 15 July 1875 to Colquhoun pointing out that the Supreme Council had specifically proposed amending, not abrogating the Treaty. He asked Sir Patrick to make this clear to Great Priory – a curious request in view of the fact that so many of the Members of Supreme Council, including Clerke himself, were themselves members of Great Priory.

Binckes was in no hurry; it was not until 16 December that he replied, saying that the proposed amendments had been passed at the Meeting of Mark Grand Lodge on 30 November. But now it was the Supreme Council which displayed some hesitant caution; then, on 13 April 1876, it was informed by the Order of the Temple that Mark Grand Lodge had abrogated the Treaty. Mark Grand Lodge still professed to wish to have an alliance of some sort between the three Orders, but no further action was taken until the demise of the Convent General eighteen years later.

While this debate was in progress meetings of the Convent General had been held on 30 October 1874 at Freemasons' Hall in Dublin and on 29 October 1875 at the City Terminus Hotel in London. According to the 'Statement' dated 28 February 1877 which the Arch-Chancellor, Townshend, submitted to the Prince of Wales:

'Certain modifications of and in the General Statutes have been made by each Convent General held between the first assembly in 1873, and that which took place in London on 20th October 1875. No objection was made by either Great Priory to any of these alterations; nor was the previous consent of either Great Priory obtained for any of them; nor was the legality of any one of them ever questioned.'

Nothing out of the ordinary was therefore expected to happen when, at the meeting in October 1875, two 'Notices of Motion' were introduced prior to the substantive Motions being moved at a meeting expected to be held in Dublin in October 1876. One was in the name of the English Great Prior, the Earl of Limerick, and seconded by his Sub-Prior, Col Shadwell H. Clerke, and the second in the name of Albert H. Royds, the Provincial Prior for Lancashire and seconded by Thomas Birchall, Constable of that Province and Past Great Chamberlain.

On 25 February 1876, before arrangements for the October Meeting were finalised, the Irish Great Prior's Council recommended to the Irish Great Priory that it should pass a resolution, in effect affirming the continued currency of the 'Anglo-Hibernian Convention', and concluding:

'And whereas certain notices of motions for altering and rescinding several of the said General Statutes were given and received at the Convent General held on 29th day of October 1875, a mode of procedure by which the mutual consent of the Two Contracting Parties, necessary for any change or modification of such Statutes, Laws, &c. cannot be obtained and which would therefore nullify the provisions of the 3rd

Article of said Convention it is therefore resolved *that the receiving of such Motions is illegal, and any change or modifications of such General Statutes, effected otherwise than by the mutual action of both Great Priories is contrary to the terms of the Anglo-Hibernian Convention and will not be recognised as legal or of any effect for the Great Priory of Ireland.'*

The Resolution, duly signed and sealed, was sent to the Arch-Chancellor with the request that it should be made known to the Members of Convent General. Unfortunately by some oversight this Resolution was not placed on the Agenda for the October meeting, but Townshend, who was in the Chair, permitted it to be read aloud by the Chancellor of the Great Priory of Ireland.

For some reason, which is not wholly clear, the Earl of Limerick's motion was deemed by Townshend to have 'fallen to the ground' and was not moved. When Royds' Motion was brought forward, there was strong objection from the Great Priory of Ireland because it was said to be in direct contravention of both the Statutes and the Convention. The Chairman ruled that these must be read together, and the motion could therefore not be brought forward because it involved a change in some essential constitutional points.

This did not satisfy the Earl of Limerick, Lord Skelmersdale, and the Earl of Shrewsbury and Talbot. They presented a Memorial to the Grand Master, the Prince of Wales, asking for a Special Meeting of Convent General to be held to consider both motions. This application the Grand Master approved, and the Special Meeting was held on 9 December 1876.

While Townshend again ruled that Royds' Motion could not be entertained, Limerick argued that Convent General had full powers to alter the General Statutes irrespective of the wishes of either Great Priory, considering that the Convention had been superseded by the Statutes. Ignoring Townshend's ruling he proceeded 'to take the opinion' of the Special Meeting of the Convent General and Royds' Motion was carried. This had three clauses –

1st. That in the Clause of the Statutes entitled 'Title of the Order' the word 'Masonic' be inserted between the words 'united' and 'Religious'.

2nd. That the Statutes headed 'Rank and Precedence' (pages 19 and 23 Statutes of the Convent General) be expunged in order that the Past Rank of the various Officers and their right to bear the insignia thereof may be restored and recognised as formerly.

3rd. That wherever throughout the said Statutes the words 'Preceptory' and 'Preceptories' shall occur, such words shall be expunged and the words 'Encampment' and 'Encampments' be inserted, and in like manner wherever the words 'Preceptor' and 'Preceptors' occur the same shall be expunged and the words 'Eminent Commander' or 'Eminent Commanders' be inserted in lieu thereof that the words in the dispensations of the Meetings and Offices of the Order may be expunged and the previous titles restored.

Regrettably there is no record of how this was viewed by the Prince of Wales, the Grand Master, whose assent to any such alteration would have been necessary.

The reaction to this attempt to restore the *status quo ante* was in marked contrast to the way in which the Ritual submitted by the Commissioners under a report (given in **Appendix I**) had been received earlier in the year, even though, when copies of this were circulated for discussion, it was found to incorporate some changes which were seen as objectionable in many English Provinces[260]. Several 'Preceptories', as they were now to be called, simply ignored the changes, even when two years later the use of this Ritual was made mandatory.

The Commissioners had been anxious for the revision so far as possible to bring the Ritual more into accordance with what they believed to be customs and procedures of the medieval Knights from whom they appear to have considered that the modern Masonic Orders directly descended. They also had taken cognisance of the medieval practice that the admission of new entrants to the Order took place in a Chapel of a Preceptory of the Order, not in the field. They therefore concurred with the substitution of the term 'Preceptory' for that of 'Encampment' as the name of a subordinate body of the Order, presided over by a Preceptor not a Commander. Elections in former times took place in the Chapter-House, but admissions were made in a Chapel; it was therefore appropriate for the meeting-room to be fitted up as a Chapel with an Altar and Crucifix. The Commissioners also made it clear that both the former English and Scottish Rituals recognised the rank of 'Novice' as did the medieval Knights, and this should be emphasised more forcibly. They also decided that a clergyman should be admitted to the Order in a different fashion from that of the admission of a Knight.

A Knightly candidate for the Order was to continue to be admitted as a Pilgrim. After his entrance he now washed his hands in token of his pureness of heart. He was then given certain Pass-words and clothed as a Novice with tunic and sword, but the ceremony of Installation as a Knight was now not directly proceeded with. The Candidate actually had to 'serve' a Novitiate of at least a month before he could have Knighthood conferred upon him.

At the end of this term he was again admitted to the Preceptory, this time in his clothing as a Novice, and he took part in an Installation Ceremony not dissimilar to that in use today, although the order of various common elements differed. The Novice first made various declarations with his hands on the Gospels, after which he signed the stone after being informed of the ancient custom 'which was nowadays dispensed with'. Then his Knightly Spurs were affixed, but less dramatically than is done in 'Antiquity' in Bath today. He retired for a vigil before 'consecration' in a Chapel of the Order. Here, now wearing a long black robe, he viewed a skeleton before perambulating holding a skull, after which he extinguished a candle, the symbolism of these actions being explained to him. He was then given an explanation of the symbols – Lamb, Dove, Cock, etc. – much as is given by an Eminent Preceptor today – before he was clothed with a white mantle, the Red Cross on which being the subject of a much lengthier exposition than is found in the present-day Ritual. After this, a portion of Scripture was read by the Chaplain[261] before the Novice was Knighted, and presented with a 'Ring of Profession' said to be a symbol of the girdle which the medieval Knights had at all times to wear. Finally he was invested with the 'Ribbon of the Order', and Installed, being then saluted by all the Knights present.

The general acceptance of this revised Ritual did nothing to resolve the somewhat depressed and confused situation into which the United Orders in England had now drifted, but this state of affairs need not necessarily be attributed solely to the conflicts within the Convent General. The latter had assumed the direction of the United Orders in England at a time of industrial depression. The textile industry in the North of England was still suffering from the effects of the American War Between The States, when cotton shipments from the Southern States to the mills of Lancashire were greatly reduced. The economic problems which England was facing may have been as responsible as was the unpopularity of the Convent General for an apparent decline of interest in the United Orders in the early 'seventies. During the nearly twenty-five years for which the Convent General survived, only thirty-six Preceptories were warranted, sixteen of these being abroad, remote from sentiments held in London, and only four in the North of England, in Chester, Blackpool, Darlington and Morecambe, none of which were in the industrial heartland where the effects of the depression were most severely felt.

The Canadian Preceptories, still under English jurisdiction, continued to seek greater independence, being increasingly disaffected by what they saw as the retrogressive views of the English Templars. Towards the end of 1875 it was at last agreed that a Great Priory of Canada should be erected with Col MacLeod Moore as National Great Prior. It is perhaps curious that for eight years the new Great Priory adhered to the Convent General, the Brother Knights, entirely satisfied with the new Statutes, apparently not yet wishing to sever all ties with the mother countries.

Lord Limerick, the Great Prior of England under Convent General, resigned in 1876, his successor, the Earl of Shrewsbury, dying no more than five months after his Installation. He was in turn succeeded by Lord Skelmersdale, later to be created the first Earl of Lathom, whom in 1877 the Grand Master, H.R.H. the Prince of Wales, appointed by Patent to be in charge of the Great Priory of

England, of which from May to December 1877 Shadwell H. Clerke had been Great Sub-Prior in Charge.

Skelmersdale was one of the dominating figures of English Freemasonry in the latter half of the 19th century. Elected a Member of the Supreme Council of the Ancient and Accepted Rite, he first became Lieutenant Grand Commander, and then in 1877, the same year as that in which he was appointed Great Prior of England, he succeeded as Sovereign Grand Commander, an Office which he occupied until his death in 1898. In 1878 he was elected Grand Mark Master Mason, presiding over Mark Grand Lodge for the rest of his life. In 1891 he was appointed Pro Grand Master for the United Grand Lodge of England. With the same Brother now at the head of each of the three bodies which had entered into the 'Tripartite Treaty', no more was heard of this for the time being, a formal Treaty of Alliance presumably being considered superfluous under the circumstances.

Under his leadership the uneasy time in the history of the United Orders in England continued. The Constitutions of the Convent General continued to be far from welcome. It was possible to bring before the English Great Priory from time to time, with proper debate, motions for amendments of these Constitutions; however the Irish insistence on the continuing validity of the Convention made the administrative machinery of the Convent General so cumbersome that few of these well-intentioned attempts to improve the situation came to fruition. That the 'Anglo-Hibernian Convention' had not been superseded by the Statutes of Convent General meant that for any such proposal even to be put forward involved asking the Irish Great Priory if it would approve what that of England proposed, and *vice versa,* a complex procedure, which not unnaturally often resulted in the proposal being abandoned.

Nowhere was the dissatisfaction with the proposals which had been put forward by the Lancastrian Knights Royds[262] and Birchall more clearly expressed than in a letter addressed by Col MacLeod Moore to Patrick Colquhoun in February 1877 –

'I am very concerned to find that at the last meeting of the "Convent General" a certain party of members had begun a very retrogressive movement without any regard to the true history of the Order which you had taken so much pains to place in a proper light. But surely the resolutions adopted will not be confirmed by the Grand Master; I look upon it as quite illegal, and shall strongly protest against these changes. There is no sense in calling Templar assemblies Encampments. The only proper term is Preceptories. It is really too bad to sweep away the improvements of late years and go back to the old hermaphrodite system of Masonic Templary – a system that cannot be sustained on either historical or antiquarian grounds..... The Statutes issued in 1873 had been most carefully drawn up and were necessary on the occasion of the amalgamation of the Irish and English Branches of the Order and were assented by all parties, and we in Canada, on *joining the Union*[263], were quite satisfied with them, and are not at all inclined to change them to please the whims of any body of Knights in England and return to a system which they know and feel is incorrect, and I much fear that it will give strength to a very discontented party in Canada who wished an entirely independent management but had become reconciled to stay under Convent General. .... A copy of the revised ritual was sent out to me, I consider it admirable and beautifully arranged. .... I intend if possible to adopt the revision. ..... I am in correspondence with the Chiefs of the Order in the U. S., who are quite pleased with our English system and I have no doubt in time will begin to adopt it but this vexed question of changing the nomenclature &c. will throw us all back again. ..... The Scottish Preceptories in New Brunswick were preparing to join the Great Priory of Canada but all this vacillating and uncertainty about the Statutes has put a stop to it for the present. The English advocates of returning to older ways can have had little idea of the effect of their proposals internationally.'

There was no further meeting of Convent General for over thirteen years, or if there was, there is no record in its Minute Book nor in its Attendance Book of its having taken place. It seems that Convent General was being run, in effect, by some kind of central 'executive' who were making such decisions as they considered themselves empowered to make without seeking ratification by any other body. There was of course much correspondence but 'democracy', never the most significant feature of Freemasonry, was conspicuous by its absence. As far as the Great Priory of Canada was concerned, by 1884 the members seemed to have recognised that Convent General had become little more than a hollow sham and they wished to withdraw from it altogether. They considered that there was little alternative to their being 'absolved from their allegiance to the Grand Master of the United Kingdom'. The Sovereign Great Priory of Canada was thereupon established, with Col MacLeod Moore as its Grand Master *ad vitam*.

Five years before the final Meeting of the Grand Convent General it was clear that the experiment had been disastrous. The restrictive rules had discouraged the newly named Preceptories to the extent that while some had ceased to meet regularly, others tried to hang on with minimal attendances, reluctant to surrender their warrants. With low membership and little or no attendance, their finances suffered, and because of their inability to settle their arrears, fifteen Preceptories were removed from the Roll in 1888.

After this, the Convent General attempted to alleviate the situation by easing some of its more restrictive rules, but the cumbersome administrative procedure involved in seeking to change anything tended to frustrate any such attempt. In spite of this the English Great Priory succeeded in implementing a few changes seen by the Brother Knights to be of importance, for example the restoration of Past Grand Rank, which had featured in Albert Royds' Motion. But it was too late for emollients; it had become evident that nothing short of more drastic action would suffice.

On 18 April 1890 Convent General met formally for the first time since 1876 of which there is any record. Shadwell H. Clerke, whom we have seen to have his own views on 'reforms', took the Chair as Great Sub-Prior of England[264] and there are sixteen signatures in the Attendance Book.

Twenty-one days after this meeting Convent General again met on 9 May 1890, once more with Shadwell Clerke in the Chair.

There is no record of its meeting again for another four years until it met on 11 May 1894, once more at Mark Masons' Hall, for what proved to be the final meeting of the Convent General. This time the Earl of Euston, now the English National Sub-Prior, was in the Chair. It was resolved to appoint a Commission to examine the future of the Convent General.

The Commission appointed at this Meeting was composed of seven from each of the English and Irish National Great Priories. They were charged with the task of discovering what had gone wrong and of devising a way to put it right. Its Report was laid before the English Great Priory a year later and was printed in its *Calendar* for 1895/6. It may well have been that some considered it ironic that it had taken a Commission a year to discover what had been set out in the *Memorials* twenty years earlier. The Commission's Report acknowledges that, from the very start, the absence of Scotland from the 'union' had diminished any chance of success that it might otherwise have had, and it went on scathingly to allege that Canada's withdrawal from its temporary attachment had come about when it discovered that 'the Convent General' was little more than a figure of speech. There were many other uncomplimentary comments in what was a lengthy document, but in spite of these, the Commission urged 'the excellent objects which it was hoped would be effected [*by the Convent General*] should by no means be abandoned'.

To this end they proposed that Ireland be invited to enter into a new Convention, into which it hoped Scotland might also enter, which, while giving each National Great Body the entire control of its own affairs, would unite the Order in the United Kingdom under one Head.

Ireland adopted the Commission's Report in every particular and there was even discussion with Scotland. One of the welcome recommendations related to the creation of Knights Grand Cross, an honour which seemed in recent years to have been rather generously conferred. (In December 1893 eight were so invested, together with no fewer than fourteen Knights Commander, but this could possibly have been a 'catching-up' process). Other than Royal personages, there were to be no more than fifteen of the higher distinction at any one time in England, and nine each in Ireland and Scotland, and these limitations have been observed ever since.

The imminent demise of the Convent General now appeared inevitable and with it a change in status of the Great Priory of England. The Supreme Council of the Ancient and Accepted Rite anticipated this situation by writing to each of its former partners in the Tripartite Treaty on 20 June 1894 to suggest that a Committee should be formed, to which each of the three should appoint three delegates, to consider the revival of the Treaty. The Grand Master of the Convent General, H.R.H. The Prince of Wales, gave his blessing to the Commission's Report and on 19 July 1895 he appended his signature to a beautifully engrossed Declaration –

> WHEREAS at an Ordinary Meeting of Convent General of the United Religious and Military Orders of the Temple and Saint John of Jerusalem, Palestine, Rhodes and Malta, holden at the Mark Masons Hall, Great Queen Street on Friday the 11th May 1894 it was resolved to appoint a Commission to enquire into the relations existing between the National Great Priories and Convent General.
>
> AND WHEREAS the Commission reported that the objects sought to be effected by the Institution of Convent General have not been attained and that the Institution itself is in no way calculated to promote the good of the Order. And that the National Great Priories of England and Wales and Ireland have in consequence presented to us a Petition praying us to dissolve Convent General and to allow ourselves to be named Sovereign of the Order in the United Kingdom.
>
> AND WHEREAS such dissolution appears to Us to be for the benefit of the Order, We have determined to give Our assent thereto in manner hereafter appearing,
>
> NOW WE ALBERT EDWARD PRINCE OF WALES, K.G., G.C.T., &c. &c. &c. &c. Grand Master of the said United Orders DO HEREBY by virtue of the power vested in us, absolve the said National Grand Priories of England and Wales and Ireland from their allegiance to Convent General and do declare that the Convent General of the said United Orders shall from and after the date hereof cease to exist.
>
> AND WE DO HEREBY consent to the request of the said National Great Priories that We should permit Ourself to be named the Sovereign of the Order in the United Kingdom.
>
> DONE at Marlborough House this
9th day of July, A.D. 1895, A.O. 777
[signed] Albert Edward, Grand Master

To repeat Frederick Smyth's eulogy 'Convent General thus took its last shuddering breath'. England and Ireland were once more independent of one another. Under the benevolent oversight of 'The Sovereign of the Order in the United Kingdom' England, Ireland, and Scotland were again in complete harmony.

The Grand Master being about to sign the death certificate of the Convent General, the Committee to consider the reinstatement of the Tripartite Treaty had held a meeting on the previous day at the Grand East of the Supreme

Council of the Ancient and Accepted Rite in Golden Square[265]. After a long discussion it was agreed –

> 'That the best means of securing the principal object in view, viz: the exclusion from all Masonic Bodies of a Brother who may be excluded or expelled from any one of them, would be for each Body to amend its Constitutions by inserting in a rule similar in its tenor and import to Paragraph 79 of the Gd. Chapter R. A. Regulations; and if this can be done there will be no need to form any Special Treaty.'

It was done in each case, and no more was heard of a formal Treaty. The consequent 'amendment of its Constitutions' is embodied today in the latter Regulation No. 5 of the present-day "Statutes for the Government of the United Military, Religious and Masonic Orders of the Temple and of St John of Jerusalem Palestine, Rhodes and Malta in England and Wales and Provinces Overseas". (**Appendix J.**)

Part Four

THE UNITED ORDERS ... TODAY

The period up to 1895 was therefore a time of great change, not only a century of internal development, and the early years of United Grand Lodge, and the other emerging Grand bodies, but also a period of developing relations with other sovereign bodies – particularly Scotland and Ireland. The year 1895 can be viewed as something of a watershed and it is now possible to see a rather less turbulent time for consolidation and development.

However, the fledgling order had also expanded in its first hundred years or so, and this expansion was to continue along much the same lines as the Craft and other English Masonic bodies would do.

The early part of this work recorded some of the history of the Chivalric Orders of Knighthood from which the modern Masonic, Military, and Religious Orders of the Temple and the Hospital obtained their inspiration, but in the earliest days the Craft lodges within which chivalric Masonic Orders emerged were often unnamed or bore names related to their meeting venue; consequently it was not until Commanderies and Preceptories separated from their Craft lodges that names were adopted which reflected the chivalric past, either through historical personages or venues. For completeness, this part, and its associated appendices, include not only the changes to the administrative structure needed to accommodate expansion, and particularly decentralisation to Provinces, but a level of detail which shows how past historical people and events have been perpetuated to this day.

But the modern era was certainly not a time of peace, and as a Military and Masonic Order with principles based on a crusading history, the examination of at least some of the main effects of global conflicts seems entirely relevant.

The development of speculative Freemasonry has also resulted in the growth of a number of Orders which require membership of the United Orders as a prerequisite qualification for entry, and so it is appropriate to mention these briefly.

Finally, some commentators have suggested Freemasonry generally has possibly reached a zenith or is even in a state of decline, and it has been found useful to try and look ahead to see what faces the United Orders in the future.

4.1 DECENTRALISATION

Decentralisation of the United Orders' administration has occurred in three main stages: Creation of large administrative Districts; Constitution of Provinces in the England and Wales and their equivalents overseas; and transfer of Preceptories to Overseas Great Priories on their seeking and being granted sovereign status.

Thomas Dunckerley was, at various times, Provincial Grand Master and also 'Grand Superintendent' of at least eighteen Provinces; whilst this latter term nowadays usually relates to superintendence of Royal Arch Chapters over which Dunckerley certainly exercised responsibility, in the earliest days the term also covered superintendence of Knight Templar activity, much of which was integral to Royal Arch Chapters and, in some cases, Craft lodges. Most of the eighteen Provinces were in the south of England, and therefore Dunckerley is not recorded as having delegated Provincial responsibility there. Surviving records suggest that Dunckerley not only acted as Provincial Superintendent, but also carried out the duties of Vice-Chancellor where there was Knight Templar activity in the following Counties:

When Provincial Grand Master:

28 Apr 1767-1776	Hampshire
1772	Isle of Wight
1777-90	Essex, Dorset, and Wiltshire,
1784-86	Bristol, Gloucestershire, and Somerset
1790	Herefordshire

When Provincial Grand Superintendent:

1776-77	Essex
1778-1807	Kent and Hampshire
1780-95	Wiltshire
1780-96	Dorset
1782	Bristol
c.1790	Suffolk
1791-95	Cornwall
1793-95	Surrey
1793-1803	Hereford and Gloucestershire
1793-96	Warwickshire
1793-1810	Isle of Wight

Dunckerley did not view these as nominal or sinecure appointments, and he is recorded as active throughout his tenure; bearing in mind travel would be on horseback or by stagecoach, long journeys would indeed be arduous and this says much for Dunckerley's enthusiasm and stamina. However, it has not been possible to establish precisely how Thomas Dunckerley viewed the development and superintendence of Knight Templar activity in the following Counties where he was neither Provincial Grand Master nor Grand Superintendent, particularly in Craft Lodges working Templar and Malta rites.

Southern England Berkshire, Bedfordshire, Buckinghamshire, Devon, London, Middlesex, Oxfordshire, Somerset, and Sussex,

The Midlands Cambridgeshire, Derbyshire, Gloucestershire, Hertfordshire, Leicestershire, Lincolnshire, Norfolk, Northamptonshire, Nottinghamshire, Shropshire, Staffordshire, Warwickshire, and Worcestershire

Western Monmouthshire, South Wales, North Wales, and West Wales

Undoubtedly journeys to the more remote counties would be extremely time consuming, and the first stage of decentralisation occurred when administrative districts were constituted to cover areas remote from London:

In 1791 Thomas Dunckerley, Grand Master, appointed Thomas Dixon, a Captain in the 1st Dragoon Guards, as 'Acting Grand Master for the north District of England' covering the Counties of Cheshire, Cumberland, Durham, Lancashire, Northumberland, Westmorland, and Yorkshire. It would seem Dunckerley used the term 'Acting Grand Master' in the same sense as District or Provincial Grand Master would be used today. Under Dixon's superintendence the earliest documented Encampments were founded as:

St Bernard of Oldham	Oldham/Werneth	Constituted 1793
Bethlehem	Carlisle	Constituted 1794

In 1793 Thomas Dunckerley, Grand Master appointed John Knight 'Provincial Grand Master for Knights Templar' in Cornwall.

In 1793 it is believed Thomas Dunckerley also appointed John Schofield, Provincial Grand Master for Lancashire, as Grand Superintendent for a KT Province covering the counties of Lancashire, Cheshire, and perhaps part of Yorkshire but documentary evidence for this has not yet been found although later (1806) evidence for this Administrative District does exist.

At about the same time, there is evidence of KT activity in the central area of the Country and circumstantial evidence suggests a similar administrative district may also have been formed covering, at times, the counties of Derbyshire, Leicestershire, Nottinghamshire, Shropshire, Staffordshire, Warwickshire, and Worcestershire. It has not been confirmed positively that

Dunckerley formally appointed an 'Acting Grand Master for the Central District of England' but is certainly likely the Provincial Grand Master and Grand Superintendent for the Counties of Nottinghamshire, Leicestershire, and Derbyshire, Col the Rt Hon. Thomas Boothby Parkyns, 1st Baron Rancliffe, a member of the Chapter and Conclave of Observance, assumed such duties before becoming Grand Master in 1796.

In 1806 an Administrative District covering the Counties of Cheshire, Lancashire, and Yorkshire, was constituted.

However, these administrative units were undoubtedly difficult to manage and it is likely that the day-to-day control was, at best, inefficient or at worst, non-existent. It would therefore soon become apparent that reorganisation along geographical lines similar to the County-based structure adopted by the Craft would be more appropriate.

The transition from totally centralised control in London to the decentralised structure we know today did not, of course, occur either instantly or as a single step process in each geographical area. Although the year 1895 was undoubtedly something of a watershed, many of the structural changes had been started in the early years of the 19th century, and, as a result, it is sensible to review the development of the decentralised organisation in a single chronological time-line.

However, in a sense all Encampments, Commanderies, and Preceptories[266] were initially brought into existence with direct administration from London; these have been progressively transferred to Provinces or Sovereign Great Priories, but some remain controlled by Mark Masons' Hall and so it is first appropriate to mention briefly the Directly Administered Preceptories which still exist today.

4.2 DIRECTLY ADMINISTERED PRECEPTORIES

Prior to the development of a Provincial Structure all Preceptories were administered directly on behalf of Great Priory by the staff of Mark Masons' Hall. As the number of such directly administered Preceptories increased, it became apparent that some form of delegated administration was required, and the development of districts, and then provinces was outlined earlier.

However, there have always been circumstances which have made it desirable to retain some preceptories under direct control. Such circumstances include:

A Grand Master's Preceptory.

London preceptories which were administered directly from Mark Masons' Hall prior to the constitution of the Province of London in 1992.

New preceptories constituted in a Country or area where no province had been constituted and where insufficient preceptories exist to justify a new district, or province.

Preceptories which, for a variety of reasons, decline to join a new district, or province on its constitution.

Preceptories which exist in an area for which a new sovereign Great Priory is constituted which decline to transfer to the new Constitution.

Preceptories formerly belonging to a province or district which ceases to exist and which remain extant but do not transfer to another body.

The lack of records makes it impossible to trace all the early Encampments or Preceptories and the earliest surviving record is dated 1868. **Appendix L** lists the known encampments which ceased to exist before that date.

On 31 August 2018 there were 25 unattached preceptories in existence with 972 members. Unattached Preceptories are listed in **Appendix M.**

4.3 PROVINCIAL PRIORIES

In earlier Chapters it was shown that it was often possible to attribute developments in the Order at specific times to initiatives by individual brethren but, after the death of Thomas Dunckerley, such initiatives cannot always be traced directly. In particular, the period between Dunckerley's death and 1836 is not well documented hence the uncertainty surrounding the creation of the administrative Districts mentioned earlier.

It was during the Grand Mastership of Colonel Charles Kemys Kemys Tynte (3 April 1846-21 November 1860) that it was finally decided that it was unwieldy to have the administration of the Order centred on very large regions of the Country, and he recommended that, wherever practical, it would be appropriate for the Knight Templar Encampments then in existence to be organised in Provinces based on the traditional Counties of England and Wales with a well-qualified and suitable person appointed by him as the (Provincial) Grand Commander.

It must be noted, however, that the designation of a Province with a County name as part of its title did not always reflect precisely the Counties actually covered. Similarly, in the early days, the inclusion of a County did not always confirm that encampments or preceptories actually existed in that geographical area.

Likewise, in the early days, the designation of a Provincial Grand Commander did not confirm there were subordinate units to be ruled in the area, or that Knight Templar activity existed in the area at all. No doubt the grant of such a title may have been in the hope that this would lead to the constitution of new separate Templar units by involving Knights who had been working formerly within Craft Lodges or Royal Arch Chapters.

It may also be observed that the constitution of a Province was not always accompanied concurrently with the appointment of a Provincial Ruler which sometimes took place only after the constitution of a second or third encampment, commandery or preceptory in the area. This is later illustrated by a mention of the preceptories known to exist when the Province was created but for convenience the date of Warrant, or in some cases an earlier Dispensation indicated by [D], or a Warrant of Confirmation [C], and earliest meeting place are shown.

Over the history a number of titles have been used to designate the rulers of subordinate units. Initially, under the Grand Mastership of Thomas Dunckerley, the designation of subordinate rulers appeared to follow Craft practice with regional rulers being designated 'Acting Grand Master' for specified Districts; progressively, other titles were adopted.

From about 1830 the title Provincial Grand Commander appeared to be in general use;

From about 1910 the title Provincial Prior was adopted;

Under the Convent General, titles were changed generally; 'Encampments' became 'Preceptories'; titles of some Officers were changed – the most significant being 'Commander' became 'Preceptor, and the 'Captains' became 'Constables'; and individual Knights were known as 'Sir Knight' or 'Eminent Sir Knight' until 1872. Thereafter this practice was retained principally in Bristol and in some other preceptories using older forms of ritual; one consequence of this change was the difficulty of interpretation of early records as Brethren who held civil, as opposed to Masonic, knighthoods, such as Baronet, Knight Bachelor, *KCB*, *KCMG*, *KBE*, etc. would also have been entitled to the prefix 'Sir'.

In 1921 United Grand Lodge introduced the Title of District Inspector for overseas Inspectorates, and Great Priory adopted a similar concept from 1923 to about 1948 when the Statutes of Great Priory authorised the appointment of a District Chancellor 'to supervise such preceptories as might be placed within his care'. As far as can be ascertained the only appointments have been in the West Indies and Caribbean areas, these were of only limited duration.

However, embryo Knight Templar activity was evident in nearly every County prior to 1791, often through the existence of *Ecossais* Lodges, Craft Lodges working degrees 'beyond the Craft' after the manner of the *Antients*, Lodges travelling with Army Regiments, and brethren having contact with seafaring knights or French prisoners-of-war. Such working was almost certainly under Craft warrants, particularly within military units with Irish, Scottish, and English (*Antients)* Lodges. It must be assumed that this activity would have been recognised by Thomas Dunckerley particularly in those Counties where he held appointments as Provincial Ruler for the Craft or the Royal Arch. Brief details of such activity preceding the constitution of a formal Provincial organisation are given in **Appendix B** and details of the structure of extant Provinces in England and Wales are shown in **Appendix N** and Overseas in **Appendix O.**

However, it must also be recognised that, in the early part of the 19th century and before the Supreme Council 33° received its Patent, most Encampments of Knights Templar also conferred the degree of the '*Rosae Crucis*' which was later regarded as equivalent to the Eighteenth Degree of the Ancient and Accepted Rite, and some also worked the degree of 'Knight Kadosh'. When, following acceptance by the Grand Conclave that the degree of '*Rosae Crucis*' should properly be regulated by the new Supreme Council 33°, Knights Templar no longer had a means to qualify for the Kadosh degree which then took its rightful place as the Thirtieth Degree of the Ancient and Accepted Rite. Details of such consequential organisational changes at preceptory level are not included in this history.

Provincial histories also show complications through administrative counties often being grouped together, or regrouped, or separated as the Order developed. Consequently, many Counties appear within several Provinces at different times; with this sentiment in mind, the development of a formal organisation in each Province is summarised in chronological order within this Chapter relating each to the Grand Master (or where appropriate a Pro-Grand Master) in office at the time and highlighting the individual initially appointed to lead each Province.

Only details of the preceptories in existence at the date each Province was constituted are shown; Full details of the preceptories existing today are shown in **Appendix N.**

Under H.R.H. Augustus Frederick, Duke of Sussex, *KG*, &c Grand Master (1812-1843)

1836 Province of Dorsetshire
Dorset was one of the Counties over which Thomas Dunckerley presided as Provincial Grand Master for the Craft (1777-90) and Provincial Grand Superintendent for the Royal Arch (1780-96) and he acted as *de facto* Provincial Grand Commander from 1777 to 1796. There is every indication that he promoted Knight Templar development at an early stage, particularly where found in military lodges temporarily deployed that area.

Durnovarian Encampment at Dorchester appears to have been one of the first to be developed, circumstantially under the influence of Thomas Dixon and Fortitude Encampment when the 1st Regiment of Dragoon Guards was stationed there in 1790. Durnovarian Encampment was later amongst those listed by Thomas Dunckerley on 27 January 1792 although it had disbanded by 1810.

A Province of Dorsetshire was constituted on 25 April 1836 with the appointment of William Williams as Provincial Grand Commander. The number of Preceptories extant at that date has not yet been ascertained as the earliest surviving today was All Souls' Preceptory at Weymouth warranted on 26 March 1847.

The Province of Dorsetshire ceased to exist on 10 January 1949 following the incorporation of Wiltshire.

Under John Christian Burkhardt, Deputy Grand Master, Acting Grand Master (1843-1846)

1846 Province of Somersetshire

In the County of Somerset, there is some evidence that Knight Templar elements were worked in Craft Lodges as early as 1770, some twenty years before the first documented organised Knight Templar activity which occurred in Royal Edward Encampment at Bridgewater (Constituted 1792.) This encampment existed for only a limited time and ceased to exist some years before the Province of Somersetshire was constituted in 1846 with the appointment of Colonel Charles Kemeys Kemeys Tynte as Provincial Grand Commander. At that date one Preceptory was in existence.

| No. 1 Antiquity | Bath | 11 Aug 1791 |

The name was changed in 1874 when it was reconstituted as the Province of Somerset.

Under Col Charles Kemys Kemys Tynte, Grand Master (3 April 1846-21 November 1860)

1847 Province of Kent

The Province of Kent was constituted 1847, but without the appointment of a Provincial Grand Commander, and without any known Preceptories, the earliest surviving today being warranted 13 May 1880.

Dr H. J. Hinxman, *MD* was appointed Provincial Grand Commander in 1856, but even at that date none of the Preceptories which survive today were in existence.

In 1880, under General J. S. Brownrigg, *CB*, Provincial Grand Commander, the Province combined with Surrey, and the two Counties remained constituted as a single Province until 14 December 1956 at which date they separated when Capt. Alexander McKenzie-Smith, MBE was Provincial Prior.

On 31 August 2018 the Province had 23 preceptories with 671 members.

1847 Province of Nottinghamshire, Leicestershire, and Derbyshire

The Province of Nottinghamshire, Leicestershire, and Derbyshire was constituted in 1847, also covering Rutland, but without the appointment of a Provincial Grand Commander until 1862 when Henry Pelham-Clinton, The Earl of Lincoln, and 6th Duke of Newcastle was appointed to that office.

At least one Preceptory appears to have been active in the County of Nottingham at this date:

A Abbey Chapter	Nottingham	Time Immemorial

The existence of other early Preceptories in the Counties of Leicestershire, and Derbyshire has not yet been ascertained as the earliest which still survive today are:

No. 152 Rothley Temple	Leicestershire	11 Apr 1884
No. 159 Peveril	Derby	8 Sep 1893

No Preceptory has been identified in the County of Rutland.

This Province nominally ceased to exist in 1856 when a separate Province for Nottinghamshire was constituted and Abbey Chapter (Time Immemorial [A]) was transferred to the new Province.

1848 Province of Hampshire.

The earliest organised Knight Templar activity recorded in the County of Hampshire is in 1791 when Royal Naval Encampment No. 2 at Portsmouth was warranted by Thomas Dunckerley on 11 March 1791. However, it is highly likely there was other KT activity in military lodges and chapters serving in the Portsmouth naval garrison or on ships in port there from time to time, and by brethren having contacts with French prisoners-of-war.

The Province of Hampshire was constituted in 1848 with the appointment of Maj. Ferris Charles Robb as Provincial Grand Commander. At that date three of the preceptories which survive to this day are known to have been in existence:

No. 2 Royal Naval	Portsmouth	11 Mar 1791
No. 27 Sepulchre Preceptory and Sandeman Priory	Christchurch	15 Jun 1840
No. 32 Royal Gloucester	Southampton	8 Apr 1845

The Province nominally ceased to exist in 1945 when the Isle of Wight was incorporated and the name was changed to the Province of Hampshire and Isle of Wight.

1848 Province of Lancashire

The County of Lancashire was one of the constituent Counties included when Thomas Dunckerley appointed Captain Thomas Dixon, 1st Dragoon Guards as 'Acting Grand Master for the North District of England' in 1791.

The earliest organised Knight Templar activity recorded in the County of Lancashire and the contiguous counties of Cumberland and Westmorland which came under Lancashire control appear to be:

St Bernard of Oldham	Oldham/Werneth	Constituted 1793
Bethlehem	Carlisle	Constituted 1794

Both encampments had probably ceased to work by 1848 and had been removed from the Roll before the Enumeration of 1868.

Subsequently the County became part of an Administrative District covering the Counties of Lancashire, Yorkshire, and Cheshire constituted by Thomas Dunckerley in 1806, but although documentary evidence for the formal constitution of a Province has not been found, Provincial Grand Commanders were appointed for Lancashire between 1794 and 1845: William Barlow (1794-1800); John Schofield (1800-1807); Joseph Heap (1807-09 Deputy in Charge); Francis D. Astley (1809-25); George Orme (1826-27 Deputy in Charge); and John Crossley (1827-45).

The Province of Lancashire was constituted in 1848 when Matthew Dawes appears to have acted informally as Provincial Grand Commander between 1848 and 1862 until Albert Hudson Royds was appointed to the office in 1862. At that date eight of the Preceptories which survive today are known to have been in existence:

No. 5	Jerusalem	Manchester	10 Oct 1786
No. 7	Loyal Volunteers	Ashton-under-Lyme	12 Aug 1796
No. 8	Plains of Mamre	Burnley	10 Mar 1806
No. 9	St Joseph	Manchester	10 Mar 1806
No. 11	Plains of Tabor	Colne	9 Sep 1805
No. 12	St Michael	Rawtenstall	10 Apr 1807
No. 17	St John of Jerusalem	Ulverston	21 Feb 1811
No. 33	St James of Jerusalem	Bolton	[D] 5 Apr 1819

On 31 August 2018 the Province had 32 preceptories with 918 members.

1848 Province of Devonshire and Cornwall

Thomas Dunckerley served as Grand Superintendent for Cornwall from 1791-1795 and some type of formal Provincial Organisation may have been created as early as 1793 when, as Grand Master, Thomas Dunckerley appointed John Knight as 'Provincial Grand Master for Knights Templar in Cornwall'.

However, no documentary evidence of the formal constitution of a Province has been found, although by then the following Encampments existed:

| Trine | Bideford | Constituted 1790 |
| St John of Redruth | Redruth | Constituted 1791 |

The Province of Devonshire and Cornwall was constituted in 1848, apparently without the formal appointment of a Provincial Grand Commander, although, at that date four of the Preceptories which survive today, together with one which has ceased to operate, are known to have been in existence:

TI F	Union or Rougemont	Exeter	Time Immemorial
No. 10	Royal Veterans	Plymouth	9 Jun 1806
No. 19	Trinity in Unity	Barnstaple	[D] 28 Feb 1812
No. 23	Cornubian	Truro	24 Nov 1826
	(Removed from the Roll 1 Jan 1888)		
No. 25	Royal Sussex	Torquay	30 Apr 1834

The first record of an appointment of a Provincial Grand Commander was in 1862 when The Revd John Huyshe was appointed.

A separate Province of Cornwall was constituted in 1870, with the appointment of the Rt Hon. Edward Granville, Lord Eliot, 3rd Earl of St Germans, as Provincial Grand Commander, but after two periods when that office was left vacant (1875-76 and 1881-95), the Province was removed from the Roll. It is assumed the administration for the County reverted to The Province of Devonshire and Cornwall.

On 31 August 2018 the Province of Devonshire and Cornwall had 11 preceptories with 351 members.

1849 Organisation of the Midlands Counties

Earlier it was mentioned that it had not been possible to establish precisely how Thomas Dunckerley viewed the development and superintendence of Knight Templar activity in the Midlands Counties, and it was in 1849 the organisation of the Counties of middle England is first encountered; this involves the incorporation of the eight Counties of Derbyshire, Leicestershire, Nottinghamshire, Rutland, Shropshire, Staffordshire, Warwickshire, and Worcestershire in the histories of 16 different Provinces, of which six exist today; these are recorded in the appropriate chronological order, but to form a guide to this fragmented history the Provinces involved are: *(Italics indicate former Provinces)*

| 1847-1856 | *Nottinghamshire, Leicestershire, and Derbyshire* |
| 1849-1884 | *Staffordshire and Warwickshire* |

1856-1883	*Nottinghamshire*
1856-1970	*Leicestershire, and Derbyshire*
1884-1895	*Staffordshire, Warwickshire, and Leicestershire*
1895-1905	*Staffordshire, Warwickshire, Leicestershire, & Nottinghamshire*
1905-1969	*Nottinghamshire, Leicestershire, and Derbyshire*
1906-1911	*Staffordshire, Warwickshire, and Worcestershire*
1911-1924	*Staffordshire, Warwickshire, Worcestershire, and Shropshire*
1924-Date	Worcestershire
1924-1966	*Staffordshire, Warwickshire, and Shropshire*
1966-Date	Warwickshire
1966-Date	Staffordshire and Shropshire
1969-Date	Nottinghamshire
1970-Date	Derbyshire
1970-Date	Leicestershire and Rutland

1849 Province of Staffordshire and Warwickshire

This Province was created in 1849 to cover the counties of Staffordshire and Warwickshire but it was not until 1857 that Henry Charles Vernon was appointed Provincial Grand Commander with three of the Preceptories that still existence today:

No. 42	Godefroi de Bouillon	Stoke-on-Trent	5 Oct 1853
No. 52	Richard de Vernon	Dudley	7 May 1857
No. 67	Howe-Beauceant	Birmingham	22 Feb 1850

In 1884, the Province was extended by the addition of Leicestershire, and it is presumed that the Province nominally ceased to exist on being reconstituted as the Province of Staffordshire, Warwickshire, and Leicestershire. The Province amalgamated with Worcestershire in 1906.

1850 Province of Cheshire & North Wales

The County of Cheshire was formerly part of an Administrative District covering the Counties of Lancashire, Yorkshire, and Cheshire constituted by Thomas Dunckerley, possibly as early as 1793 under John Schofield, and certainly by 1806, but no details have been found which confirm there was any formal appointment of an Acting Grand Master for Northern England to succeed Thomas Dixon. At that stage one preceptory was in existence:

No. 14	*Royal Edward*	*Hyde*	*13 Jul 1806*

A Province of Cheshire & North Wales was constituted in 1850 followed by the appointment in 1862 of William Courtney Cruttenden as Provincial Grand Commander. At that date two Preceptories which survive today are known to have been in existence together with another which had ceased to operate:

No. 14	*Love and Friendship*	*Stockport*	*10 Apr 1809*
	(Removed from the Roll 1 Jan 1894)		
No. 15	Preceptory of St Salem	Macclesfield	[D]1 Nov 1808
			8 Jan 1809
No. 76b	Royal Edward	Stalybridge	13 Jul 1806
	(Adopted No. 14 on 13 Jul 2006)		

On 31 August 2018 the Province consisted of 17 preceptories with 438 members. [NB. Prior to 2011 often referred to as The Province of Cheshire.]

1850 Province of Northumberland and Durham

The Counties of Northumberland and Durham were formerly part of the Administrative Unit created by Thomas Dunckerley in 1791 under Captain Thomas Dixon, 1st Dragoon Guards, Acting Grand Master for Yorkshire, Cumberland, Northumberland, and Durham. No organised commanderies or encampments have been identified at that date although circumstantial evidence of considerable activity is shown in **Appendix B.**

In 1854, The Revd Edward Challoner Ogle was appointed as Provincial Grand Commander, but not installed until first Provincial Meeting held on 11 November 1858. At that date only one of the Preceptories which survive today is known to have existed (Royal Kent Preceptory No. 20 at Newcastle) and that Preceptory was transferred to the Province of Durham when that Province was formed on 24 September 1975.

The Province nominally ceased to exist on 24 September 1975 on being separated to form the Province of Durham and the Province of Northumberland.

1856 Province of Leicestershire, and Derbyshire

A Province of Leicestershire and Derbyshire came into existence in 1856 following the separation of Nottinghamshire from the former Province of Nottinghamshire, Leicestershire, and Derbyshire which had existed since 1847; like its predecessor it exercised nominal control over the County of Rutland although that County name did not then appear in the Provincial title. None of the preceptories which survive today existed in 1856.

The Province nominally ceased to exist in 1970 when Dr Reginald Latham Brown was Provincial Prior following the separation of Derbyshire to form a separate Province.

1856 Province of Nottinghamshire

As shown earlier, The County of Nottingham features in the histories of several Provinces which are recorded later in the appropriate chronological order, but to form a record of this fragmented history this may be summarised briefly as:

1847-56 Part of Province of Nottinghamshire, Leicestershire, and Derbyshire

1856-83 Constituted as a Province of Nottinghamshire in 1856 with the appointment of The Earl of Lincoln (later from 1865 the 6th Duke of Newcastle) as Provincial Commander although the office of Provincial Grand Commander was vacant from 1879-83) and the Province ceased to exist as such in 1883.

1883-95 The County of Nottingham was not included in any Province.

1895-1905 included in the province of Staffordshire, Warwickshire, Derbyshire, Leicestershire, and Nottinghamshire.

1905-69 Combined with Leicestershire and Derbyshire to form a Province of Nottinghamshire, Leicestershire, and Derbyshire.

In 1969, the County was again constituted as a Separate Province of Nottinghamshire with the appointment of Charles Henry Venn Elliott, *TD, MA* as the Provincial Prior. At that date three of the Preceptories which survive today were in existence.

A	Abbey Chapter	Nottingham	Time Immemorial
No. 395	Wynkbourne	Mansfield	25 Jul 1964
No. 41	Pelham	Worksop	19 Mar 1969

On 31 August 2018 the Province consisted of eight preceptories with 301 members.

1857 Province of Suffolk and Cambridge
A Province of Suffolk and Cambridge was constituted in 1857, followed in 1867 by the appointment of Capt. Nathaniel George Philips as Provincial Grand Commander. At that date one Preceptory existed:

No. 16	Prudence	Ipswich	21 Feb 1811

The Province ceased in 1882 on incorporation in a Province of East Anglia.

1857 Province of Victoria, Australia
The Province of Victoria was constituted in 1857 with Dr Benjamin Archer Kent, *MD*, as Provincial Grand Commander. At that date only one of the English Encampments which exist today had been constituted:

| No. 51 | Pembroke | Melbourne | 7 May 1857 |

The Province ceased to exist in 1982 on being reconstituted as part of the Great Priory of Victoria. At that date eighteen Preceptories existed under the English Constitution and all were transferred to the new Sovereign Great Priory. These are listed in **Appendix O**.

1859 Province of Yorkshire

The County of Yorkshire possess some of the oldest records of organised Knight Templar activity in England, for in 1760 The Grand Lodge of All England recognised a fraternal Degree called 'Knights Templar' above the 3rd degree of Master Mason and before Royal Arch (*sic*).[267]

Documented Knight Templar activity has been recorded in York since at least 29 November 1779 when a Certificate records a brother admitted to the Knight Templar (5th Degree.) Later, in June 1780, The Grand Lodge of All England at York announced it was asserting authority over five degrees or orders of Masonry, the Entered Apprentice, Fellow Craft, Master Mason, Royal Arch, and Knight Templar.

In 1782, the Grand Lodge of All England at York granted Lodge No. 211(IC) working in the 14th Regiment of Foot (in Nova Scotia) a warrant for a Knight Templar Encampment dated 20 September 1782.[268]

Correspondence between Thomas Dunckerley and Templar Masons in York Conclave exists today including a letter dated 22 March 1791.

The county was formerly part of an Administrative Unit created by Thomas Dunckerley in 1791 under Thomas Dixon, (Captain, 1st Dragoon Guards) Acting Grand Master for Yorkshire, Cumberland, Northumberland, and Durham. Fortitude Encampment appears to have been established in York under the influence of Captain Thomas Dixon in or before 1790 when the 1st Regiment of Dragoon Guards was stationed there, and the encampment was certainly active in 1791 before Thomas Dunckerley became Grand Master.[269]

Subsequently Yorkshire formed part of an Administrative District covering the Counties of Lancashire, Yorkshire, and Cheshire constituted in 1806; by then the following encampments existed in Yorkshire:

| Plains of Brunswick | Haworth | Constituted 1805 |
| Union | Leeds | Constituted 1806 |

Neither was still in operation when a Province of Yorkshire was constituted on 21 October 1859. The first Provincial Grand Conclave took place on 22 February 1860 at which date the following Preceptories which survive today were in existence:

	B	Ancient York		
		Conclave of Redemption	Hull	Time Immemorial
No.	1	York Conclave	York	11 Aug 1791
No.	3	Plains of Rama	Keighley	17 Mar 1793
No.	4	Hope	Huddersfield	5 Oct 1793
No.	13	Faith	Baildon	10 Oct 1809
No.	18	Prince Edward	Todmorden	30 Oct 1811
No.	21	Salamanca	Halifax	[D] 26 Jan 1815
No.	39	Fearnley	Dewsbury	21 Oct 1859

In 1862 Dr George Fearnley, *MD* was appointed as Provincial Grand Commander.

The Province of Yorkshire nominally ceased to exist in 1864 when the Province was divided into the Province of West Yorkshire and the Province of North and East Yorkshire.

Under William Stuart, Deputy Grand Master
Acting Grand Master (22 November 1860-61)
Grand Master (1861-1872)

1862 Province of Bengal
A Province of Bengal was constituted 1862 with the appointment of Hugh David Sandeman as Provincial Grand Commander. Two preceptories were in existence at that time:

No. 64	Excelsior	21st Regiment of Foot	17 Mar 1860
	(Warrant surrendered 1 May 1886)		
No. 65	Royal Kent	Bengal (probably Calcutta)	9 Feb 1861
	(Warrant surrendered 8 Jul 1867)		

but there is also evidence of Knight Templar working in both local Craft lodges and British Army lodges in North-East India at that time. One particular lodge – Lodge No. 33 (IC) in the 21st Regiment of Foot – later worked the Royal Arch and Knight Templar degrees under Warrants for that particular purpose (issued in 1830) and saw service in India although it has not been confirmed definitively that the Regiment was in Bengal in 1862.

The Province of Bengal ceased to exist in 1916 on incorporation into a new Province of India when the Provincial Prior of Bengal, Surg. Gen. The Hon. Sir Charles Pardey Lukis, *KCSI*, *FRCS*, (later Lt Gen.) was appointed Provincial Prior of the new Province.

1862 Province of Bombay

A Province of Bombay was constituted in 1862 with the appointment of Gustavus Septimus Judge, *KCT* as Provincial Grand Commander. At that date there were at least two Preceptories in existence

No. 53	St Augustine	Lahore, Punjab	11 May 1857
	(Removed from the Roll 1975)		
No. 59	Mount Zion	Bombay	17 May 1859
	(Removed from the Roll 1 Jan 1888)		

Between 1882 and 1902 the office of Provincial Prior was vacant. It was likewise vacant from 1912 to 1914 but the Provincial Prior of Bengal, Lt. Col. Sir Arthur Henry McMahon, *GCVO, KCIE, CSI, GCT* was in charge.

From 1915 to 1916 the office of Provincial Prior was again vacant, and the Province ceased in 1916 on incorporation into a Province of India.

1862 Province of Madras

The Province of Madras was constituted in 1862 with the appointment of Lt Col William Pitt MacDonald as Provincial Grand Commander. It has not been possible to identify any commanderies then in existence. However, the Province would cover the Coromandel Coast (now Tamil Nadu) where numerous British Army units were operating, many with lodges having histories with confirmed activity 'beyond the Craft'.

The Province of Madras ceased to exist in 1916 on incorporation into a new Province of India under the former Provincial Prior of Bengal, Surg. Gen. The Hon. Sir Charles Pardey Lukis, *KCSI, FRCS*.

1862 Province of the City and County of Bristol

The earliest Knight Templar activity in the Bristol area was almost certainly associated with naval or seafaring brethren as Sea Captains' Lodges working 'higher degrees' are known from as early as 1757.[270]

Organised Knights Templar activity is known in the City of Bristol at least since 1791 when an encampment was confirmed to be in existence,[271] and a Province was constituted for the City and County of Bristol by Compact in 1862 with the appointment of William Augustus Frederick Powell, *JP* as Provincial Grand Commander with only a single Preceptory:

C	Baldwyn	Bristol	Time Immemorial

The Province of the City and County of Bristol under this name ceased in 1864 when a Province to cover Bristol and the County of Gloucestershire was constituted although no other commanderies or preceptories were known to exist. Gloucestershire separated in 1960 to form a new province, and Bristol readopted the name: Province of the City and County of Bristol.

On 31 August 2018 the Province had one preceptory with eighty-nine members.

1862 Province of Canada

In 1862 a Province of Canada was constituted with Col W. J. Bury McLeod Moore as Provincial Grand Commander. At that date six encampments formed part of the new Province:

No. 22	Hugh de Payens	Canada	12 Feb 1824
No. 44	Geoffrey de St Aldemar	Canada	11 Nov 1856
No. 46	William de la More the Martyr	Canada	28 Jul 1855
No. 47	Godfroi de Bouillon	Canada	25 Oct 1855
No. 54	Richard Coeur de Lion	Canada	29 May 1857
No. 58	Nova Scotia	Canada	11 Aug 1858

The Province ceased to exist in 1875 on the inauguration of a sovereign Great Priory of Canada.

1863 Province of China

A Province of China was constituted in 1863 with the appointment of Samuel Rawson as Provincial Grand Commander, with no preceptories but presumably in anticipation of the imminent consecration of the oldest preceptory surviving today:

| No. 78 | Victoria | Hong Kong | 8 Apr 1864 |

However, details have not been confirmed of other Knight Templar activity under military lodges, civilian Craft Warrants, or Royal Arch Charters.

The Province ceased to exist when reconstituted as Province of Far East in 1958.

1864 Province of Bristol & Gloucestershire

Following the constitution of a Province for the City and County of Bristol by Compact in 1862 the scope of the Province was extended shortly thereafter under the Superintendence of William Augustus Frederick Powell, *JP* by a Province to cover Bristol (City and County) and the County of Gloucestershire constituted in 1864.

At that time no commanderies or preceptories were known to exist in the County of Gloucestershire.

Gloucestershire separated in 1960 and the name of the Province reverted to the Province for the City and County of Bristol with Dennis Norman Frederick Tricks as Provincial Prior and one Preceptory.

1864 Province of West Yorkshire
The former Province of Yorkshire, constituted in 1859, was divided in 1864 to form the Provinces of West Yorkshire and North and East Yorkshire.

West Yorkshire was constituted 1864 under Dr. George Fearnley, *MD* Provincial Grand Commander and at that date eight Preceptories were in existence that survive today:

No. 3	Plains of Rama	Keighley	17 Mar 1793
No. 4	Hope	Huddersfield	5 Oct 1793
No. 13	Faith	Baildon	10 Oct 1809
No. 18	Prince Edward	Todmorden	30 Oct 1811
No. 21	Salamanca	Halifax	[D] 26 Jan 1815
No. 39	Fearnley	Dewsbury	21 Oct 1859
No. 66	de Furnival	Sheffield	3 May 1861
No. 89	Plains of Mamre	Haworth	17 Feb 1806

The Province celebrated its Sesquicentenary in 2010 when Province consisted of 18 Preceptories.

On 31 August 2018 the Province had 23 preceptories with 502 members.

1864 Province of North and East Yorkshire
The earliest recorded organised Knight Templar activity in the County of North and East Yorkshire relates to individual Craft Lodges working a Knight Templar degree before June 1780 when The Grand Lodge of All England at York announced it was asserting authority over five degrees or orders of Masonry, the Entered Apprentice, Fellow Craft, Master Mason, Royal Arch and Knight Templar. Documented Knight Templar activity has certainly been recorded in the City of York since at least 29 November 1779 when a Certificate records a brother admitted to the Knight Templar (5th Degree.) The Grand Lodge of All England at York is recorded as having warranted Knights Templar Encampments at Rotherham, on 6 July 1780, and in Manchester, on 10 October 1786.

Records also exist of Captain Thomas Dixon (1st Dragoon Guards) being instrumental in having founded a static Knight Templar Encampment in York around 1784 becoming the first Eminent Commander. Several items of correspondence between Thomas Dunckerley and Templar Masons in York Conclave exist including a letter dated 22 March 1791.

When the former Province of Yorkshire was divided into the Provinces of West Yorkshire and North and East Yorkshire, a Province of North and East Yorkshire was constituted in 1864 with the appointment of William Henry

Forrester Denison (Rt Hon. Lord Londesborough) as Provincial Grand Commander. At that date only a single preceptory of those extant today was active in the Province:

B Antient York Conclave of Redemption   Time Immemorial

On 31 August 2018 the Province had 13 preceptories with 365 members.

1868 Province of South Australia

A Province of South Australia was constituted in 1868 with the appointment of The Hon. Sir James Penn Boucat, *KCMG* as Provincial Grand Commander in 1869. On constitution, of the Preceptories which were transferred to the Great Priory of South Australia in 1982, only one existed:

No. 57 Percy   Adelaide   20 Aug 1858

The Province ceased to exist in 1982 on being reconstituted as part of the Great Priory of South Australia. The Preceptories transferred to the new Sovereign Great Priory are listed in **Annex O.**

1869 Province of Ceylon

A Province of Ceylon was constituted in 1869 with the appointment of Maj. Alexander Crowder Crookshank as Provincial Grand Commander. At that date one Preceptory was in existence and survives today:

No. 99 Ceylon   Kandy   29 Jul 1867

The Province was renamed the Province of Sri Lanka in 1975.

1869 Province of Staffordshire and Warwickshire

A 'Province of Staffordshire and Warwickshire' may have been reconstituted, *de facto,* in 1869 when the County of Warwickshire was added to the responsibilities of the existing Province of Staffordshire. At the time, the office of Provincial Grand Commander was vacant, and three preceptories were in existence:

No. 42 Godefroi de Bouillon   Stoke-on-Trent   5 Oct 1853
No. 67 Howe-Beauceant   Birmingham   22 Feb 1850
No. 79 Wulfruna   Wolverhampton   16 Aug 1864

The 'Province' seems to have been informally absorbed by the Province of Staffordshire, but documentation to confirm this has not been traced.

1870 Province of Cornwall

The earliest recorded Knight Templar activity in the County of Cornwall includes the Encampment of Trine at Redruth (mentioned earlier as constituted in 1791). Cornwall was one of the Counties over which Thomas Dunckerley presided as Provincial Grand Master and Grand Superintendent, acting as *de facto* Provincial Grand Commander from 1791 to 1795, after which he appeared to appoint John Knight as a 'District Grand Master for Cornwall'. Certainly organised Knight Templar activity and informal activity associated with seafaring brethren and military lodges appeared in the County at an early date.[272]

A Province of Cornwall was constituted in 1870 with the appointment of the Rt Hon. Edward Granville, Lord Elliot, 3rd Earl of St Germans, as Provincial Grand Commander, but so far as is known only one Commandery or Encampment surviving today existed at that time:

No. 90	Restormel Preceptory and St Andrew Priory	Hayle	1 Mar 1867

The Office of Provincial Grand Commander fell vacant on Lord Elliot's death in October 1877 and again in 1881-95, and the Province was removed from the Roll shortly after. No documentation has been found to show how the County was administered thereafter until the County of Cornwall was formally added to the Province of Devonshire in 1934.

Under Revd John Huyshe, GCT, Deputy Grand Master Acting Grand Master (1872-1873)

1873 Province of Oxford

The Province of Oxford was constituted in 1873, some 11 years after the appointment of Col Henry Atkins Bowyer as Provincial Grand Commander in 1862, at which date only one Preceptory is known to have been in existence.

No. 29	Preceptory of Coeur de Lion	Oxford	26 Nov 1849

The Province was renamed following the addition of Berkshire 1928, and renamed again following the addition of Buckinghamshire in 1964.

Under Rt Hon. William Hale John Charles Pery, 3rd Earl of Limerick, GCT; Great Prior of England and Wales (1873-1876)

1873 Province of Sussex

A Province of Sussex was constituted in 1873 with the appointment of Lt Col Shadwell Henry Clerke as Provincial Grand Commander; two Preceptories were extant of those which survive today.

| No. 125 | Sussex Preceptory and Southdown Priory | Eastbourne | 27 Dec 1872 |
| No. 126 | de Warenne | Brighton | 18 Jan 1873 |

On 31 August 2018 the Province had 12 preceptories with 380 members.

1874 Province of Somerset

The earliest recorded Knight Templar activity in the County of Somerset was Royal Edward Encampment at Bridgewater constituted in 1792 but, like many early encampments, had probably ceased to exist before 1810.

This Province was formerly constituted in 1846 as the Province of Somersetshire, but reconstituted as the Province of Somerset in 1874 under Captain the Hon. Arthur Wellington Alexander Nelson Hood (later Lt Col) as Provincial Grand Commander with three Preceptories that still exist:

No. 1	Antiquity	Bath	11 Aug 1791
No. 40	Bladud	Bath	23 Sep 1852
No. 121	Worlebury Preceptory of St Dunstan	Weston-super-Mare	17 Apr 1782

The Province was reconstituted in 1889 with the incorporation of the County of Monmouth; and reconstituted again as the Province of Somerset, Monmouth and South Wales on the addition of the latter in 1914. That Province was partitioned in 1952-53 and the Province of Somerset was reconstituted on 30 June 1953.

On 31 August 2018 the Province had 12 preceptories with 332 members.

1875 Province of The Mediterranean

The earliest recorded Knight Templar activity in the British Territory of Gibraltar was almost certainly related to Military Lodges attached to Regiments stationed in or passing through Gibraltar, with some of the earliest known Masonic Knight Templar activity.

There is likewise similar early evidence of Knight Templar activity in Malta associated with an *Orient of Malta* which can trace a history on the Island back to 1730 with associations with the *Orients of Marseilles, Toulouse,* and *Carcassonne* in France and working derived from the Rite of Strict Observance and the French Rite which had clear Templar elements.

Evidence also exists of Royal Arch and Knight Templar working within military lodges, with specific records of military movements around 1740-1760, mentioned earlier and in **Appendix B**, showing a clear link between service in Gibraltar and subsequent deployments to the New World.

In 1824, when Waller Rodwell Wright assumed superintendence of Masonic activity on the Island of Malta, there was certainly a wide range of activity with English, Scottish, Irish, and French prisoners-of-war lodges working there. Wright was appointed Provincial Grand Master for the Craft in 1812 and had similar appointments in other Orders. He did much to reorganise and record masonic activity on the Island.

A Province of The Mediterranean was constituted in 1875 with the appointment of Col G. Neeld Boldero as Provincial Grand Commander. Records suggest the following Preceptories existed at the time:

No. 37 Melita	Malta	c. 1815

(Name changed to Mediterranean in 1979 but restored to Melita in 1982 Now Meets Cheshunt, Herts)   *[C] 10 May 1850*

No. 60 Calpe	Gibraltar	17 Mar 1859

(Now administered as Unattached)

The Province was dissolved in 1924.

However, in recent years, the United Orders have re-established a new foothold on the Island with the blessing of the Sovereign Grand Lodge of Malta and recent consecrations have included:

No. 626	St John the Almoner	Malta	19 Jan 2001
No. 640	Waller Rodwell Wright	Malta	16 May 2003
No. 649	La Valette	Malta	29 Oct 2004

Many of the former expatriate residents, military Knights who were stationed on the Island, and members of today's Melita Preceptory No. 37 enthusiastically support this revival of United Orders activity in Malta.

Under Col Shadwell Henry Clerk;
Acting Great Prior of England and Wales (1876 -1877)

1877 Province of South Africa

The earliest recorded Knight Templar activity in the former British Colony of South Africa relates to Military Lodges stationed in, or staging through, the Colony on their journey to the Middle and Far-East around the Cape of Good Hope. However, there is also evidence that this was not only with British army and naval units but also other European forces such as Netherlands troops which also had Masonic lodges.

A Province of South Africa was constituted in 1877 with the appointment of Richard W. H. Giddy as Provincial Grand Commander, with two preceptories existing at that time:

No.	87	*Southern Cross*	*Cape Town*	*1 Sep 1866*
		[Removed from the Roll 1 Jan 1888]		
No.	133	Diamond in the Desert	Kimberley	7 May 1875

The Province ceased to exist in 1985 when divided into separate Provinces for Natal and South Africa Cape and Orange Free State when Cdr Herbert Raymond Carter was Provincial Prior.

Under Hon. Edward Bootle Wilbraham, 2nd Baron Skelmersdale;
Great Prior of England and Wales (1877-1896)

1880 Province of Kent & Surrey

The Province of Kent and Surrey was formed in 1880 by the addition of Surrey to the former Province of Kent under Gen J. S. Brownrigg, *CB*. At that date only a single preceptory was in existence:

No. 146	Black Prince	Canterbury	14 May 1880

The Province of Kent and Surrey nominally ceased to exist on 14 December 1956 when Surrey separated and was constituted as a separate province taking four of the Preceptories leaving seven in Kent.

1882 Province of East Anglia

A Province of East Anglia was created in 1882 from the former Province of Suffolk and Cambridge (constituted in 1857), with the appointment of Capt. Nathaniel George Philips as Provincial Grand Commander. At that date four of the preceptories extant today were in existence.

No. 16 Prudence	Ipswich	21 Feb 1811
No. 69 Cabbell	Norwich	3 Mar 1862
No. 80 Royal Plantagenet	Great Yarmouth	8 Nov 1864
No. 102 Tancred	Bury St Edmunds	18 Dec 1868

On 31 August 2018 the Province had 15 preceptories with 490 members.

1884 Staffordshire, Warwickshire, and Leicestershire

The Province of Staffordshire, Warwickshire, and Leicestershire was created in 1884 by the incorporation of the County of Leicestershire into the Province of Staffordshire and Warwickshire when Charles Fendelow was Provincial Grand Commander. At that time four preceptories were in existence:

No. 42 Godefroi de Bouillon	Stoke-on-Trent	5 Oct 1853
No. 67 Howe-Beauceant	Birmingham	22 Feb 1850
No. 79 Wulfruna	Wolverhampton	16 Aug 1864
No. 152 Rothley Temple	Leicester	11 Apr 1884

The Province ceased to exist under that name when, in 1893, the Province was extended to include Derbyshire.

1893 Province of Staffordshire, Warwickshire, Leicestershire and Derbyshire

This Province was created in 1893 by the addition of Derbyshire to the former Province of Staffordshire, Warwickshire, and Leicestershire with the addition of one preceptory:

| No. 159 Peveril | Derby | 8 Sep 1893 |

However, the Province as such was short-lived as it was further extended, in 1895 when the County of Nottingham was incorporated.

1895 Province of Staffordshire, Warwickshire, Leicestershire, Derbyshire and Nottinghamshire

This Province was created in 1895 by the addition of the County of Nottinghamshire (which had not been attached to any Province since 1893) to the former Province of Staffordshire, Warwickshire, Leicestershire and Derby. At that stage the Province included five preceptories spread over five separate counties:

No. 42 Godefroi de Bouillon	Stoke-on-Trent	5 Oct 1853
No. 67 Howe-Beauceant	Birmingham	22 Feb 1850
No. 79 Wulfruna	Wolverhampton	6 Aug 1864

| No. 152 | Rothley Temple | Leicester | 11 Apr 1884 |
| No. 159 | Peveril | Derby | 8 Sep 1893 |

The Province ceased to exist in 1905 when Leicestershire, Derbyshire, and Nottinghamshire separated to become part of a new Province of Nottinghamshire, Leicestershire and Derbyshire.

Under Rt Hon. Henry James Fitz-Roy, Earl of Euston, GCT Grand Master (1896-1908)

1897 Order of Holy Royal Arch Knight Templar Priests or Order of Holy Wisdom

In 1897 when the fate of the Order of Holy Royal Arch Knight Templar Priests or Order of Holy Wisdom, then administered in Newcastle-on-Tyne by the Knights Grand Cross of Jerusalem, was being considered, it was suggested that this Order the should be taken over by the United Orders. However, Great Priory decided not pursue this course and the Order was taken over by the Grand Council of the Allied Masonic Degrees.[273]

1898 Province of British Guiana & The Windward Islands

The Province of British Guiana & The Windward Islands was formed in 1898 with the appointment of Col Thomas Daly as Provincial Grand Commander. At that time two preceptories existed:

| No. 70 | Union | Georgetown, Guyana | 22 May 1862 |
| No. 77 | Star of the West | St George, Barbados | 2 Feb 1864 |

The office of Provincial Grand Commander fell vacant in 1905 and the Province ceased to exist independently in 1910 on incorporation into the Province of the West Indian Islands.

1899 Province of Somerset & Monmouth

The earliest recorded Knight Templar activity in the County of Somerset was mentioned earlier as Royal Edward Encampment in Bridgewater, constituted in 1792. (See **Appendix L**). In Monmouth, during and after the Napoleonic Wars, Abergavenny became one of the many Depots for French Prisoners of War. At one time they numbered upwards of 200, and there were sufficient brethren to form their own Lodge *Enfant de Mars et de Neptune* which lasted until 1813, undoubtedly working degrees beyond the Craft as normal in French Lodges.[274] This would result in exposure to these degrees by military brethren and well as members of local lodges.

The Province of Somerset and Monmouth was formed from the Province of Somerset by the incorporation of Monmouth in 1889 and the appointment of Lt Col Alfred Thrale Perkins, *CB* as Provincial Grand Commander. At that date four preceptories are known to have been in existence.

No. 1	Antiquity	Bath	11 Aug 1791
No. 40	Bladud	Bath	23 Sep 1852
No. 115	Gwent	Newport	1 Sep 1871
No. 121	Worlebury Preceptory of St Dunstan	Weston Super Mare	17 Apr 1872

The Province nominally ceased to exist in 1914 on addition of South Wales.

1905 Province of Nottinghamshire, Leicestershire, and Derbyshire.

The Province was formed in 1905 by the amalgamation of Nottinghamshire and Leicestershire (formerly part of the Province of Staffordshire, Warwickshire, Leicestershire, and Nottinghamshire), with Derbyshire thus reconstituting the Province of Nottinghamshire, Leicestershire, and Derbyshire originally constituted in 1847. Abraham Woodiwiss was appointed Provincial Grand Commander and three preceptories existed at that time:

A	Abbey Chapter	Nottingham	Time Immemorial
No. 152	Rothley Temple	Leicester	11 Apr 1884
No. 159	Peveril	Derby	8 Sep 1893

The Province ceased in 1969 when a Province was created for each County.

1906 Province of Staffordshire, Warwickshire, and Worcestershire

The Province was constituted in 1906 by the amalgamation of Worcestershire with the former Province of Staffordshire, Warwickshire, Leicestershire, and Nottinghamshire and Leicester and Nottinghamshire separated. Col George Walton Walker was appointed as Provincial Grand Commander and five preceptories existed at that time:

No. 42	Godefroi de Bouillon	Stoke-on-Trent	5 Oct 1853
No. 52	Richard de Vernon	Dudley	7 May 1857
No. 67	Howe-Beauceant	Birmingham	22 Feb 1850
No. 68	Preceptory of St Amand	Worcester	27 Nov 1861
No. 79	Wulfruna	Wolverhampton	16 Aug 1864

The Province nominally ceased in 1911 when Shropshire was incorporated.

1907 Province of New South Wales, Australia

The Province of New South Wales was constituted 1907 followed by the appointment of Louis Henry Mayerris Avery as Provincial Grand Commander / Provincial Prior in 1908. At that date two of the Preceptories which have survived today are known to have existed:

No. 180	Broken Hill	Broken Hill	18 Oct 1904
No. 186	Sydney	Willoughby	10 Jun 1907

The Province of New South Wales ceased to exist in 1984 on being reconstituted as part of the Great Priory of New South Wales and Australia Capital Territory.

At that date fourteen of the English Preceptories which survive today were in existence and were transferred to the new sovereign Great Priory. Details are given in **Appendix O**.

Under H.R.H. The Duke of Connaught and Strathearn, KG, GCT
Sovereign of the United Orders in Great Britain
and Grand Master of Ireland (1908-1939)

Rt Hon. Henry James Fitz-Roy, Earl of Euston, GCT
Pro-Grand Master (1908 -1912)

1910 Province of Lincolnshire

A Province of Lincolnshire was constituted in 1910 with the Appointment of Lt Col George Edward Heneage, *OBE, JP, DL,* KCT, (later 2nd Baron Heneage in 1922) as Provincial Prior. At that date two of the Preceptories which survive today were in existence:

No. 143	Temple Bruer	Lincoln	4 Apr 1879
No. 190	Sutcliffe	Grimsby	23 Apr 1910

On 31 August 2018 the Province consisted of nine preceptories with 348 members.

1910 Province of the West Indian Islands

In 1910 the Province of British Guiana and Windward Islands (constituted 1898) was renamed the Province of the West Indian Islands under The Revd Francis Bavin as Provincial Prior. At that date two preceptories which survive today were transferred to the new Province:

| No. 70 Union | Georgetown, Guyana | 22 May 1862 |
| No. 77 Star of the West | St George, Barbados | 2 Feb 1864 |

In 1923 the Province nominally ceased to exist on reconstitution as the District of British Guiana, Barbados, Trinidad, and Leeward Islands.

1911 Province of Staffordshire, Warwickshire, Worcestershire, & Shropshire

The Province of Staffordshire, Warwickshire, Worcestershire, and Shropshire was created in 1911 on the extension of the Province of Staffordshire, Warwickshire, & Worcestershire by the addition of Shropshire which added one preceptory:

| No. 193 Preceptory of St Chad | Shrewsbury | 24 Aug 1911 |

The Provincial Grand Commander of the former Province, Col George Walton Walker was appointed to take charge of the extended Province which by then had seven of the Preceptories which still exist today.

In 1924 the Province nominally ceased to exist and was reconstituted as the Province of Staffordshire, Warwickshire, and Shropshire when Worcestershire separated and was again constituted as a Province.

Richard Loveland Loveland, *KC*, GCT
Pro-Grand Master (1912-1920)

1914 Degree of Holy Royal Arch Knight Templar Priests and Order of Holy Wisdom

In March 1914 a conference was arranged in London to consider the suggestion that the United Orders should take control of the Degree of Holy Royal Arch Knight Templar Priests and Order of Holy Wisdom from the Grand Council of the Allied Masonic Degrees.[275] However, before any conclusion was reached, the Great War intervened, and it was 1920 before the subject was again considered. By that time Richard Loveland Loveland was Grand Master of the Allied Order as well as Pro Grand Master of the United Orders and he decided against it as had The Earl of Euston seventeen years previously.

1914 Province of Somerset, Monmouth, and South Wales

This new Province, formerly part of the Province of Somersetshire (constituted 1846), which had been reconstituted firstly as Somerset in 1874 and then with Monmouth added in 1889 to form the Province of Somerset and Monmouth, was reconstituted with the addition of South Wales in 1914 under Lt Col Alfred

Thrale Perkins, *CB* Provincial Prior. At that date five of the Preceptories extant today existed:

No. 1	Antiquity	Bath	11 Aug 1791
No. 40	Bladud	Bath	23 Sep 1852
No. 115	Gwent	Newport	1 Sep 1871
No. 121	Worlebury Preceptory of St Dunstan	Weston Super Mare	17 Apr 1872
No. 200	Morganwg	Penarth	21 Dec 1913

The Province ceased to exist when a new Province of Monmouth and South Wales was constituted in 1952 following the separation of Somerset which was then constituted as a separate Province on 30 June 1953.

1914 Province of South America

A Province of South America was constituted in 1914 with the appointment of Francis Hepburn Chevallier-Boutell as Provincial Prior. At that date two Preceptories existed:

No. 191	Preceptory of San Martin	Buenos Aires, Argentina	17 Mar 1911
No. 198	*Santa Rosa*	*Buenos Aires, Argentina*	*23 Apr 1913*
	(Warrant surrendered 15 May 1985)		

On 31 August 2018 the Province had 13 preceptories with 310 members.

1916 Province of India

The Province of India was constituted in 1916 by the amalgamation of the former provinces of Bengal, Bombay, and Madras (all constituted 1862), each of which ceased to exist on that date. The Provincial Prior of Bengal, Surg. Gen. The Hon. Sir Charles Pardey Lukis, *KCSI*, was appointed Provincial Prior of the new Province.

At that date seven of the Preceptories which survive today existed:

No. 53	*St Augustine*	*Lahore*	*11 May 1857*
No. 73	*Coromandel*	*Chennai*	*12 Mar 1828*
	[Formerly had Peripatetic Warrant and now meets in London		
No. 86	*Royal Deccan*	*Hyderabad*	*1 Aug 1866*
No. 137	*Himalaya*	*North West Provinces*	*20 Nov 1877*
No. 153	*Connaught and Strathearn*	*Meerut, NWP*	*1 Nov 1884*
No. 177	*Ardvorlich*	*Rwalpindi, India*	*20 Jan 1903*
No. 181	*Royal Kent*	*Calcutta, India*	*6 Jan 1905*

Between 3 April 1950 and 1 April 1960 Pakistan was included in the Province of India.

The Province was dissolved in 1968 and the transfers of some of the listed preceptories are shown in **Appendix O**.

However, in 2007 Knight Templar activity saw something of a revival in India (along with the introduction of other Degrees and Orders), with the first three being constituted in 2007 with two others more recently:[276]

No. 663	Unity and Brotherhood	Trivandrum, Kerala	21 Mar 2007
No. 664	Kottayam	Kottayam, Kerala	21 Mar 2007
No. 665	Bombay	Mumbai	19 Mar 2007
No. 696	Karnataka	Karnataka & Goa	14 Nov 2015
No. 709	St John's Preceptory	Andhra Pradesh	9 Dec 2017

Maj-Gen Thomas Charles Pleydell Calley, *CB, CBE, MVO*, GCT Pro-Grand Master (1920-1932)

1923 District of British Guiana, Barbados, Trinidad, and Leeward Islands.

In 1923 the former Province of British Guiana and Windward Islands (Incorporated into the Province of West Indian Islands, constituted 1910) was reconstituted as the District of British Guiana, Barbados, Trinidad, and Leeward Islands with William Heather Parratt as District Chancellor.

The District has now ceased to exist and the constituent preceptories are administered directly from Mark Masons' Hall as Unattached Preceptories.

1924 Province of Staffordshire, Warwickshire, and Shropshire

The Province of Staffordshire, Warwickshire, and Shropshire was created in 1924 from the former Province of Staffordshire, Warwickshire, Worcestershire, & Shropshire when Worcester separated and was again constituted as a Province. The Provincial Prior of the former Province, George Charles Kent assumed responsibility as the new Provincial Prior and three preceptories were transferred to the newly-reconstituted Province of Worcestershire.

The Province nominally ceased to exist on 5 July 1966 when Warwickshire separated to form a new Province.

1924 Province of Worcestershire

In 1924, the former Province of Staffordshire, Warwickshire, Worcestershire and Shropshire (constituted 1911) was sub-divided with the separation of Worcestershire in 1924 with the appointment of William Thomas Page as

Provincial Prior. At that date three of the Preceptories which survive today were in existence.

No. 52	Richard de Vernon	Dudley	7 May 1857
No. 68	Preceptory of St Amand	Worcester	27 Nov 1861
No. 212	Richard Coeur de Lion	King's Heath	23 Apr 1920

On 31 August 2018 the Province had 16 preceptories with 424 members.

1925 Province of Northampton, Huntingdon, and Bedford
A Province of Northampton, Huntingdon, and Bedford was constituted in 1925 with the appointment of Thomas Phipps Dorman as Provincial Prior. At that date there were four Preceptories in existence:

No. 207	Victory	Northampton	27 Dec 1918
No. 218	Perseverence	Kettering	6 Jan 1921
No. 236	Wendlynburgh	Wellingborough	24 Feb 1925
No. 240	United Priors	Huntingdon	18 Oct 1925

On 31 August 2018 the Province had 14 preceptories with 433 members.

1927 Province of Queensland, Australia
A Province of Queensland was constituted in 1927 with the appointment of Alexander Corrie as Provincial Prior. At that date three preceptories had been constituted:

No. 171	Duke of Albany	Brisbane	11 Jun 1900
No. 241	Beauceant	Toowoomba	1 May 1926
No. 242	Carpentaria	Gordonvale	21 Dec 1926

The Province ceased to exist in 1983 on being reconstituted as the Sovereign Great Priory of Queensland. At that date Flt Lt Harold Edmund Doe, RAAF was Provincial Prior and thirteen of the English Preceptories which survive today were in existence and all were transferred to the new sovereign Great Priory. Details are given in **Appendix O**.

1928 Province of Oxford & Berkshire
This Province was formed in 1928 by the addition of Berkshire to the Province of Oxford (constituted 1873) with the appointment of Sir Philip Colville-Smith, *CVO*, as Provincial Prior.[277] At that date four of the Preceptories which survive today were in existence.

| No. 29 | Preceptory of Coeur de Lion | Oxford | 26 Nov 1849 |

No. 204 Wellesley	Sindlesham	23 Apr 1918
No. 258 Crusaders	Maidenhead	30 Jan 1929
No. 264 Cressing	Gerrards Cross	24 Feb 1930

The Province ceased to exist in 1964 when reconstituted following the addition of Buckinghamshire.

1929 Province of Western Australia

The Province of Western Australia was constituted in 1929 with Alexander Cunningham McCallum, *MBE*, as Provincial Prior. At that date three Preceptories had been constituted there:

No. 167 Westralia	Perth	18 Oct 1897
No. 215 Geraldton	Geraldton	20 Nov 1920
No. 255 Burwell	Perth	1 Nov 1928

The Province ceased to exist in 1983 on being reconstituted as the Great Priory of Western Australia. At that date sixteen of the English Preceptories which survive today were in existence and were transferred to the new sovereign Great Priory. Details are given in **Appendix O**.

1930 Province of Essex

Essex was one of the Counties over which Thomas Dunckerley presided as Provincial Grand Master and Grand Superintendent and acted as *de facto* Provincial Grand Commander from 1776 to 1790. Unquestionably there was Knight Templar activity in both Essex and surrounding Counties within Military Lodges from the earliest times.

The Province was constituted in 1930 with the appointment of the Revd Felix Eustace Crate as Provincial Prior at which date two preceptories had been consecrated:

| No. 256 Maplestead | Colchester | 30 Nov 1928 |
| No. 261 de Mandeville | Chingford | 21 Dec 1929 |

On 31 August 2018 the Province had 23 preceptories with 714 members.

1930 Province of New Zealand

This Province was constituted in 1930 with the appointment of William Thomas Charlewood as Provincial Prior. At that date two of the four preceptories which had been consecrated in New Zealand were still in existence.

| No. 246 Royal Canterbury | Christchurch | 15 July 1927 |

| No. 254 | Wattemata | Auckland | 14 Feb 1927 |

(later renamed Selwood Preceptory of St John)

In 1958, the Province ceased to exist when separated to form the Provinces of New Zealand (North) and New Zealand (South).

1933 Province of Hertfordshire
A Province of Hertfordshire was constituted in 1933 with the appointment of John Frederick Cleeves as Provincial Prior. At that date, three of the Preceptories which survive today are known to have been in existence.

No. 28	Stuart	Watford	13 Apr 1840
No. 266	St Alban	St Albans	24 Feb 1930
No. 269	Temple Chelsin	Hertford	1 May 1931

On 31 August 2018 the Province had 16 preceptories with 428 members.

Under Rt Hon. Henry George Charles Lascelles, 6th Earl of Harewood, *KG, GCVO, DSO*, GCT Pro-Grand Master (1932-1939), Grand Master (1939-1947)

1942 Province of Transvaal, South Africa
A Province of the Transvaal was constituted in 1942 with Reginald Shaw Rigg as Provincial Prior. At that date five Preceptories, all formerly part of the Province of South Africa, which survive today were in existence.

No. 133	Diamond in the Desert	Kimberley	7 May 1875
No. 160	Johannesburg	Johannesburg	21 Sep 1893
No. 273	Keystone	Boksburg	25 Jun 1933
No. 288	Kosmos	Johannesburg	25 Jan 1936
No. 289	Transvaal	Pretoria	26 May 1940

On 31 August 2018 the Province had 13 preceptories with 250 members.

1945 Province of Hampshire & Isle of Wight
The Province of Hampshire, constituted in 1848, incorporated The Isle of Wight in 1945 under Col George Nowers Dyer, *CBE, DSO*, Provincial Prior who had been appointed in 1944. At that date the one Preceptory on the Isle of Wight was incorporated in the new Province thus giving a total of six preceptories:

| No. 2 | Royal Naval | Portsmouth | 11 Mar 1791 |

No.	27	Sepulchre & Sandeman Priory	Christchurch	15 Jun 1840
No.	32	Royal Gloucester	Southampton	8 Apr 1845
No.	76A	William Stuart	Alton	20 Jan 1864
No.	194	Loveland	Bournemouth	30 Sep 1911
No.	237	Vectis	Ryde, IOW	17 Mar 1725

On 31 August 2018 the Province had 12 preceptories with 404 members.

Under Rt Hon. George St Vincent,
5th Baron Harris of Seringapatum and Mysore, *MC, DL*, GCT
Grand Master (1947-1973

1949 Province of Dorset and Wiltshire

Wiltshire and Dorset were two of the Counties over which Thomas Dunckerley presided as Provincial Grand Master and Grand Superintendent, acting as *de facto* Provincial Grand Commander from 1777 to 1795. The earliest recorded Knight Templar activities in the County of Wiltshire were the Encampments of:

| Harmony of Seven Degrees | Salisbury | Constituted 1792 |
| Science of Seven Degrees | Salisbury | Constituted 1794 |

It is interesting to speculate on these choice of names and the nature of their working for the French Rite of Seven Degrees, the fifth degree of which was Scots Master or Knight of St Andrew with Royal Arch and Knight Templar elements, made its appearance in Britain as early as 1733. Later, in the Salisbury area, the degree could either have been taken there by French Prisoners of War who were members of French Military Lodges which worked that Rite and released on parole in that area, or through the introduction of his Rite by Pierre Lambert de Lintot, or by British Army regimental lodges. Both encampments had disbanded by 1810 and were removed from the Roll before 1868, which may explain why the County of Wiltshire did not join a modern Province until comparatively recently.

The Province of Dorset and Wiltshire was constituted on 10 January 1949 following the incorporation of Wiltshire into the Province of Dorsetshire (Originally constituted 1836) with the appointment of Col Montague James Raymond as Provincial Prior. At that date three of the Preceptories which survive today were in existence:

No. 31	All Souls	Weymouth	26 Mar 1847
	(From Dorsetshire)		
No. 98	Hyde	Wareham	1 Oct 1867
No. 322	William Longespee	Salisbury	29 Sep 1948

On 31 August 2018 the Province had nine preceptories with 240 members.

1952 Province of Monmouth and South Wales

This Province was formerly part of Province of Somerset, Monmouth, and South Wales.

    The Province of Monmouth and South Wales was constituted 1952 with appointment of Richard William Bartlett as Provincial Prior and at that date three of the Preceptories which survive today were in existence.

No. 115	Gwent	Newport	1 Sep 1871
No. 200	Morganwg	Penarth	21 Dec 1913
No. 319	Giraldus Cambrensis	Llanelli	25 Jul 1948

On 31 August 2018 the Province had 15 preceptories with 496 members.

1953 Province of Somerset

This province has a complex history having, at times, formed part of the Provinces of Somersetshire (1846-74), Somerset (1874-89), Somerset and Monmouth (1889-1914), Somerset, Monmouth, and South Wales (1914-1952).

    The Province separated in 1952 from the Province of Somerset, Monmouth, and South Wales and was constituted as a separate Province on 30 June 1953 with the appointment of Maj. George Travers Biggs, *DSO, TD* as Provincial Prior. At that date five of the preceptories which survive today were in existence.

No. 1	Antiquity	Bath	11 Aug 1791
No. 40	Bladud	Bath	23 Sep 1852
No. 121	Worlebury Preceptory of St Dunstan	Weston-super-Mare	17 Apr 1872
No. 211	King Ina	Taunton	4 Dec 1919
No. 244	Selwood Preceptory of St John	Frome	14 Feb 1927

On 31 August 2018 the Province had 12 preceptories with 332 members.

1956 Province of Surrey

Knight Templar activity in the County of Surrey was formerly administered by the Province of Kent and Surrey constituted in 1880. Surrey separated on 14 December 1956 when a new Province of Surrey was constituted and Sir George Townsend Boag, *KCIE, CSI* appointed as Provincial Prior. At that date five of the Preceptories in existence today became part of the new Province:

No. 162	Temple Court	Guildford	1 May 1894
No. 196	Preceptory of Croydon	Croydon	14 Feb 1912
No. 225	Kyngstun	Surbiton	6 Jan 1923

No. 304	Chertsey	Chertsey	11 Jun 1946
No. 338	St Saviour's	Sutton	19 Mar 1953

A sixth preceptory (No. 360 Gascoigne was warranted a week after the separation date on 21 December 1958 to meet at Croydon.

On 31 August 2018 the Province had 18 preceptories with 427 members.

1958 Province of New Zealand (North)

Originally formed part of the Province of New Zealand (Constituted 1930) which ceased to exist in 1958 when the North and South Islands separated to form the Provinces of New Zealand (North) and New Zealand (South).

The Province was constituted in 1958 followed by the appointment of Norman Berridge Spencer, *MSM* as Provincial Prior in 1959 with the transfer of four Preceptories:

No 254	Waitemata	Auckland	1 Nov 1928
No 285	St George	Auckland	23 Apr 1938
No 287	Royal Taranaki	Taranaki, NZ	21 Sep 1938
No 291	Aotea	Taranaki, NZ	24 Aug 1942

The Province ceased to exist on the constitution of the Sovereign Great Priory of New Zealand in 1983 with the transfer of six Preceptories to the new sovereign body. Details are given in **Appendix O**.

1958 Province of New Zealand (South)

Originally formed part of the Province of New Zealand (Constituted 1930) which ceased to exist in 1958 when the North and South Islands separated to form the Provinces of New Zealand (North) and New Zealand (South).

The Province of New Zealand (South) was constituted in 1958 with the appointment of Ernest Julius Woolf as Provincial Prior with the transfer of four Preceptories:

No 246	Royal Canterbury	Christchurch	15 Jul 1927
No 342	Tuarangi	Ashburton	24 Feb 1955
No 353	Amuri	Amberley	21 Dec 1956
No 355	Aurora	St Andrews	25 Jul 1957

The Province ceased on the constitution of the Sovereign Great Priory of New Zealand in 1983 and the transfer of these Preceptories to the new sovereign body.

1958 Province of Far East

This Province was originally constituted as the Province of China in 1863 and reconstituted as Province of Far East in 1958. David Smith Hill was appointed

Provincial Prior in 1959. At that date two of the Preceptories which survive today were then in existence in Hong Kong:

No. 78	Victoria	Hong Kong	8 Apr 1864
No. 195	Preceptory of Shanghai	Hong Kong	6 Dec 1911

Provincial Sub-Priors were formerly appointed for Hong Kong and Malaysia and Singapore until Malaysia and Singapore separated in 1991 to form a Province of South East Asia.

On 31 August 2018 the Province had three preceptories and 156 members.

1960 Province of Gloucestershire and Herefordshire

This Province was originally part of a Province covering the City and County of Bristol and the County of Gloucestershire constituted in 1858. Gloucestershire separated from Bristol in 1960, forming a separate Province which incorporated Herefordshire on 14 June 1960 with the appointment of Percy Harold Creese as Provincial Prior. At that date three of the Preceptories which survive today were in existence:

No. 72	Coteswold Preceptory of St Augustine	Cheltenham	12 Feb 1863
No. 341	King Richard I	Downend	21 Sep 1954
No. 365	Dean Forest Preceptory of St Mary	Newnham	29 Dec 1959

On 31 August 2018 the Province had nine preceptories with 276 members.

1962 Province of Rhodesia

A Province of Rhodesia was constituted in 1962 with the appointment of Ferdinand Farrant Duckworth as Provincial Prior. At that date two Preceptories which survive today were in existence:

No. 347	Rhodes	Bulawayo	21 Sep 1955
No. 370	Le Crac des Chevaliers	Harare	24 Dec 1960

The Province was renamed the Province of Zimbabwe in 1980 when Eric Edgar Spence became Provincial Prior.

1964 Province of Oxfordshire, Berkshire, and Buckinghamshire

This Province was formed in 1964 by the addition of Buckinghamshire to the Province of Oxfordshire and Berkshire under Col Alexander Denis Burnett Brown, *OBE, MC, TD*, Provincial Prior. At that date seven of the Preceptories which survive today were in existence:

No. 29		Coeur de Lion	Oxford	26 Nov 1849
No. 204		Wellesley	Sindlesham	23 Apr 1918
No. 258		Crusaders	Wokingham	30 Jan 1929
No. 264		Cressing	Beaconsfield	24 Feb 1930
No. 314		St Hugh	Banbury	30 Nov 1947
No. 323		Beaumont	Oxford	18 Oct 1948
No. 389		Aylesbury	Aylesbury	24 Feb 1964

On 31 August 2018 the Province had 17 preceptories with 511 members.

1966 Province of Staffordshire and Shropshire

Although the original Province covered Preceptories in Staffordshire, Warwickshire, and Worcestershire, it has at various times been linked with six other geographical counties, namely, Derbyshire, Leicestershire, Nottinghamshire, Shropshire, Warwickshire, and Worcestershire. It has been linked with five but never all six at the same time. The addition or removal of the different geographical areas has not always been reflected in the formal reconstitution or renaming of the Province.

The Province of Staffordshire and Shropshire in existence today, although not formally constituted until 1966, can therefore claim the following precedents:

1849-69	Staffordshire
	Staffordshire, and Worcestershire
1869-	Staffordshire, Warwickshire, and Worcestershire
1906-24	Staffordshire, Warwickshire, Worcestershire, and Shropshire
1924-66	Staffordshire, Warwickshire, and Shropshire
1966	Staffordshire and Shropshire

In 1890 the Godefroi de Bouillon Preceptory presented to Lichfield Cathedral a magnificent statue of Godefroi de Bouillon which is still there today. It can be seen externally on the South Transept. It cost £35!!

A new Province of Staffordshire and Shropshire was created from the former Province of Staffordshire, Warwickshire, and Shropshire when Warwickshire separated to form a new Province on 5 July 1966. This occurred during the tenure of Col The Earl of Powis, *CBE, TD* who had been appointed as Provincial Prior in 1963 and remained as Provincial Prior for Staffordshire and Shropshire following the separation.

At the date of Constitution (5 July 1966) six of the Preceptories which survive today were in existence:

No. 42		Godefroi de Bouillon	Stoke-on-Trent	5 Oct 1853

No. 79	Wulfruna	Wolverhampton	16 Aug 1864
No. 170	Bernard de Tremelay	Walsall	30 Nov 1899
No. 193	St Chad	Shrewsbury	24 Aug 1911
No. 369	Sir John Kent	Stafford	24 Dec 1960
No. 398	Saint Clement	West Bromwich	17 Mar 1965

On 31 August 2018 the Province had 17 preceptories with 531 members.

1966 Province of Warwickshire

Formerly part of the Province of Staffordshire, Warwickshire, and Shropshire, constituted 1924, the Province of Warwickshire was constituted on separation on 5 July 1966 following the appointment of Leslie Burnett as Provincial Prior on 24 January 1966. At that date six of the Preceptories which survive today were in existence.

No. 67	Howe-Bauceant	Birmingham	22 Feb 1850
No. 229	Peter de Erdington	Sutton Coldfield	15 Jul 1923
No. 293	Holy Rood	Warwick	30 Nov 1942
No. 331	Holy Trinity	Coventry	1 Nov 1950
No. 340	Temple Balsall	Temple Balsall	24 Aug 1954
No. 361	Ascalon	Rugby	26 Dec 1958

On 31 August 2018 the Province had 14 preceptories with 412 members.

1969 Province of Nottinghamshire

The County of Nottingham was first constituted as a Province in 1856 but ceased to exist as such in 1883 following which it had a complex association with several other provinces until 1969 as described earlier. The County was formerly part of Province of Nottinghamshire, Leicestershire, and Derbyshire constituted 1847.

A separate Province of Nottinghamshire was (re)constituted in 1969 with the appointment of Charles Henry Venn Elliott, *TD,* as the Provincial Prior. At that date three of the Preceptories which survive today were in existence:

A	Abbey Chapter	Nottingham	Time Immemorial
No. 395	Wynkbourne	Mansfield	25 Jul 1964
No. 413	Pelham	Worksop	19 Mar 1969

On 31 August 2018 the Province had eight preceptories with 301 members.

1970 Province of Leicestershire and Rutland

The Province of Leicestershire and Rutland came into existence in 1970 following the separation of Derbyshire from the former Province of Nottinghamshire, Leicestershire, and Derbyshire which had existed since

1885; David Neil Foister, *TD* was appointed Provincial Prior and there were four preceptories existing at that time:

No. 152	Rothley Temple	Leicester	11 Apr 1884
No. 294	Ivanhoe	Leicester	20 May 1944
No. 410	Sir John Babington	Loughborough	12 Apr 1968
No. 420	Ulverscroft	Leicester	28 Nov 1969

On 31 August 2018 the Province had seven preceptories with 214 members.

1970 Province of Derbyshire

Formerly part of Province of Leicestershire and Derbyshire constituted in 1847 which was divided in 1970 when Derbyshire was constituted as a separate Province following the appointment of Dr Reginald Latham Brown as Provincial Prior in 1968. At that date four of the Preceptories which survive today were in existence.

No. 159	Peveril	Derby	8 Sep 1893
No. 348	Abbeydale	Dore	24 Feb 1956
No. 399	St Laurence	Long Eaton	1 Mar 1965
No. 423	Bertram de Verdun	Burton-on-Trent	16 Mar 1970

On 31 August 2018 the Province had eight preceptories with 253 members.

1970 Province of Middlesex

The Province of Middlesex was constituted in 1970 with the appointment of Col Bernard Stuart Horner, *OBE* as Provincial Prior. At that date five of the Preceptories which survive today were in existence.

No. 253	Staines	Staines	1 Nov 1928
No. 268	Herga	Harrow	21 Sep 1930
No. 388	Twickenham	Twickenham	26 Dec 1961
No. 394	Uxbridge	Uxbridge	23 Jul 1964
No. 429	Southgate	Southgate	14 Oct 1970

On 31 August 2018 the Province had 12 preceptories with 286 members.

Under Lt Col John Leighton Byrne Leicester-Warren, *TD*, *VL*, GCT, Grand Master (1973-1975)

No Provinces or Districts were created during the very brief Grand-Mastership of Lt Col Leicester-Warren.

Under Harold Devereaux Still, GCT,
Great Seneschal /Acting Grand Master (1975-76)
Grand Master (1976-1996)

1975 Province of Durham

Durham was formerly part of Province of Northumberland which included the County of Durham, which separated and was then reconstituted on 24 September 1975 with the appointment of Charles Henry Swann, JP as Provincial Prior. At that date eight of the Preceptories which survive today were in existence.

No. 118	Mount Grace	Hartlepool	6 Apr 1872
No. 139	St Cuthbert's	Darlington	15 Feb 1878
No. 222	Finchale	Sunderland	1 May 1922
No. 233	Haliwerfole	Old Elvet, Durham	0 Nov 1924
No. 275	St Lawrence	South Shields	31 Oct 1934
No. 292	Wycliffe	Darlington	1 Nov 1942
No. 316	Tees	Stockton-on-Tees	21 Dec 1947
No. 339	De Umfraville	Gateshead	24 Aug 1953

On 31 August 2018 the Province had 14 preceptories with 434 members.

1975 Province of Northumberland

The Province of Northumberland was formerly part of the Province of Northumberland and Durham constituted in 1850. Durham separated as a separate Province in 1975 with responsibility for eight Preceptories and The Province of Northumberland was Reconstituted on 24 September 1975 with the appointment of Harold Frederick Lockwood Mavity as Provincial Prior. At that date six preceptories became part of the new Province:

No. 20	Royal Kent	Newcastle-upon-Tyne	16 Apr 1812
No. 226	Lindisfarne	Berwick-upon-Tweed	25 Apr 1923
No. 232	Chibburn	Whitley Bay	1 Nov 1924
No. 239	Brandling	Gosforth, North'd.	24 Aug 1925
No. 284	Brinkburn	Morpeth	21 Sep 1937
No. 461	St Wilfred of Hexham	Hexham	21 May 1975

On 31 August 2018 the Province had 16 preceptories with 488 members.

1975 Province of Sri Lanka

In 1975 the Province of Ceylon (constituted 1869) was re-designated the Province of Sri Lanka during the tenure of Brig. Christopher Allan Hector Perera Jayawardana, *CMG, CVO, OBE, KStJ, ED, ADC,* KCT as Provincial Prior with two Preceptories:

| No. 99 | Ceylon | Kandy | 29 Jul 1867 |
| No. 164 | Colombo | Colombo | 6 Jan 1895 |

On 31 August 2018 the Province had two preceptories with 36 members.

1980 Province of Zimbabwe
A Province of Zimbabwe was constituted by the renaming of the Province of Rhodesia under Eric Edgar Spence as Provincial Prior in 1980 at which date there were two Preceptories:

| No. 347 | Rhodes | Bulawayo | 21 Sep 1955 |
| No. 370 | Le Crac des Chevaliers | Harare | 24 Dec 1960 |

On 31 August 2018 the Province had two preceptories with 33 members.

Independent Great Priories in Australia:
In 1982 Great Priories were constituted for Victoria and South Australia and the former Provinces of Victoria, constituted 1857, and South Australia, constituted 1868 ceased to exist. At that date twenty-six English preceptories which survive today were in existence; eighteen were transferred to the new sovereign Great Priory of Victoria, and eight to the new sovereign Great Priory of South Australia. Details are given in **Appendix O**.

In 1983 a Great Priory of New South Wales and Australia Capital Territory was constituted and the former Province of New South Wales, constituted 1907, ceased to exist. At that date fourteen of the English preceptories which survive today were in existence and all were transferred to the new sovereign Great Priory. Details are given in **Appendix O**.

In 1984 a Great Priory of Western Australia was constituted and the former Province of Western Australia, constituted 1929, ceased to exist. At that date nineteen of the English preceptories which survive today were in existence and all were transferred to the new sovereign Great Priory. Details are given in **Appendix O**.

In 1985 a Great Priory of Queensland, was constituted and the former Province of Queensland, constituted 1927, ceased to exist. At that date thirteen of the English preceptories which survive today were in existence and all were transferred to the new sovereign Great Priory. Details are given in **Appendix O**.

1983 Province of The Netherlands
The Province of The Netherlands was constituted in 1983 with the appointment of Henri Anton van den Akker as Provincial Prior. At that date 5 preceptories existed:

No.417 Olivier-de-la-Marche	Leiden	20 Jun 1969
No. 486 St George's	Eindhoven	10 Feb 1978
No. 503 St Bernard de Clairvaux	Terneuzen	18 Mar 1981
No. 504 St Peter's	Leiden	20 Mar 1981
No. 505 St Maartens	Gronigen	20 Mar 1981

The Province ceased to exist on 23 November 2013 when a Sovereign Great Priory of The Netherlands was inaugurated with the transfer of the former preceptories of the United Orders in the Netherlands being transferred on that date.

1985 Province of Natal
In 1985 the former Province of South Africa (Constituted 1877) separated into Natal and South Africa (Cape and Orange Free State).

A Province of Natal was constituted in 1985 with the appointment of Douglas William Harris as Provincial Prior. At that date four preceptories existed:

No. 148	Natalia	Pietermaritzburg	19 Jul 1880
No. 156	Victoria Jubilee	Durban	27 Dec 1886
No. 509	Acre	Empangini	30 Jul 1981
No. 535	Coeur de Lion	Newcastle, Natal	17 Jul 1985

On 31 August 2018 the Province had four preceptories with 41 members.

1985 Province of South Africa (Cape and Orange Free State)
In 1985 the former Province of South Africa (Constituted 1877) separated into Natal and South Africa – and Orange Free State

A Province of South Africa (Cape and Orange Free State) was constituted in 1985 with the appointment of Cdr Herbert Raymond Carter as Provincial Prior. Six preceptories were transferred to the new Province:

151	Vasco da Gama	Port Elizabeth	20 Dec 1883
168	Mount Zion	Cape Town	18 Oct 1897
270	The Bloemfontein	Bloemfontein	18 Oct 1931
405	St Andrew's	Durban	23 Aug 1966
444	Rougemont	Durban	30 Apr 1973
511	Phoenix	Simonstown	13 Oct 1981

The Province nominally ceased to exist in 2006 on being reconstituted as the Province of South Africa (Cape).

1991 Province of South East Asia

Originally part of the Province of China constituted in 1863 with Samuel Rawson as Provincial Grand Commander. It then became part of the reconstituted Province of the Far East from 1958 with Maurice John Baptiste Montargis as Provincial Prior and two Provincial Sub-Priors appointed for Hong Kong and Malaysia and Singapore.

That Province split to form a Province of South East Asia in 1991 at which date the Preceptory in Singapore and that in Kuala Lumpur were transferred to the new Province, for which Capt. Eidwen Frederick Mullan was appointed as Provincial Prior.

On 31 August 2018 the Province had three preceptories with 214 members.

1992 Province of London

The first documented Knight Templar activities in London were the encampments of:

No. 6	St George	London	20 Oct 1795
	Boyne	Woolwich	Constituted 1805
	(Removed from the Roll before 1868)		

A Province of London was constituted in 1992 with Jack Lodewyck Charles Dribbell as Provincial Prior, and the transfer of twenty-five previously unattached preceptories meeting in the London area. Details appear in **Appendix N**.

On 31 August 2018 the Province had 29 preceptories with 964 members.

Under Leslie Felgate Dring, GCT, Grand Master (1997 – 2011)

2005   Province of Bolivia

This Province was constituted in 2005 with the appointment of Carlos Bedregal Soria as Provincial Prior; three preceptories existed at that date:

No. 604	General Jose Ballivian	La Paz	2 Nov 1996
No. 624	Civis Mundi	La Paz	19 May 2001
No. 646	Mariscal Andres de Santa Cruz Calahumana	La Paz	4 Oct 2003

On 31 August 2018 the Province had seven preceptories with 219 members.

2006 Province of South Africa (Cape)

The former Province of South Africa (constituted 1877) was reconstituted in 1985 as two Provinces: The Province of Natal and Province of South Africa (Cape and Orange Free State). In 2006 the latter was reconstituted as the Province of South Africa (Cape) with the appointment of Alasdair Bruce Duthie as Provincial Prior. Seven preceptories became part of the newly constituted Province:

No. 151	Vasco da Gama	Port Elizabeth	20 Dec 1883
No. 168	Mount Zion	Cape Town	18 Oct 1897
No. 270	The Bloemfontein	Bloemfontein	18 Oct 1931
No. 511	Phoenix	Simonstown	13 Oct 1981
	[In abeyance since 28 Feb 2018]		
No. 534	Lord Roberts	Somerset West	8 Feb 1985
No. 542	St George	George	13 Mar 1987
No. 688	Port Alfred	Port Alfred	31 Mar 2012

On 31 August 2018 the Province had six preceptories with 88 members.

Under Timothy John Lewis, GCT, Grand Master (2011-2017)

No new Provinces or Districts were created during the brief Grand-Mastership of Timothy John Lewis.

Under Paul Raymond Clement, GCT Grand Master (2017-Date)

2019 Province of River Plate

On 9 August 2019, a Province of the River Plate was constituted with four preceptories formerly part of the Province of South America:

No. 191	Preceptory of San Martin	Buenos Aires	17May 1911
No. 701	Santa Rosa	Buenos Aires	26 Feb 2016
No. 702	St Philip and St James	Montevideo	27 Feb 2016
No. 703	Santiago Apostol	Mendoza	27 Feb 2016

Today's Structure

These successive constitutions and the consequent delegation of responsibility to Provincial Priors, and in some cases, the transfer of preceptories and Provinces to Sovereign Great Priories have resulted in today's structure with the number of preceptories and membership shown against each existing Province. Further details for each Province are given in two Appendices:

Appendix N   :   England and Wales

Appendix O   :   Developments Overseas

No doubt further developments can be expected in the future.

4.4 THE EFFECT OF WAR

In every sense, of course, the Crusading Orders, both Military and Hospitaller, were born of International conflicts, as were the minor chivalric Orders founded during the lesser crusades. The same may be said for other chivalric orders which developed in many cases to recognise the contribution made by individuals in war.

The impact of military activity and the movement of lodges associated with military and naval forces has already been mentioned, but there were not only impacts on both masonic lodges and preceptories but also discernable impacts on non-masonic activities which are interesting in the context of this history. The general impacts which apply to all wartime conflicts may be summarised under five main headings:

Travelling to theatres of conflict brought British Military forces into direct contact with civilian populations and naval and civil maritime personnel during deployments both within Britain and during deployments overseas.

Armed conflicts brought British military and naval forces into direct contact with the armed forces of many other Nations and Masonic individuals and Military Lodges amongst their ranks.

Deployments in overseas theatres brought direct contact with civilian populations of other Nations which resulted in cultural as well as masonic changes.

Most armed conflicts result in the taking of prisoners-of-war on all sides; British forces interned in overseas theatres undoubtedly acquired experience of foreign Freemasonry; foreign prisoners were often interned in the British Isles and this brought not only contact with British military and naval personnel escorting or guarding them but also contact when 'on parole' with civilian brethren and lodges.

Armed conflict often resulted in psychological effects on both participants and their families. On the negative side, today this may be termed 'Post Traumatic Stress' with long-term effects, but the discussion of this is outside the scope of this history. A somewhat lesser impact reveals itself on the direct impact on Masonic lodges, etc. as individuals finding at least some relief from the trauma of war in Masonic companionship resulting in an increase in Masonic activity after major conflicts.

Wars of the Spanish Succession (1700-13), Austrian Succession (1740-48) and The Jacobite Uprisings (1715-16 and 1745-46)

It is hardly possible to better the summary of the impact of European wars on the British army as penned by Brig. P. R. Sharpe.

> The war of the Spanish Succession (1702-13) saw the first real test abroad of the post civil war Army. The rise of John Churchill to become the Duke of Marlborough and his four great victories of Blenheim, Ramilies, Oudenard and Malplaquet established the British Army as a major fighting force in Europe. The expansion of British interests in its fledgling colonies also became a major focus for military activity. America, India and the West Indies began to call for garrisons of substantial troops. The Army therefore began to shape itself around continental and colonial commitments. The continental army fought along side coalition partners and both Marlborough in Europe and Wellington in the Peninsula 100 years later, commanded more foreign formations than British ones. Both elements of the Army found themselves involved in the Seven Years war that had European, North American and Indian theatres of operation.
>
> A distinction must be made between this Army and the home force of the militia, fencible regiments and yeomanry. For the most part the home force focussed on policing type duties, counter insurgency tasks, and assisting revenue officers in preventing smuggling on the coast. They did not serve overseas indeed, there were laws throughout the period that expressly forbade it. It is interesting to note that the reverse was not true, during the war of Austrian succession (1740- 48) some British forces had to return from Europe to deal with the Jacobite rebellion of 1745. The Seven Years War (1756- 63) is one worth dwelling on due to its imperial importance with the resultant expansion of British interests in Canada, India and the West Indies. (Brig. P. R. Sharpe. *Short History of The Armed Forces And Masonry*)

It can therefore be established that the introduction of military lodges at the very time the role of the British Army was changing in this way combined to change the way Freemasonry itself developed. It is therefore fair to say that many Masonic changes came about directly from the effects of war.

In addition to the general interactions mentioned above, one direct, but over-looked impact on 'higher degrees' was the influence of the Wars of the Spanish and Austrian Successions and the Jacobite Uprising on Andrew Michael Ramsay, and although the impact of his 'Oration' on the Chivalric Orders and their influence on speculative Freemasonry was considered earlier, his military history has not perhaps been considered sufficiently.

Andrew Ramsay, who only added the Christian name Michael (or Michel) around the time he became a Knight of St Lazarus in 1723 after which he became known as Chevalier Andrew Ramsay, went in about 1707 with the English auxiliaries to the Netherlands, where he fought under Marlborough during the War of the Spanish Succession. Later he gained further military experience through joining the Jacobite army, probably in Glasgow about 1715, then fighting at the battle of Preston (9-14 November, 1715), after which he was captured and imprisoned but escaped. He was recaptured and held in Wigan jail until he was deported along with other Jacobite prisoners in June 1716. Their destination was the Island of St Kitts in the West Indies[278], but they managed to overpower the ship's crew and were landed in France.

During his stay in France he had several period of employment as tutor to the children of wealthy and influential families. These included the family of a direct descendant of Godfrey de Bouillon and Ramsay compiled a history of the Turenne family which increased his knowledge not only of the Crusades but also the histories of other Orders of Chivalry. His tutoring duties also brought close contact with senior members of the Jacobite Court, and it must be assumed he then became aware of the involvement of Scottish brethren with the early Knights Templar mentioned previously.

It may therefore be concluded that the background to Ramsay's 'oration' included a lifetime of sound military, chivalric, social, and historical studies drawn from a wide variety of cultures over a time scale of several hundred years.

Late-Eighteenth Century Conflicts (1778-1815)
This was a period when Britain became embroiled in a number of conflicts including the Bourbon or Anglo-French War (1778-83), the Anglo-Dutch Wars (1780-84), the French Revolutionary Wars (1792-1802, and the Napoleonic Wars (1803-1815). Leaving aside any of the political reasons for these various conflicts the impact on speculative and chivalric Freemasonry as a result of military involvements may be reasonably summarised under three headings:

Such conflicts took British Military forces into direct contact with many European countries and, through deployments both within Britain and to the New World, to many overseas cultures.

Such conflicts brought British military and naval forces into direct contact with the armed forces of many Nations including French, German, Spanish, Dutch, Belgian, Scandinavian, American and Canadian Forces.

These conflicts resulted in at least 122,000 prisoners-of-war being interned in the British Isles. Smaller numbers of British forces were interned in France, and although the extent of their Masonic activity is uncertain, some Brethren certainly acquired experience of continental Freemasonry.

Such evidence as exists confirms these eighteenth century conflicts did much to develop military travelling lodges and promote their involvement with many degrees and orders. This did not apply only to British forces and their Lodges:

The first Dutch Field Lodge was established at Maastrict in 1745.

The first German military lodges were constituted about 1745.

The majority of French military lodges were constituted between 1750 and 1800.

Whilst the earliest lodges in the New World were constituted in the 1720s and 1730s, period 1750-1800 saw a considerable increase in their distribution and popularity.

The interactions mentioned earlier between individual brethren and travelling and static lodges were undoubtedly facilitated by the military conflicts and that these interactions contributed most significantly to the spread of speculative Freemasonry in general, and the Royal Arch, and Chivalric Orders in particular. It is particularly noticeable that those Nations which had participated in the knightly crusades and subsequent lesser crusades were those whose cultures had perpetuated chivalric concepts and history providing fertile ground for speculative chivalric Freemasonry to take root.

The Great War (1914-18)
A few statistics usefully illustrate the impact of the Great War:

At 31 December 1913, there were 134 preceptories on the Roll of the United Orders;

In the preceding decade (1904-1913) 18 new preceptories were consecrated;

During the period 1914-1918, only 4 new preceptories were consecrated, one of which was in Bermuda;

In the following decade (1919-1928) 52 new preceptories were consecrated.

Interpretation of these simple figures must necessarily be subjective, but such a resurgence of interest is also reflected in the development of Freemasonry generally. Leaving aside the consecrations during the war, it can be seen that almost three times as many consecrations occurred in the decade after the war as before. Speculative Freemasonry may therefore be judged, perhaps, to provide a therapeutic haven for brethren returning from the trauma of conflict. However, War, of course, changed attitudes in other ways.

A Revival of Medieval Chivalry: The Most Noble Order of Crusaders
Established in London in 1921 by three ex-servicemen among the chaos of delayed demobilisation, million-strong unemployment, and the attempts of the British Government to return to a peacetime footing, The Most Noble Order of Crusaders was designed to be a secret society of British men gathered to tackle the social problems of the Country.[279]

Describing its inception, *The Tenth Crusade* (the Journal of the Order) relayed that:

> 'inspiration came to [the founder] to revive the Crusades, to appeal yet again to the innate chivalry, the sense of self-sacrifice, the love of fellowship, in short to all that we call the "Spirit of 1914", and once more make a Crusade, but this time against all the powers of evil which are threatening England.'

The Order saw itself as being engaged in a new social crusade, but *The Tenth Crusade* was more than a title of its journal; it located their activities in sequence with previous crusades. In this schema 'The Ninth Crusade' was the First World War, in which the 'indomitable Spirit of the British' won the war, and was equated with that of the crusaders.

As a self-styled Order of Chivalry, The Most Noble Order of Crusaders, sought to take up the mantle perceived to have been held by the medieval crusaders, the exemplars of chivalrous knighthood. The Order was organised into Conclaves, and by 1926 about 48 existed with a membership of around 5000, of which 80% were of working class.

After December 1936, when the Order affiliated with The Royal Society of St George, an English patriotic Society, it dwindled to become a charitable organisation and rapidly faded from view.

World War II (1939-45)
Examining the period before and after World War II for comparison with the Great War data:

At 31 December 1938, there were 255 preceptories on the Roll of the United Orders;

In the preceding decade (1929-1938) 31 new preceptories were consecrated;

During the period 1939-1945, only 11 new preceptories were consecrated, six of which were overseas;

In the following decade (1946-1955) 45 new preceptories were consecrated.

For comparison with the Great War, and leaving aside the consecrations during the war, it can be seen that in the decade after the war although there were more consecrations the post-war impact was nothing near as dramatic.

The actual period of the war itself was necessarily a time of national austerity, and indeed, a directive was issued on behalf of Great Priory in 1941 which, in effect, suspended meeting of Preceptories of the United Orders for the duration of the war. In any cases meetings would have been rendered impractical as many Masonic Halls were taken over in part or in whole for civil defence purposes. Where meetings did take place, many events were scheduled for daylight hours so as to minimise lighting and heating and to make travelling easier, and often there were no festive boards; when the suspension was actually lifted is not known precisely, but by 1947, individual Preceptories were being encouraged to resume a normal programme of meetings.

4.5 EXPANSION OVERSEAS

In 1977 a most extensive tour was undertaken by the Grand Master and the Great Marshal, Brigadier Geoffrey Galloway, which included Sri Lanka, Singapore, Hong Kong, New Zealand and every Province of Australia. The report thereon made fascinating reading and the Grand Master was, as he put it, 'made aware of the great strength of the bonds of the Order'. Those bonds were not weakened when, in more recent years, the Provincial Priories in Australasia became sovereign jurisdictions.

It is clear from such comments, and from the analysis of the membership of early encampments that much of the impetus for the development of Freemasonry in general and the chivalric orders in particular came not from local residents but mainly from expatriate British immigrants, seafaring brethren, or members of military lodges.

Details of specific Provincial developments within the United Orders were given in the previous Chapter, and **Appendices N and O** give more details of the Order today, so in this Chapter confines itself to a brief outline by Country or Region (in alphabetical order) of the main overseas developments.

AUSTRALIA
Although Ireland issued Warrant No. 227 in 1814 to the 46th Regiment of Foot stationed in New South Wales, records indicate that the earliest Preceptory of Knight Templar Masonry was formed in New South Wales when Ireland issued a permanent Warrant on 29 January 1845, for the St Elmo Encampment No. 267. It was still working strongly in 1866 but became defunct sometime prior to the founding of the Grand Lodge of New South Wales in 1888. Scotland issued a Warrant in 1869 for a Priory of the Temple in Sydney, but there is no record of it after 1875.

The first English preceptories to be consecrated in New South Wales were Broken Hill No. 180 in 1904, and The Preceptory of Sydney No. 186 in 1907. Preceptories have been consecrated in South Australia from the 19th century onwards, the first being the Pembroke of Australasia Preceptory, No. 51 in Melbourne in 1857. By the turn of the century eight preceptories had been consecrated, although three did not survive beyond 1894. Development continued throughout the 20th century and records show The Great Priory of Scotland was also consecrating preceptories in Australia during these early days.

Development of a Provincial structure for the United Orders in Australia was erratic to say the least; in 1857 a Province of Victoria was constituted, but a period of over ten years elapsed before the next province was constituted for South Australia in 1868, and an even greater period passed before a Province of New South Wales was constituted in 1907. A further twenty years passed before the next Province (Queensland) was constituted in 1927.

Nevertheless, by the 1980s it was perceived that the United Orders were strong enough to merit their own sovereign bodies and Independent Great Priories were constituted in Australia:

    1982   Victoria
    1982   South Australia
    1984   Western Australia
    1984   New South Wales and Australian Capital Territory
    1985   Queensland

A period of 125 years therefore elapsed between the first warranting of a United Orders encampment in 1857 and the creation of the first Australian Sovereign Great Priory in 1982. For general interest, **Appendix O** also gives some additional details about the continued development of the United Orders in our former Provinces.

BOLIVIA

The first United Orders preceptory for Bolivia was constituted in 1996 and a steady increase of interest has been observed in that Country with a Province being constituted in 2007. By 2018 the number of preceptories had increased to seven with over 200 members.

CANADA

Despite the early introduction of the Royal Arch and Knight Templar degrees to Canada by British Army brethren in the 1750s and 1760s, it was 1824 before the first encampment was chartered by The United Orders in Canada under the Grand Mastership of H.R.H. Augustus Frederick, Duke of Sussex. However, three decades then elapsed before the next encampment was chartered; and, during this period, the Royal Grand Conclave of Scotland also chartered an encampment. From 1854 growth was steady and by 1862 it was possible to constitute a Province of Canada with the appointment of Colonel W. J. Bury McLeod Moore as Provincial Grand Commander. At that time six English encampments existed, but under his inspiring leadership development continued steadily with a further fourteen encampments or preceptories being created over the next thirteen years.

An Independent Great Priory of Canada was constituted in 1875 under the Grand Mastership of Rt Hon. William Hale John Charles Pery, 3rd Earl of

Limerick who was Great Prior of England and Wales within the ill-fated Grand Conclave of which the Canadian Preceptories were part. At that date, twenty of the English Preceptories which survive today were in existence, and were transferred to the new sovereign Great Priory just fifty-one years after the warranting of the first United Orders encampment.

FAR EAST AND SOUTH EAST ASIA

In 1863 a Province of Far East was constituted and again it may be deduced that the impetus for the spread of Freemasonry in general and of the chivalric orders in particular was essentially through the influence of expatriate British immigrants, seafaring brethren, or members of military lodges deployed there or en-route to the antipodes. Today two Provinces exist for The Far East and South East Asia and details appear in **Appendix O**.

FINLAND

The United Orders gained a foothold in Finland in the 1980s with three Preceptories having been warranted from London in 1983-84 and a Sovereign Great Priory for Finland was constituted by the Grand Master at Helsinki in 1985. At that date three English Preceptories were transferred to the new sovereign Great Priory thus showing the development of a sovereign Great Priory in just two years.

INDIA

Despite the early appearance of chivalric Masonry on the Indian sub-continent amongst British Army brethren mentioned earlier in the days of the British Raj, it was not until 1857 that the first separate United Orders encampment was consecrated (in the Punjab). Some five years later, in 1862, three Provinces were created in Bombay, Bengal, and Madras. These had a somewhat precarious existence, and were dissolved to form a single Province of India in 1916. The Province did survive partition in 1947 and the departure of Britain from India, but at best the United Orders struggled there and the Province was dissolved in 1968.

Although Freemasonry continues throughout India under a Grand Lodge and four Regional Grand Lodges, until recently these did not have a Knight Templar element. However, since 2007 there has been something of a resurgence of interest on the sub-continent with the constitution of five preceptories. It might also be noted that other degrees and orders have also gained a recent foothold – including Red Cross of Constantine, the Order of the Secret Monitor, the Order of Royal and Select Masters, and the Order of the Allied Masonic Degrees amongst others.

NEW ZEALAND

Although the first Preceptories were constituted in New Zealand in the closing years of the 19th century, a Province of New Zealand was not constituted until 1930 when eight preceptories had been formed, many under the influence of expatriate British immigrants, seafaring brethren, or members of military lodges deployed to the antipodes. This Province ceased to exist in 1958 when separate Provinces were created for the North and South Islands of New Zealand, and these two Provinces ceased in turn when an Independent United Great Priory of New Zealand was constituted in 1984. At that date all the surviving preceptories which were transferred to the new sovereign Great Priory – some 106 years after the first United Orders encampment was warranted.

RHODESIA – ZIMBABWE

In common with many other former British colonies, Rhodesian brethren have showed an interest in chivalric Masonry but the first United Orders preceptory was not constituted there until 1955. A second preceptory was constituted in 1960 along with a Province which still survives today (having been renamed Zimbabwe in 1980). At best this must be described as a mere toe-hold with United Orders Brethren numbering just thirty-one in a countrywide population of nearly 17 Million.

SOUTH AFRICA

Developments in South Africa started with a Province of South Africa being Constituted in 1887 and again it can be shown that much of the impetus came from expatriate British immigrants, seafaring brethren, or members of military lodges deployed to that area or in transit to the Far East.

Several different provinces have been constituted since that date and today, Provinces exist for Natal, the Transvaal and the Cape Province. Details are given in **Appendix O.** However, there does not appear to have been sufficient gain in popularity of the United Orders to warrant any move to found a sovereign Great Priory in South Africa.

SOUTH AMERICA

Significant interest in the United Orders appeared in Bolivia as mentioned earlier, but was also noticeable in Argentina as early as 1911 and Brazil by 1913, resulting in the constitution of a Province of South America in 1914. Since then interest has also been apparent in Uruguay and in 2019 a new Province of the River Plate was created with responsibility for four of the preceptories from the Province of South America.

THE NETHERLANDS

Olivier-de-la-Marche Preceptory No. 417 was constituted at Leiden, the first in Holland in 1969 and the constitution of a Province with the Appointment of a Provincial Prior for the Netherlands occurred in 1983. A Sovereign Great Priory of The Netherlands was inaugurated on 23 November 2013 with the transfer of all of the former Preceptories of the United Orders being transferred on that date – forty-four years after the first preceptory was constituted.

THE MEDITERRANEAN – GIBRALTAR AND MALTA

Throughout this history, Gibraltar has been mentioned many, many times, and the earliest recorded Knight Templar activity in the British Territory of Gibraltar was almost certainly related to Military Lodges attached to regiments stationed in or passing through Gibraltar. The same comment applies to the Island of Malta, and from 1875 to 1924 these two outposts of the British Empire came under a Province of the Mediterranean. However, it was always noticeable that Freemasonry in both Malta and Gibraltar was much influenced by expatriate British immigrants, seafaring brethren, or members of military lodges resident there for long periods. As military presence has reduced in recent years so has Masonic activity and the single Gibraltar preceptory is now administered as an unattached preceptory.

The situation in Malta is somewhat different however; from perhaps as early as 1730 the interest in Freemasonry and the Chivalric Orders was intimately related to the Knights Hospitallers of St John who held sway in Malta until 1798. Freemasonry then thrived under the English, Irish, and Scottish Constitutions until c.1964 when Freemasonry in Malta came under the control of a sovereign Grand Lodge of Malta, and most foreign Masonic bodies either ceased to operate, joined the Maltese Grand Lodge, or returned to the United Kingdom. However, the interest in the Knights Templar and Knights of Malta was sustained and although there is no longer any English Provincial organisation on the Island between 2001 and 2004 three new preceptories were consecrated and interest in the United Orders continues.

4.6 RELATIONS WITH OTHER CONSTITUTIONS

It has long been the custom of the United Orders to maintain cordial interaction with other Constitutions in a formal way and such international contacts can now be summarised under three distinct headings:

The Tripartite Biannual Conferences

International Conferences of Great Priories

Exchange of Representatives with other Constitutions

The Tripartite Biannual Conferences
It was during Lord Euston's Grand Mastership (1896-1908) that England, Ireland and Scotland agreed to hold annual meetings to discuss questions of mutual concern and also agreed that henceforth each Great Priory would be free to pursue its own course. These have continued to the present day, usually held alternately in London, Dublin, and Edinburgh.

International Conferences of Great Priories
1905 In 1905 a deputation headed by the Grand Master attended the Triennial Convention of the Grand Encampment of the United States. The visit led to a Concordat and in 1907 both the United States and Canada were represented at the annual conference of the United Orders.

International conferences have taken place at intervals over the years, and from time to time, reports of the involvement of Great Priory have featured in the annual address to Great Priory by the Grand Master. This topic is really outside the scope of this history except for some brief examples of recent events:

On 25 August 2000 the 5th International Conference of Great Priories was held in Stirling, hosted by the Great Priory of Scotland.

In 2009 the Knights Templar Triennial International Conference was held at Winchester from 3-5th September 2009 hosted by the Great Priory.

In 2012 the Knights Templar Triennial International Conference was held in France.

2019 The 9th Triennial International Conference of Great Priories was held in Avignon between the 6th and 8th September 2019 hosted by France.

On many occasions similar less formal visits have been exchanged with members of other Great Priories and it is a pleasure to welcome our brother knights from America at Great Priory and in our preceptories.

Appointment of Representatives

It is the normal custom to exchange representatives with other Sovereign Great Priories and similar Grand bodies with responsibilities for Knight Templar and Knight of Malta degrees.

Out of courtesy, it is usual for a senior member of the order appointed to represent another Sovereign body at our Great Priory to be a Knight Grand Cross or Knight Commander and similar courtesy is customary with the appointment of a representative of the Great Priory of England to attend other Sovereign bodies. In order of the date of the original appointments, representatives have been exchanged with the Great Priories listed in **Appendix P.**

4.7 OTHER RELATED ORDERS

No review of the Chivalric Masonic Orders would be complete without at least a brief mention of Orders active today which require membership of the United Orders as a prior qualification in their candidates. These are

The Rectified Scottish Rite or Knights Beneficent of The Holy City;

The Grand College of Holy Royal Arch Knight Templar Priests and Order of Holy Wisdom; and

The Commemorative Order of St Thomas of Acon.

The Rectified Scottish Rite or Knights Beneficent of the Holy City
The Grand Priory of *Helvetia* (Switzerland) and the *Grandes Prieures de Galles (*France) *et Belgique,* who are also listed as 'other Great Priories', work according to the Rectified Scottish Rite. There is a long and most interesting history of this rite, which was derived from the Rite of Strict Observance which has been more fully described earlier. That story cannot be told here, but it should be mentioned that the mother Grand Priory, that of *Helvetia*, dates from 1779.

The Rite is nominally structured as a six-degrees rite but, as with the Ancient and Accepted Rite, the first three are regarded as having been conferred in a candidate's Craft lodge.

The fourth degree of the rite is in two parts, Scottish Master, and Scottish Master of St Andrew. It is noteworthy that in Switzerland and France, where some of the regular lodges work the Craft degrees of the Rectified Scottish Rite, there are St Andrew's lodges in which the rite is taken a stage further, and it is from these that the candidate progresses.

The fifth degree of Squire Novice leads into the last, *Chevalier Bienfaisant de la Cité Sainte* (Knight Beneficent of the Holy City), by which title the rite is often identified and can, like the Orders of the Temple and Malta, be seen to have a link with the medieval knights of Jerusalem.

There are today Grand Priories of the Rite in the United States (constituted in 1934), France (1935), England (1937), Germany (1959) and, of more recent date, Belgium.

The Grand Priory of England was created and installed in London on 2 April 1937 by letters Patent from the Independent Grand Priory of Helvetia.

Until 2007 it existed within the Great Priory of the United Orders but meetings were only held rarely and membership, by invitation only, was very restricted.

At a meeting of the Grand Priory on 28 May 2008, the Order in England became independent of the Great Priory of the United Orders and was reorganised into four Prefectures with three Scottish Masters of St Andrew Lodges in each; membership is still by invitation only, and is restricted to members of Knight Templar Preceptories recognised by the Great Priory of England and Wales and Royal Arch Chapters recognised by the Supreme Grand Chapter of England

During the last ten years the popularity of the Rite has increased and by the end of 2018 the four Prefectures administered eighteen Lodges:

> Anglo-Saxon Prefecture
> Avalon Prefecture
> Heart of England Prefecture
> Brigantes Prefecture

It is to be noted that the Martinist Order and the Swedish Rite also include some of the CBCS degrees.

The Order of Holy Royal Arch Knight Templar Priests and Order Of Holy Wisdom

Although it has no official connection with the United Orders of today, the Grand College of Holy Royal Arch Knight Templar Priests of Great Britain And Tabernacles Overseas deserves mention.

This Order has historical links which cannot here be pursued in depth. It is, however, interesting to note among the degrees worked under the Irish Early Grand Encampment and the Early Grand Rite in Scotland there were those of the Temple and Malta and several which now survive only in the list of thirty-one 'Appendant Degrees' which are communicated by name to a Knight Templar Priest.

It is one of only two regular masonic organizations in England ('regular' in the sense that no objection to it has been raised by Grand Lodges and Chapters, or by any of the authorities centred upon Mark Masons' Hall) which requires its candidates to be Knights Templar; they must also be subscribing members of the Craft.

In the 18th century the one degree which is now conferred in full crops up under various names and within several rites from the 18th century onwards. Perhaps the most important and long-lived of these is best known under the name of The Priestly Order (or sometimes *Ne Plus Ultra*).In the Early 1800s there existed *The Mother Tabernacle of the Order of High Priesthood*[280] at

Manchester which was known to be working a Royal Arch Knight Templar Priest Degree containing a version of the Grand High Priest Degree similar to that used in the USA both then and now.

On 9 May 1819 the Second Lancashire Union Band, Bury issued a form of Warrant to the Brethren of The (Craft) Lodge of Prince George (Now No. 308) authorising them to form the First Yorkshire Union Band. The Warrant is still in existence, and in the possession of Prince George Lodge, and records show The Priestly Order was worked continuously at Bottoms until May 1871 with more than 100 'consecrations' of named individuals from Lancashire and Yorkshire. Members of this Degree were referred to as Priests and Pillars, and colloquially it was referred to as the 'Pillar Degree'. The following list associated with the seven pillars may be of interest:

Pillar	Lamp	Door
Wisdom	Knowledge	Hope
Strength	Prayer	Faith
Beauty	*Holy Desires*	Mercy
Truth	Purity	Utterance
Light	*God's Word*	Salvation
Power	Peace	Perseverance
Glory	Joy	Life

Admission to the Degree was restricted to Knights Templar who had been 'created' Knights of the Red Cross of Babylon, and most extant contemporary records indicate the Priestly Order and Red Cross of Babylon Degree were worked in one Council in the 1800s, as are the degrees of Grand High Priest and Red Cross of Babylon (*et al*) in a Council of the Allied Masonic Degrees today.

During the period 1819 to 1871 minutes exist for meetings of that Priestly Order at Bottoms and this activity clearly predates, by some 78 years, the transfer of control of the Knight Templar Priest degree to the Grand Council of the Allied Masonic Degrees in 1897. It also suggests the working of the degree at Bury and, perhaps Bottoms, may antedate the working of the degree by the Royal Kent Tabernacle at Newcastle-upon-Tyne; contemporary records from the Newcastle area exist which cite Bottoms activity as an authoritative source for degree working and ritual. Evidence for Priestly Order activity is extant today not only in the records of Prince Edward Council of the Allied Masonic Degrees, but also in those of Prince Edward Preceptory No. 18 and High Greenwood Rose Croix Chapter No. 124. Clearly brethren in this area still worked after the manner of the *Antients* with close relations between Knight Templar, Rose Croix and other degree working.

From 1812 there was at Newcastle-upon-Tyne a Council of Knights Grand Cross of the Holy Temple of Jerusalem which included among its degrees that of Knight Templar Priest. This seems to have operated throughout the century until 1894 when the sole survivor admitted nine members of the Royal Kent Preceptory as Knight Templar Priests. Conscious, no doubt of the difficulties of continuing as an independent body, the revived body adhered to the Grand Council of the Allied Masonic Degrees which had been formed in London in 1880. It was to retain a measure of self-government but its activities seem to have been very limited for a number of years.

In 1897, when the fate of the Order then administered in Newcastle-on-Tyne by the Knights Grand Cross of Jerusalem was being re-considered, it was suggested that the Holy Royal Arch Knight Templar Priests or Order of Holy Wisdom should be taken over by the United Orders. However, the Grand Master decline to assume this control, and the Order was taken into the care of the Order of Allied Masonic Degrees.

A significant point in the history was the admission as Knight Templar Priest of Colonel C. W. Napier-Clavering in 1913. When he became Grand Master of the Allied Masonic Degrees in 1920 he encouraged a change, already in train, by which the Newcastle Tabernacle formed itself into a Grand College and took over from the Allied Degrees Grand Council in 1923 or 1924 (there is some doubt as to the operative date) the control of the Knight Templar Priests.

By 1930 seven more tabernacles had been constituted, one of them in New Zealand from which came the knight priests who, in 1933, established a regular and sovereign Grand College in the United States. There followed in England some years of 'consolidation' but in the 1940s began an expansion which has continued. Of more than 140 tabernacles now working, many are in Commonwealth countries and South Africa, and there are others in the Netherlands and Germany, and a recently-formed tabernacle in Edinburgh.

Whereas all other masonic degrees and Orders emanating from England have always been administered from London, the Grand College of Knight Templar Priests has had its seat in the north, for long at Newcastle-upon-Tyne, but now at York.

The Commemorative Order of St Thomas of Acon

The traditional history of this Order relates an origin in 1189 during the time of The Third Crusade; on 8th June 1191, Richard Coeur de Lion with his forces arrived before the seaport of Acre which had been besieged for two years by other Christian princes.

Richard captured the city in five weeks, and among his followers was one William, the chaplain to the Dean of St Paul's who, on sighting the many

Christian corpses about the walls of Acre, had compassion on them. With the aid of a small band of helpers he buried a large number of dead and tended the wounded, and subsequently founded an Order for the specific purpose of burying Christians who fell in the Holy Land. Later he added a second purpose – the ransoming of Christians taken capture by the Saracens.

The Order came to England at the time St Thomas of Canterbury was popular and so the Order was named after him; however, the Order having been formed in Acre the name also embodied an Anglicised, form of Acre – Acon. Richard Coeur de Lion patronised the Order and, to facilitate its protection, authorised a Knightly element, which, it is claimed today, played its part in the defence of the Holy Land as a lesser chivalric Order.

The Order was 'revived' as The Commemorative Order of St Thomas of Acon in 1974 with E. Kt John E. N. Walker, PGtA-de-C of the United Orders as the first Grand Master

Today it is claimed that the Order is based on historical facts recorded in 13th century records held in the library of the City of London in Guildhall; in accordance with time immemorial traditions, Members of the Order take part in an Annual Pilgrimage to the shrine of St Thomas of Canterbury after whom the Order is named.

Membership of the Order is restricted to subscribing members of the United Religious, Military and Masonic Order of the Temple and of St John of Jerusalem, Palestine, Rhodes and Malta, or the recognised equivalent body in other jurisdictions. Candidates are admitted as Knights Templar, installed and invested with the insignia of the Order.

4.8 A LOOK AHEAD

The farther backward you can look, the farther forward you can see.
Winston Churchill

When, to mark the two hundredth anniversary of the establishment in England of a Grand Conclave, the original governing body of our United Masonic Orders, a history was published, its detail was somewhat limited by the relative paucity of readily-available archival material.

Since then, more material has come to light, and this work represents a completely fresh look at the history, not only of those valiant Knights who fought in the Crusades whose exploits provided the inspiration to today's Masonic, Military and Religious Orders, but also the culture of many European countries which have enabled our United Orders to develop within our British culture. The account of the warfare in the Holy Land provides, of course, the basis for our history, but its later developments have been related to events in later, lesser crusades and the environment not only in which they emerged but also their lasting impact on more modern interpretation of chivalric ideas and concepts traceable back to the romance of the Crusades.

A complex history cannot always be set out in strictly chronological order, and in particular, the suppression of the Knights Templar Order effectively removed most primary sources, and this account has attempted to trace the development of the United Orders including deductions from the history of contemporary organisations and events.

Whilst the history of the Medieval Orders of Knighthood, from which the modern Masonic, Military and Religious Orders of the Temple and the Hospital have derived their names, is well enough documented, the different interpretation of these events has inevitably led to alternative ideas about their traditions and legacies, and generally these have appeared in very different ways during the intervening seven hundred years since the Templar order was suppressed.

This account considers how the military, and seafaring legacies of the crusading Orders are reflected in activities of such orders as the Portuguese Order of Christ, the Order of Teutonic Knights, the Hospitaller Order of St John, and The Hanseatic League noting that it is certainly possible that individual former chivalric Knights Templar could well have found haven in such organisations. It is, however, worth reminding readers that today's Masonic Chivalric Orders of the Temple and Malta are not the same as the Crusader Orders of the Temple and St John from which they draw their inspiration, and the numerous attempts in the past to claim otherwise must be firmly discounted.

The residual elements of the Chivalric Orders of Knighthood are also examined, both in terms of the contemporary global environment which permitted their survival, and the development of more modern orders of Chivalry and honour systems which perpetuate the concepts to the present day. The impact of cultural changes, the reformation, some aspects of technological change including the industrial revolution, and social developments are also considered; these appear in the emergence of clubs and societies, universities, trade guilds, and livery companies which embraced all levels of society setting the scenes for the birth of operative and speculative masonry up to the end of the 17th century and the emergence of Masonic orders of chivalry. Whilst the account generally considers these developments in Britain, the various environments which allowed such developments to spread world-wide are also examined briefly, particularly through global trade, colonialisation, and the use of military and naval forces to not only facilitate such developments, but also defend British interests and spread cultural and masonic ideas globally.

The story then outlines the development of the modern speculative Masonic orders of chivalry in England and Wales and the establishment of 'the Great Priory of the United Religious, Military and Masonic Orders of the Temple and of St John of Jerusalem, Palestine, Rhodes and Malta of England and Wales and its Provinces Overseas' up to the end of the 19th century.

The success of the 19th century development resulted in an organisation of increasing size and complexity, and so to complete this history, the expansion of the United Orders is reviewed with a detailed account of organisational changes up to the present day. However, in parallel with the earlier spread of British military, colonial, and trading interests across the globe, the United Orders have spread similarly, and so the account also summarises how other Countries – particularly former British Colonies and English-speaking Nations – have now benefited.

But the United Orders do not stand in isolation; as the membership of the Order requires membership of the Craft and the Royal Arch, other Masonic Orders exist which require members to hold Knight Templar qualifications, and so these too are reviewed briefly, noting that one Order in particular – Knight Beneficent of the Holy City or *Chevaliers Bienfaisant de la Cité Sainte* – has a pedigree as old as, or even older than, the United Orders, and traditions which cover the same period of 900 years after the first recorded development of The Poor Fellow-Soldiers of Christ and the Temple of Solomon in AD 1118. In this context, it may be observed that this Order (The Rectified Scottish Rite) culminating in the degree of Knight Beneficent of the Holy City, was introduced into England from Switzerland in 1937 and therefore has direct parallels with other orders recently introduced from other Countries; however, this order remained essentially dormant for many years, and although previously administered by the United Orders, since 1937 it had an extremely restrictive qualification requirement resulting in very limited recruiting of new members so producing a less-than-viable self-sustaining membership. Recently however, during the writing of this history the Order has undergone a massive revival, not only with a clear lead from the Grand Master of the United Orders, but also with a specific strategy for regional development and a somewhat less-restrictive qualification policy. This Order, today, demonstrates that a Masonic Order that has complex qualifications requiring membership, not only of the Craft but also the Royal Arch and the United Orders can still attract a new following with prospects for future development. It does, however, suggest that there are lessons to be learned which may be useful for future survival.

Further on the question of isolation, Freemasonry itself has had to weather repeated attacks over its history. This is not the place to examine fully this complex topic, but two examples illustrate such external attacks:

In 1799, the introduction of the Unlawful Societies Act mentioned earlier put all fraternal institutions under threat, and the impact of this provision was still being felt as recently as 1968. Whilst a legal remedy was obtained through an exemption clause for Masonic bodies, nevertheless there was an on-going impact on the Chivalric Orders – one aspect being the perceived need to wear aprons to confirm Masonic affiliation.

In 1988, the introduction of the Criminal Justice Act posed a specific threat to the Chivalric Masonic Orders with Section 139 relating to the possession of offensive weapons and the carrying of swords to meetings. This led to Great Priory reporting the legal opinion of the Great Chancellor in the following terms for distribution to each preceptory:

'Under Section 139 of The Criminal Justice Act (1988) it is an offence to have any article which has a blade or is sharply pointed in a public place, except a folding pocket-knife, but it is a defence to prove that the person charged had a good reason or lawful authority to have the article with him in a public place, or that he had it for religious reasons, for use at work, or as part of any national costume. I cannot doubt that any impartial court, that is one not composed of anti-masonic fanatics, would accept that a Knight, on his way to a Preceptory or Priory, had a good reason for having his sword with him particularly when it is sheathed and, as is usual, carried in some kind of outer container.'

It must be presumed that this is still valid, so it would be interesting to assess how many members of the United Orders today are aware of this Counsel opinion. More recently, of course, the current decade has seen a burgeoning public debate about knife-crime, and although it is now customary to minimise the number of attendees required to carry swords to Great Priory and Provincial meetings, this must be a matter which needs careful watching.

The question of the decline of modern Freemasonry has often been asked in recent years; this has usually referred to both the Craft and the Royal Arch, which are essential requirements for membership of The United Orders. Undoubtedly the pure statistics do not leave much doubt about this.

However, the Craft and the Royal Arch are only part of the story. What we can also see today is that a number of 'new' Masonic Orders have either emerged, or been imported from other constitutions, or greatly expanded in Britain during the last decade or so. These include both non-chivalric and chivalric Masonic Orders, and some can be traced to the earliest days of speculative masonic history.

The Order of Knight Masons (a rite similar in historical content to the degree of Red Cross of Babylon worked under the Order of the Allied Masonic Degrees) and the Order of Pilgrim Preceptors have recently been imported from Ireland; the Degree of Excellent Master has been introduced from Scotland; and the Order of the Silver Trowel has come to Britain from the United States. All of these also require qualification by membership of other degrees and Orders, so clearly speculative masonry still has something to offer in the 21st century.

One very recent development is designated The Order of the Scarlet Cord, a name which like many Masonic degrees, has historically more than one application. Perhaps the older, also formerly called the Knight of Rahab, first appeared as an appendant degree within a Priestly Order well established in the early 19th century both in Britain and on the Continent. From 1897 the degree was retained as an (unworked) appendant degree within the Order of Holy Royal Arch Knight Templar Priests nominally controlled by the Grand Council of the Allied Masonic Degrees until formally transferred in 1923 to the Grand College of Holy Royal Arch Knight Templar Priests, where it exists today.

The more recent Order, now designated The Ancient and Masonic Order of the Scarlet Cord is also based on an earlier Order, The Royal Order of Knights of the Scarlet Cord, developed in the British Isles in 1889, which was itself derived from 18th century documents from the Amsterdam Masonic archives based on a traditional biblical Old Testament history related to the period of Joshua, the fall of Jericho and the story of Rahab. Following major revision, the Order was adopted by the Order of the Secret Monitor and worked from about 1895 to 1929. A revival of interest then occurred in 2006 when a new Secret Monitor Conclave was consecrated with the sole purpose of reviving the old Order and interest was so great that the Order was inaugurated as a separate Sovereign body in July 2010. Whilst this Order, in either form, has no direct Chivalric background, or Knight Templar qualification, its revival and success clearly illustrates a continuing interest in knightly themes with a sustained appeal in the modern Masonic environment.

A similar revival can be seen in the case of The Order of Holy Wisdom. This Order, traceably working in Lancashire and possibly elsewhere with a long, complex ritual in the early 19th century, and formerly included within the Order of Holy Royal Arch Knight Templar Priests or Order of Holy Wisdom, has in the last decade been revived with a shorter working. This degree now a fundamental part of that Order, being an essential qualification for higher offices, and it too necessarily depends upon its members having a Knight Templar qualification. However, this Order is so closely-bound to the Order of Holy Royal Arch Knight Templar Priests and its basic qualification, and its development is so recent, it would not at present possible to speculate on its popularity or offer a reliable estimate of the success of the recent initiatives.

The Commemorative Order of St Thomas of Acon, with a traditional history related back to the Fall of Acre during the Crusades, appeared in England – claiming its emergence as a 'revival' quite recently. Expansion has been rapid and the Order can now been found in other Countries besides England.

Whilst this is not the place to comment on detail on these recent changes, we can make two general and important observations. Firstly, the impetus for all of these degrees and orders and the selection of their illustrative 'traditional histories' has undoubtedly come from looking back at the historical events of the past, including crusading and biblical history. And secondly, when mooted, not only were these degrees and orders favourably received but also their (re) introduction was widely acclaimed and their subsequent development has been sustained.

Perhaps this suggests these innovations refreshed the attitudes to varieties of Freemasonry which benefited from such changes to prevent their decline as observed in the Craft. However, in a sense, the Craft has also benefited from a form of innovation in recent years – not in ritual or philosophical terms but in social terms. In particular more publicity, less secrecy, and better eduction in Craft Lodges and Royal Arch Chapters. Specifically, in his the address to United Grand Lodge in April 2007 H.R.H. The Duke of Kent not only emphasised that:

.. pure Ancient Masonry consists of three degrees and no more; viz. those of Entered

Apprentice, the Fellow Craft, and the Master Mason including the Supreme Order of the Holy Royal Arch.,

"This has been the position for nearly 200 years and will remain unchanged.

But also continued:

However, since many members of the Craft are members of these Orders, I am pleased to acknowledge formally their existence and regularity, and in particular their sovereignty and independence.

The best known of these Orders are: Mark, Ancient and Accepted Rite, Knights Templar, Royal and Select Masters, Royal Ark Mariner, Red Cross of Constantine, Allied Masonic Degrees, Order of the Secret Monitor, and Knight Templar Priests,

…. I also accept the valuable role they play in providing additional scope for Brethren to extend their Masonic research in interesting and enjoyable ways."

Hence this shows not only something of a softening of the attitude of the Craft to other orders, but also recognition of their enduring nature; whether or not intended, this one statement undoubtedly provided publicity for the orders beyond the Craft. When looking at overseas developments, it was observed that there was a revival of interest in speculative Knight Templar Masonry in India in 2007; that increase of interest was also evident in several other degrees and orders and can be traced directly to the statements made by H.R.H. The Duke of Kent.

Economic and demographic changes are also apparent; today an increasing proportion of the population undergoes further education and university training but working careers are shorter, retirement comes earlier, and lasts longer. The current working population is more mobile, does not remain in a large family group with several generations, and does not remain in one place for long. Work patterns are also changing; working days are longer and there is more travelling,

The changes can be seen to have several obvious effects on masonic activity.

Education patterns mean fewer members join in the 20-30 age bracket, and employment mobility means fewer Lewises[281] are 'at home' to join Freemasonry. On the contrary many Universities now have lodges able to recruit before the age of 21, but such activity is mostly restricted to the Craft and the Royal Arch.

The general increase in education perhaps means a smaller proportion of members are content with just the social aspects of our ceremonies and more wish to participate actively, which may explain why degrees and orders with multiple ceremonies and increased participation of younger members taking smaller ritual parts seem to be increasingly successful.

Effective recruiting requires modern marketing; gone are the days when families were a major source of new members. Modern marketing requires the product to be advertised to the potential recruits – which is exactly the opposite of conventional Freemasonry – and lodges, etc. taking this outdated approach are in decline.

Longer retirement perhaps explains a greater interest in 'themed' lodges which have enabled members to combine their masonic interests with former hobbies. Such lodges include lodges related to schools and universities, former military associations, professions, scouting, sports, and motor-cycling to name but a few.

An ageing population, particularly in an environment of increased traffic congestion and reducing public transport, alters interest in evening meetings and travelling during hours of darkness; likewise older members dislike 'late evening eating'; which undoubtedly explains both the clear popularity of 'daylight meetings' and recent increases in Saturday meetings.

Increasing prosperity has resulted in a gradual move away from large towns and cities with a decline of urban lodges, etc.; however, the corollary is that modern meeting places must have easier and better communications links and car parking facilities.

So what are the implications for the membership of the United Orders; and what initiatives might be beneficial to a speculative Masonic Order nearly 300 years of age with a traditional history containing elements 900 years old? Looking ahead is always difficult, and despite our lengthy history, it would seem a past perspective might be of only limited value.

First, in terms of the qualifications required of new members, there is little evidence that the current requirements limit recruiting; the other orders with similar requirements seem to be successful; but members must continue to support our Craft and Royal Arch and improve the education of potential members as to the attractions and benefits of the Templar Order.

Secondly, it is vital to avoid preceptories declining with an increasingly aged membership to a point where the membership is too small to remain viable. Initiatives must include an assessment of the strength and weakness of the masonic population supporting each preceptory, and the development of alternative target populations.

Thirdly, the Order must avoid making increasing demands on its members which might cause increased reluctance to support the Order. This must include financial commitments, time burdens through excessive or late meetings, limiting undue ritual participation.

Lastly, the Order must continually remain aware of the balance between members' aspirations and rewards. This is particularly relevant to an Order requiring membership of two others which necessarily results in a higher age profile than some orders. Whilst rewards through promotions must avoid developing a 'top-heavy' structure it is also clear some of the recent successful orders achieve a reward structure that does not leave members with the view that increasing age and infirmity will prevent rewards being earned.

The effect of even a proactive application of such initiatives, will of course depend, to a large extent on the survival of the Craft and the Royal Arch. However, the apparent success of other newer orders and the continued development of those Sovereign Great Priories which have recently separated from the United Orders suggest there is no reason to suppose the United Orders will not continue to go from strength to strength and that current and future Freemasons will still walk *in the steps of the Templars*.

Appendicies

APPENDIX A

IN THE STEPS OF THE TEMPLARS – TIMELINE

Date	Event and location
1095	First Crusade: Instigated by Pope Urban at Council of Auvergne (18 Nov 1095).
1113	Pope Paschal II promulgated a Bull, *Pie Postulatio Voluntatis*, dated 13 Feb 1113 in effect giving authority to found a new Order, 'The Hospitallers'.
1118	Supposed Founding of Military and Religious Order of the Poor Knights of the Temple of Jerusalem (Knights Templar).
1147	Second Crusade (1147-49) fails in attack on Damascus.
1147	Lisbon Crusade (1147): capture of Moorish-held Lisbon which then became part of the Christian kingdom of Portugal.
1147	Wendish Crusade (1147): first of the Northern Crusades by German crusaders campaigning against pagan Wendish Slavs settled around the Elbe River.
1157	Crusade in Spain.(1157-1158) Muslim occupiers of the Iberian peninsula since 718 were progressively driven out in a long series of crusades known as the Wars of the Reconquest.
1170	Almohad dynasty (1170-1296) having occupied Seville between 1130-1170, defeated King Alfonso VIII of Castile in the Battle of Alarcos (1195) but were then defeated by Christian forces from Leon/Castile, Navarra, and Aragon in the Battle of Las Navas de Tolosa (1212), and forced back to Africa. Their rule in Morocco ended in 1269.
1183	Third Crusade (1183-1197).
1193	Baltic Crusade (1193) Order of the Teutonic Knights engage in a permanent crusade in Prussia following a call by Pope Celestine III for a crusade against pagans of the Baltic.
1198	Livonian Crusade (1198-1212) Following the establishment of a new German Military Order, the Brothers of the Sword, in present-day Latvia, by Pope Innocent III to aid in the establishment of Christian rule in Livonia and the pagan Baltic.
1199	'Sicilian' Crusade (1199). The first 'political' Crusade. Pope Innocent III called a crusade against Markward of Anweiler, Margrave of Ancona and Count of Abruzzo in central Italy and Lord of Palermo in Sicily, which posed a threat both to the Papal States and to the pope's claim to supremacy over Sicily.
1200	Fourth Crusade (1200 – 1204).
1204	Fifth Crusade (1204-1220).
1208	The Albigensian Crusade (1208-29) which aimed to root out the heretical or Albigensian sect of Christian Cathars in France.
1211	The Baltic Crusades (1211-25) which sought to subdue pagans in Transylvania.
1221	Final Palestinian Crusades (1227-1277).

Date	Event and location
1243	Novgorod Crusades (1243-15th century). While authorized by, and fought on behalf of, the Church, these wars were prosecuted by Danish, Saxon, and Swedish princes as well as by military orders such as the Sword Brothers and the Teutonic Knights.
1248	Seventh or Egyptian Crusade.
1312	Hungarian Crusade (1314) Crusade in Hungary against Mongols and Lithuanians. This crusade was renewed by the papacy in 1325, 1332, 1335, 1352, and 1354.
1314	Oral tradition that when Robert Bruce reinstated Royal Order of Scotland he admitted all known Knights Templars to it.
1321	Italian Crusade (1321) Crusade against political opponents of the papacy.
1325	Polish Crusades (1325-1369) Crusade in Poland against Mongols and Lithuanians. This crusade was renewed by papal order in 1340, 1343, 1351, 1354, 1355, 1363, 1369).
1328	German Crusade (1328) Crusade against King Louis IV of Germany.
1340	Bohemian Crusade (1340) Crusade against heretics in Bohemia.
1348	Finnish Crusade (1348) Crusade of King Magnus of Sweden against pagans of Finland.
1386	Battle of Kosovo (1386) Christian Serb forces defeated by Egyptian Mameluk forces which had, during the 14th century taken over from the Ottoman Turks as the impetus for Islamic expansion throughout most of Asia Minor into Macedonia and Bulgaria.
1396	Relief of Constantinople (1396-).
1453	Relief of Belgrade (1453-1456).
1521	Relief of Belgrade (1521-1526).
1530	Emperor Charles V gives Island of Malta to Knights Hospitallers (with approval of Pope Clement VII); Templar relics transferred to Malta with The Order of the Hospital.
1659	Traditional Date for Creation of Order of Scottish Master of St Andrew and transmission of Knight Templar traditions of Knights Beneficent of the Holy City /CBCS in Scotland.
1732	Alleged working in Norwich of Ark, Mark, and Link, Royal Arch, and Knight Templar degrees in 1732.
1733	*Ecossais* Lodges established in England with Knight Templar elements.
1740	Lodges under High Knights Templar of Ireland alleged to have wide-spread working of Knight Templar degree.
c. 1743	Chapter of Clermont in Paris develops a type of Templar system, allegedly originally devised about 1743 in Lyon including 5th degree of Illustrious Knight or Templar.

Date	Event and location
1744	Baron Von Hund (1722-76) claims admission into (an) Order of the Temple in presence of William, 4th and last Earl of Kilmarnock (Grand Master Mason, Scotland 1742-43).
1745	By Laws preserved at Stirling record fees to be charged: Excellent and Super-Excellent: five shillings sterling and Knights of Malta five shillings sterling.
1745	On 30 September 1745 the Duke of Perth wrote to David, Lord Ogilvy with account of admission of Prince Charles Edward Stuart as Knight Templar. Lord Ogilvy fled to Gothenburg, Sweden and later, in exile, after Battle of Culloden raised a regiment in France.
1751	Founding of Grand Lodge According to The Antient Institutions (*The Antients*) with lodges permitted to work degrees 'beyond the Craft'
1756	Swedish Rite established with subsequent inclusion of degrees VII-X of Knight Templar character.
1759	Canadian Records show Royal Arch and Knight Templar degrees worked by military lodges from 1759.
1760	Francis Drake, Junior Warden, Grand Lodge of All England at York announces a fraternal Degree of 'Knight Templar' within Craft – Royal Arch context.
1765	Sir Edward Gilmore recorded as admitted to KT 24 March 1765 according to Rules of High Knights Templar in Ireland as first in list of 93 members.
1769	The records of St Andrews Royal Arch Chapter show the conferring of the order or degree of Knight Templar on first of about 50 candidates admitted between the years 1769 and 1794.
1769	Earliest existing minute regarding KT (Boston, Massachusetts) when members of three Military Lodges stationed at Boston, Massachusetts, conferred higher Degrees, including Templar Grades.
1772	KT meeting allegedly held in Rose & Crown, Temple St Bristol after which 'Home to spend an Evening under the Rose with Knights Templars'.
1778	Evidence of Knight Templar degree being conferred by Lodge of Scone & Perth, Now No. 3 (SC), in St Stephen's Lodge, No. 145(SC), Edinburgh.
1778	(RA) Chapter of Friendship Minutes of 21 Oct 1778 notes that 'Dunckerley had advised them in writing that they "might make Knight Templars" if they wanted to and so resolved'.
1779	Munster Fusiliers bring Royal Encampment (now Jerusalem Preceptory No. 5) to Manchester between 1779 and 1780.
1779	Mount Moriah Lodge (35th Regiment of Foot) issues KT Certificate dated 14 April 1779 in St Lucia.
1779	Grand Lodge of All England (1725-c.1796) conferred the KT degree on 29 November 1779 in York.
1780	The records of the Grand Lodge of all England at York, of date June, 1780, announced that lodge as asserting authority over five degrees or orders of Masonry, the Entered Apprentice, Fellow Craft, Master Mason, Royal Arch and Knight Templar.

Date	Event and location
1780	Bristol Knights constitute themselves into the 'Supreme Grand & Royal Encampment of the Order of Knights Templars of St John of Jerusalem, Knights Hospitallers and Knights of Malta etc'. [20 Dec 1780.]
1783	Reference to KT in Sea Captains' Lodge No. 445 at Bristol [Letter from Secretary to Grand Secretary 3 April 1783].
1786	Founding of Early Grand Encampment of Knights Templar in Ireland.
1789	St John's Lodge of Secrecy and Harmony (No. 539) Warranted in Malta with petition signed by several distinguished Knights Hospitaller of the Order of St John. (Erased at The Union in 1813.)
1791	In January 1791, Thomas Dunckerley, being Grand Superintendent of Royal Arch Masons at Bristol was invited by the Knights Templar to be their Grand Master.
1791	Thomas Dunckerley appoints Captain Thomas Dixon, 1st Dragoon Guards, Acting Grand Master for Yorkshire, Cumberland, Northumberland, and Durham.
1791	Thomas Dunckerley issues Patent dated 1 January 1791 for KT Encampment named of 'Eminent Chapter of Antiquity', Bristol.
1791	Grand Conclave of the Royal, Exalted, Religious and Military Order of H.R.D.M.. Grand Elected Masonic Knights Templars K.D.S.H. of St John of Jerusalem, Palestine Rhodes etc. came into being 24 June 1791. First Statutes issued.
1793	*Freemasons Magazine* (Oct 1793) refers to Duke of Kent as His Royal Highness, Prince Edward, Patron of the Order.
1793	John Schofield, Provincial Grand Master for Lancashire, appointed as Grand Superintendent for a KT Province consisting of the counties of Lancashire, Yorkshire and Cheshire.
1795	Death of Thomas Dunckerley, First Grand Master.
1796	The Rt Hon. Thomas Boothby Parkyns, Lord Rancliffe Installed as Grand Master.
1798	Order of the Hospital evicted from Malta by Napoleon (with loss of Templar relics); Napoleon enters Valletta on 12 June 1798.
1799	Publication of *The Unlawful Societies Act* 'for the more effectual suppression of Societies established for seditious and treasonable purposes' (39 Geo. III, c.79).
1800	Robert Gill, Deputy Grand Master acts as Grand Master until 1804.
1805	HRH Prince Edward Augustus, Duke of Kent & Stratharn, Grand Patron Installed as Grand Master.
1807	Waller Rodwell Wright Installed as Grand Master.
1812	Royal Grand Patron, the Duke of Kent, presides over 'Grand Conclave of Emergency of Grand Officers' on 30 January 1812.
1812	H.R.H. The Duke of Sussex Installed as Grand Master 6 August 1812.

Date	Event and location
1813	United Grand Lodge of England formed at 'The Union' with Duke of Sussex as the first Grand Master.
1836	First Knight Templar Province constituted (Dorsetshire 25 April 1836).
1843	Death of The Duke of Sussex.
1846	Colonel Charles Kemeys Kemeys Tynte installed Grand Master on 3 April 1846. Fresh Statutes of the Order approved.
1847	A Supreme Council of England for the Ancient and Accepted Rite established with move to deny KT Encampments authority to confer *Rosae Crucis* and *Kadosh* degrees.
1853	Revised Statutes sanction appointment of Provincial Grand Commanders.
1868	Encampments owing allegiance to the English Grand Conclave, those in Canada among them, were re-numbered.
1871	Grand Conclave adopts 'Treaty of Alliance' with Supreme Council and the Grand Lodge of Mark Master Masons (*The Tripartite Treaty*) on 12 May 1871.
1873	Installation of the H.R.H. Prince of Wales as the Grand Master of the Convent General on 7 April 1873.
1873	First appointments of Knights Grand Cross and Knights Commander.
1895	Convent General effectively ceases 19 July 1895, and H.R.H. Albert Edward Prince of Wales, Past Grand Master, becomes Sovereign of the United Orders in Great Britain and Ireland.
1896	Issue of the Statutes of the Great Priory of England & Wales and The Dependencies Thereof, adopting Revised Title of Order: The United Religious and Military Orders of the Temple and of St John of Jerusalem, Palestine, Rhodes, and Malta.
1897	Great Priory considers, but rejects, suggestion of taking control of the degrees of Knight Templar Priest and Order of Holy Wisdom from the Newcastle-on-Tyne Knights Grand Cross of Jerusalem.
1920	Great Priory considers, but rejects, suggestion of taking control of the degrees of Knight Templar Priest and Order of Holy Wisdom from the Order of the Allied Masonic Degrees.
1937	On 2 April 1937 The Great Priory of the United Orders received a Patent for The Rectified Scottish Rite and Knights Beneficent of the Holy City in England and Wales, etc.
1991	Great Priory celebrates Bicentenary of the founding of the United Orders.
2007	Great Priory of the United Orders relinquishes control of the Rectified Scottish Rite and Knights Beneficent of the Holy City in England and Wales, etc.
2018	900th Anniversary of the traditional date of Founding of Military and Religious Order of the Poor Knights of the Temple of Jerusalem from which the Masonic Order of Knights Templar drew their inspiration.

APPENDIX B

THE BASE FOR THE GRAND CONCLAVE

In January 1791, Thomas Dunckerley, being Grand Superintendent of Royal Arch Masons at Bristol having accepted an invitation[282] from the Knights Templar to be their Grand Master, wrote in one of his first letters:

'I accept with gratitude the confidence you place in me as Grand Master by the Will of God, of the Most Noble and Exalted Religious and Military Order of Masonic Knights Templar of St John of Jerusalem. I must request that as soon as possible you send to me the Names, Ages, Proffession (sic) & Residence of your Encampment as I intend to have a regular Register of our Order. Being Grand Superintendent of Royal Arch Masons at Bristol, I was requested by the Knights Templar in that City (who have had an Encampment Time Immemorial) to accept the office of Grand Master, which I had no sooner complied with than Petitions were sent to me for the same purpose from London 1, Bath 2, the first Regiment of Dragoon Guards 3, Colchester 4, York 5, Dorchester 6, and Biddeford (sic) 7. I suppose that there are many more Encampments in England, which with God's permission I may have the happiness to revive & assist. It has already been attended with a blessing for I have been but two months Grand Master & have already 8 Encampments in my care.'

There can be no doubt this record of Encampments known to Dunckerley in 1791 was correct, but likewise his supposition '*I suppose that there are many more Encampments in England...*' was equally valid – at least so far as there is evidence of Knight Templar activity elsewhere, perhaps worked under Craft Lodges and Royal Arch Chapters rather than formal Encampments.

Recent research, particularly into the movements of military lodges and their interactions with 'static' lodges implies there was much more Knight Templar activity than Dunckerley suggested. This Appendix therefore amplifies Dunckerley's supposition in the light of more recent research and then reviews known activity of military lodges and brethren to establish the probably incidence of Templar brethren in each County which, prior to 1791 formed the cadre from which the Grand Conclave would then rise.

These include, not only actual KT records, but also evidence of *Ecossais* Lodges, Scotch Master Working, and Military Lodges with known KT interactions.

It will be seen that, prior to Dunckerley writing in 1791, virtually every County had either evidence of Knight Templar activity or itinerant military lodges and brethren who had had realistic opportunities for contact with known KT activity between 1769 and 1791, including French prisoners-of-war incarcerated in the United Kingdom.

Incidence by County

Bedfordshire
1744   The 14th (Bedfordshire) Regt of Foot after Dettingen and Fontenoy in 1744, had in 1750, Lodge No.211(IC) which by 1760 worked RA and KT degrees. It is therefore possible individual brethren possessing these degrees may have been present as early as 1744.

1769   Brethren of the 14th (Bedfordshire) Regt of Foot were in Boston (St Andrews Lodge) working a Knight Templar degree.

1782   The 14th (Bedfordshire) Regt of Foot with links with the County for recruiting purposes and by then the Regt Lodge No.211(IC)[1750]; Lodge No.245(IC)[1754]; Lodge No 58(EC - Antients) [1782]; had records of RA and KT working so senior personnel on recruiting duties would probably have included KT brethren.[283]

Berkshire
1759   Early Antients Lodges 73A(ECA) Reading [1759-1760]; 3B(ECA) Reading [1771-]; 80(ECA) Reading [1759-1763] may well have had visitors from 1760 prisoner-of-war camp at Windsor and military brethren guarding them.

1760   14th Regt (With Lodges 211(IC) and 58(ECA) [1750-1818] and known record of KT members deployed Reading/ Windsor (for prisoner-of-war duties).

Pre-1790   Royal Edward of the Seven Degrees Encampment at Hampton Court had name suggesting strongly an earlier connection with *Ecossais* Lodges working a Seven Degree Rite with Knight Templar elements.

1791   29th Regt with Glittering Star Lodge No. 322 (IC) [1759] with known record of RA and KT degrees (1760-68)1 deployed to Windsor in 1791.

Bristol, County of Bristol [Thomas Dunckerley PGM (Craft) 1786 PGSupt(RA) 1782-]

1740   On 18 July 1740 (et al) a Lodge held at The Rummer, Bristol referred to the Scotch Master Degree;

c.1756   French prisoner-of-war activity recorded in the Stapleton area.

1757   Sea Captain' Lodges known to be working 'higher degrees'.

1772   Meetings recorded as Knights Templar at the historic Rose and Crown Inn, Temple Street, Bristol in January 1772.[284]

1780   The Supreme Grand and Royal Encampment of Knights Templar of St John of Jerusalem, Knights Hospitallers, and Knights of Malta, recorded.

1780   Knights Templar in Bristol constituted themselves into The Supreme Grand and Royal Encampment of Knights Templar of St John of Jerusalem, Knights Hospitallers, and Knights of Malta, etc., etc.[285]

Pre-1790   Encampment Eminent of Seven Degrees (at Bristol) is listed in The 1794 List of Encampments as a Time Immemorial which suggests an origin based on The French Rite of Seven Degrees or *Ecossais* Masonry. Although a later chapter covers the history of Bristol Knights Templary in more detail, it is useful to note here that, even today, the Baldwyn Rite works the degrees of Scots Knights of Kilwinning, Scots Knight Grand Architect, and The Knights of The East, The Sword, and The Eagle in addition to Knights Templar, which further suggests such an *Ecossais* origin.

Cambridgeshire
1765   Early Antients Lodge 137(ECA) Isle of Ely.

1782   30th (Cambridgeshire Regt) had recruiting contacts with that County. The 30th Regt Lodges No.30/85(IC)[1738 to 1823] had known RA and KT activity and senior recruiting personnel could well have included KT brethren.

Peterborough was on the normal military route of march for troops moving north from South coast ports or garrison towns such as Colchester or Chatham, particularly en route to Northern garrison towns of York, Newcastle, or Berwick and to Scotland. Records also exist of French prisoners-of-war being housed near the City.

Cheshire
1774-75   The 22nd (Cheshire) Regt served on Garrison duties in England after periods deployed to the Americas including a presence in 1769 in Boston Massachusetts where the first KT ceremony was recorded. The 22nd Regt had Lodge No.251a (IC)[1754 to 1871] and Morian Lodge No. 132(SC) [1767 to 1809] at that time. Whilst the Regt was not deployed to Chester, it is possible brethren and knights who had been recruited there visited on leave, recruiting duties, or retired there.

1760   Oldest Antients Lodge 83A (ECA) Stockport [1760-]; 47B (ECA) Macclesfield [1764-].

1780   The History of Freemasonry in Cheshire[286] records KT activity in the province around 1780, namely in the minutes of Royal Chester Lodge No. 180 when a minute recorded a member 'took Royal Arch and Templar- no fees'.

Cornwall [Thomas Dunckerley PGSupt(RA) 1791-95]
1720s   There was considerable maritime trade between west country ports and Ireland,[287] France, and Gibraltar and early circumstantial evidence of a number of Sea Captains' Lodges exists showing working of *Ecossais* or 'higher degrees' in the 1720s; such working included Knight Templar elements, and at least one such lodge existed at Falmouth as early as 1757. It has been suggested Cornish seafarers were instrumental in taking *Ecossais* degrees to French ports in the 1720s.

c.1756   Falmouth, Launceston, Penryn, and Redruth in Cornwall have records of French prisoner-of-war activity between 1756 and 1814.

Pre-1790   St John of Jerusalem Encampment meeting in Redruth is recorded by Thomas Dunckerley in letter dated 22 Mar 1791 to Conclave of Redemption at York.

Cumberland
1750-51   The 14th Regt with Lodge: No.211(IC)[1750]; later recorded as working RA and KT (1760-68) returned from Scotland after the Jacobite uprising (1745-46) and deployed to Carlisle possibly with KT brethren by then.

1756   Carlisle, Cumberland has records of French prisoner-of-war activity after 1756.

1791   Thomas Dixon [Captain, 1st Dragoon Guards) as 'Acting Grand Master for the north District of England' included Westmorland & Cumberland so it is likely Dunckerley knew of KT activity there by then.

Derbyshire
1745 onwards   It is recorded that a detachment of Irish troops (from a Nottingham base) were stationed in North Derbyshire / South Yorkshire for several years after the Jacobite uprising to intercept renegades escaping through the Peak District, and anecdotal evidence suggests 'higher degrees' reached the area through Irish military brethren at that time.

1756   Chesterfield, Derbyshire has records of French prisoner-of-war activity from 1756 and two French prisoner-of-war lodges: *Loge De L'espérance* and *Loge De St Jerôme Et L'espérance.* It is recorded that Scarsdale Lodge members made eight Visits To *Loge De St Jerome Et L'espérance,* while the Scarsdale Lodge minutes record that on 5 March 1810, 'Hy. Vinclair and R. De La Croix, two foreigners, visited this night.' Both were prominent French Masons.

1759   Records exist of French prisoners-of-war from Basingstoke relocated to Derby in 1759.[288] Derby has records of French prisoner-of-war activity from 1759 and one officer of high rank passed most of his captivity as the honoured guest of the Duke of Devonshire at Chatsworth House.

1762   Early Antients Lodges including No. 106(ECA) Chesterfield [from 1762] would have been sympathetic to French prisoner-of-war visits.

Devon
c.1756   From 1756 French prisoners-of-war were imprisoned in naval 'hulks' at many south coast ports including Plymouth but also inland at Bideford, Dartmoor, Okehampton, Tavistock, and Tiverton and later up to 6,000 were housed on Dartmoor. One observer, commenting about Dartmoor as a residence, was 'amazed at the selection of such a place as the site for a (French prisoners-of-war) prison – the most inclement climate in England; for nine months there is no sun, and four and a half times as much rain as in Middlesex. The regiments on duty there have to be changed every two months.' Ashburton, Devon, located twenty miles from Plymouth and close to Dartmoor, recorded the existence of a French prisoner-of-war Lodge *Des Amis Reunis* as late as 1810 although earlier records have not been found. Tiverton certainly recorded both unorganised French prisoner-of-war activity before 1810 and from that year until at least 1814, they had their own lodge *Les Enfants De Mars A L'o*.

1776   In 1775 John Knight was Exalted in the Royal Arch Chapter of Sincerity, Peace and Prosperity at Devonport in which town it is also probable that he was Installed as a Knight Templar, probably in 1776.

1778   A Knight Templar Degree in 1778 at Portsmouth, Devon in 'a quasi-military Lodge', has been noted in connection with Irish Military Lodges[289] and activity under the High Knights Templar of Ireland from as early as 1740.

1780   The First Regiment of Dragoon Guards deployed to Exeter, Devon in 1780 for military review.

1783   After action at Quebec with possible contact with HMS *Vanguard* in 1759-60 and many years of service in Gibraltar, the 56th (West Essex) Regiment with King George III Lodge No. 101(SC) [1760] and Lodge No. 420(IC)[1765] left Gibraltar, and embarked for England, landing at Portsmouth in December; it marched from thence to Chatham where it remained until 1784. The Regt almost certainly included KT brethren by this time.

1790   Trine Encampment is listed at Biddeford, Devon meeting in *The New Ring of Bells* in the 1794 List of Encampments as Warranted in 1790.

Dorset [Thomas Dunckerley PGM(Craft) 1777-90 PGSupt(RA) 1780-96]
c.1756   Between 1756 and 1814 Portchester Castle, Dorset was used as a prison for French prisoners-of-war and Dorset and Denbighshire Militia performed garrison duty.

1757   Kings Dragoon Guards deployed to Dorchester, Devon in 1757 and in 1778-9 (and certainly had KT brethren by that time).

1782   The 35th Regt of Foot (originally raised in Belfast) designated Dorsetshire Regt in 1782 had recruiting contacts with that County, and included Lodges No. 205a(IC)[1750 to 1763]; Lodge No. 205b(IC)[1785 to 1790]; Lodge 205 has records of the Royal Arch as part of its Craft working and Lodge Banner depicts EA-RA-KT symbols by 1790; Lodge No.8 (ECM PGL (Quebec)];[1760-63] almost certainly worked RA and KT.

1765   The 1st Batt. 39th Regt of Foot (Dorsetshire Regt) although stationed in Castletown, IOM between 1765 and 1813, is assumed to have had contacts with the County of Dorset for recruiting purposes, and the Regt with its associated Lodge No. 290(IC) has a history of interactions with many regiments in Gibraltar in 1727 but, in particular with the 14th Regt of Foot in Gibraltar between 1752 and 1759 with proven KT working.

Pre-1790   Thomas Dunckerley in his letter dated 22 March 1791 to the Conclave of Redemption at York, mentions Dorchester where there is evidence of Durnovarian Encampment at the Dorchester, *Royal Oak* before that date.

Durham
1745-46   Many Regts staged through the Newcastle Garrison on deployments to and from Scotland. Newcastle was a major port for troop movements to/from Scotland and the Continent and regiments with known interactions with continental brethren would have been frequently in transit.

1757   The earliest Knight Templar activity in Northumberland and Durham was probably taken there by naval or seafaring brethren and Sea Captain's Lodges working 'higher degrees' are known from as early as 1757; Lanes List of Lodges records at least one such lodge: Sea Captains' Lodge, Sunderland, warranted 14th January 1757, and with considerable military movements and maritime trade with Scotland and the Continent, it is not surprising that their working included Knight Templar elements.

1786   1st Regt of Dragoon Guards with Lodge 520(ECM)/426(ECM)/ 342 (ECM) [1768-1813] deployed from York to Durham and Newcastle, and then continued northwards to Scotland in 1787. The Regt had known Knight Templar Brethren by that time.

1791   Thomas Dixon [Captain, 1st Dragoon Guards) as 'Acting Grand Master for the north District of England' which included Durham and Northumberland so perhaps Dunckerley knew of KT activity there by then.

Essex
Evidence certainly exists of Knight Templar activity in East Anglia in the later years of the 18th century, possibly under the influence of Thomas Dixon of the 1st Regt of Dragoon Guards which was stationed in Colchester.[290] It may also be noted that a Thomas Dixon was also Scribe E of a Colchester Royal Arch Chapter which almost certainly worked Knights Templar and other degrees.

1744   The 14th Regt of Foot deployed to Colchester, Essex in 1744 between engagements at Dettingen and Fontenoy. At that time the 14th Regt is not known to have had a travelling military lodge but shortly thereafter, in 1750, Lodge No.211(IC) was Warranted and by 1760 that lodge was recorded as working RA and KT. It is therefore possible individual KT brethren may have been present then.

1784   The 1st Regt of Dragoon Guards deployed to Colchester, Essex, and had KT brethren by that time.

Gloucestershire [Thomas Dunckerley PGM (Craft) 1784-86 Gloucestershire, and Somerset PGM (Craft) 1786 Gloucestershire PGSupt(RA) 1793-1803 [Gloucestershire and Herefordshire]
c.1773   The 28th Foot, 1st Battalion, (later named Gloucestershire Regt) with Lodges No. 35(IC) [1734-1801] and No. 510(IC) [1773-1858] had known interactions with proven KT activity in the 14th and 29th Regts including Gibraltar, Culloden, Boston, and Louisburg.

c.1782   The 27th Foot (in 1782 designated the West Middlesex Regt) was raised in Gloucestershire and Somerset and had the first Military Lodge Warrant issued by the Antients Grand Lodge (Lodge No. 41A (ECA) when the Regt was in the New World (Charlesburg, Canada) [1755-1756]. Undoubtedly there would be contacts with this County for recruiting after 1782.

Gwynedd
Carnarvon, (now Gwynedd) has records of French prisoners-of-war activity after 1756.

Hampshire and Isle of Wight
c.1756   Between 1756 and 1814 French prisoners-of-war[291] were imprisoned in prison 'hulks' in many south coast ports and throughout Hampshire including Alresford, Alton, Basingstoke, Fareham, Odiham, Petersfield, Portchester, Forton (near Portsmouth), Winchester; and Yarmouth, Isle of Wight. Specific records exist of French prisoners-of-war visits to Lodge of Economy No. 88 at Winchester up to 1810.

1758   In 1758 French prisoners-of-war[292] were imprisoned in Petersfield, formed their own Lodge which remained active there until relocated in 1759.

1778   Knight Templar degree noted in 'quasi-military' lodge in Portsmouth.[293]

Pre-1790   Naval Encampment at Portsmouth, is listed in the 1794 list of Encampments and is still working as No. 2.

1776   14th Regt of Foot (With Lodges 211(IC) and 58(ECA) [1750-1818] and Known KT activity from 1769 returned from USA to Turkey Point near Portsmouth for a few months before returning to the New World.

I782   The 36th Regt of Foot (designated Herefordshire Regt) with Lodge No 36(IC)[1777 to 1815]; Lodge No. 542(IC)[1777-80]; Lodge No. 559(IC)[1778 to 1815];Lodge No. 31(IC) ; [recorded by Jenkyns as working Royal Arch and Knight Templar degrees under Craft Warrants] deployed from Ireland to Hilsea Barracks near Portsmouth.

1782   The 37th Regt of Foot (originally raised in Ireland) designated North Hampshire Regt and would have had recruiting contacts with the County from that date. The 37th Regt Lodges : No. 52ECA) [1756 to 1813][recorded as working Super Excellent and Royal Arch degrees]; Solomon Lodge ECA in New York)[1776-81]; and later North Hants Lodge No.726(EC)[1844 to 1862]; Earliest Antients Lodge 52(ECA) warrant was granted when 37th Regt of Foot was in Halifax Nova Scotia [1756 onwards].

Hereford, Herefordshire Thomas Dunckerley PGM (Craft) 1790; PGSupt(RA) 1793-1803 [Gloucestershire and Herefordshire]
1782   36th Regt, originally raised in Ireland in 1701, was designated 36th (Herefordshire) Regt in 1782 and would therefore have had contacts for recruiting purposes with that County. 36th Regt Lodges included Lodge No 36(IC)[1777 to 1815]; and Lodge No. 542(IC)[1777-80]; Lodge No. 559(IC)[1778 to 1815]; and Lodge No. 31(IC). [Jenkyns records the Regt working Royal Arch and Knight Templar degrees under Craft Warrant.]

Pre-1790   Royal Edward Encampment meeting in Hereford at '*The Bowling Green*' is recorded by Thomas Dunckerley in his letter dated 22 March 1791 to the Conclave of Redemption at York.

Isle of Man[294]
1765   Lodge No. 290(IC) associated with the 1st Batt. 39th Regt of Foot (Dorsetshire Regt) met in Castletown, IOM between 1765 and 1813. The Manx Museum has no records to confirm this, and there is no evidence to show what working was carried out but working 'beyond the Craft' was normal practice in Irish Military Lodges at this time.[295]

***Kent* [Thomas Dunckerley PGSupt(RA) 1778-1807]**
1756 onwards   Chatham, Kent has records of French prisoner-of-war activity after 1756, and Dover, has records of French prisoner-of-war activity between 1756 and 1814.

1762   Lodge constituted at the '*Bunch of Grapes*', Chatham (Antients Warrant of Constitution: 8 Dec. 1762) and others with Marine military connections.

1769   Presence of Kent Regimental Brethren may be indicated in the recorded St Andrews Lodge Minute of 28 August 1769 where KT was worked.

1783   After action at Quebec with possible contact with HMS *Vanguard* in 1759-60 and many years of service in Gibraltar; the 56th (West Essex) Regiment with King George

III Lodge No. 101(SC) [1760-1809] and Lodge No. 420(IC)[1765-1817] left Gibraltar, and embarked for England, landing at Portsmouth in December, it marched from thence to Chatham where it remained until 1784.

Lancashire

c.1756   From 1756 French prisoners-of-war were imprisoned near Liverpool and at a number of other sites in Lancashire.

1781   Knights Templar established and working within Lodge No. 37 meeting at Bolton.[296] Their Rules and Regulations are still extant.

1786   Grand Lodge of All England at York receives Petition dated 11 June 1786 from Bro John Hassall and other Brethren in Manchester and grants a Charter dated 10 Oct 1786 for Jerusalem Encampment at Manchester [No. 5].

1786   Knights Templar degree recorded in Antiquity Lodge No. 146 at Bolton.[297]

1789   St Bernard Chapter and Conclave, Hollywood, Lancs mentioned in a KT Certificate issued by Lodge No. 37 at Bolton to Henry Mills.

Leicestershire

1760-82   The 59th Regt of Foot, originally raised in Leicestershire and Northamptonshire would have had recruiting contacts with those Counties prior to being re-designated 2nd Batt (Cambridgeshire Regt) in 1782. The Regt Lodges included Lodge No. 243(IC)[1754]; Lodge No.5 (Nova Scotia Antients Grand Lodge)[1765]; and Lodges in this Regt were recorded as working RA and KT (1760-68) along with Lodges in 14th, 29th, and 44th Regts.

Leicestershire has records of French prisoner-of-war activity from 1769 to 1810 at Ashby-De-La-Zouch, Leicester, and Syston;[298] a prisoner-of-war Lodge *Vrai Amis De L'ordre* existed at Ashby-De-La-Zouch until 1810 and there are records of visits to local lodges by French prisoners-of-war and/ or French prisoners-of-war as joining members.

1784   The 17th Foot, (later named The Leicestershire Regt) with Lodges 136(IC) [1743] and 158(IC) [1743-] had contact with other Regiments at Louisburg and has documented records of KT activity at least as early as 1784.

Lincolnshire

1756 onwards   Kings Lynn and Humber ports were important staging posts for troops travelling to and fro to Scotland and the Continent and for landing French prisoners-of-war who then deployed throughout the County with noted prisoners-of-war activity recorded at nearby Wisbech (now in Cambridgeshire).

c.1758   The 10th Regt of Foot,(Col Pool's Regt) (later named The Lincolnshire Regt) with Lodges 177(IC) [1748-1755], 299(IC) [1758-1818] and 378(IC) [1761-1815] had, in Ireland in 1758, contact with 29th Regt which, shortly afterwards had known KT activity.

c.1776   The 30th Regt of Foot was raised in Lincolnshire and presumably maintained contact with the County. Lodges No. 30(IC); No. 535(IC)[1776]; and St John's

Lodge No.628(EC)[1822]. The Regt known to have worked RA and other degrees in Dominica in 1787].

1783-85   The 1st Regt of Dragoon Guards with Lodge 520(ECM)/426(ECM)/ 342 (ECM) [1768-1813] deployed throughout Lincolnshire in 1783 and then Lincoln, Boston, and Stamford in 1785. (With Known KT members.)

London
1733   Lodge No. 115 meeting at *Devil Tavern*, Temple Bar, London (Rawlinsons Manuscript describes as 'Scotch Masons Lodge, Pines Engraved List of 1734 shows 'Scotts Masons Lodge) an *Ecossais* Lodge was working Knight of the East and KT degrees.

1740   Old Lodge No. 1 (Lodge held at *The Mourning Bush*, Aldersgate) on 17 June 1740 recorded nine members made Scotch Masons.

1751   Many Antients Lodges were formed in London from 1751 onwards, most were short-lived; one of the earliest with any longevity was: Lodge No. 4A(ECA) London [[1751-1765]. Although tenuous, a number adopted names reminiscent of Knight Templar rather than Craft activity including Mount Moriah (Now No. 34); Temple Lodge (Now No. 101); and Lodge of Joppa (Now No. 188).

1751   Sea Captains Lodge No. 212, St Andrew's Cross, Hermitage, Wapping, London members would have had undoubted contacts with marine and military brethren.

1759   The 7th Foot, (later named Royal Fusiliers (City of London) Regt with Lodges No. 38(IC) [1750-1801], No. 231(IC) [1752-1801] and No. 53(ECA) [1768-?] had had known inter-actions with 14th and 29th Regts including service in Gibraltar by 1759.

c.1760   Pierre Lambert de Lintot carries French Rite of Seven Degrees (or a modified version 'de Lintot's Rite' with KT elements) to London.

Pre-1790   Encampment Observance of Seven Degrees London) is listed in the 1794 List of Encampments as a Time Immemorial at London Coffee House, Ludgate Hill, which name strongly suggests an origin based on *Ecossais* Lodge / The French Rite of Seven Degrees or de Lintot's Rite.

1784   The 1st Regt of Dragoon Guards deployed from York to London Area (including Greenwich, Deptford, and Blackheath) with known KT members by that date.

Middlesex
1782 The 27th Foot (in 1782 designated the West Middlesex Regt) were raised in Gloucestershire and Somerset and are noted for The first Military Lodge Warrant issued by the *Antients* Grand Lodge – Lodge No. 41A (ECA) when the 57th Regt of Foot were in the New World (Charlesburg, Canada) [1755-1756]. The Regt had known interactions with Regt Lodges working RA and KT and undoubtedly there would be contacts with this County for recruiting after 1782.

Monmouth
1756 onwards Early prisoner-of-war activity was noted in Chepstow and Monmouth, and

Abergavenny recorded the existence of a prisoner-of-war Lodge *Enfant De Mars Et De Neptune* as late as 1813 although earlier records have not been found. Records also exist elsewhere in Wales with, for example, known French prisoner-of-war activity from 1769 to 1814 including a prison at Llanfyllin, Pembroke.

Norfolk

1759   Sea Captains Lodge No. 236, *White Swan*, South Quay, Great Yarmouth, Norfolk and from 1761 early *Antients* Lodge No. 95 (ECA) Norwich [1761-1762]; No. 97 (ECA) Lynn Regis Norfolk [1762-1763]; and No. 99 (ECA) Norwich [1762-1777] are all likely to have worked degrees 'beyond the Craft.'

1760   In 1760, an Angel Lodge, Yarmouth, minute records it was 'unanimously agreed to allow Bro. Mercer, a French prisoner, seven pence per week towards his support for lodging.'

1769   From 1769 the 9th Regt of Foot, (later named Royal Norfolk Regt) with Lodge No. 246(IC) [1754-1817] had known inter-actions including Culloden, and Boston with the 14th and 29th Regts which recorded KT activity by 1769 and ample evidence of repeated contact with the County, including deployments in 1781-82, when back in England including Norwich, Lowestoft, and Yarmouth to recruit replacements; senior recruiting personnel would almost certainly have included KT brethren.

1773   Evidence exists of a Certificate dated c.1773 issued as a KT Certificate to (Possibly) Robert Caldwee By Lodge No. 167 (ECA).

1774-75   The 1st Regt of Dragoon Guards with Lodge No. 520(ECM)/426(ECM)/ 342 (ECM) [1768-1813] undertook several deployments in the East Anglian area including, on 8 May 1775, deployment to Norwich; Such duties possibly included escorting French prisoners-of-war from Harwich and Kings Lynn ports to internment camps across Eastern England as far north as York. Further deployments were made to Ipswich in 1784-85 and Bury St Edmunds in 1785 (with Known KT Brethren by that time).

1788   On 11 Jan 1788 the (Norfolk) Provincial Grand Secretary, James Bullivant, wrote to the Grand Secretary: *'Several Gentlemen wishing to form a Grand Chapter of Knights Templar have desir'd me to make an enquiry if a grant can be given from the Grand Lodge for that purpose ..... '*

Northamptonshire

1760-82   The 59th Regt of Foot, originally raised in Leicestershire and Northamptonshire would have had recruiting contacts with those Counties prior to being re-designated 2nd Batt (Cambridgeshire Regt) in 1782. The Regt Lodges included Lodge No. 243(IC)[1754-1815] and Lodge No.5 (Nova Scotia *Antients* Grand Lodge) [1765-1774]; Lodges in this Regt. were recorded as working Royal Arch and Knight Templar degrees (1760-68) [as were Lodges with 14th, 29th, and 44th Regts with which they were in repeated contact].

1782   The 48th Regt of Foot, 1st Battalion, (In 1782 named Northamptonshire Regt) with Lodges No. 86(IC) [1750-1858] and No. 218(IC) [1738-1784] had repeated inter-actions with the 14th and 29th Regts including Fontenoy, Culloden, Boston, and Louisburg;

these Regts had known KT activity by that time.

1786   Northamptonshire had a major prisoner-of-war prison at Norman Cross near Peterborough which housed up to 6,000 foreign internees, and Northampton recorded the existence of prisoner-of-war Lodge *La Bonne Union* until at least 1810.

Northumberland
1744   The 14th Regt of Foot deployed from York to Berwick which was a major Garrison town and a significant staging post for many Regts passing to and from Scotland.

1742-49   The 46th Regt of Foot was originally raised in Newcastle (as Col Price's Regt) so presumably always maintained contacts with the County. Served 1742-49 in Berwick and Scotland.

1745   The 5th Regt of Foot, (later named Royal Northumberland Fusiliers) with Lodges No. 86a(IC)[1738] and No. 86b(IC)[1738-1815] had known inter-actions with proven KT activity in 14th and 29th Regts including Culloden, Boston, and Gibraltar.

From c.1756   French prisoners of war[299] were imprisoned at Tynemouth and a number of anecdotes exist, some associated with escape attempts.

1786-7   1st Regt of Dragoon Guards with Lodge No. 520(ECM)/426(ECM)/ 342 (ECM) [1768-1813] having served in York and Durham in 1786 deployed to Newcastle, and then continued deployment northwards to Scotland in 1787. [The Regt had known Knight Templar Brethren by that time.]

1791   Thomas Dixon [Captain, 1st Dragoon Guards) as 'Acting Grand Master for the north District of England' which included Durham and Northumberland, so perhaps Dunckerley knew of KT activity there by then.

Nottinghamshire
1744-45   It has been claimed that a Nottinghamshire encampment supposedly worked a seven degree system including Rose Croix, Kadosh and Knights of the Red Cross under the umbrella of Knights Templar, and by 1745 conferred the Templar degree on visitors.

1746   The 46th Regt of Foot deployed to Nottingham from Scotland via Berwick in 1746. [Later Regt had Lodge No. 227(IC) [4 Mar 1752 – Still Extant as Quebec No.1].

1760-82   The 59th Regt of Foot, originally raised in Leicestershire and Northamptonshire would have had recruiting contacts with those Counties prior to being re-designated The 59th (2nd Nottinghamshire) Regiment of Foot in 1782. The Regt Lodges included Lodge No. 243(IC)[1754-1815] and Lodge No.5 (Nova Scotia Antients Grand Lodge)[1765-1774]; and Lodges in this Regt. were recorded as working Royal Arch and Knight Templar degrees (1760-68) as were Lodges with 14th, 29th, and 44th Regts].

1783   There is speculation that an Encampment was formed in 1783 in Nottinghamshire under the first Provincial Grand Master, The Rt Hon. Thomas Boothby Parkyns, 1st Baron Rancliffe, who then became the KT Grand Master in 1797.

1785   There is also evidence of members of KT in the area in 1785, and it has been published that the militia of Nottingham took the Order to Edinburgh in 1798.

Oxfordshire

This is really the only County for which evidence of KT activity before 1791 has not yet been found.[300]

Certainly, records exist of prisoner-of-war activity at Wantage in Oxfordshire with the establishment of a French Lodge *Coeurs Unis* sometime before 1810, but earlier records have not yet been found.

Shropshire

Shropshire has records of early French prisoner-of-war activity at Oswestry and one interesting anecdote: 'On 20 May 20, 1813, a French officer on parole who is supposed by himself and countrymen to possess strength little inferior to Samson. (He is Monsieur Fiarsse, he follows the profession of a fencing-master, and is allowed to have considerable skill in that way) had been boasting that he had beat every Englishman that opposed him in the town where he was last on parole (in Devonshire), and he sent a challenge … to a private of the 64th Regt.'

Somerset [Thomas Dunckerley PGM (Craft) 1784-86 Bristol, Gloucestershire, and Somerset PGM (Craft) 1786 Somerset]

1732   Lodge of Antiquity [TI] Bath (still extant) and Royal Cumberland Lodge (ECM).

1733   *Ecossais* Lodge working Scots Master, Knight of the East, and Knight Templar degrees recorded at Bath, Somerset and, in 1735, The Lodge held at *The Bear*, Bath on 28 Oct 1735 Lodge of Masters admitted ten Scots Master Masons.

c.1756   Between 1756 and 1814 records exist of French prisoner-of-war activities in Wincanton, Somerset including the existence of a French Lodge *La Paix Desiree* until at least 1810.

1781   The 1st Regt of Dragoon Guards deployed from York to Bath, Somerset. On 7 November 1781 the Regiment was reviewed at Bath by Major General Ward.

Pre-1790   Royal Cumberland Encampment meeting at *The Bear Inn* in Bath, Somerset is recorded by Thomas Dunckerley in his earliest writings.

Pre-1790   Encampment Antiquity of Seven Degrees (Bath) is listed in The 1794 List of Encampments as Time Immemorial which suggests an origin based on *Ecossais Lodge* / The French Rite of Seven Degrees.

1788-94   The 13th Regt of Foot deployed home to Bath after 6 years in the West Indies (where KT activity was recorded by then) with Lodge No.153ECA)[1768 to 1810]; Lodge No.637(IC)[1784-1818]; and Lodge No.661(IC)[1787-1819];

Staffordshire

c.1756   Between 1756 and 1814 records exist of French prisoner-of-war activities in Staffordshire including two French Prisoner-of-War lodges in Leek (*De L'Amite* and *Reunion Desiree*).

Suffolk [**Thomas Dunckerley** PGSupt(RA) c.1790 – Suffolk]
1760   The 9th Regt of Foot with Lodge No. 246(IC)[10 April 1754] - by 1760 known to work degrees beyond the Craft including Knight Templar and Holy Royal Arch Knight Templar Priest (or Priestly Order). Later returned to England from the New World and in 1781-82 redeployed back to Lowestoft, Yarmouth, to recruit replacements.

1784-85   The First Regiment of Dragoon Guards deployed to Ipswich in 1784, and Bury St Edmunds in 1785 (With known KT Brethren by that time).

Surrey [**Thomas Dunckerley** PGSupt(RA) 1793-95 Surrey]
Although no specific evidence has been found, the County would have had many military units and their lodges in transit before 1791, circumstantially, KT brethren must have been there.

Sussex
1784   1st Regt of Dragoon Guards with Lodge 520(ECM)/426(ECM)/ 342 (ECM) [1768-1813] deployed to Sussex.

Warwickshire
1750   The First Regt of Dragoon Guards deployed to Birmingham to quell Riots.

1770   The 6th Regt of Foot, (later named Royal Warwickshire) Regt with Lodges No. 45(IC) [1735-1801], No. 643(IC) [1785-1800] and No. 646(IC) [1785-1818] had had inter-actions with known KT activity in 14th and 29th Regts by c.1770.

1783   The 1st Regt of Dragoon Guards with Lodge No. 520(ECM)/426(ECM) /342 (ECM) [1768-1813] deployed to Coventry and then York.

Wiltshire [**Thomas Dunckerley** PGM (Craft) 1777-90 PGSupt(RA) 1780-95]
1746   A Lodge met In Salisbury in 1746 'when certain members there were made 'Scott's Masons' cited in 'History of Freemasonry in Wilts, F. H. Goldney,1880.

1774   Known connections between 36th Regt of Foot and 28th Regt of Foot at Salisbury probably with KT brethren at that time.

1782   The   1st   Regt   of   Dragoon   Guards   with   Lodge   No. 520(ECM)/426(ECM)/342 (ECM) [1768-1813] deployed to Devizes in 1782. (With known Knight Templar Brethren by that time).

Pre-1790   Harmony of Seven Degrees Encampment meeting in Salisbury, Wiltshire at *The White Hart* recorded by Dunckerley. [Circumstantially this could suggests involvement with *Ecossais* KT working as early as 1733 and with military KT brethren in transit to the coastal ports.]

Pre-1790   Science of the Seven Degrees Encampment meeting in Salisbury at The Parade Coffee House recorded by Thomas Dunckerley.

Naming of these early Encampments suggests most strongly an earlier connection with *Ecossais Lodges* working a Seven Degree Rite with Knight Templar elements.

Worcestershire

1751   The 29th (Worcestershire) Regiment of Foot with 2 Militia Batts. [5th Batt. The 1st Worcestershire Militia and the 6th Batt. The 2nd Worcestershire Militia] [Formed from 1694 Colonel Thomas Farington's (or successive Colonels' names) Regiment of Foot. Granted a Warrant for Lodge 322(IC) [1759 and still working as Glittering Star Lodge] with probably Knight Templar Activity from Ireland and Caribbean deployments in 1759-61 and known KT activity from Boston (1769-75).

1769   Presence of The 29th (Worcestershire) Regt Brethren recorded in the St Andrews Lodge Minute of 28 August 1769 in Boston, Massachusetts.

Yorkshire

1745   Minutes of York Lodges record visits by Brethren of 14th Regt *en route* from Fontenoy, Flanders to Culloden[301] with some suggestion of 'higher degrees' being worked.

1745   Plausible anecdotal evidence suggests Knight Templar Masonry may have appeared in the Sheffield area just after the Jacobite uprising.[302]

1754   The 1st Regiment of Dragoon Guards deployed to York, Leeds, and Wakefield.

1756   From c.1756 to 1814 a number of Yorkshire towns have records of French prisoner-of-war activity including Bedale, Boroughbridge, Knaresborough, Pontefract, Richmond, and Wakefield where prison ships (hulks) on the River Calder were used.

1756-63   The 21st (Granby's) Light Dragoons were chiefly employed in the County escorting French prisoners of war from Scarborough to prison barges at Hull up to 1763.

1759   Records of prisoner-of-war activity exist in Leeds from 1759 including records of visits to Talbot Lodge by French prisoners-of-war, some of whom became joining members.

1762   In York, although the earliest prisoner-of-war activity has not been dated, on 10 June 1762, The Grand Lodge of all England at York constituted Lodge No. 1 to meet at *The Punch Bowl*, Stonegate, York[303], a lodge referred to locally as 'Frenchmans' Lodge', which P. O. Preston (sometime Provincial Vice-Chancellor, Province of North and East Yorkshire) asserted worked Knight Templar degrees before that date leading to the insertion of the following clause in the June 1762 warrant which specifically stated:

   'Prohibiting, nevertheless them and their successors from making anyone a Brother who shall be a subject of Great Britain or Ireland ....'

1779   The Grand Lodge of all England at York announced that Lodge asserted authority over five degrees or orders of Masonry, the Entered Apprentice, Fellow Craft, Master Mason, Royal Arch, and Knight Templar.[304] and in the same year the first known Certificate for KT in York Signed by John Brown, G. Sec, GL of All England recording that, on 29.11.1779, a brother was admitted to the Knight Templar (5th Degree).[304]

1780   Charter dated 6 July 1780 for a KT Encampment to meet in Rotherham (associated with Druidical Lodge)[306] granted by Grand Lodge of All England at York.

1782   Grand Lodge of All England at York granted Lodge No. 211 (in Nova Scotia) a warrant for a Knight Templar Encampment dated 20 Sep 1782.[307]

1784   Capt. Thomas Dixon recorded as Eminent Commander of Ancient York Conclave of Redemption.

1786   Minutes of Minerva Craft Lodge No. 250 in York in 1786 include reference to Knight Templar working under the Craft Warrant[308] a year when The First Regiment of Dragoon Guards was stationed in York.

1786   Thomas Fletcher recorded as Eminent Commander of Ancient York Conclave of Redemption

Pre-1790   Encampment of (Ancient York Conclave of) Redemption (York) is listed in the 1794 List of Encampments as a Time Immemorial Encampment.

1790   John Watson is recorded as Eminent Commander of Ancient York Conclave of Redemption.

1791   Ancient York Conclave of Redemption at York received response to a petition sent to Thomas Dunckerley at Bristol, stating, the existence of 8 Encampments by that date. York should have been allocated No. 5 but declined and retained name without number.

1791   John Watson received Warrant for a Conclave or Chapter of Encampment at the City of York from Thomas Dunckerley, Grand Master, dated 11 March 1791. *[Signed R. W. Whalley, Grand Chancellor; W. Hannam, Acting Grand Master.]*

1791   Ancient York Conclave of Redemption has handwritten letters dated 22 March 1791, 21 April 1791, 21 May 1791, 15 June 1791, and 28 June 1791 from Thomas Dunckerley. The letter dated 15 June 1791 confirms the appointment of Thomas Dixon (see above). Records exist of visit by Thomas Dixon [Captain, 1st Dragoon Guards) who intimated that Thomas Dunckerley was about to form a Grand Conclave of which he was to be the first Grand Master.

1791-94   The 14th Regt of Foot returned to York following service in the West Indies at St Vincent, during the American War of Independence. When the French Revolutionary army invaded the Netherlands the 14th Regt was part of the Duke of York's army, fighting at Famars in 1793, Valenciennes and Tournai.

Scotland
1779   A body of Dublin Freemasons existing under the title 'The High Knight Templars of Ireland' applied for and received a charter from Lodge Kilwinning in

Scotland.[309]... initiating 'Black Masonry' which eventually became the degree of Knight Templar. Gould notes '... it was to their intercourse with brethren belonging to the regiments serving in Ireland ... that Scotch lodges owed their acquaintance with Knight Templarism.'

In Scotland French prisoners-of-war were incarcerated at Edinburgh, Hawick, Jedburgh, Melrose, Montrose, Peebles, Perth, Sanquhar (Dumfries), Selkirk, and Valleyfield (Esk Mills and Penicuik) with many records of visits to local lodges by French prisoners-of-war and/or French prisoners-of-war as Joining Members. Specific records of prisoner-of-war Lodges exist at Montrose (*Bienfaisance*) to 1813; Sanquhar (*La Paix Desiree A L'o*); and Valleyfield (*De L'infortune* ['Misfortune']. Kelso has records of French prisoner-of-war activity including visits to Kelso Lodge No. 58 between 1810 and 1814 but earlier records have not been found.

Canada

1782　　　In 1782, six brethren then living in Halifax, Nova Scotia, conferred the Royal Arch and Knight Templar degrees upon several candidates acting under the authority of the warrant of St John's Lodge, No. 211(GLAE), now No. 2. The minutes from 1782 to 1806, and from 1839 to 1856, along with other evidence, are still extant and help to establish the origin and continuity of the present day Antiquity Preceptory No. 5, Halifax, Nova Scotia.[310]

1789　　　Lodge No. 213/9 ER(A) in the 4th Battalion, Royal Regiment of Artillery has its minute book in existence dating from 1789 and containing 'Marks' of Mark Master Masons who had been made in the Lodge. Although these minutes date from the time the Regt and Lodge were at Woolwich, it indicates that the Mark degree was likely being worked prior to that time and there are collateral indications that Royal Arch and Knight Templar degrees were known to the Lodge when in Montreal in 1791.

RELATED MILITARY ACTIVITY

In addition to the details given above where Knight Templar or other chivalric activity has been recorded, there are a number of military deployments by regiments with lodges and brethren which are almost certainly relevant as these allowed interaction between the Regts with known KT activity and other Regts and brethren.

Similar interactions occurred at sea during deployments and when awaiting embarkation at major ports. Initially four cartel ports were designated for the reception of the prisoners arriving in England: those of Lynn, Plymouth, Dartmouth, and Portsmouth. Later, Great Yarmouth also became an exceedingly busy receiving port.

Prisoners were then distributed throughout England and Wales, usually marched on-foot, but also on canals escorted by units drawn from many regular army and militia regiments. One example amongst many relates to Sissinghurst Castle, Kent. Between 1760 and 1766 the 14th Regt of Foot was deployed to several locations in the South of England including Dover, Maidstone, Windsor, and Sissinghurst Castle in Kent guarding French prisoners-of-war.

Military Lodges Established By 1791[311]

(With known Interactions with 14th and 29th Regts working KT at Boston in 1769.)
Key:
B1 Boston (1769);
B2 Boston (1775)
B3 Belle Isle (1761)
C1 Caribbean (1759)
F1 Fontenoy (1745)

G1 Gibraltar (1727)
G2 Gibraltar (1752-59)
H1 Halifax, Nova Scotia (1765-68)
J1 Jacobite Uprising (1745-46)
L1 Louisburg-Quebec 1758-62
V1 HMS Vanguard (1756-59)

Regiments of Foot

Unit	Lodge(s)	Constituted	Interactions
1st Regt Foot, Royal Scots 1st Batt.	11(IC) 381(IC)	1732–1847 1762–1817	L1; J1; V1
1st Regt Foot, Royal Scots 2nd Batt.	74(IC)	1737–1801	J1
2nd Foot, Queen's Royal Regt (West Surrey)	244(IC) 390(IC)	1754–1825 1762–1815	C1
5th Foot, Royal Northumberland Fusiliers	86a(IC) 86b(IC)	1738-1784 1784–1815	G1; B2; C1
6th Foot, Royal Warwickshire	45(IC) 643(IC) 646(IC)	1735–1801 1785-1800 1785-1818	G2
7th Foot, Royal Fusiliers (City of London)	38(IC) 231(IC) 153(ECA)	1750-1801 1752–1801 1768-?	G2
9th Foot, Royal Norfolk	246(IC)	1754–1817	B3; C1
10th Foot, Lincolnshire (Col Pool's Regt)	177(IC) 299(IC) 378(IC)	1748–1755 1758–1818 1761–1815	Ireland 1758 with 29th Regt
11th Foot, Devonshire	72(ECA) 604(IC)	1758-1767 1782-1794	F1
13th Foot, Somerset Light Infantry	153(ECA) 637(IC) 661(IC)	1768-1810 1784-1818 1787-1819	C1; F1; G2
14th Foot, West Yorkshire (Prince of Wales Own)	211(IC) 58(ECA)	1750-1818	B1; B2; G2; L1; J1
15th Foot, East Yorkshire	245(IC)	1754-1801	C1; L1
16th Foot, Bedfordshire & Hertfordshire	293 (IC) 300 (IC)	1758–1817 1758–1801	J1; H1
17th Foot, Leicestershire	136(IC) 158(IC)	1743-1801 1743-	L1
18th Foot, Royal Irish (Col Folliott's Regt)	168(IC) 351(IC)	1747-1801 1760-1793	B2; F1; G1; G2
19th Foot, Green Howards	156(IC)	1747-1779	B3; C1; F1
20th Foot, Lancashire Fusiliers, 1st Batt.	63(IC)	1737-1869	F1; J1

Unit	Lodge(s)	Constituted	Interactions
21st Foot, Royal Scots Fusiliers	33(IC) 936(IC)	1734-1801 1772-1864	B2; C1; G3; J1
22nd Foot, Cheshire [Founded GL of New York in 1781]	251(IC) 132(SC)	1754-1817 1767-1809	G2; L1
25th Foot, King's Own Scottish Borderers	92(IC)	1738-1815	F1; G2; J1
26th Foot, 1st Batt., The Cameronians	26(IC)	1758-1823	B3; C1; V1
27th Foot, 1st Batt., Royal Inniskilling Fusiliers [Col Hamilton's Regt]	23(IC) 205(IC) 528(IC)	1734-1801 1750-1785 1787-1815	J1
28th Foot, 1st Batt., Gloucestershire Regt	35(IC)	1734-1801	B3; C1; G2;
29th Foot, 1st Batt., Worcestershire	510(IC) 322(IC)	1773-1858 1759	L1 B1; B2; B3; C1
30th Foot, 1st Batt., East Lancashire [Col. Harward's Regt]	85(IC) 30(IC) 535IC)	1738-1793 1793-1823 1776-1823	C1; B2; B3; G2
32nd Foot, 1st Batt., Duke of Cornwall's Light Infantry	61(IC) 73(SC) 617(IC)	1736-1792 1754-1809 1783-1815	B2; C1; F1; G2; V1
33rd Foot, 1st Batt., Duke of Wellington's	12(IC) 90(ECA)	1732-1817 1761-1815	B3; C1; F1
34th Foot, Cumberland Regt	466(ECM)	1783-1813]	C1; F1; J1; V1
35th Foot, 1st Batt., Royal Sussex	205(IC)	1749-1790	C1; L1; V1
36th Foot, Herefordshire Regt	542(IC) 36(IC) 559(IC)	1770-1780 1777-1815 1778-1815	B3; C1; J1
38th Foot, 1st Batt., South Staffordshire	38(IC) 441(IC)	1734-1801 1765-1817	B2
39th Foot, 1st Batt., Dorsetshire	128(IC) 290(IC)	1742-1886 1758-1804	G1; G2
40th Foot, 2nd Somerset Regt	128(IC) 42(ECA)	1742-1758 1755-	C1; L1; V1
42nd Foot, 1st Batt., Black Watch (Royal Highlanders)	195(IC)	1749-1815	F1; G2; J1
45th Foot, 1st Batt., Sherwood Foresters	445(IC) 272(ECA)	1766-1815 1791-1804	L1
48th Foot, 1st Batt., Northamptonshire	86(IC) 218(IC)	1738-1784 1750-1858	B2; F1; L1; J1
49th Foot, 1st Batt., Royal Berkshire	354(IC) 616(IC)	1760-1846 1783-1817	C1; B2
50th Foot, 1st Batt., Queen's Own Royal West Kent	112(IC) 113(IC)	1763-1786 1764-1830	B3; C1

Unit	Lodge(s)	Constituted	Interactions
51st Foot, 1st Batt., King's Own Yorks. Light Infantry	94(IC) 690(IC)	1761-1805 1788-1796	
52nd Foot, 2nd Batt., Oxford and Bucks Light Infantry	370(IC) 7(PGLQ) 226(ECM)	1761-1832 1769 1770-1813	B2
53rd Foot, 1st Batt., King's Shropshire Light Infantry	236(IC)	1773-1815	B3; G2
56th Foot, 2nd Batt., Essex	101(SC) 420(IC)	1760-1809 1765-1817	B2; F1; G2; L1
58th Foot, 2nd Batt., Northamptonshire	218(IC)	1750-1759	C1; G2; L1
59th Foot, 2nd Batt., East Lancashire	243(IC)	1754-1815	B1; B2
62nd Foot, 1st Batt., Wiltshire (Duke of Edinburgh)	407(IC)	1763-1786	F1; J1
63rd Foot, 1st Battalion, Manchester	512(IC)	1774-1814	C1; V1
64th Foot, 2nd Staffordshire Regt	106(SC)	1761-1816	B2; B3; C1; V1
66th Foot, 2nd Batt., Royal Berkshire	392(IC) 538(IC) 580(IC)	1763-1817 1777-1811 1780-1823	C1; G2
76th Foot, 2nd Batt., Gordon Highlanders	359(IC) 248(ECA)	1760-1807 1788-1828	C1
77th Foot, Atholl Highlanders	578(IC)	1780-1813	C1

Whilst this anthology of known or suspected Knight Templar activity prior to 1791 is acknowledged to be incomplete, and occasionally circumstantial, it nevertheless indicates that, at the time Thomas Dunckerley became Grand Master, relevant activity existed in virtually every County and in most Garrison Towns and seaports.

During the writing of this work many Provincial and Lodge histories, usually written from a Craft perspective, have been examined and, often with reading 'between the lines', much evidence of a tenuous or circumstantial nature is discernable; no doubt further research will reveal more such activity.

Even this brief summary also suggests that Dunckerley's efforts to establish the new organisation for the Order were probably welcomed widely throughout the Country by many more knights who existed than his letter of 1791 implies, and that those included a high proportion of knights with military backgrounds who welcomed the discipline introduced by the new organisation.

APPENDIX C

BRISTOL CHARTER OF COMPACT OF 1780

In the Name of the Great Architect of the Universe
The Supreme Grand and Royal Encampment of the Order of Knights Templars of
St. John of Jerusalem, Knights Hospitaller
and Knights of Malta, &c., &c.,
To all Knight Companions of that Noble Order
Health - Peace - Goodwill

Whereas by Charter of Compact our Encampment is constituted, the Supreme Grand and Royal Encampment of this Noble Order, with full Power, when Assembled, to issue, publish and make known to all our loving Knights Companion, whatever may contribute to their knowledge, not inconsistent with its general LAWS. Also to constitute and appoint any Officer or Officers to make and ordain such laws, as from time to time may appear necessary to promote the Honour of our Noble Order in general and the more perfect government of our Supreme degree in particular. We therefore the MOST EMINENT GRAND MASTER, the Grand Master of the Order, the Grand Master Assistant General, and two Grand Standard Bearers and Knights Companions for that purpose in full Encampment Assembled, do make known,

First, According to ancient custom, that a complete Encampment of this degree consist of the Most Eminent Grand Master, the Grand Master of the Order, the Grand Master Assistant General, and two Grand Standard Bearers, who when in Encampment Assembled are to be considered as such, and no regular Encampment of this Degree can consist of a less number than five.

Second, That to this Order none be admitted but men of the best character and education – open – generous and liberal in sentiment, which have passed the four Degrees of Masonry – have been duly proposed and recommended by a Knight Companion of the Encampment, balloted for and approved of, but none to be admitted if there is more than one negative.

Third, That the first Grand Officer be stiled, the Most Eminent Grand Master – The second the Grand Master of the Order – the third, the Grand Master Assistant General – fourth and fifth two Grand Standard Bearers, and the rest worthy Knights Companions.

Fourth, that the Most Eminent Grand Master wears a robe or mantle and the insignia of the Order – and all the Knights Companions to wear the Insignia of the Order. The robe of the Most Excellent Grand Master to be black velvet with crimson satin, trimmed with gold lace and black fur, a black ribbon with gold fringe, a star and dagger pendant, and a shield on his arm with the proper arms emblazoned thereon. The Grand Master of the Order to wear a crimson velvet robe trimmed with gold lace and ermine, – a crimson ribbon with gold fringe, a star and dagger pendant, a shield with the arms emblazoned thereon, and a sword by his side. The Grand Master Assistant General to wear a blue velvet robe trimmed with gold lace and white fur, a blue ribbon with gold fringe, a star and a dagger pendant, a shield and a sword, the same as the most Eminent Grand Master.

Fifth, that as soon as any Encampment is opened and the Knights Companion are seated the minutes of the last meeting are to be read by the Secretary and then rejected or confirmed after which ballots are to be taken and the elected Candidates Installed.

Sixth, That in an Encampment any Knight Companion who has anything to propose must rise and address himself to the Most Eminent Grand Master – nor in such address is he on any account to be interrupted, but he who intends to reply must wait until the speaker resumes his seat.

Seventh and whereas this Encampment is by Charter Constituted the Supreme Grand and Royal Encampment. Be it therefore known that no Encampment within the Kingdom of England will be acknowledged by us, unless they admit of our Supremacy and conform to the Statutes, nor any received as Knight Companions except those installed in an Encampment constituted by us, or in some foreign Prince's dominions, or was Installed before A.D. 1780.

Eighth that the mode of application for a Charter be by Petition addressed to the Supreme Grand and Royal Encampment at our Castle in Bristol, signed by five companions of the order specifying, the time when, and the place where to be held, with the names of the first three officers, and the title they would chuse to have their Encampment known by.

Ninth, and be it further ordained, that one guinea and a half shall be paid for every Constitution. One guinea for every Installation fee to our Supreme Grand and Royal Encampment, and not less than one guinea to any other Encampment where they are Installed, and five shillings for every Grand Certificate from this Supreme Grand and Royal Encampment.

Tenth. That every subordinate Encampment shall have power to make such Byelaws as to them shall seem meet for their own private government, provided they are not incompatible with the general Statures established by this Supreme Grand Royal Encampment.

Eleventh. That an Encampment be held the first Thursday in every quarter at 7 o'clock in the evening in the summer, and six in the winter which shall be deemed public Encampments, but that the Most Eminent Grand Master – the Grand Master of the Order, and Grand Master Assistant General shall have power to convene a private Encampment as often as they shall find it expedient.

Twelfth, That every visiting Knight Companion shall pay, if a Member of a lodge two shillings and sixpence, if not a member of a lodge, four shillings.

Thirteenth. That the cash or fund as well as the furniture, &c. belonging to the Supreme Grand and Royal Encampment shall, and is, hereby vested in and deemed the property of the Most Eminent Grand Master, the Grand Master of the Order, and the Grand Master Assistant General for the time being so that any action or suit that shall happen to be necessary for the preservation or recovery of the same or any part thereof may or shall be brought or commenced, or prosecuted in their names, in trust for the use and benefit of the Supreme Grand and Royal Encampment, and be paid, applied, and disposed of as the Encampment in due form from time to time shall think proper to direct.

Fourteenth, That every member of this Supreme Grand and Royal Encampment shall sign these laws and shall observe and keep the same as well as any future laws that shall be found necessary to be made.

Fifteenth. That this Charter of Compact shall be read at least once a year.

Sixteenth. That all presents made to this Supreme Grand and Royal Encampment be entered in the Minute Book with the Knight Companion's name in token of his esteem for this Most Noble Order.

Seventeenth. That if any doubt should arise in the respective Encampments concerning the Construction of these Statutes or other Matters relative to this Degree which cannot be amicably adjusted amongst the Knight Companions thereof – the subject shall be fairly stated, and laid before the Supreme Grand and Royal Encampment whose determination shall be final.

Eighteenth. That every Subordinated Encampment be stiled a Grand Encampment, the first Officer Grand Master, the second Master of the Order – the Third Master General Assistant and two Standard Bearers.

Nineteenth. That every Encampment, including the Supreme Grand and Royal Encampment, has power to Elect two Captains Commanding and four inferior Captains which with the Officers forms the Most Complete Encampment.

Twentieth. That no resolution or Decree can pass the Supreme Grand and Royal Encampment unless two of the first three Officers and two-thirds of all the other members agree to the said resolution and that no motion can be made for any alteration in our Laws, but in a Public Supreme Grand and Royal Encampment, and which shall not be determined until the next Public Meeting and must then be by ballot.

Done at our Castle in Bristol 20th day of December 1780

(signed) Joshua Springer M. E.   Jno Maddick, G. M. of the O.
          Wm. Trotman G. M. A.   Wm. Lewis, Equerry
          Robt. Wasborough, Steward   J. Ferris, Treasurer
          Wm. Mason, Grand Actuary

(This document bears the signatures of subsequent Grand Masters and Commanders who appear to have signed it on appointment to Office as an acknowledgement that they are bound by its provisions and would act in accordance therewith.)

APPENDIX D

JOHN KNIGHT'S EARLY CORNISH CEREMONIES

John Knight documented in considerable detail a sequence of twenty-six degrees of which Knight Templar was the 19th, Knight of Malta the 21st, and *Ne Plus Ultra* the 26th. Earlier, the existence of *Ecossais* Lodges in England was noted from about 1733, the Rite of Perfection in France and the New World and among French prisoners-of-war not long after, and the appearance Priestly Order and Holy Royal Arch Knight Templar Priest degree sequences by the 1760s. These possibly suggest the source of John Knight's Knight Templar and *Ne Plus Ultra* rites. There are also a number of instances of such degrees being carried around by Sea Captains' Lodges from as early as 1722 and by lodges attached to Army Regiments, both being active in Cornwall and the West Country.

A Comparison of John Knight's sequence of degrees with these possible earlier sources is instructive:

John Knight Sequence	Possible Earlier Sources
1° Entered Apprentice	
2° Fellow Craft	
3° Mark Man or Foreman of Fellow Crafts	Scottish Fellow Craft (9°Adonhiram Rite)
4° Master Mason	
5° Mark Master Mason	'*Old Mark*' and *Antients* Mark Ceremonies
6° Master of Arts and Sciences	Master Elect (4° *Ecossais* Rite) or 'Passing the Chair' (*Antients* working)
7° Architect	Architect (Rite of Perfection)
8° Grand Architect	Grand Architect (9°Adonhiram Rite alternative designation)
9° Excellent or 81 Deputy Grand Masters	Excellent Master
10° Super Excellent or Nine Supreme Deputy Grand Masters	Super Excellent Master
11° Red Cross	Knight of the Red Cross
12° The Sublime Degree of Royal Arch Masons	Royal Arch
13° Preparing	
14° Dedicated	
15° Decorated	
16° Advanced	
17° Circumscribed	
18° Royal Ark Masons, Mariners or Noachites	Ark, Mark & Link (Irish and *Antients* Lodges)
19° Military Order of Masonic Knights Templar	

John Knight Sequence	Possible Earlier Sources
20° Mediterranean Pass	
21° Knight of Malta	
22° Eastern Knight	Knight of the East (6° *Ecossais* Rite) and other Rites
23° Western Knight	Knight of the East and West
24° Northern Knight	Knight of the North (Priestly Order or HRAKTP)
25° Southern Knight	Knight of the South (Priestly Order or HRAKTP)
26° *Rosae Crucis* or *Ne Plus Ultra*	

John Knight later extended this sequence to thirty-seven degrees, and although he himself confessed he was dubious about some, he retained the 20th Degree of 'Mediterranean Pass' and the 21st 'Knight of Malta'. These seemed to be worked as a 'Rite' although there is no evidence the sequence was referred to as such.

APPENDIX E

JOHN KNIGHT'S KT CEREMONY OF 1805

The first entry in the earliest of John Knight's transcriptions of the Degree of Knights Templar (in the Note Book catalogued as 'No. 27' in the John Combe's Masonic Library at Hayle in Cornwall) is a list of those present at the Meeting on 11 March 1805. They included John Knight 'E.D.G.M.' and P.G.M., the other Officers of the Encampment (1st Captain, 2nd Captain both 'at foot', two Standard Bearers 'one on each side of E.D.G.M.' and 'Gd. Scribe Registr.', together with "equerries at the Door") and ten Knights.

The 'furniture' of the Encampment consists of a "Table set apart with proper lights viz. 3 large lights representing John, Peter and James, 8 small lights (the other apostles) 1 small Candle extinguished Judas" and on a small table covered with a white cloth a skull and crossbones, "with bread, wine etc.", and three swords arranged in a triangle..

Evidently those present were wearing hats, for the first command of the E.D.G.M. in the Opening is 'Be uncovered' and then after the Opening, 'Order. Hats on and swords drawn'.

The 'Opening' differs considerably from that in use today. After the usual Masonic precautions to make sure that the gathering is secure from interruption and a Prayer has been said, the E.D.G.M. asks what is the hour (the 'clock') as in the opening of the First Point in the 18th Rose Croix Degree, and receives a similar answer to that given there – 'The instant that the Veil of the Temple is torn, ... ', culminating in '. . . . the W--- was lost'. The 'Word' is at once searched for and found, E----- being given to the E.D.G.M., but with no indication of what this search and discovery entailed.

Hats are then put on and swords again drawn, and the 'Knights Companions march round the Encampment Singing the Canticles', examples of which are given later, which occur at intervals during the ceremony, after which hats are again removed and swords returned. The E.D.G.M. says –

> 'In commemoration of our Gd. M (aster) J (ohn) D (e) M (olay)
> Let us Eat the Bread of Thankfulness and Drink the Cup of Cheerfulness.'

and then goes on to say –

'Let the Watchword of the Day be	The Will of God'
Give the Gd. S(ign) & G. Word	E-------- God with Us
Take B(read) & W(in)e All Say	Happiness here, Eternal Happiness Hereafter'

The Encampment is then open for business.

If a candidate is to be installed he is presented in much the same way as is done in Preceptories today, except that during his preparation he washes his hands and he is blindfolded before entering the Conclave. At his introduction he is said to be in possession of three passwords which are given for him, and which are still used today in either the Craft or Knight Templary. He is admitted on 'the St George's Guard' (of which there is no explanation) after his conductor on his behalf (and later the candidate himself) made a declaration that he was

'Born under Wedlock, baptized in the faith of Christ, a believer and professor of the Holy Gospel and Religion of Christ, enlisted under his Banner to be a faithful Soldier, never to deny his name among Jews, Turks or Infidels'.

He then entered the room after which he was 'led over the Sands twice round', and it must be noted that although the subsequent explanation to the newly installed Knight suggests this was important, there is no explanation of what this means. He then has to reply to the same lengthy interrogation to which his conductor has already replied on his behalf. The E.D.G.M. then instructs his conductor to

'Lead him three times round, at each time blow out the candle (sic) ... place him at the bottom of the Conclave. Advance Five Steps and Kneel with right hand on the Bible and left on Simn's ....

[These brief instructions cannot be sensibly interpreted today, firstly because 1 candle was said to be extinguished before the opening, and even had it been re-lit it can hardly have been blown out three times; and secondly a likely explanation of 'Simn's .....' is that it refers to the skull noted in the opening instructions and, although this was probably considered symbolically to represent that of Simon of Syracuse, the earlier instructions suggest furnishings were placed on two separate tables.]

While the candidate is in this position he attends to a reading of the 2nd Chapter of the 1st Epistle of St Peter, in the middle of which occurs the passage familiar to us in our Ceremony today commencing "Dearly Beloved, I beseech you as strangers and pilgrims . . . . ". Today we do not read the earlier part of the Chapter which refers to 'living stones' and 'the chief corner-stone to be laid in Sion' as was then done.

After this reading the candidate has to assent to a lengthy Obligation similar in the main to that taken today, but including the Penalty which has now been removed from today's Ritual. In this early ritual the Penalty is related to John the Baptist and not to Simon of Syracuse. The phrases relating to this have been interpolated, the original 'Penalty' having been firmly scratched out. It seems to have read 'and that the Spirit which once inhabited the Body to which this belongs appear against me in the day of judgment'.

The pilgrim-candidate is then refreshed with a Crust of Bread and a Glass of Wine with which he drinks to the immortal Memory of the original three Grand Masters and to 'S. John of Jerusalem the faithful Soldier of the Lord'. Only after this is the Novice 'Restored to Light' Then, holding the skull ('Simn'), the E.D.G.M. makes a further short declaration, and then repeats two verses from the Book of Revelations, the first containing the passage familiar to us concerning 'a White Stone and in the Stone a new name written', the second more familiar to members of the Order of Holy Royal Arch Knight Templar Priests ("Him that over cometh (sic) will I make a Pillar in the Temple of my God". (Revelations, iii, verse 12). The final elements in the Installation ceremony may be set out at length:

Draw (?) the Sword five times over the Head saying each time I dub you a K . . . t T. . . . r Hospr & of Mal. and of the Holy Sacred R . . .E. . . R & Military order of Masonic Knights Templar St John of Jerusalem, Palestine, Rhodes &c &c.
Raise him under the right Arm and Say . . . . Rise Sr. Knight

With the new Knight appropriately clad once more, and apparently having been made a Knight of Malta of which he has been told nothing but the 'Sign and Gripe', with Swords drawn and with Hats on the Knights march round 'in due form' again singing a Canticle, after which 'Refresh – Glass of Wine & Crust of bread' apparently then drinking the health of 'the Duke of Kent &c &c'.

The salient points of the ceremony are then explained to the newly-made Knight as follows:

EXPLANATION OF THE CEREMONY TO THE NEW- MADE KNIGHT

Why you blow'd out the Candle
When Judas betrayed Christ, he put out his light of Faith. Therefore you have now cast out Judas's light that is the Light of Darkness.

Why you sho'd Wash
This is an emblem of purifying ourselves with the Blood of Faith (Heb. Ch. 10th – Vs 20 & 22)

By a new and living way which he hath consecrated for us thro' the Veil, that is to say the Flesh, let us draw near with a true Heart in full Assurance of faith having our Hearts Sprinkled from an Evil Conscience and our Bodys Washed with pure Water.

Why you were Cloah'd (sic) in the Garment
The white Garment Indicates that we ought to be particularly careful to keep ourselves free from Vice, Spotless like the Linen Garment from the Whitners* (sic) Field, thinking nothing too great, nothing too hard, if it tends to promote the Honour of the Knights and the Service of True Religion. – Supporting the Dignity of the order must be the constant practice of every Knight Templar to render him Sacred to the cause of Virtue, Gentleness and Humility.
*'Whitner's', presumably what would today be called the 'Fuller's'.

Why you were led & Walk'd on the Sands
This represents the Earthly colour of the Subteranious (sic) Mansion to which we must all shortly retire, and from whence we cannot return, until (sic) we have put on Corruption – this sho'd. teach us humility and Modesty, for a proud Knight is a Scandal to the Order and a reproach to human Nature.

Why you had a White Sash
This indicates that we are carefully to preserve an unspotted purity, despising Luxury of every Kind, for a true Knight Templar sho'd. be irreproachable in his Conduct, and intrepid in every action that has a tendency to promote the Cause of Virtue.

Why you had a Sword girt about your loins
With the Sword you are to defend the Holy Sepulchre of Christ (that is to say the Christian Religion) against all … infidels and punish the Champions of Vice and Immorality. Its two Edges intimates the Motive that regulates a Knights Templars conduct which is uprightness. The first Animates him to assist the Weak when oppressed and the Second is to defend this Country against all attempts of its

perfidious Enemy's (sic) and like the rapid Courier fly to the assistance of every Brother and Knight Companion in distress and lay prosterate (sic) before you all those who trample on the Sacred Laws of our Order.

Why you were invested with a Star & Garter
In the name of the great omnipotent being, and in memory of St John of Jerusalem wear on thy neck for thy renown this noble Garter, as a Symbol of this Illustrious Order never to be forgotten or laid aside wereby (sic) thou mays't be admonished to be Courageous and having undertaken a part that was against the enemies of our Lord & Saviour, you may ever Stand fast and firm to it and Valiantly and safely conquer through the Cross,

Why was the image of St John presented to you?
Wear this Star and Garter arrayed with the Image of St John of Jerusalem by whose emulation you may ever pass thro' every Adventure and having vanquished the enemies both of body and Soul be crown'd with the palm of eternal Victory. Amen. Amen.

After the Installation Ceremony, but before the Encampment is closed once more the Bread of Thankfulness is eaten and the Cup of Cheerfulness drunk – ('Each Kt. Compn. takes a glass of wine, Happiness here and Eternal Happiness hereafter').

There is no statement of the Precepts of the Order, but its place is taken by the E.D.G.M. saying – Let us bear in mind the Solomon (sic) introduction into this our Holy Sacred and Religious order – and the Ob. which we have taken, and be always particularly careful whom we recomm. to become Knights Companions of this our Order, and be well assured of his integrity towards our King, our Laws, and our Religion, and that he will ever be ready to guard our City and Holy Cell. (sic) and may we ever Keep in mind the Three Grand Principals (sic) of Masonry, Brotherly Love, Relief and Truth.

The E.D.G.M. gave a short exposition of these before closing the Conclave after a Prayer sufficiently remarkable to be worth quoting in full –

Thou Great and Almighty Architect of the Universe who made Man of the Visible Creation Lord, and endued him with reason to adore thine infinite Power, Wisdom and design, we beseech thee to replenish us with thy Heavenly Grace that when assembled in the Conclave or not, teach us to Glorify thy sacred name Jehovah and rejoice before him . . . . Amen

The E.D.G.M. declares the Conclave closed in the name of the Holy and Undivided Trinity with five knocks from himself and from each of the two Captains, and five from the equerry.
   It is perhaps curious that 'Solomon' for 'solemn' appears so frequently in manuscript rituals of this date and earlier; this probably suggests a rather closer relationship between the Craft and Knight Templary than exists today. However, John Knight was using this Ritual comparatively early in his Masonic career and that he considered it the 'fifth' Degree (EA, FC, MM, RA, KT) may be indicated by the five knocks in the closing. The ceremony contains much of the material worked in our present Knights Templar Degree, but there are several

omissions. The 'Lecture', or recapitulation of the Degree which appears in the 1810 Note-Book is already more sophisticated and in many respects closer to that in use today.

In this version no longer is the candidate admitted on three words which today feature within the Ceremony itself, but, as today, on a Royal Arch word. At his admittance a Rough S.w was placed to his naked F..e H..d. Ephesians vi. v. 10 – 17, ('Put on the whole Armour of God'),which was omitted from the earlier version, was then repeated to him. He took a similar Obligation to that in use today which was, however divided into three parts. After the first, his pilgrim's staff was removed, and a sword placed in his hand while he took the second part. He was then told that he had to undertake a part in guarding the sepulchre before he could take the third part, and he was 'conducted 5 times round the R.... E....... the worthy Knights guarding and defending the same with their faces outwards'.

The Obligation completed, the candidate was raised 'By the Angle Triangle' (of which no explanation is given), having been shown the 'Scaunce with 12 Lights one Extinguish'd', and he is the entrusted with the Penal Sign of a Knight Templar and the Grand Sign and Word.

The newly Obligated Knight was then conducted seven times round the Conclave, before being seated in the West and where he was instructed to drink to the memory of the three Grand Masters and that of St John. After this he was invested with a Star and Garter, the Garter being worn round the neck, the Star apparently bearing the image of St John and appendant to it. Finally he was invested with a white sash.

After some further instruction 'The Porch belonging to the Palace of the High Priest on which is the representation of a Cock' was explained to him by recounting the whole story of St Peter's denials. He was also told that the Sword and Sceptre were the Sword of Faith and the Sceptre of Righteousness, an explanation which is nowadays omitted, but 'The Star in the East' is explained at considerable length. He was told that the "Ladder with 5 Steps resting on the Holy Bible alludes to the different degrees in Masonry four of which have been already explained in the Royal Arch – the fifth is the illustrious order of K. . . . . T . . . . .s". This is followed by the explanation first of the White Stone with the Word 'E . . . . . ' and then by that of 'A Lamb on Mount Sion'. Finally there is a long exposition of the Cross on Mount Calvary and Our Lord's five sufferings together with a detailed account of the Crucifixion. There is no mention of the Dove

A further transcription by John Knight is noted as having been amended in 1812 and 1815; it appears that other additions may have been made later. Knight had by then extended his Rite not only to twenty-five Degrees, but has added twelve additional of some of which he confesses himself to be somewhat dubious. The Illustrious Order of Knights Templar is no longer the fifth Degree but the 19th but it was still worked according to the Ritual set out above; however there had now been added after it the 20th Degree of 'Mediterranean Pass' and the 21st 'Knight of Malta'.

In this transcription the ceremony is set out only in outline and is followed by the note 'N.B. for Installation (sic), Lecture, Canticles, Odes, Toasts &c . . . . see Knight Templars Book', presumably referring to that from which the procedures above have been taken.

The summary of the Knights Templar ritual is followed by that of the Mediterranean Pass. The Candidate appears "As a Warrior (sic) and Knight Templar, Spurs &c. Carrying a Speaking Trumpet, Triangle and Holy Bible" He enters by twelve knocks – seven slow, three quick and two slow, and having entered is 'led round twenty-three times . . .advancing by twenty-three steps'. The only additional information given is that the Sign is "To hail a Bror: with: a Speaking Trumpet", the Token is 'Hook both hands and thumbs to form a Triangle' and the encoded word appears to be 'Mortoree' or 'Mourtore'.

This Degree is followed by the 21st Degree, Knight of Malta, set out with equal brevity. The Opening and Closing as today involve 33 knocks, five from each of the five officers followed by eight single knocks. However the candidate entered 'As a Knight Templar – Sandals, Scrip, Staff, Sword, Mantle & Cord' by twenty-four knocks and was led twenty-four times round. The Obligation is curious –

'!, A.B....In addition to all my former Ob. may I ever Act with honor in Conjunction with my Colleagues of the Seven Nations, thus encorporated for the Common Good. If I do not, may they all unite against me equally with the Jew, Turk, and Infidel to crush the Wretch so lost to himself, to honor, and to his God. . . . So h. me God... K.5.'

The Sign is given as 'The Arms on the Breast Crossed so as to hide the Thumbs & Arms & Body forming an X', the Token as shaking the Viper from the Hand, and the Word as 'Meleta, or Malta, or Capharsalem, in English'.

How typical was this process of evolution of the ritual it is impossible to say; it is probable that something of the sort was occurring in each of the early Encampments with a measure of cross-fertilisation, but all the evidence indicates that at this time there were no more than rudimentary ceremonies both of the Mediterranean Pass and the Knight of Malta.[312]

John Knight's Canticles

One particularly interesting feature of John Knights ceremony was the inclusion of a series of Canticles specified to be sung during various parts of the Knight Templar proceedings. None of these appears to have survived in modern rituals. The following are among the 'Canticles' recorded in the Ritual Books written by John Knight and which were presumably sung by the Knights in the Encampment of St John of Jerusalem at Redruth in the early 19th century:

Ode – Jesus, Hominum Salvator

Hail hail Divine, heal Sacred Art
Descended from above
Whose mystic order fills the heart
With ever blooming love.
With what extatic (sic) joy we meet
Where pious hands unite
No Spicy groves are half so Sweet
Or yield such pure delight
What Streams of Cordial pleasure flow
From Virtues fairest spring
What Heavenly breezes gently blow
With peace upon the Wing.
A Turk! Mahomitan (sic)! or Jew!
Can ne'er approach our Shrine
All, all that's to a Saviour due
Bespeaks the whole divine
A branch from Jesse's* Sacred root
"With fragrance fills the Skies"
To us it yields immortal fruit
And Crowns of lasting joys.
Our great Messiah Lord and King
Demands our ardent lays

To Him let Ev'ry Mason Sing
And sound Jehovah's praise.

*Isaiah in his 11th Ch. prophys. our blessed Lord and Saviours Coming on Earth

Knights Templar

At the bright Temples awful dome
Where Christian Knights in Arms are drest,
To that most Sacred place we come
With Cross and Star upon the breast.
Pilgrims inspired with zealous flame
Through rugged ways & dangers past
Our Sandals torn, our feet were lame
But Faith & Hope O'ercame at last
Remember Knights the noble cause
Let Cymon's fate prevent your fall,
Be firm and True obey the Laws
Nor let the Cock unheeded call,
Let none the Sacred Word profane,
Nor e'er let Peter christ (sic) deny.
Your conduct still preserve from blame,
Nor let the Urn be placed on high.
Unite your Hearts, unite each hand,
In friendship, Harmony and Love,
Connected thus, Knights Templars Stand
Our love and charity to prove.
Until that awful final day,
When fire shall melt this earthly ball,
Your courage and your faith display
Attend to Freedom's Sacred Call.
True to our God, our Laws, our King,
Devout, obedient, Loyal, free
The Praise of Royal Edward Sing
The Patron of our Mystry (sic).
In uniform each Knight is drest,
Distinguished all by Black, Red, blue
The Cross and Star upon the breast
Adorn the heart that's just and true.

Knights Templar

On, on my dear Knights pursue the great Lecture
Approach to the Temple that formd Architecture
Advance to the + if shield Templars ye be
To sing praises in Honour of great Masonry.

-2d-
When David the Father of the Wisest of Kings

With Hyram and Solomon prepared all things
To Erect the great Temple for the Work of the Lord
With Harmony finish'd not the sound of a Word.

-3d-

The Master and Craftsman besought a degree
The Orich (sic)[313] Domatic and all did agree
Jehovah's great name to erect (sic) within side
And Join'd with their Hands though extended and wide.

-4th-

View the Angles, Right Angles, Triangles I mean
Observe well its Lustre 'twill purchase you fame,
Not like Judas Iscariot whose light amongst men
Was darkened for *[314] falsely betraying the same.

-5th-

With the sword of your faith you'll defend his great name
Remember twas Wonderful first call'd the same
Messiah the last ★ [315] Still remember that He
Emanuel was born to save Templars free.

-6th-

From the West you must travel look up to the East,
When a star blazing brightly of which ye are possess'd
Advance still to Golgotha[316] there you'll perceive
Emblems of what prepared Templars believe.

-7th-

Remember you Templars that's made Templars free
With Arms wide extended 'twas Heavens decree,
Who patiently suffered for Remission of Sins,
To prepare a seat with the great King of Kings.

-8th-

Then Brother Knights Templars observe the great cause
Subdue Jews and Heathens to Gods Holy Laws
In Triumph We'll March the Grand Turk to dethrone,
And prove to his shame Gospel truths he must own.

-9th-

The Grand Masters and Knights renowned by Name,
The Royal Encampment will purchase you Fame,
In the name of Jehovah Halleujah W'ell (sic) sing
And welcome the Pilgram (sic) that glad tidings bring.

-10th-

Noble Knights of the Island of Malta agree,
That none but a Master and Masters that's free,
Shall take up their sword that was once laid aside,

To renew the Grand Secret with Arms strech'd out Wide.

(The poetic muse or whoever wrote these various lines must have been having some off-days; further there seem to be Masonic (or possibly Biblical) references among them which today are obscure. It is curious that David is brought in but no Hiram Abiff. Perhaps all would have been clear to the Masons of the time, but these references and their context are certainly not so obvious today.)

APPENDIX F

DAVYD NASH'S 'CIRCULAR LETTER' (1857).

[EXTRACT of Paragraphs Concerning Degrees of The Ancient And Accepted Rite]

One feature which pre-eminently distinguishes those Encampments from those holding under the London Grand Conclave is this, that while the latter has abandoned an important portion of the rights and authority which it exercised previous to the year 1844[317], selling its birthright for a mess of pottage, the Supreme Grand and Royal Encampment maintains its ancient constitution intact and unimpaired. We refer especially to the degree of Knights Rosae Crucis, or Sov. Princes Rose Croix of Heredom, a Chapter of which, according to the Ancient constitution of Masonic Knights templar in England, of which and the privileges belonging to it, the Encampments holding under the Grand Conclave have been deprived, that body having yielded its authority over the Degree of Knights Rosae Crucis to another and different Masonic body . . . . . . The degree of Knights Rosae Crucis has been held in Bristol uninterruptedly for nearly a century and for the last 50 years with a splendour and completeness of ritual unapproached in any other Encampment in England.

In the Encampment of Antiquity at Bath, the degree is known to have been held as early as 1793.

The degree of Grand Elected Knights Kadosh (K.D.S.H.) has not for many years been conferred in Bristol. The late Eminent Commanders F. C. Husenbeth, Richard Smith and others possessed the degree and a Grand Council of the Knights K.D.S.H. was held at Bristol on Good Friday, March 29, 1839.

APPENDIX G

AGREED ARTICLES IN THE 1862 'CHARTER OF COMPACT'

Now therefore Know ye that we the said contracting parties do hereby mutually covenant declare and agree as follows

1   That from and after the day of the date of these presents the said Encampment of Masonic Knights Templar of Baldwyn at Bristol from time immemorial shall and doth hereby enrol itself under the Banner of the Grand Conclave of Masonic Knights Templar of England and Wales and doth submit itself in all things to the Laws and General Statutes thereof and to the rule and government of Sir Knight Wm. Stuart the Most Eminent and Supreme Grand Master thereof and his lawful successors to the intent that from and after the day of the date of these presents a full perfect and perpetual union shall subsist between the said Grand Conclave of Masonic Knights Templar of England and Wales and the said Grand Encampment of Baldwyn at Bristol from time immemorial and that the same shall be thereafter held under one and the same constitution and authority –

2   That the City and County of Bristol shall be constituted and created a separate and distinct Provincial Commandery the limits thereof shall be the limits of the Masonic Province of Bristol as constituted by the Grand Lodge of Free and Accepted Masons of England and Wales –

3   That the said Encampment of Masonic Knights Templar of Baldwyn at Bristol shall retain its ancient and accustomed style and title of 'from time immemorial' and shall take precedence of all Encampments holding Warrants under the Grand Conclave of Masonic Knights Templar of England and Wales of later date and shall be entered accordingly in the Register of the Order –

4   That the following Encampments established by and meeting under Warrants granted by the said Encampment of Baldwyn at Bristol from time immemorial (that is to say)

> The Encampment of Antiquity at Bath
> The Encampment of Ascalon at Birmingham
> The Encampment of the Holy Rood at Warwick
> The Encampment of the Vale of Jehoshaphat at Highbridge
> The Encampment of the Vale Royal at Salisbury
> And the Percy Encampment at Adelaide, South Australia

shall from the day of the date hereof and are hereby recognised and adopted and the several Knights Companions thereof affiliated by the Grand Conclave of Masonic Knights Templar of England and Wales and the said Encampments shall take precedence in the official Registers amongst the Encampments of the Grand Conclave of England and Wales according to the dates of their respective Warrants –

5   That all the property and effects of the said Encampment of Masonic Knights Templar of Baldwyn of Bristol from time immemorial and the other Encampments before mentioned and all deeds, documents, papers, books and other articles and things now in their possession respectively shall remain in the custody of the Treasurer for the time being of the

several Encampments respectively or of such person or persons as shall be from time to time appointed by the members thereof respectively on behalf of and in trust for the members of the said several Encampments –

6   That no fee for registration in the books of the Grand Conclave of Masonic Knights Templar of England and Wales shall be demanded of or payable by any Sir Knights Companion who shall at the date of these presents be members of the said Encampment of Masonic Knights Templar at Bristol from time immemorial or of any of the hereinbefore mentioned Encampments –

7   That all present and future members of the said Encampment of Masonic Knights Templar of Baldwyn at Bristol from time immemorial and of the Encampments hereinbefore mentioned shall from the date of these presents be subject to the annual payment of one shilling each to the Funds of the Grand Conclave of Masonic Knights Templar of England and Wales pursuant to Law 3 of the Statutes thereof Given under our hands this 9th day of May A.D. 1162 A.O. 744 A.L. 5862

(L.S.)   (triple cross)   WILLIAM STUART M.E.S.G.M.

  Signed and delivered in the presence of

GEORGE VERNON, Deputy Grand Master
H. CLARK, Grand Registrar

APPENDIX H

SUPREME COUNCIL LETTER OF 24 MARCH 1875

From The S.C. Of The A. & A. Rite Signed By Shadwell Clerke Drawing Attention To The Changed Circumstances Regarding The Tripartite Treaty

To 'The Acting Authority of the Temple and the Hospital'
and to the 'Grand Lodge of Mark Master Masons'.

'1. The United Orders of the Temple, Hospital and Malta now include the Irish Branch of these Orders, over which the M. E. & S. G. M. is the Head; & the Chief. Government in the Convent General is composed of English and Irish Kts. Templar.

2. In each Nationality the M. E. & S. G. M. appoints a Great Prior to represent him. This Great Prior exercises within his own Jurisdiction powers analogous to those of the GD. M. over the Collective Body. He is in effect the Dep^y of the M. E. & S. G. M.

In the Statutes of the Convent General under the Heads 'Grace and Appeals' a reservation is made in favour of existing or future Treaties, between the Order of the Temple and other Chivalric or Masonic Bodies, but no other allusion has been made to Treaties.

There does not appear, therefore, to be anything in these Statutes to prevent the Convent General (a body consisting of English and Irish Knights) passing some Law, which might be contrary to the Spirit of the Tripartite Treaty; and, which Law would, by the Statutes, be binding on the Great Prior & Great Priory of England & Wales.

Again in Article IV of the Tripartite Treaty, the Acting Authorities of the Three Parties to the Treaty are defined, as the Grand Chancellor of the Order of the Temple, the Grand Secretary Gen, 33° and the Grand Secretary of the Grand Lodge of Mark Masters. It is assumed that the Grand Chancellor of the Order of Kts. Templar is the G. Officer now styled the Arch Chancellor and who is an Irish Knight Templar, and in no way concerned with the Tripartite Treaty.

The Gt. Priory of England and Wales is no longer a Supreme Body to the same extent as the Grand Conclave (existing when the Treaty was made) as it is subject to the M. E. & S. G. M. and the Convent General.

For the above reasons it appears to the Su. Co. 33° of England & Wales very desirable that two Plenipotentiaries should be appointed by each of the three Parties to the Treaty with a view of considering what alterations to the Treaty, the change in the Constitutions of the Order of the Temple may have rendered necessary.

And also, what further alterations as experience in the working of the Treaty may have shown to be advisable, especially as regards the working of Article IV, and to the powers of the Judicial Council.

Should this proposal be accepted, the Sup. Co. 33° of England & Wales are prepared to nominate Plenipotentiaries as proposed.'

APPENDIX I

THE 1876 REPORT OF THE RITUAL COMMISSION

The Commission has the honour to report that under the powers delegated to it of giving effect to the provisions of the General Statute as to Ritual, a Ritual has been drawn up and signed by the Commissioners including the English and Irish Plenipotentiaries.

Considerable difficulty was experienced in reconciling the claims of conflicting Rituals, *viz.,*

1. The Ritual of the ancient Templars founded on the Benedictine Canons.

2. The Scottish Ritual, very closely copied from it.

3. The present English Ritual, which is comparatively new, having been drawn up in 1851, in place of that previously existing, and

4. The Irish Ritual.

It would have been an easy task to have formed an entirely new Ritual, but it was exceedingly difficult to combine a Ritual out of these discordant elements and yet render it homogeneous.

A General Meeting of the Commissioners, under the presidency of the Great Prior of England and Wales, was held in April 1873, all the Commissioners but one being present, including the Plenipotentiaries under the Anglo-Hibernian Convention. At that General Meeting it was determined to reject novelties or innovations of recent date, and every paraphrase of Rituals other than those already mentioned, and certain resolutions were *unanimously* adopted as a basis on which the new Ritual should be drawn up.

The Ritual drawn up by the Commission is in accordance with these said conditions and resolutions, it is suited to the *Three Kingdoms*, and is consistent with the nature and traditions of the Order. *No novelty has been introduced and every clause of it is to be found in actual words or in substance in one or other of the Templar Rituals.*

The parts into which the Ritual is divided correspond, in general, with those of the Scottish Ritual, as being more nearly allied to the ancient forms.

Both the English and Scottish Rituals recognise the class of Novice, and the latter requires a term of novitiate. This is in accordance with ancient rule and practice; but the Commissioners in establishing a short term of novitiate have done so chiefly because they believe that such a regulation will conduce to the interests of the Order, while the power of dispensation reserved to the Great Prior and to the Sub-Prior provides for cases in which such a term of novitiate may be considered undesirable.

In drawing up the Ritual the Commissioners kept in mind the necessity of arranging the ceremonies so as to suit the limited accommodation at the disposal of many Preceptories, and were also most careful in avoiding the retention or introduction of any portions of present or past Rituals calculated to create confusion or to produce ridicule or irreverence.

The Conclave or Meeting is supposed to be a *Chapter* of the Preceptory, and not an *Encampment* of Knights Templar, and to take place in the Chapel of the Preceptory, hence the place of meeting is fitted up as a Chapel, the Altar being in its usual place; but in Part II an Altar or Sepulchre, as at present arranged in English Receptions, is retained. The Cross or Crucifix, Bible, &c, are all retained. The Preceptor's chair is placed on the left of the Altar.

The Installation of the Knights Templar, as also of the Knights of Malta, took place in their Chapels. The Knights, having consulted in the Chapter-house, elected the Candidate. Certain communications having been made and questions asked in an adjoining room, he was led to the Chapel, where the Reception, and consequently the Consecration, took place.

The Commissioners have endeavoured to follow this precedent, and, with this view, have combined the Altar, before which the Aspirant kneeled, with the Sepulchre, since if the Aspirant was received in Jerusalem, the Holy Sepulchre and the Altar were identical; and, at the present day, the Knights of the Holy Sepulchre are knighted at the Holy Sepulchre with the sword of Godefroi de Bouillon. The Knights were never received in the Field, but in the Church of Jerusalem, or its representative, the Preceptory Chapel, which, by a fiction, was supposed to be the Church of the Holy Sepulchre 'at home'[318], the home of the Order being Jerusalem; for this reason the modern introduction of the term 'Encampment' has been rejected as incorrect and unwarranted by any authority.

The opening and closing forms in the English Ritual of 1851 were mere servile adaptations of the Craft Ritual, and quite at variance with chivalric or religious ceremony. The forms approved are more simple and appropriate, and are based on the Scottish Ritual.

The part of Pilgrim is retained, as it is found in the Rituals heretofore used, and as it was considered that the Aspirant might be so termed, though he was never so described in the ancient Canons.

The Scottish Vow of Profession is according to the ancient Canon, and a modified form of it is introduced.

In accordance with the General Statute, and also with the Scottish Ritual, a Ring of Profession is introduced.

In accordance with the General Statute, and with present English and Irish Rituals, the Ribbon and Star are introduced.

The Imprecations, which may be considered another name for Vows, are retained, being in the Scottish and English Rituals, and formerly in that of Ireland.

Perambulation in a modified and more consistent form, as in Scottish Ritual, is retained, although there is no reference to it in the ancient Canons. It is not in the Irish Ritual.

Chaplains were a special class of the Order, and were eligible for various offices, including that of Preceptor, which was not necessarily a military one. Following this precedent, it is proposed that every clergyman, on inception, shall become, *ipso facto*, a Chaplain of the Order, in general, and of his Preceptory in particular, and shall be eligible, as heretofore, for the office of Preceptor and every other office not necessary military, with all rights and privileges pertaining thereto. No novitiate is required, and provision to that effect is made in the Ritual. Clergymen will thus be relieved from the necessity of wearing a military costume, and of holding offices and performing duties inconsistent with their sacred profession; their rights as Members of Preceptories of the Great Priories, and of the Convent General being in no way interfered with.

The prayers hitherto in use are retained, as also those portions of Scripture usually read. In addition, the Lord's Prayer, and a prayer for the Queen, the Grand Master, and the brethren are introduced. This is in accordance with ancient practice, the recitation of the Noster, and of a prayer for the Grand Master and the Brethren, being formerly inseparable from Templar Meetings. Such prayers are also found in modern Rituals.

The mode of 'Standing to Order', at present in use, is a mere copy of a modern military regulation; it is replaced by that assumed, in the time of the Crusades, by the Knightly Champions of the Cross at certain portions of their religious services. The position is simple, and assumed only at the most solemn portions of the ceremonies.

The mode of salute, the pass-words, &c, as in use in England and Wales, the Commissioners recommend for adoption throughout the Order. They do not differ in essential points from those of the Irish Branch of the Order.

A short Ritual for the installation of a Preceptor, corresponding in all essential points with that of now in use in the English Preceptories, has been drawn up.

A short Ritual for the Reception of a Serving Brother has also been drawn up.

It is recommended that a Cross be prefixed to the word 'Frater' or 'Brother' when denoting a Brother of the Temple, as distinguishing the Templar Brother from that of other Orders or Societies; such was formerly the practice, and it ought not to be abandoned. A Cross should also be prefixed to the signatures of all professed Brethren when signing as Templars; the Patriarchal Cross as heretofore being used by Preceptors.

The Commissioners recommend that the Ritual now formally signed and lodged in the respective Chanceries, according to Statute, shall be used from and after the next Convent General, at every Convent General, and every Chapter of the Great Priories; but that in order to avoid inconvenience, and to afford due time for its study, its use in preceptories shall be optional until January 1st, 1877, from and after which date "no deviation shall be permitted from such authentic Ritual except authorised by a Commission appointed by the Convent General *ad hoc*".

(Signed)

‡ **J. F. TOWNSHEND,**   }   Plenipotentiaries
     Arch-Chancellor of the Temple }   under the
                                     }   Anglo-Hibernian
‡ **P. Mac. C. DE COLQUHOUN**   }   Convention of
     Arch-Registrar of the Temple   }   1868

‡ **R. W. SHEKLETON,**
     Past Sub-Prior, Ireland

‡ **W. H. WRIGHT,**   **Past Grand Captain, England and Wales. and Past
                      Deputy Provincial Grand Commander, Lancashire**

‡ **R. B. DE BURGH,**   **Chancellor, Great Priory of Ireland**

‡ **EMRA HOLMES,**   **Past Grand Provost, England and Wales.**

‡ **JOHN RINGLAND, MD,**   **Constable, Great Priory of Ireland**

‡ **BENJAMIN TERRY HODGE, MD,**   **Past Grand Standard Bearer,
                                      England and Wales.**

‡ **GEORGE CHATTERTON**

APPENDIX J

EXTRACTS FROM THE UNITED ORDERS STATUTES OF 2018

(quotation from) The Statutes for the Government of the United Religious, Military and Masonic Orders of the Temple and of St John of Jerusalem, Palestine, Rhodes and Malta in England and Wales and Provinces Overseas.[319]

5. Great Priory possesses the supreme superintending authority, and alone has the inherent power of enacting laws and regulations for the government of the Orders, and of altering, repealing and abrogating them. Great Priory also has the power of investigating, regulating and deciding all matters relative to the Orders, or to particular Preceptories, or to individual Knights which it may exercise either itself, or by such delegated authority as in its wisdom and discretion it may appoint, but in Great Priory alone resides the power of erasing Preceptories and expelling Knights from the Orders, except in all cases of expulsion passed by the United Grand Lodge of England, the Supreme Grand Chapter of Royal Arch Masons of England, the Supreme Council of the Ancient and Accepted Rite, or any Order administered at Mark Masons' Hall, of a brother who is a member of the United Orders, when in such cases, he shall also be expelled from these Orders,

…. subject to appeal under Statute 134.

APPENDIX K

ENCAMPMENTS OVER WHICH THOMAS DUNCKERLEY PRESIDED

[while Grand Master of the Grand Conclave][320]

There has been much disagreement about the number of Conclaves or Encampments which were on Dunckerley's Register when he erected Grand Conclave on 24th June 1791. 'Baldwyn' at Bristol was presumably one of the number because it was from thence the idea of Dunckerley becoming 'Most Eminent and Supreme Grand Master' of the Order first emanated. It is hard to say precisely what Dunckerley means when he states that he 'Constituted' the 11 conclaves which he lists in this letter – in addition to these he seems to have 'constituted' another short-lived Conclave in Bristol which he does not mention. Some, for example St John of Jerusalem at Redruth, did not exist until Dunckerley gave them a Warrant of Constitution. Others, for example 'Observance of the Seven Degrees' (a relic of the former Seven Degree Rite) and 'Redemption' at York, could well claim to be of Time Immemorial constitution, that is they were already working when the Grand Conclave itself was Constituted. Which of the others were in recognisable existence before 24 June 1791, and became, as it were, founder members of Dunckerley's Grand Conclave, is uncertain. 'Constituted' in Dunckerley's letter seems to have a dual meaning; some of these Conclaves were not working before they received a Warrant from Dunckerley and were thus 'Constituted' by him as the word would be understood today, while others, already in existence in one form or another, Dunckerley 'Constituted' by recognising them as 'Regular'.

Of those which are not noted in the footnotes as 'working today', only 'Observance', 'Trine', and 'St. John of Jerusalem' figure in the 'Roll of Encampments recognised by Grand Conclave' in 1809. 'Trine' and 'St. John of Jerusalem' do not appear in the 'List of Encampments' published in the Minutes of the 1855 Meeting of Grand Conclave. 'Observance of the Seven Degrees' was erased in 1888.

Moreover, the details at Appendix B show how diverse was the activity distributed around the various countries, and it is understandable why the list compiled by Dunckerley may be considered less then definitive.

APPENDIX L

ENCAMPMENTS REMOVED BEFORE 1868

In 1868 all Encampments owing allegiance to the English Grand Conclave, those in Canada among them, were re-numbered, closing up the gaps caused by Encampments which had ceased to exist. This is the so-called 'Enumeration of 1868' and there has been no further 'closing-up' to the present day, although in one or two cases the Grand Master for the time being has exercised his prerogative of allocating a lower vacant number to an existing Preceptory in place of its '1868' one where for some special reason he has considered this to be desirable. The following encampments have been identified as having existed but ceased working before the 1868 re-numbering:

Encampment	Meeting	Constituted	Removed
Trine	Bideford	1790	-
St John of	Redruth	1791	-
Royal Edward	Bridgewater	1792	
Saint Bernard	Oldham/Werneth	1793	c.1811
Bethlehem	Carlisle	1794	
Boyne	Woolwich	1805	
Plains of Brunswick	Haworth	1805	
Fortitude	1st Dragoon Guards		Not Known
Durnovarian	Dorchester		Not Known
Harmony of Seven Degrees	Salisbury		Not Known
Science of Seven Degrees	Salisbury		Not Known
Holy Trinity	Hereford		Not Known
Royal Edward of the Seven Degrees	Hampton Court		Not Known
Royal Gloucester	Southampton		Not Known
Holy Sepulchre	Chichester		Not Known
Mount Carmel	London	1806	1867
Union	Leeds	1806	-
Sinai	Hampton Court	1808	-
Patriotic	Colchester	1808	-
Concord	Harwich	1808	-
Holy Cross	Whitehaven	1809	-
St Patrick	Liverpool	1809	-
True Friendship	Bristol	1809	-
Gethsemane	Bristol/Cardiff	1809	
Holy Trinity	Whitehaven	1811	1867
Joppa	Sunderland	1811	1865
La Reunion Desiree	Port-au-Prince, Haiti	1811	-
Trine	Portsea	c.1812	-
Mount Calvary	St Kitts, WI	c.1812	
Frederick of Unity	London	1847	1867
Almeric de St Maur	Bolton	1853	1854 (Note 1)
Ascalon	Birmingham	1867	(Note 2)
Vale of Jehoshaphat	Highbridge	1862	(Note 3)

Vale Royal	Salisbury	1862	(Note 3)
St John	Simla	1860	1865
St Michael & St George	Corfu	1861	1865
Eastern Conclave of Redemption	Scinde	1866	1867

Notes:

1 United in1854 with St Geoffrey de Omer, later No 35 Warrant Surrendered 1904.

2 Warranted by Baldwyn at Bristol during period of Independence before 1862.

3 These Encampments, also warranted by Baldwyn, were placed on the Roll of Grand Conclave in 1862 when relations with Baldwyn restored; by then they had already ceased to meet.

It may also be observed that these locations are either seaport towns or on navigable inland waterways.

APPENDIX M

ROLL OF PRECEPTORIES NOT ATTACHED TO PROVINCES

	Preceptory:	Meeting in:	Date of Warrant:
6	Preceptory of St George	MMH, London	20 Oct 1795
38	Bermuda	Bermuda	27 Jun 1851
			23 Jun 1890 Warrant of Revival
60	Calpe	Gibraltar	17 Mar 1859
64	*Excelsior*	*1st Batt. 21St Regt*	*17 Mar 1860*
		Fusiliers 1 May 1886 Warrant Surrendered	
70	Union	Guyana	22 May 1862
77	Star of the West	Barbados	2 Feb 1864
189	Jamaica	Jamaica	24 Aug 1909
203	*Sir George Somers*	*Bermuda*	*1 Mar 1918*
		May 2012 Warrant Surrendered	
280	St Helier	Jersey, CI	1 May 1936
456	Royal Victoria	Bahamas	14 Feb 1975
491	St George of Guernsey	Guernsey, CI	4 Apr 1979
498	St German's Preceptory of Mann	Isle of Man	12 Dec 1980
516	Northern Territory	Darwin, Australia	28 Jan 1982
588	Iyanola	St Lucia, West Indies	28 Feb 1995
626	St John the Almoner	Malta	19 Jan 2001
640	Waller Rodwell Wright	Malta	16 May 2003
649	La Valette	Malta	29 Oct 2004
663	Unity and Brotherhood	Trivandrum, India	21 Mar 2007
664	Kottayam	Kottayam, India	21 Mar 2007
665	Bombay	Mumbai, India	19 Mar 2007
666	St James	MMH, London	13 Oct 2011
676	Seychelles	Seychelles	10 Mar 2010
678	The Grand Master's	MMH, London	4 Sep 2009
679	Francis Bavin	Jamaica	22 Oct 2009
683	Carantania	Brezovica, Slovenia	4 Feb 2011
684	Kolossi	Limmasol, Cyprus	25 May 2012
696	Karnatka Preceptory and Priory	Karnatka and Goa, India	14 Nov 2015
709	St John's	Andhra Pradesh. Teangana and Tamil Nadu, India	9 Dec 2017
111	Observance	Chennai, India	*17 Oct 1853*
		Removed from The Roll 1 Jan 1888; Reponed August 2018	

APPENDIX N

PROVINCIAL STRUCTURE IN
ENGLAND AND WALES

In Part 4, the development of Districts and Provinces was summarised as a natural part of the decentralisation of the United Orders in chronological order, and this Appendix records for each Province in the British Isles, in more detail and, where applicable, local masonic developments in each geographical area and the evolution of earlier decentralised bodies into the structure of today. For consistency, former Provinces are included. Provinces constituted under the United Orders which are geographically located overseas appear in **Appendix O.**

Dates of Warrant are shown and when preceded by:

[C] = Date of Warrant of Confirmation   [D] = Date of Dispensation;

PROVINCE OF CITY AND COUNTY OF BRISTOL
Constituted by Charter of Compact with the appointment of Samuel Bryant, MD as Provincial Prior in 1862; Reconstituted as Bristol (City and County) and Gloucestershire in 1864; Reconstituted 1960 on separation of Gloucestershire and inauguration of Province of Gloucestershire under the title of Bristol (City and County) with Dennis Norman Frederick Tricks as Provincial Prior.

Preceptory:	Meeting in:	Date of Warrant:
C Baldwyn	Bristol	(Time Immemorial)

Currently known under the title of Province of City and County of Bristol.

PROVINCE OF CHESHIRE AND NORTH WALES
Originally Constituted: [sometime between 1793 and 1806] as the Province of Lancashire, Yorkshire and Cheshire. Constituted as the Province of Cheshire in 1850; William Courteney Cruttenden appointed Provincial Prior in 1862. Renamed Province of Cheshire and North Wales in 2011.

Preceptory:	Meeting in:	Date of Warrant:
14 Royal Edward	Hyde	13 Jul 1806

[No 14 formerly held by Love and Friendship at Stockport Warranted 10 Apr 1809; Erased 1 Jan1894 and re-allocated to Royal Edward, Stalybridge formerly No 76b]

15 Preceptory of St Salem	Congleton	1 Nov 1808
		[D] 8 Jan 1909
91 Geoffroy de Bouillon	Birkenhead	2 Apr 1867
100 de Tabley	Wilaston	3 Apr 1868
132 Grosvenor	Chester	9 Apr 1875
184 Preceptory of St Hilary	Birkenhead	30 Nov 1906
217 Palestine	Wallesey	27 Dec 1920
231 Menai	Rhyl	30 Nov 1924
234 de l'Isle Adam	Chester	2 Nov 1924

272 Love and Friendship	Neston	23 Apr 1933
318 St George	*Christleton*	*26 May 1948*
(In abeyance from 10 May 2017 to 3 May 2018)		
326 Preceptory of Faith	Sale	17 Mar1949
327 Temple	Sandbach	17 Mar1949
454 Preceptory of St David	Rhewl Mostyn	1 Nov 1974
558 Northwich	Macclesfield	16 Jan 1990
560 Cheshire Preceptory of Hope		*7 July 1990*
[Amalgamated Apr 2007 with Faith Preceptory No 326]		
578 The Cheshire Bodyguard	*Knutsford*	*17 Feb 1993*
[Warrant surrendered Aug 2011]		
584 The Preceptory of Charity	*Timperley*	*7 Jan 1994*
[Warrant surrendered 1 May 2015]		
603 The Croes Newydd	Wrexham	7 Jun 1996
605 St Werburgh	Christleton	31 Oct 1996
685 The Llewelyn Fawr	Llandudno	12 Nov 2011

PROVINCE OF DERBYSHIRE

Formerly part of the Province of Nottinghamshire, Leicestershire, and Derbyshire constituted in 1847, a separate Province of Derbyshire was constituted 1970 with Dr Reginald Latham Brown as Provincial Prior.

Preceptory:	Meeting in:	Date of Warrant:
159 Peveril	Derby	8 Sep 1893
348 Abbeydale	Dore	24 Feb 1956
399 St Laurance	Long Eaton	19 Mar 1965
423 Bertram de Verdun	Burton-on-Trent	16 Mar 1970
473 The High Peak	New Mills	1 Jun 1976
520 Round Table	Chesterfield	18 Jan 1983
523 The Stydd	Belper	4 Sep 1983
620 The Derventio	Belper	5 May 1999

PROVINCE OF DEVONSHIRE & CORNWALL

Constituted as The Province of Devonshire in 1848 and Revd John Huyshe was appointed Provincial Prior in 1862; Reconstituted as Province of Devonshire and Cornwall in 1934 with the addition of Cornwall with Revd Preb. Stanley Roots Carden MA, HCF as Provincial Prior.

Preceptory:	Meeting in:	Date of Warrant:
F Union of Rougement	Exeter	Time Imm.
		[C] 8 Aug 1811
10 Royal Veterans	Plymouth	9 Jun 1806
	[C] 25 Nov 1948 and [C] 17 Mar 1969	
19 Trinity in Unity	Barnstaple	28 Feb 1812
		[D]16 Apr 1812
23 Comubian	*Truro*	*24 Nov 1826*
[Erased 1 Jan 1888]		
24 Loyal Brunswick	*Stonehouse*	*25 Nov 1830*
[Amalgamated 17 Jan 1929 with Royal Veterans Preceptory No 10		
25 Royal Sussex	Torquay	30 Apr 1884

30	*Holy Cross*	*Axminster*	*13 May 1844*

[1893 Warrant Surrendered]

90	Restormel	Hayle	1 Mar 1867

(With power to meet at any MH in Cornwall May, Sep, & Nov)

480	Launceston Castle	Launceston	6 Jan 1977
561	The Holy Cross	Seaton	10 Aug 1990
611	St John of Jerusalem	Newquay	2 May 1998
625	Tamar	Exeter / Launceston	25 Oct 2000
628	The Mandylion	Ivybridge	24 Oct 2001
654	The Vera Crux	Exmouth	21 Jan 2005

PROVINCE OF DORSET AND WILTSHIRE

Constituted with the Appointment of William Williams as Provincial Prior as the Province of Dorsetshire in 1836; Reconstituted with Incorporation of Wiltshire on 10 January 1949 with Col Montague James Raymond as Provincial Prior.

Preceptory:	Meeting in:	Date of Warrant:
31 All Souls'	Weymouth	26 Mar 1847
98 Hyde	Wareham	1 Oct 1867
322 William Longespee	Salisbury	29 Sep 1948
379 St Peter and St Paul	Marlborough	27 Dec 1962
492 St Aldhelm	Malmesbury	1 May 1979
595 Vale of Dorset	Kinson	13 Dec 1994
615 Royal Durnovarian	Salisbury	6 Feb 1999
669 St Lawrence	Warminster	15 Nov 2007
708 Geoffroi de Charny	Warminster	6 Sep 2017

PROVINCE OF DURHAM

Formerly part of the Province of Northumberland and Durham constituted in 1850; Reconstituted with the appointment of Charles Henry Swann, JP, as Provincial Prior on separation from Northumberland on 24 September 1975.

Preceptory:	Meeting in:	Date of Warrant:
118 Mount Grace	Hartlepool	26 Apr 1872
139 St Cuthbert's	Darlington	15 Apr 1878
		[C]15 Feb 1951
222 Finchale	Sunderland	1 May 1922
233 Haliwerfolc	Old Elvet, Durham	30 Nov 1924
275 St Lawrence	South Shields	31 Oct 1934
292 Wycliffe	Darlington	1 Nov 1942
316 Tees	Stockton-on-Tees	21 Dec 1947
339 De Umfraville	Gateshead	24 Aug 1954
479 Strathmore	Burnopfield	10 Dec 1976
550 The Marmaduke Lumley	Chester-le-Street	23 Aug 1988
559 Bishop Antony Bek	Shildon	26 Feb 1990
567 Durham Preceptory of Installed Preceptors	Durham City	17 Dec 1990
589 Prince Bishops	Durham City	29 Apr 1994
622 Palatine Guards	Durham City	18 Apr 2000

PROVINCE OF EAST ANGLIA

Constituted in 1857as Province of Suffolk and Cambridge; Capt. Nathaniel George Philips appointed Provincial Prior in 1867. Constituted as Province of East Anglia in 1882.

Preceptory:		Meeting in:	Date of Warrant:
16	Prudence	Ipswich	21 Feb 1811
69	Cabbell	Wroxham	3 Mar 1862
80	Royal Plantagenet	Great Yarmouth	8 Nov 1864
102	Tancred	Bury St Edmunds	18 Dec 1868
179	Holy Rood	Cambridge	24 Jun 1904
330	Lynn Regis	Kings Lynn	9 Apr 1950
418	St John	Diss, Norfolk	2 Jul 1969
439	Hereward the Wake	March	5 Jun 1972
451	Walter Short	Thetford	25 Jun 1974
497	The Walsingham	Fakenham	20 Oct 1980
538	The Dunwich	Southwold	21 Jan 1986
544	Martyn	Sudbury	6 May 1987
667	Beeston Regis	Sheringham	2 Aug 2007
677	The Isle of Ely	Ely	27 Jun 2009
692	The Peter Cannon Meridian	Bury St Edmunds	20 Sep 2014

PROVINCE OF ESSEX

Constituted in 1930 with the appointment of the Revd Felix Eustace Crate as Provincial Prior.

Preceptory:		Meeting in:	Date of Warrant:
256	Maplestead	Colchester	30 Nov 1928
261	de Mandeville	Upminster	21 Dec 1929
271	St Chad's	Chingford	25 Jul 1932
274	Chelmersforde	Chelmsford	25 Jul 1934
295	St Katherine's	Southend-on-Sea	29 Jun 1944
309	Pymmes Park	Loughton	6 Jun 1947
310	Hubert de Burgh	Southend-on-Sea	6 Jun 1947
382	Felix E. Crate	Upminster	23 Apr 1963
434	Arthur Dentith	Saffron Waldon	2 Aug 1971
441	Essex	Braintree	28 Sep 1972
442	Sir Peter de Tany	Harlow	19 Dec 1972
453	St Thomas a Becket	Loughton	31 Oct 1974
467	Hugh de Payens	Rochford	23 Dec 1975
489	Essex Jubilee	Upminster	5 Jan 1979
496	St Osyth	Clacton-on-Sea	16 Sep 1980
507	*Waltham Holy Cross*	*Chingford*	*18 May 1981*
	[In abeyance from 4 Dec 2017]		
562	Essex Bodyguard	*Itinerant*	15 Aug 1990
563	Langdon Hills	Orsett	13 Sep 1990
564	Frederick C. Hughes	Russell Sq. London	11 Oct 1990
583	Ambresbury	Chadwell St Mary	7 Jul 1993
623	Cressing Temple	Braintree	18 Nov 1999
631	Plantagenet	Hutton	21 Nov 2001
641	Sir William St Clair	Orsett/Braintree	20 May 2003

| 645 Mistley Towers | Manningtree | 17 Sep 2003 |

PROVINCE OF GLOUCESTER & HEREFORDSHIRE

Gloucester was originally part of the Province of Bristol (City & County) and Gloucestershire constituted in 1864; Gloucestershire separated from Bristol and incorporated Herefordshire on 14 May 1960 with the appointment of Percy Harold Creese as Provincial Prior.

Preceptory:	Meeting in:	Date of Warrant:
72 Coteswolde Preceptory of St Augustin	Cheltenham	12 Feb 1863
341 King Richard I	Downend, Bristol	21 Sep 1954
365 Dean Forest Preceptory of St Mary	Newnham	29 Dec 1959
376 Sir Thomas Docwra	Hereford	24 Sep 1961
406 Stroud Preceptory of St Michael	Stroud	12 Sep 1966
493 Corinium Preceptory of St John the Baptist	Cirencester	16 Jul 1979
501 The Avon Preceptory of St Andrew	Stapleton, Bristol	15 Jan 1981
506 Gloucester Preceptory of Saint Nicholas	Gloucester	24 Mar 1981
616 Preceptory Jean Parisot de la Valette	Stroud	28 Nov 1998

PROVINCE OF HAMPSHIRE & ISLE OF Wight

Constituted as Province of Hampshire with the appointment of Maj. Ferris Charles Robb as Provincial Prior in 1848; Reconstituted in 1945 with Incorporation of the Isle of Wight when Col George Nowers Dyer, *CBE, DSO* was Provincial Prior.

Preceptory:	Meeting in:	Date of Warrant:
2 Royal Naval	Portsmouth	11 Mar 1791
27 Sepulchre Preceptory and Sandeman Priory	Christchurch	15 Jun 1840
32 Royal Gloucester	Southampton	8 Apr 1845
76a William Stuart	Alton	20 Jan 1864
194 Loveland	Bournemouth	30 Sep 1911
237 Vectis	Ryde, IOW	17 Mar 1925
357 Pilgrim	Portsmouth	23 Apr 1958
432 St Michael and St Mary	Andover	4 Mar 1971
569 Emmaus	Petersfield	20 May 1991
574 Excalibur	Botley	9 Dec 1991
575 Frescewatre	East Cowes, IOW	24 Oct 1992
617 Parsifal Preceptory and Priory	Chandler's Ford	16 Jan 1998

PROVINCE OF HERTFORDSHIRE

Constituted with the appointment of John Frederick Cleeves as Provincial Prior in 1933.

Preceptory:	Meeting in:	Date of Warrant:
28 Stuart	Watford	13 Apr 1840
37 Melita	Cheshunt	c. 1815 and 10 May 1850
[Originally met in Malta; Renamed 1982 Mediterranean; Name reverted to Melita]		
266 The Preceptory of St Alban	St Albans	24 Feb 1930
269 Temple Chelsin	Hertford	1 May 1931
281 St John the Evangelist	Southgate	1 Nov 1936
283 Temple Dinsley	Royston	24 Aug 1937
315 John F. Cleeves	Cheshunt	30 Nov 1947
383 Joseph Moffett	Watford	25 Jul 1963
409 Charles Herbert Perram	Radlett	12 Oct 1967
416 Royston	Royston	11 Apr 1969
424 Hatfield	Radlett	2 Aug 1971
463 MacLeod	Radlett	18 Jul 1975
543 The Harold Devereux Still	Radlett	16 Mar 1987
581 Standon Priory	Sawbridgeworth	15 May 1993
618 Crossed Swords	Bishop Stortford	5 May 1999
670 Jacques de Molay	Cheshunt	13 Oct 2007

PROVINCE OF KENT

Constituted in 1847; Reconstituted on Joining with Surrey 1880; Reconstituted when Surrey separated on 14 Dec 1956 with the appointment of Capt. Alexander McKenzie-Smith, *MBE* as Provincial Prior.

Preceptory:	Meeting in:	Date of Warrant:
146 Black Prince	Canterbury	14 May 1880
155 Lullingstone	London (Duke St)	12 Jun 1885
224 Roffa's Camp	Wigmore	24 Aug 1922
257 Crystal Palace	London (MMH)	25 Dec 1928
286 Bromley	Penge	17 Apr 1938
325 Temple Ewell	Dover	21 Dec 1948
333 St Vincent	Tunbridge Wells	23 Apr 1951
371 West Kent	Sevenoaks	24 Feb 1961
373 Axstane Preceptory of St John of Jerusalem	Wrotham	1 Mar 1961
391 Preceptory of the Holy Trinity	Gravesend	26 May 1964
392 Pilgrims' Way	Wilmington	26 May 1964
401 Thanet	Margate	19 Jan 1966
402 Boxley Abbey	Maidstone	25 Jan 1966
433 Westwood	Hoo	10 Jun 1971
436 St Michael's	Sittingbourne	30 Nov 1971
475 Lord Harris	Ashford	5 Jul 1976
484 Frederick Friday	Chatham	12 Jul 1977
500 Shirley Woolmer	Sidcup	15 Jan 1981
552 The Kent Bodyguard	Gillingham	1 Feb 1989
555 Oakley	Bromley	28 Jul 1989
596 The Galloway Preceptory	Gillingham	10 Feb 1995
597 Richard Plantagenet	Welling	21 Feb 1995

629 Kent Preceptory of St George   Dartford   22 Jan 2002

PROVINCE OF LANCASHIRE

Constituted in 1806 within the Province of Lancashire, Yorkshire, and Cheshire. Cheshire separated on 1 October 1809 and separate Provinces of Lancashire and Yorkshire were constituted on that date. Province of Lancashire re-constituted in 1848 with the subsequent appointment of Albert Hudson Royds as Provincial Grand Commander in 1862.

Preceptory:		Meeting in:	Date of Warrant:
5	Jerusalem	Manchester	10 Oct 1786[321]
7	Loyal Volunteers	Ashton-under-Lyne	12 Aug 1796
8	Plains of Mamre	Burnley	10 Mar 1806
	[De Lacy Preceptory, Burnley joined 1 May 1874]		
9	St Joseph	Manchester	10 Mar 1806
	[Centenary Warrant dated 1935]		
11	*Plains of Tabor*		*7 Apr 1805*
	[Warrant Issued but Preceptory Never Consecrated][See No 110 below]		
12	St Michael	Breightmet	10 Apr 1808
	[Consecrated Bury – Moved to Rawtenstall in 1932]		
17	St John of Jerusalem	Ulverston	21 Feb 1811
	[Consecrated Todmorden 20 Oct 1810 – Moved to Ulverston in 1892,		
	Barrow-in-Furness in 1902, and Ulverston in 1955]		
33	St James of Jerusalem	Westhoughton	5 Apr 1819
			[D] 5 Jan 1849
34	Prince Albert	Ormskirk	31 Aug 1849
35	*United Lane*	*Manchester*	*3 Nov 1853*
	[Amalgamated with Geoffrey de St Aldemar, Great Priory of Canada in 1904]		
36	Jacques de Molay	Liverpool	8 Mar 1850
41	Faith	Wigan	6 Jan 1853
43	St George's	Mossley	11 Mar 1854
			[C] 20 Mar 1878
49	William de la More	St Helens	22 Mar 1856
56	Hugh de Payens	Darwen	23 Dec 1857
61	Edmund Plantagenet	Warrington	11 Aug 1859
95	de Lacy	Southport	30 May 1867
	[Consecrated in Burnley but joined Plains of Mamre Preceptory 1 May 1874; with		
	sale of Warrant to Southport Masons – still in existence]		
97	Prince of Peace	Preston	1 Jul 1867
110	Plains of Tabor	Colne	8 Apr 1805
	[Adopted No. 11 8 Oct 2005]		
123	St Bernard *[formerly Alpass]*	Bury	1 Nov 1872
149	Royds	Morecambe	23 Jul 1880
			[C]8 Nov 1897
157	Rose of Lancaster	Garstang	17 Mar 1887
161	Robert de Sable	Carlisle	30 Nov 1893
210	Pax	Widnes	24 Aug 1919
313	Edmund Grindal	Cleator Moor	1 Nov 1947
428	Maples	Leyland	30 Sep 1970
440	The Earl of Lathom	Liverpool	3 Jul 1972

494 de ffaryngton	Leyland	5 Sep 1979
515 Robert de Bruys	Keswick	15 Jan 1982
592 The Northern Light	Fleetwood	18 Nov 1994
606 The Westmorland	Kendal	3 Sep 1997
621 Praetorian	Leyland	5 Nov 1999
630 Saint Edmund	Rochdale	4 Jan 2002
694 John o'Gaunt	Milnthorpe	3 Jul 2015
Preceptory of Installed Preceptors		

PROVINCE OF LEICESTERSHIRE & RUTLAND

Former Province of Nottinghamshire, Leicestershire, and Derbyshire constituted in 1847; Reconstituted as Province of Leicestershire and Rutland in 1970 with the appointment of David Neil Foister, *TD* as Provincial Prior..

Preceptory:	Meeting in:	Date of Warrant:
152 Rothley Temple	Leicester	11 Apr 1884
294 Ivanhoe	Leicester	22 Mar 1944
410 Sir John Babington	Loughborough	12 Apr 1968
420 Ulverscroft	Leicester	28 Nov 1969
613 de Verdun	Lutterworth	11 Dec 1998
660 Sir Richard Hastyngs	Ashby-de-la-Zouch	13 Sep 2006
661 Militia Templi	Leicester	20 Dec 2006

PROVINCE OF LINCOLNSHIRE

Constituted in1910 with Lord Heneage, *OBE* as Provincial Grand Commander..

Preceptory:	Meeting in:	Date of Warrant:
143 Temple Bruer	Lincoln	4 Apr 1879
190 Sutcliffe	Grimsby	23 Apr 1910
		[C] 30 Nov 1934
301 Heneage	Grantham	1 Mar 1946
320 All Saints'	Gainsborough	25 Jul 1948
349 Carmelite	Boston	23 Apr 1956
466 St Paul's	Skegness	4 Dec 1975
553 Wolds	Louth	16 Feb 1989
609 Chapter House Preceptory of Past Preceptors	Lincoln Cathedral	30 Jan 1998
680 Lincolnshire Centenary Daylight	*Moveable*	1 Mar 2010

PROVINCE OF LONDON

Until 1992 Preceptories consecrated in the London area were administered directly from Mark Masons' Hall as Unattached Preceptories and were not considered to be part of a Province. A similar position applied in other directly administered Orders. As the number of Orders and Units within the different Orders increased such administration became too burdensome for the staff of Mark Masons' Hall and so a decision was taken to create a Province for London in the majority of the Orders administered directly.

In the United Orders, a Province of London was constituted with the appointment of Jack Lodewyk Charles Dribble as Provincial Prior in 1992, and although two Preceptories are still administered directly by MMH (See **Appendix M**) the following are now considered part of this Province:

Preceptory:		Date of Warrant:
D	Mount Calvary	17 Nov 1842
26	Faith and Fidelity	12 Sep 1838
45	United Preceptory of Kemys Tynte and Temple Cressing	9 May 1856
73	Coromandel	12 Mar 1828[322]
		[C] 12 Jul 2002
117	The New Temple	13 Apr 1872
127	Bard of Avon	28 Feb 1873
		[C] 1 Mar 1955
128	Oxford, Cambridge and United	Mar 1873
131	Holy Sanctuary	12 Feb 1875
140	Studholme	14 Jun 1878
154	Shadwell Clerke	14 Nov 1884
163	Ascalon	27 Dec 1894
172	Connaught Army and Navy	1 Nov 1901
173	King Edward VII	8 May 190
178	Empress	1 Oct 1903
183	Sancta Maria	23 Apr 1906
185	Preceptory of Galilee	1 Mar 1907
188	Preceptory of Baluchistan	21 Sep 1908
206	Annus Mirabilis	30 Nov 1918
		[C] 14 Dec 1948
209	Public Schools	25 Jul 1919
219	Golden Square	24 Feb 1921
251	Sydenham	29 Jun 1928
		[C] 24 May 1962
282	Britannic Preceptory of Madeira	27 Dec 1936
300	The Military Lodges	18 Oct 1945
321	Royal Colonial Institute	Sep 1948
512	Guild of Freemen	14 Oct 1981
576	St John at Ealing	16 Nov 1992
614	The London Bodyguard Preceptory	11 Dec 1998
632	Londinium	5 Dec 2001
695	Secretum Templi Londinium	24 Oct 2015

PROVINCE OF MIDDLESEX

Constituted in 1970 with the appointment of Col Bernard Stuart Horner, *OBE* as Provincial Prior.

Preceptory:		Meeting in:	Date of Warrant:
253	Staines	Staines	1 Nov 1928
268	Herga	Harrow	21 Sep 1930
388	Twickenham	Twickenham	26 Dec 1961
394	Uxbridge	Uxbridge	23 Jul 1964
429	Southgate	Southgate	14 Oct 1970
449	Gauntlet	Harrow	26 Mar 1974
450	All Hallows	Twickenham	30 Apr 1974
485	Lanfranc	Harrow	19 Aug 1977
518	Middleseaxe	Twickenham	7 Apr 1982
573	Mount Lebanon	Twickenham	16 Oct 1991

| 591 Arch of Steel | Twickenham | 18 Jul 1994 |
| 627 Thomas Dunkerley | Twickenham | 1 Oct 2001 |

PROVINCE OF MONMOUTH & SOUTH WALES

Constituted in 1889 to cover Monmouth, Somerset and South Wales; reconstituted with the appointment of Richard Wilson Bartlett as Provincial Prior in 1952; Somerset separated on 30 June 1953

Preceptory:	Meeting in:	Date of Warrant:
115 Gwent	Newport, Gwent	1 Sep 1871
200 Morganwg	Penarth	27 Dec 1913
319 Giraldus Cambriensis	Llanelli	25 Jul 1948
427 Menevia	Aberaeron	9 Sep 1970
502 Holy Palestine	Swansea	TBC
547 The Owain Glyndwr	Llanelli	11 Aug 1987
Preceptory of Installed Preceptors		
556 Sant Madoc	Porthcawl	22 Sep 1989
568 St David's	Narberth	8 Jan 1991
577 Castell Nedd	Neath	3 Oct 1992
579 Cefn Ydfa	Bridgend	3 Apr 1003
582 Fforest Preceptory	Treharris	4 Jun 1993
602 Temple Slebech Preceptory	Llanelli	9 Dec 1995
of Provincial Bodyguards		
668 Sir William Marshall	Chepstow	15 Sep 2007
673 The Lord Swansea	Swansea	30 May 2008
704 The Brecknock Castle	Brecon	7 Oct 2016

PROVINCE OF NORTHAMPTON, HUNTINGDON AND BEDFORD

Constituted in 1925 with the appointment of Thomas Phipps Dorman as Provincial Prior.

Preceptory:	Meeting in:	Date of Warrant:
207 Victory	Northampton	27 Dec 1918
218 Perseverence	Kettering	6 Jan 1921
236 Wendlynburgh	Wellingborough	24 Feb 1925
240 United Priors	Huntingdon	18 Oct 1925
243 St Oswald	Peterborough	13 Jan 1927
260 Ampthill	Bedford	4 Jul 1929
513 Norman Wright	Stamford	10 Dec 1981
554 The Holy Cross	Daventry	16 Feb 1989
557 The Kingsbury	Dunstable	9 Jan 1990
572 The Peter George	Kettering	14 Oct 1991
601 Sir Richard de Montfitchet	St Neots	1 Sep 1995
610 The George North	Kettering	28 Feb 1998
671 Heritage	Corby	3 Nov 2007
681 Hugh de Payens	Luton	27 Nov 2010

PROVINCE OF NORTH AND EAST YORKSHIRE

Originally formed part of the Administrative District of Lancashire, Yorkshire and Cheshire. Province of Yorkshire constituted in 1806, and then sub-divided into the Provinces of North and East Yorkshire and West Yorkshire in 1864. William Henry Forrester Denison (Rt Hon. Lord Londesborough) was appointed Provincial Grand Commander for the Province of North and East Yorkshire

Preceptory:	Meeting in:	Date of Warrant:
B Ancient York Conclave of Redemption	Hull	Time Immemorial (c.1784)
101 Ancient Ebor	York	18 Dec 1868
187 Erimus	Saltburn-by-the-Sea	6 Jan 1908
202 Londesborough	Bridlington	24 Jun 1917
223 Humber	Hull	1 May 1922
238 Scardeburg	Scarborough	15 Jul 1925
381 Royal	Filey	19 Mar 1963
385 St John of Beverley	Beverley	18 Oct 1963
403 Anchor	Northallerton	25 Jul 1966
452 Salebeia	Selby	25 Jul 1974
608 Servitas	Bridlington	4 Oct 1997
656 Walter de Gant	Bridlington	23 Apr 2005
690 Ashbrooke	Middlesborough	11 Sep 2012

PROVINCE OF NORTHUMBERLAND

Originally constituted as the Province of Northumberland and Durham in 1850. Reconstituted in 1975 with the appointment of Harold Frederick Lockwood Mavity as Provincial Prior.

Preceptory:	Meeting in:	Date of Warrant:
20 Royal Kent	Newcastle-upon-Tyne	16 Apr 1812
226 Lindisfarne	Berwick-upon-Tweed	25 Apr 1923
232 Chibburn	Whitley Bay	1 Nov 1924
239 Brandling	Seaton Delaval	24 Aug 1925
284 Brinkburn	Morpeth	21 Sep 1937
461 St Wilfred of Hexham	Hexham	21 May 1975
469 St Aidan	Amble	28 Jan 1976
481 St Oswald	Newcastle-upon-Tyne	17 Feb 1977
522 The Prior's Haven	North Shields	25 Apr 1983
525 St George of Throckley	Throckley	23 Apr 1984
537 Wudcestre	Ashington	30 Oct 1985
580 St Ronan	Blyth	5 Jun 1993
586 Templar Segedunum	Wallsend	29 Jan 1994
590 Northanhymbre	Shiremoor	13 Jun 1994
600 Northumbria Guards	Whitley Bay	13 May 1995
633 Tutelage	Morpeth	9 May 2002

PROVINCE OF NOTTINGHAMSHIRE

Constituted in 1856; Reconstituted in 1960 with Charles Henry Venn Elliott, *TD, MA,* as Provincial Prior

Preceptory:	Meeting in:	Date of Warrant:
A Abbey Chapter	Nottingham	Time Immemorial
395 Wynkbourne	Mansfield	25 Jul 1964
413 Pelham	Worksop	19 Mar 1969
415 Candia	Nottingham	21 Mar 1969
443 Clermont	Nottingham	19 Dec 1972
462 Corpus Christi	W. Bridgeford	9 Jun 1975
495 The Pilgrim	Newark on Trent	30 Jul 1980
510 Nottinghamshire	Nottingham	25 Sep 1981

PROVINCE OF OXFORDSHIRE, BERKSHIRE AND BUCKINGHAMSHIRE

Constituted 1964 under the Provincial Prior for Oxfordshire and Berkshire, Col Alexander Denis Burnett Brown, *OBE, MC, TD.*

Preceptory:	Meeting in:	Date of Warrant:
29 Preceptory of Coeur de Lion	Oxford	26 Nov 1849
204 Wellesley	Sindlesham	23 Apr 1918
258 Crusaders	Wokingham	30 Jan 1929
264 Cressing	Beaconsfield	24 Feb 1930
314 St Hugh	Banbury	30 Nov 1947
323 Beaumont	Bicester	18 Oct 1948
389 Aylesbury	Aylesbury	24 Feb 1964
430 Sir Oliver Starkey	Slough	17 Dec 1970
438 Robert Loyd	Caversham	19 May1972
464 Cygnet	Beaconsfield	11 Aug 1975
474 *Outremer*	Newbury	4 Jun 1976
487 Terra Sancta	Chipping Norton	21 Jul 1978
499 Robert de Turnham	Milton Keynes	15 Dec 1980
514 Preceptory of Friendship and Care	Sindlesham	15 Dec 1981
637 Leslie Felgate Dring Preceptory of Installed Preceptors	Oxford	12 Sep 2002
691 Bisham Abbey	Marlow	21 Jan 2014

PROVINCE OF SOMERSET

Originally Constituted in 1846; reconstituted 1952 with the appointment of Maj. George Travers Briggs, *DSO, TD,* as Provincial Prior in 1953

Preceptory:	Meeting in:	Date of Warrant:
1 Antiquity	Bath	11 Aug 1791
40 Bladud	Bath	23 Sep 1852
121 Worlebury Preceptory of St Dunstan	Weston-super-Mare	17 Apr 1872
211 King Ina	Taunton	4 Dec 1919
244 Selwood Preceptory of St John	Frome	14 Feb 1927
354 Estune Command	Nailsea	30 Jan 1957
455 Keynsham Preceptory of St Keyna	Keynsham	14 Jan 1975
476 Cumba	Crewkerne	6 Jul 1976

551	King Arthur of Avalon	Glastonbury	8 Dec 1988
638	Exmoor	Minehead	28 Apr 2003
672	Our Lady of Walsingham	Crewkerne	11 Apr 2008
686	Templecombe Preceptory	Yatton	24 Jan 2012

PROVINCE OF STAFFORDSHIRE AND SHROPSHIRE

Constituted in 1849 to serve Staffordshire, Shropshire and Warwickshire. Warwickshire separated on 5 July 1966 and a separate Province of Staffordshire and Shropshire was constituted with the appointment of Col The Earl of Powis, *CBE, TD* as Provincial Prior.

Preceptory:	Meeting in:	Date of Warrant:
42 Godefroi de Bouillon	Stoke-on-Trent	5 Oct 1853
79 Wulfruna	Wolverhampton	16 Aug 1864
170 Bernard de Tremelay	Walsall	30 Nov 1899
193 Preceptory of St Chad	Shrewsbury	24 Aug 1911
369 Sir John Kent	Stafford	24 Dec 1960
398 Preceptory of St Clement	West Bromwich	17 Mar 1965
404 Preceptory of St Alkmund	Whitchurch	18 Aug 1966
407 Roger de Clinton	Wolverhampton	12 Dec 1966
411 Robert de Stafford	Stoke-on-Trent	18 Jun 1968
431 Powys	Wellington	7 Jan 1971
457 Sir Robert Mavesyn	Tamworth	7 Mar 1975
465 Ralph Le Strange	Alverley	24 Sep 1975
524 Ranulph de Blundeville	Leek	22 Sep 1983
530 William de Ferrars	Burton-on-Trent	15 Oct 1984
545 The Staffordshire and Shropshire	Wolverhampton	15 Jun 1987
546 John O'Gaunt	Kidsgrove	24 Jul 1987
682 Mercia Praetorian	Penkridge	22 Jan 2011

PROVINCE OF SURREY

Constituted in 1864; Joined with Kent from 1880 to 14 December 1956 when Kent separated and Sir George T. Boag, *KCIE, CSI* was appointed Provincial Prior.

Preceptory:	Meeting in:	Date of Warrant:
162 Temple Court	Guildford	1 May 1894
196 Preceptory of Croydon	Croydon	14 Feb 1912
225 Kyngstun	Surbiton	6 Jan 1923
304 Chertsey	Chertsey	11 Jun 1946
338 St Saviour's	Sutton	19 Mar 1953
360 Gascoigne	Croydon	21 Dec 1958
364 Preceptory of St George at Stoneleigh	Surbiton	29 Dec 1959
378 Preceptory of St John at Stoneleigh	Surbiton	24 Jun 1962
425 Sacryham	Croydon	11 Jun 1970
446 Emmaus	Surbiton	14 Aug 1973
447 Whyte Stone	Farnham	26 Nov 1973
478 Stephen Langton	Redhill	6 Sep 1976
517 Agincourt	Camberley	7 Apr 1982

570	Praesidium Legati	Surbiton	24 May 1991
594	The Pride of Surrey	Sutton	27 Sep 1994
598	Nuffield	Redhill	31 May 1995
607	St Catherines	Godalming	7 Jun 1997
693	St Michael at Bisley	Brookwood	8 May 2015

PROVINCE OF SUSSEX

Constituted in 1873 with the appointment of Lt Col Shadwell Henry Clerke as Provincial Grand Commander.

Preceptory:		Meeting in:	Date of Warrant:
125	Sussex Preceptory and Southdown Priory	Eastbourne	27 Dec 1872
126	De Warenne	Brighton	18 Jan 1873
137	Duke of Connaught and Strathearn's Himalaya	Littlehampton	20 Nov 1877[323]
174	Holy Sepulchre	St Leonard's on Sea	28 Oct 1902
201	Preceptory of St Richard	Chichester	24 Aug 1914
208	Thornton	Brighton	26 May 1919
400	Crux Christi	Horsham	28 Sep 1965
470	Holy Cross	Uckfield	5 Feb 1976
477	Bright Morning Star	Brighton	3 Sep 1976
488	William of Normandy	Battle	12 Dec 1978
571	The Jerusalem Cross	Peacehaven	5 Jun 1991
619	The John Forest	Peacehaven	5 May 1999

PROVINCE OF WARWICKSHIRE

Constituted in 1849 to cover the Counties of Staffordshire, Shropshire, and Warwickshire. Warwickshire separated on 5 July 1966 and was constituted as a separate Province with Leslie Burnett as Provincial Prior.

Preceptory:		Meeting in:	Date of Warrant:
67	Howe-Beauceant	Birmingham	22 Feb 1850
			[C] 17 Feb 1894
229	Peter de Erdington	Sutton Coldfield	15 Jul 1924
293	Holy Rood	Warwick	30 Nov 1942
331	Holy Trinity	Coventry	1 Nov 1950
340	Temple Balsall	Temple Balsall	24 Aug 1954
361	Ascalon	Rugby	26 Dec 1958
448	Edgebaston	Edgebaston	25 Jan 1974
458	Warwickshire	Warwick	12 Mar 1975
529	St Alphege	Solihull	10 Sep 1984
541	The Abbey	Nuneaton	2 Feb 1987
565	Praetorian	Edgebaston	5 Nov 1990
566	Guy of Warwick	Warwick	27 Nov 1990
647	Leamington Priors	Leamington Spa	3 Apr 2004
662	Omnis Sanctus	Birmingham	6 Jan 2007
689	The Preceptory of Light	Knowle	21 May 2012

PROVINCE OF WEST YORKSHIRE

Re-constituted in 1806 as part of the Province of Lancashire, Yorkshire, and Cheshire. Yorkshire separated in 1859 and in 1864 was sub-divided in to the Provinces of North and East Yorkshire and West Yorkshire. The Province of West Yorkshire was constituted in 1864 under George Fearnley, MD, Provincial Grand Commander.

Preceptory:		Meeting in:	Date of Warrant:
3	Plains of Rama	Keighley	17 Mar 1792
4	Hope	Huddersfield	5 Oct 1793
13	Faith	Baildon	10 Apr 1809
18	Prince Edward	Todmorden	30 Oct 1811
21	Salamanca	Halifax	16 Apr 1812
			[D] 26 Jan 1815
			22 Feb 1860
39	Fearnley	Dewsbury	21 Oct 1859
66	de Furnival	Swinton	3 May 1861
			[C] 7 Jun 1861
89	Plains of Mamre	Haworth	17 Feb 1806
			Warrant of Revival 1 Mar 1867
114	Fidelity	Leeds	2 Jun 1871
158	Amphibious	Heckmondwike	12 Mar 1892
199	King George V	Leeds	23 Apr 1913
205	Integrity	Morley	1 Nov 1918
213	De Ros	Harrogate	29 Jun 1920
214	Chantry	Wakefield	18 Oct 1920
216	Wharfedale	Otley	27 Dec 1920
230	Airedale	Bingley	15 Jul 1924
235	Temple	Barnsley	25 Jan 1925
259	Trafalgar	Batley	26 May 1929
265	Grey Friars	Doncaster	24 Feb 1930
298	Saint Laurance	Pudsey	30 Nov 1944
324	Preceptory of St Paul	Bradford	21 Dec 1948
390	Craven	Skipton	24 Feb 1964
587	Cohors Praetoria	Morley	16 May 1994

PROVINCE OF WORCESTERSHIRE

Formerly a part of the Province of Staffordshire, Warwickshire, and Worcestershire constituted in 1849, a separate Province of Worcestershire was constituted in 1924 with the appointment of William Thomas Page as Provincial Prior.

Preceptory:		Meeting in:	Date of Warrant:
52	Richard de Vernon	Dudley	7 May 1857
68	Preceptory of St Amand	Worcester	27 Nov 1861
212	Richard Coeur de Lion	King's Heath	23 Apr 1920
278	Temple	King's Heath	24 Jan 1936
332	Preceptory of the Holy Cross	King's Heath	1 Mar 1951
367	St Mary and All Saints	Kidderminster	21 Sep 1960
396	Preceptory of St John the Baptist	Stourport on Severn	27 Dec 1964
408	Hales Abbey	Halesowen	2 Jan 1967

414	Simon de Montfort	Evesham	19 Mar 1969
421	Bernard de Frankley	Northfield	24 Dec 1969
482	Trinity	King's Heath	12 Apr 1977
519	Preceptory of King John	Worcester	19 Oct 1982
531	St Stephen	Redditch	6 Nov 1984
549	The Worcestershire	Worcester	24 Mar 1988
585	The Varangian	Worcester	30 Nov 1993
612	St Michael and All Angels	Tenbury Wells	29 Sep 1998

APPENDIX O

DEVELOPMENTS OVERSEAS

Earlier, the development of Districts and Provinces overseas was summarised as a natural part of the decentralisation of the United Orders in chronological order, and this Appendix records for each Overseas geographical area, more detail and, where applicable, other masonic developments in that Country and the transfer of English Provinces and Preceptories to one or more National Sovereign bodies.

English Freemasonry has spread throughout the English-speaking world for many different reasons, but the principal causes can be identified as

Establishment and security of British Colonies.

Major trading activities and the shipping routes connecting these outposts with Great Britain.

Military activity arising through warlike conflict, policing operations to secure former colonies or trading interests, or support of international treaties and agreements. In many cases such Encampments and Preceptories were short-lived and ceased to function when the sponsoring military unit or brethren were redeployed.

One result is that development of devolved Freemasonry occurred primarily in the centres of English-speaking peoples, and this Appendix details not only the decentralisation of the United Orders, but also, where relevant, the interactions with other English-speaking organisations such as our sister constitutions in Scotland, and Ireland. Preceptory numbering is that of the United Orders but later numbering following transfer to another sovereign body is given where known.

PROVINCES OF THE UNITED ORDERS

BOLIVIA
Constituted as the Province of Bolivia with the appointment of Carlos Bedregal Soria as Provincial Prior in 2005

Preceptory:	Meeting in:	Date of Warrant:
604 General Jose Ballivan	La Paz	2 Nov 1996
624 Civis Mundi	La Paz	29 May 2001
646 Mariscal Andres de Santa Cruz Y Calahumana	La Paz	4 Oct 2003
674 Caballeros de la Santa Cruz	Santa Cruz	30 May 2008
697 Cyril Howell Rees	La Paz	24 Oct 2015
698 Inti	Oruro	14 Nov 2015
699 Caballeros del Santo Grial	Santa Cruz	7 Nov 2015

BRITISH GUIANA AND THE WINDWARD ISLANDS
Constituted as a Province of British Guiana and the Windward Islands in 1898 with the appointment of Lt Col Thomas Daly as Provincial Prior. The office of Provincial Prior was

vacant from 1905 to 1910 at which time the Province ceased to exist when incorporated into a Province of West Indian Islands where Preceptories are listed.

BURMA
Constituted as the Province of Burma in 1866 with the appointment of Col A. T. Greenlaw as Provincial Prior.

Preceptory:	Meeting in:	Date of Warrant:
81 Loyal Burham	Rangoon	5 Jun 1865
[Warrant Surrendered 1902]		
166 St George in Burma	Moulmein	25 Apr 1896
[Warrant Surrendered 12 May 1924]		
182 Iles	Rangoon	29 Jun 1905
[Removed from the Roll 9 May 1976]		

The Province ceased to exist in 1926.

CANADA
The first Preceptory to be chartered by The United Orders was in 1824 but a period of 30 years then followed until the next Preceptory was chartered; however, during this period, the *Royal Grand Conclave of Scotland,* chartered a Preceptory. From 1854 growth was steady and a Province of Canada was inaugurated in 1862 with Col. W. J. Bury McLeod Moore as Provincial Grand Commander. Growth continued and a total of 19 Preceptories were constituted by the United Orders before a Sovereign Great Priory was established in Canada in 1875:

Preceptory:	Meeting in:	Date of Warrant:
22 Hugh de Payens	Canada	12 Feb 1824
44 Geoffrey de St Aldemar	Canada	11 Nov 1854
46 William de la More the Martyr	Canada	28 Jul 1855
47 Godfroi de Bouillon	Canada	25 Oct 1855
54 Richard Coeur de Lion	Canada	29 May 1857
58 Nova Scotia	Canada	11 Aug 1858
(Originally Chartered in 1839 as St John's by Royal Grand Conclave of Scotland)		
75 Coeur de Lion	Canada	5 Dec 1863
88 Plantagenet	Canada	14 Nov 1866
96 Plantagenet/Sussex	Canada	30 May 1869
103 Hurontario	Canada	10 May 1869
104 Union de Molay	Canada	21 May 1869
106 King Baldwin	Canada	7 Jun 1861
108 Mount Calvary	Canada	15 Apr 1870
109 Moore	Canada	27 May 1870
113 Harrington	Canada	14 Apr 1871
116 St John the Almoner	Canada	8 Mar 1872
119 Gondemar	Canada	3 Mar 1872
120 Ode de St Amand	Canada	7 May 1872
122 Palestine	Canada	31 May 1872
130 St Bernard de Clairvaux	Canada	16 Oct 1874

All the Preceptories shown were transferred to the Independent Great Priory of Canada on its constitution in 1875 thus predating the establishment of the United Orders as a Sovereign body on 19 July 1895.

FAR EAST
A Province of China was constituted with the appointment of Samuel Rawson as Provincial Grand Commander in 1863; thus predating the establishment of the United Orders as a Sovereign body on 19 July 1895.

   The Province was reconstituted and renamed as Province of Far East in 1958 with the appointment of David Smith Hill as Provincial Prior in 1959. In 1991 the Province was divided with the separation of a Province for South East Asia in 1991 with the appointment of David James Roads as Provincial Prior.

Preceptory:	Meeting in:	Date of Warrant:
78 Victoria	Hong Kong	8 Apr 1864
195 Preceptory of Shanghai	Hong Kong	6 Dec 1911
675 Hong Kong	Hong Kong	19 Jun 2009

FINLAND
The United Orders gained a foothold in Finland in the 1980s with three Preceptories having been warranted from London in 1983-8. A Sovereign Great Priory for Finland was constituted by the Grand Master at Helsinki in 1985 and the following Preceptories were transferred:

Preceptory:	Meeting in:	Date of Warrant:
521 Alpha	Helsinki	2 Mar 1983
526 Beta	Helsinki	15 May 1984
527 Gamma	Helsinki	2 Jun 1984

GIBRALTAR
There is every indication that Knight Templary was known well before 1791 in Gibraltar through the influence of seafaring brethren and many military lodges holding Irish, Scottish and *Antients* warrants.

Preceptory:	Meeting in:	Date of Warrant:
60 Calpe	Gibraltar	17 Mar 1859

This Preceptory is not attached to any Province but is administered as an Unattached Preceptory directly from Mark Masons' Hall.

INDIA
Masonic activity in many different degrees and Orders was initiated on the Indian sub-continent during the days of the British Raj, and this included Preceptories constituted by the United Orders. Many of these were in the territory which became Pakistan at the date of Partition in 1947 and, following the proscription of Masonic activity in that Country, some were transferred back to the United Kingdom.

INDIA – BENGAL
Constituted in 1862 as the Province of Bengal with the appointment of Hugh David Sandeman as Provincial Grand Commander. The Province ceased to exist in 1916 with the incorporation of a Province of India where Preceptories are listed.

INDIA – BOMBAY
A Province of Bombay was constituted in 1862 with the appointment of Gustavus Septimus Judge, KCT as Provincial Grand Commander. At that date two of the Preceptories which survive today were in existence and these are listed under The Province of India. Between 1896 to 1902 the office of Provincial Prior was vacant. It was likewise vacant from 1912 to 1914 but the Provincial Prior of Bengal. Hon. Col. Sir Arthur Henry McMahon, *GCVO, KCIE, CSI*, GCT was in charge. From 1915 to 1916 the office of Provincial Prior was vacant. The Province ceased to exist in 1916 on incorporation into a new Province of India

INDIA – MADRAS
Constituted with the appointment of Lt Col William Pitt MacDonald as Provincial Prior in 1862. Reconstituted as part of the Province India in 1816 where former Preceptories are shown.

PROVINCE OF INDIA
Former Provinces of Bengal, Bombay & Madras constituted in 1862 were incorporated in a new Province of India with the appointment of Surg-Gen The Hon. Sir Charles Pardey Lukis, *KCSI*, as Provincial Prior in 1916. Pakistan was incorporated on 3 April 1950 and detached on 1 Apr 1960. The Province was dissolved in 1968.

Preceptory:	Meeting in:	Date of Warrant:
53 St Augustine	Lahore	11 May 1857
[Removed from the Roll in 1975]		
59 Mount Zion	Bombay	17 May 1859
[Removed from the Roll on 1 Jan 1888]		
73 Coromandel	Chennai (Peripatetic|)	12 Mar 1828
[Now meets in London]		*[C]12 Jul 2002*
86 Royal Deccan	Hyderabad	1 Aug 1866
[Warrant Surrendered 1918]		
93 Mount Calvary	Bombay	10 May 1869
[Removed from the Roll on 1 Jan 1888]		
94 Mount Moriah	Scinde	10 May 1869
[Removed from the Roll on 1 Jan 1888]		
111 Observance	Madras	17 Oct 1853
[Removed from the Roll on 1 Jan 1888; Reponed August 2018]		
112 Mount Lebanon	Bombay, India	16 Jan 1871
[Removed from the Roll on 1 Jan 1888]		
124 Royal Mysore Excelsior	Bangalore, India	4 Nov 1872
[Removed from the Roll on 10 May 1907]		
136 Mount Carmel	Bengal, India	20 Nov 1877
[Removed from the Roll on 1 Jan 1888]		
137 Himalaya	North West Provinces	20 Nov 1877
[Amalgamated with Connaught and Strathearn Preceptory No. 153 as Duke of Connaught and Strathearn's Himalaya Preceptory No. 137 on 1 June 1931 and Transferred to United Kingdom now meeting at Littlehampton, West Sussex]		
138 Acre	Allahabad, Bengal	20 Nov 1877
[Warrant Surrendered 18 Dec 1889]		
141 Ardvorlich	Rwalpindi, India	18 Oct 1878
[Warrant Surrendered 8 July 1887]		

153 *Connaught and Strathearn Meerut, NWP*   *1 Nov 1884*
       [Amalgamated with Himalaya Preceptory No 137 as Duke of Connaught and
       Strathearn's Himalaya Preceptory No 137 on 1 June 1931 and Transferred to United
       Kingdom now meeting at Littlehampton, West Sussex]
177 *Ardvorlich*   *Rwalpindi, India*   *20 Jan 1903*
       [Removed from the Roll on 8 Dec 1922]
181 *Royal Kent*   *Calcutta, India*   *6 Jan 1905*
       [Removed from the Roll on 8 Dec 1922]
197 *St Thomas*   *Bombay, India*   *23 Apr 1912*
       [Warrant Surrendered 18 May 1966]
227 *Eagle of Taxila Preceptory &*   *Rwalpindi, India*   *22 Nov 1923*
       Priory of St Thomas
       [Warrant Surrendered 17 May 19672]
312 *Wordsworth*   *Calcutta, India*   *25 Jul 1947*
       [Removed from the Roll on 8 Dec 1982]

The Province was dissolved in 1968, but recently five new Preceptories have been constituted:

663	Unity and Brotherhood	Trivandrum, India	21 Mar 2007
664	Kottayam	Kottayam, India	21 Mar 2007
665	Bombay	Mumbai, India	19 Mar 2007
696	Karnataka	Karnataka & Goa	14 Nov 2015
709	St Johns	Andhra Pradesh	9 Dec 2017
		Telangana & Tamil Nadu	

and one Preceptory has been recently reponed:
111 Observance   (Formerly Madras reponed August 2018]

These Preceptories are not attached to any Province and are administered as Unattached Preceptories directly from Mark Masons' Hall.

MEDITERRANEAN
Constituted as The Province of The Mediterranean with the appointment of Col G. Neeld Boldero as Provincial Prior in 1875.

Preceptory:	Meeting in:	Date of Warrant:
37 Melita	Malta	Approx 1815

       [1979 name changed to Mediterranean; 1982 name Melita restored]
       [Now meets in Cheshunt, Herts]

60 Calpe	Gibraltar	17 Mar 1859

       [Now administered by MMH as Unattached Preceptory]

Province dissolved in 1924.

NATAL
The Province of Natal was constituted in 1985 with the appointment of Douglas William Harris as Provincial Prior and four preceptories which form the Province today:

Preceptory:	Meeting in:	Date of Warrant:
148 Natalia	Pietermaritzburg	19 Jul 1880
156 Victoria Jubilee	Durban	27 Dec 1886
405 St Andrew's	Durban	23 Aug 1966
Warrant Surrendered 15 Aug 2000		
444 Rougemont	Durban	30 Apr 1973
Warrant Surrendered 9 Feb 2000		
509 Acre	Empangini	30 Jul 1981
535 Coeur de Lion	Newcastle, Natal	17 Jul 1985

RIVER PLATE

A Province of the River Plate was constituted in 2019 with four preceptories which were formerly part of the Province of South America; namely:

Preceptory:	Meeting in:	Date of Warrant:
191 Preceptory of San Martin	Buenos Aires	17 Mar 1911
701 Santa Rosa	Buenos Aires, Argentina	26 Feb 2017
702 St Philip & St James	Montevideo, Uruguay	27 Feb 2017
703 Santiago Apostol	Mendoza, Argentina	27 Feb 2017

SOUTH AFRICA

Developments in South Africa started in 1866 and a Province of South Africa was Constituted in 1887 under W. J. Hoskins Giddy as Provincial Grand Commander, thus pre-dating the establishment of the United Orders as a Sovereign body on 19 July 1895.

Subsequent separations occurred with Province of Transvaal Constituted in 1942, Province of Natal Constituted in 1985, and Province of South Africa (Cape & Orange Free State) constituted and renamed South Africa (Cape), in 2006. Preceptories are listed under these separate entries.

SOUTH AFRICA (CAPE) [Formerly the Province of South Africa (Cape and Orange Free State)

Following the constitution of the Province of Natal in 1985 The Province of South Africa was reconstituted in 2006 as the Province of South Africa (Cape and Orange Free State) under Cdr Herbert Raymond Carter as Provincial Prior. The Province was renamed as The Province of South Africa (Cape) in 2006 under Alasdair Bruce Duthie, Provincial Prior

Preceptory:	Meeting in:	Date of Warrant:
87 Southern Cross	*Cape Town*	*1 Sep 1866*
[Removed from the Roll 1 Jan 1888]		
151 Vasco da Gama	Port Elizabeth	20 Dec 1883
168 Mount Zion	Cape Town	18 Oct 1897
[Resuscitated 27 Apr 1931]		
270 The Bloemfontein	Langerug, Worcester	18 Oct 1931
511 Phoenix	Simonstown	13 Oct 1981
[In abeyance since 28 Feb 2018]		
534 Lord Roberts	Somerset West	8 Feb 1985
542 St George	George	13 Mar 1987

| 688 Port Alfred | Port Alfred | 31 Mar 2012 |

SOUTH AMERICA

Constituted as the Province of South America in 1914 with Francis Hepburn Chevallier-Boutell as Provincial Prior.

Preceptory:	Meeting in:	Date of Warrant
191 Preceptory of San Martin	Buenos Aires	17 Mar 1911
[Now Province of River Plate]		
198 Preceptory of Santa Rosa	*(formerly Buenos Aires)*	23 Apr 1913
[Warrant Surrendered 15 May 1985]		
412 Crux Meridionalis	Sao Paolo, Brazil	26 Jul 1968
532 Rio de Janiero	Rio de Janiero, Brazil	8 Jan 1985
634 Santa Catarina	Florianopolis, Brazil	17 May 2002
635 Espirito Santo	Vitoria, Brazil	16 May 2002
636 Sao Sebastiao	Rio de Janiero, Brazil	20 Jun 2002
639 Campo Salles	Sao Paulo, Brazil	18 Oct 2002
655 Wanderers	Santos, Brazil	8 Feb 2005
706 Cavaleiros Da Abolicao	Fortaleza, Brazil	4 Feb 2017
707 Serra Gaucha	Caxia do Sul, Brazil	8 Jul 2017

SOUTH EAST ASIA

A Province of South East Asia was constituted 1991 with Capt. Eidwen Frederick Mullen as Provincial Prior. [Formerly part of the Province of Far East and up to 1958 under the Province of China]

Preceptory:	Meeting in:	Date of Warrant:
71 Celestial	*Shanghai*	*10 Oct 1862*
[Removed from the Roll 11 May 1900]		
85 Star of the East	*Singapore*	*20 Dec 1866*
[Warrant Surrendered 14 Apr 1897]		
277 Star of the East	Singapore	27 Dec 1935
290 Golden Chersonese	Kuala Lumpur	29 Jun 1941
657 Borneo	Sabah	2 Dec 2005

SRI LANKA

Constituted as The Province of Ceylon with the appointment of Maj. Alexander Crowther Crookshank as Provincial Grand Commander in 1869 and renamed Sri Lanka in 1975.

Preceptory:	Meeting in:	Date of Warrant:
99 Ceylon	Colombo	29 Jul 1867
164 Colombo	Columbo	6 Jan 1895

TRANSVAAL

Constituted in 1942 with the appointment of Reginald Shaw Rigg as Provincial Prior.

Preceptory:	Meeting in:	Date of Warrant:
133 Diamond in the Desert	Kimberley	7 May 1875
160 Johannesburg	Johannesburg	21 Sep 1893

273 Keystone	Boksburg	25 Jun 1933
288 Kosmos	Johannesburg	25 Jan 1936
289 Transvaal	Pretoria	26 May 1940

[The above 5 Preceptories were formerly Part of Province of South Africa]

334 Northern Transvaal	Pietersburg	25 Jul 1951
419 Far West	Carltonville	21 Nov 1969
460 Park Lane	Johannesburg	30 Apr 1975

[Preceptory formerly Part of Province of South Africa]

| 471 Concordia | Manzini, Swaziland | 26 Mar 1976 |
| 528 Omega | Johannesburg | 14 Jul 1984 |

[Preceptory formerly Part of Province of South Africa]

536 Coeur de Lion	Boksburg	17 Jul 1985
658 Lumier	Rustenburg	29 Jul 2006
676 Seychelles	Mahe, Seychelles	10 Mar 2010

ZIMBABWE

The Province of Rhodesia was Constituted in 1962 with the appointment of Ferdinand Farrant Duckworth as Provincial Prior and renamed as the Province of Zimbabwe in 1980.

Preceptory:	Meeting in:	Date of Warrant:
No 347 Rhodes	Bulawayo	21 Sep 1955
No 370 Le Crac des Chevaliers	Harare	29 Dec 1960

SOVEREIGN GREAT PRIORIES

AUSTRALIA

Knight Templar Preceptories have been consecrated in Australia from the 19th century and six of these came into existence before the dissolution of the Convent General and the establishment of the United Orders as a Sovereign body on 19 July 1895.

Preceptory:	Meeting in:	Date of Warrant:
51 Pembroke of Australasia	Melbourne	7 May 1857
57 Percy (Baldwyn Warrant)	Adelaide	20 Aug 1858
62 Jacques de Molay	Australia	9 Nov 1859

[Removed from The Roll 1 Jan 1888]

| 82 Hinxman | Brisbane | 1 Aug 1865 |

[Removed from The Roll 1 Jan 1894]

| 107 St George | Australia | 12 Nov 1869 |

[Removed from The Roll 1 Jan 1888]

| 144 Tyrawley | Launceston, Tasmania | 17 Nov 1879 |

[Removed from The Roll 1 Jan 1894]

After the establishment of the United Orders, consecration of Preceptories in Australia continued although in a somewhat erratic manner until 1982.

In 1857 a Province of Victoria was constituted in Australia, but a period of over ten years elapsed before the next province was constituted for South Australia in 1868, and an even greater period passed before a Province of New South Wales was Constituted in 1907. A Further 20 years passed before the next Province (Queensland) was Constituted in 1927.

Independent Great Priories were constituted in Australia based primarily on the Provincial structure established by the United Orders, but with additional external influences, for example from Scottish Preceptories. Generally speaking, on the constitution of the several independent Great Priories these absorbed individual Preceptories on an entirely amicable basis. The resulting structure that can therefore be observed today is as follows:

1982 GREAT PRIORY OF SOUTH AUSTRALIA

The Great Priory of South Australia was constituted in 1982 with the simultaneous transfer of the following Preceptories from the Great Priory of England:

Preceptory:	Meeting in:	Date of Warrant:
57 Percy (Baldwyn Warrant)	Adelaide	20 Aug 1858
169 Earl of Euston	Adelaide (now Norwood)	21 Sep 1898
328 Fellowship	Adelaide	24 Aug 1949
336 Port Adelaide	Port Adelaide	25 Jul 1952
377 Port Pirie	Port Pirie	30 Nov 1961
426 Whyalla	Whyalla	24 Jul 1970
468 Trinity	Adelaide	28 Jan 1976
472 St John the Baptist	Strathalbyn	30 May 1976

1982 GREAT PRIORY OF VICTORIA

The Great Priory of Victoria was constituted in 1982 with the simultaneous transfer of the following Preceptories from the Great Priory of England

Preceptory:	Meeting in:	Date of Warrant:
51 Pembroke of Australasia	Melbourne	7 May 1857
175 Australasian	*Melbourne*	*27 Dec 1902*
[Amalgamated with Pembroke Preceptory]		
176 Metropolitan	Melbourne	27 Dec 1902
228 Ballarat	Ballarat	23 Apr 1924
245 Earl of Stradbroke	Melbourne	17 Apr 1927
247 Geelong	Geelong	5 Aug 1927
250 Star of the Valley	Shepparton	26 May 1928
252 Ivalda	Darebin	21 Sep 1928
262 Werrigar	Warracknabeal	26 Dec 1929
263 Western	Warrnambool	9 Jan 1930
305 St John's	Caulfield	29 Jun 1946
343 Chaffey	Mildura	1 Mar 1955
344 Ringwood	Ringwood	1 Mar 1955
345 Victoria Centenary	Camberwell	1 Mar 1955
375 Bendigo	Bendigo	25 Jul 1961
397 Dandenong St Paul's	Dandenong	24 Feb 1965
422 St Andrew's in Gippsland	Moe	9 Feb 1970
437 Melbourne	Melbourne	22 Feb 1972
508 Lily of the Dale	Lilydale	17 Jun 1981

1984 GREAT PRIORY OF WESTERN AUSTRALIA

The Great Priory of Western Australia was constituted in 1984 with the simultaneous transfer of the following Preceptories from the Great Priory of England

Preceptory:	Meeting in:	Date of Warrant:
167 Westralia	Perth (now Freemantle)	18 Oct 1897
215 Geraldton	Geraldton	20 Nov 1920
255 Burwell	Perth	1 Nov 1928
297 Talpioth	Northam	30 Nov 1944
302 Athlit	Nedlands	25 Mar 1946
303 Golden Cross	Boulder	26 May 1946
306 Narrogin	Narrogin	27 Dec 1946
307 Joppa	Freemantle	1 Mar 1947
311 Sanctuary	Victoria Park	20 Apr 1947
346 Talisman	Swanbourne	26 May 1955
351 Duke of Sussex	Busselton	25 Jul 1956
352 Armadale	Armadale	24 Feb 1956
356 Crusader	Morawa	30 Jan 1958
358 Ascension	Leederville	25 Jul 1958
359 Lakemba	Merredin	21 Sep 1958
386 Wongan Hills	Wongan Hills	30 Nov 1963
445 Rockingham	Rockingham	30 Aug 1973
459 Swan	Guildford	3 Apr 1975
490 West Australia Jubilee	Katanning	8 Jan 1979

1984 GREAT PRIORY OF NEW SOUTH WALES AND THE AUSTRALIAN CAPITAL TERRITORY

The Great Priory of New South Wales and the Australian Capital Territory was inaugurated in 1984 by the Great Priory of England & Wales, following agreement between Preceptories of the Provincial Grand Priory of NSW (England) and the District Grand Priory of Australia (Scotland). At Constitution the following Preceptories were transferred from the Great Priory of England:

Preceptory:	Meeting in:	Date of Warrant:
180 Broken Hill	Broken Hill	18 Oct 1904
186 Sydney	Sydney (now Willoughby)	10 Jun 1907
221 Avery	*Seaforth*	*25 Jul 1922*
249 Riverina	Wagga Wagga	25 Apr 1928
299 Newcastle	Newcastle	1 Apr 1945
317 St Swithin	*Turramurra*	*1 Mar 1948*
329 Albury	Albury	24 Aug 1949
335 St Michael	*Narrandera*	*21 Sep 1951*
337 St Paul's	*Murrumburra*	*21 Dec 1952*
362 Tamworth	Tamworth	19 Mar 1959
366 Illawarra St George	Hurstville	1 Mar 1960
368 Agnus Dei	Casino	18 Oct 1960
374 St John Canberra	Canberra	25 Jul 1961
483 Castle Hill	Castle Hill	25 May 1977

Today it contains 20 Preceptories, being seven metropolitan and 13 regional, three of which were consecrated in April 2000, April 2002 and April 2003. A number of former English preceptories (indicated by *) were, by 2014, in some form of voluntary suspension, or are 'Not Meeting', or have been erased.

1985 GREAT PRIORY OF QUEENSLAND

The Great Priory of Queensland was inaugurated on 1 June 1985 by the Great Priory of England & Wales. At Constitution four Scottish and the following thirteen Preceptories were transferred from the Great Priory of England taking precedence according to the date of their warrants:

Preceptory:	Meeting in:	Date of Warrant:
171 Duke of Albany	Brisbane	11 Jun 1900
220 North Queensland	Townville	25 Jul 1921
241 Beauceant	Toowoomba	1 May 1926
242 Carpentaria	Gordonvale	21 Dec 1926
248 Capricorn	Rockhampton	14 Feb 1928
267 Vexillum Belli	Brisbane	1 May 1930
276 Mackay	Mackay	29 Jun 1935
279 Wilde Bay	Maryborough	25 Apr 1936
372 Cooroora	Yandina	24 Feb 1961
380 Burnett	Bundaberg	19 Mar 1963
384 De Conlay	Warwick	24 Aug 1963
387 Central Highlands	Emerald	26 Dec 1963
393 Alpha	Kedron, Brisbane	25 Jul 1964

One Preceptory of the United Orders does not come under an Australian Sovereign Great Priory but remains Unattached administered directly from Mark Masons' Hall:

516 Northern Territory	Darwin, Australia	28 Jan 1982

1985 GREAT PRIORY OF NEW ZEALAND

The first 2 Preceptories were constituted in New Zealand in the closing years of the 19th century, thus pre-dating the establishment of the United Orders as a Sovereign body on 19 July 1895.

Preceptory:	Meeting in:	Date of Warrant:
142 Royal Canterbury	*Christchurch*	*20 Nov 1878*
[Removed from the Roll 1 Jan 1894]		
150 Plantagenet	*Timaru*	*22 Nov 1882*
[Removed from the Roll 1 Jan 1894]		

The Province of New Zealand was constituted until 1930 with the appointment of William Thomas Charlewood as Provincial Prior.

   The Province ceased to exist in 1958 when separate Provinces were constituted for the North and South Islands.

Province of New Zealand (North)

This Province was constituted in 1958 with the appointment of Norman Berridge Spencer, *MSM* as Provincial Prior.

Preceptory:	Meeting in:	Date of Warrant:
254 Waitemata	Auckland	1 Nov 1928

285 St George	Auckland	23 Apr 1938
287 Royal Taranaki	Taranaki, NZ	21 Sep 1938
291 Aotea	Taranaki, NZ	24 Aug 1942
363 Preceptory of St John	Auckland	1 Nov 1959
435 Tamehana	Matamata	23 Aug 1971

Province of New Zealand (South)
This Province was constituted in 1958 with the appointment of Ernest Julius Woolf as Provincial Prior

Preceptory:	Meeting in:	Date of Warrant:
246 Royal Canterbury	Christchurch	15 Jul 1927
342 Tuarangi	Ashburton	24 Feb 1955
353 Amuri	Amberley	21 Dec 1956
355 Aurora	St Andrews	25 Jul 1957

The Provinces of New Zealand (North) and New Zealand (South) nominally ceased to exist in 1983 with the constitution of a sovereign United Great Priory of New Zealand but the new Great Priory adopted essentially the same structure with separate provinces for North and South Islands and transfer of all the former United Orders Preceptories.

THE NETHERLANDS
Olivier-de-la-Marche Preceptory No 417 was constituted at Leiden, the first in Holland in 1969; others followed and in 1983 Henri Anton van den Akker was appointed Provincial Prior for the Netherlands .

The Province ceased to exist on 23 November 2013 when The Great Priory of The Netherlands was inaugurated, at which time the following Preceptories were transferred:

Preceptory:	Meeting in:	Date of Warrant:
417 Olivier-de-la-Marche	Leiden	20 Jun 1969
486 St George's	Eindhoven	10 Feb 1978
503 St Bernard de Clairvaux	Terneuzen	18 Mar 1981
504 St Peter's	Leiden	20 Mar 1981
505 St Maartens	Gronigen	20 Mar 1981
533 Toison d'Or	Zaandam	2 Feb 1985
540 St Michael	Bilthoven	3 Sep 1986
548 Taciturnus	The Hague	22 Feb 1988
593 The Netherlands Bodyguard	Leiden	22 Oct 1994
599 Saint Romain Preceptory of Installed Preceptors	Bilthoven	22 Sep 1995
659 Graaf Otto Van Gelre	Velp	18 Nov 2006
687 Hertog Valram van Limburg	Herkebbosch	19 Nov 2011

APPENDIX P

EXCHANGE OF REPRESENTATIVES

It is the normal custom to exchange representatives with other Sovereign Great Priories and similar Grand bodies with responsibilities for Knight Templar and Knight of Malta degrees, and in order of the date of the original recognition or inauguration, representatives are or have been exchanged with the following Sovereign Grand Bodies:

[1760]   Grand Lodge of Sweden

[1770]   Grosse Landesloge Der Freimaurer Von Deutschland

[1778]   Great Priory of Ireland

[1811]   Great Priory of Scotland

[1814]   Grand Lodge of Norway

[1816]   Grand Encampment of the United States of America

[1853]   Danish Order of Freemasons Grand Lodge of Denmark

[1876]   Grande Prieuré Independend D'Helvétie (Founded 1779)

[1881]   Grand Lodge of Iceland, The Icelandic Order of Freemasons

[1883]   Great Priory of Canada

[1981]   Great Priory of Greece

[1982]   Great Priory of Germany

[1982]   Great Priory of South Australia
         [Recognition withdrawn 20 May 2015]

[1982]   Great Priory of Victoria, Australia

[1984]   United Great Priory of New Zealand

[1984]   Great Priory of New South Wales and Australian Capital Territory

[1984]   Great Priory of Western Australia

[1985]   Great Priory of Queensland
         [Recognition withdrawn 20 May 2015]

[1985]   Great Priory of Finland

[1986]   Grande Prieuré de Belgique

[1994]   Great Priory of Spain

[1995]   Great Priory of Lusitania

[1999]   Grande Prieuré du Togo

[2002]   Grande Prieuré Rectifié de France (CBCS)

[2003]   Grande Prieuré des Ordres Unis Pour La France

[2008]   Great Priory of Brazil

[2013]   Great Priory of The Netherlands

[2013]   Great Priory of Portugal

[2014]   Gran Priorato D'Italia

[2014]   Great Priory of Peru

[2015]   Great Priory of Benin

SELECT BIBLIOGRAPHY

Addison, C. G., *The History of the Knights Templar* (G. J. Palmer, Savoy Street, Strand, London: 1842), p.6, citing the document *De Aedificiis* by the 5th century Byzantine historian Procopius of Caesarea as '*Procopius de Oedificiis Justiniani*, Lib. 5'. and pp.4-5, citing a Vatican document by Pope Urban IV (Jacques Pantaleon, 1195-1264), Latin Patriarch of Jerusalem, as '*Pantaleon, Lib.* iii, p.82'.

Barber, M. & Bate, K., *The Templars:* Selected Sources, Manchester University Press (2002)

Broadley, A. M. *The History of Freemasonry in the District of Malta,* London, George Kenning (1880)

Campbell, D. G., *Committee on Ritual, Handbook for Candidate's Coaches,* Grand Lodge of Free and Accepted Masons, California (2007), "*The Master Mason: Irregular and Clandestine Lodges*".

Carlile, R., *Manual of Masonry* (The Republican, 1825) and subsequent published editions *Manual of Freemasonry* (Reeves and Turner, London)

Chaucer, G., *The Canterbury Tales* (Middle English: Tales of Caunterbury) (1387-1400) (ISBN-13: 9780679601258)

Chilvers, R. W., *Melita Preceptory and Priory – The Shadows of Truths Suspected (A Celebration of more than 200 years of Masonic Templary under the Banner of Melita Preceptory and Priory* (Privately Printed for Melita Preceptory No. 37, Cheshunt, 2015)

Chudley, R., *Thomas Dunckerley, A Remarkable Freemason,* (London, Lewis Masonic 1982) ISBN 0853181292

Collier's Encyclopedia, Thomson Gale (1985), 1985 Edition, Macmillan Library Reference (1990), '*Knights Templars*'.

Collins, R., *The history and working of British C.B.C.S. ... and the Consecration on May 1, 2007, of St James Lodge of St Andrew No. 2.* (The Square September 2007)

Cooley, R. & Knowles, M. *The Priestly Order, The History of the Order of The Holy Royal Arch Knight Templar Priests* (York, The Grand College, 2009 Edition)

Cryer, The Revd N. B., *The Arch and the Rainbow*, Ian Allan Regalia, Surrey 1996), (ISBN: 9780853182115)

de Villehardouin, Geoffrey, *Memoirs or Chronicle of The Fourth Crusade and The Conquest of Constantinople*, [trans. Frank T. Marzials] (London: J. M Dent, 1908)

Dollinger, P., *The German Hansa*. Translated and edited by D. S. Ault and S. H. Steinberg. Stanford: Stanford University Press, 1970. (ISBN, 0804707421, 9780804707428.)

Frale, Barbara, The Chinon Chart: Papal Absolution to the last Templar, Master Jacques de Molay, Journal of Medieval History, 30 (2004)

Gould, R. F., *Military Lodges. The Apron and the Sword*: or, *Freemasonry under Arms*. Being an account of lodges in regiments and ships of war, etc. (London: Gale & Polden, 1899).

Hamill, J. & Gilbert, R., *Freemasonry*, AQC (2004), Glossary, p.247.

Hughan, W. J., *The Old Charges of British Freemasons* (London, Simkin, Marshall & Co 1872)

Hughan, W. J., '*Origin of Masonic Knight Templary in the United Kingdom*' AQC 18 (1905)

Jenkyns, S. Michael, *History of British and Colonial Regiments and their Military Lodges* (Col By Council, Allied Masonic Degrees, Canada, (Ottawa, 1977) [UGLE Library A175 JEN 1]

Josephus, Titus Flavius, *Jewish War, Rome (78 AD); Translation by William Whiston (1736), Loeb Classical Library (*1926), Volume II, Book 5, pp.212, 217.

Kahler, Lisa, *Freemasonry in Edinburgh*, 1721-1746, St Andrews University, Unpublished. PhD Dissertation (1998)

Laidler, Keith, *The Head of God: The Lost Treasure of the Templars*, 1st Edition, Weidenfeld & Nicolson, London (1998), p.177.

Le Strange, H., *History of Freemasonry in Norwich 1724-1895*, (Agas H. Goose, Norwich, 1896)

Lloyd, T. H., *England and the German Hanse, 1157-1611.* Cambridge University Press, 1991)

Lonnqvist, Minna and Kenneth, *Archaeology of the Hidden Qumran: The New Paradigm*, Helsinki University Press, Helsinki (2002).

Maidment, James (Ed), *Templaria* Papers relative to the History, Privileges, and Possessions of SCOTTISH KNIGHTS TEMPLARS and their Successors, the Knights of St John of Jerusalem &c (1828-29) [Copy Privately printed for George Stirling, Lord Drummond of Blair &c (1870) in Library of KT Priory of West Yorkshire]

Mandleberg, C. John, *Ancient and Accepted: The First One Hundred Years of the Supreme Council 33 Degrees for England and Wales, 1845-1945*, (QCCC, London, 1 July 1995) ISBN-10: 0907655297 ISBN-13: 9780907655299

Mandleberg, C. John, and Davies, L. W., *Royal Arch Masons & Knights Templar at Redruth, Cornwall, 1791-1828*, QCCC Ltd. (Hamilton House Publishing}, (2005).

Mandleberg, C. John, *Morton Edwards, Sculptor, and the Honourable Society of Royal Ark Mariners*, Mark Masons Hall Ltd. (2012)

Marcombe, David, *Leper Knights.* (2003, Woodbridge: Boydell Press.) p. 34. ISBN 1843830671.

Mathie, Dr A. G., *The Provincial Priory of Cheshire (1850-2000)* (privately printed for The Province 2001),

Meyers, Eric, *The Oxford Encyclopedia of Archaeology in the Near East*, Oxford University Press, Oxford (1997), Vol.2, pp.268-269.

Nicholson, Helen J., *The Knights Templar on Trial*, (The History Press, The Mill, Brimscombe Port, Stroud, Gloucestershire GL5 2QG, 2009) App. 1 205–217. ISBN 9780750946810.

Nicholson, Helen, J., *The Knights Templar: A new history*. (Phoenix Mill Thrupp, Stroud, Gloucestershire UK: Sutton Publishing Limited, 2001) pp. 12, 191-92. ISBN 0750925175.

Nicholson, Helen, J., *The Crusades*. (Greenwood Publishing Group. ISBN 9780313326851, 2004)

Powell, Arthur C. and Littleton, Joseph, *A History of Freemasonry in Bristol*, Provincial Grand Lodge, Bristol (Bennett Brothers Ltd. Bristol,1910)

Price, B. W., *Metamorphosis, The Evolution of Price Edward Council 'G'* (Ripon, Privately Printed for the Bi-Centenary of the Council 2003)

Read, Piers Paul, *The Templars: The Dramatic History of the Knights Templar, the Most Powerful Military Order of the Crusades*, (2006 Edition Perseus Books Group (first published 1999) ISBN 030681496X (ISBN13: 9780306814969)

Rengstorf, Karl Heinrich, *Hirbet Qumran and the Problem of the Library of the Dead Sea Caves*, German edition (1960), Translated by J. R Wilkie, Leiden Press, Brill (1963).

Renwick, E. D*., A Short History of the Order of St John*, (St. John's Gate, 1958) (6th Ed. 1971).

Runciman, Stephen, *A History of the Crusades, Vol. III, the Kingdom of Acre*, (Cambridge University Press, 1951, reprinted 1988)

Schildhauer, J., *The Hansa: History and Culture*. Translated by Katherine Vanovitch. (New York: Dorset Press, 1988)

Schuchard, M. K., *Secret Agent on Earth and in Heaven*, (Brill, Leidon, 2012)

Seward, D., *Monks of War, The Military Orders* (Eyre Methuen, 1972) (2000, The Folio Society)

Sharpe, P. R., *A Short History Of The Armed Forces And Masonry*, (Website of the Circuit of Service Lodges retrieved 22 Aug 2018)

Sire, H. J. A., The Knights of Malta, p.25 (Yale University Press, New Haven & London, 1993)

Smyth, Frederick H., *Brethren in Chivalry, 1791-1991* (Lewis Masonic, London, 1991) ISBN 0853181810

Sommers, S. M., *Thomas Dunckerley and English Freemasonry* (London, Pickering & Chatto, 2021)

Stevenson, D., *The Origins of Freemasonry Scotland's century (159-1710)* (Cambridge University Press, 1988)

Swinson, Arthur, *A Register of the Regiments and Corps of the British Army*. (London: The Archive Press,1972) ISBN 0855910003.

Theodoric, *Description of The Holy Places. (Circa 1172 AD)* (Trans. Aubrey Stewart,) (Published for Palestine Pilgrims' Text Society, London 1891)

Thorp, J. T., *French Prisoners Lodges* (Gibbons, Leicester, 1900)

Tunbridge, P., The Climate of European Freemasonry 1730 to 1750, AQC 81(1968),88-128.

Unidentified French author, *De la Maçonnerie Parmi Les Chretiens* ('*On Masonry Among Christians*'), Germany (ca. 1750), quoting the 12th century Italian Abbot Joachim of Flora (Calabria), a friend of Richard the Lionheart, in: Frank Sanello, *The Knights Templars: God's Warriors, the Devil's Bankers,* Taylor Trade Publishing, Oxford (2003), p.223.

Urban, W., *The Prussian Crusade*. London: University Press of America, Inc., 1980.

Urban, W., *The Teutonic Knights and Baltic Chivalry*. Historian 57 (Summer 1995)

Wickes, H. L., *Regiments of Foot: A History of the Foot Regiments of the British Army.* (Reading, Berkshire: Osprey Publishing,1974). ISBN 0850452201.

William, Archbishop of Tyre, '*A History of Deeds Done Beyond the Sea*' (Emily Atwater Babcock and August C. Krey, trans.,) (Columbia University Press, 1943)

Wolfram, R., *The Weapon Dances of Europe*. (University of Illinois Press on behalf of Society for Ethnomusicology: Ethnomusicology. Vol 6, No. 3 (September 1962). 186–87. ISSN 00318299

Wise, T., *The Knights of Christ*. (Osprey Men-At-Arms Series. London: Osprey Publishing Ltd, 1984)

Yarker, John, *The Arcane Schools*, Manchester (1909), pp.341-342.

General Sources
United Orders, *The Statutes for the Government of the United Religious, Military and Masonic Orders of the Temple and of St John of Jerusalem, Palestine, Rhodes and Malta in England and Wales and Provinces Overseas. (Liber Ordinis Templi, Mark Masons' Hall,* Various Editions 1900-2018).

The web sites of the British Army Regiments cited in the text.

A number of Provincial Priory Histories and Web Sites where these exist.

Lane, J. *Masonic Records 1717-1894* (London: Freemasons' Hall, 1895)

ENDNOTES

[1]   Smyth, Frederick H., *Brethren in Chivalry*, 1791-1991 (Lewis Masonic, London, 1991).

[2]   Renwick, E. D., *A Short History of the Order of St John*, p. 7. (6th Edition, 1971).

[3]   Allegedly the oldest public house in England, believed to have been founded in Nottingham, around 1068 when Nottingham Castle was built, is named '*Ye Olde Trip To Jerusalem*' as many pilgrims and crusaders reputedly rested there on their way to Jerusalem.

[4]   Seward, D. *Monks of War, The Military Orders*, 15 quotes a document of 1123 which refers to Hugues as 'master of the Knights of the Temple'.

[5]   Theodoric, *Description of The Holy Places*. Indeed Theodoric, a German Monk visiting the Holy Land in 1171-73 wrote 'This building ... has passed into the hands of the Knights Templars, who ... have below them stables which ... according to our reckoning, could take in ten thousand horses with their grooms.

[6]   It is recorded that, in 1123, Hugh of Champagne attended the Lateran Council opened by Pope Callistus II, a known advocate of the Knights Templar.

[7]   This word used also for a piebald horse was later found used for a battle-standard – for example the red '*baucents*' of the Brittany pirates.

[8]   The following year, Matilda of Boulogne, the wife of King Stephen of England, (not King Stephen's rival claimant, the 'Empress' Matilda) gave the Templars the Manors of Cressing, Essex and Cowley, Oxfordshire.

[9]   They were named 'The Evil Neighbour' and 'God's Own Sling'.

[10] They included two great catapults, the 'Victorious' and the 'Furious'.

[11] Runciman, Stephen, *A History of the Crusades*, Vol. III, the Kingdom of Acre, (Cambridge University Press, 1951, reprinted 1988), p.423.

[12] Sire, H. J. A., *The Knights of Malta*, (Yale University Press, New Haven & London, 1993), 25

[13] According to the account written by John of St Victor; there are conflicting accounts of this meeting.

[14] '*De Unione Templi et Hospitalis Ordinum ad Clementem Papam Jacobi de Molayo Relatio*'

[15] Baigent, M. & Leigh, R. *The Temple and the Lodge*, Guild Publishing (Jonathan Cape Ltd), London 1989, p.65

[16] *Ibid*. p.67.

[17] *Ibid, passim*. The enterprising Scots have taken full advantage of the publicity given to this discovery by Baigent et al. and the churchyard and its surrounds to which many of these tombstones have been brought together to form what is now virtually a 'theme park' with souvenirs on sale at 'tourist' prices. A similar lesser collection on the further bank of the sea-loch can be viewed without such distractions.

[18] *The Conquest of Lisbon: De Expugnatione Lyxbonensi* (New York: University of Columbia Press), (2nd ed) (A supposed eyewitness account by Osbernus).

[19] Christiansen, Eric, *The Northern Crusades*. (London: Penguin Books, 1997) (ISBN 0140266534.), 287.

[20] Fletcher, R. A., '*Reconquest and Crusade in Spain c.1050-1150*', Transactions of the Royal Historical Society (1987), 31-47.

[21] Riley-Smith, Jonathan, *The Crusades: A History*. (Continuum International Publishing Group, 2005) ISBN 0826472699., 161.

[22] Power, Daniel, Who Went on the Albigensian Crusade? (*The English Historical Review*, Vol. 128, Issue 534, October 2013), 1047-1085.

23 Christiansen, Eric, The Northern Crusades (London: Macmillan, 1997) (2nd Ed).
24 Pope Callixtus III, *Bulla Turcorum*, 20 June 1456 [*Cum hiis superioribus annis* announces the Fall of Constantinople and seeks funding for another crusade against the Turks].
25 Pope Martin V, *Sane charissimus*, 4 April 1418 issued after the seizure of Ceuta calling on all to support John I of Portugal in his war against the Moors.
26 Pope Clement V Bull, *Ad Providam*, dated 3 May 1312, granted all of the Order's lands and wealth to the Hospitallers 'so that its original purpose could be met'.
27 Nicholson, Helen J., *The Knights Templar on Trial*, App 2, 218-249.
28 Nicholson, Helen J., *The Knights Templar: A new history*. pp. 12, 191-92.
29 Haagensen, Erling and Lincoln, Henry, *The Templars Secret Island* (Cassels & Co, London, 2000) ISBN 1841881902.
30 '*Switzerland*'. Encyclopaedia Britannica. 26. 1911. p. 247. Retrieved 14 Nov 2014.
31 Nicholson, Helen, J., *The Knights Templar on Trial*, App1, 205-217.
32 Frale, Barbara, *The Chinon Chart: Papal Absolution to the last Templar, Master Jacques de Molay*, Journal of Medieval History, 30(2004), 127
33 d' Aigrefeuille, Charles, *Histoire de la ville de Montpellier*, Volume 2, p. 193 (Montpellier: J. Martel, 1737-1739).
34 *Processus Contra Templarios, Exemplaria Praetiosa*, published on 25 October 2007.
35 The preliminary work by W. Bro. David Peck of Quatuor Coronati Lodge, No. 2076 during a recent visit to Malta is gratefully acknowledged.
36 Pope Clement V Bull, *Vox in excelso.*
37 Nicholson, Helen, J., *The Crusades*. p. 98.
38 Pope John XXII Bull *Ad ea ex quibus* (1319) Created Portuguese Order of Christ. (*Ordem dos Cavaleiros de Nosso Senhor Jesus Cristo*).
39 Paine, L., *The Sea and Civilization: A Maritime History of the World*. (New York: Random House, LLC, 2013), 316-38.
40 Pope Nicholas V, Bull to Alfonso V for all conquests in Africa with authorisation to build churches and extended Portuguese dominion over all the seas from Africa to India. That Bull (*Romanus Pontifex* 4 Jan 1455) granted the Portuguese perpetual monopoly in trade with Africa also allowing enslavement of natives. Pope Calixtus III (Bull *Inter Caetera*, 13 Mar 1456) confirmed the earlier Bull and gave the Order of Christ the spiritualities of all lands acquired and to be acquired.
41 Frale, Barbara, '*The Chinon Chart: Papal Absolution to the last Templar, Master Jacques de Molay*', Journal of Medieval History, 30 (2004), 127.
42 Franson, Jennifer M., Essay Sep 2000 quoting from Dollinger, Philippe, *The German Hansa*, translated and edited by D. S. Ault and S. H. Steinberg, Stanford, Stanford University Press (1970); Lloyd, T. H. *England and the German Hansa 1157-1611*, Cambridge University Press, 1991; Schildhauer, Johannes, *The Hansa: History and Culture*, translated by Katherine Vanovitch, New York, Dorset Press 1988; Urban, William, *The Prussian Crusade*, London University Press of America, Inc. 1980; Urban, William. *The Teutonic Knights and Baltic Chivalry*, Historian 57 (Summer 1995), 519-530; Wise, Terrance, *The Knights of Christ*, Osprey Men-at-Arms Series, London, Osprey Publishing Ltd. 1994.
43 Von der Porten, Edward, 1994. *Hanseatic League: Europe's First Common Market*. National Geographic Magazine. (October 1994) No: 05953. Retrieved 12 June 2018.
44 Chilvers, R. W., *Melita Preceptory and Priory – The Shadows of Truths Suspected, 2*
45 Inquisitor for Malta (1706-11) and records held in the Archives of the Metropolitan Cathedral of Mdina, Malta concerning *The Ordre du Temple /Society d'Aloyeau.*

[46] Cavaliero, R., *The Last of the Crusaders: The Knights of St John and Malta in the Eighteenth Century* (Hollis and Carter, 1960), 72.

[47] Library and Museum of Freemasonry, UGLE SN 1136 contains the annual returns up to 1792.

[48] Broadley, A. M., *History of Freemasonry in The District of Malta* (London, Kenning, 1880), 5.

[49] *Ordem Militar de Cristo*, previously the Order of the Knights of Our Lord Jesus Christ (*Ordem dos Cavaleirros de Nosso Senhor Jesus Cristo*).

[50] Maidment, James (Ed), Templaria Papers relative to the History, Privileges, and Possessions of Scottish Knights Templars.

[51] [Author's Note: Part of the briefing by tour guides given today to tourists visiting the tomb of Tsar Paul I includes his acceptance of this Grand Mastership.]

[52] Seward, D., *Monks of War, The Military Orders* (2000, The Folio Society, revised Ed.), 286.

[53] *Associazione dei cavalieri italiani del sovrano militare ordine di Malta*, ACISMOM (www.orderofstjohn.org)

[54] *Corpo Militare dell'Esercito dell'ACISMOM* (Army Military Corps of the ACISMOM),

[55] www.johanniter.org

[56] www.johanniter.nl

[57] www.johanniterorden.se

[58] Savona-Ventura, Charles (2014). *The History of the Order of Saint Lazarus of Jerusalem*. New York: Nova Publishers.

[59] Giovanni Lami (1697-1770) was an Italian jurist, Church historian, and antiquarian.

[60] Sanctioned by the Papal Bulls: *Valdarno* (Anastasius IV of 1154), *Valdinievole* (Alexander III of 1169), and *Pistoia and Prato* (Innocent III of 1198).

[61] Harwood, W. S., *Secret Societies in America*, New American Review 164 (May 1897), 617-624.

[62] Gist, N. P., *Culture Patterning in Secret Society Ceremonials*, Social Forces 14 (May 1936), 497-505.

[63] Merz, C., *Sweet Land of Secrecy: The Strange Spectacle of American Fraternalism* The Harper's Magazine 154 (1927), 329-34.

[64] Stevens, A. C., *Fraternal Insurance (1900) Review of Reviews 21 (1900).*

[65] Knoop, Jones, and Hamer (Ed), *The Two Earliest Masonic MSS* (2nd Edition 1938) The instruction is quite specific in providing a bridge from the recognised religious framework to a more generalised one: '*Let a man's religion or mode of worship be what it may, he is not excluded from the order, provided he believe in the glorious architect of heaven and earth and practice the sacred duties of morality.*' Equally specific in the Regius MS is the link to charity as it closes with the words: "Amen! Amen! So mote it be, So say we all for charity".'

[66] Batham, C. N., *The Grand Lodge of England According to the Old Institutions*, Prestonian Lecture 1981, 61 records that, after The Union in 1813, The Antients regarded ''Omitting to read the Ancient Charges to Initiates .... as another landmark that was being violated'.

[67] Marcombe. David, *Leper Knights*. (2003, Woodbridge: Boydell Press.) p. 34.

[68] Hughan, W. J., *The Old Charges of British Freemasons,* 6 records. Some of the Masonic 'Old Charges' discovered in later years were found in Pontefract Castle in Yorkshire. [Author's Note: Later evidence suggests these may have reached there through descendants of the Townley family of Burnley where Christopher Townley ('the Transcriber'), known to have had an interest in such documents, was active in the 17th century.]

[69] In Rastel's Chronicle, I. vi. under the life of Edward III is the following curious passage: 'About the 19 yere [sic] of this kinge, he made a solempne feest at Wyndesore, and a greate justes and turnament, where he devysed, and perfyted substanegally, the order of the knyghtes of the garter; howe be it some afferme that this order began fyrst by kynge Rycharde, Cure de Lyon, at the sege of the citye of Acre; where, in his great necessyte, there were but 26 knyghtes that fyrmely and surely abode by the kynge; where he caused all them to were thonges of blew leyther about theyr legges. And afterwarde they were called the knyghtes of the blew thonge.' I am obliged for this passage to John Fenn, Esq; a curious and ingenious gentleman of East-Dereham, in Norfolk, who is in possession of the most rare book whence it is taken. Hence some affirm, that the origin of the garter is to be dated from Richard I and that it owes its pomp and splendour to Edward III.

[70] Another popular legend, with perhaps less of a pedigree, involves the 'Countess of Salisbury', whose garter is said to have slipped from her leg while she was dancing at a court ball at Calais. When the surrounding courtiers sniggered, the king picked it up and returned it to her, exclaiming, *'Honi soit qui mal y pense!'* ('Shame on him who thinks ill of it!'), the phrase now regarded as the motto of the Order.

[71] Florescu, Radu, and Raymond McNally, *Dracula: Prince of Many Faces, His Life and His Times*. (Boston, Little Brown, 1989 ISBN 0316286567), 40-42.

[72] Hugh, Chisholm, Encyclopaedia *Britannica*. 5 (11th ed.). Cambridge University Press.

[73] Charles XIII & II also Carl, Swedish: *Karl* XIII (7 October 1748-5 February 1818), was King of Sweden (as Charles XIII) from 1809. and King of Norway (as Charles II) from 1814 until his death.

[74] See Chapter 2.11.

[75] Pope Gregory IX (Bull 13 Apr 1231 *Parens scientiarum* 'The Mother of Sciences') guarantees the independence of the University of Paris.

[76] Theodoric, *Description of The Holy Places* (c.1172AD) (Trans Aubrey Stewart,) (Published for Palestine Pilgrims'Text Society, London 1891), 59-60

[77] The single extant manuscript of the Song of Roland in Old Anglo-Norman French, is in the Bodleian Library at Oxford. This copy dates between 1129 and 1165. Eight further manuscripts, and three fragments of other poems, exist on the same subject.

[78] Gaunt, Simon and Pratt, Karen (Trans), *The Song of Roland, and Other Poems of Charlemagne* (1st Ed) (2016) New York, USA, Oxford University Press ISBN 9780199655540.

[79] Young, K., *The Drama of the Medieval Church* (2 vol., 1933); and anthologies by Pollard, A. W. (Ed) (8th ed. 1927) and Hopper, V. F. and Lahey, G. B.(1962).

[80] Cryer, The Revd N. Barker, *Drama and the Craft*, The Prestonian Lecture 1974 (AQC 87(1974),76.

[81] Pearson, A. H., *The Sarum Missal, in English*, Ed.2 (1884, Oxford University Press) As an example, an early text, still extant, refers to the 3rd century martyrdom of St Lawrence, in the Sarum Missal, or *Sarum Use* introduced to England by St Osmund, a Norman nobleman, appointed in 1078, by William of Normandy, as Bishop of Salisbury (the modern name of the city known in Latin as *Sarum*). *The Sarum Use* was later translated into English and appeared in York area late in the 13th C, and the St Lawrence story is the base for one of today's Masonic degrees.

[82] Wolfram, R., *The Weapon Dances of Europe*. (University of Illinois Press on behalf of Society for Ethnomusicology: Ethnomusicology. Vol 6, No. 3 (September 1962). 186-87.

[83] Cawte, E. C., The Morris Dance in Hereford, Shropshire and Worcestershire/ Journal of the English Folk Dance and Song Society. 9 (4)(1963), 197-212.

[84] Chaucer, Geoffrey, *Canterbury Tales*, 'General Prologue' II 43-6, 51-4. This likely reflects the participation by Henry, Earl of Derby (son of Chaucer's patron John of Gaunt) in the years of 1390-1391 and 1392-1393.

[85] Young, K., *The Drama of the Medieval Church* (2 vol. 1933): and anthologies by Pollard, A. W. (Ed) (8th ed. 1927) and Hopper, V. F. and Jahey, G. B.(1962).

[86] Ward, A. W., *A History of English Dramatic Literature...*, I (Macmillan & Co, London, 1899); quoted by Warren, K. M. (1911) Moralities. In The Catholic Encyclopedia. (New York: Robert Appleton Co.) A Morality has been defined by Dr. Ward as 'a play enforcing a moral truth or lesson by means of the speech and action of characters which are personified abstractions – figures representing vices and virtues, qualities of the human mind, or abstract conceptions in general'.

[87] Cameron, Charles, '*On the Origin and Progress of Chivalric Freemasonry in the British Isles*', AQC, 13 (1900), 167.

[88] Crowe, Frederick J. W., AQC 24(1911), 185-198.

[89] The cipher is derived from divisions of the Templar Cross somewhat in the same manner as the 'Mark' cipher is derived from a blank 'noughts and crosses' layout.

[90] A number of scholars have claimed that the codex, once deciphered, appears to be a more modern, scholarly Latin, and not ecclesiastical Latin used during the period of its supposed origin. Although this would not confirm it as a total forgery it would suggest later adaptation, amendment, or embellishment sometime between 1314 and 1804.

[91] According to Mackey's *Lexicon of Freemasonry* The Charter records the Grand Masters by date of accession: from 1313, John Mark Larmenius; 1324, Francis Thomas Theobald (Alexandrinus); 1340, Arnold de Braque; 1349, John de Claremont; 1357, Bertrand du Guesclin; 1381, John Arminiacus; 1392, Bernard Arminiacus; 1419, John Arminiacus; 1451, John de Croy; 1472, Bernard Imbault; 1478, Robert Lenoncourt; 1497, Galeatius de Salazar; 1516, Philip Chabot; 1544, Gaspard de Galtiaco Tavanensis; 1574, Henry de Montmorency; 1615, Charles de Valois; 1651, James Ruxellius de Granceio; 1681, James Henry, Duc de Duras; 1705, Philip, Duke of Orleans; 1724, Louis Augustus Bourbon; 1737, Louis Henry Bourbon Conde; 1741, Louis Francis Bourbon Conty; 1776, Louis Hercules Timoleon, Due de Cosse Brissac; 1792, Claude M. R. Chevillon; and 1804, Bernard Raymund Fabre Palaprat.

[92] See Chapter 2.6 – Joint Author of *Magna Carta*

[93] Gould, R. F., *History of Freemasonry*, Vol II, (Edinburgh, Grange Publishing), 140.

[94] Yarker, J., AQC 1 (1886-88), 100, 151.

[95] Preston, Peter O., (Unpublished notes compiled when Vice-Chancellor, Province of North and East Yorkshire, United Orders, York, 1997).

[96] Gould, R. F., *English Freemasonry before the Era of Grand Lodges*, AQC1 (1886), 70.

[97] Stevenson, D., *The Origins of Freemasonry, Scotland's Century 1590-1710*, Cambridge, Cambridge University Press (1988), 225.

[98] Hughan, W. J., *Masonic Sketches and Reprints*, Part II, 14.

[99] Stevenson, D., *The Origins of Freemasonry*, Scotland's Century 1590-1710, 225

[100] Lane, Masonic Records No, 161 notes: Dates from about 1717. Has Minutes of 1725.

[101] For details of the long connection between Scotland and Bordeaux see Murdock, Steve 'The French Connection: Bordeaux's "Scottish" networks in context, c.1670-1720' in Gilles – Leydier (ed.) *Scotland and Europe, Scotland in Europe* (Cambridge: Cambridge Scholars Publishing, 2007).

[102] Tunbridge, P., *The Climate of European Freemasonry 1730 to 1750*, AQC 81(1968), 88-128.

[103] Earlier confusing examples exist: such as: The Venerable Bede (673-735 AD) uses the term *Scottorum nationem* (word-for-word: Scots nation) to refer to the people from Ireland who settled on part of the Pictish lands ('*Scottorum nationem in Pictorum parte recipit*'). This can be interpreted as the arrival of the people called Gaels in the kingdom of Dal Riada on the west coast of Scotland.

[104] Stevenson, D., *The First Freemasons: Scotland's Early Lodges and Their Members* (Aberdeen, 1988).

[105] Powell, C., AQC 49(1939), 160 and quoted by Ward, E., AQC 75 (1962), 131-132.

[106] The Auxiliaries were quartered in Cambrai on the lands owned by François Salignac de la Mothe-Fénelon, Archbishop of Cambrai (1651-1715) and circumstantial evidence suggests it was around 1707 that Ramsay and Fenelon became acquainted. On leaving the army Ramsay travelled to France and resided with Fénelon until his death in 1715 and during which period Ramsay was converted by him to Roman Catholicism.

[107] See Fresh evidence on the early life of Chevalier Andrew Michael Ramsay, AQC 131 (2018), 309-318.

[108] Fleury's disapproval cannot have been on account of the Papal Bull *In Eminenti*, because this was not published until 28 April 1738.

[109] Bodleian Library Carte MSS 226, f.419.

[110] Brodsky, Michel, *Les Mythes et les legendes de las Grande Loge d'Angleterre*, Renaissaance Traditionelle, No. 129, (January 2003), 133.

[111] Lasislas de Malczovich considered that Ramsay 'established three degrees, viz. (1) Ecossais; (2) Novice; (3) Knight Templar' (AQC 5 (1892), 187 but he adds nothing to support this statement, which is generally disregarded.

[112] Gould, R. F., *History of Freemasonry throughout the World* (Vol 4), 321.

[113] Vatcher, S., *A Lodge of Irishmen at Lisbon*, 1738, AQC 84 (1971), 88 (and Ferrer Benimeli, José Antonio, *Masoneria, Inglesia e Illustracion*, Madrid, 1982, Vol II, 440-468, App. 45 X.).

[114] Baron von Hund asserts in his diary, which may be considered as good as the evidence in the diary of Elias Ashmole, that he received the Templar degrees from the hands of the Grand Master of Scotland in 1743.

[115] It is posible Lord Kilmarnock had a political motive for promoting a Templar Rite, as an instrument working on behalf of the exiled House of Stuart; certainly later events bear this out and Lord Kilmarnock was beheaded in 1746 on Tower Hill, London, for his part in the Jacobite uprising. It is, however, probable that von Hund know nothing of this and naively took the Templar background at face value.

[116] Kahler, Lisa, *Freemasonry in Edinburgh 1721-1746*, St Andrews University, unpublished. PhD Dissertation (1988) 207-14.

[117] Schuchard, M. K., *Secret Agent on Earth and in Heaven* (Brill, Leidon, 2012), 396-397 records 'On 30 Sep 1745, the Duke of Perth wrote to David, Lord Ogilvy with an account of the admission of Prince Charles Edward Stuart as a Knight Templar.

[118] Bushnell, N. S., *William Hamilton of Bangour, Poet and Jacobite*, (Aberdeen, Aberdeeen UP, 1957) 72, 81-83.

[119] Hughan, W. J., '*Origin of Masonic Knight Templary in the United Kingdom*' AQC 18 (1905)., 91 Also Yarker, J., *The Arcane Schools*, 435.

[120] Gould, R. F., *Military Lodges*, (London: Gale and Polden,)(1899), 130.

[121] See, for example, Gould, R. F., *Military Lodges*, 130, 153.

[122] National Archives Records – *Registers of Prisoners of War 1755-1831*, (ADM 103).

[123] de Malezovich, L., *The Earlier History of Masonry in Austria and Hungary* (AQC, vol. v).

[124] Hughan, W. J., *Unpublished Records of the Craft*, (Kenning, 1871), Part II, pp.16-17.

[125] Ward, Eric, AQC 71(1958), 32.

[126] It is interesting to find that an engraved plate of 1785 made for his Rite by de Lintot (who was by trade an engraver) was adopted, with certain adjustments, by Dunckerley for use on Knights Templar Certificates when the Grand Conclave was established in 1791. It remained in use for many years, and appears to this day (1991) on the Summonses of the Royal Kent Preceptory No. 20, constituted in 1812 at Newcastle-upon-Tyne.

[127] Gould, R. F., *History of Freemasonry*, Chap XVIII, 418 quotes names as Bros. Du Fresne, Le Pettier, Julian Vilfort, Pierre Le Villaine, Louis Brusle, and Francis Le Grand.

[128] Jackson, A. C. F., A. & A. R., *The Intermediate Degrees* (Matthews, Drew & Shelbourne, London 1982), 35.

[129] Cameron, Sir. Charles, AQC 13 (1900), 157.

[130] Turnbull, E. R. and Denslow, R. V., *A History of Royal Arch Masonry* (1956) [UGLE lib].

[131] The Lodge No. 58 in the 14th Regiment of Foot (it appears to have had no other name), Warranted on 17 January 1759, had been posted to St Augustine's, Florida by March 1776. Its Warrant was renewed in 1777. It appears to have ceased to exist by 1804. ('Lane's List' p.78.)

[132] That Lodge, a revival of an earlier Lodge of the same name, survives by amalgamation within today's The Royal Sussex Lodge of Hospitality No. 187 dated from 1796.

[133] Berman, R. A., *Over the Hills and Far Away – Irish and Antients Freemasonry in Middle America*, AQC 132 (2019).

[134] For readers less familiar with Masonic terminology it is worth mentioning that such lodges were generally warranted under the Irish Constitution (IC), the Scottish Constitution (SC) or the English Constitution. For clarity this work cites the Warrants issued by the latter as: by the Premier Grand Lodge (or *Moderns*) (ECM), the *Antients* from 1751-1813 (ECA), or the United Grand Lodge of England from 1813 (EC).

[135] Jenkyns, S. Michael, *History of British and Colonial Regiments and their Military Lodges* (Col By Council, Allied Masonic Degrees of Canada, (Ottawa, 1977); although Ray Sheppard, the historian for Glittering Star Lodge No. 322(IC), disappointingly states that there is nothing in the minutes of the lodge mentioning KT prior to 1769, individual brethren were undoubtedly knights.

[136] Cameron, Sir Charles, AQC 13 (1900), 157

[137] Turnbull, E. R. and Denslow, R. V., *A History of Royal Arch Masonry* (1956) [copy in G.L. library]

[138] Lodge No. 213/9 (ECA) in the 4th Battalion, Royal Regiment of Artillery has its minute book in existence dating from 1789 and containing 'Marks' of Mark Master Masons who had been made in the Lodge. Although these minutes date from the time the Regt and Lodge were at Woolwich, it indicates that a Mark degree was likely being worked prior to that time and there are collateral indications that Royal Arch and Knight Templar degrees were known to the Lodge when in Montreal before 1791.

[139] Lane lists a Lodge at *The King's Head* in Norwich warranted in 1736 (No. 146) [In 1817 named Union Lodge Now No. 52] which is known to have worked the Royal Arch, Knight Templars, Ark and Mark degrees.

[140] Harris, Reginald V., *The Hugh de Payens (Premier) Preceptory No. 1, Kingston, Ontario, 1823-1953* (The Heritage Lodge No. 730,A.F. &A.M., G.R.C., 1986.)

[141] Harris, Reginald V., *Freemasonry in Canada before 1750*, Canada.

[142] *Régiments francais de la Guerre d'Amerique* [French Regiments in the American War (for Independence)], Comte de Trentinian, Executive Vice-President, French State Society, Sons of the American Revolution, (downloaded from http://xenophongroup.com/mcjoynt/regts.htm 15 February 2017.

[143] Gould, R. F., *Military Lodges*, 133-35

[144] George Draffen of Newington, *Prince Hall Freemasonry*, (AQC 89(1976) App. 1, 70-91 lists British Regiments Stationed Near Boston *c*.1775 as:

Regt	Colonel /Regt Name	Lodge No./Name	Dates
4th	(2nd Tangier)Kings Own Royal Lancashire	United No. 147(SC)	6 Feb 1769
10th	Greville /The Lincolnshire Regt	No. 299 (IC)	3 Aug 1758
		No. 378(IC)	5 Nov 1761
18th	Folliot /The Royal Irish Regt	No. 168(IC)	3 Sep1747
		No. 351(IC)	7 Aug 1760
22nd	Duke of Norfolk /The Cheshire Regt	No. 251(IC)	8 Nov 1754
23rd	Herbert/Royal Welch Fusiliers Regt	No. 137(SC)	26 Dec 1767
38th	Lillingston /South Staffordshire Regt	No. 441(IC)	4 Jul 1765
43rd	Fowkes/Oxford & Bucks LI St Patrick's Regt	RA No. 156(SC)	17 Nov 1769
49th	Trelawney/Royal Berkshire Regt	No. 354(IC)	4 Dec 1760
52nd	2nd Batt, Oxford & Bucks Light Inf Regt	No. 370(IC)	6 Aug 1761
59th	2nd Batt, East Lancs Regt	No. 226(EC)	17 Jun 1769
63rd	1st Batt, Manchester Regt	No. 512(IC)	6 May 1774
64th	1st Batt, North Staffordshire Regt Duke of Yorks	No. 106(SC)	2 Feb 1761

[145] For a brief period (1661-65) the Islands of St Kitts, St Croix, St Martin and St Barthelemy were owned by the Knights of St John of Jerusalem, then the sovereign power in Malta, which purchased them on 21 May 1661 from the bankrupt *Compagnie des iles de l'Amerique* and sold them to the French West India Company in 1665.

[146] Gould, R. F., *Military Lodges*, 199.

[147] Gould, R. F., *History of Freemasonry*, Vol 1, 151.

[148] Rylands, W. H. *Freemasonry In Lancashire and Cheshire. (XVII Century.)* (Read 20 January 1895 to Quatuor Coronati Lodge No. 2076), 187.

[149] Fort, George F., *Early History and Antiquities of Freemasonry* (London, 1878), 136-7.

[150] The 29th Regt of Foot, which features repeatedly in this narrative, was originally raised by Colonel Thomas Farrington of the Coldstream Guards under a Royal Warrant dated 16 February 1694 and was known as 'Farrington's Regiment' (in some records 'Farrington's Foot') in accordance with the existing practice of calling regiments after their Colonel. In 1702 the Regt was transferred to Ireland; from 1704-06 it fought under the Duke of Marlborough, including the great victory of Ramilles.

[151] Gould, R. F., *History of Freemasonry*, Vol 2, 384.

[152] Jenkyns, S. M., *Freemasonry in Gibraltar, 1727 – present* (1999-2000 and 2005-2006, Acacia Lodge, No. 561 GRC, Ottawa, Canada).

[153] John Lane, in his *Masonic Records 1717-1894*, Second Edition, provides the following entry for the Lodge on page 52: 'Gibraltar Lodge. St John's Lodge, 1768. Mother Lodge of St John, 1785. The Rock, Gibraltar, (Malaga), Spain 1728. Lodge at Gibraltar is referred to in G. L. Min. 10 May 1727. Deputation to constitute 9 March 1728/9. (G. L. Warrant) Nov. 1728 No. 51B18. 9 March, 1729 No. 51. No. 51 1740. No. 30, 1755. No. 28, 1760. No. 25, 1780. No. 25 1781. No. 24 1792. Warrants of Confirmation, 12 Mar. 1785 and 22 Nov. 1786. Last payment 1800. Lapsed before the Union 1813.'

[154] Gould, R. F., *Military Lodges*, 24.

[155] Gould, R. F., *Military Lodges*, 207 states 'The first Dutch Field Lodge was established at Maastrict in 1745'.

[156] York was, and is, a major garrison city and Regiments of Foot associated with the city included: Col Herbert's Regiment (1645), Col Price's Regiment, Col Clayton's Regiment, Col Tidcomb's Regiment, Col Beveridge's Regiment, Col Sir Edward Hales's Regiment, The East Yorkshire Regiment (The Duke of York's Own), Col Jordan's Regiment, Col Henry Harrison's Regiment, Col the Earl of Hertford's Regiment, Col Howe's Regiment, Col Leslie's Regiment, Col Tufton's Regiment, Col Earl of Torrington's Regiment, Sir William Clifton's Regiment, The Royal Dragoon Guards, and The Yorkshire Regiment.

[157] As Price's Regiment they fought at Falkirk and Culloden.

[158] Gould, R. F., *Military Lodges*, 129.

[159] Thorp, J. T., *French Prisoner Lodges (1756-1814)* (Leicester, 1900), includes the following: Abergavenny, Alresford, Ashburton, Ashby-de-la-Zouch, Bandon, Basingstoke, Bedale, Bideford, Boroughbridge, Bristol, Carlisle, Carnarvon, Chatham, Chepstow, Chesterfield, Dartmoor, Derby, Dover, Edinburgh, Esk Mills, Falmouth, Fareham, Hawick, Jedburgh, Kelso, Knaresborough, Launceston, Leeds, Leek, Leicester, Llanfyllin, Melrose, Montrose, Northampton, Okehampton, Peebles, Pembroke, Penrith, Penryn, Perth, Peterborough, Petersfield, Plymouth, Pontefract, Portchester, Portsmouth, Redruth, Richmond, Sanquhar, Dumfries, Selkirk, Sissinghurst, Tavistock, Tiverton, Tynemouth, Wakefield, Wantage, Wincanton, Winchester, Wisbech, Yarmouth, and York.

[160] Thorp, J. T., *French Prisoners' Lodges (1756-1814)* (Leicester, 1900), 131

[161] Gould, R. F., *History of Freemasonry*, Chap XXVII, 243

[162] Sharpe, P. R., *A Short History of The Armed Forces And Masonry* (Website of The Circuit of Service Lodges) (retrieved 22 Aug 2019)

[163] First Regt of Dragoon Guards Lodges included No. 520 (ERM /No. 426(ERM / No. 342 (ERM).

[164] The York Conclave records include handwritten letters dated 22 March 1791, 21 April 1791, 21 May 1791, 15 June 1791, and 28 June 1791 from Thomas Dunckerley. York should have been allocated No. 5 but declined and retained its name without a number.

[165] R. F. Gould, *Military Lodges*, 191

[166] It will be seen in Part Four and Appendices that many modern Knight Templar preceptories adopted the names of former chivalric knights or known Templar houses. If any genuine historical connections of this nature existed it would not be unreasonable to expect such links to have been perpetuated in preceptory histories or rituals. One such example is the history of De Ros Preceptory No. 213; although the name is derived from Robert de Ros, a, Knight Templar at the time of the First Crusade and the family exists to this day, there is no known involvement of any actual Crusader Knight with speculative Freemasonry.

[167] Smyth, Frederick H., *Brethren in Chivalry, 1791-1991* (Lewis Masonic, London, 1991)

[168] A well-known local landmark consisting of a leaden statue of Neptune then standing at the end of Temple Street but later removed to make room for street improvements.

[169] Possibly a reference to the *Rose* or *Rose and Crown* tavern in Temple Street where the artist William Bird, RA had painted a rose on the ceiling of the principal room used for festivities.

[170] *Freemasonry in Bristol, Part IV*, 10.

[171] James Heseltine was a member of Old Horn Lodge No. 2 which later became the Somerset House Lodge. He was Grand Secretary 1769-83 and Grand Treasurer 1785-1864 [Carr, Harry and others *Grand Lodge 1717-1967*, OUP for UGLE (1967)].

[172] *Some early Irish certificates and their story*, AQC 16,(1903), 69.

[173] *The Freemason* published 30 September 1882 Historical Calendar records Birth of Thomas Dunckerley as 23 Oct 1724.

[174] Sommers, S. M., *Thomas Dunckerley and English Freemasonry*, 107 records Dunckerley joined the Honourable Society of Cymmrodorian in 1788 and is listed of being of Welsh descent.

[175] Sommers, S. M., *Thomas Dunckerley: A True Son of Adam*, AQC 124(2011), 95-120.

[176] *Ibid. passim.*

[177] *Ibid.* p.110 quoting photocopy of original letter in Library and Museum of Freemasonry (London).

[178] Sadler, Henry, *Thomas Dunckerley, his life, labours, and letters.* (London, 1891)

[179] Other amounts have been quoted; this is the sum in the Privy Purse records.

[180] Report by Major Charles Shirreff, Deputy Provincial Grand Master of Shropshire, to Grand Secretary on meeting held at Shrewsbury on 31 August 1790.

[181] Sommers, S. M., *Thomas Dunckerley and English Freemasonry*, ibid, 130.

[182] Dunckerley, in a letter in Jan 1792 to John Knight, refers to 'the Masonic knowledge which I have gleaned in Europe, America, and Africa over 40 years past'.

[183] *Freemasons Magazine* (Oct 1793).

[184] Sommers, S. M., *Thomas Dunckerley and English Freemasonry*, 79-80.

[185] The first Sea Lodge No. 254 was held in HMS *Vanguard* at Quebec under a warrant dated 16 Jan 1760 granted by the Premier Grand Lodge of England.

[186] Jenkyns, S. M., *History of British and Colonial Regiments and their Military Lodges*, (quotes from Milbourne) (1st, 3rd, 4th, 14th, 15th, 17th, 22nd, 26th, 27th, 28th, 32nd, 34th, 35th, 38th, 40th, 42nd, 43rd, 44th, 45th, 46th, 47th, 48th, 49th, 54th, 55th, 56th, 58th, 60th, 62nd, 63rd, 64th, 65th, 78th, and 90th Regts of Foot and Brethren of at least 1 Canadian Lodge and Lodges No. 192(IC)[47th (Lascelles' Regt)]; No. 218(IC)[48th (Webb's Regt)]; No. 245(IC) [15th (Amherst's Regt); No. 1, (Louisburg)[28th (Bragg's Regt) warrant from the PGL Massachusetts (Moderns)]; and Lodges held in the 43rd (Kennedy's Regiment) and the Royal Artillery, under Irish lodges dispensations.

[187] John Lane *Masonic Records 1717-1894* ('Lane's List' Reprinted Lewis Masonic, 2000) shows Warranted No. 451 (Moderns) on 14 August 1773 meeting successively at various Inns in Bristol, renumbered 358(1780), 359(1781), and 291(1792). The Lodge lapsed in c.1797 and because of the restrictions in *The Unlawful Societies Act*, its Warrant and Number were taken over on 26 February 1799 by a new lodge meeting at Wotton-under-Edge which lapsed in about 1807.

[188] Ward, Eric, AQC 71(1958), 36.

[189] After the erection of Grand Conclave, reference was generally made to such a presiding Officer as an 'Eminent Deputy Grand Master' (EDGM); (see letter Dunckerley/John Knight dated 27 January 1792 below.)

[190] For example, in that for the year 1958, p.750 (The pagination commences with Page 739 for reasons which today are not immediately apparent!)

[191] [Author's Note: It is disappointing that, to date, it has not been possible to discover if, when, and where this last interesting piece of ceremonial took place!]

[192] Presumably 'grand scribe and registrar' is intended; this Office is frequently spelled

'register' in contemporary documents.

¹⁹³ Mandleberg, C. J., and Davies, L. W., *Royal Arch Masons & Knights Templar at Redruth, Cornwall, 1791-1828*, QCCC Ltd. (Hamilton House Publishing, 2005).

¹⁹⁴ 'About 1745' in *Rose Croix*, p.126 (Cosby Jackson op. cit.) is not correct.

¹⁹⁵ The word 'Druids' in the names of both the Redruth Lodge and its Chapter was acquired after a member of the Lodge had given a well-received lecture on the ancient Cornish Druids at a meeting of the Provincial Grand Lodge of Cornwall several years earlier.

¹⁹⁶ The Officers and Knights Companions attending the meeting of the Encampment at Redruth on 11 March 1805 appear to have their ages at the date of their admission to the Order appended to their names.

¹⁹⁷ Mandleberg, C. John, and Davies, L. W., *Royal Arch Masons & Knights Templar at Redruth, Cornwall, 1791-1828*,.21.

¹⁹⁸ At this early date this was a White Sash.

¹⁹⁹ On opposite recto is written in a different hand 'Since this was written the Sashes are charged 7/- which make it to be 22/- instead of 21/-'

²⁰⁰ Mandleberg, C. John, and Davies, L. W., *Royal Arch Masons & Knights Templar at Redruth, Cornwall, 1791-1828*, 23

²⁰¹ [Author's note: It has not been possible to trace 'where Dunckerley 'glean'd his Masonic knowledge of Africa' although his naval travels included Mediterranean voyages and he might have visited Tunis where there is a history of British expatriate and Military Freemasonry from an early date.]

²⁰² Still working as No. '**B**'.

²⁰³ Still working as No. 2.

²⁰⁴ A 'Frock Coat', that is.

²⁰⁵ Mandleberg, C. John., and Davies, L. W., *Royal Arch Masons & Knights Templar at Redruth, Cornwall, 1791-1828*, 24-26.

²⁰⁶ 'The Will of God' was the 'Word of the day' communicated during the opening of an Encampment of Knights Templar.

²⁰⁷ In 1798 a short-lived Lodge No. 302 was warranted in this regiment by the *Antients* Grand Lodge. Rancliffe himself was a 'Modern', so presumably he had little to do with this Lodge.

²⁰⁸ Thorp, J. T., *Lord Rancliffe*, (The Transactions of the Leicester Lodge of Research, Tenth Meeting, 28 May 1894)

²⁰⁹ This provision remained in force until finally repealed by the 1967 Criminal Justice Act and many think that it would have saved a great deal of trouble if it had been retained. However, it may be noted that most Clerks of the Peace did not bother saving them in the middle of the 19th century.

²¹⁰ Smyth, F. H., *Brethren in Chivalry*, 31.

²¹¹ The full text of the Charter of Compact can be found in C. F. Matier's *The origin and Progress of the Preceptory of St George 1795-1895* (1910).

²¹² It may be relevant to point out that the Duke, involved with both the Premier Grand Lodge, 'the Moderns' and its rival, 'the *Antients*', was one of the leading Brethren who wished to see a Union of the two Grand Lodges. His Election as Grand Master of 'the *Antients*' in 1813 at the time when his brother the Duke of Sussex was Grand Master of 'the Moderns' undoubtedly facilitated the formation of the United Grand Lodge of England.

²¹³ Recorded in one of John Knight's small manuscript notebooks formerly held by Quatuor Coronati Lodge (445-1.5B) (now held in the Library of United Grand Lodge).

[214] Catalogued as Note Book No.27 John Coombe Masonic Library, Hayle Masonic Hall, Cornwall

[215] Powell, C., *Sheffield Knights Templar Ritual (c.1800), Edition and Introduction (2010)*, privately printed for the Author, Sheffield (2010)

[216] Songhurst, W. J., AQC XXXVIII(1925), 183.

[217] That is to say the Charter given by the Duke five years earlier.

[218] Part IV of *Freemasonry in Bristol* 1910, p.35.

[219] Springer's resignation was caused by advancing years; he died in 1812.

[220] Duckett, Thomas E., *The Baldwin Saga*, p.7 (privately printed under the authority of the Council of Bristol, 1980)

[221] The Chaplain to the Duke of Sussex who, in 1835, was to play a major part in revising the Ritual of the Order of the Holy Royal Arch.

[222] It is, perhaps reasonable to speculate that the extensive troop movements in the area and the activities of regimental lodges and brethren may have justified this appointment.

[223] Nos. 12, St Michael (Rawtenstall); 13, Faith (Bradford); 15, Preceptory of St Salem (Congleton); 16, Prudence (Ipswich); 17, St John of Jerusalem (Ulverston); 18, Prince Edward (Todmorden); 19, Trinity in Unity (Barnstaple); and 20, Royal Kent (Newcastle upon Tyne – which may have been working somewhat earlier.)

[224] One can still meet such Brethren even today; the Author is aware of a recent incident when a Brother, on his way to a Knights Templar meeting (a meeting which was also to be attended by as distinguished a member of the Craft as the Provincial Grand Master in the Craft of each of the two Brethren concerned), was accused in a forthright and heated manner of betraying his obligations by going to such a meeting.

[225] This Act gave exemption from its provisions to all Freemason's Lodges provided that they complied with the Rules and Regulations contained in the 1799 Act. The Act did not specify that these exemptions applied only to existing Masonic bodies, nor that they applied only to Craft Lodges.

[226] Now No. 25.

[227] Three encampments are known to have been warranted between 1824 and 1830: Hugh de Payens No. 22 (1824) in Canada, which transferred its allegiance to the Great Priory of Canada in 1875; Cornubian No. 23 meeting in Falmouth and Truro (Erased 1888); and Loyal Brunswick No. 24 (1830) meeting in Plymouth (erased 1927), all of which appear in the 'Enumeration of 1868'. Others may have been warranted but erased before that date.

[228] Now the Preceptory of St George No. 6.

[229] MMH archives, [formerly labelled Shelf A2 No. 875].

[230] W. H. White was also Grand Secretary of the United Grand Lodge of England, 1838-57, having been Assistant Grand Secretary 1810-13, and Joint Grand Secretary (with Edwards Harper) 1813-38. He retired at the age of 80.

[231] Grand Prior, Grand Sub-Prior, Grand Prelate, First Grand Captain, Second Grand Captain, Grand Chancellor, Grand Vice-Chancellor, Grand Registrar, Grand Director of Ceremonies, Grand Banner Bearer, Grand Almoner, Grand Sword Bearer, Grand Herald, Second Grand Herald, First Grand Expert, Second Grand Expert, First Grand Standard Bearer, Second Grand Standard Bearer, First Grand Aide-de-Camp, Second Grand Aide-de-Camp, Assistant Grand Director of Ceremonies, Grand Equerry, Grand Superintendent of Works, Grand Organist, Grand Treasurer, Grand Almoner, Grand Hospitaller, Grand Chamberlain, First Grand Captain of Lines, and Second Grand Captain of Lines (*But still no Grand Orator!*)

²³² Col Tynte, Somerset (Grand Master); William Stuart, Hertfordshire (Deputy Grand Master); Sir F. Fowke, Leicestershire; Lord Suffield, Norfolk; William Tucker, Dorset (Past 1st Grand Standard Bearer); Dr, Crucefix, Kent (Member of Grand Conclave Committee); and J. Wyld MP, (Cornwall).

²³³ Udall was Henry Leeson's immediate predecessor as Second Grand Captain.

²³⁴ It has also been noted that important masonic historians such as the late Brigadier Cosby Jackson in his various writings on the Ancient and Accepted Rite, and the late Frederick Smyth in *Brethren in Chivalry* do not discuss the topic.

²³⁵ This Ritual was probably largely (or may even have been wholly) the result of editing work of John Masson who was appointed First Grand Captain at the meeting.

²³⁶ The Chancellor at this time was Henry Emly, one of the earliest Sovereign Grand Inspectors General in the newly-formed Supreme Council of the Ancient and Accepted Rite, and the Vice-Chancellor was a barrister, John Halsey Law, of Lincoln's Inn.

²³⁷ Evidently the Brethren who framed this regulation thought of the 'Dependencies' as 'English', ignoring the fact that they formed part of the 'British' Empire. This was common practice in the Statutes and Regulations of many of the Ruling Bodies of English Degrees and Orders in the second half of the 19th century.

²³⁸ Colonel Tynte (Somerset); William Stuart, soon to be Tynte's successor as Most Eminent and Supreme Grand Master, (Hertfordshire); Sir. F. G. Fowke, Bart. (Leicestershire); the ill-fated William Tucker (Dorset); J. Wyld (Cornwall); the Revd. John Huyshe (Devon); Major Ferris C. Robb (Hampshire); Matthew Dawes (Lancashire); Colonel G. A. Vernon (Staffordshire); and W. C. Cruttenden (Cheshire). Of these, Tucker, Dawes and Vernon were members of the Supreme Council of the A. & A. Rite. Other members of the Supreme Council on the Committee at this time were Henry Emly (Grand Chancellor), J. A. D. Cox (Grand Registrar) and Henry Udall (nominated by the M. E. Grand Master). The resolution of any problem caused by the separation of a Rose Croix Chapter from the Encampment of which it had hitherto formed a part was presumably considerably facilitated by this representation on the Committee.

²³⁹ Perhaps £350-£400 in early 21st century money. However, this same sum (£3.15) is specified unaltered (item 5) in the 'Concordat 'between England, Ireland and Scotland, last reaffirmed in 1971 and amended in 1978! (In the Statutes of the United Orders in England and Wales, the minimum fee for Installation of a Candidate is now 'the Registration Fee plus VAT. [Regulation 108].)

²⁴⁰ Today the signatures of twelve Knights are required (Regulation 57).

²⁴¹ For example Baldwyn in Bristol (see earlier Chapter) and some of John Huyshe's Encampments in Devonshire.

²⁴² These can be seen, for example, in the Preceptory of Coeur de Lion No. 29 where they are surreptitiously worn on occasions!

²⁴³ In the archives of the Supreme Council 33° for England and Wales etc. there is a Rose Croix Ritual, written on the title page of which is 'S.E.T. 1862 – Jacques de Molay'. The margins are optimistically endorsed at intervals, presumably by its original owner, 'Stolen from S. E. Taylor'. The Ritual is that of the *Rosae Crucis* degree presumably being worked at that time in the Camp of Baldwin; it is almost identical with that in use today. It was presumably the personal copy of Eminent Knight Major (later Lt Col) Samuel E. Taylor, Deputy Grand Superintendent of the Camp of Baldwyn.

²⁴⁴ In the Circular Letter this date is given as '1790' but this is an evident misprint.

[245] Masson neither quoted sources for his history nor went so far as to claim specifically that the Masonic rituals approved by Grand Conclave were derived from such chivalric Templar sources.

[246] Mark Shuttleworth was a cousin of Robert James Shuttleworth, elected to the Supreme Council of the A. & A. Rite on 10 April 1861. Each was said to be a descendant of Dr. Desaguliers.

[247] These included, *inter alia*, Union No. 70 (Guyana); Celestial No. 71 (Shanghai); Star of the West No. 77 (Barbados); Victoria No. 78 (Hong Kong); Loyal Burmah No. 81 (Rangoon); Southern Cross No. 87 (Cape Town); and Mount Calvary No. 93 (Bombay).

[248] *Freemasons' Magazine and Masonic Mirror* (May 17, 1862), 396.

[249] Prior to 1962 the Provincial Priory was that of 'Bristol and Gloucestershire', but Gloucestershire was separated in 1962.

[250] In Baldwyn and in Ireland this is still the case.

[251] Supreme Council Letter Book II, No.252.

[252] See, Mandleberg, C. J., *Morton Edwards, Sculptor, and the Honourable Society of Royal Ark Mariners*, Mark Masons Hall Ltd. (2012)[ISBN: 9780957216709]

[253] The Plenipotentiaries were the Reverend G. R. Portal, the Earl of Limerick, Sir Patrick Colquhoun, Captain Nathaniel Philips and J. M. P. Montagu.

[254] Mandleberg, C. J., Ancient and Accepted, (QCCC, London, 1995), 213.

[255] Notes of G. E. W. Bridge in the Archives in Mark Masons' Hall.

[256] For readers unfamiliar with Masonic terminology, see Endnote 266 .

[257] The building was destroyed during World War II by enemy bombing.

[258] See MacLeod Moore's letter to Patrick Colquhoun of 27 February 1877 below.

[259] Mandleberg, C. J., *Ancient and Accepted*: 501.

[260] Col Shadwell H. Clerke, Provincial Prior of Sussex and Sub-Prior for England and Wales, would not sign the Report in which the revised Ritual was set out, declaring 'I regret that I am unable to concur in this Report, or to give my approval to the Draft of the New Ritual submitted by the other Members of the Commission'.

[261] 'Put on the whole armour of God', Epistle to the Ephesians, vi, 10-18.

[262] Albert Hudson Royds was the leading, if not to say dominating, figure in the Christian Orders in Lancashire in the latter part of the 19th century. Such was his pre-eminence among his Brethren that for many years the Prince Albert Preceptory No. 34 was known simply as the 'Albert Preceptory' and considered to have been named in Royds' honour, an erratum which was not revealed until the 150th anniversary of the Preceptory in 1999 which was attended by the Grand Master, M. Em. Kt Leslie Dring, GCT. A necessary reference to the Warrant of the Preceptory at this time demonstrated beyond doubt that it was named in honour of the Consort of Queen Victoria, H.R.H. Prince Albert and this historical basis featured in the oration prepared for the occasion by C. John Mandleberg who acted as Great Prelate for the presentation of a Banner!

[263] Authors' Italics.

[264] Shadwell H. Clerke was also at this time Great Captain-General in the Supreme Council of the Ancient and Accepted Rite.

[265] For the Order of the Temple, Richard Loveland-Loveland, Colonel Noel Murray and General J. C. Hay; for the Mark Grand Lodge, the Earl of Euston, Viscount Dungarvan, and C. Fitzgerald Matier (who was to succeed Frederick Binckes as Grand Secretary); and for the A. & A. Rite, (of which all the other six apart from Matier were also prominent Members), Captain Nathaniel Philips, Hugh Sandeman

and Frank Richardson. Of these only Loveland Loveland was absent from the Meeting on 18 July 1895.

[266] For readers unfamiliar with Masonic terminology the basic unit within the United Orders, formerly an Encampment, Commandery, Conclave or Chapter, is today called a Preceptory and works the Masonic degree of Knight of the Temple under the supervision of an Eminent Preceptor (equivalent to the Craft office of Worshipful Master); every Preceptory may also work the degrees of Knight of Malta and a short intermediate degree of Knight of St Paul and the Mediterranean Pass for which a Priory of Malta is opened under the supervision of a Prior of Malta. The offices of Eminent Preceptor and Prior of Malta are usually held by the same knight. The Priory normally uses the same name and number as the Preceptory, but there are Priories in existence which have a separate name. Preceptories are grouped within a Province under the supervision of a Provincial Prior and meet, usually once a year in a meeting of the Provincial Priory. Each Province may also hold meetings of a Provincial Priory of Malta under the supervision of a Provincial Sub-Prior of Malta.

[267] Hughan, W. J., *Unpublished Records of the Craft*, (Kenning, 1871), Part II, pp.16-17.

[268] Robertson, J., Ross, *History of Knights Templar in Canada*, (Toronto, 1890).

[269] T. Dunckerley letter dated from Hampton Court Palace on 27th January 1792.

[270] Lane's List of Lodges records Old Sea Captains' Lodge of Hospitality, Bristol, warranted 12 August 1769.

[271] Thomas Dunckerley letter from Hampton Court dated 27 January 1792.

[272] Lane's List of Lodges includes Lodge of Fortitude No.131 Warranted 1772 Falmouth, Cornwall with former connections to 67th Regt of Foot, which almost certainly had exposure to Knight Templary in the West Indies well before that date.

[273] NB. The Earl of Euston was also Grand Master of the Order of the Allied Masonic Degrees.

[274] Thorp, J. T., *French Prisoners Lodges* (Gibbons, Leicester, 1900), 27-48.

[275] It will be remembered that a similar suggestion had been made in 1897.

[276] These are currently administered from Mark Masons' Hall as Unattached Preceptories.

[277] Grand Secretary, United Grand Lodge of England 1917-37.

[278] Powell, C., *See Fresh Evidence on the Early Life of Chevalier Andrew Michael Ramsay*, AQC 131 (2018), 309-316.

[279] Kitchen, M., *Europe between the Wars*, 2nd Ed, (London: Pearson Longman, 2006), 278.

[280] Prestige, H. H .C., *A Century of the Allied Masonic Degrees*, London 1979.

[281] A Lewis is the son of a Freemason.

[282] Ward, Eric, AQC 71, p.36 (1958).

[283] For this and all regiments with County connections it must also be assumed that some brethren completed their military service and retired to the County from which they were recruited and therefore provided a source of Masonic knowledge to local brethren after their return.

[284] Duckett, T. E., *The Baldwyn Saga*, (privately printed, The Council of Baldwyn, Bristol 1980), 6.

[285] Charter dated 20 December 1780 (Text at **Appendix C**).

[286] *The History of Freemasonry in Cheshire*, Armstrong, J., (1901) quoted by Mathie, A. G., *The Provincial Priory of Cheshire 1850-2000* (privately printed 2001).

[287] Bandon, County Cork has records of the Antient Boyne No. 84(IC) of 1746 which record visits by French prisoners-of war and/or French prisoners-of war as Joining Members.

[288] Hughan, W. J., *An article in The Freemason* (1886), 556.

[289] Chetwood Crawley, W. J., *Some early Irish certificates and their story*, AQC 16 (1903), 69.

[290] In a letter dated from Hampton Court Palace on 27 January 1792, Dunckerley says: '*I was selected Grand Master to revive the Order in England in February 1791 and have had the pleasure to constitute the following Conclaves ....* ' He then listed ten Conclaves, including six of the seven which had petitioned him to form a Grand Encampment, and a further four, including Harmony Encampment in Salisbury. At that time, therefore, the Grand Encampment appears to have had jurisdiction over eleven Templar units. The original eight were: Baldwyn (Bristol), Observance (London), Royal Cumberland (Bath), Fortitude (York), Colchester (Colchester). Redemption (York), Durnovarian (Dorchester) and Trine (Bideford).

[291] Thorp, J. T., *French Prisoners' Lodges*, Leicester (1900), 20.

[292] Thorp, J. T. *ibid.*

[293] Chetwode Crawley, W. J., *Some Early Irish Certificates and their Story*, AQC 16 (1903), 69.

[294] *The History of the Provincial Grand Lodge of the Isle of Man (1886-2006)*, privately printed for the Province, Douglas 2006) and Records of Grand Lodge of Ireland.

[295] However, on visits to the IOM the Author has seen Gravestones bearing engravings of straight 'Templar' swords not unlike those identified by Baigent and Leigh at Kilmartin (and elsewhere) in Scotland.

[296] Preston, P. O., unpublished notes made as Provincial Vice-Chancellor, North and East Yorkshire (c.1997 source not stated).

[297] Venning, Lt Col H. C. W., *History of the Priory of Lancashire* (Littlebury Bros, Liverpool, 1956),34, 46; Lanes List shows Antiquity Lodge No. 146 Warranted 1776 but located at Bolton in 1786.

[298] French prisoners-of war artefacts including an apron and certificate are displayed in Syston Masonic Hall.

[299] Thorp, J. T., *French Prisoner Lodges (1756-1814)* (Leicester, 1900), 15].

[300] This must be regarded as an anomaly as two Army Regts associated with the County – the 43rd Regt and the 52nd Regt – have a history of interactions with Regts with known Knight Templar activity, such as that in Boston in 1775.

[301] As Price's Regiment they fought at Falkirk and Culloden and had interactions with other Regts.

[302] Songhurst, W. J., AQC XXXVIII(1925), 183.

[303] Gould, R. F., *History of Freemasonry*, Chap XVIII, 418

[304] Source not stated by P. O. Preston [but later quoted as 'records of date June 1780' by W. Redfern Kelly, GCT, in a series of articles in the Toronto Freemason] [*Author Note – perhaps the latter is the date the minutes were signed.*]

[305] Preston, P. O. Unpublished Notes made as Provincial Vice-Chancellor, North and East Yorkshire (c.1997 source not stated but later found to have been quoted by Shepherd and M. P. Lane, Jerusalem Preceptory No. 5 Bi-Centenary History (privately printed S. H. Cliffe Ltd, Dukinfield, Cheshire, 1986)

[306] *The Freemason*, letter by W J Hughan published in August 1900.

[307] Source not stated by P. O. Preston [later found quoted by Robertson, *History of KT in Canada* (Toronto, 1890)

[308] *Bicentenary History of Ancient York Conclave of Redemption* [B] TI (York, 1991), 74

[309] Gould, R. F., *History of Freemasonry* Vol 2, 291.

[310] Jenkyns, S. M., *History of British and Colonial Regiments and their Military Lodges*,

contains extensive details of military lodges and their deployments, not only in Canada but also throughout the world.

311 Sources include: Gould, R. F., *Military Lodges. The Apron and the Sword* or, *Freemasonry under Arms*. Being an account of lodges in regiments and ships of war, etc. (London, Gale & Polden, 1899). J. Lane, *Masonic Records 1717-1894* (London, Freemasons' Hall, 1895); Grand Lodge of Ireland, Register of Warranted Lodges; and Sharpe P. R., *A Short History of The Armed Forces and Masonry* (website of The Circuit of Service Lodges retrieved 22 August 2018); and Jenkyns, S. M., *History of British and Colonial Regiments and their Military Lodges*.

312 [It is certainly difficult to interpret these instructions today – it certainly rather improbable to us to lead a candidate round 23 or 24 times - as does the rubric in John Knight's final 37th Degree where his ritual instructs the candidate to advance to the East on not one but on two occasions with the penal signs and words 'of each of the preceding (36!) degrees'].

313 The original text is clearly 'O-r-i-c-h' and not 'Arch' as one might expect, and despite repeated attempts, it has not been possible to find an explanation of the term.

314 A sketch of a triangle with three dots outside the top of the left side, and one in the middle of the figure.

315 A pencil sketch of (apparently) a star.

316 A sketch of a Skull and Cross Bones.

317 That is, the year before the Supreme Council of England and Wales received its Patent from the Northern Jurisdiction, USA.

318 *vide* Round Church of the Holy Sepulchre in Bridge Street, Cambridge.

319 *Liber Ordinis Templi* 2018/2019 'Statutes', 2018, page 290, 291.

320 'Appendix K' from Mandleberg, C. John, and Davies, L. W., *Royal Arch Masons & Knights Templar at Redruth, Cornwall, 1791-1828*, 123.

321 [Minutes exist from 20 May 1795 and a Centenary Warrant is dated 27 December 1888] [The History of the Province of Lancashire states that it is possible that 'the Royal Encampment, as it was then known, apparently originated in Ireland in the County of Munster and was brought to Manchester by the Munster Fusiliers who were stationed in the city between 1779 and 1780']. A Charter dated 10 October 1786 was granted by the Grand Lodge of All England at York to Jerusalem Encampment and given the number 5].

322 From 1863 to 1916 St John of Jerusalem & Malta Preceptory and Pitt Macdonald Priory No. 73 in Chennai (Peripatetic).

323 Duke of Connaught and Strathearn's Preceptory No. 153 (Meerut, North West Provinces, India) amalgamated with Himalaya Preceptory No.137 on 1 June 1931.

ALPHABETICAL INDEX

The Unlawful Societies Act (39 Geo.III, c.79) 245, 262, 292, 374
Theresa, Queen of Portugal 30, 31, 93
Time Immemorial (in Masonic usage) 16
Tyre 39, 45-47, 49, 51, 53-56, 62, 64

U
Union Bands 188, 369
United Orders, Current Provinces and Districts
    [1847] Province of Kent 315, 331
    [1848] Province of Devonshire and Cornwall 317, 318
    [1848] Province of Lancashire 317
    [1850] Province of Cheshire & North Wales 319, 320
    [1856] Province of Nottinghamshire 319, 320, 321, 347
    [1857] Province of East Anglia 321, 331
    [1862] Province of City and County of Bristol 324, 325
    [1864] Province of North and East Yorkshire 323, 326
    [1864] Province of West Yorkshire 323, 326
    [1873] Province of Sussex 329
    [1874] Province of Somerset 315, 329
    [1910] Province of Lincolnshire 335
    [1914] Province of South America 337, 353, 363
    [1924] Province of Worcestershire 338
    [1925] Province of Northampton, Huntingdon and Bedford 339
    [1930] Province of Essex 340
    [1933] Province of Hertfordshire 340
    [1942] Province of Transvaal, South Africa 341
    [1945] Province of Hampshire and Isle of Wight 316, 341
    [1949] Province of Dorset and Wiltshire 342
    [1952] Province of Monmouth and South Wales 342
    [1956] Province of Surrey 343
    [1958] Province of Far East 325, 344, 363
    [1960] Province of Gloucestershire and Herefordshire 345
    [1964] Province of Oxfordshire, Berkshire and Buckinghamshire 345
    [1966] Province of Staffordshire and Shropshire 346
    [1966] Province of Warwickshire 347
    [1970] Province of Derbyshire 348
    [1970] Province of Leicestershire and Rutland 347
    [1970] Province of Middlesex 348
    [1975] Province of Durham 320, 349
    [1975] Province of Northumberland 349
    [1975] Province of Sri Lanka 327, 349
    [1980] Province of Zimbabwe 344, 350
    [1985] Province of Natal 331, 350, 351
    [1991] Province of South East Asia 345, 351
    [1992] Province of London 311, 352

[1908-1912] Rt Hon Henry Fitzroy, Earl of Euston [Pro GM] 335

[1912-1920] Richard Loveland Loveland, KC [Pro GM] 336

[1920-1932] Maj-Gen Thomas Calley, CB, CBE, MVO [Pro GM] 338

[1932-1947] Lord Harewood, KG, GCVO, DSO [Pro GM 1932-1939][GM 1939-1947] 341

[1947-1973] Rt Hon. George St Vincent, 5th Baron Harris, MC, DL 342

[1973-1975] Lt Col John Leicester-Warren, TD, VL 348

[1975-1996] Harold Devereux Still [Acting GM 1975-76][GM 1976-96] 349

[1997-2011] Leslie Felgate Dring 352

[2011-2017] Timothy John Lewis 353

[2017-Date] Paul Raymond Clement 353

United Orders, Initial Provincial Grand Commanders and Priors

Bavin, The Revd Francis, (West Indian Islands) [1910-23] 335

Bedregal Soria, Carlos (Bolivia)[2005-14] 352

Biggs, Maj. George Travers (Somerset) [1952-65] 343

Boag, Sir George Townsend, KCIE, CSI (Surrey) [1956-69] 343

Boldero, Col G Neeld, (Mediterranean) [1875-96] 330

Boucat, The Hon Sir James, KCMG (South Australia) [1869-1912] 327

Bowyer, Col Henry Atkins (Oxford) [1862-77] 328

Brown, Col Alexander D. B., (Oxfordshire, Berkshire and Buckinghamshire) [1963-66] 345

Brown, Dr. Reginald Latham (Derbyshire) [1968-85] 320, 348

Brownrigg, Gen. John Studholme, CB (Kent & Surrey) [1880-89] 315, 331

Burnett, Leslie (Warwickshire) [1966-75] 347

Carter, Cdr Herbert Raymond (South Africa, Cape and Orange Free State) [1985-93] 331, 351

Charlewood, William Thomas (New Zealand) [1930-31] 340

Chevallier-Boutell, Francis Hepburn (South America) [1914-20] 337

Cleeves, John Frederick (Hertfordshire) [1933-48] 341

Colville-Smith, Sir Philip, CVO, (Oxford & Berkshire) [1928-38] 339

Corrie, Alexander, (Queensland) [1927-30] 339

Creese, Percy Harold (Gloucester and Herefordshire) [1960-64] 345

Crookshank, Maj. Alexander Crowder, (Ceylon) [1869-75] 327

Cruttenden, William Courtney (Cheshire & North Wales)[1862-69] 319

Daly, Col Thomas, (British Guiana & The Windward Islands) [1898-1905] 333

Denison, William, Rt Hon. Lord Londesborough (North & East Yorkshire) [1864-89] 327

Dixon, Capt. Thomas, (North District of England) [1791] 211, 212, 309, 314, 317, 319, 320, 322, 326

Dorman, Thomas Phipps (Northampton, Huntingdon & Bedford) [1925-30] 339

Dribbell, Jack Lodewyck Charles (London) [1992-97] 352

Duckworth, Ferdinand Farrant (Rhodesia) [1962-63] 345

Duthie, Alasdair Bruce (South Africa (Cape)) [2006-09] 352

Dyer, Col George Nowers, CBE, DSO (Hampshire and Isle of Wight) [1945-55] 341

BV - #0008 - 050922 - C0 - 248/168/28 - CC - 9780853185963 - Gloss Lamination